FROM SOLON TO SOCRATES

FROM SOLON TO SOCRATES

Greek History and Civilization during the sixth and fifth centuries B.C.

Victor Ehrenberg

Second Edition

LONDON and NEW YORK

First published 1968 by Methuen & Co. Ltd
Second edition 1973
Reprinted three times
Reprinted 1986

Reprinted 1989, 1991, 1993
by Routledge
11 New Fetter Lane, London EC4P 4EE
29 West 35th Street, New York, NY 10001

© *1967 and 1973 by Victor Ehrenberg*

Printed in England by Clays Ltd, St Ives plc

ISBN 0–415–04024–8

to the memory of
Madge Webster
(A. M. Dale)
and
A. H. M. Jones

CONTENTS

MAPS

ABBREVIATIONS

AP   Aristotle, *Athenaion Politeia*

ASAI   *Ancient Society and Institutions.* Studies presented to
             V. Ehrenberg (Oxford 1966)

ATL   *The Athenian Tribute Lists*, ed. B. D. Meritt, H. T. Wade-
             Gery, M. F. M. Gregor. 4 vols. Cambridge, Mass.
             1939–53

BICS   Bulletin of the Institute of Classical Studies

CAH   *Cambridge Ancient History*

CHJ   *Cambridge Historical Journal*

D   *Anthologia Lyrica*, ed. E. Diehl

DK   H. Diels and W. Kranz, *Die Fragmente der Vorsokratiker*
             (Berlin 1934⁵, 1952⁶)

DSDA   H. Bengston, *Die Staatsverträge des Altertums*, vol. 2
             (Munich 1962)

FGrH   F. Jacoby, *Fragmente der griechischen Historiker* (Berlin
             1929. Leiden 1954–57)

Gomme   A. W. Gomme, *Historical Commentary on Thucydides*,
             vols. 1–3 (Oxford 1945–56), vol. 4 (ed. A. Andrewes
             and K. J. Dover), Oxford 1970

GRBS   *Greek, Roman and Byzantine Studies*

Hdt.   Herodotus

Hill³   G. F. Hill, Sources for Greek History 478–451, new ed.
             by R. Meiggs and A. Andrewes (Oxford 1951)

HSt   *Harvard Studies in Class. Philology*

HZ   *Historische Zeitschrift*

ML   R. Meiggs and D. Lewis, *A Selection of Greek Historical
             Inscriptions to the End of the 5th cent. B.C.* (Oxford 1969)

NumChr.   *Numismatic Chronicle*

P   *Poetae Melici Graeci*, ed. D. L. Page (Oxford 1962)

PI   Victor Ehrenberg, *Polis und Imperium* (Zurich 1965)

RE   Pauly-Wissowa-Kroll, *Real- Encyclopaedie f. d. klass.*
          Altertumswissenschaft
SB   *Sitzungsberichte*
SEG   *Supplementum Epigraphicum Graecum*
Tod   M. N. Tod, *Greek Historical Inscriptions* I², II (Oxford
          1946, 1948)

PREFACE TO THE FIRST EDITION

In this book I am dealing with a period which has often been covered and is generally regarded as the most important in Greek history. That alone would not justify another attempt. Apart from the fact that there have been new discoveries, archaeological and otherwise, that could not have been dealt with in earlier works, I had two reasons of my own, or rather two aims, in undertaking to write this book. The first was to show the unity of Greek history in every phase, a unity of political, economic, religious, and cultural aspects. Even though in my view political, military, and social history must be the framework, indeed the centre, of any general history, it ought to be shown that this cannot be separated from the world of the mind. In all, however, that I have to say on works of literature, philosophy, science, or art, I beg to point out that I am not writing as an expert on any of these subjects, nor indeed do I attempt to cover the whole ground, but only to show the multifarious picture of Greek life at any given moment. It goes without saying that a severe, and perhaps not always fair, selection is inevitable. I make no apologies for things left out.

The other aim was, not simply to give a narrative, but to reveal the uncertainties of modern scholarship on many important questions; it ought to be clear that a mere enumeration of (alleged) facts is misleading. Thus, the book is not a general textbook, though it may still show traces of that earlier plan, and though I hope that it will be useful for the younger student of history no less than for the scholar.

Writing today on even comparatively well-known periods of ancient history is, in fact, like entering a jungle – a jungle of ancient traditions and modern conjectures, with very few undisputed facts. We have long ago lost the beautiful innocence of those whose love for Greece was combined with an unperturbed belief in the truth of at least the chief traditions of the Greeks themselves. We may be less critical than our immediate predecessors in our search for absolute historical truth, not least because we no longer believe in the possibility of discovering that truth. We are a generation in between, no longer sure of critical positivism, nor, on the other hand, of the rationalist intuition now so much in vogue. I myself cannot claim that my love for the ancient Greeks has found a safe route through the jungle, much as I have tried.

During my lifetime, progress in the study of Greek history has been considerable, though progress does not necessarily mean advance in only one direction. Whatever tangled web we weave, we do not practise to deceive. Honest research always pays, and the Greeks still have, and always will have, much to tell us about man's fate and man's achievements. Greek history remains an exciting story, and not something to be left to the discussions and quibbles of the so-called experts. If I have succeeded in showing some of the excitement as well as some of the difficulties involved, I shall have done as much as I can.

In the necessary selection of modern literature to be mentioned in the notes, I have tried to quote the most important contributions; but for the sake of younger students of history in this country or the United States, I have laid stress, whenever I could, on books and articles in English. Anything published in 1967 could be only exceptionally included. In the spelling of Greek names, I have followed the publishers' wish to stick to the Latinized forms, although that involves the usual lack of consistency.

The book has kept me busy for a number of years, and while I have been working on it, I have learned much – not only about the Greeks. Now that it is finished, I feel that it is not finished at all, and never will be. My years and my obligation to the publishers induced me to stop.

I had the advantage of valuable help. Dr J. P. Barron read and corrected all but the last chapter at an earlier stage; much has been added or altered since, and he cannot be held responsible for any faults in the book. The same holds true for the last chapter, which Professor W. K. C. Guthrie was good enough to read, providing several invaluable suggestions and corrections. Dr Barron also helped me later with the revision of some passages and with the reading of part of the proofs. A good deal of correcting my English was done by the publishers' readers, and Dr and Mrs J. A. North; also by my wife. To all of them I am most grateful. Thanks are also due to Mr Peter Wait and Miss Janice Price of Methuen for their unwavering interest in the book.

I am grateful to Mr F. H. Jenkins of the London Institute of Classical Studies for his indefatigable work on the maps. They are intended to help the reader; they cannot replace the use of a historical atlas. Any faults or omissions in the maps are my own.

V. E.

London, December 1966/June 1967.

PREFACE TO THE SECOND EDITION

This new edition has provided the opportunity, not only to correct a large number of minor errors, but also to revise the text and to include many additions, while at the same time I tried to shorten the Notes and to bring them up-to-date. I am grateful to a number of critics, friendly or less so, for having pointed out some of the mistakes and weaknesses, many of which I had realized myself. I hope I shall be forgiven for not mentioning names, as they were so many. The fundamental outlook of the book has remained the same, but I trust this can be called an improved edition. Some books were published too late for me to use them, among them such important ones as R. Meiggs, *The Athenian Empire* and G.E.M. de Ste Croix, *The Origins of the Peloponnesian War*.

I am conscious of the fact that I had not really fulfilled my own aims; even now this goal seems out of reach. But I should like to describe once more the scope of my aims. The unity of Greek history and civilization is centred on the Polis. Thus, political and social history still are the core of the story, though at the same time part of the history of the mind. Traditional military history just as pure economics are specialist subjects, while their effects are essential for any general history; that means that the tactics of single battles or the statistics of import and export do not belong to it, nor do the technique of the dramatist or of the artist. I have made an exception for Marathon and Salamis, for they – like Cannae – deserve a detailed description. I repeat Professor Momigliano's quotation from John Stuart Mill (A.M., *Studies in Historiography*, London 1966, 60): 'The battle of Marathon, even as an event of English history, is more important than the battle of Hastings. If the issue of that day had been different, the Britons and Saxons might still have been wandering in the woods'.

The first edition of this book was dedicated to the memory of Mrs A. M. Webster. I have now added the name of A. H. M. Jones whose premature death deprived the world of a great scholar and myself of a cherished friend.

I wish to thank the publishers, and especially Mr Anthony Forster who took a very helpful interest in my book.

London, March 1972.   V. E.

I. Greece a

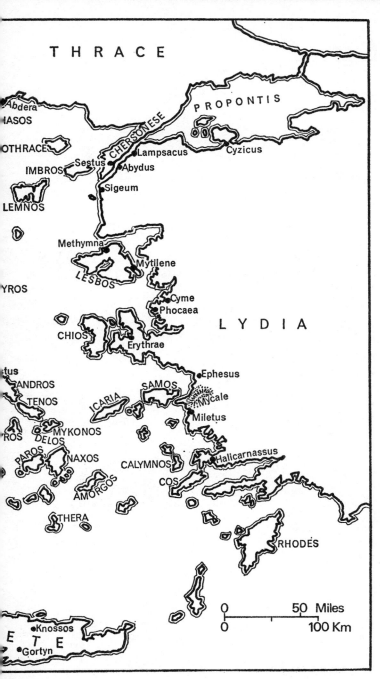

THRACE

PROPONTIS

•Abdera

IASOS

OTHRACE

Lampsacus

Cyzicus

IMBROS

Sestus

Abydus

Sigeum

LEMNOS

Methymna

Mytilene

YROS

LESBOS

Cyme

Phocaea

LYDIA

CHIOS

Erythrae

Ephesus

tus

ANDROS

SAMOS

Mycale

TENOS

ICARIA

Miletus

ROS

MYKONOS

DELOS

PAROS

NAXOS

CALYMNOS

Halicarnassus

COS

AMORGOS

THERA

RHODES

| 0 | | 50 Miles |
| 0 | | 100 Km |

Knossos

ETE

Gortyn

Aegean

I

INTRODUCTION

1 · *From Solon to Socrates*

The title of this book has several implications. The first is purely
chronological. The period between Solon and Socrates includes the
sixth and fifth centuries, that is to say, the culmination and the end
of the archaic age, and the finest flowering of the classical age. I do
not include the fourth century, in spite of Plato and Praxiteles, because of the decline and change in politics during that period. The
second point is that both men, Solon and Socrates, were Athenians.
The present book is intended to describe the most important period
of *Greek* history; but its chief political and cultural centre is Athens.
We shall be compelled, both by the evidence of our sources and by
the force of historical facts, to emphasize again and again the part
played by Athens. Thirdly and finally, the two men of the title, by
their natures and activities, give a clear indication of what will be
the main contents and the scope of the history with which we are
dealing. Solon was a poet and a statesman; he is the first Greek
politician who still speaks to us. In his person is reflected the whole
aspect of the culture of his time, the unbroken connexion between
art and politics, between word and action. The unity of Greek life
was manifest in the man who wrote elegies in Ionic language and
metre, who loved the good things in life and passionately loved his
city, who firmly believed in the guidance of the gods, while at the
same time recognizing the political, social, and economic problems
of the day and courageously planning how to solve them. With him
begins the long line of 'political animals', of men who were great
citizens, but at the same time great men in their own right.

In a sense, the same can be said of Socrates, although his personality was infinitely more complex. He served as a soldier in war,
he believed in the rule of law, even to the point when it became a

1

question of life and death for himself. He was also the man who revolutionized Greek thought and died for doing so. With him one epoch ends, and another begins. His execution was the first unforgivable crime of the restored democracy, which traced its origins back to Solon. That crime, which remains a crime, even though some of the accusers were acting in good faith, made Plato despair of his city, and set him on the path to his own 'Utopian' state and his ideal of the philosopher-kings. Once again we detect the unity of the spiritual and political spheres, though in reverse order. Plato's contemporary was Isocrates, who in his numerous books combined a fervent Athenian patriotism with a growing distaste for petty polis politics and a longing for a greater Panhellenic unity. The polis community had been the *Leitmotif* of Solon's life and thought; now men began to turn away from the everyday life of the community towards the realities of larger political issues, or to the problems of the personal existence of the individual, or to the realms of pure thought. The last chapter of this book is concerned with these aspects.

It can be said that in the two centuries from Solon to Socrates the Greek city-state, the polis, reached its zenith and went beyond it. The polis started before Solon and survived Socrates; but in the sixth and fifth centuries it was at its greatest, its citizens were most loyal to it, and the community most nearly approached its ideal. This was true not only of Athens but of her in particular. The nature of the whole development is also reflected in the fact that Solon was a nobleman who in his professional activity as well as in his political aims represented a kind of middle class between the landowners and the manual workers, and that Socrates was a man of modest social origin who by his teaching tried to give the aristocratic youth of his time a new lease of life and a new purpose. The two men, neither of them an extremist, tried to create new bonds between the extremes in society, a new unity within the state, or a new picture of man. Neither of them was completely successful, but both are symbolic of that moderation and clarity of mind which are the mark of Athenian greatness.

2 · The Early History of the Greeks

The Greeks, like other Indo-European peoples then first entering upon the stage of history, invaded the Mediterranean area from the north, migrating in several waves between the late third and the early second millenium B.C. The facts of that early history are much disputed and our view of it frequently changes according to new discoveries or new interpretations.[1] It is, however, certain that the sea, which became the very life-blood of Greek existence, had been unknown to the invaders; the word for the sea, *thalassa*, belonged to a pre-Greek Mediterranean language. The other word (*hals*) simply meant the salt water in contrast to the fresh water of springs and rivers. The Greeks, after prehistoric beginnings, passed through their first historical period in the Mycenaean age (roughly between 1600 and 1100), when they built formidable fortresses, combined with modest palaces and small towns, in various districts of the Greek mainland. One of these sites, the place where Homer's Agamemnon ruled, was Mycenae in the Argolis, which gave its name to the whole era. Walls of enormous strength (the later Greeks called them Cyclopean) and narrow gateways protected an area in which the royal palace was the most important building; its main parts were built to the 'Megaron' plan, the same which later was inherited by the Greek temple. The 'Mycenaean' Greeks soon came under the strong influence of the unique civilization of 'Minoan' Crete, called after the mythical king Minos. Sea-power and domestic peace favoured the growth of a rich cultural and wordly life in which women, both human and divine, played a decisive part. While accepting the advanced art and technique as well as some of the habits and fashions of Crete, the Mycenaeans maintained their own way of life and their warlike strength. From about 1400 B.C. or possibly somewhat later, they seem to have been masters of Crete, perhaps after a disastrous volcanic eruption on the island of Thera.[1a] As raiders and traders the Mycenaeans ranged over large parts of the Mediterranean, and even founded colonies on the Aegean islands and the shores of Asia Minor. They survived the Minoan civilization for about two centuries. Whether there was a large 'Achaean' empire, possibly spreading from its centre Mycenae with its radiating roads to other parts of the Peloponnese or even to central Greece, remains doubtful. If Pylos was an important centre, it is more likely that it was an independent kingdom ('Nestor's') than part of a larger empire. Although a uniform Mycenaean civilization undoubtedly existed, and although in the *Iliad* Agamemnon is the commander in war over many minor rulers, we ought to hesitate before speaking of an Achaean or Mycenaean 'empire' or even 'nation'; the name of the Achaeans (like that of the Danaoi) will have been not more than an expanded tribal name. Where the land Aḫḫijava (= Achaea) of the Hittite sources was situated is still unknown; its king was technically on equal terms with the Hittite king, but that need not have meant that he was really very powerful; anyway, it seems unsafe to regard his state as a large realm in the Greek motherland.[2]

The Trojan war, whether a full-size war or a major raid, belongs to the period before 1200 B.C.; it is one of the last great events of the Mycenaean age and even shows features (such as the large 'bodyshield') which belong to pre-Mycenaean times. To Homer the Trojan war was the background rather than the theme of his stories of heroic deeds and men; there were other epics, or at least other oral traditions, which recounted events such as the sailing of the Greek fleet from Aulis, perhaps the events of the first nine years of the war, certainly the end of the siege and the sacking of the city. History is to some extent revealed in the catalogue of ships (*Il.* 2, 484 ff.), though only to some extent; the general setting will have been provided by the weakening of the Hittite empire.[3] After the war the Mycenaeans rapidly declined. We do not know whether that is a case of cause and effect; even the archaeologists cannot answer that question, at least not yet.

The Mycenaean period of the history of the Greeks was in many ways of lasting influence on later centuries. It was the age in which Greek mythology was born, the tales of gods and heroes, which were bound to the main sites of Mycenaean Greece, as, for instance, the sagas of the Seven against Thebes or the *nostoi*, the return of the Greek leaders from the Trojan war. It was the age when the gods of the invaders shared the pantheon with Cretan and even Asiatic gods, and above all goddesses, when the family of the Greek immortals grew into their final shape. Herodotus (2, 53) tells us that Hesiod and Homer 'made' the Greek gods. These two were not only the oldest poets known to later generations, but also the greatest, and the poet (*poietēs*) was the true 'maker', and always the teacher of the Greek world. It was the age from which the oral tradition of epic poetry sprang which culminated in Homer who, however, is no reliable witness to Mycenaean society. The records in Linear B, on the other hand, which were written in an early Greek otherwise unknown, but clearly a precursor of Homeric Greek, have taught us that there existed some literacy, though confined to the royal palaces, and that the rulers of the age were the heads of elaborate households with an extensive bureaucracy and a complex partition of labour among free people and slaves.[3a] The whole system was completely alien to Homeric kingship and most likely followed eastern models for which Minoan Crete was the intermediary; it did not survive the Mycenaean age, which ended during the twelfth century, when the creative force of those early Greeks was dying. What happened then is obscure. The destruction of the Mycenaean fortresses and the abandonment of many sites in Greece is usually explained by assuming a number of invasions. It seems, however, that parts of the Mycenaean population dispersed over the Aegean and farther east, while no traces of the alleged (Indo-European) invaders have been found who would have replaced them. Thus it is possible that the final upheaval was caused by a force stronger than human invaders, i.e. by climatic conditions causing drought, famine and emigration, or possibly even a revolt against the palaces with their well-stocked storerooms.

After almost two centuries, invaders did enter Greece, the Dorians and their relatives, the north-western Greeks, with an admixture of Illyrians. That migration (probably during the eleventh century) is usually called the Dorian invasion and is reflected in the legend of the return of the Heraclids; sometimes it is called the Aegean migration, because about the same time Thracian tribes such as the Phrygians and Mysians entered Asia Minor and destroyed the realm of the Hittites, while the general upheaval of migration even reached Syria and 'the peoples of the sea' threatened Egypt. Another distant effect was the migration to the west of some pre-Greek Aegean peoples, in particular the Tyrrhenians, the later Etruscans.

We know almost nothing about the dark centuries which followed (eleventh to ninth), and archaeology is lifting the curtain only slowly and haphazardly. Yet it was then that the historical Hellenic people took shape, and the foundations were laid for a new beginning, the very beginning of European history. It was then that in Greece and the Aegean the Bronze Age ended and the Iron Age began. It really was a beginning, as the Mycenaean legacy was no longer strong enough to impose itself on the newcomers; even so, many links across those dark centuries connected the past with the future. Quite a long time elapsed before the Greeks finally settled. There was a period of inner migration, and of emigration. Some of the pre-Doric Greeks in Laconia, for instance, settled in the northern Peloponnese, which thus acquired the name of Achaea; others went to Cyprus and farther. A number of tribes colonized the islands and the west coast of Asia Minor, settling roughly in the same order from north to south (Aeolians, Ionians, Dorians) as in the eastern parts of the motherland; the north-western tribes settled in the western districts of Greece. The 'Ionian migration' (probably about 1000 B.C.) brought Greeks from Attica and other places to Asia; it was the most important of the later movements, though it might be better to regard the whole process as a continuous and more or less coherent migration without clear tribal distinction. The name of the Ionians – as Iavan or such like – became the name for the Greeks in general throughout the east. The moves from north to south had come to an end, the division into tribes was of comparatively small importance, and the eternal Mediterranean theme of east–west relations imposed itself on the Greeks. Ever after the Aegean was a Greek sea, though for several centuries the sea routes were generally dominated by the Phoenicians. Greek history henceforth included the Asiatic Greeks as well, although for long periods they were under the rule of eastern empires. In fact, the Greeks of Asia Minor, especially the Ionians, largely freed as they were from ancient tribal and traditional bonds, and compelled by circumstances to adopt urban life, were the first to raise post-Mycenaean Greek culture to a high level, though for a long time they had little contact with the motherland.[4]

The geographical nature of Greece and the islands, and to a lesser degree also of the Asian shores, was a prime factor of the division into many small and independent political units.[5] That is true of Mycenaean and Hellenic times alike. Some Mycenaean rulers, as we have seen, may have temporarily attained pre-eminence over their neighbours, but so did rulers and states in later years as well. The general feeling of belonging to one and the same people did exist, because of the same gods, the same language, and the common Homeric heritage. What, however, is typical of the Greeks throughout their history is their 'particularism', their division into many small states. These belonged to two main types. Among the invaders, though they usually mixed with the previous population, the traditional tribal organization remained strong. Many tribes did not outgrow a form of settlement in villages and hamlets, loosely held together by the adherence to a common cult centre. That form of political community, or rather tribal society, was called *ethnos*; it still played a part in Homer's poetic world,[5a] but afterwards only prevailed in the western and northern parts of Greece. Historically far more important was the trend towards settling round one central town, mostly where there had been a major Mycenaean seat. The internal structure of such a community preserved many features of tribal organization and differed strongly from its Mycenaean predecessor. The settlement was no longer built round a royal palace. Increasingly, the settlement acquired an urban character; normally a wall enclosed residential areas as well as one or two cult centres, and a market-place. The tribal order of the people was maintained, or sometimes artificially reconstructed. The phratries (brotherhoods) preserved the ancient Indo-European word (*frater*) which no longer existed in Greek, while the phylae were tribes within a tribe; both groups went back to early times; so was the *oikos* – the family unit, though tribe and family were subordinated to the urban community. This was to be the polis, not quite appropriately translated as the city-state, since it always included the agrarian countryside outside the town. It was, in fact, both more and less than a state, rather a human community, often very small indeed, always held together by narrow space, by religion, by pride, by life. We shall have more to say about it later. Monarchy was no longer the autocratic and bureaucratic rule of the Mycenaean king as known from the Linear B tablets; it continued rather the popular tribal chieftainship. Gradually it lost its position and had to give way to the growing power of an aristocracy of rich and independent families ('clans') of landowners and warriors. That happened in

Greece itself, though also in Asia Minor, where the traditional tribal order with its phylae and phratries was without roots and to some extent artificial.[6] In some places monarchy was replaced by a dynastic oligarchy, a regal clan such as the Bacchiadae in Corinth, who shared among themselves the rule of the state. Monarchy as an institution survived in a few states only; but even then its power was more and more restricted. The chief, though not the only, example of this kind of development is Sparta. It is significant that the Greek language did not possess the Indo-European root denoting royalty (reg-); the words used for kingship were of non-Greek origin, such as (w)anax or basileus, the latter originally only a lower grade of rulership,[6a] or an expression merely meaning the 'founder' or the 'leader in war' (archagetes).

All the time, even before the Greeks finally settled in Asia Minor, they were becoming well acquainted with the east. The evidence for such relations has recently increased most conspicuously; here it must suffice to say that they were both friendly and hostile, some-times political, sometimes largely economic and cultural. Whenever the Greeks were influenced by more advanced civilizations, such as that of Babylon or Egypt or Lydia, they always shaped the eastern legacies in their own creative manner and started new developments. It seems that the Greeks learned in particular from Lydia what they knew and thought about the nature of despotic monarchy; the word tyrannos was of Lydian origin. A field of special interest is cosmology or rather cosmic mythology; there the analogies be-tween oriental and Greek stories – which will rarely have been direct borrowings – are often most surprising. Our present know-ledge is still very scanty; but it seems just as much a mistake to make the Greeks a mere outer fringe of the oriental world as to regard them as completely independent. Their creativeness was no less great for using and incorporating alien ideas and achievements.

3 · The Eighth Century

The Greek world which emerged from the dark centuries went through a period of great creative activity.[7] First, both in importance and in time, was the invention of the alphabet. Greeks who came in touch with the Phoenicians, perhaps in one of the trading settlements on the Syrian coast, adapted the Semitic alphabet just as they learned other things from Phoenician sailors, traders, and artisans. As with all Semitic peoples, the Phoenician alphabet consisted of consonants only; by using for the vowels some of the signs not needed in Greek, by changing the sound of others, and by adding a few signs, the alphabet was adapted to the Greek language. Though the regional Greek alphabets later differed in a few features, essentially the Greek alphabet was one, used by all Greek dialects and soon spreading far and wide, above all to Italy. It was the first essential instrument of literacy and intellectual activity, which the other European peoples inherited from the Greeks. Its making was a stroke of genius, of the creative and at the same time adaptable genius of the Greek people.

Another remarkable feature of the period was the development of a new style in art, especially in vase painting. The break caused by the last Greek migrations completed a change which had started before. It must be regarded as the transformation to a new primitiveness, most notable in the protogeometric style which seems to have been independent of the vicissitudes of tribal migrations. In the place of the declining Mycenaean realism an abstract or stylized art emerged, culminating in the geometric style, in which abstract ornaments and eventually human figures and scenes of severely geometric design covered the various vessels in a number of bands or friezes. The last and most perfect phase of the geometric style is found in the so-called Dipylon vases, chiefly from the Kerameikos cemetery at Athens (middle eighth century). Of the many symptoms of that great general transformation, which must have taken place, the geometric style is the one which we can still see and thus study. It shows that Athens played an essential part in that early development, as also stated by Thucydides (1, 10). The only important Mycenaean state in Greece which had not been destroyed by the migrations, Athens became a haven for refugees and probably the centre of migration from the motherland to Asia Minor.

It seems likely that at least some of the scenes depicted on geometric vases refer to heroic stories as told in epic poetry. Homer, as the poet of the *Iliad*, is more or less contemporary with the Dipylon vases, and the *Odyssey*, whether or not by the same poet, was probably composed a few decades later; the limits are roughly between 750 and 700. The remarkable fact that Homer and the geometric style were contemporaries has frequently perturbed modern scholars, who found a profound contrast between the mature art of epic poetry and the primitive style of painting and clay figures. In fact, what looks primitive is of high and to some extent even sophisticated artistic standards; it was a new start after the artistic tradition had reached a low level during the dark centuries since the decline of the Mycenaeans. It was different with poetry. The epic tradition was never interrupted; it lived on, chiefly in Asia Minor, and was handed down orally from one generation to the next. That made it possible that the first surviving expression of the Greek mind was at the same time its greatest. In Homer, whose home was among the Asiatic Greeks, the oral tradition which went back to Mycenaean times reached its culmination and its end; it makes no difference whether he wrote himself or dictated to a scribe. Centuries of history have gone into the making of *Iliad* and *Odyssey*, memories of the Mycenaean age as well as impressions of the surrounding contemporary world of proud aristocrats. The most 'historical' section of the epics, the catalogue of ships in *Iliad* II, clearly derives from Mycenaean times, though it is equally certain that it includes features of the period after the Dorian migration. The bards (*aoidoi*) were the connecting link throughout the centuries. They had sung the 'deeds of men' to the rulers in the Mycenaean palaces; they did the same for the later chieftains and noble lords. Memory and creative innovation, poetic genius and the tradition of the craft, all joined to keep epic poetry alive – in fact, to take it to its highest perfection when Homer produced his great poems.[8] He became the eternal teacher of the Greeks.

Whatever the Trojan war had been like, for Homer, and for all time to follow (down to Heinrich Schliemann, who, in the late nineteenth century, discovered the sites of Troy and Mycenae), it had become part of Greek history, roughly belonging to the twelfth century, a panorama of heroic men performing heroic deeds, of their all-too-human gods, of their rich, exuberant lives. To speak of a Homeric society can be misleading, because Homer pictures a composite world; he does not simply depict the aristocracy of his own time nor, in fact, the world of the Mycenaeans or of any period in between. In his lifetime, during the eighth century, everywhere a closed aristocratic society was held together by its firm solidarity, its great wealth, and its proud traditional code of behaviour. It was built upon a number of clans (*genē*) which at times fought each other, but were also bound together by common interest and family bonds, even beyond the boundaries of the single state. Many inter-state marriages took place, though it would be misleading to speak of a Panhellenic society. If the Trojan war was supposed to be a common Greek enterprise, it remained a struggle of allied, but independent states, and if it was all about the elopement of an adulterous woman, that too may have been significant for a society whose masculine pride was at stake. The position of women in the epic tradition was in general higher than in later times, but this did not so much apply to the whole sex as to the legal wife and mother. During the same eighth century, however, society was to undergo changes in which the aristocrats became conscious of the possibilities and the duties which the new polis community opened up for them. In possession of most of the land, relying on dependent peasants or even serfs, the nobles, freed from any royal interference, exercised political power. Though owners of comparatively large estates, they began to concentrate in towns whose political and economic importance slowly increased. The market-place (*agora*) became the centre for meetings and jurisdiction as well as a place of worship and trading. The non-nobles, too, mostly farmers and tenants, tended as far as possible to live in town where most of the artisans and other professions, up to then migrant, also settled. It was in the towns, as is shown, for example, by the recent excavations at Smyrna,[9] that, probably still during the eighth century, the polis started its long life as a completely new form of human community, a community of citizens – or those who were to become citizens – living either in the city or the countryside, ruled over by a class of noble land-owners. Homer, in his description of the shield of Achilles (*Il.* 18, 478 ff.), depicts the life of an early polis in peace and war.

Speaking of 'the polis', we must not forget that there were very many of such city-states, and that to some extent they differed. But the Greeks themselves regarded the polis as one particular type of state. Aristotle was by no means the first to teach that historical truth. Perhaps first on colonial ground in Asia Minor, walled cities became the rule, particularly as they were surrounded by a non-Greek population. The cities of the motherland relied for quite a long time on a citadel, which served as a home for the gods and a refuge in time of war. The noblemen, though divided into clans and families often at loggerheads with one another, learnt to become part of the political community of the polis, even if the ruling part, rather than a self-contained class, while the non-nobles soon began to demand personal and eventually political rights. The struggle between the nobility and the lower classes, that is to say, between rich and poor as well, was to last a long time; it could not be decided, if at all, without some hard bargaining and even fighting. That conflict is first clearly reflected in the work of Hesiod, the last of the great epic poets and the first to write about himself and about his class, the hard-working poor farmers who suffered injustice and oppression. Living in Boeotia, about 700 B.C., he produced in his *Works and Days* a document of humanity and at the same time a picture of society. Justice, or 'Just Retaliation', Dike, the divine daughter of Zeus, came down to earth among the just and the unjust. This is part of the process of 'personification', by which the abstract concept and the goddess (whichever is earlier) form a unit,[9a] a process that was to become a common feature of Greek thought and belief. Hesiod's world was separated from that of Homer geographically as well as socially. Yet he learnt his poetry from the old bards, who at his time began to be replaced by the rhapsodes, men who no longer sang to the lyre but held a staff and recited poetry which in general was no longer their own, though it was probably still a kind of musical rendering. It is likely that the rhapsodes were chiefly responsible for preserving the epics which were to become the Bible of the Greeks. The audience too might have been different – no longer Homer's noble warriors but 'the people'; the occasions were now not so much the banquets of the rich as the gatherings and festivals of the community. Hesiod also wrote the *Theogony*, a poem on the origin and the genealogy of the gods; in it he made Homer's Olympians part of a larger number of deities seen in a sort of systematic theology. In his myth of the ages of mankind (*Erga* 109 ff.) he constructed, as it were, the first philosophy of man's history, a deeply pessimistic philosophy with its symbols of the metals declining from gold to iron, and its nostalgic pictures of the heroes inserted between the Bronze and Iron Ages.[10] Herodotus' statement (2, 53) that Homer and Hesiod had taught the Greeks everything about the gods is in a sense true.

Constitutionally, the polis continued the tribal order with its personal subdivisions: phylae, phratries, clans. That order was only partially replaced by a regional structure, and the polis always retained the three original elements of the political order: the king or chieftain, the council of the elders, and the assembly of the warriors.[11] In the gradual process whereby aristocratic rule replaced monarchy an important stage was reached when kingship, from being a 'charismatic' position ('by the grace of the gods'), was changed into an elected office. This office had different names in different states; but it always meant the position of the 'first man' in the state. At the same time the regal power tended to become divided among several officials, three in particular, corresponding to the chief functions of a ruler: priestly, military, judicial. The whole development took place as a kind of peaceful revolution; monarchy in Greece – apart from *tyrannis* – never became the hated concept it was to be in Rome.[12]

The polis was a religious as well as a political community. Civic officials performed religious rituals, and there never was – with the exception of the staff of a few oracles – a priestly class, a clergy. Thus, although state and religion were one, it is quite wrong to speak of an established church. There was no such thing. The local main deity became the monarch in an unmonarchical state, a fact which strengthened the forces of isolation in every state, its self-sufficiency (*autarkia*). This principle was broken, probably for the first time, in Ionia, where the Greeks must often have felt the need of joining hands against external foes. We hear of an inter-state union, a league of clearly religious as well as political character. Its origin is obscure. The most surprising feature of this Ionian League is a kingship which may have been the relic of a real central authority. It was natural for the Ionian cities to join hands, separated as they were from one another by mountains or the sea, and open to attacks from the hinterland. They had a common sanctuary of Poseidon, on the promontory of Mycale. Other Greek leagues followed in the motherland, all starting on a religious basis, but with a political, and possibly economic, purpose. Whether the combination of a religious league (*amphictiony*) and a rudimentary monarchy can throw some light on the emergence of the independent city-state in Asia Minor seems doubtful.[13]

4 · The Great Colonization (c. 750–550)

The urbanization of Greece and the Aegean led to that large number of independent 'city-states' of which we have spoken. At the same time the Greeks grew more conscious of being one people. Homer and Hesiod gave them a common treasury of language, gods, and human behaviour, which had sufficient strength to counteract the dividing forces of the dialects, the local cults, and the multitude of states. The 'Panhellenic' aspects of the Greek mind found expression largely outside politics, for instance, in the competitions at the festivals at Olympia, recorded from 776 B.C., whose oracle of Zeus, however, never reached Panhellenic significance, and at other sacred places, or in the growing authority of the Delphic oracle. The intercommunication between various parts of the Greek world was socially supported by an aristocracy which, as we have mentioned before, upheld many inter-state connexions and generally shared the same code of honour, hospitality, and prowess.

The colonization of the west coast of Asia Minor during the eleventh to ninth centuries was a prologue to later adventures.[14] The Panhellenic links, however, we have mentioned had very little to do with the great movement by which, from the middle of the eighth century onwards, new Greek cities were founded on most of the Mediterranean coasts. The movement, which followed occasional precedents by Greek travellers, traders, and artisans, was almost contemporary with the Phoenician move of founding trading places as far west as Spain. The prosperity of the ancient Phoenician cities in Syria suffered greatly under the harsh rule of the Assyrians, and the Phoenician trade began to decline. Only in the west was a new great centre rising, Carthage, founded by men from Tyre, late in the ninth century according to tradition, though archaeology seems to indicate a somewhat later date. Egypt went through a long period of decline and inactivity. In Asia Minor, Phrygians and Lydians were building their new realms, so far without threatening the Greeks there. The onslaught of the Cimmerian hordes from the northern steppes about the middle of the seventh century destroyed the Phrygian empire, but was repelled by the Lydians, who thereafter became less friendly neighbours to the Greek cities, till new powers arose, the Chaldaeans, the Medes, the Persians, who one after another gained supremacy over the Near East. All these events contributed to make the sea an open field for Greek adventure and expansion. When, from the middle of the sixth century, Persia ventured westwards, Greek colonization had run its course.

There were comparatively few 'mother-cities' whence colonists frequently set out.[15] In most areas of colonization the first to go out were the Euboeans, closely followed by Corinth. Thus, Eretria and Chalcis, Corinth and Megara in central Greece, Miletus, Phocaea, and Rhodes in Asia Minor were among the foremost. The leader of a colonial expedition, the 'founder' (oikistes), was always a citizen of the mother-city, but people from other states usually joined in the enterprise. In general, the colony kept good relations with the mother-city; cults and social structure were usually the same, though there were exceptions, and power politics played their part. The sequence of foundations hardly ever followed a fixed geographical scheme; an earlier colony, as, for instance, Cumae in Italy, was frequently farther away than later ones lying on the route, and the colonists – for whatever reason – might pass by the most fertile agricultural land. The ethnic tradition persisted; Ionian cities founded Ionian colonies, Dorian cities Dorian. At the same time each colony was an independent polis of its own, and colonisation was something entirely different from what it meant in modern times.

The Greek city-state spread over a large area. It is time to discuss at greater length the type of state it was.[16] With the growing urbanization of which we have spoken, the emergence of town-centred states was a natural development that started during the eighth century in Ionia, and soon reached the motherland. The Greek polis was a city as well as a state, and there were more than a hundred of such units. Within the narrow boundaries of a territory rarely larger than 400 square miles – in Greece itself only Sparta and Athens held larger areas – it had all the characteristic features of limited space. It centred round the common 'hearth' just as the *oikos* centred round its own hearth, and its goddess Hestia was worshipped in the market-place as in the individual home. One town, usually walled, with its immediate countryside formed that 'community of place' which Aristotle (*pol.* 1260b, 41) mentions as the first essential quality of a polis. Above all, however, it was the community, the state, of its citizens. The official name of any Greek state was the name of its people and not of the city; where we say 'Athens', the Greeks said 'the Athenians'. Within the narrow space the citizens were able to build a community under the rule of the city god or goddess. Its membership gradually changed and grew, and it found its spiritual basis in the ideas of justice and good order (*dike, eunomia*). That meant at the same time that, through its community life, the polis educated and civilized its members. In a climate which, by the open-air existence at least of the men, provided natural and easy ways of human communication, work and leisure, politics and the matters of the mind, and also, of course, less dignified pleasures and activities, all were blended into one. At first, only the nobles had been citizens; gradually other free men gained partial or full rights of citizenship. Foreigners, women, and slaves were excluded, though the latter in general were well treated, and could even acquire certain rights of legal standing.

Limited space also meant that the polis on the whole looked inwards rather than outwards, though for the same reason different states were often close neighbours, and as neighbours do, they frequently quarrelled about some border district. We hear of a number of such disputes in subsequent centuries; the most famous was the Lelantine war between Chalcis and Eretria in Euboea, which is even supposed to have led to large coalitions of allies on either side (late eighth or, less likely, early seventh century). We realize that overpopulation might easily have arisen because of the small amount of arable land available within the polis boundaries. This was one and perhaps the most important cause of that trend towards emigration which made the Great Colonization possible. The hunger for land was not confined to poor farmers who might have got into economic difficulties, or to landless people, trying to find a better living. There were also the second and third sons of noblemen, who had no claim to the family estate; they would be eager to live on a new estate of their own. Other causes of discontent were civil strife among the citizens of a polis, or within the noble class alone; also the mere lust for adventure and gain, or the urge for discovering unknown lands and peoples; the latter was often the effect rather than the cause of colonization. To some extent, and sometimes even as the primary reason, the increased possibilities of trade caused people to leave their native cities; many of the new sites were chosen because they had good harbours as well as fertile land. The need for importing grain was great in most states. The leadership of all the colonizing expeditions was in the hands of aristocrats, but the body of colonists was as a rule composed of people from all social strata.

Everywhere the colonists settled near the sea, though several colonies had no harbour at all. There usually was some form of agreement with the natives, though not always without the use of force. In general, the colonies brought benefits to the natives too. The coasts of the Near East were mostly in the hands of big powers and therefore not free; one attempt to settle in Cilicia was frustrated by the Assyrians. A very successful Greek foundation was at Al-Mina in northern Syria. It may have been founded about 800 B.C. by Euboeans, but had close connexions with the Greeks on Cyprus. It was essentially a trading post and developed into a lively centre.[17] The approach to the west, on the other hand, was practically free, and the finds of Greek vases show that some trade reached the shores of Sicily as well as Etruria and Latium in the early eighth century, before any permanent settlement was established.[18] With the short-lived settlement on Pithecusae (Ischia) and with Cumae, the Chalcidians began the long series of Italian colonies; Cumae was to be the main gateway for Greek civilization (e.g. the alphabet) to reach Etruscans and Romans. Later it became itself the mother-city of Naples. In Sicily, various mother cities founded colonies, covering all the shores, though the process did not follow any preconceived plan; only the west remained in the hands of the Phoenicians, and the interior belonged mainly to the natives. The Sicilian Greeks were, on the whole, just as divided among themselves as the poleis in the motherland. The cities founded chiefly by Chalcis and Megara covered first the eastern and then the northern and southern coasts, culminating in the most western Greek cities of Himera in the North and Selinus in the South (see map, p. 116). Syracuse, on the other hand, founded by Corinth, followed an aggressive policy both towards neighbouring Greek cities and towards the Sicels.

For the acquisition of extensive fertile land, South Italy provided an even better opportunity. Here a different mother-country took the main initiative, Achaea with its small cities in the northern Peloponnese. The Achaeans had never known large fertile plains; now they found them amply in Italy. They founded Sybaris, Croton, and Metapontum, while Locris established another Locri (Epizephyrii), and Sparta, as we shall learn in more detail (p. 37), founded Taras (Tarentum). Many other colonies followed, among them the Sybarite foundation of Poseidonia (Paestum). The many flourishing cities in southern Italy with their comparatively large territories caused the whole area to be given the name of 'Greater Greece' (*Magna Graecia*); it was here that the Hellenes received the name they held in Latin and in most languages ever since: Graeci, the Greeks.

Even bolder expeditions brought some Greeks farther west. They discovered the ancient country of Tartessus in Spain beyond the straits of Gibraltar; its silver, as well as the tin of Britain, became a major object of trade. Phocaean traders founded Massilia (Marseilles) at the mouth of the Rhone (about 600 B.C.); it was to become, especially after Spain and the Atlantic had been closed to the Greeks (see below), one of the greatest centres of Greek trade and influence, both of which spread from there overland. In contrast to the east and even the north-east, the Greeks did not meet here with any older and possibly superior civilization. Their own influence in Sicily, Italy, and even Gaul was enormous; Etruscans, Romans, Celts became their disciples.[19]

In the early sixth century the colonization of the west began to lose impetus. Much earlier, during the seventh century, Greeks had approached the northern coast of Africa; colonists from Thera founded Cyrene, which was an isolated Greek stronghold among Libyans, between Egypt and Carthage.[20] Naucratis in the Nile delta was a Milesian foundation, essentially a trading post which soon developed several different quarters of Ionian origin, and above all the Hellenion, a centre for all kinds of Greek traders who monopolized all Greek trade with Egypt. For two early foundations (seventh and sixth century respectively) we have written decrees, for Cyrene (ML 5) and for the settlement of Opuntian Locrians at Naupactus (ML 13). They reveal different aspects of the colonists' position.[20a]

Colonization in the east, though perhaps never quite broken off since the Ionian migration, was, on the whole, later than the colonization of the west. The main efforts from the middle of the seventh century onwards, with Miletus as the chief colonizer, were directed towards the shores of the Black Sea. That sea had long been an 'unfriendly' sea (pontos axeinos) before it finally became the friendly and hospitable sea (euxeinos). We hear of no support by the Delphic god, as it had become increasingly important in the west, but Apollo of Didyma was a neighbour of Miletus and was naturally interested in Milesian colonization.[21] Again, trade considerations were the chief incentive, though it was largely the corn trade which decisively supported the domestic economy in Greece. Olbia (Odessa) and Panticapaeum (Kertsch) in the north, Phasis in the east (Medea's Colchis), Sinope and Trapezus in the south were prominent. Soon Miletus found a competitor – though one with whom a friendly agreement may have been concluded – in Megara, which not only founded Heracleia, the mother-city of Chersonesus in the Crimea, but above all Calchedon and Byzantium, the two cities dominating the Bosporus, the entrance to the Black Sea. Calchedon, with its rich hinterland, was founded first; Byzantium, with its wonderful harbour, later – a fact among others that should warn us not to regard colonization as a coherent and planned process, and trade as its primary stimulus. These and further colonies in the Hellespont and the Propontis, that is, in the passage leading to the Black Sea, were among the later foundations. In the same period, sometimes even earlier, various cities founded colonies along the southern shores of Thrace, thus closing the gap in the circle of Greek cities round the Aegean sea, and opening up a region which was particularly rich in mines and timber, and from where, especially from Thasos, excellent wine was exported. Corinth, which founded Potidaea in the Chalcidice, at the same time secured her route to the west by establishing colonies at Corcyra (Corfu) and other places along the Adriatic coast which, as for instance Epidamnus, also served as the terminal points of trade routes across the Greek mainland. Increased trade was attracted to the regions which exported corn, such as Sicily, Egypt, and the Black Sea. The greatest need was to feed the people.

The upper classes, who were the leaders both at home and in the colonies, were no longer a pure nobility by birth; descent, though still important for a long time to come, slowly gave way to the importance of wealth, a process which the Greeks called the transition from aristocracy to oligarchy. However, the rise of non-nobles to the upper classes took time, and though some nobles began to enrich themselves by trading, their chief aim remained to keep, and if possible to extend, their hold on the land. It is significant that the ruling class was frequently known as the 'landowners' (*geomoroi*), or, as in Chalcis, as the 'horse-breeders' (*hippobotai*). Many poor peasants were forced into dependence or even serfdom. Naturally there were counter-moves, and the growing importance and wealth of people who did not own land were bound to have their effect on the social scene.

5 · The Seventh Century

Jacob Burckhardt, in his *History of Greek Civilization*, calls the era roughly coinciding with the seventh century the age of the 'agonal and colonial man'. There is a good deal of truth in this. *Agon* means competition, and the word *agonistic* describes the world of athletic competitions which played an increasing part in the life of the aristocracy and the polis. The agonistic idea gave an outstanding position to the athletic victors, in particular to those in the Olympian stadion race, and later in the chariot race as well. By the word *agonal*, however, a wider concept is indicated, the spirit of fair competition in all spheres of life, even in warfare. The love of competition is common among early societies,[22] but, as far as I know, we never find it, as with the Greeks, permeating life as a whole, private and public, artistic and political, within the state and between the states. The realities of economic and social life kept their importance, sometimes at the expense of agonal fairness; but the spirit of the latter was real too. The 'colonial' man was the Greek citizen in foreign surroundings, who was usually thrown into close contact with fellow citizens of different origins. His outlook was less traditional, though hardly less Greek, than that of the average citizen in the Aegean. Throughout the seventh century colonization was an outstanding event. It showed, among other things, that the polis under the leadership of an aristocracy was a body very much alive, that its social and political structure, like its gods, could be transferred to distant parts, and that in foreign surroundings it generally proved a stronghold of Greek civilization, spreading it among the native population. Where the Greek settlers were a small minority, and the natives a half-civilized and receptive majority, as, for instance, on the northern shores of the Black Sea, a mixed society and a mixed civilization still preserved much of the Greek legacy.

In the extended Greek world some places were prominent in various cultural achievements. First Crete, later Corinth and Rhodes were centres of art. In Crete eastern influence started the orientalizing style of vase painting, with its animals and monsters, which reached its fullest expression in Corinthian pottery. In Crete probably also originated the earliest stone sculpture, called 'daedalic' after the mythical Cretan sculptor and inventor Daedalus. Largely inspired by Egyptian art, Greek sculpture started here on its triumphal road. Towards the later part of the century Ionia's advanced and refined civilization began to exercise a strong influence on the mind, and especially the art, of the islanders and the people of the motherland.

During the same period the polis underwent changes which were chiefly brought about by two developments, the gradual rise of the free non-nobles and subsequently a new military structure and secondly, the rise of the individual. The interrelation of politics and military service led to a change both of tactics and constitution. What gradually emerged was the 'polis of hoplites', when all who could afford their own armour and weapons, and also leave home for a certain period – they were mainly the owners of medium-sized estates – would serve as heavily armed soldiers (hoplites), fighting in closed ranks, the 'phalanx'. They were a new type of soldier, subject to strict discipline and much training; they replaced the single combatants of Homeric battles, and to some extent also the cavalry of noblemen. It took time for the hoplite phalanx to become an established fact, but in the end the ability, both physical and economic, to serve as a soldier made the citizen. Even so, political, social, and economic differences persisted, and often became even stronger and more clear-cut. They opened the door to a new kind of political leader.

It was a period in which the individual for the first time found the means of expressing his or her personal feelings and experiences by writing lyric poetry. Archilochus, Alcman, Sappho, Alcaeus, Tyrtaeus, Mimnermus belong to the seventh century, great names although little more than fragments of their poems have survived. Archilochus and the two poets from Lesbos, Sappho and Alcaeus, all members of the aristocracy, though Archilochus was a bastard, put into words their private and individual emotions and their political adventures and feelings; Alcman and Tyrtaeus, both writing their poetry in Sparta, the one choral lyrics, the other warlike elegies, were firmly linked with their community and belonged essentially to the political sphere. The lyric poets are impressive witnesses of men's (and even women's) liberation as individual personalities. At the same time political individualism developed out of the tensions of social life. There must have been many people who were looking for somebody to provide a new and better response to their needs and experiences, and common sense or ambition or both would bring about new forms of political leadership. There was, on the one hand, the urgent demand of the ordinary peasants no longer to be the victims of the arbitrary jurisdiction of the aristocrats. From Hesiod onwards oppression and injustice were causes of growing complaint, and the first remedy was the codification of law. Some of the lawgivers of whom we hear may be legendary, but there can be no doubt that in various parts of the Greek world laws were written down for the first time. These codes will in general have contained the current customary law, and that means that they favoured the nobles; but the mere fact that rules of law were laid down and could be known by all was a help and probably prevented a good deal of injustice. Juridical progress is also manifest, for instance, in the Athenian Dracon's distinction between murder and manslaughter (see p. 57). Most important of all is that the community began to take the place of clan and class in the task of jurisdiction. Laws relating to the family, the rights of inheritance, and the position of slaves and foreigners were among the matters which increasingly became the concern of the state. The 'Law of Gortyn', largely preserved in an inscription of the early fifth century, contains much that goes back to earlier times, showing remarkable progress in legal knowledge. Of most of the legislations, e.g. of Zaleucus in Italian Locri and Charondas in Catane, very little is known; but the general tendency was to give the state a larger share in jurisdiction, and to weaken the arbitrary decisions of the noble judges who might even be bribed. Sometimes the nobles themselves were either sensible enough, or compelled by circumstances, to acknowledge and even to promote the new developments. Blood-vengeance, with its curse of constant feuds among the clans, and the dangerous right of taking the law into one's own hands, slowly gave way to the growing legal supremacy of the state and its officials.[23] Hence eventually sprang the idea, fostered by a deepening belief in divine justice, that the community of the polis was based on the rule of law.

However important the codification of law was, it proved insufficient in the long run to satisfy the rising class of non-nobles, to solve the difficult economic problems, and to create the peaceful atmosphere which was badly wanted. The community needed a stronger supreme authority, a unified domestic and foreign policy, and above all social peace and economic prosperity. In various cities the opportunity was seized by individual leaders, strong personalities who gained power by usurpation. The Greeks called them 'tyrants', a word which was imported from the Lydian language, and which originally had no implication of cruelty and was synonymous with 'king'. Actually most of the tyrants were excellent rulers who brought social and cultural progress to their states. The hatred of *tyrannis* was at first the expression of the feelings of the other aristocrats, who felt the hostile impact of a popular leader. Later it was caused by the moral decline of the dynasties which never survived their third generation. As a result of that hatred, in fifth- and fourth-century democracy, freedom was regarded as identical with non-monarchical rule.

The tyrants[24] were mostly members of the ruling class, who based their power on the support of mercenaries and of the majority of the people. In particular they helped the peasants in their economic difficulties. Ambitious men who aimed at personal power, they always tried to found a ruling dynasty; but in general they knew how to combine such aims with the interest of their states. An early example is Pheidon of Argos, usually known as a king rather than a tyrant. His power in the Peloponnese was considerable, and he was famous for introducing regular weights and measures.[25] Other outstanding rulers during the seventh and early sixth centuries were the Orthagorids in Sicyon, especially Cleisthenes, grandfather and namesake of the later Athenian statesman; the Cypselids in Corinth, Cypselus and his son Periander; Thrasybulus in Miletus; Phalaris of Acragas, who seems to have earned by particular cruelty the title of tyrant in its later meaning. Later in the sixth century came Polycrates of Samos, Lygdamis of Naxos, and Peisistratus of Athens. The tyrants, by inter-marriage and common interests, formed a small international society of their own; they were able to look beyond the frontiers of their polis and promoted trade and colonization. Perhaps the most remarkable man among them all was Periander, who was responsible for the policy of Corinthian expansion and colonization; his foundations were far more dependent on the mother-city than usual.[26] The colonies of Corinth and Corcyra secured the entrance to the Adriatic, and Corinth, famous or notorious for her pottery and her hetaerae, was for a long time the Greek city outstanding in trade, art, and manufacture, as well as in influence on the wider Greek world, until Athens took over.

The urgent dangers of social disruption and economic distress were the greatest help the tyrants found when they seized power. Sometimes, however, the parties involved in the social struggle came to an agreement to elect an arbitrator (*aesymnetes*) who was to find a solution to which both sides could consent. That happened, for instance, at Mytilene, where civil strife brought several men to the position of tyrant, only to lose it again. Eventually Pittacus was generally acclaimed as supreme leader, though not by his former friend, the poet Alcaeus, who regarded him as a tyrant. The distinction between the two positions of tyrant and aesymnetes was by no means always clear, although as a rule the aesymnetes was a special official, appointed for a fixed period; in fact, Pittacus did not conform to this pattern, though he resigned after a rule of ten years, and Aristotle (*pol.* 1285a, 31) called aesymnety an 'elective tyranny'. Solon, who was clearly elected as a mediator, expressly refused to become a tyrant. He was at the same time one of the great lawgivers. We have therefore three different names – tyrant, aesymnetes, lawgiver – for a position which in all its forms reflected the same historical phenomenon, the rise of the political individual and his ascendancy within the state.

There can be no doubt that the work of lawgivers, tyrants, and arbitrators had the greatest effect on the development of the polis. Although one tyrant might support the other, the bonds between one polis and another, as established previously by aristocratic solidarity, weakened, and the 'personality' of each single polis became more distinct.[27] Most states flourished under their temporary rulers, and the peasantry acquired a better economic position. As stressed above, the establishment of written laws was the first decisive step in the rise of the non-nobles, a means of saving the people from unjust judgements, such as those of which Hesiod had complained. Thus, the power of the nobles was somewhat restricted, and trade became an important and more respectable profession. Gold and silver became highly valued, and this form of mobile wealth soon competed with land ownership; but it took time till metal, first counted in weight, replaced 'oxen' as the measure of value. Pheidon of Argos is supposed to have issued the first coins in Greece itself, following the example of Lydia and some Ionian cities. But this tradition about Pheidon is almost certainly not true. With the 'turtle' coins of Aegina, on the other hand, issued hardly earlier than c. 600 and probably later, there began the silver coinage of the Greek motherland. Since the development of coinage largely resulted from the economic conditions of the late seventh century, we may be allowed to speak of its beginnings here. The names *drachme* (a handful) and *oboloi* (spits) reveal that the coins replaced an earlier iron money in the shape of spits, which might be of practical use, but were rather unsuitable for trading.[28] For a time, coins were minted in larger units only (staters=two drachmas), and the full impact of a money economy cannot be dated earlier than the sixth century, a fact confirmed by the few significant hoards that have been found. It is therefore a mistake to attribute the social upheavals of the later seventh century to the introduction of coinage. Trade and manufacture certainly expanded during that time, though probably to a lesser degree than is frequently believed.

Slavery had always existed among the Greeks, though it rarely meant more than that the wealthy had several domestic slaves, and the less wealthy a few. With the growth of trade and manufacture, slaves were increasingly used in business and in mining, hardly in agriculture, though their numbers anyway remained small, and free labour was at the core of economic life.[29]

The fact that for a time the whole population of a polis was governed by one man contributed to a growing feeling of equality among the people, or at least to the longing for it. It became more and more the leading aim of the non-nobles. It would be going too far to speak of an anticipated democracy, but when one-man rule everywhere came to an early end, the budding institutions of the city-state survived, and the constitution which emerged usually showed more democratic features. However powerful the tyrants had been, in the long run the polis and its society were stronger than the individual. The trend towards more democratic forms of government showed itself in oligarchies as well, for instance, at Chios. An inscription from the first half of the sixth century[30] clearly reveals a constitution with a democratic council and other democratic features, and a highly advanced stage of jurisdiction with money penalties, that is to say, penalties in staters which could be weights in silver as well as coins. Among the eastern Greeks in particular money economy was spreading, and other property besides land began increasingly to provide an additional qualification for social and political status. The old *oikos*-economy that was bound to landed property began to give way to an economy which, though never state-directed, involved the polis community as a whole. The composition of society changed, and *nouveaux riches* frequently took the place of the impoverished scions of the nobility. In the sixth-century poet Theognis of Megara (as far as we can separate his verse from many later additions) we have an eloquent and strongly biased witness of the struggle of the old aristocracy, for its traditional ideas and ideals which were partly adopted and partly destroyed by the rising lower classes.

Few among the many Greeks states, during the seventh century, played an important part in the general Greek scene; this is certainly true of those two states which were chiefly to determine the further course of Greek history. In Athens tyranny came late, and only after

Solon had tried an agreed solution. Sparta never had a tyrant. These are special cases which demand special treatment. We know more about these two states than about any other Greek polis, though we must realize that there were others whose development was not interrupted by the rule of powerful individuals. They were mostly states in more remote areas, and their domestic history generally consisted of the gradual change from a long-lasting aristocracy to a moderate oligarchy. The history of Sparta and Athens during the sixth century and afterwards cannot be understood without going back to their beginnings. That is the reason why the next two chapters had to be written as they have been written.

II

EARLY SPARTA

1 · Creation of a State

The early history of Sparta, like that of most Greek states, is hidden by the clouds of legend. In the case of Sparta, however, it is not simply the story of a mythical founder or some other mythical story. With Sparta, history and legend are more closely interwoven than anywhere else because the fame of her institutions and the outstanding qualities of her citizens gave later writers the chance of idealizing the picture and creating an artificial historical phenomenon, 'the Spartan Mirage'.[1] Of Lycurgus, the lawgiver, if not the founder, of that ideal Sparta, Plutarch states that 'nothing can be said that is undisputed'. In spite of this statement, he then continues to write the life story of the man whom the Greeks themselves did not know whether to call a man or a god. Plutarch's illogical attitude only confirms that his account of the *Life of Lycurgus* is legend rather than history, and so is most of the post-Herodotean evidence. The conservatism of later Sparta, on the other hand, retained a good many early elements, and that is another reason why a chapter on early Sparta is needed if we want to understand her later character.

Today, with the help of linguistics and archaeology, critical scholarship is a little more able to distinguish between history and legend – though even now modern historians disagree widely, and essential questions are still unanswered. Most of what we can say about early Sparta remains hypothetical, and will probably always remain so. I shall try to find a path between the few facts and the many possibilities and assumptions with which ancient tradition and modern scholarship tend to illuminate (or to obscure) Spartan history, but I am well aware that my reconstruction may seem to some people no more satisfactory than all the rest.[2]

Laconia or Lacedaemon,[3] the central region of the southern

Peloponnese, includes the fertile valley of the Eurotas between the mountains of Taygetus and Parnon. It had been an Achaean realm in Mycenaean times, which left traces of survival, e.g. in cult names such as *Pohoidan* (Poseidon). Whether Laconia, like the Argolis and Messenia, was invaded round about 1200 B.C. is doubtful; but at any rate the period meant the end of the Mycenaeans here, and it was

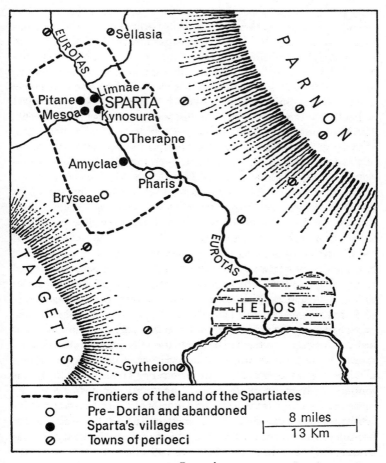

2. Laconia

followed by severe depopulation. Almost two hundred years later Dorian invaders settled in Laconia, and a new epoch began. This invasion found its mythical and propagandist reflection in the legend of the 'Return of the Heraclids', although Heracles was not originally a Dorian hero, and only the two royal families, and perhaps a few others in Sparta, claimed him as their ancestor.[4] The way the invaders took is not known, though the situation of Sparta makes it clear that they entered the valley from the north. The legendary route from the straits of Rhion–Antirhion up the Alpheios valley is not impossible, but it is perhaps more likely that they came across the Corinthian Isthmus and entered Laconia from the Argolis.[5] The occupation took a long time. A few Achaean centres survived depopulation and invasion, especially Amyclae, about five miles south of Sparta; others, like Therapne, had been destroyed earlier. It is impossible to write an historical account of the conquest. The pre-Dorian population was either subjugated or expelled; most of them will have left before and emigrated as far as Cyprus. Some of the Dorians occupied Crete and later the islands of the Dode-canese and the south-west coast of Asia Minor.

The Dorians were members of a migrant warrior tribe, the last to shatter the Mycenaean kingdoms. They were not used to agriculture, still less to the methods of royal bureaucracy as they existed in Mycenaean times. In fact, there seems to have been very little indeed left for the Dorians to learn from their predecessors. Sparta did not become the heir to a living cultural heritage. The Spartans started almost from scratch. The new settlement was decisively shaped by these circumstances. The new masters took over the Achaean name of Lacedaemon, and the Laconian dialect always contained some non-Dorian elements; but the political and social conditions owed little, if anything, to the earlier population. The place called Sparta, on some low mounds near the Eurotas river, was a conglomeration of villages even as late as the fifth century (Thuc. 1, 10, 2). It was founded early in the tenth century, probably some time after the invasion, at a site previously not inhabited;[6] practically no My-cenaean sherds were found there, the earliest finds belonging to the protogeometric period. Amyclae, the Achaean sanctuary of Hya-cinthus (who was later identified with Apollo), situated about five miles south of Sparta, was probably the centre of the Laconian

Achaeans; it resisted for a long time and was captured as late as the middle of the eighth century; this added a fifth to the existing four villages of Sparta.[7]

It seems that even before the new state was fully established, and certainly before it included the whole of Laconia, the conquerors went beyond the frontiers and turned against the Argive Dorians in the east and south-east as well as against the Achaeans in Arcadia in the north and north-west. Such wars for the frontier regions went on for centuries; there is little trustworthy historical tradition about them. Helos on the coast and the island of Cythera were later conquests; like the east coast of the peninsula, they may have been, for a considerable time, part of the realm of Argos. The frontier wars confirm that the rule of the new masters was soon fairly safe; the settlement of Sparta remained without any fortification. It can also hardly have been later than the first half of the eighth century, perhaps even earlier, that the growing community was able to send out colonists, first into the surrounding districts, establishing them – like some of the Dorian or non-Dorian population in those areas – as the people 'living around', the perioeci; soon the Spartans went overseas as well. Some later claims are unlikely to be true, but the islands of Melos and Thera appear to be Spartan foundations, though it is not entirely impossible that the colonists were pre-Dorian Laconians. What the conditions were under which Sparta was enabled and induced to go overseas is obscure; we have hardly any archaeological evidence, and everything else remains guess-work.[8]

The Dorians, wherever they settled, were divided into three tribes (*phylae*); that division therefore must go back to pre-immigration times. They were the Hylleis, Dymanes, and Pamphyloi – the last, the 'all-tribesmen', according to their name, represented an earlier union of several small tribes. In some other Dorian states these phylae were mixed with other tribes, but at Sparta the settlement, though it probably included Illyrian elements as well, upheld the pure Dorian tribal division, showing that the Dorians completely dominated the new state. The conquerors were a warrior race, displaying some of the features of primitive societies of which the anthropologists tell us. The men, for instance, lived in common huts and had common meals; they were divided into a number of age groups, and, as is natural in a male society such as this, paederasty was widespread. Similar social conditions existed in Crete.[9] The three phylae were the units of the army, probably as late as the seventh century; Tyrtaeus (fr. 1, 51 D) speaks of the Spartans fighting in the separate units of the three phylae.[10] There were subdivisions such as would emerge from the general cohabitation of men. The people who became the masters of Laconia showed a social structure similar to other Greek communities, though they differed in certain aspects both social and political.

They had, in particular, their own system of public education, with the main emphasis on military training and discipline; they were also the first to do their athletics naked, and their custom spread to Olympia. Socially, they were a whole people, and not only a ruling class. Leadership rested with the kings as the successors of the tribal chieftains. There were two, belonging to two royal families which never inter-married, the Agiads and the Eurypontids. The origin of the double monarchy is obscure; it may have had something to do with the two tribes of the Hylleis and Dymanes originally being two separate groups. The Agiads were regarded as the older and somehow nobler house, the Eurypontids tended to be closer to the people, the *damos*. The kings, called *archagetae*, had supreme power as leaders in war, priests and judges.[11] As far as we can see, there was always an aristocracy distinct from a non-noble peasantry. We have already seen that some social conditions originated in the early period, and that is also true of the relations between the conquerors and the conquered. The warrior community, undoubtedly small in numbers, changing over from nomadic animal-breeding to settled agriculture, could only exist if there were others to work the land for them. From the beginning the new masters must have owned most of the land; it was divided into lots (*klaroi*) – whether they were roughly equal seems doubtful – and was tilled by 'serfs', the helots, who provided for the common meals of their masters and the livelihood of their families. There will also have been a stratum of free smallholders. The helots were part of the conquered, pre-Dorian population.[12] It is significant that they had an asylum – later extended to private slaves – at the pre-Dorian sanctuary of Poseidon on Cape Taenaron.[13]

We can assume that the primitive sovereignty of the warriors' assembly (*Wehrgemeinde*) survived in the 'apella',[14] and the elder noblemen acted as advisers to the kings. At what time they gained an official standing as members of a council of elders (*gerousia*) is unknown, though it must have happened fairly early. The apella, on the other hand, had the final decision by acclamation on such questions as peace and war. The earliest real evidence of the Spartan constitution is the 'Great Rhetra' (Plut. *Lycurg.* 6), a document widely and diversely discussed as to its date, significance, and even to some extent its text. It is called 'great' in contrast to three 'small' Rhetras also mentioned by Plutarch, which are probably nothing more than formulations of traditional customs; when we speak of *the* Rhetra, it is always the great one that is meant. Plutarch quotes it as an oracle given by the Delphic Apollo to Lycurgus; a further item is supposed to be an addition by the kings Polydorus and Theopompus thus contradicting the Delphic origin of the Rhetra itself. 'Rhetra' is a Dorian expression, indicating anything pronounced. It could be a divine oracle, though later it is normally used for a law or a treaty. As to the date of the Great Rhetra, the only clear indication is that Tyrtaeus (fr. 3, b) paraphrases its wording – with certain differences – and thus provides a certain *terminus ante quem*, the second half of the seventh century.

A translation would run somewhat like this: '(1) Found a sanctuary of Zeus Syllanius and Athena Syllania; (2) arrange the phylae and obae; (3) establish as the gerusia thirty [men] including the archagetae [= kings]; (4) hold the assembly from season to season, between Babyka [a bridge] and Knakion [a stream]; (5) thus put proposals [to the damos] and decline to do so. The damos shall have the right of refusal (?) and the power.' Rider: 'If the damos speaks crooked, the elders and archagetae shall refuse it (?).'

This seems the essential meaning of the Rhetra: it gives orders to somebody who had asked the oracle, hardly the mythical lawgiver, but either the damos itself, or as the last sentence (5) of the Rhetra suggests, the gerusia. In any case, the tradition about the oracle is most likely a later invention. The Rhetra deals with the creation of a new cult (1), the organization of phylae and obae (2), and that of the gerusia as a body of thirty including the two kings (3); it fixes the place and time for regular meetings of the apella (4), and it regulates the relations between the damos, the elders, and the kings (5). The

general tendency is to give power (*kratos*) to the gerusia,[15] to make
the kings little more than its presidents and first speakers (though
that may mean quite a lot), and formally to acknowledge the
sovereignty of the damos. It cannot have meant to give the damos
full and final power, partly because a real sovereignty of the 'people'
is historically impossible at any early date, and partly because the
wording would actually anticipate the concept of democracy.[16]
The rider ascribed to the kings contemporary of the First Messenian
War made the (unanimous?) will of elders and kings supreme over
any 'crooked' decision of the apella. The rider cannot be much later
than the Rhetra itself; with its stress on the importance of the kings
it could not belong to the late seventh century.[17] Its aim was to
deprive the damos of any real power which might still derive from
the last sentence of the Rhetra. In all this a good deal remains uncertain or obscure; but the whole document, written in a somewhat
old-fashioned language, however much altered till the text reached
Plutarch, represents the act of reorganizing the state, thought almost
exclusively its constitutional elements. They all, as far as they are
mentioned in the Rhetra, seem to have existed before, but were
then put on a new basis. The phylae were the three Dorian tribes,
and the obae were the local units of the settlement of Sparta, its
'villages'.[18] A possible moment for the reconstruction, that is to say,
for the inclusion of all citizens in both kinds of units, would have
been the creation of Amyclae as the fifth of the Spartan villages. The
Amyclaeans, who were Achaeans, would previously not have belonged to any of the Dorian phylae.[19] Thus, the tribal and the
territorial divisions were combined. It is very possible that the whole
action had something to do with the army, though only the phylae,
not the obae, were later army divisions.

In order to find a possible date for the Rhetra, it is necessary to
find it a possible place in the history of Sparta. Perhaps the most
remarkable fact about this remarkable document is the absence of
the ephors.[20] The later list of eponymous ephors began with the
year 754–753. It is not certain whether this date can be trusted. If
it is historical, depending naturally on the recent introduction of
writing, the ephors at that time would have been religious sky-
watchers of little, if any, political importance. We know (from
Plut. *Agis* 14) that the five ephors had to observe the night sky,

waiting for a sign which could be used to end the rule of one of the kings; that happened every ninth year, and the term of eight years may have belonged to an ancient ritual.[21] The political implications must belong to later times, perhaps as late as the sixth century, but they would hardly have been practicable, unless the ephors had a certain religious significance in the past. The ritual may have been part of the original activities of those whose title could mean 'inspectors' or 'surveyors', or in a very literal sense, 'observers'.[22] It is also possible that the five men responsible for certain religious acts were originally at the same time village headmen; the year 754 may indicate that by then their position became of more general importance.[23] Whatever the implications of that year, or, on the other hand, of the tradition (Arist. *pol.* 1313a, 26) that the ephors were introduced by the king Theopompus later in the eighth century, the argument from silence is cogent. The Rhetra reveals a state in which the gerusia (including the kings), and not the ephors, held supreme power. The position of the damos, as indicated there, would have been impossible after the ephors gained ascendency. The leadership of the kings and the primitive democracy of the warriors' assembly survived only within the limits of a narrow oligarchy.

The position of the kings was strongest as leaders in war. The political expansion of Sparta was clearly led by them, though it remains doubtful whether there was a special bond between the kings and the perioeci. These, the 'people living around', that is, around the land of the Spartans, inhabited towns, each enjoying a kind of local autonomy, but politically completely dependent on Sparta. The number of these poleis eventually increased to about one hundred. It is unlikely that the people there had all the same ethnic origin. The upper class was Dorian; some may have settled there as early as the time of the invasion, others came later, some as Spartan colonists.[24] The extension of the state territory to include the perioeci took centuries, but it seems to have been an essentially peaceful process; sometimes it followed as an aftermath of war.

Fighting did take place again and again on all frontiers. The increasing numbers and the natural acquisitiveness of the Spartan aristocracy led to advances not only in the north and east but also in the west, that is to say, north and south of the mountain barrier of

Taygetus. This eventually resulted in the First Messenian War about which we know from Tyrtaeus who wrote two generations later. The war lasted, he tells us (4, 4), nineteen years; its date is roughly between 735 and 715 B.C., since in the list of the Olympian victors in the stadium race the last Messenian appears in 736, the first Spartan in 720. After a long struggle, especially for the mountain fortress of Ithome, the Spartans were victorious and appropriated the fertile Pamisus plain, though at that time probably only the northern half. They turned the inhabitants, most of them Dorians, into helots. Hereafter these vastly outnumbered their masters, and became a menace to the state. Tyrtaeus (5) described them 'like asses burdened with big loads'; they had to deliver half of their crops to their masters. This was a very heavy burden indeed; although the Messenian *klaroi* may have been larger than those in Laconia, the economic situation of the Messenians was far worse than that of the Laconian helots. It was the Messenians who ever afterwards threatened to revolt against Sparta.[25] In that first war the king Theopompus was a leading figure; as he is also connected with the Rhetra, we may ask whether the war had something to do with the Rhetra. It seems quite possible that after that dangerous and terrible war an attempt was made to limit the regal power in favour of the gerusia, and even to some extent to strengthen the position of the damos. Theopompus' younger fellow king Polydorus was murdered; he was long remembered as a friend of the people. It is unlikely that he was really responsible, together with Theopompus, for the 'reactionary' rider to the Rhetra.

Anyway, there was a period of inner strife and lawlessness in Sparta, of which both Herodotus (1, 65) and Thucydides (1, 18) knew. They date it to the ninth century, which is impossible and is based on the Lycurgus legend.[26] On closer investigation the years round 700 B.C. seem most likely. The gap between rich and poor had grown very wide, and the eternal cry of agrarian revolt – redistribution of land – was raised even in Sparta, as Aristotle (*pol.* 1306b, 38) concluded from Tyrtaeus.[27] It was the common situation in most of the Greek states at that time when colonies were sent out and tyrants rose to power. This was the right moment for an attempt at political reform as revealed in the Rhetra, though the rider seems to indicate that it led to further trouble. The most likely date for the

Rhetra is the late eighth or the early seventh century.[28] For a time a narrow oligarchy was in power as in so many Greek states, and naturally the damos resented the oligarchic rule. The general unrest is confirmed by the story of the *partheniai*, 'the sons of virgins', who after one version are supposed to have been illegitimate sons, born during the First Messenian War. Whether that is true or not, or which of the different stories contains some truth at all, they certainly were discontented people who had no part in the war, and therefore probably no share in the new land; perhaps they were younger sons without a *klaros*, though that would not explain their name. Land hunger was a sign of the time, natural enough with an increase in population and the rise of the peasantry everywhere. It is unlikely that in Sparta, after the extension of citizens' land into Messenia, this was still of major significance, and it cannot have been the main cause of the migration of the parthenii. Their discontent will also have been caused by political and social grievances, and they may have proved strong indeed. The men left Laconia and sailed west; they founded Taras (Tarentum) in southern Italy, the only colony Sparta sent out during the centuries of the great colonization; that was about 705 B.C. Archaeological evidence at Tarentum shows sufficient Laconian pottery of the seventh century to prove that relations between the mother-city and the colony were not particularly bad, as is sometimes assumed.[29]

During the same period Sparta suffered external setbacks. It was probably in the first half of the seventh century that Argos had a great and successful ruler, Pheidon. It will have been he who defeated the Spartans (under Polydorus?) at Hysiae in 669.[30] He even occupied Olympia temporarily, thus extending his power right across the Peloponnese. After his death, Argos declined, and soon Sparta again made progress along her frontiers. The Rhetra had consolidated the early state as an 'alternative to tyranny', but it had not solved the serious problems of Spartan society.[31]

2 · *Towards Social Reform*

Our main source for the political situation in seventh-century Sparta is Tyrtaeus. He wrote his 'elegies', clearly following the Ionian tradition in both language and motifs, as represented, for instance, by Callinus, but centred on Sparta and the present situation. The latter was shaped by the dangerous revolt of the Messenians, known as the Second Messenian War (between c. 650 and 620).[32] Tyrtaeus sang his war songs to rouse the Spartans in the fight against the Messenians, who, under their (legendary?) leader Aristomenes, found allies in Pisa and Arcadia, while Sparta's only ally was Elis, which wanted to acquire the Pisatis with Olympia. It is certain that Sparta's expansion and the methods of her rule had caused fear and hatred. Tyrtaeus (fr. 1 D) describes the fighting of the 'phalanx', the massed lines of heavily armed soldiers which had replaced the single fighters of earlier times. He speaks of the need to fight in the 'first line' (fr. 6, 1.9, 16), and also mentions light-armed soldiers (fr. 8, 35); both facts seem to indicate that the phalanx was not yet finally established.[33] In praising 'our fathers' fathers' of the First Messenian War (fr. 4, 6) as a model for the present youth, Tyrtaeus does not suggest what their tactics actually had been. We cannot be sure when exactly the new tactics were introduced at Sparta, but the most likely date seems early in the seventh century,[34] and in that case the Rhetra could easily be a result of the social changes involved. They would have taken some time, and the battle of Hysiae as well as the history of the Messenian revolt revealed Sparta's military weakness at that early stage of the hoplite army. After a certain period, however, the citizen-soldiers became the backbone of military strength, and they began to ask for equal rights with the nobles. In Sparta, with her old traditions of the warriors' assembly and the common life of the damos, the ground was well prepared; but the damos had to overcome the resistance of kings and elders, that is to say, the state as represented in the Rhetra had grown out of date.

Tyrtaeus used the words of the Rhetra as the foundation of his ideal of *eunomia*, of good order, a satisfactory distribution of power, and a loyal attitude on the part of the citizens. He belongs to the early stages of the damos' reaction; he is, as it were, the bridge between the Rhetra and the final reforms.[35] The old order had started to deteriorate and even to disintegrate, as became evident during the Messenian revolt. To preach and to prepare for the revival of ancient Spartan valour and efficiency was to Tyrtaeus a sacred mission he had to fulfil. We can be sure that he did not stand alone. Tyrtaeus was not a lame Athenian schoolmaster, as later legend had it, but a Spartiate deeply concerned with the needs of the moment. He was one of those members of the damos who felt (fr. 9 D) that efficiency in athletics, wealth, noble descent, or the ability to speak, counted little, compared with being 'a brave man in war'. It is to 'the common good for both the state and the damos', when a man fights without fear against the enemy. Tyrtaeus again and again exhorts the Spartans to be brave, to fight, and if necessary to die, but never 'to tremble'.[36] It took the Spartans about thirty years to overcome the Messenians, and the obstacles to victory were not only in the strength of the enemy. Even the Sparta which, towards the end of the seventh century, emerged from war and victory was, as is confirmed by the unsuccessful fighting against Tegea in the early sixth century, still far away from full military efficiency.

During the seventh and sixth centuries, Sparta shared in the wide-spread prosperity of the Greek world. Trade connexions overseas are mentioned more than once, and foreign traders, artists, and poets were attracted to a place where cult and festivals were, on the whole, joyful, and payment good. Choral songs were a special feature of the festivals; choruses of boys and girls were traditional, and this branch of poetry flourished in Sparta. The first to introduce lyric poetry to the Greek mainland was Terpander from Lesbos, whom the Spartans had invited; but there is little genuine evidence about him, and the poet best known to us, and most typical of the age, is Alcman, who may have been an Ionian Greek from Sardes (fr. 13 D, 16 P; cf. 13 P), but was more likely a genuine Spartan. He wrote in Laconian dialect, and was completely imbued with the spirit and life of the Spartan people. He was probably an elder contemporary of Tyrtaeus, living to an advanced age (fr. 94 D, 26 P), enjoying some of the peaceful periods of the seventh century.[37] The evidence of his poetry is fragmentary and scanty, but sufficient to show a Sparta full of culture and pleasures.[38] Alcman largely accepts the ethical standards of the past, and it is possible that he was influenced by Delphi. It can probably be said that his Sparta was not very different from other Greek centres of the seventh century. Traces of an original spirit of discipline might have survived, but there is nothing in Alcman of the rigid austerity of later times,

though there is some indication of a new importance of the damos.
Alcman was not a political poet, but with this difference he sings of
the same Sparta as the bellicose Tyrtaeus. He could claim that
'a rival to the iron is the beautiful playing of the cithara' (fr. 100 D,
41 P). The standards of military prowess and honour had weakened,
the wealthy lived a life the majority of the damos resented, but to
the poet and his audience life could be easy and enjoyable. This
'relaxed' state of Spartan society seems to be confirmed by the
development of vase-painting and sculpture. There was no sudden
break in the cultural history of Sparta, but archaeologists have
noticed a surprising change of style in the late seventh century,[39]
and about half a century later the beautiful Laconian pottery,
inspired as it was by Corinthian ware and widely dispersed in the
Greek world, disappeared together with the Corinthian vases.[40]
To the sixth century belongs also the erection of the temple of
Athena Chalkioikos with its metal-covered walls, and the throne
at Amyclae, decorated by an Ionian artist. Many small works in
bronze or ivory have been found at Olympia, which are today
regarded as Laconian. It seems that Spartan art was still going strong
as late as the beginning of the fifth century. The marble figure of a
crouching warrior (the so-called 'Leonidas') belongs to that date,
but it is perhaps an exception; while almost certainly the work of a
foreign artist, it continues a Laconian tradition representing warriors
and armed athletes.[41] In general, a decline can be observed, and it is
unlikely that the decline both in art and trade simply resulted from
Athenian competition, although that will have played its part.[42]
Spartan art did not suddenly die during the sixth century, but it
clearly lost its prominence and became 'provincial'. We must not
forget that most of the craftsmen and traders were perioeci or
foreigners; for a time they may have upheld traditions which had
become alien to the life of the Spartans themselves. The contents of
the poetry of Alcman and Tyrtaeus prove that there was a change
from an easy life to one of austerity, and afterwards Spartan literature practically ended. Bent on a military ideal, and hostile to all
personal luxury, in fact to every sign of individuality, Sparta was
bound to become culturally barren.[43]

The Rhetra, though stressing the traditional role of the damos,
had failed to take notice of its new position in society; it was

probably too early for that. After the change in military tactics the damos came more and more into the foreground, even in Alcman's unpolitical poetry. It needed a social as much as a political reform to turn the former oligarchy and its prospering society into something else. Against gerusia and kings the damos needed new leaders. They were found in the five ephors, who, annually elected by and from the people, gradually gained power. That process probably began during or shortly before the Messenian revolt, that is, towards the middle of the seventh century, but the peak of the ephors' rule was reached much later. The collegium of the ephors, as we have seen, had existed before; but it was only now that, to an ever growing degree, they became the decisive leaders of the community. Ever afterwards their position was supreme, though challenged now and then by their chief rivals, the kings.

3 · *The State of the Ephors*

Tyrtaeus is the earliest and at the same time the most impressive witness for the ideal of the citizen-soldier. Though probably never quite absent from Spartan political concepts, this ideal needed to be reinvigorated and made real to become the only basis of state and society. It was after the Second Messenian War that, under the leadership of the ephors, the community acquired the structure which was supposed to be the work of a single lawgiver, Lycurgus. The final increase in citizens' land by the conquest of all Messenia made a new and fairer distribution of land practicable; equal *klaroi* belonged to the Lycurgan ideal, and the *klaros* was known as 'the ancient lot'.[44] That was the basis on which Sparta in the following decades became the state of *eunomia* (cf. Hdt. 1, 66); but that meant at the same time the severe and rigid community that aimed at training its citizens to an ever higher degree of prowess and courage, at the suppression of the individual, at absolute discipline and obedience, at unconditional service to and for the state. This state, however, was no longer an oligarchy. The Spartiates, as the citizens were now called, were regarded as a body of equals, the *homoioi*. That implied a roughly equal political standing within the damos, while economic equality remained an ideal never achieved. Differences of wealth remained, and later increased again. We also hear frequently of the 'first families', remnants of an aristocracy which even in the egalitarian society retained some influence.[45] All Spartiates, however, now lived in Sparta itself; they were 'absentee landlords', and their land was inalienable and hereditary; the helots who worked it were attached to an individual *klaros*. There were no longer any citizen peasants outside the land tilled by the helots, and the helots belonged to the state; the state alone, that is to say, the ephors, could let helots free or allow them to be sold or killed. Hatred against their masters was strong among them, particularly in Messenia, and the Spartiates lived in constant fear of revolts.[45a]

The perioeci served in the army as hoplites, though in separate units. As they were not trained in the same way as the Spartiates, they must have come from an upper class who would have the time and the means for military training. The lower classes among the perioeci were either peasants or traders and manufacturers, occupations forbidden to the Spartiates; this group must have been most useful to the community. Obviously there were also slaves in the cities of the perioeci. At the same time the ring of the cities of the perioeci, extended even to the south and west of Messenia, kept the land of the citizens with their helots isolated from the outer world, separating them from possible contacts which might be dangerous to the state. The perioeci became – though probably not before the sixth century – an essential part of the state and were included in its name; that, as was common with the Greeks, was the name of the people, and it was not the Spartiates, it was 'the Lacedaemonians', including all free men of the country, Spartiates as well as perioeci.

There were five ephors, and they have been regarded as the leaders of the five obae of Sparta. This is not impossible, but there is no clear evidence for the connexion, still less for that with the five *lochoi* into which the army was later subdivided; the ephors were never army leaders.[46] They are not mentioned in Tyrtaeus' fragments; that may be accidental and is not, at any rate, a valid *argumentum e silentio* as it is with the Rhetra. It may even have been deliberate, as the whole tendency of the reform movement was to revive an alleged form of early society, which was eventually regarded as the work of Lycurgus. There can be no doubt that the ephors took the lead in bringing about the changes in Spartan society. The only famous ephor, Chilon, who was counted among the Seven Sages, lived around 550. There is no certain evidence to connect him with the work of reform; but since this was attributed to the legendary Lycurgus, we cannot expect any such evidence, and Chilon was known as a successful soldier as well (*FGrH* 105 F 1). He may easily also have had a late share in the reform, and the cult of the heroized Chilon is most likely due to his political activity. The final shape of state and society, as it emerged latest in the second half of the sixth century, was of such imposing consistency that we can easily understand ancient and modern historians alike tending to regard it as the achievement of a single statesman. The consistent tradition of past centuries, and the adherence to that tradition by the reformers, may easily have worked together to give the impression of a unique and coherent work. It is, on the other hand, impossible to produce a history of the development of 'Lycurgan' Sparta; we can only trace the results as we visualize the Sparta of the classical age. Even this Sparta is not fully known, partly because of its own secretiveness (of which already Thucydides complained), and partly on account of the mist of legend which later spread over it.

Sparta's social structure and the firm leadership of the ephors, which henceforth competed with the traditional role of the kings, prevented the state from ever being ruled by a tyrant, as in fact the rise to eminence of any individual was excluded, except for a few great powerful military leaders. This is what is usually called the Sparta of Lycurgus. It is perhaps significant that Pindar in 470 (*P.* 1, 64), in describing Sparta as a model for Hieron's new city of Aetna, speaks of the laws of Aegimius, an unknown mythical king; on this basis he could claim that a kingdom, and not a tyrannis, was established at Aetna. The legend of Lycurgus hardly started before the sixth century, and its impact does not become manifest before the fourth century.

Socially the community was based on a system of education, the *agogē*, by which all boys from the age of seven and all young men were subjected to a strict and austere way of life. As we have already noted, much of the social system derived from early times. The age groups, the common meals (*andreia* or *phiditia*), the cohabitation of men, the paederasty, and other features of a primitive past, all served the one purpose of turning the Spartiates into first-class

soldiers and passionate patriots. Family life was hardly possible,
though when a man had reached the age of thirty he could at least
sleep at home. Boys and girls had their separate physical training,
and could be seen naked at their exercises and games. Women
counted as healthy mothers of healthy sons, but they also enjoyed
a freedom unusual elsewhere in Greece. No doubt the Spartiates
were proud of their new order, and the individual was, in general,
eager not only to comply with its rules but even enthusiastically to
support it and to out-rival his fellow-citizens. They called freedom
what by others would be called authoritarian rule. They were
deliberately kept isolated from the outer world, and it is significant
that at a time when the general Greek fashion for men was to wear a
beard and moustache, and no longer to shave the upper lip, the
ephors, at the beginning of their year of office, made the startling
announcement (Arist. fr. 539) that the citizens must 'shave their
moustaches and obey the laws', thus emphasizing what we may call
the traditional approach. For some time export trade flourished, as
can be seen by the Laconian vases found in east and west; but that
trade, no less than the making of the vases, was probably largely in
the hands of foreigners or perioeci. Many of their towns were busy
harbours. The part played by the perioeci, and especially by foreign
artists, is one of the reasons why the general picture is somewhat
ambiguous. The archaeological evidence provides comparatively
little for the Spartiates themselves. Naturally, the Spartans still
knew how to dance and to make music. That was part of their
education, and both sexes joined in such activities at religious
festivals; but when we compare with the spirit of Alcman's poetry
we see how much had been lost in gaiety, glamour, and popular
appeal. It was now largely a matter of official arrangements. Moreover, as far as the Spartiates were concerned, foreign connexions
were cut down to a minimum; not one of the victors at Olympia
came from Sparta after the middle of the sixth century, and very
few later on; it was the time of Chilon, who is supposed to have
said (Hdt. 7, 235) that it would be better if the island of Cythera
had sunk into the sea, an utterance probably dictated by the desire
to have the Lacedaemonians, that is to say, the perioeci as well, cut
off from any connexion overseas. No personal luxuries were
allowed, and in a period of increasing money economy in the

Greek world, Sparta stuck to her traditional form of iron money (in the shape of *obeloi*, spits?), which was of no use in trading abroad. There was gold and silver in Sparta; the state owned much, and some people grew rich in such possessions. However, this was against the law and could be punished. Sparta had no coins of her own before the third century B.C. Even the strictest ideal can never be fully attained, but in Sparta the hold by the state on everybody and everything was very firm indeed, and eventually included the perioeci as well.[47]

The middle of the sixth century is remarkable also for another change. After the Second Messenian War Sparta defeated her old enemy Argos in a famous battle, and won the frontier districts of Cynuria and Thyreatis (Hdt. 1, 82). Her territory was larger than that of any other Greek state, but by then her expansive force had been largely spent. This must have been one of the main reasons why she turned her face so determinedly away from the outer world. Military setbacks against the Arcadians led to a definite change in foreign policy. Just as Elis (probably soon afterwards) made an alliance with the west-Arcadian town of Heraea (*ML*, no. 17), so Sparta concluded with Tegea, and later with other states, treaties of alliance which bound her partners to military support in time of war, while they remained free and autonomous, even to a large extent in foreign policy. From such individual treaties a league was gradually built up. Instead of trying to conquer the Peloponnese, Sparta became its *hegemon*. In the end the whole peninsula was included, with the exception of Argos, which always remained hostile, and Achaea, the most northern area, separated by high mountains from the south and practically outside all Greek politics. With the backing of a proud and disciplined people, Sparta grew into the leading power of all Greece, soon to be recognized as such by Greek and non-Greek states. It was symbolic that even earlier, on the advice of the Delphic oracle, the bones of Orestes had been brought from Tegea to Sparta (Hdt. 1, 67 f.). Thus, the image of a continuation of Agamemnon's rule was established. It is probably from this kind of policy that the belief arose that the Spartan kings were Achaeans, not Dorians.[48] The Peloponnesian League, called 'the Lacedaemonians and their allies', emerged as a loose confederation of autonomous states, without constitutional bonds, but

providing a safe instrument of power politics under Spartan leadership, largely directed against democracy and tyrannis. The influence
exercised by some of the allies, especially by Corinth, was sometimes
strong, but what really counted were Sparta's military strength and
her great prestige.

It seems certain that the whole constructive policy up to the
middle of the sixth century was the work of the ephors, and Chilon
may have played an important part. Despite the annual change of
office, the ephors had early developed a firm tradition of power.
Constitutionally their leadership was safely established. They were
elected 'from all citizens' (Arist. *pol.* 1270b, 27 f.); how 'democratic'
this 'very childish' form of election by acclamation was may be
doubtful. As a collegium, the ephors represented an anonymous
rule, even a kind of tyranny, sanctioned by the gerusia. It was the
ephors who decided state policy and supervised the whole life of the
community. They shared some jurisdiction with the elders, and they
left the command in the field to the kings, though normally they
were responsible for the call-up of the army, and it soon became the
rule that some ephors accompanied king and army. Most legal and
moral matters were directed by the ephors, and they could interfere
in the private lives of the citizens, to say nothing of perioeci and
helots. The former stood under their direct jurisdiction. The only
rivals of the ephors were some of the kings, especially among the
Agiads; but the ephors knew how to play one king off against the
other. Still, strong personalities among the kings were bound to
clash with the ephors. This happened for the first time towards the
end of the sixth century when Cleomenes I tried to extend the
Peloponnesian league to include Athens and Argos. His ambitious
and very personal policy was opposed to the policy favoured by the
ephors, a policy essentially defensive and isolationist. In the end he
quarrelled with some of the allies as well as with his fellow king
Demaratus; ever afterwards it was the law that only one king was
to lead an army abroad. In general, the kings enjoyed the full
prestige and honours of their hereditary position; they represented
state and people before the gods, but there was little left of their
legislative and judicial powers. Significant for the relations between
kings and ephors even under normal conditions was the monthly (!)
exchange of oaths (Xen. *rep. Lac.* 15, 7): the kings swore 'to reign

according to the laws', the ephors in the name of the state 'to uphold monarchy as long as the kings kept their oath'. Their mutual position could not be made clearer.

The gerusia consisted of men over sixty who were elected for the rest of their lives by popular acclamation, a method again called childish by Aristotle (*pol.* 1271a, 9), but probably well suited to preserve the aristocratic character of the gerusia. Its members were not responsible to anybody, and formed the highest court of justice. Its composition and power possibly still depended on some of the 'first families', and thus maintained an oligarchic character.[49] The gerusia may have held the right of *probouleusis*, that is to say they prepared any proposal put before the apella, which retained the right of refusal.[50] In practice, there must have been a good deal of co-operation between gerusia and ephors, though the latter held the initiative. A good example during the sixth century is their common intervention when the king Anaxandridas had no son, and they allowed him to take a second wife (Hdt. 5, 39 ff.).

Later admirers regarded Sparta's constitution as a mixture of the three main forms – monarchy, aristocracy, democracy, represented respectively by kings, gerusia, and apella with the ephors. There is some truth in this theory, though the 'mixed constitution' was not the cause of Sparta's stability. There was no equal distribution of power among the elements of the constitution; the conflicts between the kings and the ephors never ceased, while oligarchy was restricted by the authority of the ephors; the ephors were also responsible for the fact that under their leadership the assembly was to play a more important part, though it is unlikely that the body of well-drilled Spartiates would ever try to act independently. The 'ecclesia' appears officially in the peace treaty with Argos (418–417; Thuc. 5, 77, 1), and its meetings in 432 and 415 are described in detail by Thucydides (1, 67 ff.; 6, 88, 10 ff.). In these cases it was always the question of peace or war that was debated, and we cannot be sure whether final decisions were taken by the assembly on other questions as well.[51] Sparta has been called a military camp or, on the other hand, a police state. Again there is some truth in either description, but not the whole truth, which cannot be put into a short formula. As far as the constitution goes, the equality of the Spartiates as well as their rule over the non-Spartiates are fundamental.

Officially, and especially in the descriptions by later writers, the rule of law, of *nomos*, was proclaimed; it was what Tyrtaeus, perhaps the first to do so, called *eunomia*, good order. However, as there were no written laws, their application by ephors and gerusia could be very arbitrary. Tradition and discipline, both based on a firm belief in divine sanction, had created a state which might be called authoritarian.[52] Authority was chiefly in the hands of the ephors; but usually they had to get the assembly's consent. As they changed annually, theirs was not a personal authority: they were the powerful tools rather than the masters of the system, and the old men of the gerusia were the guardians of the tradition.

In one respect, already mentioned, Sparta was clearly an oligarchy. The harsh rule of the Spartiate minority over the helots, who were pre-Dorian or even Dorian Greeks and not foreign slaves, and also the political non-existence of the perioeci, bore the signs of a strictly oligarchic state. That was the reason why Sparta's foreign policy supported oligarchies whenever possible, and was equally hostile to tyrants and democracies. In her period of new strength during the sixth century, and with the help of the growing Peloponnesian league, Sparta initiated in particular an aggressive policy against tyranny. In pursuance of such a policy, even an expedition overseas took place against Polycrates of Samos; it failed (Hdt. 3, 46 ff., 54 ff., see below, p. 104). This remains a surprising move, though it clearly shows that the deliberate isolation of the Spartiates did not prevent the state from carrying out an active foreign policy as the 'leader of Hellas' (*prostates Hellados*). There are indications that it included the awareness of possible danger from the expanding Persian empire.[53]

Seventh-century tradition survived in the 'city of lovely choirs', which is still mentioned in Lysander's dedication at Delphi;[54] that is to say, music and cult held their own far into the fifth century and beyond. That culture, however, was no longer really alive. Whatever her ancient roots, Lycurgan Sparta was an artificial creation. It was bound to fall into misuse and corruption. Even apart from such a decline, it must be realized that further developments could not possibly be prevented. Later philosophers might praise Sparta's consistency and grandeur, and embody their own ideas in their description; but all this was out of date long before they wrote.

This can be said of Plato in particular. After the later fifth century a new aristocracy of rich families emerged from the Spartan damos, and the foundations of state and society soon proved to be unstable. The first signs of this can be discerned around 500, but on the whole it was a later development which belongs to a different chapter of Greek history.

III

ATHENS BEFORE
AND UNDER SOLON

1 · *The Aristocratic State*

Athens, practically – though not entirely – untouched by the
various invasions after 1300 B.C., had been actively involved in the
Ionian migration (see p. 6), and Athenian pottery had flourished
in the ninth and eighth centuries; after that there is no evidence that
Athens was of importance till the time of Solon. What the Greeks
themselves later wrote about early Athenian history is partly legend
and partly the story of the transition from monarchy to aristocracy,
which was general among Greek states. Some conclusions, however,
can be drawn from later sources.[1] If we concentrate here on Athens,
it is not only because of her later importance but also because we
have so very little evidence for other states. In general they will
have developed along similar lines, though Athens was never really
typical. The most important fact is that the whole of Attica,
originally divided among many *poleis* (cf., e.g., the 'Tetrapolis'
round Marathon), was united under the rule of Athens at an early
date. This was later described as a single act of synoecism, and regarded as the work of Theseus, mythical hero and king of Athens.
Thucydides (2, 15) tells us that Theseus did away with the independent poleis and created one *bouleuterion* and one *prytaneion*, that is,
one council chamber and one seat of government. It can be accepted
as historical that a political unification took place without any large
transfer of population. It is, however, out of the question that it all
happened in one single move; we must rather assume that there
was a lengthy process, probably ending when the ancient sanctuary
and town of Eleusis with its fertile hinterland, the Thriasian plain,
lost its independence in the late eighth century (or even the early

seventh), after having been an independent state under kings of its own. Like Sparta, Athens held a comparatively large territory; but unlike Sparta, Athens did not rule over subjects free or bond, rather

3. Attica and Surroundings

the whole of Attica was citizens' land. In Homer, Attica is never mentioned; it was identical with Athens (*Il.* 2, 546 ff. *Od.* 3, 278), a view necessarily based on the fact of synoecism.[2]

The city-state which emerged from the process of unification preserved to some extent earlier tribal features, as in fact every polis did, more or less. Athens, just like Thebes and Syracuse, had a name that indicated a plurality of communities (*hai Athenai*); the fact has never been explained, though it probably derives from an original synoecism.[3] There were four phylae, some of which also appear in other Ionian cities; but there was less uniformity among Ionians than Dorians. The names of the Athenian phylae cannot be explained.[4] Each was headed by a tribal king (*phylobasileus*), whose title shows that he was subject to the king of Athens. Smaller communities within each phyle were the phratries (brotherhoods), to which originally only members of the noble families were admitted. These families, based on the household unit of the *oikos*, were bound together in a clan or *genos* by common mythical ancestry. While the phratries had a common cult of Zeux Phratrios and Athena (perhaps Phratria), the clans worshipped, apart from special deities, Zeus Herkeios (the god of the hearth) and Apollo Patroos (the family god), that is to say, they bound their members, living and dead, together in one sacred tradition of kinship which gave the whole body of clans a firm basis of solidarity. The clans with their patronymic names were the natural units of the aristocracy, and sometimes a particular clan might dominate a phratry; the clans exercised power in local districts, and sometimes villages (demes) would be called after a clan, though that could also happen with a phratry. The main distinction between clan and brotherhood is that the former were related, at least in theory, by blood, their members being parts of a *genos* (*gennetai*) or milk-brothers (*homogalaktes*), while the phraters were not brothers in any sense of real kinship.[5] The phratries, in fact, were the link between clan and state; every child within a clan was to be admitted to a phratry and thus became a future citizen. Clans may have not come into existence before the settlement of the tribe, while the phratry belongs to an earlier past when phylae and phratries were also military divisions (as in *Il.* 2, 362 f.) of the tribe.

Athenian society under the rule of kings and the bonds of religious worship was an aristocracy of the clans. Later tradition saw its rise chiefly in terms of constitutional changes; the transition was put into a scheme such as recorded by Aristotle (*AP* 3), which is clearly not historical. We are told that after the kings there were first life-long archons ('rulers'), followed by decennial, and finally,

annual officials of that name. Whether the life-long archons represented a stage of elected instead of hereditary kingship is at least
doubtful; the ten-years archons are pure invention. The name
archon indicates that a magistrate has taken the place of the king.
At an early date the office was divided into three; the first was the
basileus, a title which could never be abolished as it involved the
ruler's duties towards the gods. The second office was the *polemarchos*,
the leader of the army, the third that of the (first) archon, the eponymous official.[6] This is the order given by Aristotle and it has rightly
been doubted. Both the archon *basileus* and the first archon can only
have come into being when there was no longer a king. The later
list of eponymous (and therefore annual) archons probably began
with the year 682–681.[7] It is not certain whether this year also marks
the introduction of annual archons, but it is at least not unlikely.
The polemarch as the leader in war could represent a later division;
but since in the Linear B tablets an army leader (*lawagetas*) is mentioned beside the king (*wanax*), it seems possible that there may
have been an army leader also at Athens, while monarchy was still
in existence; the analogy of the Spartan kings who remained military leaders is not conclusive, especially as there were two. 'Many
years afterwards,' Aristotle tells us (3, 4), six further archons were
added, the 'law-setters' or *thesmothetai*, who were responsible for
jurisdiction and the preservation of the laws, that is to say, the
knowledge of the customary law.[7a] The offices of the various
archons remained individual offices; it was only the thesmothetae
who formed a board like most of the other officials at Athens. Other
similar magistrates were introduced in the course of time and thus
the power of the archons was gradually limited; there were,
e.g., the treasurers (*tamiai*) of the temple of Athena, the *kolakretai*,
who administered the treasury of the community, that is to say,
the growing amount of public revenue and expenses, the *poletai*,
who were responsible for public sales and tenancies, the eleven
(*hendeka*), who served as police and also as judges. Probably all the
officials were elected by the 'people', the *ekklesia*, i.e. an assembly
of landholders, rather than being chosen by the council on the
Areopagus, as Aristotle maintains (*AP* 8, 2). When he stresses
that the archons were chosen 'from among the nobles and the
rich' (*aristinden kai ploutinden*) he states a historical fact, not a

constitutional rule. Of the procedure of the election we know nothing; for the rest, the *ekklesia* is unlikely to have had any rights except that of saying Yes or No to questions of decisive importance. The Areopagus (as we usually call the council, from the hill where it met) consisted of the traditional elders; what exactly their functions were, apart from generally giving advice and, of course, carrying out judicial duties, is difficult to know. Aristotle's views are clearly influenced by the romantic conservatism of Isocrates' *Areopagiticus*; but there can be no doubt that the council had great power and a prestige unrivalled by any other constitutional element, as the only institution created by the gods.

Archons and Areopagus were the exclusive domain of the nobles. They were called *eupatridai*, the sons of good (i.e. noble) fathers; they were the 'high-born', the aristocracy consisting of many clans.[8] There were two other classes or groups in early Athens, the farmers (*agroikoi*) and the artisans (*demiourgoi*). It seems unreasonable to doubt the early existence of the three 'classes', though they will not have been legally acknowledged separate units.[9] The nobility were the large landowners, mainly corn-growers and to some extent cattle-breeders, later cultivators of olives and vines; olive oil became one of the chief sources of Athenian prosperity. These wealthy families were a clear minority of the people, but they held most of the fertile land in the Attic plains, while the small farmers generally lived on the poorer land in the hills.[10] The Eupatrids, in every sense the high and mighty, held not only the great offices of state but also the few official priesthoods; they ruled the community as the heirs to the power of the kings. The clans were not always a united body; there were just as in other states many regional and personal conflicts among them, but they were an essentially uniform society featuring, as we can see from the vase paintings, athletics, paederasty and wine drinking.[10a] The main thing, however, was that they formed a more or less united front of the wealthy and powerful against those who had no political rights, the free peasants and the landless. At the same time the contrast was, or at least grew, even stronger between those – whether noble or non-noble – who held some land and those who did not, and therefore had no share in public life at all.

Two facts show that the rule of the aristocracy and the hereditary principle based on noble birth were not uncontested. First, there were similar cult associations whose members (*orgeones*) were non-nobles.[11] They aimed at getting into the phratries or to have equal rights with their members, in order to gain full citizenship; they eventually succeeded, though the final achievement may have been as late as the time of Solon. At some time other cult associations (*thiasoi*) were introduced as parts of the phratry, probably as a means of mixing nobles and non-nobles. The decisive general factor was the change of military tactics of which we have spoken before (p. 21). With the introduction of the phalanx, those who could afford it served in war as hoplites; most of the *georgoi* must have been among them. The effect on both aristocrats and peasants will have been strong indeed, especially as phylae and phratries had been the army divisions in the field. When the heavily armed soldiers, the hoplites, became the main strength of the army, its units must have included the non-nobles as well – in fact, as the largest contingent. They gradually intensified their claims, and the nobles began to give way; indeed, whether compelled to do so or by voluntary action, they now played a decisive role within the whole community, not only as a ruling society. They began to accept the existence of a state authority, though this still remained essentially in their hands, and the law developed in the direction as described before. The archons may at first have had the task of restraining and supervising the use of self-help by the clans, but soon this proved insufficient, as the ruling class had to recognize that arbitrary jurisdiction by noble judges, such as we know it from Hesiod, would no longer be possible.

The second important fact which influenced the aristocratic order were the local ties of neighbourhood and the regional nuclei of clannish power. Local and family interests became more and more intertwined. Some of the clans had their estates chiefly near the city, others far away. Obviously the situation was bound to create different political trends and opposing groups.[12] Moreover, a territorial division of the whole state became inevitable, and this must have altered the purely personal character of the phylae. It seems that most members of a phyle had settled near to one another. When Aristotle (*AP* 8, 3) tells us that each phyle had three subdivisions, the *trittyes*, and each of these four *naukrariai*, it is clear that this is

a regional division. The number of twelve *trittyes* corresponds with
the tradition of twelve poleis in early Attica, and with the altar of
the twelve gods regarded as the centre of the state.[13] In the forty-
eight naucraries the citizens were registered for financial and administrative purposes. According to Herodotus (5, 71, 2), their
presidents (*prytaneis*) played an important political part of which
otherwise nothing is known; they may have actually been the heads
of the trittyes. Anyway, the *naukraros* meant originally the master
of a ship; as the leader of a naucrary he will have been the head of
a body of citizens responsible for the means of building and equip-
ping a warship. As the naucraries were parts of the trittyes, and they
of the phylae, the latter must have had some regional meaning. On
the other hand, they did not lose their traditional personal bonds.
Their heads, the four tribal kings (mentioned above, p. 52), had
once judicial power in cases of bloodshed; that was primarily a
religious duty to avoid pollution of the community. They later lost
this power, but had other religious tasks. We never hear of any
political or administrative action taken by them, another indication
that the four phylae remained essentially 'personal', not local, units.

2 · *The Social Crisis*

The nobility, firmly entrenched in the security of their political
power and their bonds of kinship, cult, and neighbourhood, and so
far not yet seriously affected by the slow rise of the peasantry, were
to face an economic and social crisis which not only undermined
their own power but also severely shook the whole community.
Our evidence is scanty and partly obscure; but the essential out-
lines are frequently reported.[14] Like other states, Athens faced the
danger of being ruled by a tyrant. In 632 (or 636) a young nobleman, Cylon, a former Olympic victor and the son-in-law of the
tyrant Theagenes of Megara, seized the Acropolis, but was prevented from further success by the remarkable action of the peasants
who flocked into town, were armed, and saved the situation for the
authorities. The people were probably incensed by the fact that
Megarian soldiers helped Cylon, as the Athenians in general may
have feared the predominance of Megara; but the support by the

peasants will also have been due to their dependence on the upper class and, on the other hand, to promises made by the latter which materialized shortly afterwards in Dracon's legislation. Cylon's attempt failed; he himself escaped, but his followers were dragged from the altar to which they had fled and were killed. This sacrilege was chiefly attributed to the archon Megacles, the head of the Alcmaeonid family, and the memory of his crime played some part in later Athenian history.[15]

The enmities among the noble families and the blood-bath that ended the Cylonian affair were symptoms rather than causes of general conditions otherwise hardly known to us. There was more to it than the failure of a conspiracy. 'After that,' Aristotle writes (*AP* 2, 1), 'there was for a long time civic struggle between the nobles and the people.' That conflict must have been simmering under the surface for some time past. The events surrounding Cylon, whatever their significance, showed general disturbance and unrest, though at the same time a united front against tyranny. The people in arms had become a serious danger to the ruling class. Only a few years later Dracon (about 624) gave Athens the first written codification of laws and thus granted the people some safety against arbitrary jurisdiction. The only part of his code which survived Solon's legislation was his laws on homicide, which were renewed late in the fifth century, and preserved on stone.[16] Dracon was the first to distinguish between murder and manslaughter. We know nothing of his further laws, though they must have existed; after Solon the Greeks themselves had practically no knowledge of that earlier legislation. Their belief that more or less every crime down to theft and larceny was punished by the death penalty is nonsense, and probably the whole story that Dracon 'wrote his laws in blood' was later invention. On the other hand, part of the social crisis which Solon was to overcome, must have been caused by laws of a clearly severe nature. When Solon (24, 9 D) speaks of the men sold into slavery, about whom we shall have to say more, as enslaved 'wrongly' (*ekdikōs*) or 'rightly' (*dikaiōs*), the meaning is not moral but legal. It was the question whether the sale into slavery was based on law or not. That law can hardly have been anything else but one of Dracon's. That remains true, although his extant law on manslaughter was mild and progressive, showing that even for unpremeditated murder the penalty was only exile. This law is the beginning of the end of the long history at Athens of blood-vengeance and private punishment, although the consent of the family or phratry was still needed for the return of the exiled killer. Deliberate murder was still a matter in which the family took a decisive part, though probably only after the state authority had spoken.[17] The formal constitution ascribed to Dracon in *AP* 4 is unhistorical.[18]

We have so far noted the outbreaks and effects of unrest rather than its causes. These were the economic and social conditions in which a large part of the people were living; their specific character, however, is highly disputed.[19] In general, the lower classes were in a sorry plight; what their situation exactly was depends on some facts which cannot be regarded as clearly established. One thing we now know is that down to Solon, money economy hardly began to exert any influence at Athens. It was a question of land and its produce. Aristotle (*AP* 2) tells us that 'the poor with their wives and children were in servitude to the rich', 'that all the land was in the hands of the few', and Plutarch (*Sol.* 13, 4) says, 'the whole demos was in debt to the rich'. These are exaggerated and generalizing statements, obviously based on Solon's poems, which only speak of those who needed his help; they leave out the bulk of the free peasantry which must have existed, though we do not hear of them. We know, after all, of two groups which will have consisted chiefly of the free yeomen class, the hoplites and the orgeones; to a large extent they will have been the same people, the *zeugitai* (see below, p. 65). What we do not know for certain is whether their farms were alienable, as the estates of the nobles most decisively were *not*. Solon seems to have given a law to prevent the unlimited accumulation of land (Arist. *pol.* 1266b, 16), and that may partly have been directed against the usurpation of public land by the wealthy; but that alone would not explain the urgency of the social situation. We must assume that the rich could actually buy out a farmer; their farms will therefore have been alienable. For Hesiod (*Erga* 336 ff.) it depends on piety and the blessing of the gods whether one can buy another *kleros* or somebody else one's own; the Boeotia of Hesiod cannot provide a definite proof for Attica, though it may strengthen our argument. Obviously land freshly put under cultivation would be free, but it remains doubtful what happened when a farm was regarded as a family *kleros*.[19a]

Even if we accept the view that farms outside the noble family estates could be sold, it still remains an open question whether at Athens the family estate could be divided among several sons. Analogies again from other regions (e.g. Hesiod's Boeotia or the law of Gortyn) are inconclusive; but the fact that the plight of the peasantry was so widespread, and also that Athens did not send out colonies (but see p. 401, note 25), makes it likely that there was no bar to dividing the ordinary lot, except that it may frequently have been too small for further division. Thus the number of very small farms would increase and make it more likely that so many peasants fell into debt. It is also possible that some farms stood on public land and that the nobles usurped parts of it and forced the smallholders into service or expelled them. Even at their worst, however, conditions in that country of limited size somehow managed to avoid the extremes. There never were *latifundia* as in Italy, and the means of improving the social and economic situation proved to be comparatively simple.

Yet a man of wisdom and courage was needed. In a famous poem in iambics (24), Solon renders, as it were, account of what he has done. The first thing is that he freed the land from the *horoi* which 'were erected in many places'. Mother Earth herself will be witness 'before the tribunal of Time' that she who had been 'in servitude before, was now free'. The *horoi* were pillars or stones, neither purely boundary nor mortgage stones, but set up to show that a particular piece of land and its crop were under a pledge. It is likely that there was a kind of class-war going on, when noble landowners forced peasants into dependence and into serving as labourers on their estates. Or a farmer in need of corn or seed or anything else would ask a wealthier neighbour for help. He would borrow with the intention to pay back in kind, or the loan may have been only fictive. Anyway, as a security, the creditor got hold of the land. What name we give to the form of contract by which a debtor gave his land, or part of it, to a creditor is of little importance. It is, at any rate, the situation to which Aristotle refers.[20] Solon, in the following verses, goes on to mention three different groups of people; the last were those who were in servitude in Attica. They must have been the same as those on whose land the *horoi* were erected. From other sources we know that they were called *hekte-morioi* ('sixth parters'); they could also, though probably later when the meaning of *hektemorioi* was no longer clear, be called *pelatai* (clients?) or thetes which was the general name of the land-less. They were unable to repay the loans they had accepted or provide sufficient labour, and were forced to pay one-sixth of their produce to the creditor.[21] The *horos* made it clear that the debtor, his family, and his land were in the power of the creditor, as long as the pledge was not redeemed, and that the land could not be claimed or sold by himself or any relative of his. As Solon implies, it was the lack of freedom which weighed most upon the hecte-morii, but in their state of poverty the rate of payment was often a heavy burden. Moreover, there must have been increasing econo-mic pressure because of the growth of the population. Like every-where else, at Athens too the signs of land-hunger became evident, and that frequently caused grazing land to be turned into poor arable land, with the danger of soil erosion.[22]

There were other forms of oppression which Solon mentions. Before the line on the hectemorii, he speaks of those 'many who, lawfully or not,[23] had been sold abroad', and others who had fled from Attica because of debts and 'had even forgotten their Attic speech – so widely had they been wandering' (and, we may add, for such a long period). We learn that it was possible to sell a man into slavery for debt. Aristotle maintains that loans were on the security of the persons of the debtor and his family. Sale into slavery was the ultimate consequence of that rule. It also meant that less people had to be fed at home, though it is unlikely that this fact influenced the deportation of enslaved peasants. Moreover, there were foreign slaves in increasing numbers, who were part of the property of the wealthy.

The distinction made by Solon between those at home and those abroad is at the same time a distinction (as stressed by Plutarch, *Sol.* 13) between the hectemorii, that is to say, free peasants in financial bondage, and those who either had become slaves abroad or had fled Attica in order not to be enslaved. The two groups were not men of different origin or even different social status, who for that reason would have been treated differently. Rather, they represented two different phases in the treatment of the debtors, a milder one and a more severe one; the second stage would probably be reached if and when one of the hectemorii was unable to pay his sixth. That is the explanation which Aristotle gives in his rather confused chapter (*AP* 2). It is probably not more than a guess, but it makes sense.[24]

We may still ask what caused the state of affairs in which a great many people had fallen into dependence. A few bad harvests or some hostile raids from neighbouring areas might be bad enough, but could hardly account for such deep and widespread distress among the farmers. We shall discuss Solon's reform of weights and measures. Coins – though only staters, i.e. two drachma pieces – had perhaps by then been introduced in Corinth and Aegina, though even that is not certain, and most trading was still on a barter basis or dealt with money weights and not with coins. Even so, economic competition generally increased, and it did influence the Athenian market as well. This must have made life more difficult for the Attic farmers, while the larger landowners who chiefly grew olive trees and vines could easily exchange their produce against imported corn or even luxury goods. When a peasant tried to get help from a wealthy neighbour, it was quite common, as Solon expressly states (fr. 3, 7 ff.), for the rich to make the most unfair use of their opportunities. Solon reproaches them for 'avarice and arrogance' (4, 4), thus condemning on moral grounds what, he knows, was at the same time a grave social danger. The opening-up of overseas trade routes and the need for cutting down home consumption may even have made the sale abroad of slaves a really profitable, if contemptible, form of business, while it also reduced the number of the poor.

The general situation therefore was that the rule of an oligarchy of noble and wealthy landowners had become so oppressive that a revolution did not seem far away. It was the situation which in so many Greek states led to the rise of a tyrant. The Athenians, after the lesson of Cylon's attempt, behaved once again with remarkable political wisdom. The lower classes would naturally applaud anybody who was going to help them. They were not only the really poor (hectemorii and many of the thetes) but also farmers who as non-Eupatrids were excluded from holding office. The wealthy, on the other hand, must have realized that any intervention would mean losses for them, but that a revolution would be worse. The number of the hectemorii will have greatly increased at the end of the century, and differences among various noble clans may have strengthened the wish for a peaceful settlement. It was also a question of maintaining the military strength of Athens, which suffered by the decline of the free peasantry. An additional reason will have been that in the late seventh century wealth from other sources than land began to play a considerable part. The men who sailed the seas, although a small minority in an overwhelmingly agricultural society, must have been some of the most energetic and ambitious people from both the nobles and the non-nobles. With the wealth thus acquired, and used if possible to buy land, those not belonging to the nobility gained a higher social status. The old social barriers were beginning to break down. All classes of the people had the greatest interest in achieving a peaceful solution to the troubles within the community, and were prepared to accept the decision of a mediator.

3 · Solon: Seisachtheia and Constitution

What was it that made Solon a possible and, as it seems, the only possible candidate for the role of mediator? Born in the early thirties of the seventh century, he was neither too young nor too old. He belonged to a clan of highest nobility, but was – if we may trust Plutarch (2), who most likely made an obvious conclusion from some of Solon's verse – a man of moderate means. Probably a younger son, he did not inherit the ancestral estate and was engaged in trade; he had travelled a good deal and therefore might have a better understanding of economic affairs in general than most of his fellow noblemen. However, these qualities would hardly have sufficed to single Solon out for the great task of putting the state in order. It seems that he became known to his fellow citizens by his actions in the war which had been going on for a long time between Athens and Megara for the possession of Salamis. It may have helped to alleviate the situation of the poor farmers, when the island of Salamis was added to the available land.[25] The stories told later about the capture of the town of Salamis and Solon's part in it are mainly invention; the only reliable source is the few fragments of an elegy (2) in which Solon exhorted the citizens to fight for the island and not to be among the *Salaminaphetai*, the betrayers of Salamis.[26] It seems certain that soon after the public appearance of Solon reciting his elegy, the island was conquered or reconquered, possibly under his leadership. The war with Megara, however, did not end till eventually Sparta was asked to arbitrate between the two states and gave Salamis to Athens – a clear indication of Sparta's acknowledged leadership in Greece.

A public recital in the agora was the most effective, if not indeed the only, means for a man to spread his views and to become known among the people. Solon, 'using the ordered song of verse instead of mere speech' (2, 2), wrote, and undoubtedly recited, other poems which must have carried even greater weight than the Salamis elegy to induce the Athenians to make him their political mediator (*diallaktēs*), poems which in general terms expressed Solon's views on gods and men, on wealth and poverty, on right and wrong, on the punishment of evil-doers by divine justice. These and other subjects are the themes of his first elegy, in which he really speaks of his 'mission' as a poet, and produces a kind of moral and pious programme for the life of men.[27] In a language more poetical than that of most of his other extant poetry, and with deep religious fervour, he warns his fellow men not to rely on wealth and power but to fear fate's punishment. Even closer to the point is the elegy called *Eunomia* (fr. 3), which shows his deep concern for the fate of his beloved Athens. The state is threatened by the people themselves, especially by the unjust aims of the leaders and the rich. He foretells servitude and civil war, he speaks of the poor sold abroad into slavery. 'Bad order' (*dysnomia*) brings evil to the polis, while 'good order' (*eunomia*) saves the state from ruin, 'straightens crooked judgements', and 'stops the works of factional strife'. We must assume that the nobles played a decisive part in electing Solon. Economic reasons will have played their part. The rich (like Solon himself) frequently traded their own produce abroad, but that was no longer sufficient, and they were in need of traders and potters for their oil export. The epoch of the exclusive rule of the narrow-minded land-owners was coming to an end, and the wealthy class must have realized that the danger of revolt and possibly tyranny was so great that any alternative was preferable. Here was the man who told them the bitter truth, and therefore had the confidence of the lower classes, the man who dared reverse the usual concepts of class description, calling many of the rich 'bad', and claiming that the poor were 'good' (4, 9).[28] What chiefly angered the lower classes was no longer as in Hesiod's Boeotia the crooked judgements by the squires but their illgotten wealth.[29] It must have been clear, at the same time, that Solon had no radical views. He was the man who knew the answer to, and the way out of, the dangerous distress. As Tyrtaeus in Sparta spoke of *eunomia* in an hour of crisis, so did Solon – though they did not mean the same thing – and the whole people responded. Whether Solon was an outstanding poet or not, he was a real 'maker' (*poietes*), a creator, and the moral passion of his poetry as well as his general moderation carried conviction as the expression of a just and determined man, and of a statesman at that. As he says himself, he did his work thanks to his power (*kratos*), bringing into harmony both force and justice.[30] Most remarkable at the same time was the kind of piety which ruled his mind and actions. In all his poetry we find nothing of mythology or of theological discussion; he had a simple belief in the final justice of the gods and in the particular protection of his beloved Athens by Pallas Athena (esp. fr. 3). He was able to fill the position which archaic and to some extent even classical Greece offered to the poet, and that meant fulfilling the task of guiding the people.

Solon was elected archon for the year 594–593 and was given full power.[31] The foremost thing to do was to free the debtors and their land. He did this by cancelling all debts, and this was called *seisachtheia*, the 'shaking-off of burdens'. It certainly was a radical measure, but the loss for the creditors did not touch the substance of their wealth. At the same time he forbade for the future all loans on the security of the person (*epi sōmasi*) so that never again could a man, or his wife and family, be enslaved for debt. It is possible that he cancelled thereby a law of Dracon's. A law like this, with its effects reaching into the future, was a kind of *habeas corpus* act, rare if not unique in the Greek world. It must also have included any cases of selling citizens into slavery for reasons other than debt. When the stones on the land were removed, and 'Mother Earth made free', the creditor lost his hold on the debtor, and the master on his dependent labourer, obviously without any recompense. The hectemorii disappeared, and we never hear of them again.[31a]

This act of liberation must have been comparatively easy, compared with the task of bringing back to Athens those who were enslaved abroad. We do not know how Solon was able to buy them free from their owners. Did their former master know where they were? Could those who had sold them be forced to pay for their liberation? Or was public money used, and if so, where did it come from? It is not impossible that the reform of measures and coinage, about which we shall have more to say, provided some means for state business. Solon could not sell the land of exiled opponents, as other reformers often did, though there may have been a few farms the owners of which could no longer be traced. Those who had voluntarily exiled themselves in order to find a livelihood elsewhere will have gladly returned as soon as they heard of the *seisachtheia*. The free peasantry of Attica was thus fully restored, though Solon did not provide the means the liberated people would need to start their new lives, and we may also ask whether it was possible fully to restore the land to the previous owners. What he did was to improve the general economic situation by banning all export of natural produce except oil of which there must have been plenty. Thus, he prevented precious corn from going abroad, and helped those who were better off, but had lost some of their wealth. He also tried to strengthen non-agricultural activities, and to foster trade and manufacture by various measures such as his reform of weights and measures (see p. 73), and the creation of a new market-place.[32] Some of the former peasants who returned from exile will have taken up other professions; there may even have been a more widespread move from the rural areas to the city.

The economic reforms were followed by a remoulding of the constitution on a new economic basis. Even before Solon the introduction of the new military tactics which we have mentioned several times had led to a new division of the people. According to their military position they were divided into horsemen or knights (*hippeis*), the yoke-men (*zeugitai*), and the *thetes*, that is to say, cavalry, phalanx of hoplites, and men without military duties.[33] The three groups had an economic and social significance as well since the keeping of a horse and the providing of heavy armour required certain economic standards. The new groups to some extent replaced the ancient division into eupatrids, geomori, and demiurgi, though only to some extent. The old division survived, not least because it was based on ancient cult communities; besides, the natural pride of the nobles in their ancestry prevented the eupatrids from disappearing. In order to deprive them of their constitutional monopoly, Solon used the military division on a purely economic basis as the framework of constitutional qualifications. He found it, however, necessary to put a first 'class' above the *hippeis*, the *pentakosiomedimnoi*, the 'men of 500 bushels'. Aristotle (*AP* 7) explains that the four 'classes' were distinguished according to the return from their property of 500, 300, 200, and less than 200 bushels, respectively. For several reasons this is a most unlikely scheme, and it will be advisable to take for granted only the nature of the *pentakosiomedimnoi*, as their name is self-explanatory. They were the cream of the *hippeis*; they would naturally serve in the cavalry. In using the four property groups for his work on the constitution, Solon clearly intended to base his constitutional reform on the facts of Athenian agrarian economy. Landed property and its income, not birth, was to be the basic principle. Whether that would mean a considerable change in the composition of the governing class is another question.

Was it possible, however, to find out the exact, or even the average, number of measures yielded by the crop, especially as production must have fluctuated from year to year? Even if that could be done, what would it mean, since it was not possible to count liquid produce in *medimnoi*, still less the possession of cattle, sheep, and goats, to say nothing of the income from trade?[34] A solution might be that *medimnos* was the symbol for pre-coinage valuation, just as in Homer and even in Dracon's laws (Poll. 9, 61) it was the ox;[35] but that is purely hypothetical, and there is no other evidence for it. Thus it seems better to try to explain the matter without the help of such a theory. All we can say is that an estate of comparatively large size, whether mainly corn-growing land or vineyards and olive groves, or partly even grazing ground for cattle, would be regarded as producing 500 *medimnoi*, without any serious attempt at counting. Social connexions and public opinion would probably settle the point safely enough. The exact limits for the other classes are therefore likely to be pure invention, though it is just possible that a grading took place very much on the same general lines as the selection of the *pentakosiomedimnoi*. The three less wealthy groups would be respectively those rich enough to serve in the cavalry, those able to equip themselves with a hoplite's armour and to leave their farms during a campaign or during training, and finally, those below these standards. Aristotle tells us that Solon's classes had existed before him. This is certainly true of the military division. If the name of the *pentakosiomedimnoi* was in earlier use, it could only have been as a kind of nickname for the most wealthy. What was completely new was that Solon used the four groups as a basis for constitutional rights, and that the military divisions as well as the *pentakosiomedimnoi* – the latter for the first time officially recognized – served on account of their economic standing.

Any constitution in which the rights of citizenship, and in particular the qualification for high office, were graded according to economic standards was no longer fully aristocratic.[36] Neither was it democratic, as was the view of fourth-century Greeks who regarded Solon as the father of Athenian democracy. Any reform would and could only be based on traditions which went far back, but were still alive. Solon's constitutional and social work was possible only as the continuation of the atistocratic state and society of the past, but it went far beyond that. If it can be said that democracy was, as it were, the goal of the Athenian political development, it means that it could be approached only step by step. Solon, with no idea of democracy in his mind, was predestined by his whole nature to advance slowly, without making too much of a break. The principle of his constitution was not as revolutionary as it might look, but it certainly opened the way for more social changes. It can best be explained as the necessary political result of the change in military structure, which itself resulted from the changing economic capability of the citizens. Athens had reached the stage of the 'hoplite polis', though the hoplites had by no means yet equal rights with the upper class. When in the later fifth century the oligarchs relied on the notion of those 'able to provide their arms', they were looking back to Solon's timocracy.[37]

Solon did more than create a timocracy, even in the constitutional field. He cleared the way by proclaiming a law of amnesty (see below, p. 70); he then granted the citizens new political rights. He almost certainly opened the ecclesia to the thetes, who thus for the first time had a share in public affairs. In this, as in other constitutional changes, our knowledge is restricted by the fact that the evidence, above all *AP*, is strongly influenced by later events, and it is not always possible to arrive at the original facts. High offices were reserved for the two upper classes, though archons and treasurers were elected from the *pentakosiomedimnoi* only.[38] All officials were elected by the ecclesia; according to *AP* 8, 1, the archons were chosen by lot from forty previously selected men, ten from each phyle, an assertion in conflict with Aristotle's own views elsewhere, and difficult to combine with later constitutional developments. The problem is not yet finally solved.[39] The Areopagus was filled by the ex-archons, and thus became a council of the wealthy rather than the old and noble. This method of recruiting the members of the Areopagus was probably first introduced by Solon, though it is not quite impossible that it existed before under different conditions. The rich and the noble were, as has been said before, to a large extent the same people, and any change in the composition of the Areopagus can have been only slow. The prestige and power of that body remained strong. Solon will have defined more strictly its rights of jurisdiction and general supervision; in particular, all cases of premeditated homicide were now judged by the Areopagus, while Dracon had left all capital jurisdiction to another early court, the 51 *ephetai*. According to *AP* 8, 4, Solon also granted the Areopagus the power to retaliate against any attempt at destroying the constitution.[40] To what extent the archons and treasurers, or as to that, any other officials, depended on the advice of the council is obscure; in general, an increase in the power of magistrates, especially the first archon, and a slow decrease in that of the Areopagus, are likely. In one short reference Aristotle (*AP* 8, 4) mentions the creation by Solon of a new council of the 400, one hundred from each phyle. Plutarch (*Sol.* 19, 1) repeats this and adds that it acted (as the Cleisthenic council of the year 507) as a 'probuleutic' body, before anything was put to the assembly. A similar 'democratic' council existed in Chios towards the middle of the sixth century. Plutarch speaks of two Athenian councils as the two anchors on which the polis was safely riding. There is, however, no record of anything the council of the 400 did or could have done, and doubts about its very existence are not without justification.[41] Any decision largely depends on whether we believe that Solon wanted to break the power of the Areopagus, or only slightly to limit it. Athenian history before Cleisthenes shows no sign of a second council; the one which resisted Cleomenes (Hdt. 5, 72, 2, s.p. 87) was most likely the Areopagus. There were opportunities to speak of the council if it had existed, and thus the *argumentum e silentio* has some force.

Areopagus, ecclesia, and magistrates in Solon's constitution, taken as a whole, kept their previous positions, though some restrictions were laid down. The decisive difference was in their composition, which had largely changed. Aristotle (*AP* 9, 1) describes three elements as 'the most democratic' in this constitution; above all, the law forbidding loans on personal security, secondly, the right of any citizen to claim redress for anybody who had been wronged, and thirdly, 'the right of transfer to the court'. From his own knowledge of the fourth century Aristotle anachronistically adds, 'When the people are masters of the judicial vote, they become masters of the state.' The first item refers, of course, to the *seisachtheia* (see p. 64). Of the two others we might say that in general they aimed at a stronger legal protection of the citizens against arbitrary, or at least authoritarian, treatment by magistrates. It is practically certain that the word *ephesis*, which in the fourth century meant an appeal from one court to a higher one, was in Solon's time simply the transfer from the single judge, before any verdict of his, to the people's court.[42] The latter received the name *heliaia*, which is another word for assembly. It is possible, though not very likely, that it was merely the ecclesia acting as a court. Perhaps the court will have been elected by lot from the ecclesia; no other details are known about the 'people in court'. But the famous, almost revolutionary basis of the judicial system was that any citizen could now raise a charge when anybody – whether free or slave, whether man, woman, or child (Dem. 21, 47) – had been wronged by an unlawful action. 'Anybody's wrong was everybody's business.'[43] The state and, with its help, the individual citizen took over where so far it had been for the family to act, or for the noble society as a united whole. Freedom and responsibility of the citizen went hand in hand. This was a revolutionary reform.

Solon was a man of the middle road. That will have been a trend of his nature, but it was also the result of a reasoned approach to politics rather than an *a priori* principle. Solon learnt the wisdom that 'in great things it is hard to please everybody' (fr. 5, 11). He proudly claimed (5, 1 ff.): 'To the demos I have given such honour as is sufficient, neither taking away nor granting them more. For those who had power and were great in riches, I equally cared that they should suffer nothing wrong. Thus I stood, holding my strong shield over both, and I did not allow either side to prevail against justice.' Such verse (and there is more in a similar vein) confirms that he believed himself to have succeeded in his work of mediation. He had probably started it by issuing an amnesty law (Plut. 19, 4) by which all who had lost their citizenship (the *atimoi*) were given it back, except those condemned for major crimes by one of the ancient courts.[44] After his legislation, stories were told which show that neither side was satisfied, and also that he refused to follow the advice of some of his friends to become a tyrant; he had enough insight and irony to see himself through the eyes of one of those friends (fr. 23). He had the conviction of his own mission, and he remained faithful to his aims and principles. His constitution was never put down in writing as one coherent concept; but the ecclesia must have accepted certain special laws. It needed, however, more than merely economic and constitutional measures. Social peace largely depended on reasonable laws, and a jurisdiction bound to them. Dracon's work had to be repeated and improved, that is to say, new laws had to be given which would be in harmony with the spirit of Solon's whole work. That could only last, if at all, if it were built upon a new code of written laws. As Solon tells us himself (24, 18), 'Laws I wrote, alike for nobleman and commoner, awarding straight justice to everybody.' The word 'I wrote' (*egrapsa*) is clearly stressed, but the reference to noblemen and commoners is even more important. Solon's concern was the whole people.

4 · Solon's Legislation

The orators of the fourth century quote a large number of laws which they attribute to Solon. It is generally accepted that only some of them are really Solonian, while others belong to later times, though early as seen from the fourth century. 'Solon's laws' at that time largely meant traditional laws, *corpus iuris Atheniensium*. Like Dracon's they were called *thesmoi*, as rules 'set' by an acknowledged authority, whether divine or human, and usually written down; they were contrasted with the later political laws, the *nomoi*. Once again we have to face the fact of a tradition distorted or at least exaggerated; the early history of Athenian law is greatly obscured. What happened to the written code of Solon's laws in the many vicissitudes of Athenian history during the sixth and fifth centuries is quite unknown. In 410–409, and continued in 403, after two olig- archic revolutions, a revision of the extant laws was carried out. Dracon's law of homicide was renewed. The rest of the laws were regarded as 'Solonian', or at least called so because of the authority of his name; many of these laws undoubtedly *were* Solonian, and Aristotle most likely still read some of them.[45]

It is unlikely that Solon's code of law included much about the constitution, which was probably settled by popular decrees; it is certain that the *seisachtheia* was not mentioned in the laws, as it was a unique measure not to be repeated, and other matters were simply part of customary law and did not need to be freshly formulated. These matters, especially the duties of the magistrates, have to a great extent been included in the previous section, although it is not possible to single out certain laws, quite apart from the fact that we do not know their wording. The Greeks at that time, and still later on, did not distinguish between constitution and laws, not even between public and private law. Moreover, Solon did not arrange his laws according to their subject matter but rather after the magistrates responsible for their observance. It must have been easy to add new laws to the extant ones since, at any rate, a very mixed lot was assembled under the title of one office, e.g. that of the first archon, and therefore on the same tablet. Solon's laws were origin- ally published on wooden slabs, called *kyrbeis* or *axones*, probably shaped like prisms and revolving round (vertical?) axes so that they could be easily read without taking up too much space. It seems that they survived, however precariously, the sacking of 480.[46]

The greatest number of laws likely to be Solonian is concerned with family law. This may be partly due to the fact that most of the cases dealt with by the orators belonged to that sphere. It is, however, probably quite true that Solon regarded as one of his most urgent tasks the establishment or re-establishment of what was the very foundation of Athenian society, the permanence of the family. It is typical of him that he gave various rules to bind both parents and children, thus, as in politics, taking the middle line. Of great importance was his law on heiresses (*epikleroi*), who, especially when orphaned, were protected in order to continue the existence of the family (*AP* 9, 2. 56, 6. Plut. 20). Therefore the heiress did not enter her husband's family but was to produce the legitimate male heir to her father's family. A similar purpose was served by Solon's law on adoption, allowing under certain conditions a man without legitimate male offspring to adopt a man and thus make him his heir. This law chiefly concerned the upper class; it was to prevent a family from dying out, as is said in one speech (Dem. 43, 11. 76) 'that the *oikos* be not made destitute (of heirs)'. The law was at the same time a first small step towards freeing the individual property from the clan. It was still far from being private property, especially as the adopted son could only leave the estate to his actual son, not again to an adopted man.[47] Marriage, naturally most important in this context, was generally to be protected, adultery and unchastity of women were severely punished; so were, though less severely, violation, procuring, and the prostitution of boys. There was a definitely moral trend in Solon's legislation, for instance, in the strict rules to control women and boys, and the law against exaggerated display at funerals, laws about slander and calumny, and others concerned with private life. In criminal law Solon retained Dracon's laws on homicide.[48] Theft was heavily punished when committed in the dark or from a public place such as market or harbour, or if the value of the stolen goods exceeded fifty drachmas,[49] a law which showed a discrimination understandable under the conditions of non-existing public security. Solon took the trouble of regulating such things as the water supply of each farm, or the distance between trees and beehives; he knew that for the small farmer these could be questions of economic survival. Olive oil was plentiful, and Solon, as mentioned before, made it the one agricultural product that could be exported; he strictly forbade the export of corn, which the larger landowners had probably practised. In exchange for the export of oil – and of the fine pottery that went with it – barley and wheat, both badly needed, could be imported. Thus, the owners of large olive groves, the traders, the potters, no less than the poor in town and country, would all benefit from his measures. In particular, he favoured the development of crafts; it is reported that he made it an offence if a father did not see to it that his sons learned some kind of craft.

With the last laws mentioned we are again in the field of economics. Even before Athens acquired a money economy, trade grew rapidly, and with it agriculture began slowly to change over from farming merely for livelihood to commercial farming, that is to say, to working for export. Athenian Black Figure vases of the early sixth century have been found in the West as well as the Black Sea area, confirming the growth of Athenian trade. Solon, for some time a trader himself, understood the importance, for a poor country such as Attica, of trade, and therefore of manufacture and good craftsmanship. He also made it easier for foreign craftsmen to settle at Athens and even to become citizens; surely this chance must have attracted many, and it will have substantially contributed to the swift rise of art and craft at Athens.

Aristotle (*AP* 10) mentions also that Solon after his legislation caused 'the enlargement of measures, weights, and the coinage. Under him the measures became larger than those of Pheidon, and the mina, which formerly had a weight of seventy drachmas, was increased to a hundred. The old type of money (*charaktēr*) was the didrachmon. As weights for the coinage he made sixty-three minae equal to the talent, and the three minae were apportioned to the stater and the other weights.'[50] The law behind these enigmatic sentences has been a matter of debate even before Aristotle, and ever since the *AP* was recovered. The Pheidonian measures and weights had nothing to do with coinage, and Pheidon cannot have been responsible for the coins of Aegina, even if it had been part of his realm. Aegina, however, could have been the one state in the Greek motherland, apart from Corinth, which at Solon's time had issued coins, though it is now believed that coins were not introduced from Asia Minor before *c.* 575.[51] Recent discussion, on the other hand, suggests that the earlier standard which Solon changed was not Aeginetan but Euboean, i.e. Chalcidian. According to this theory, Solon – or some later man whose work was then called Solonian – introduced a new weight of 100 compared with the old 70.[52] If the primary purpose of coinage was for the use of governments rather than private traders, it nevertheless fostered overseas trade more than anything else. The change of standards would make Athens adopt the standard of another trading country, but in the long run, the Attic, i.e. the new Solonian, standard, and with it Athenian trade, conquered the Mediterranean world in both the east and the west. It is clear that Solon, by fighting the trade competition of places such as Corinth, Aegina, Megara, and perhaps Chalcis, prepared the way for the prosperity of sixth- and fifth-century Athens.

The whole tenor of Solon's legislation (and here we include the measures treated in the previous section), of which no survey could be complete, is one of moderate conservatism. We would not expect anything else from a man such as he. Any revolutionary measures like the *seisachtheia* would be compensated by the adherence to traditional ways wherever possible. Behind this mild conservatism there was, however, a great mind and a strong will. In many ways a typical product of his time, he stood high above the politics of the day by his absolute integrity, the clarity of his intellect, and the passionate fervour of his ethics. He bound the community as a whole to its laws, that is to say, he founded the state on justice. He made the people its executant, and secured the personal freedom as well as the political responsibility of every citizen. Although he did not and could not use the expression, he was the first deliberately to proclaim 'freedom under the law', the rule of what was to be called the 'King Nomos'.[53] Even so, justice and freedom did not include equality among the citizens, neither economically nor politically. Solon believed in a divine justice that would always put matters right in the end, and in man's duty to justify the justice of the gods; but he was aware of the need of rational action in order to create social solidarity.[54] Many of his laws did little else than put customary rules under the state's authority, but he succeeded in creating an atmosphere of legality. It could perhaps be said that, under the leading lights of piety and justice, Solon (with others) finally changed the Homeric set of values, modernized the ethics of the aristocrats, which they had partly forgotten themselves, and adapted them so that they could serve as guidance for the whole people.[55] He was enough of a traditionalist not to become a revolutionary, though too much of a reformer not to change the face and indeed the very nature of state and society. He had a strong sense of the possible, and at the same time a deep feeling for that balance between freedom and responsibility, which was to be the principle in all further developments of the state.[56] He never imagined a democratic form of constitution, but his *eunomia* implied the rule of *dike*, of justice. While his work in practically all its aspects remained, as it were, unfinished, he paved the way into the future, and made it possible for Peisistratus and Cleisthenes to continue and to improve his work, so that eventually it did lead to democracy, with its ideal of a state of law, liberty, and equality.

Solon had outgrown the bonds of aristocracy of which his younger contemporary Theognis of Megara was a fervent champion. His verses reflect the traditional life and education of the aristocrats, with their emotional centre in paederasty, that is to say, love between man and boy, and their outlets in resentment and hatred of an emerging and different world. It is significant that, and how, Theognis varied some of Solon's verses to suit his own ideas.

It need hardly be stressed that all this was true only as far as the citizens were concerned. Women and slaves never had any standing in the polis, though foreigners at Athens acquired an improved status, and a chance of becoming citizens. Slavery had been with the Greeks, just as with all early peoples, mainly as a natural result of warfare, after the initial stage, when an enemy was killed and no prisoners were taken, had largely passed. At Athens, so far, slaves played no important economic part, though the newly discovered silver mines at Laurium, essential for the new coinage, were always worked by slaves – if not exclusively, at least mainly.[57] The need for giving legal status to the slaves hardly occurred to Solon. When later they were granted some power to make business agreements, this was possible only when they were employed by someone not their master, or when they eventually had an independent business of their own. As far as we know, this did not happen before the late fifth century, after a lengthy process of development that cannot be traced here. The decline, on the other hand, of the position of women since Homeric times is remarkable. From Hesiod onwards there was a great deal of misogynic poetry, while the great figures of Penelope or Nausicaa, or of the Phaeacian queen Arete, or the overwhelming if evil part played by Helena or Clytaemnestra, survived in Greek myth and memory. There are indications that the Greeks in pre-historic times lived in a matriarchal society; its remnants can still be traced in epic poetry. The great change must have happened by the time of the invasions, during or after the Mycenaean age. When the polis arose, in the eighth century, Greek society was completely dominated by masculine standards; if Sappho somehow seems to indicate an exception, it is the exception that proves the rule. At the same time, the greater freedom of women in Sparta remains remarkable. Such matters must not be forgotten, when we come to deal with the further development of democracy, though they should not be judged by standards and views of later times.[58]

IV

THE SIXTH CENTURY

1 · Tyrannis at Athens

Even during his term of office Solon had met with criticism and hostility. Refusing to become a tyrant, as some of his supporters suggested, he tried to safeguard his work by imposing an oath on the archons of each year to maintain his legislation (*AP* 7, 1. Hdt. 1, 29). He himself went travelling abroad – for ten years, we are told.[1] His hope that the Athenians would settle down and give his constitution and legislation a period of trial was soon to be disappointed, though the freedom of the peasantry was never again endangered. After a few years of calm, political and social issues combined to start civil strife again. Though it is a mistake to say that Solon achieved nothing, his attempt at creating a peaceful society had certainly failed. The office of first archon provided the position of power on which the struggle turned, which shows that individual noblemen were fighting against the very principles of Solon's constitution. The assembly had not yet gained the strength to impose its own decisions, and we do not hear of any political activity by the Areopagus. The little we know of these years comes from *AP*, and it does not allow us to fill the gaps between the few events mentioned.[2] Probably in 590–589 no archons were elected,[3] and the same happened in 586–585. This can only mean that there were riots which made elections impossible. A few years later, most likely in 583–581, one Damasias was archon and remained in office for two years and two months, until he was expelled by force. This was clearly an attempt to seize supreme power, using the archonship as a spring-board for tyranny. Resistance to Damasias would have come mainly from the aristocracy, as is confirmed by the peculiar events which followed, though their general meaning is much disputed. Aristotle tells us (*AP* 13, 2) that for one year after

Damasias, that is 580–579, ten archons were elected, as in a similar way about a century later, five from the Eupatrids, three from the *agroikoi*, and two from the *demiourgoi*. It is remarkable that a board of ten, a 'decemvirate', was elected to fill the position of the highest magistrate,[4] but the composition of the board is even more remarkable. While the election of a 'collegium' probably implied an attempt to stop the struggle for the highest office, it also meant a return to the ancient division of the people into nobility, peasantry, and the landless. It was a unique event, a step backward, never to be repeated; even so it disclosed the persistent vitality of the society of the pre-Solonian state. The complex and to some extent artificial order of 580 was a reaction to the threat of tyranny. While constituting a return to the old classes, it shows at the same time, through its numerical scheme, the impact of the spirit of more recent times. As the Eupatrids could never be in a minority, they will have been largely responsible for the whole matter; on the other hand, their position was no longer so powerful that they could act without the agreement of either the non-noble farmer or the merchants (rather than artisans). We do not know whether the two latter groups were wealthy people, but it is more likely than not that they were; Solon's constitutional changes could not simply be ignored.[5] They may all have been *pentakosiomedimnoi*, which would reveal the social rise of the non-noble rich; but whatever the exact significance of the ten archons, they were a sign of social developments in which the unity and preponderance of the noble class were more and more weakened.

After this short interval the struggle went on. It is practically certain, even though many points of detail remain doubtful, that regional and social conflicts combined with the feuds of the clans and the ambitions of individual leaders. Some of these might aim at tyrannical power; others would try to prevent tyranny from coming into being. In our tradition these struggles are regarded mainly as conflicts between three different regions of Attica, called *pedion*, *paralia*, and *diacria* – plain, shore, and hill. The men from these parts were the pediaei (or pediaci), the paralii, and the diacrii, whom Herodotus calls hyperacrii. The conventional view is that they represented groups of distinct social, professional, and political character. The men of the plain would be the rich landowners who politically were reactionaries; the men of the shore would be mainly traders and fishermen who kept to a moderate line in politics, adhering on the whole to Solon's ideas; the third group were the small farmers and shepherds of the hills. On this basis it has become a widespread habit to speak of the three groups as political 'parties'. The Greeks themselves called them *staseis* (Hdt. 1, 59, 3. *AP* 13, 4), factions in domestic strife, and that name is much more appropriate to the historical context as we can reconstruct it than the name of parties. It may remain open for the moment how far the factions were regionally or socially determined, how far just following individual leaders; but it can be said at once that the view – already expressed by *AP*, but not by Herodotus – that they represented clearly distinguished political opinions and aims is mistaken.

The three regions undoubtedly existed, although they were by no means as accurately defined as is often assumed, and as was indeed assumed later by the Athenians themselves.[6] There is a good deal of vagueness about the possible frontiers of the regions, not entirely due to our incomplete knowledge, as they were by no means clear in the minds of contemporary Athenians either. The regions frequently overlapped, especially in the mesogaea, the plain of the interior. They are best understood as popular concepts, and therefore not clear-cut geographical units; it is significant that they never served as administrative areas. Nevertheless, if we avoid any strict definitions, it may still be right to divide sixth-century Attica into these three parts.[7] It is less certain to what extent each region contained its own special type of people; they certainly were not as clearly distinguished as is often supposed. The main fault of the division, however, seems to be that the city had no place in it, or rather belonged to both pedion and paralia; moreover, it is known that Peisistratus as the head of the diacrii found substantial support in the city. Most of the real clashes among the groups must have occurred just there.

All further features of the struggle, social as well as political, largely depend on the kind of leaders the three groups found. We are told (Hdt. 1, 59. *AP* 13, 4. 14, 3) that the pediaei were led by Lycurgus, son of Aristolaidas, perhaps, like his namesake in the fourth century, a member of the noble clan of the Eteobutadae. They seem to have centred on 'the' plain, that of Athens itself; but they also held the Phaleron harbour. The paralii were led by Megacles, the Alcmaeonid. His family mainly farmed south of Athens near the shore, though without a good harbour; they had a great many supporters in the city. Finally, the hillmen were led by Peisistratus, son of Hippocrates, whom Plutarch (*Sol.* 10, 3) connects with Brauron, a place on the east coast, which can probably be regarded as part of the diacria.[8] Peisistratus, we are told, actually created his 'party', that is to say, the regional bonds were even less strong in his case than with the other two groups.

Each of the groups, as we saw, had a share in the others' areas; even so, they may have consisted of people bound together locally and by the leadership of one man and his clan. The pediaei and paralii will also have included other clans and their followers, but it cannot be maintained that the two groups were very different in composition. There were large landowners, farmers and merchants in both, and they were both factions within the nobility. The diacrii were geographically least definitely fixed, for there are hills everywhere in Attica and some of the hill-dwellers clearly belonged to one of the other groups. It is likely that the original *diakria* was north-east Attica, including the plain of Marathon, the town of Brauron, and possibly the old harbour of Prasiae. Whether the later descriptions of the social status of the diacrii are historically reliable is most doubtful, though in general it will be true that they included people who were very poor, perhaps also foreigners recently admitted to citizenship (cf. *AP* 13, 5). Peisistratus, who eventually succeeded in seizing power, and whose family had had no great influence previously, found followers among those who needed protection from the wealthy and economic security for themselves.[9] Among them must have been many in the city of Athens itself, for without the support of its population and of the ecclesia, Peisistratus would never have succeeded.

In short, there were three factions, led by individual members of the aristocracy and loosely connected with regional areas, where they probably found the bulk of their respective supporters. On the whole, it is the old picture of feuding clans, but the conflicts within the noble class went deeper now, as the aristocrats were facing a new developing society in which the non-nobles played a decisive part. Economic standards became increasingly important, and in various ways the nobles tried to keep their leadership in the new circumstances. Moreover, the danger of a one-man rule had, by then, complicated the issues. We cannot be sure whether Lycurgus, or even Megacles, aimed at becoming tyrants, though we know from Solon that the idea was in the air.[10] The rivalry of the great clans was probably as strong as ever, and we know of other families such as the powerful Philaids, the family of Miltiades. They came originally from Brauron or its immediate neighbourhood, but farmed in the Athenian plain; they were probably connected, in friendship and in rivalry, with Peisistratus.[11]

Peisistratus had won renown in the war against the Megarians; he even for a time occupied their harbour town of Nisaea. About the same time Athens lost Sigeum and had trouble with Aegina. Its increasing trade and the outstanding beauty of its pottery made Athens a dangerous competitor to other trading centres, but so far its economic progress was not backed by political strength, although victory in the First Sacred War, which secured the independence of Delphi, strengthened Athenian (as well as Spartan) influence in central Greece. In general, Solon's legacy was largely squandered by the feuding nobility, and the chance of adapting Solon's order to a changing economic situation was missed. Most likely, Solon was still alive and his warnings against the threat of tyranny (fr. 8 D) may have been caused by the rise of Peisistratus. When the latter seized the Acropolis (in 561–560), after being granted a body-guard by an official decree of the assembly, Solon was too old to resist, though he still wrote poetry (fr. 10 D) in which he described monarchy as an evil, which overcame the city like a thunderstorm from a serene sky. Solon must have died soon afterwards. The struggle, however, did not cease.[12] Peisistratus was expelled, probably twice; first, by a coalition of Lycurgus and Megacles; the second time, after he had concluded an alliance with Megacles and staged a return to the Acropolis.[13] But then he quarrelled with him again and went into exile in the region between Macedon and Thrace, where he was able to exploit some gold and silver mines. With the wealth he thus amassed he built ships and hired mercenaries; the latter were mainly Scythian archers, who henceforth frequently appear on Athenian vases; democracy was to take them over as the city police. Peisistratus also found allies among various

Greek states, eventually invaded Attica, and defeated his opponents in the battle of Pallene between Athens and Marathon. It was of outstanding importance that he now had money at his disposal, with which he could fight poverty, especially in the city, and at the same time steadily strengthen his own position.[14] He regained supreme power, the only Greek tyrant, apart from those under Persian suzerainty, who did so with the decisive help of foreign powers – a fact which largely determined his future policy. It was as a statesman of more than local importance that he ruled Athens, a great and wise ruler. His power was never again questioned; he died in 528–527 and was followed by the two sons of his first marriage, Hippias and Hipparchus.[15]

It is not possible to write a real history of Peisistratus' reign, but we know of its most important features. After his early failure he made his rule safe by foreign as well as domestic support. He was on friendly terms, or at least at peace, with most Greek states. While a great friend of Argos (where he found his second wife, the mother of his two younger sons), he was able to become an official 'guest friend' (*proxenos*) of Sparta. In a similar way many of his external connexions were of a personal kind – for instance, the friendship with Lygdamis, who with his help became tyrant of the flourishing island of Naxos, and through whom he also became a political friend of Polycrates of Samos. Although he had friendly relations with a hereditary kingdom such as Macedon or with aristocracies such as Eretria and Thebes, common interest brought the tyrants even closer together; their families often intermarried, and Peisistratus could use Lygdamis for holding as hostages some of his own opponents (Hdt. 1, 64, 1). He regained Sigeum and installed there his son Hegesistratus as a more or less independent ruler (Hdt. 5, 94). He allowed the elder Miltiades to occupy the Thracian Chersonese and thus removed a possible rival from Athens (cf. Hdt. 6, 35), at the same time gaining new land for Athenian citizens and securing the position around the Hellespont, which was of increasing importance for Athenian trade, especially the growing trade in grain from the Black Sea.[16] He kept his mining property at Mt Pangaeum, and with the Attic mines at Laurium at his disposal, his rule rested on a very solid financial basis. In all these matters personal and state policies went hand in hand.

At home he tried to win the permanent support of the non-nobles, and in particular of the increasing city population. The old clans lost some of their privileges, for instance, the right of issuing coins (if they ever had it),[17] and local jurisdiction. Their wealth, their social position, their virile splendour, on the other hand, were undiminished, as can be concluded from the fact that so many noble Athenians won victories at Olympia, especially in the chariot race. By appointing district judges and by going about a good deal himself (*AP* 16, 5), Peisistratus reduced the hereditary power of the squires and made life easier for the ordinary farmer. To them he sometimes advanced money, perhaps for settling on new ground that previously had been only used for grazing and was now to be used for growing olive trees and vines. He also gave some new land from a few confiscated estates of exiled nobles. He completed Solon's work for the peasants whose small holdings became the typical and predominant form of agriculture, and he succeeded to such an extent that he could afford to impose a tax on produce, perhaps even a tithe (*dekate*).[18] An anecdote (*AP* 16, 6) makes it likely that the collection of this tax was not always carried out with great strictness. At any rate, from this time onwards, in spite of much hardship, Athenian farming remained strong, centring on the cultivation of olives and vines; as this was slow business, demanding great care, peace and security were essential for the peasantry. Peisistratus' reign could appear to later generations, especially to the peasants, as a golden age, 'the life under Kronos' (*AP* 16, 7).

This would never have happened, in view of democracy's hatred of tyranny, unless Peisistratus' policy in general was one of reconciliation as well as of economic and cultural progress. It is quite unlikely that he had to disarm the citizens (*AP* 15, 4), though Hippias afterwards did so (Thuc. 6, 58). Even many of the noble families, apart from those in exile (later even they, as we shall see), were won over by his moderation and his success. He maintained Solon's laws and constitution, though he saw to it that the higher offices were held by his relatives and close supporters (Hdt. 1, 56. Thuc. 6, 54). The Areopagus continued to serve as a court in murder cases, and Peisistratus himself appeared before it (*AP* 16, 8. *pol.* 1315b, 21); but it is significant that the accuser did not dare to come forward. Whether the Areopagus also had a share in government, we do not know; though, with the archons being all on Peisistratus' side, it is quite likely that this body of former archons remained active. Superficially, and not only superficially, the Solonian constitution continued to work; in fact, it now worked even better, as Peisistratus embodied that strong and unified power which had been missing in Solon's constitution. Peisistratus became very popular indeed; later tradition again and again emphasizes his humanity and wisdom. He tried by all possible means to raise the living standards of the people, and his active foreign policy went hand in hand with the growth of Athenian trade and the beginnings of an Athenian navy. It was during his reign that Attic black-figured vases, whether as containers for oil or wine, or as highly accomplished works of art and craftsmanship, went out all over the Greek world, and displaced the Corinthian ware.

Perhaps Peisistratus' greatest asset, apart from the real power he held, was his religious policy. In full accord with the trends of the time, he was deeply religious, even with a tendency towards mysticism. It does not reduce the strength of these convictions that they fitted in with his determined statesmanship and were supported by the amount of money at his disposal. His relation to the state goddess Athena was very close indeed. It is most likely he or, shortly after his death, his son Hippias who issued the first coins with Athena's head and her bird, the owl; they remained the permanent symbols on Athenian coinage. The 'owls', especially the much valued tetradrachms, spread far beyond Attica, carrying Athenian trade and Athenian prestige everywhere, the most important export article beside oil and wine to provide Athens with urgently needed grain and timber. Peisistratus also built or at least greatly embellished Athena's temple on the Acropolis. The details are disputed, but it is certain that it was he who first made the sacred rock a beautiful place and a witness to the greatness of Athens and her goddess.[19] He also started a huge temple of Zeus outside the city, the Olympieum, which remained unfinished till the time of the emperor Hadrian. He greatly favoured the rural cults of Demeter and Dionysus. He built the first telesterion at Eleusis, the centre for the mystery cult there, and created other sacred precincts. By purifying the sanctuary of Apollo at Delos, the holy place for all the Ionians (Thuc. 3, 104, 1), he renewed the claim of Athens as the leading city among the Ionians, and gained at the same time a strategic stronghold. He, as well as Hippias later, strongly relied on oracles, and a man like the soothsayer Onomacritus played quite an important role under Peisistratus. The tyrant's grandson dedicated altars to the Twelve Gods and to Apollo (Thuc. 6, 54, 6), and Hipparchus even left an inscription of dedication at the Ptoion in Boeotia.[20]

Building activities and religious policy in general went together with the extension of the Great Panathenaea and the inauguration of the Great Dionysia. Our tradition about the early history of the Panathenaea is either obscure or unreliable.[21] It seems, however, likely that towards the middle of the sixth century something decisive was done for the quadrennial ('Great') Panathenaea, and we have every reason to believe that Peisistratus took a strong interest in a festival which at the same time served the goddess Athena and the whole people of Athens.[22] It must have been he who tried – with chariot racing as perhaps the oldest feature of the annual Panathenaea, which continued to exist together with the quadrennial festival – to make this a rival to the Panhellenic festivals of Olympia, Isthmus, and Delphi. He showed complete lack of interest in those older institutions which attracted so many of the noble and wealthy from all parts of Greece, and his relations with the Delphic oracle were definitely cool. That was perhaps another reason why he took a strong interest in Delos and its sanctuary, a competitor for Delphi in the worship of Apollo. Again we notice the peculiar mixture of religion, patriotism, and self-aggrandizement. The Great Panathenaea never succeeded in reaching the level of the great Panhellenic festivals, but they were important and popular; they helped to strengthen the unity of Attica and thus Peisistratus' own position, and the vast number of Panathenaic vases we still can see in our museums, which, filled with oil, were rewards for the athletic and musical victors, were at the same time a means of helping the Athenian potters and of displaying, in honour of Athena, a peculiar beauty of their own. The Great Panathenaea also provided the opportunity for recitals from Homer, which must have caused a wider and deeper appreciation of the epic legacy; but the story of a 'Peisistratid redaction' of the two epics can hardly be true, although many scholars have accepted it.[23]

The Great or City Dionysia, on the other hand, brought the agrarian god of wine, music, and fertility to the city. The god was celebrated in a number of annual festivals such as the Rural Dionysia and the Lenaea; but the transfer of his greatest festival to the city not only revealed the growing importance of the urban population, but also the city's significance as a cultural centre. This annual festival was to provide the framework for the greatest achievements of the Attic genius, tragedy and comedy. It derived from various aspects of Peisistratus' policy, his support of the peasantry and their cults, his aim of reconciling the city and country populations, his wish to raise the cultural standards of Athens generally. In 534 Thespis wrote a play in which for the first time an actor appeared, separate from the chorus, and it was probably then that the iambic trimeter was introduced. He created what has been called – rightly or wrongly – the first Attic tragedy.[24] It may have been about the same time that phallic dances and songs, some perhaps imported from Dorian states such as Megara, and obscene and comic processions from various festivals, especially rural ones, invaded the city. From all this, later Attic comedy originated. The Athenians had Peisistratus to thank for making them a people of keen theatre-goers, and their god Dionysus the god of the theatre.

Equally important for his popularity were Peisistratus' practical plans for Athens, for instance, a better water supply from the famous well of the *Enneakrounos*. He and his sons also added to Solon's new market-place, the *agora*, which soon grew into the very centre of city life. It has rightly been said that under Peisistratus, Athens changed from what was little more than a village into a city, and a flourishing and beautiful city at that. Naturally, for all these activities he needed a good deal of money. It seems that his considerable personal resources went into a common state treasury, probably as the largest contribution; obviously he had to supervise the state finances himself. There were also custom duties, which increased with the growing trade, and some other public income, in particular from the Laurium mines. The man whose reign witnessed a vigorous naval and trading policy was at the same time a man of wide intellectual interests and deep religious feelings. He truly laid the foundations of Athenian greatness.

Politically, the mere fact of monarchical rule increased the impact of the idea of equality among the people, especially as, at least for some time, many noble houses were exiled. The former ruling class began to change its character, as were the *nouveaux riches* whose wealth was based on trade rather than land, a fact which lowered the barrier between the nobles and the non-nobles. A new society had started on its career. The *tyrannis* was a necessary and creative antecedent of democracy. Peisistratus' own position was such that after his death in 527, his elder sons Hippias and Hipparchus could follow him in joint rule without any difficulty. This hereditary succession was a purely personal matter and often occurred in the first generation of other tyrannies. The two sons seem to have ruled in complete amity, although Hippias was the political leader, keeping to his father's policy. From a late fifth-century inscription, containing part of a list of archons, we know that Hippias held office in 526–525, Cleisthenes in 525–524, and Miltiades in 524–523 – thus, one after another, a Peisistratid, an Alcmaeonid, and a Philaid.[25] These names reveal, first, that it was worth while for the ruler to fill the highest office himself for a year; it might be regarded as a show of legality. Secondly, the list reveals that there was a real, if temporary, reconciliation of the ruling family with parts of the aristocracy. This is the more surprising as Herodotus (6, 103, 3) speaks of the murder of Miltiades' father Cimon, who had several times won the chariot race at Olympia and had become very popular; the assassination was obviously planned by the Peisistratids, but their part in it remained secret. Soon afterwards Miltiades went out to the Chersonese to continue and confirm the work of his uncle, the elder Miltiades, and his brother. Hippias, by more radical measures than his father, rid himself of potential or real rivals.

At that time the situation in the Aegean began to deteriorate. The extension of the power of the Persian empire, of which we have more to say later on, began to threaten the Greeks in the Aegean, among them the outposts of Athenian settlements. Polycrates, with his ambitions for a wider thalassocracy, perished (*c.* 520), and a few years later Samos was occupied by the Persians. Lygdamis met a similar fate, and Peisistratus' hostages won their freedom and joined his opponents in exile. Then Sigeum and the Chersonese, one after the other, fell, and all these events led to much bloodshed and misery. The situation in the motherland was no less dangerous. Sparta, though unsuccessful against Polycrates, had strengthened her position in Greece as the leader of the Peloponnesian League, to which by this time Corinth and Megara belonged, the two states holding the key positions between the Peloponnese and Attica. Argos, closely bound to the Peisistratids, was badly weakened by Spartan predominance in the Peloponnese. Hippias, who had taken Plataea under Athenian protection, thereby provoked the permanent hostility of Thebes, which aimed at uniting Boeotia under her leadership (Hdt. 6, 108; cf. Thuc. 3, 55. 68, 4).[26] As Sparta refused to help Plataea, Thebes was now on good terms with Sparta. Athens lost ground, and Hippias' rule became less and less popular. He was a lesser man than his father, and with enemies rising from without and within, tyranny went the way it went everywhere after one or two generations, for the hereditary principle contradicted the very basis of a tyrant's rule, his own genius.

It seems, however, that the event which later was regarded as outstanding, the assassination of Hipparchus by Harmodius and Aristogeiton, had little, if anything, to do with the end of Hippias' rule.[27] Two young aristocrats, a pair of lovers, felt offended either by Hipparchus or his stepbrother Thessalus and killed the former at the Panathenaic procession in 514. They were both killed afterwards, and neither the event nor its motives were ever made clear. We cannot completely deny the possibility that the violent deed was actually directed against tyranny as such, but it is unlikely. The immediate consequence, at any rate, was that Hippias' rule became harsh and oppressive (Hdt. 5, 55. Thuc. 6, 56 ff. AP 18 f.). To meet the threat of revolt he needed mercenaries, and therefore more money. He introduced, for instance, a number of taxes such as one on birth and death, which hurt practically every family (Arist. oec. 1347a, 16). In 511–510 he fortified Munichia, the hill dominating the Phaleron bay. In the following year his rule broke down. The deed of the tyrannicides became later on the symbol of the liberation. Thucydides, by stressing that the whole affair was a matter of love and jealousy, made it clear that he disbelieved the popular legend, which had led to a cult of the two men and to the erection of their statues in the market-place soon after 510. The 'legend' must have been of very early origin. It was most emphatically voiced in the famous drinking-song 'the Harmodius', a *skolion* in which Hipparchus is called 'the' tyrant, and his murderers are praised for having made Athens *isonomos*, which is the word indicating equality, the principle of democracy.[28]

Actually Athens was liberated by the intervention of Sparta and the action of some exiled noble families, especially the Alcmaeonids. This was a fact which cannot have been popular with the people, any more than were the Alcmaeonids themselves later. It is possible that the legend of the tyrannicides sprang from a source both anti-Spartan and anti-Alcmaeonid. Herodotus leaves no doubt that he thinks the Alcmaeonids, and not the tyrannicides, were the true liberators (6, 123, 2).[29] The first attempt by the exiled aristocrats led to a defeat at Leipsydrion near Mt Parnes, where a great many of the noble youth were killed, an event which was described in another of the drinking-songs (24 D). It was then that the aristocrats, and especially Cleisthenes, the head of the Alcmaeonids, realized that they needed help against Hippias. The plot centred on Delphi, where the Alcmaeonids had won favour with the priests (and money for themselves) by restoring the temple of Apollo. The Pythia, Apollo's prophetess, was bribed, as Herodotus frankly admits,[30] and she urged the Spartans at every possible occasion to free Athens from her ruler. Perhaps Sparta was not much in need of being urged; her foreign policy was generally hostile to tyrants, and the friendship of the Peisistratids with Argos must have been reason enough for an action against them, despite their *proxenia*, which, after all, had been a piece of opportunist policy. Moreover, at that time the Agiad king was the great Cleomenes I, who, ambitious for himself and for his state, tried to free himself from the restraining influence of the ephors and wished to force Athens and Argos to become members of the Peloponnesian League. A small Spartan expedition by sea failed, and then Cleomenes took command of a strong land army and joined hands with the Athenian exiles. Their leaders were Cleisthenes and Isagoras, the latter a man from an old noble family of which Herodotus knows nothing more than their obscure cult. Both men were united in their determination to overthrow Hippias,[31] though otherwise they held very different political views. Isagoras represented the reactionary aristocracy, while Cleisthenes was to show that he was a man of new and radical ideas.

Hippias largely relied on the cavalry of his Thessalian allies, but they were powerless against the Spartan hoplites; after having suffered defeat, they went home. Cleomenes entered Athens, where he found support, and Hippias was besieged in the Acropolis. The Spartans, not used to fighting against fortifications, were on the point of withdrawing, when Hippias' children were captured on their way out of Attica (*AP* 19, 6). To save them, Hippias and his followers surrendered and left the country; they found a refuge at Sigeum. That was the end of tyranny at Athens, and of the war with Sparta.

It was not yet the end of civil war. Isagoras and Cleisthenes led two opposing factions among the aristocracy. The former, elected archon in 508, at first obviously backed by a powerful section of the nobility, was confronted with a man, supported by another group of noble clans and soon gaining the support of the broader masses of people, especially in the city, by revealing plans of a new democratic order.[32] Isagoras, who was on good terms with the Spartan king, both personally and politically, recalled him, and Cleomenes forced the Athenians to expel the Alcmaeonids and with them seven hundred other families. The old charge of a religious curse because of the killing of Cylon's followers was used against the Alcmaeonids, and government was put into the hands of a body of three hundred. For a short time probably, Athens was a member of the Peloponnesian League.[33] The whole affair looks very much like a radical purge, in order to establish a narrow oligarchy, which was also in the interests of Sparta. Cleomenes and Isagoras met, however, with the resistance of the council (Hdt. 5, 72, 2. *AP* 20, 3) which they had tried to disband and which most likely was the Areopagus (see above, p. 68). The Spartans withdrew, Isagoras was powerless, and many of his followers were executed. The field was free once again for Cleisthenes, and he returned with his family and the other exiles.

2 · Cleisthenes

Cleisthenes was not, like Solon, a man to whom extraordinary power was granted. Having been first archon in 525 (see p. 87), he could not aim at that office again.[34] Everything he wanted to carry out had to be confirmed by the assembly, so that his reforms were at the same time the first example of democratic methods. He was opposed by the relatives and supporters of the Peisistratids, and above all by the majority of the aristocracy; his struggle against Isagoras continued the traditional *stasis* among the noble clans. But if he certainly tried to gain and to maintain power for himself and the Alcmaeonids, that was not his only, probably not even his chief aim. Power was to him a means of creating the constitutional framework for a society on the verge of becoming democratic, and of securing the unity of the state without a tyrant. Naturally he tried to find support among the non-nobles, by outlining plans which would give them a decisive say in the state. At the same time he never thought, even in his most radical moods, of destroying the traditional organization of cult and kinship. To combine it with, and subject it to, a new and different order, purely revolutionary action would not do. His plans were complex and comprehensive, and to carry them out he needed time. He seems to have started immediately after his first return, but he could not freely act before his opponents had been decisively weakened. He soon restored law and order, and then embarked on the creation of a new social order and a new form of government. How long it took to complete his work, we do not know. Nor do we have evidence of the gradual progress he must have made; we see only the final picture of a new organization of the state, and we must try to understand it.[35]

Every Greek polis is an entity composed of a number of human groups. Kinship, cult, and neighbourhood were the basic factors. So far the organization of the Athenian people had largely rested – through the clans and phratries – on the first two, though we have seen that regional influences had also played a part. With Cleisthenes, the local principle became predominant, but he immediately found ways and means to restrict it. The local principle predominated over the state organization, through the new ten phylae of which we shall say more soon; it prevailed, above all, through the small communities, the demes, which were to form the basis on which a new order of a largely artificial character was to be erected. The ancient social and religious bodies were preserved, though they were deprived of all political power. It was this union of different elements, the combination of theory and tradition, of a new division of the people, based on the villages and boroughs, with essential old institutions, that gave Cleisthenes' new order the chance of keeping city and rural population together and building up a new democratic society. He was to provide the framework within which the Athenian community was to live for centuries. Cleisthenes, no doubt, was a great innovator; but even he could not have done what he did without the steps taken in the same direction by Solon and Peisistratus.

The demes were local communities of very different size. Many had been ancient places of human habitation, and had naturally gathered a certain amount of local traditions; others were created by Cleisthenes, partly by uniting several villages into one new deme. It is an open question to what extent, or whether at all, the boundaries of the demes were fixed. The essential thing with the demes was the people, and not the land.[35a] Even so, a good deal of preparation was needed, especially in the way of a general survey of the land. According to later sources (cf. Strabo 9, 396), the total number of demes was 174; we do not know how many of these existed in Cleisthenes' time, but the majority probably did. Each was made into a political unit with a local assembly, a treasury, and a leading official, the demarchus.[36] There is no evidence as to what the original method of the latter's election was, but there is little doubt about the democratic character of these small political units. Each deme kept a register in which every citizen was inscribed when he reached the age of eighteen.[37] This was now the necessary legal procedure by which a man would become an Athenian citizen. It is possible that Cleisthenes used the demes and their registration for the admission of new citizens as well; but Aristotle's rather obscure passages on this subject do not justify the view that this was one of Cleisthenes' chief aims, or that the new citizens were an important section of the demos. Cleisthenes may have been glad to get some support from such people and, like Solon, probably did enfranchise a number of aliens.[38] Some 'new' citizens were probably those who had lost their citizenship under the Peisistratids. They, on the other hand, had made some people citizens without legal sanction; that led to a revision of the citizen roll (*AP* 13, 5) which cannot be separated from Cleisthenes' reforms. The decisive point for him, at any rate, was that everyone admitted, whether a man of the city or a farmer in the country, was a citizen in his own right, as a demesman and consequently as a member of one of the new phylae. The registration with the phratry, after birth and again on gaining maturity, was not abolished, simply because the cult connexions of the people made that impossible; but it was henceforth without political or constitutional significance. The name of the deme, the *demotikon*, was in future to be put after a man's name, instead of his father's name, the *patronymikon*, so that no social differentiation resulted from the nomenclature. Though it took a considerable time before this rule became common use, it was the seal on Cleisthenes' largely successful attempt to create only one type of citizen.[39]

The demes were allocated to ten local phylae or tribes, which, as the structural foundation of practically all political business, were to replace the ancient four phylae. The latter survived like the phratries, but even their religious and social importance was on the decline. The new phylae had each an eponymous hero with a cult, sanctioned by Delphi; even so, they were never genuine sacred communities. The whole character of the new order was secular and rational. The phylae served as the framework for the elections to practically all political institutions, above all to the council and to the increasingly numerous boards of magistrates. For the first time in history, as far as we know, a state was organized according to the decimal system, though the system as such had played a part in Greek thought, and to a small extent even in constitutional life. It is possible that the 'acrophonic' system of writing numerals, which was based on the decimal system and goes back to earlier times, began to be used in official records in Cleisthenes' day.[40] The duodecimal system with the traditional figures of three, four, and twelve lost its political, though not its religious, importance, and to fit the nine archons into the new scheme, the scribe of the thesmothetae was added as the tenth (*AP* 55, 1. 59, 7. 63, 1). The army too was organized on the basis of ten regiments, one from each phyle, and the local principle made the call-up and formation of the army units far easier. The decimal structure, with its freedom from traditional bonds, representing a union of political and scientific thought, became a symbol of democracy.

In creating the ten phylae, Cleisthenes was chiefly guided by two principles: one was that the phylae should be roughly equal in population; the other that each should represent a mixture of all classes, a cross-section of the whole people. If that were achieved, it would mean the destruction of the preponderance, local as well as general, of the large landowners, most of whom belonged to the Eupatrids, and would create the unity of state and people which the country so badly needed. In order to secure these aims, Cleisthenes divided the whole of Attica into three sections called city (*asty*), shore (*paralia*), and inland (*mesogaia*). Each phyle was composed of three parts, the *trittyes* (= thirds), one from each of the three sections of the whole country. It seems obvious that Cleisthenes depended on, but also deliberately altered, the traditional division into plain, shore, and hill. The city received the place it deserved in any division, while the two other parts more or less followed an easy and definite regional separation. The city part included a fair amount of land outside the walls, namely the plain of Athens, but also some coastline including Phaleron harbour. The urban trittyes served at the same time as demes (or the other way round), while the other trittyes usually received their names from the largest deme within their frontiers. Size and distribution of the trittyes, and therefore the geographical shape of the phylae, have been and still are a matter of discussion and research.[41] It seems likely that there were a number of anomalies, such as particular demes being enclaves outside their trittyes, some trittyes of the same phyle being contiguous and others widely separated, some boundaries following natural conditions and others not. Even so, it is certain that the arrangement was not haphazard, and Aristotle's view (*AP* 21, 4) that the three parts of each phyle were put together by lot is clearly mistaken. In many cases we can still recognize the tendency to match larger and smaller trittyes, and that is what we should expect. An additional factor may have been a desire to cut through territories in which individual clans or religious ties had a particularly strong hold, or, on the other hand, to strengthen the position of Cleisthenes' own clan, the Alcmaeonids. The main issue was the will to bring together in each phyle men of very different social standing, above all, the urban and rural populations. The general description by Aristotle that Cleisthenes wanted 'to mix the people', and thus to create a unified body of citizens, fits the traceable facts best. His laws were

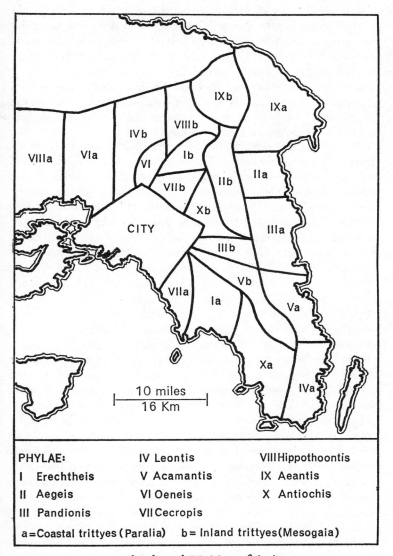

PHYLAE:

I Erechtheis	IV Leontis	VIII Hippothoontis
II Aegeis	V Acamantis	IX Aeantis
III Pandionis	VI Oeneis	X Antiochis
	VII Cecropis	

a = Coastal trittyes (Paralia)   b = Inland trittyes (Mesogaia)

4. Cleisthenes' Division of Attica

called *nomoi* as an expression of norms imposed on and by the people; they were the 'statutes' of Athens. That is also confirmed by the name which Cleisthenes gave his new order: *isonomia*, equal distribution and thus equality among the citizens, equality before the law as well as equal political rights, equal share in the state.[42] The unity of the state again found its living symbol in the goddess Athena. Cleisthenes finally established the uniform coinage of the 'owls' which, in spite of minor changes, kept its general archaic character throughout the fifth century.

A man was to belong to his deme for all time to come, and his descendants kept the same *demotikon*, whether he or they were still resident in that deme or not. Thus the local community was no longer of the same importance in the future, while the original mixture within the electoral and administrative bodies was preserved. This was most important because gradually a considerable number of people must have moved to the city, where all major public affairs were dealt with. If a man still belonged to his deme, no matter where he lived, the neighbourhood principle was no longer in full force, but neither had it been replaced by new bonds of kinship. If anything now counted beside the local principle, it was the individual citizen whose political activity had sometimes few ties left with any larger groups. The administration of the state was both centralized and locally dispersed, but essentially unified.

The city, as we said, became the very centre of all state affairs. There was the ecclesia, the sovereign assembly of the people, ruled by the principle of 'one man, one vote'. It soon found a new meeting-place on the Pnyx, west of the hill of the Areopagus, where about 500 B.C. a platform terrace with the *bema*, the speaker's stone, was carved out of the rock. There were the archons, still elected from the upper class, as the highest officials, and the Areopagus, the council of ex-archons, whose activities (though hardly its prestige) were reduced by Cleisthenes' new council of the Five Hundred (*boulē*), which was to become the truly ruling body of the democratic state. It found its home in a new house at the agora, which saw much building activity in the early fifth century. Every phyle sent fifty men to the council, chosen by lot from and by the demes and according to the size of the population of the deme. The council acted both as a probuleutic body to bring proposals before the assembly, and as an advisory body to the magistrates. Naturally it was bound by the final decisions of the ecclesia, but in practice it acted as the central administrative committee. For the day-to-day business, however, a body of five hundred men was far too large. For that reason, and also in order to give as many citizens as possible a share in the government, the fifty members from each individual tribe, the *prytaneis*, served in turn for one tenth of the year, and each prytany took the name of its phyle.[43] No citizen was allowed to sit more than twice in the council. Each prytany of fifty had a chairman (*epistates*) who served for twenty-four hours. Thus there was a general and continuous turnover, and there were comparatively few citizens who had not sat at least once in the council as one of the prytans. The system became a political school for the majority of Athenian citizens.

This, of course, is more or less the ultimate shape of the Five Hundred in the fifth century, but most of its characteristic features go back to Cleisthenes. In the early years the Areopagus, filled with and upheld by the ruling families, kept much of its prestige and power; it went, at least to some extent, with the times, and remained an important body even after the creation of the council of the Five Hundred. Archon and Areopagus, both still in the hands of the upper class, were practically the rulers of the state; however, that proved only to be the transition to a new constitutional order. It was later that the new council surpassed its rival completely. Cleisthenes could not build up his council in one year, and in modern works his reforms are frequently compressed into too short a time; it is possible that the council was not fully established before the solemn oath of the councillors was introduced, an oath still in use in Aristotle's time; its introduction, according to *AP* 22, 2, happened in the twelfth year before Marathon, which would mean 501–500.[44] Probably in the same year, ten new army leaders, the strategi, were elected for the first time; more will be said about them later. Perhaps another oath, that of the ephebes, known to us by later sources only, was also introduced at this time; the institution of the *ephebeia* itself, the military training of the young men, was a common and traditional feature in Greek states.[45]

The higher and lower offices – higher and lower in their importance and competence, not as parts of a hierarchy, for there was none – were filled by election in the assembly; voting was in tribal units taken from the demes. Apart from the archons and some technical, especially military, offices, the magistrates were chosen by using the lot. This method, as applied to the sphere of politics, had a precedent in the religious sphere, where sortition represented a divine decision. It is a question of dispute who first introduced it as a secular instrument of politics. Perhaps it was Solon in the election of the jurors to the heliaea (see above, p. 69). Cleisthenes, at any rate, extended the same method of appointment to a number of newly created popular courts (*dikasteria*). Sortition was also used, in combination with a preceding selection by vote (*prokrisis*), if not by Solon, certainly before Cleisthenes. That alone should suffice to show that election by lot was not necessarily a democratic measure. Its political character depended in each single case on the size and composition of the body from which people were chosen by lot. When, for instance, in *AP* 47, 1, it is said that 'the treasurers of Athena are chosen by lot, one from each phyle, from the penta-cosiomedimni according to the Solonian law which is still in force', we understand that Solon caused the treasurers to be elected by lot from the highest income class only; possibly there was a preselection as well.[46]

Cleisthenes used the same method on a far larger scale as the basis of his new order. When there was a *prokrisis*, it took place in the demes. But the general rule now was direct appointment by lot, and it is obvious that, with social divisions largely removed, the method had definitely become a democratic one. The officials, while increasing in numbers, lost a good deal of importance; whether the lot was the cause or the result of this process is an academic question. The effect was the same. As far as possible, personal influence and abuses were prevented, and the only restric-tion (if we may call it so) was that nobody could be put up as a candidate who had not presented himself for the election. Appoint-ment by lot was an expression of the equality of the citizens, and though it left much to chance, it did work. This was made possible because the average citizen who applied for an office would have at least a minimum of political and administrative experience, either from frequent attendance in the assembly or from a year's service on the council; above all, he belonged to the various community bodies of deme and tribe, of phratry and guild.[47] Moreover, in any office he would only be one out of ten, and the individual official, usually elected for one year, was of minor importance. The officials were the executive organ of the will of the people and of the council as its committee, and after their term they had to render account of their use of public money. In this way a method which might look almost senseless could be justified as a good and useful democratic measure. Within that mixed society which Cleisthenes had created and which was most effective in the *prytaneis*, deriving from one phyle only, democracy began to work almost at once. At the same time the archons kept their power, or indeed regained what they had lost under the tyrants. Thus the policy of the state was still determined by members of the upper class, though they had to get the consent of the assembly and its steering committee, the council.

Among Cleisthenes' democratic measures Aristotle (*AP* 22, 1) mentions especially the law of ostracism. Later in the same chapter and in his *Politics* he defines it as a measure against men who were too powerful, and in particular against possible tyrants and their followers.[48] We know that a corresponding institution existed in other states as well, probably all of them democracies at the time when it was introduced. The rules at Athens were that each year in the main assembly of the sixth prytany the people were asked whether they wanted an ostracism; if the vote (probably without debate) was in the affirmative, the decisive voting would take place later that year. By ostracism one man was sent into exile for ten years, without losing either his citizenship or his property. The procedure was that every citizen could write a name on a sherd (*ostrakon*); it was a secret ballot, and simple majority decided. A quorum of six thousand votes was needed, a fairly high figure and a reasonable safeguard against easy misuse. As an appeal to public opinion, it was a measure which combined resoluteness of purpose with mildness of means; but it is by no means self-evident what its purpose really was.

The first time ostracism was practised was in 488-487, when a member of the Peisistratid family was expelled. More ostracisms followed in the next ten years. At that time Cleisthenes must have been dead for some years (see below); that is the main reason why many scholars believe that it was not he who invented the whole device but somebody nearer in time to its first use. Against this view, however, strong arguments can be put forward. The removal of one man from the political scene must have derived from a situation in which this man threatened the peace of the community. As Aristotle expressly tells us, ostracism was designed to prevent internal strife, a *stasis*. Thucydides (8, 73, 3) states that normally the measure was practised because of the power and authority of some individual. It is, of course, possible that the use of ostracism changed with the changes of political conditions; but nobody could risk asking the people, unless he was himself in a strong position and very popular, while his opponent threatened the unity of people and state. That was indeed Cleisthenes' own situation when he was the champion of the people, and possible danger threatened either from a possible tyrant or a faction under a hostile leader.[49] Cleisthenes naturally wanted to protect democracy, which was his own work, and to prevent a return of *tyrannis* or oligarchy. At the same time by his new measure he stopped the expulsion of whole clans, which had been frequent in former struggles. He actually managed well enough with his reforms without using the law of ostracism, but he could never be sure whether a more dangerous situation might not rise again. The nature of the new law, on the other hand, its boldness, its rational clarity, its moderation, fits well into the general picture of Cleisthenes' statesmanship. It is likely that the other states, such as Syracuse, where a similar device was practised, simply imitated Athens. Despite Androtion's possible contradiction, we have no reason to reject the tradition about Cleisthenes' authorship of the law, and if ostracism later became a dangerous political instrument, this cannot be put down to its originator.[50]

Earlier we have mentioned that in, or shortly after, 501–500 ten strategi were elected for the first time (*AP* 22, 2). It is generally assumed, and is likely in itself, though Aristotle does not make it clear, that henceforth the election was made by the whole people, not by each tribe separately as before. The army at that time was led by the polemarch, one of the archons, who changed every year. However, since the army must have been divided into ten units, according to the ten phylae, it is reasonable to assume that the institution of ten regimental commanders goes back to an early stage of Cleisthenes' reforms. We do not know for certain what they were called at first; but since it is unlikely that the posts were at once doubled, we can assume that the ten strategi were the original ten army commanders.[51] The fact that they were elected year by year, and not chosen by lot, gave them a standing that was eventually to overreach that of the polemarch, as became to some extent clear in the battle of Marathon. It is unlikely that they immediately gained political influence as well; the decisive change occurred as late as 487–486, when the archons were first chosen by lot and lost most of their power (see below, p. 146).

In the years in which Cleisthenes' reforms took root the foreign relations of Athens underwent great trouble. Aegina, an island of traders close to the harbour of Athens, was hostile chiefly because of economic jealousy, and warfare between the two states dragged on for a long time; Athens, without a strong fleet, was unable to gain victory.[52] In 506 Cleomenes, called in again by Isagoras, marched over the Megarian border into Attica, while the Boeotians and Chalcidians threatened from the north. Thebes had been an enemy since Athens had agreed to protect Plataea against enforced membership of the Boeotian league, which was by then under Theban leadership. Athens was saved when opposition to Cleomenes arose in the Peloponnesian army, both from his fellow king Demaratus and from the Corinthian contingent (Hdt. 5, 74 ff.; cf. below), and he was forced to withdraw. The other enemies were defeated by the Athenians, allegedly in two battles on the same day. In memory of this event a bronze quadriga was erected on the Acropolis, showing an epigram which reveals the pride of the young democracy.[53] The event was the more remarkable since shortly before, after failing to win allies among the Greeks, and facing an anti-Athenian front, Athens – and that could only mean the Alcmaeonids and not possibly the Peisistratids – had tried to get support from the great expanding power in the east, the Persian empire. According to Herodotus (5, 73), the Athenian envoys were told by the satrap at Sardes that they had to give earth and water to the Great King, as symbols of surrender; after that, they could conclude a treaty of alliance. The envoys accepted, but seem to have been disavowed at home, when the situation there had improved. This story, though based on a historical embassy, was most probably later changed in an attempt to remove a stain from the Athenian tradition; but in about 507 'medism', in the sense of treacherous dealing with the Persians, was non-existent; it became high treason only after the Ionian revolt. Another attempt by Cleomenes, this time with the intention of actually bringing Hippias back to Athens, also failed because of Corinthian resistance.[54]

Athens was in the pangs of becoming a democratic state and at the same time fighting enemies from within and without. She showed astonishing strength, and we can be sure that, apart from Cleisthenes' leadership, this was due to the introduction of freedom and democracy (cf. Hdt. 5, 78). New forces were released when new strata of society emerged. There was a first flowering of a specific Attic art; the Alcmaeonids continued the patronage of Peisistratus. Hand in hand with the growth of the numbers of citizens went the growth of the hoplite army, a process which reflected a higher standard of living. It was also during this period that the Athenians first founded a new type of colony, the cleruchies, where the colonists remained citizens of Athens; such a colony was not an independent polis but rather an extension of Athenian territory and power. We hear of such imperialist beginnings in Euboea, where the aristocrats of Chalcis had to give up land, in Lemnos and Imbros, founded by Miltiades, and possibly in Salamis.[55] A driving force behind these movements may have been the need of reducing the numbers of people to be fed at home, and at the same time the chance of importing food from those colonies. Athens also extended her frontiers by including two places near the Boeotian border, the small town of Hysiae, north of Cithaeron and on the way to Plataea, and Oropus with its fertile plain along the Euripus, though the Oropians never became Athenian citizens.[56] We do not know how long Cleisthenes was at the helm. He must have died about 500 at the latest; he did his great work as a man approaching the seventies, displaying wisdom no less than energy. The Alcmaeonids and some other noble families kept a prominent position for the time being; they could do so within the framework of a state and a society which were both growing more democratic all the time. Cleisthenes' *isonomia*, equality of rights among all the citizens, was not yet rule by the people, that is democracy, but it was speedily approaching it. Resting on religious as well as local community life and working through the sovereign assembly of the whole body of citizens, it was indeed rule by majority, however shy and inhibited this majority may still have been for some time. It was helped by the two councils, both bearing great responsibilities, by the wealthy citizens accepting special obligations from time to time, the *leitourgiai*,[57] and by many ordinary citizens serving as temporary officials. There were to be constitutional and social changes, but Cleisthenes had provided the essential framework for centuries of Athenian democracy.

3 · The Wider Greek Scene

Colonization and the natural position of the Greeks between east and west had made them aware of a world which was non-Greek. Wherever they had settled along the shores of the Mediterranean they had met, and sometimes fought, people who did not speak Greek, who had different gods, different customs, different forms of political organization. They came to consider them as 'barbarians', a word which originally merely implied that they spoke an unintelligible language (see below, p. 178). In general, these foreign people remained outsiders who hardly interfered with the life of the Greeks, who could therefore concentrate on their own small affairs. There were, however, various centres and events of more than local significance, even apart from Sparta's Peloponnesian League and Peisistratus' foreign policy. In both fields, political as well as spiritual, the achievements of the sixth century were such that they cannot be neglected; they will now be discussed within the framework of the whole Greek world.

Athens was not the first democracy, but for quite a time she was the only one of major importance. By far the majority of the Greek states were oligarchies, and the most powerful among them, though of a special nature, was Sparta. Her 'guardianship of Hellas' (*prostasia Hellados*) was unchallenged, and recognized inside as well as outside the Greek world; it was not a legalized form of leadership, but it was leadership nevertheless. On the other hand, Sparta's position as the head of the Peloponnesian League was based on mutual treaties and therefore a legal as well as a factual leadership.

In various states the old aristocracy fought a rearguard action against the rising lower classes and their ideas of democratic developments. The chief witness of this process is Theognis of Megara, of whom we have spoken before (p. 75). Megara, however, was one of the many states with little say on larger political issues, while Corinth was really important. Second in importance within the league, she usually exercised considerable influence.[58] This city, situated near the Isthmus connecting the Peloponnese with central Greece, had reached, under its tyrants Cypselus and Periander, great power and prosperity. It was now ruled by a moderate oligarchy, and its material civilization was on a high level till at least the end of the sixth century. With its colonies in the Adriatic, Corinth had built up an intensive trade with the west; it had a strong fleet, and Corinthian coins and Corinthian pottery spread far and wide. The latter, remarkable for its acceptance of oriental motifs and its baroque mixture of animals and men, ended in a decline of craftsmanship, caused by mass production. Obviously there was little, if any, clash of interests between Sparta and Corinth, while the growing prosperity of Athens and the competition of her artists and artisans would confirm Corinth in her loyalty to Sparta. The two states were also agreed in their enmity towards Argos, though the merchants and sailors of Corinth might hesitate to be involved in any war on land. The Corinthians showed independence, for instance, when they refused to follow Cleomenes against Athens; they might be afraid of a policy so clearly bent on dangerous adventures.

It had been different with Polycrates, the powerful tyrant of Samos, whose domestic opponents received help from both Sparta and Corinth (c. 524; Hdt. 3, 44 ff.). Polycrates had made Samos a very flourishing place, though largely by an aggressive policy of war and piracy; the latter at that time usually went together with trade. He competed with Peisistratus in trying to win influence over Delos, by occupying the neighbouring island of Rhenaea (Thuc. 1, 13, 6. 3, 104, 2); Delos was a place not only of religious but also of strategic importance.[59] Polycrates was famous for his building activity as well as for his fate, which is reflected in the tales of his good fortune, his splendid court, and his final disaster.[60] His end came about as a result of a much wider development, namely the threat of Persian expansion towards the Aegean. Polycrates' belated attempt at changing sides and supporting the Persians did not save him from being enticed to Asia where he was assassinated by the local satrap.

Polycrates' fate was an outstanding example of what Persian rule might mean to the Greeks. The 'Ionians' (a name rather loosely transferred from their leading group of cities to describe the Greeks of Asia Minor generally) had always felt the impact of the neighbouring empires of the east. Most of their cities, situated at the western parts of valleys leading from the interior to the shore, and thus at the ends of important caravan routes, were essential outlets for the Asiatic empires. At the same time they were isolated from one another except by sea, and suffered from a dangerous strategic situation as well as from lack of unity. Their cultured and often luxurious life led to increasing refinement, as can be seen in the Ionian influence, e.g. on Athens, but also to diminishing military and civic strength. Such decline became very obvious when the Ionians turned against Persian rule. After Hittites and Phrygians, it had been the realm of the Lydians which exercised a kind of over-lordship over the Asiatic Greeks. The Lydians had weathered the storm of the invasion by the Cimmerians, nomads from the north, and under their king Gyges gained new strength. In need of a direct approach to the coast, they made increasingly inroads into the autonomy of the Greek cities; but they accepted Greek civilization and in general treated the Greeks with leniency, even with friendship. It was probably from Lydia that the Greeks first learned the use of coins. The last Lydian king Croesus went to Delphi and other Greek oracles for advice, and his own fate became part of Greek legend.[61] By then a far more frightening enemy to both Lydians and Greeks had arisen, since Cyrus the Achaemenid king of the Persians (559–530) had overthrown the supremacy of the Medes and thus united the two Indo-European peoples who were to rule the Near East for many years.[62] Croesus, fortified by the famous ambiguous reply of the Delphic oracle (Hdt. 1, 53), that if he fought the Persians he would destroy a great empire (an oracle which after the event must have looked to many Greeks like the betrayal of a generous friend), crossed the Halys river, the eastern border of his own realm, and met Cyrus in battle (c. 547). The outcome was indecisive, but in the following winter when Croesus as usual had discharged his troops and none of his potential allies (among them perhaps Sparta) was able to help, Cyrus invaded Lydia and captured the strong fortress of Sardes. Croesus was taken prisoner, and the Lydian empire, after a short-lived revolt, came to an end. Soon the Greek cities in Asia Minor, always disunited, fell one after another to Persian attacks. The Phocaeans alone took to their ships and emigrated to join their fellow colonists in Corsica (see p. 119f.). The possibility of the west receiving emigrants from the east became, as it were, a natural outlet as the Persian pressure increased. To the Greeks who remained in Asia, this slow drain of men who more often than not were an élite either of intellect or of adventurous efficiency must have been a serious loss. We shall hear of other cases.

Herodotus tells us (1, 74 f.) that Thales of Miletus, who in an earlier war between Lydia and the Medes was supposed to have predicted an eclipse of the sun (585 or 582 B.C.), helped Croesus by devising a scheme of dividing the waters of the Halys, in order to make an easier crossing for the army. Herodotus does not believe the story, but gives no reasons, and we need not doubt it; Thales was still alive at a later date when he gave the Ionians the advice to create a common political centre in Teos (Hdt. 1, 170); it is hardly necessary to say that his advice was not followed. Thales is known as the first of the Milesian philosophers. He combined various different abilities. He gained some technical and astronomical knowledge from the Chaldaeans in Babylon, but without accepting the connexion with astral religion or astrology; he was able to regard politics in a way that went beyond the walls of one's own polis, and thus fully to realize the Persian danger; finally and chiefly, by turning away from mythical cosmology, and conceiving the idea of a rational theory of the *kosmos*, he became the first 'natural' philosopher. He and his followers Anaximander and Anaximenes, like him men of action as well as of thought, were looking for a single moving force in the natural world, the *archē*, which meant origin and principle at the same time. It was a completely new way of questioning, and the beginning of scientific thinking, though it was not yet science. What Thales called 'water', Anaximenes 'air', and Anaximander 'the Infinite' (*apeiron*), were irrational concepts in rational and non-mythical terms. These men found their principles not by mere guessing but by using observation and speculation combined. 'Their ideas form a bridge between the two worlds of myth and reason.' They wrote in prose, a new literary form which even within philosophical writing had for some time to battle against the tradition of poetry. With the Milesian school of natural philosophers the history of philosophy started; human search for knowledge and truth began its eternal pilgrimage. Greek had indeed become 'the language of human reason'.[63] It was nature, not yet man, that became the object of intellectual investigation. Anaximander, in many ways the most remarkable among those early thinkers, applied the moral human standards of his time, right and wrong (*dike* and *adikia*), which he saw at work as the decisive forces in his own polis, to the rivalling forces in his grandiose picture of the universe; he thus created a border zone between what were to be natural and social sciences.

It was hardly mere chance that this happened at Miletus, the largest of the Ionian cities, which as far as we know greatly prospered during the sixth century, especially after the fall of Samos. Here goods and ideas were imported from Egypt and the east; here was a natural climate for rational progress and the transition from *mythos* to *logos*. Man and the world, *mikrokosmos* and *makrokosmos*, met where life was full of new experiences and possibilities. This is also true of a late successor of the Milesian philosophers, Heraclitus of Ephesus. His 'obscurity' was to become proverbial. An aristocrat by descent and conviction, contemptuous of others, of his fellow citizens (*DK* 22 B 121) no less than of most of his predecessors, he uttered dark 'hints', oracular like the Delphic god who 'neither speaks nor hides things, but indicates' (B 93). Heraclitus was guided by intuition rather than observation. He believed in a governing principle of the universe, which he called *logos*. The word had for him many meanings. It could be the everlasting fire which he identified with the world (B 30), following perhaps Iranian ideas; it could be eternal truth, it was 'word and thought together', even human knowledge, although that depended entirely on divine knowledge. Even so, Heraclitus found the way to individual self-contemplation. 'Man's character is his daemon', his destiny (B 119); 'I searched for myself' (B 101). The same man who visualized human self-knowledge believed in a world of 'becoming', of eternal change. The idea expressed in the simile that nobody could enter the same river twice (B 91) was crystallized in the famous, though not genuine, saying 'All is in flux' (*panta rhei*). Harmony is the final aim, but it consists in the union of opposites. That is why 'war is the father of all things' (B 53), i.e. the struggle going on within every living and always changing being. No systematic thinker, this inspired and extremist philosopher found enthusiastic admirers, from the Stoics down to Nietzsche. He was the most brilliant example of that kind of thinker in whom natural science and the knowledge of man met and combined, before they were finally separated.

Another witness of the process which we have tried to indicate is Hecataeus, also from Miletus, the first to study history and geography on a rational basis. His proud claim (*FGrH* 1 F 1) that he tells the truth 'as I see it', while the other Greek stories seem to him ridiculous, continued the tradition of Hesiod's prooemium, and finds more sober successors in Herodotus and Thucydides. History at that time could hardly be anything but geneaology bridging the gap between myth and the human past and present, since family traditions everywhere led back to a divine ancestor; local chronicles provided another link. Thus, the mythical tradition could be interpreted in purely human and rational terms. This is what Hecataeus did as the first of the forerunners of true history writing. They all are usually, but to some extent, misleadingly, called *logographoi*, though they differ a good deal from one another in subjects and in methods.[63a] Hecataeus' rationalism may to us sometimes sound rather trivial, but it was a necessary step to be made. Hecataeus also collected, partly by his own experience, partly from travellers' tales, in his description of the earth (*perihēgesis gēs*), a sober and factual knowledge of the known parts of the world. Following Anaximander's example and improving on it, he also designed a map of the earth. It was he who first used the word *historia* in the meaning of 'research', displayed the knowledge of widening horizons, and worked out the unity, at that time essential, of geography, ethnography, and history. Herodotus, whether agreeing or polemizing, learnt from him the basic facts of his profession.[64]

Hecataeus followed, and went beyond, the work of several writers of books called *periplous*, that is, a description of the shores of the sea, along which the sailors – still without any technical instruments – would find their way. Such books were of immediate practical use, and one of them was written by Scylax of Caryanda in Caria, who explored for the Persian king Darius the Indus river and the Indian Sea, anticipating the voyage of Alexander's admiral Nearchus.[65] This is an early example of the influence the Persian empire could have even on Greek literature. The connexions between Persia and the Greeks naturally varied; it was closest and also most oppressive in Asia Minor, where the Greek cities were ruled by citizens chosen by the Persian satrap ('tyrants'), more or less vassals of the king. Meanwhile the Persian empire grew in various directions, while Greek and Carian mercenaries served in the Persian army. Cyrus had conquered the neo-Babylonian realm of the Chaldaeans, and thus freed the Jews from their exile 'by the waters of Babylon'. His son and successor Cambyses (530–522), embarking for the first time on a combined operation of land and naval forces (a scheme henceforth typical for Persian advances towards the west), turned Egypt into a Persian satrapy and made even Cyrene tributary, weakened as it was by domestic conflicts. He finished Cyrus' work of destroying the old balance of power in the Near East. The Persians now ruled the greatest empire that had ever existed. There was no independent fleet left in the eastern Mediterranean, except for the small navies of a few Greek cities. The Greek trading centre at Naucratis suffered a serious setback, though to some extent it later recovered. After the death (possibly murder) of Cambyses and the short rule of a priestly impostor, the revolt of an aristocratic 'Junta' (as it would be called today) brought Darius to the throne (522 B.C.), a young Achaemenid, but not a descendant of Cyrus, whose two daughters he married. This great ruler, after putting down all revolts and restoring peace throughout the empire, gave it an organization which combined a strong central government with powerful regional governors of twenty provinces, the satrapies.[66] The old conflict between despotism and feudalism was to some extent replaced by the creation of a (more or less) loyal bureaucracy, by a system of fixed tributes paid by every satrapy, and by a network of roads and royal courier services as a means of centralization. Though this is not the place to speak in detail of Darius' achievements, it is important to know what kind of enemy the Greeks had to face. Darius' reign not only established a prosperous empire, whose golden coins, the *dareikoi*, with the picture of the king as an archer, were soon highly valued far beyond the Persian frontiers, even among the Greeks, but his rule was also based on high moral principles, and that can be said of Persian society as a whole. The king thought of himself piously as the instrument of the great divine power of good, Ahura-Mazda, though he was also able to impose his will by the most ruthless methods. For quite a time the Greeks had regarded this empire as 'barbarian', but not as an enemy. Envoys went to Susa, and we find Greek traders, artists, and physicians at the court of the Great King.

His empire, however, enormous as it was, tended like all empires to expand even farther and became an imperialist power. Having conquered the neighbouring countries in the east and south, it then turned to the west and north. After gaining most of the eastern Aegean islands and thus securing the Asiatic seaboard, Darius turned north (about 513), crossed the Bosporus with land and sea forces, and managed to proceed even beyond the Danube. We do not know how far north he went; Herodotus' account is quite unbelievable. We can only guess what the purpose of a campaign against the Scythians and into the unknown may have been, if it happened at all. As there had been Scythian inroads into Armenia, it is just possible that Darius, ignorant of the vast distances, hoped to overcome them from the west and thus to protect the northern frontier of his empire. According to Herodotus, his army almost met with disaster, but was saved after its retreat by the Ionian commanders who were guarding the bridge over the Danube.[67] The main campaign had been a failure, and the Greek cities at the Bosporus used the moment to revoke their submission to the Persian king; otherwise the results were by no means negligible. Two of Darius' generals, Megabazus and Otanes, one after another, subjected southern Thrace from the Bosporus and the Black Sea coast in the east to Macedon in the west; two new satrapies were established on European soil. Amyntas, king of the Macedonians, was able to retain his rule only by submitting to Persia. The ring round the eastern Mediterranean was almost closed, except for Greece. Darius now was on her doorstep, and the menace to the

Greeks had become much closer. For the time being, however, peace prevailed. Darius, after his absence, found a good deal to do to strengthen his rule, but it seems that he also sent a number of spies to Greece to find out what the powers there were like. The threat – for some exiled Greeks the hope – of an intervention by Persia had become very real; it is in the light of this situation that we must understand the attempts of Greek states to open diplomatic relations with the Great King.

In fact, the situation meant more than a purely military threat to the Greeks, although that was most strongly felt, and the vast resources and the numbers of the Persian army and fleet were well known, even exaggerated. What the Greeks did not realize, were the moral forces embedded in Persian beliefs and standards. They saw the rule of a despot and a barbarian society. The stronger the Greek feeling for freedom and independence grew, the more they feared Persia, and the greater, on the other hand, the Persian menace became, the more Greek consciousness of freedom grew; but they had still to learn that it was first necessary to lay aside their own quarrels. We have mentioned the wholesale emigration of the Phocaeans, but there must have been a good many individuals as well who found it advisable to emigrate. One of them was Xenophanes of Colophon, a rhapsode and a thinker of great intellectual force. He left Ionia – just as Pythagoras had done in protest against Polycrates' rule – in order to be a free man; he wandered about Greek lands and ended his long life in Italy. The breach with the tradition was as complete as possible. Xenophanes, a man with no polis of his own, vigorously displayed an intellectual autonomy so far unknown. He challenged the general adulation of the athletic victors as well as the anthropomorphic conception of the gods.[68] He attacked indeed the most beloved traditions, especially of the upper classes, though he was dining and wining with them. He was a rationalist, anticipating later thinkers, though the times were hardly ripe for his thoughts. Above all, he dared to speak of the one god who rules nature – 'the greatest among gods and men', as he said with forceful simplicity, if with a significant lack of logic. He was, it is true, an exception, but the story of his life reflects the change that took place, even from a geographical point of view, in the Greek mind. The Ionians, having lost their freedom, also lost the cultural leadership of the Greeks, which was taken over by the motherland and the west.

We have mentioned Pythagoras, who settled at Croton in Italy. He united in his teaching two opposite trends of his time, which we may generally call scientific and mystical. He is, of course, famous for his mathematical discoveries, but presently more important was his leadership of a circle of disciples, united by social and religious bonds and an ascetic communal life. To his followers he was a kind of prophet, and through them he exercised strong political influence. The union of philosophical and cosmological thought, also of ethical considerations, on the one hand, with irrational and even mystic beliefs on the other, claiming a prophetic authority for their teaching, was characteristic of leading minds in the west during succeeding decades. Following and opposing Heraclitus, there were men like Parmenides of Elea in Italy and Empedocles of Acragas in Sicily. Parmenides discovered the contrast and conflict between 'being' and 'seeming', truth and opinion (*aletheia* and *doxa*), and thus established the principle of logical thought over and against perception through the senses, a contrast at the core of all future philosophy. He anticipated Descartes' unity of being and thinking,[69] but he failed to find a real status for the world of seeming which he described in detail. His monism was a fight against common sense. With his poetical imagination he accepted and enriched the old concept of Dike or Ananke as the binding force of world order, while man had hardly any say in his *kosmos*. His paradoxical philosophy, continued and extended by his school, the Eleatics, served as a stimulant for very different trends of thought.

The genius of men like Heraclitus and Parmenides – of Empedocles we shall speak later – reflected what, on a lower level, was a general phenomenon. Moreover, the parallelism of minds and the exchange of ideas were equalled on the material side. The standard of living went up everywhere, trade and craft flourished, and the artists, especially the sculptors, went through a great period which made their works not only the predecessors of the accomplished art of the fifth century but also a magnificent product of the archaic spirit. During the sixth century the Greeks, deeply impressed by what they saw in Egypt, began to learn how to build stone temples and developed the 'Doric' and 'Ionic' styles in architecture. The temples, quite different from the Egyptian ones, had a megaron-type cella for the statue of the god and surrounding rows of columns; they were rarely a place of cult and prayer, rather a house for the god; for the statue *was* the god. Sculptors, again adapting Egyptian models, started on life-size or even colossal statues and discovered the beauty of the nude male body, as so frequently displayed in Greek athletic sports. The *kouroi* were a frequent type of a young man, originally deriving from the islands, especially Naxos; very soon it proved to be far more alive than the Egyptian statues. Nude female bodies were not quite unknown in Greek art, since there had been imitations of eastern Astarte figures in ivory or clay; but even Aphrodite soon appeared clothed. A more independent imitation of eastern fashion were mirror handles in the shape of a nude girl, significantly first favoured in Sparta. In general, and especially in stone sculpture, the shape of the female body came increasingly to life in the folds of refined dresses. A new field for sculptural work was found in the adornment of the temples. Vase-painting began to reach a perfection of grace and simplicity, never surpassed in later times. The cultural atmosphere, as described earlier for the reign of Peisistratus, can by and large be attributed to most Greek cities, although the strong influence of Ionian refinement and afterwards the predominance of Athens are beyond doubt. Society in most states was oligarchic, but democratic ideas made progress, and everywhere the peasantry, however backward, played a major part. Rural traditions survived, and some of the ancient rural gods, such as Demeter and Dionysus, gained new importance with the move of many peasants to the cities. There was, however, more than that. The revival of the mysteries of Eleusis and the ecstatic worship of Dionysus, as well as the ascetic teaching of an after-life by the Orphics, the Pythagorean doctrine of reincarnation, the spread of chthonic hero-worship and the appearance of wonder-workers and prophets are all witnesses for a more general movement which responded to deeper religious needs of the community or the individual human being.[69a] It was at the same time a movement of liberation, but a liberation attained only after death. In contrast to traditional religion, these movements were originally not state cults, and often not even tied to a fixed community. There is evidence, for instance, in late sixth-century vase-paintings, of fierce and brutal rituals in Dionysiac religion, but they were gradually put under state control and adapted to more humane standards. In that era of irrationalism the division of human nature between body and soul became one of the strongest sources of mystical knowledge. The famous slogan that the body is a tomb (*sôma sêma*) was the expression of an urgent desire to secure an existence after death. 'Many bear Dionysus' wand, but few are inspired.'[70]

At the same time, ever since Hesiod, the traditional Greek religion had increasingly accepted ethical standards. It did not mean individual morality, which was a growth of later times. What it did mean was justice and fairness between men and gods as well as between men and men. This trend found its clearest reflection and its strongest promoter in the policy of Delphi.[71] Whatever the pre-history of the cult of Apollo there, its great time began towards the end of the seventh century, as is reflected in the Delphic section of the Homeric hymn to Apollo. The oracle and the protecting union of the neighbouring states and tribes (amphictiony), though both far older, gained general importance after the First Sacred War (about 590) which led to Delphi's independence from Krisa; the latter was destroyed (see above, p. 81). To what extent Delphi influenced Greek colonization is not clear, though it certainly favoured and fostered it in its later stages, in particular in the west; that fact caused the tradition of the earlier colonies to be reshaped to the greater glory of the Delphic god. The priests and their mouthpiece, the oracle-giving Pythia, were clever politicians, frequently open to bribery, but they were more than that. While they usually favoured aristocratic constitutions, they had little general influence on inter-state politics – like the Panhellenic festivals with their temporary truce, of which one, the Pythian, belonged to Delphi. But Delphi largely succeeded in imposing, at least on the members of the amphictiony, humane rules of inter-state warfare.[72] That was possible because the priests, without clinging to a narrow doctrine, preached a wisdom centred round the idea of human limitations. It was to some extent traditional ethics, practised by men like Solon, the wisdom of the middle line, of the 'never too much!' (*medén ágan*). Behind this teaching of moderation on a purely human level, as expressed in the sayings of the Seven Sages, and especially in the inscription on the temple itself, 'Know Thyself' (*gnôthi seautón*), which implied the sequence 'and follow the god', was the great son of Zeus, acting as a moral and purifying power. The Delphic message was essentially religious, and its first purpose was to propagate the cult of Apollo and the image of his wisdom. It has well been said of the Homeric hymns (poems mostly of the sixth century) that 'they enshrined a religious belief which was completely anthropomorphic and anthropomorphically complete'.[73] If that is true, it is equally true that Delphi surpassed this form of religion and supported the growing trend towards belief in a higher ethical nature of the gods. This put certain obligations on man, and Delphic influence can be traced, for instance, in the development of law and purification which were both submitted more definitely to moral rules. The same spirit was manifest in Aeschylus and Pindar (of whom we shall have more to say), who both, especially the latter, shared and advanced beliefs predominant in the late archaic age and filled with deep awe of the greatness and nature of the gods. From many of Pindar's odes and paeans we can learn something about the possible loftiness of Delphic religion, but we must not forget that Greek religion never demanded 'all or nothing';[74] we must also accept what Herodotus, who was a strong believer in the divine wisdom of Delphi, tell us us about Delphic oracles, politics, and even bribery.

The Delphic amphictiony was not the only one, though it was the most important of its kind. The Panionion on Cape Mycale opposite Samos, Delos as the centre of 'the union of the Ionians and the population of the isles nearby' (Thuc. 3, 104), Calauria, an island in the Saronic gulf with a sanctuary of Poseidon, and other places were the nuclei of common cults, common sacrifices, and festivals in honour of the god concerned. As always in Greece, however, religious ties had their impact on political and social issues. Above all, protection for the sanctuary implied peace among the member states of the amphictiony. In Calauria and Cape Mycale the central god was Poseidon, that is to say, it was largely a union of small maritime states intent on checking piracy. The centre, in particular Delphi, had powers of religious punishment and of imposing money fines. With its increasingly strong organization this type of inter-state union represented an early and by no means unsuccessful attempt to improve the relations within the world of Greek states. Its importance weakened decisively when, during the fifth century, the Peloponnesian League and other political unions gained power, while the Delphic oracle lost some of its influence.

It is, however, not true that Delphic religion and Dionysiac cult dominated all life. There was, especially among the upper class, a tradition in which boys and hetaerae and symposia, with beautiful love-songs and drinking-songs, were symptoms of an easy-going cultural and sexual life. Its outstanding poet was Anacreon, whose songs we still read and whose life was largely spent at tyrants' courts. In this kind of society, as well as among most of the lower classes, the Homeric gods were still supreme.

We now turn to the west.[75] Greek colonization here (see above, p. 17f.) reached its peak about 600 B.C., though some more daughter colonies were founded after that date. In general the cities of Sicily and South Italy, more than ever, were magnificent centres of trade and art and high cultural standards; they also provided excellent opportunities for the sale of the refined pottery, first of Corinth and then of Athens. Still today the imposing temples of Selinus and Poseidonia (Paestum), to mention only two places, and the magnificent metopes in the museums of Palermo and Paestum tell the story of a flourishing culture during the ripe archaic age, which displayed a great deal of creative originality. This is true of architecture and art, and even more so of philosophy and literature. It was the period in which Pythagoras founded his circle of disciples at Croton, while Parmenides of Elea and his school discovered the conflict between truth and opinion; that is to say, it was the period in which western thought was dominated by the contrast, or the union, of science and mysticism. From Rhegium came the lyric poet Ibycus, even earlier from Himera Stesichorus, who gave a new form and new contents to many of the old myths. Epicharmus of Syracuse wrote mythical burlesques, naturalistic scenes of everyday life, and more serious allegorical discussion-plays. Croton was famous for her medical school and for the successes of her athletes, Sybaris for her wealth and luxury; the large number of Olympian victors from Croton was probably due to the aristocratic and Panhellenic attitude of the Pythagoreans. Syracuse developed into one of the largest commercial and artistic centres. Greeks and Etruscans sometimes lived together, especially in places on the northern Adriatic. At Spina, in the ancient part of the Po delta, large amounts of Athenian pottery of the late sixth and early fifth century have been found, some with Greek and Etruscan inscriptions. Here probably was a Greek community within an Etruscan city which served as a harbour for its fertile hinterland.[76] Essentially, however, the civilization of

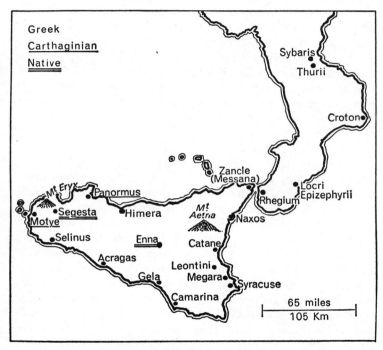

5. Sicily and South Italy

Greek Sicily and Greek Italy was purely Greek and in constant connection with the motherland, by immigration, trade and traffic of men, goods and ideas.

Though the list of cultural achievements in the west could easily be extended, and their influence on the Greek mainland emphasized, it will suffice as a background to a political scene far less edifying. In regions all of which were much richer in fertile land than any part of the motherland, where wine, corn, and cattle were produced on a large scale, and works of art either created or imported, the standards of life were very high indeed, and Pythagoreanism can to some extent be understood as an ascetic reaction against this kind of life. In most of the cities the big landowners, sometimes joined by the rich merchants, formed a ruling oligarchy which more than once met with the opposition not only of the natives who had frequently been robbed of their best land, but above all of the lower classes in the cities. A tyrant like Phalaris of Acragas might come and go, but normally oligarchic rule prevailed. There had also been some of the most influential lawgivers, Zaleucus of Locri and Charondas of Catane, who may belong to the seventh century (see p. 23). Their laws gradually spread to other cities, to some extent helping the poor against the rich, though in general preserving oligarchic constitutions and preventing the rise of tyrants, who seem to have been a constant danger, especially in Sicily.

At the same time, conflicts and wars among the various Greek cities never really ceased. The best-known event was the battle in which the men of Croton with the help, it seems, of an adventuring Spartan prince, Dorieus, stepbrother of Cleomenes,[77] won an overwhelming victory over Sybaris, followed by the complete destruction of that city (511–510 B.C.). The event came as a shock to the Greek world, and the people of Miletus, attached to Sybaris by close trade relations, went into mourning (Hdt. 6, 21). The largest Greek city in Italy had disappeared, and it counted for very little that a small town of the same name continued to exist as a dependent place under the rule of Croton. For some time the latter was the leading Greek state in Italy. There can be no moral justification for the annihilation of a neighbouring Greek city, even though life in Sybaris may have been dissolute and in Croton austere. Politically the fratricidal war was a disaster for the western Greeks, in view of the rising hostile forces everywhere, and a sad epilogue to their independent history.

For several decades the western Greeks had been increasingly threatened by various non-Greek powers. The Italic peoples were never quite content to leave the Greek cities in their favourable and important positions. We find, for instance, the Iapygians fighting against Tarentum, but above all the Etruscans, with their rising power, commerce, and expansion, had become a serious menace to Cumae and other Greek cities in south-western Italy. Perhaps even more important was the natural rivalry of Carthage, the seafaring and trading city in North Africa, which during the sixth century grew into an aggressive power as the largest Phoenician colony in the west.[78] The Phoenicians had founded ports of call for trading purposes (*emporia*) along most of the shores of the western Mediterranean. When the Greeks in Sicily pushed westwards along both the northern and the southern coasts, with Himera and Selinus as their spearheads (cf. Thuc. 6, 4 f.), the Phoenicians withdrew, but firmly held the western part of the island as well as part of Sardinia. The opening of the route to Tartessus in south-western Spain[79] led to more competition between Greeks and Phoenicians. The Carthaginians, on the other hand, while most efficient in sailing and trading, only slowly developed something like an 'imperial' policy. They sent out expeditions round north-western Africa and to the Scilly Islands, but their aristocracy of merchants and absentee plantation landlords was ruled by economic interests rather than by aims of political expansion. Even so, the Greeks had to face a formidable power, based on a well-organized political structure at home, and owning a strong fleet and well-trained mercenary armies. Selinus, the most western of the Greek cities in Sicily, was for a long time at war with the combined forces of the Carthaginians in western Sicily and the native Elymians, whose main city was Segesta. In spite of occasional setbacks, however, the Hellenization of Sicily made steady progress, even in the interior, while in Italy Greek influence outside their own cities was largely confined to the mediating activities of the Etruscans, whose own civilization was more and more enriched and changed by the acceptance of Greek achievements.

Matters came to a head through the advance of the Phocaeans, and to some extent also of the Rhodians who had founded Acragas (*c.* 580) and then made an attempt, together with some Cnidians under their leader Pentathlus, to settle on the west coast of Sicily; the attempt led to nothing. The Phocaeans, on the other hand, after the foundation of Massilia (*c.* 600), which soon grew into a prosperous and important city, sending out colonies to the French and Spanish

Mediterranean coasts, founded (*c.* 560) Alalia in Corsica; perhaps they also settled in Sardinia.[80] It is significant that in 540, when the Ionians came under Persian rule, Bias of Priene suggested a common emigration to Sardinia (Hdt. 1, 170). Obviously neither Carthage nor the Etruscans could suffer further advances by the Greeks into their own spheres of interest, in particular into the sea north of Sicily known as the Tyrrhenian (= Etruscan) sea.[81] When the Phocaean newcomers in Sardinia carried on indiscriminate piracy, the two non-Greek powers joined hands and defeated the Phocaeans in a naval battle off Alalia (*c.* 540), an event which has rightly been regarded – though perhaps not by contemporary Greeks – as the end of Greek colonization in the west. From then on the western Greeks were mostly on the defensive. Corsica became Etruscan, Sardinia finally Carthaginian, and Massilia for the time being was almost isolated. Carthage, although in general cautious in her anti-Greek policy – the Greeks would be much stronger in numbers if they ever united – was able to close the Straits of Gibraltar to Greek shipping, and soon after to destroy the rich realm of Tartessus. Etruscan power reached the south of Italy and was at its height, though it soon began to decline. Carthage (in 509, according to Polybius 3, 22) concluded a treaty about mutual trade and traffic with the small country town of Rome, which was about to emerge from Etruscan rule. A new situation was developing in the western Mediterranean. The wealth of the Greek cities both in Italy and in Sicily was in general unimpaired, and the evidence of their art remains most impressive. There was, however, no attempt at united action, rather the opposite. The destruction of Sybaris by Croton was only one example, though one of the worst, of warfare between polis and polis. Oligarchies began to give way to the rise of tyrants, at least in Sicily; this meant a strengthening of military power which could easily lead to new clashes with the Carthaginians. That happened at a time when tyranny in Greece and the Aegean had practically ceased to exist.

The Greek states in east and west, though culturally probably in closer contact than ever before, were generally as divided in political matters as they could be. Few major wars had been fought during the sixth century, but plenty of small conflicts occurred both within and between the states. For every Greek polis, any other polis was just as much a foreign power and a potential enemy as the 'barbarian' Lydian or Persian empire. The Persian advance into the Aegean, however, naturally had its impact on the Greeks. The Ionians, including Miltiades, ruler of the Thracian Chersonese, helped Darius during the Scythian expedition, and Athens twice sent embassies to Susa. Persia was a power with whom one had to reckon, though not necessarily as an enemy; her rule over the Straits seems not to have impeded Greek corn trade in any substantial way. Eventually the situation changed, and Persia's support of the exiled Hippias made Athens her enemy. Still, Athens did not mean Greece, and attitudes differed greatly. Delphi was quite unable, even if it had been willing, to impose a common policy on the Greeks. That indeed was urgently needed, when the menace of Persia as well as of Carthage began to throw its dark shadows over the Greek lands.

V

THE WARS FOR FREEDOM

1 · *The Ionian Revolt and the Motherland* (500–491 B.C.)

Our main source for this chapter is Herodotus (bks. 5–6). He wrote more than one generation after the events, and we shall have more to say about him against the background of his own time. Here we ought to mention that the variety of his sources, written as well as oral, his generally non-political attitude, his interest in individuals rather than in states, his strong religious beliefs, and last not least the fact that he frequently leaves to his reader to decide what really happened – all that combined with his genius as a story-teller – makes it impossible to extract a strictly coherent and factual historical narrative from his work. However, he can still help us to see the Greeks as a whole, but also to discern the individual merits of either Athens or Sparta in the wars for freedom. That is, in fact, what the Persian wars were fought for, and to Herodotus, whatever each state or person did for Greek freedom is the *Leitmotif* in the multifarious symphony of his work.

We have seen (p. 105) how the Persians strengthened their hold on the Greeks in Asia Minor. The area had been for a long time under the influence of eastern empires, and at the same time always closely connected with the Greek world, a borderland if ever there was one. Still, all the cities along the Aegean shores, apart from a few Carian ones in the south, were Greek. Herodotus (5, 2, 1) says of the people of Perinthus on the Propontis that they 'had been brave men fighting for their freedom'. It was freedom that the Ionian cities had lost, not so much through direct Persian rule, although they had to pay tribute, but because they were, as already mentioned (p. 109), governed by local 'tyrants'. These men maintained their positions by the backing of the Persian satraps as well as the support of at least some of their fellow citizens. At that time *tyrannis* had practically disappeared in the motherland, and when soon afterwards it had a new start in Sicily (below, p. 165f.) it was under completely different conditions; the tyrants there, while pursuing their own policy, defended the Greeks against external dangers. The Ionian Greeks had other complaints as well; they had suffered economic setbacks under Persian rule, as shown by the loss of trade to the west (Sybaris!) and the decline of the trading centre at Naucratis, which was partly caused by competition from other Greek states, but also by the Persian control of the Straits to the Black Sea, and in general by the strong development of Phoenician as well as Athenian trade. The Greek upper class suffered also under the rule of Persian officials.[1] It is not justifiable to ascribe the discontent of the Ionians to any kind of 'national' feeling, and it was almost by chance that from their general discontent an actual revolt developed. For this and the following war years we have no other but Greek sources, and Herodotus makes the intrigues of two men, Histiaeus and Aristagoras, the cause of the outbreak of hostilities. Though it is usual with him to provide personal reasons for general happenings, in this case he may not be far from the truth. We shall see that Herodotus undoubtedly omitted essential facts, and it is also important to recognize how strongly biased against the Ionians he was, although the reasons for this attitude remain obscure. Anyway, the widespread discontent among the Ionians, as well as their lack of unity, needed leadership.

Histiaeus, tyrant of Miletus, whom the Great King regarded as responsible for keeping the Ionians loyal while he fought the Scythians (above, p. 110), had been rewarded with the land of Myrcinus in the Strymon valley (Hdt. 5, 11. 23 f.). With its rich resources of silver and timber, and a mixed population of Greeks and Thracians, it could provide a strong base for an ambitious man such as Histiaeus. We are told that Megabazus, when campaigning in Thrace, realized the danger and persuaded Darius to take Histiaeus with him to Susa, where he was kept in a kind of honourable detention at the court. Meanwhile, Aristagoras, his son-in-law, ruled in his stead at Miletus.

Frustrated for many years as one of Darius' counsellors, and longing to return to Ionia where he hoped to play an active and independent part, Histiaeus managed to send a secret message to

Aristagoras, exhorting him to raise a revolt.[1a] This action derived
from Hisiaeus' hope to be sent to Ionia as a peacemaker, if and when
there was trouble. Aristagoras, though apparently on good terms
with the Persians, was at that moment in difficulties with the satrap
in Sardes, Darius' brother Artaphrenes. A body of aristocrats from
Naxos had been expelled by a democratic rising and asked for his
help. Naxos was the most flourishing of the Cyclades, and would
provide an excellent stronghold for any further advance by Persia
into the Aegean. Aristagoras, hoping at the same time to ingratiate
himself with the satrap, to acquire increased power for himself, and,
in particular, to mobilize a Greek fleet, persuaded Artaphrenes, and
through him the king, to prepare a powerful expedition. It sailed
(probably in spring 499), but the Naxians had been forewarned,
and the campaign, after a siege of several months, ended in complete
failure. A great deal about the whole affair is obscure, but it certainly brought Aristagoras into disrepute with the Persians, and he
decided on revolt.[2]

It is not unlikely that this decision was not the outcome of the
moment but had been in his (and Histiaeus') mind for a long time.
In fact, he could not have embarked on a revolt without having
probed the conditions and minds of the people in other cities and
found a reassuring response. Now, he called a council of war – for
the moment, it seems, of his friends in Miletus only. He found full
support, except from Hecataeus, who as a widely travelled geographer knew of the extent and the power of the Persian empire;
he is said (Hdt. 5, 36, 2) to have enumerated all the peoples under
Persian rule. When his warning went unheeded he suggested that
they should seize the treasures of the temple of the Branchidae, and
with their help gain the mastery of the sea. He was right, though
only partially, in maintaining that by the latter alone could the
Ionians hope to succeed, and that such a scheme was impossible
without vast financial resources. What he proposed, however, was
a sacrilege of the first order. His realistic and secular mind did not
shrink from such a deed; but we can understand why his advice
was not accepted. However 'progressive' the Ionians in general
were, the majority would never dare to provoke the wrath of the
gods.

Any success against the great empire could be achieved only, if at all, by a quick combined action on land and sea, and the establishment of a *fait accompli* in Asia Minor before the cumbersome machinery of the empire got going. Some hope might derive from the fact that the Greek hoplite was certainly superior to the Persian infantryman, though there always was the excellent Persian cavalry; at sea Persia had relied, at least for more northern regions, on the Ionians themselves, though to a greater extent on the Phoenicians, the foremost sailing nation of the time. The Greek fleet, after the expedition to Naxos, was still assembled at Myus near Miletus, and the proposal of rebellion was accepted with enthusiasm. In many cities the tyrants were removed, and Aristagoras proclaimed *isonomia* for Miletus, thus abandoning his position as an irresponsible tyrant. We may doubt whether that gesture made a great change in war time, but the demos, suffering from the general economic decline, was restless everywhere; at the same time it is likely that the example of Cleisthenian Athens had its impact. That can perhaps also be seen in the fact that *strategi*, so far unknown in Ionia, were elected throughout the cities, though it may only mean that elected military leaders, as might be expected, were now supreme everywhere. More important was the fact that the ancient Ionian league was to some extent revived; a common council was to sit at the Panionion (Hdt. 5, 109. 6, 7). The leaders of the revolt, on the other hand, realized that they needed help from the motherland. With the decision to ask for such support, the whole affair lost its character as a domestic concern of the Persian empire and became involved in the developing conflict between east and west.

Aristagoras, armed with a bronze map, probably made by Hecataeus, first went to Sparta as the leading power in Greece. According to Herodotus, he pleaded before Cleomenes (who appears as the only representative of Sparta, which is significant for his unique position), stressing the obligation of Sparta to free the Ionians from 'slavery', and at the same time the possible riches to be gained. To some extent his inducements seem to have been of the right kind, appealing as they did to Spartan hostility towards tyrants as well as to Cleomenes' personal ambitions. But the king refused. Herodotus reports this in a charming story about the king's little daughter, but we may believe that anyway even Cleomenes could not decide for himself, and it is certain that neither the ephors nor the other king Demaratus, who was on very bad terms with Cleomenes, would ever support such an adventurous enterprise.[3]

Aristagoras then went to Athens. Here the new democracy, led by aristocrats, though probably no longer by the Alcmaeonid clan, had gained a number of successes against hostile neighbours, but had still to fear the return of Hippias, who found open support in Persia. That probably was the strongest argument in favour of a movement by which the local tyrants in Asia were to be deposed. In contrast to Sparta's isolationism, the Athenians had some knowledge of Asia Minor, as a result of the struggle for Sigeum; they would know, even without Aristagoras' map, that to help the Ionians would not mean marching as far as Susa. Cultural relations with Ionia had been very strong, in particular among the ruling classes at Athens, and it was only in the last decade of the sixth century, about the time of Cleisthenes' work, that a new Attic spirit was revealed in sculpture and vase-painting. An additional reason will have been the need to import corn through the Straits, which might be threatened as long as the route was dominated by the Persians. Even so, the decision, it seems, had not an easy passage in the assembly, a fact which reflected the factional divisions among the people, and foreshadowed future events. At the moment, however, it was decided that a squadron of twenty ships should be sent to Ionia. This was quite a considerable force for the Athens of those days, when she probably had no more than fifty warships. Eretria in Euboea was the only other Greek state that helped – not a negligible power and, as a friend of Athens and an enemy of Chalcis, probably a democracy; the Eretrians may also have remembered the help Miletus had given during the Lelantine war. But they provided only five more ships, rather a poor contribution. We do not know whether Aristagoras approached any other states, though it is not unlikely. It must not be forgotten, however, that the Greek states were deeply divided among themselves, and ships might be needed nearer home.[4] Herodotus, in a famous passage (5, 97) recalling Homer,[5] calls the dispatch of the ships from Athens and Eretria 'the beginning of the evil for both Greeks and barbarians'. He blamed Athenian democracy, which he otherwise praised, for that unfortunate decision. The clash would have come at any rate, but that particular event served as a pretext for the Persian attackers;

Darius' intention to make the Aegean a Persian sea was confirmed and strengthened. Herodotus, in those words, thinks of the long wars and heavy losses which followed. He regards the support of the Ionian revolt as a grave mistake; at the same time he realizes that it was this event that put Athens into the centre of the unfolding story of the Persian wars. He knows all about the great Greek victories, and the final goal of establishing freedom against despotism; and yet he is impartial enough to see the 'evil' which came to either side. So remote was he from any nationalist thought.[6]

That would have been less remarkable at the time of the events we are dealing with than when Herodotus wrote his book about half a century later. The Ionians, as we have seen, were hardly moved by strong 'Greek' feeling, and Herodotus came from Halicarnassus, which, like the other Dorian cities, kept out of the revolt, though the Carians in the hinterland did not. Greek patriotism, at that time, was exclusively polis patriotism, and the many embassies sent to Sardes or Susa confirm that the Persians were not necessarily regarded as enemies of the Greeks. Moreover, men like Theognis and Pindar displayed a hatred of war, a kind of pacificism, which excluded any 'Greek' patriotism. It was the same, if not even more so, with the Asiatic Greeks. These people betwixt and between the enormous empire of the East and the Greek world of scattered states, which were fighting one another, could never find a cause strong enough to bind them together and to give them a real political purpose. Although the revolt led to a temporary revival of the Ionian league and perhaps to a common coinage,[7] there never was a determined patriotism, never complete unity, or even a full knowledge of the real situation.

During the winter 499–498 both sides were occupied with preparations for war. Persia had been utterly unprepared for the event, and it can easily be understood that the first round went to the Greeks, although it eventually led to disaster. After the twenty-five ships had arrived from Greece and joined the Ionian fleet near Ephesus, a bold attack was made overland against Sardes, while Miletus was perhaps already under siege by the Persians (Plut. de malign. Her. 24). The city of Sardes was burnt, but the citadel was held by Artaphrenes, and when Persian and Lydian troops approached, the Greeks retreated, obviously after some time had passed, as the enemy's reinforcements could hardly have been at hand. The unexpected participation by the Lydians may have been caused by the burning of their ancient capital; it will have contributed greatly to making the failure of the revolt inevitable. Near Ephesus the Greeks were forced to make a stand and were defeated. The Eretrians lost their general, and soon after the Athenians, though not the Eretrians, went home. That was a heavy blow for the Ionians, who now dispersed into their cities. It is reasonable to assume that it was not the one setback alone which, despite Aristagoras' desperate entreaties, caused the early defection of the Athenians. Neither they nor he would at that moment have expected the burning of Sardes to make such a great impression everywhere, and, in consequence, the revolt to spread so rapidly. It also shows that the defeat at Ephesus was only a minor affair. The Ionians succeeded in bringing Byzantium and other cities along the Straits to their side as well as most of Cyprus in the south. It was the crucial moment of the whole rebellion (498–497).

The Athenian withdrawal must have been mainly determined by the influence of home affairs, even though the obvious weakness and disunity of the Ionians were soon again manifest; they received, for example, no support from the states between the Hellespont and the Black Sea. We know nothing about that particular year at Athens, but we do know that the archon for 496–495 was Hipparchus, most likely the son of Charmus, who in 488–487 was the first to be ostracized (see below, p. 147), and whose sister had married the tyrant Hippias. Although free from any suspicion of favouring *tyrannis* (otherwise he would not have been able to stay in Athens),[8] this Hipparchus is likely to represent a trend in Athenian policy opposing the support given to the Ionians. The wavering assembly might regard him as somebody who could possibly pacify the dreaded hostility of Hippias and the Persian king. More important still was the attitude of the leading families at Athens. Whatever family may have been responsible for the support of Ionia, it is likely that they had to give way to some of their opponents; the Alcmaeonids were either entirely removed from any leading position or had joined hands with the 'loyal' members of the Peisistratid clan in liquidating their former policy.[9]

In Asia the Persian counter-offensive had started. The details of the fighting, and in particular the chronology, are quite uncertain. In a long campaign, despite a naval victory by the united Ionian fleet, Cyprus was recovered by the Persians, and a number of Ionian and Carian cities were recaptured, some after heavy resistance. From both sides, north and south, the Ionians were threatened, and they could do little but wait and see where the next blow would fall. It now became clear that neither Histiaeus nor Aristagoras was a competent leader. The former had been released by Darius after he had promised to quell the revolt, but was suspected by Greeks and Persians alike. Aristagoras had abandoned Miletus and refused to accept Hecataeus' advice to bide his time in the nearby island of Leros; he went to Thrace to find a refuge for himself and other Greek fugitives. He tried to found a colony where Athens sixty years later founded Amphipolis; but he was soon killed there in battle. Histiaeus, whom the Milesians had refused to accept in their city 'after having tasted freedom' (Hdt. 6, 5), got a squadron of eight ships from Lesbos and took to piracy in the Bosporus. Then and later, however, he tried to support the Ionian cause, sometimes by very crude actions; eventually he was captured and executed by the Persians. If the two men were largely responsible for the outbreak of the Ionian revolt, they were in fact little more than adventurers who tried to get the best out of a situation not of their making. It would be unfair to take Herodotus' description as entirely true. He was generally biased against the Ionians, and at least some of their leaders were of a different stamp, as for instance, the wise and active Hecataeus whose own (truthful?) record Herodotus must have read, or the brave sailor Dionysius, of whom we shall hear in a moment.

The Persians now put Miletus under siege and at the same time got together a strong Phoenician fleet.[10] The Ionians, on the other hand, at a meeting of the delegates to the Panionion, decided to let Miletus defend itself and no longer to fight on land; all available ships were to be sent to the island of Lade off Miletus. Some of the islands provided strong contingents, but the mainland cities contributed surprisingly little; we do not know whether they had already submitted to the Persians or simply withdrawn from the Greek cause. Herodotus (6, 8 f.) describes in detail the battle line and also the training which the crews voluntarily, at least for some time, underwent under the guidance of Dionysius of Phocaea, who himself commanded only three ships. A Persian attempt by their former tyrants to persuade the Greeks to submit had no effect. But fatigue and the lack of a supreme command undermined the spirit of the Ionian crews, and in the final battle some contingents deserted, while others fought bravely. In the end few Greeks escaped from the defeat; soon afterwards Miletus was taken and sacked, and its surviving people enslaved or transferred to the east. It was the end of the greatness of Miletus and the end of the Ionian revolt. Many cities suffered through the conquerors' reign of terror. One man who fled at the last moment was Miltiades, ruler of the Thracian Chersonese (Hdt. 6, 41). He reached Athens in 493 to be involved at once in the feuds prevailing among the leading politicians and families there (see below).

The revolt, after all, had lasted for six years, though that was probably due to Persian slowness rather than to Ionian effectiveness. Soon peace was restored, and Darius displayed a magnanimous and wise policy, rare among victors; he probably revoked the severe measures by the local commanders. It was essential for the empire to make its open north-western frontier safe and secure; more than ever, the position and attitude of the Ionian Greeks remained a matter of Persian domestic policy. Artaphrenes, undoubtedly acting on Darius' orders, forced the Ionian cities into mutual treaties by which disputes were to be settled peacefully; he also fixed a tribute which was still the same in Herodotus' time.[11] These measures, however, were only a first step. In spring 492 Mardonius, a gifted young general and one of Darius' sons-in-law, reached Asia Minor with an army and fleet of considerable strength. Before he marched on to the Hellespont he introduced democratic rule in the Ionian cities (Hdt. 6, 43). There were exceptions, especially on some islands, but it can hardly be doubted that it was the wish of Darius to do away with those tyrants 'by the grace of the king', whom he rightly regarded as one of the chief causes of the revolt. However, it must not be forgotten that such a democracy, granted by and connected with Persian suzerainty, was something very different from that of a fully autonomous polis. To strengthen the loyalty of the Ionians was also essential in view of Darius' plans against Greece which were to become clearer during that year; in fact, many Ionians fought in the great war loyally on the Persian side. Incidentally, the mild treatment by Persia will have contributed to the fact that Ionian activity in the field of intellect and general culture was not interrupted, but politically the independent history of the Asiatic Greeks had reached its end.

Mardonius crossed the Hellespont and went into Thrace. The magnitude of the enterprise is clearly exaggerated in the Greek tradition; but one way or another the campaign was directed against Greece. Whether that meant, as Herodotus maintains, that the real purpose was to punish Athens and Eretria, or even to conquer Greece, seems doubtful, to say the least. It is more likely that it was a preparatory move to make sure of Thracian and Macedonian submission, to complete the hold on the Aegean, and to bring the Greeks face to face with the power of the Persian empire. This campaign of 492 was only partly successful. The fleet was severely damaged by a storm when it tried to round Mt Athos,[12] and the army suffered a defeat by a Thracian tribe, the Brygi, though they were subdued before Mardonius returned home, himself seriously wounded. Thasos with its rich mines had been reduced by the fleet; when in the following year the Thasians planned a revolt, they immediately obeyed an order by Darius to dismantle their walls and to bring their ships to Abdera, which was in Persian hands. Everywhere along the shores of the empire ships were being built and war was being prepared. The Greeks could be in no doubt that Persia was aiming at their subjection.

The news of the destruction of Miletus had come to the Athenians as a grievous shock. In spring 493, under the immediate impression of the event, the performance of the *Capture of Miletus* by the tragedian Phrynichus caused an outburst of sorrow, pity, and shame among the audience. Phrynichus was severely fined, and the play was never again to be performed (Hdt. 6, 21). It was the first time that a play had reflected an actual recent event. Though myth and reality will have been intermingled as they did in the mythological plays (see below, p. 176), the theatre was just as much as the assembly a place in which political issues could be aired. In the same year Themistocles held office, though hardly the first archonship.[13] He was of noble, though somewhat obscure origin, according to one tradition the son of a slave woman; anyway, he was opposed to the

leading families and their policy. From his later history we know
that his mind was dominated by the aim of turning Athens into a
naval power, which meant at the same time a more democratic
state. His first move was to create a new and safe harbour, using
the bays between the rocky hills of the Peiraeus instead of the
flat and indefensible beach of Phaleron. Themistocles must have
fought against the wavering policy which had ended in the Ionian
débâcle. It is quite possible that the future archon was behind
the performance of Phrynichus' provocative play, just as he
was much later (476) the choregus of another of the poet's political
tragedies.

The time, however, was not yet ripe, and it was, at any rate,
a long-term policy. In the same year Miltiades returned to Athens;
a man who as the ruler of the Chersonese and a Persian vassal had
outgrown the status of an Athenian citizen, and had had no share
in the Ionian revolt, but who recommended himself at that moment
by his intimate knowledge of Persian military matters. An attempt
was made to remove this *grandseigneur* from the political scene. He
was accused of *tyrannis* over the Chersonese, rather a ridiculous
accusation; for in legal terms *tyrannis* was aiming at the overthrow
of democracy, and even the prosecution did not charge him with
that. He was acquitted, and soon after elected one of the strategi
(Hdt. 6, 104). It is obvious that the people wanted him as a military
leader. Probably he was chiefly supported by the rural population
and the hoplite class; Themistocles, whose supporters were above
all the common people in the city, was for the time being forced
into the background, and the Athenians, especially the noble
families, closed their ranks against a threat which every day became
more imminent.

Events in other parts of Greece point to the same situation. In
Sparta the king Cleomenes had further strengthened his position
by inflicting a crushing defeat at Sepeia on the old rival state of
Argos (Hdt. 6, 76 ff.).[14] The city and acropolis of Argos were not
taken, and for that reason Cleomenes was accused at home of
bribery; he was acquitted, as was only reasonable, but the event
shows that his enemies were still active. Perhaps it had been a
mistake to spare Argos itself, and thus open the way for a kind of
counter-revolution. Argos had lost thousands of her citizens, and the

dependent towns of Mycenae and Tiryns now broke away. Herodotus also speaks of a local slave revolt; anyway, the dismembered state which emerged and gradually regained some power was a democracy in which people formerly suppressed – the perioeci mentioned by Aristotle (*pol.* 1303a, 6) – became citizens, though not without some internal struggle. For the time being Argos was no longer a power that counted, but for several decades its anti-Spartan attitude was strengthened.

About this time (491) Darius is said to have sent envoys to the Greek states to demand earth and water as a symbol of submission. At Sparta and Athens, by a breach of the most elementary international rules and the commands of religion, the envoys were put to death. Herodotus tells this in a different context, when the event seemed to set a dangerous precedent (7, 133); he might feel that it spoiled his picture of the Greeks suffering aggression. Most of the other states complied with the Persian demand, especially the islands which were most exposed to the danger of a naval attack. Among these was Aegina, a member of the Peloponnesian League and a thorn in the side of Athens for a long time past as well as a possible stepping-stone for a Persian campaign. It may have been for Aegina's sake in particular that Darius sent his envoys.[15] Athens used the opportunity to complain of Aegina in Sparta; whether they were actually accused of 'being traitors to Hellas' may be doubted, although Herodotus claims (6, 61) that Cleomenes was acting 'for the common good of Hellas' when he tried to take hostages from Aegina. It was then that the smouldering conflict between him and his fellow king Demaratus burst into flames, as the latter had secretly supported the Aeginetan refusal to Cleomenes. In an intrigue, in which the oracle of Delphi played a rather sinister part, Cleomenes managed to declare Demaratus' birth illegitimate, to deprive him of his kingship, and to put in his place another Eurypontid, Leotychidas, who acted in agreement with Cleomenes. Demaratus later fled to the Persian court. Aegina gave hostages whom Cleomenes handed over to the Athenians. A weak spot in the Greek armour had been eliminated, and so was some of the disunity among the Greek states. Cleomenes held more power than any Spartan king before him, and with Sparta's friendship behind them, the Athenians prepared to meet the enemy.

2 · *Marathon*

Darius decided to change the strategy against Greece, largely because of the dangers of the long northern route which had been experienced in 492, perhaps also because he had limited aims. There was a change in the command of the expedition as well. Mardonius, on account of his wound rather than from disgrace, stayed at home, and two new commanders were chosen, Datis, an experienced soldier of Median origin, and Artaphrenes, the youngish son of the satrap in Sardes. The new plan was to sail across the Aegean, to subdue the islands, and then to punish Athens and Eretria for having intervened in the Ionian revolt. It is more than doubtful whether any further aims were contemplated for the moment.[16]

The fleet was to be manned with an adequate number of soldiers, and a new special type of transport ship was used for sending the horses over (Hdt. 6, 48. 95). How strong were the Persian forces? Herodotus (6, 95) speaks of a total of six hundred triremes; but that is his conventional number for any Persian fleet (except in 480), and even in his own description the horse transports were included in that number, and they were not triremes. The fantastic figures of later writers are no help; we really do not know, though we can make a reasonable guess. If we accept a fleet of one hundred triremes as possible, and a fair number of transports in addition, this should be a likely maximum; but it is also possible that there were hardly any warships, as there was no danger of naval fighting during the whole campaign. The number of fighting men, both foot and horse, may have been around twenty thousand, rather less than more.[17]

The fleet assembled in Cilicia and then sailed against Naxos, the first objective in this campaign of vengeance. The Naxians took to the hills, but a few were taken prisoner, and the town with its temples was burnt. The Delians could see the smoke rising above Naxos, and before the Persian fleet approached their island the people fled to Tenos. Datis, however, landed at Rhenaea and sent a message to the Delians that he only wished to pay homage to Apollo. This was mainly a political manoeuvre, one of several examples to show that the Persians did not wish to alienate the Ionians, who had close relations with the god of Delos.

As on other occasions, Herodotus, in an emphatic phrase, stresses the fact that Darius sailed against Eretria, 'taking with him Ionians and Aeolians'.[18] Some of these were soldiers and hostages taken from the other islands; it seems that there was still room enough on board, and that might confirm that the fleet had more transports than warships. The most important Greek in the fleet was Hippias, a very old man, who hoped to regain his position as the ruler of Athens, and who could naturally give the Persians plenty of good advice. His presence proves that it cannot have been their aim simply to destroy Athens, rather that they wanted to make it a subject state. If Datis succeeded in this, Persia would have a stronghold from which it might seem possible later to conquer all Greece.

The Persians landed on Euboea, after having subdued the islands along their route. The nearest city in the south of the island, Carystus, at first refused to give hostages or to march against her neighbours, but when the enemy laid siege to the city and devastated the countryside, the Carystians agreed to the terms of surrender and the fleet moved through the Euripus against Eretria. A considerable time must have passed since the Persians had left Asia. As there was no Greek fleet large enough to intervene, the slow progress of the Persians must have been deliberate. It could never have been their intention to take the Greeks by surprise; but neither was there a deliberate display of both severity and clemency on the part of Persia.[19] Datis and Artaphrenes simply had to make sure that their route across the Aegean – which was also the route for a possible retreat – was safe.

Eretria was in grave danger, but the citizens were divided among themselves whether to resist or not. We are told that four thousand Athenian cleruchs from Chalcis were dispatched to help Eretria, but never got there and went instead to Attica to save themselves. If the story is true, these men must have joined their tribal units and fought at Marathon; nothing, however, is said about it, and the story may be a later invention to cover the fact that Athens sent no help at all. There was even now little feeling of solidarity among Greek states. Moreover, the Athenian attitude is more than understandable; for Athens needed every soldier herself, and to send troops over to Euboea would mean their complete loss.[20] Eretria fell after a few days' siege and was sacked; the people were enslaved and taken away.

There can be no doubt that the Athenians, too, were not of one mind. Had Hippias friends there, had he perhaps already been in contact with such people? This is not unlikely, though we do not know for certain; all theories about pro- and anti-Persian factions miss the point. Any division of the people rested exclusively on

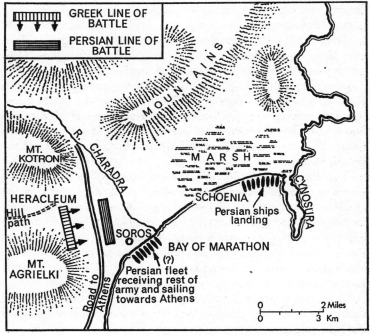

6. Battle of Marathon

domestic issues of which, of course, one was Hippias' possible return. Herodotus seems to have heard a number of stories, e.g. against the Alcmaeonids; some of them may be well-founded, but most of such stories only reflect earlier or later domestic divisions. All we can say is that, when the emergency occurred, Athenian democracy rose to the occasion.

The Persians, 'after waiting for a few days, sailed for the land of Attica' (Hdt. 6, 102). This sentence, simple as it seems to be has caused havoc in the minds of modern historians. Without going into the details of the various conclusions, it will suffice to say that: (1) the Persians needed a few days to rest their troops, to keep the horses fit after the long voyage, to take water and provisions on board, and to take the Eretrian prisoners on board and disembark them on a nearby small island; (2) that they landed at the nearest place in Attica where a plain gave them the opportunity to use the cavalry. There were two other possible plains in Attica; but it would have been rather dangerous to attempt a landing at Phaleron, in view of the city and its army, and the Thriasian plain at the bay of Eleusis would have meant not only a long voyage but also the danger of being hemmed in and possibly cut off from the return route to Asia. Moreover, if the Persians succeeded in luring the Athenian army away from Athens, they could hope to conquer the city without much trouble, even perhaps with the help of Hippias' friends there. It is possible that Hippias advised Datis as to the place to land, but even without such advice, the bay of Marathon offered itself as the natural landing site. Surrounded by steep hills, but opening southwards for a road to Athens, the plain behind the wide curve of the bay was one of the finest and, as it were, most attractive sites, pleasant to the military eye.[21] The Persians safely disembarked along the 'Schoinia', a narrow strip of coast along the big marsh in the north of which part at least was probably a fresh-water lake in ancient times; disembarkation here was protected by the Cynosura promontory against both storm and interference. By not landing farther south – there may have been several reasons for not doing so – Datis gave the Athenians the chance to cover the opening of the plain towards Athens.

Herodotus' account of the working of the Athenian command (6, 103) is anachronistic and impossible; he assumes rotation among the ten strategi, and regards Miltiades as 'the tenth', a formula very similar to the one used by Thucydides.[22] The commander-in-chief was the polemarch Callimachus, though it is likely that the strategi by then had grown in stature. While still the commanders of the tribal units they formed a kind of council of war, and the polemarch would largely depend on their common judgement. Miltiades, thanks to his personal reputation and greatness, was, however, the leading spirit, and he persuaded council and polemarch to accept his strategy. It is, in fact, the last time we hear of a polemarch as a military leader. When the news of the enemy's landing reached Athens it had already been decided not to defend the city behind the walls but 'to march out'.[23] The hoplites had their arms and rations ready, and the nobles had left their horses behind and fought on foot, proof enough that the hoplites' training was negligible. Probably the army had been assembled ever since the fall of Eretria, which must have come as a great shock to the Athenians. A number of slaves were to accompany their masters as armour- and baggage-bearers; some of them were killed in battle and honourably buried. At short notice the army marched out – either by the rough paths through Mt Pentelicum into the Vrana valley or more likely by the longer, but easier, road south of the mountains, which reaches the plain of Marathon from the south. Earlier, a professional runner, Philippides or Pheidippides, was sent the 140 miles to Sparta which he reached within about 36 hours. This famous first 'Marathon race', however, was wasted, as the Spartans, celebrating their great festival of the Carneia, were unable to send their promised help before the full moon, which was probably six days away.[24]

When the Athenians were about to take up their position, a contingent of Plataeans arrived. That small Boeotian town had remembered the help Athens had given it against Thebes (above, p. 88). Although the Plataeans had been given protection ever since and might expect to need it again in the future, their present action was much less a matter of politics than of genuine gratitude and friendship. Herodotus maintains (6, 108) that the Plataeans came 'in full force'. This sounds almost too good to be true. Anyway, how strong was the Greek army? The traditional figure of 10,000 Athenians (with or without 1,000 Plataeans) seems too large; at any rate, the round figures are suspicious. We can only say that the Greeks were considerably smaller in numbers than the Persians, so that their battle line at normal depth would be very much shorter. The position they held was, however, favourable; it was slightly above the level of the plain, and it could cover both the main road to Athens on their right flank, where the polemarch Callimachus and Miltiades were in command, and the mountain path on their left, where the Plataeans formed the end of the line.

Herodotus' description of the battle itself leaves many things obscure, and other sources, including the paintings in the Stoa Poikile (Paus. 1, 15), are more confusing than helpful, but with the results of modern topographical and archaeological studies a fairly certain reconstruction of the fighting seems possible. It was – apart from the fighting near Ephesus in 498 (see above, p. 128) – the first open battle on land between Greeks and Persians, and though comparatively small forces were engaged on either side, the event was in many ways most remarkable and deserves a detailed description.

The Persians had left their camp on the Schoinia, had marched south along the shore, crossed the bed of the Charadra, which in summer was practically dry, and formed a line of battle opposite the Greek position. For several days both armies faced each other without moving. For the Greeks in their position, it was the natural thing to wait for a Persian attack, the more so as they were hoping for the arrival of the Spartans. The Persians, too, would certainly know of that forthcoming help for the Greeks; nevertheless, they did not attack, perhaps because it would have cost a great deal of blood to drive the Athenians out of their strong position, perhaps also because there may have been some earlier fighting, in which the Persians displayed cavalry as well as infantry, but were beaten.[25] Datis, now at any rate, chose a strategy which he may have had in mind the whole time: to keep the Greek army where it was, and meanwhile to move against the undefended city. To achieve his aims he had to act before the Spartans arrived. Now, Herodotus in his story of the battle never mentions the Persian cavalry. As it was in many ways the most important part of the army, on which the whole expedition with its horse transports was based, the sole explanation is that the horsemen actually had no share in the final fighting. This could be explained by the fact that cavalry was useless against the elevated position of the Greeks. That is confirmed by a curious and very late source, the only source that explains what Datis' intentions were. In the Byzantine lexicon of the *Suda* (formerly known as Suidas) a Greek proverb 'the horsemen are away' is discussed with a reference to the battle of Marathon, when some Ionians from the Persian side revealed to the Greeks that the cavalry had embarked or was embarking.[26] That could only happen during the night, and before daylight part of the Persian fleet with the cavalry on board, together with some ships carrying the Eretrian prisoners taken from their

island, was sailing south to round Attica and enter the Saronic gulf.
The rest of the ships will have anchored along the shore near the
mouth of the Charadra, in order to take the army on board, if
necessary.[27]

Miltiades will at once have realized what the disappearance of the
cavalry implied. The moment had come for a bold attack by the
Greek hoplites, the more so as he must have been in continual fear
of some counter-move by Hippias' partisans at Athens. The distance
between the two battle lines was eight stadia, i.e. about a mile. It
seemed a mad thing to advance against the enemy through the open
plain with its scattered trees; but when the Greeks came within
reach of the archers they proceeded 'at a quick step'.[28] In order to
equal the width of the Persian front, Miltiades had weakened his
centre, while keeping the wings strong. It meant running a serious
risk, but it worked. The Greek centre gave way, while the wings
put their opponents, among them the Ionians, to flight and then
converged on the élite troops of the victorious Persian centre. It was
a masterstroke, anticipating – though without cavalry – Hannibal's
tactics at Cannae. Heavy hand-to-hand fighting ended in a general
flight on the part of the Persians; they suffered great losses, the rest
were taken on board ship. The Greeks succeeded in capturing only
seven ships.[29] Several thousand of the enemy were killed; the dead
Athenians numbered only 192; nothing is known about the numbers killed among the Plataeans and the slaves.

Immediately after victory was won, the Athenian army, though
they must have been desperately tired, returned home to be in time
for any Persian attempt at landing at Phaleron. The Persian fleet
was heavily laden and could move only slowly; thus, the Athenian
army was in time. When Datis realized that the hoplites were there
he gave up, and the fleet returned to Asia. The Eretrians were settled
in the neighbourhood of Susa. The Greek victory was complete,
Miltiades was the hero of the day; but the hoplites, citizens chiefly
of the Zeugite class, shared the honour. Among the many stories
told about the battle is the rumour of a shield signal, obviously a
reflection of the sun, given to the Persians from Mt Pentelicum
(Hdt. 6, 115. 121 ff.). It is not clear when this signal was supposed
to be given, nor for what purpose; later the Alcmaeonids were
blamed for it, probably because they had fallen from popular favour

(above, p. 128). Nobody can deny that there may have been some communication between Hippias' friends at Athens and the enemy; but nothing about it is certain, though anything was possible in view of the fierce domestic intrigues. We must never forget that 'medism' had not yet been invented.[30]

Three days after the full moon, that is probably the second day after the battle, a Spartan contingent of 2,000 arrived, visited the battlefield, 'praised the Athenians and their achievement, and then returned home' (Hdt. 6, 120). The dead Athenians were buried in one common grave, in a mound (the *Soros*) which has lately been excavated; ashes and bones as well as funeral vases and armour have been found. It is likely that the tomb was erected where many of the slain had been lying; it is therefore a crucial point in the topographical reconstruction of the battle. As it stands not far from the shore, it cannot have been the place where the Greek centre had its heaviest losses, when it had to retreat. The tomb will rather have been the place of the last Persian resistance before the final flight, when among others the polemarch was killed.

The victory by a small army, won chiefly by the Athenians, seemed little short of a miracle. It is only natural that soon there spread the legend of help given by a number of gods and heroes. Pious gratitude was stronger even than civil pride, though that too was manifest. Both found expression in the many dedications to the gods, which could still be seen in Pausanias' day, at Marathon and Athens, at Delphi and Olympia and Plataea, some of them of later origin or at least later completion. The excavations at Olympia have recently brought to light a wonderfully preserved oriental bronze helmet with the inscription 'To Zeus, the Athenians who took it from the Medes'.[31] On another helmet, this time Greek, the inscription runs 'Miltiades dedicated'. It is likely that the former commemorated Marathon, while the second may have been dedicated by the 'tyrant' of the Chersonese.[32]

The effect of the victory was more manifest in the increased self-confidence of the Greeks in general than in any serious damage done to the enemy. Both sides had learnt a good deal about one another. The Persians, in particular, must have realized the error of their strategy; it was the obvious thing for them to return to Mardonius' plans. The invasion, however, was certainly to come. On the Greek side the weakness of the Persian infantry, compared with their own well-armed, well-trained hoplites, made a deep impression, and the belief that Persian superior power was not invincible created a false idea of the enemy, though in 480 it at least helped to induce those states not in immediate danger to join the common cause. For Athens, the miracle that had happened opened the way into a new future.

3 · Between the Wars

In the year after Marathon, Miltiades asked the assembly 'for seventy ships, an armed force, and money, without informing them what country he was going to attack' (Hdt. 6, 132). This was a most unusual procedure, and the figure of seventy ships seems far in excess of what Athens at that time was able to put to sea, even though most of the ships were probably old-fashioned fifty-oarsmen boats (*pentekonteroi*). What followed makes the story hardly less curious. The people, induced by the prospect of material gains ('gold'), decided on an expedition of which they did not know the purpose, and which must have strained Athenian resources very considerably. Their confidence in Miltiades is obvious, and he may have given a hint why it might be better not to disclose where he was going. In fact, he sailed against Paros, which in the early fifth century was not yet known for its marble and was of little economic or political importance. The whole affair remained a puzzle even for the Greeks later on. As early as Herodotus, several versions of what happened were known, and it does not help that Herodotus tells only an anecdotical Parian version which involved a sacrilege by Miltiades, and remains silent on the Athenian version. On the other hand, what Ephorus says (*FGrH* 70 F 63) of a major strategic plan to occupy all the Cyclades, a plan which failed because the leader of the expedition became a traitor, is clearly anachronistic and seen through the eyes of a man who knew about Athenian imperialism and about Themistocles' life and fate.[33] Miltiades, whose personal interest and responsibility in the enterprise were manifest, was not interested in Athenian naval supremacy, in securing a trade route, or in the conquest of an island without natural resources; but he had his connexions in the northern Aegean, and he knew from personal experience the importance of the mines of Thrace and Thasos. The latter was a colony of Paros, and relations between the two islands seem to have been fairly close. That is all we know, but it is possible that Paros was to be only a kind of preparatory station for the conquest of Thasos. The attack on Paros, however, proved a failure, and Miltiades himself was severely wounded. The Athenian fleet sailed for home.[34]

Miltiades had not kept his promise to the people; moreover, the expedition had cost some lives and a good deal of money. He had many enemies, and they seized the opportunity. Xanthippus, married to an Alcmaeonid and father of an infant son Pericles, charged Miltiades with 'deceiving the people'. At the trial, with the accused on a stretcher, unable to speak, the death penalty was proposed, but the court rejected it and punished Miltiades by the enormous fine of fifty talents. Soon afterwards he died of his wound, and the money was paid by his son Cimon. Even for so rich a family as the Philaids this payment cannot have been easy.

Was the punishment simply an act of ingratitude on the part of a democracy towards its leader? It has often been called so, and later examples may support the view. In some way this is even fair; for the people, the sovereign of the democratic polis, had first sanctioned the expedition, and then held its leader responsible. The 'ancient law', quoted by Demosthenes (20, 100. 135), prescribing the death penalty for a mere breach of promise to the people, can hardly have been in existence then, and it is even doubtful whether it was introduced to meet Miltiades' case; democracy was not yet as strong as that. But the state exercised its power over the individual and indeed over a man who – with all his great merits – had more than once flouted state authority.

This, however, is only part of the picture. The legal sovereignty of the Cleisthenian demos must be seen against the background of the feuds between various noble families and their individual leaders, feuds which persisted because aristocrats were, and remained for a long time, the only trained politicians and therefore held, or were struggling for, the power within the democratic constitution. Miltiades, however popular he had been with part of the people, had fierce enemies among the nobles. Envy and ambition were

strong allies against a man who seemed more independent than any
of the rest. Moreover, there were traditional clan feuds which
neither the tyrants nor Cleisthenes had been able completely to
remove. Xanthippus, who acted as the prosecutor, represented one
faction; others were one way or another attached to the Peisistratids.
There was also a man such as Aristeides, with his strict ideals of
justice and legality, who would oppose anybody breaking the rules
of Cleisthenes' reforms. It was he who was elected first archon in
489–488. And then there was Themistocles, who is supposed to have
said 'that Miltiades' trophy kept him awake at night' (Plut. *Them.*
3, 4), who was, as it were, a faction of his own and in opposition
to everything Miltiades had stood for. The victory of Marathon
was a glorious fact of the past; with Miltiades' disappearance, the
way was open for new developments which eventually were to
supplant, or at least to supplement, the lessons of Marathon.

In the following year (488–487) ostracism was used for the first
time (*AP* 22, 3). The man expelled was that Hipparchus who had
been archon in 496–495. There is no evidence as to who suggested
the action to the people, nor why it was done. Hipparchus, as far
as we know, though belonging to the Peisistratid family, was
hardly a dangerous man, and the idea must have been to hit out at
those who had been in favour of that clan. That could be popular
enough even without a strong lead by an individual politician, but it
must have been somebody's initiative, the more so as it was a new
and almost revolutionary method.[35] In the next year Athenian
democracy made a decisive step forward; but before we come to
that it seems right to look at the situation outside Athens.

If Marathon at first caused little change in the general policy of
Athens, we should certainly not expect greater effects in other
states. In Sparta, after Cleomenes had beaten Argos and secured his
royal position by forcing his fellow king Demaratus into exile
(above, p. 133), his machinations, especially the bribing of Delphi,
became known; he had to leave and stayed away for some time.
Although he was not officially banned, it seems that his position
was seriously undermined. He went first to Thessaly, and then to
Arcadia, where he tried to stir up trouble against Sparta and to
win personal supporters. The question remains open whether he
was only thinking of gaining a stronger position for himself, a

position far beyond that normally granted to a Spartan king, or whether he primarily thought of creating a strong power against another Persian attack. There is also a tradition, though disputed, that he stimulated a revolt of the Messenian helots; it would be this revolt which had its effects far in the west when Messenian refugees were received at Rhegium and then settled at Zancle, which was renamed Messana (see above, map 5). To Sparta, in particular to the ephors, Cleomenes was a traitor. He was lured back with false promises, and soon afterwards died, either by suicide or by murder (Hdt. 6, 74 f.). His successor was his half-brother Leonidas. The ephors were in full power again, and Sparta's hegemony over the Peloponnese was restored.

Aegina had kept quiet during the war, since her hostages were still in Athenian hands. When Athens, despite intervention by the Spartan king Leotychidas, refused to return them (Hdt. 6, 85 ff.), war broke out again between Aegina and Athens.[36] The latter was too late in supporting a democratic rising at Aegina, which was completely crushed. It is significant for the weakness of Athens at sea that the Athenians 'bought' – at a nominal price – twenty ships from Corinth; as before, Corinth showed the same friendly attitude towards Athens, which at that moment seemed a less dangerous competitor than Aegina. Success and defeat were following each other, and the war was dragging on, a fact that provided a credible pretext for Themistocles' naval policy.

Apart from him (and perhaps Cleomenes), the Greeks were acting in these years (about 488–484) as if there was no possible threat of a new Persian attack. They were fortunate and to some extent justified in this attitude. For Darius, although he made preparations for a larger expedition, did not really get on with it. A revolt in Egypt started in 486, and there was trouble in other parts of the empire. Darius, now an old man, died in the same year, to be succeeded by his son Xerxes, whose mother was Atossa, daughter of Cyrus. The new Great King, a true Achaemenid if ever there was one, was the heir not only to the throne but also to his father's military plans.

The trend towards a more advanced democracy at Athens went hand in hand with naval policy, for the oarsmen of the fleet would be recruited from the classes of non-hoplite status, who thus gained

an important share in the defence of the state. First, however, constitutional change had to come at the top. It is from *AP* 22, 5, that
we learn what happened. In 487–486, under the archonship of
Telesinus, the archons were for the first time appointed by lot, one
(including the secretary) from each phyle, but out of 500 candidates
elected by the demes.[37] They would still be men of the two upper
classes (perhaps the *hippeis* had been admitted as early as Cleisthenes), but the chance of the draw deprived the office of its real
importance. It still remained an honour to be an archon, but no
ambitious politician would henceforth aim at being the first archon.
There was no longer a single office, the holder of which would
occupy a unique and powerful position, and what was true of the
first archon was valid also for the polemarch, the military leader.
Men of respectability, but without political status, would in
the future fill the archonships. This meant at the same time that the
archons gave way to boards of officials; most significant was the
change-over to the collegium of the ten strategi, whose strengthened
position could be noticed even before Marathon. They were elected
officials and could be re-elected an unlimited number of times, and
they were now in full charge of army and navy; there was never a
distinction between general and admiral. This new position gave
to the strategi (or at least to some of them who were able and
ambitious) the leadership in politics as well. That meant that the
people themselves would elect their politicians and statesmen, if
necessary to hold office over a number of years.

Another result of the new method of appointing the archons was
that in the long run the composition of the council on the Areopagus
would change, since every year the nine archons became its members
for life. As the years passed, they would be in ever-larger proportion
citizens of the upper classes, but of little political ambition, and the
general importance of the Areopagus might gradually be reduced.
Taken all in all, the reform of 487–486 – it could almost be called
a constitutional revolution – continued the work of Cleisthenes;
first, in the important part given to the demes, but above all, in the
way it combined radical ideas with moderation.

It seems clear that behind this reform was a single mind. None
of the factional leaders could be interested in such measures, but a
man like Themistocles could. He had held high office and perhaps

was a member of the Areopagus; he had also been one of the strategi at Marathon and knew all about the position of the polemarch. After Miltiades' death, his only important rival among candidates for further strategies, though perhaps for some time his ally, was Aristeides. The way was open for Themistocles, and where it was not he would see to it that nobody remained to obstruct his plans. Our tradition about Themistocles, beginning with Herodotus, is frankly hostile; that is largely due to his later, rather chequered career, though he may early have shown certain qualities, such as love of money, which gave him a bad name. Among later writers it is only Thucydides who fully recognized the genius of the man, above all, his outstanding intellect and clear foresight as a statesman (1, 138, 3). Themistocles had at the same time exceptionally strong willpower and a great ability to impose his will on others. We now have in the famous Ostia bust a realistic portrait of the man; it gives the impression, not of an aristocrat, rather of a thick-set, perhaps even coarse man with a determined and thoughtful mind; what it does not show is his cunning and his vanity.[38]

In the next few years, after the expulsion of Hipparchus, ostracism was used several times. In 487–486 Megacles the Alcmaeonid, and in 485–484 his brother-in-law Xanthippus, were expelled; there was one more whose name we do not know. In all these ostracisms a large number of votes was given against Themistocles; it was he who challenged the aristocrats.[39] The predominance of the Alcmaeonids was over, and their earlier attempt at coming to terms with Persia may in popular opinion have become a policy of support for Hippias. We even know from a large number of ostraca of an Alcmaeonid, otherwise unknown, Callixenus, who comes from a different deme from that of the main part of the clan, and who on one ostracon is called 'traitor'.[40] It is theoretically not impossible that one or other of the ostracisms was originally directed *against* Themistocles. He was an obvious target for the old-style politicians, but who but Themistocles could count on sufficient popular support to risk an ostracism? He could rely on the urban lower classes, and he will also have found friends among the convinced democrats of other groups. The use of ostracism went beyond Cleisthenes' original intentions, but it still tended in the same direction, though it was his own family, the Alcmaeonids, who provided most of the victims. To what extent it had become an instrument of organized group politics, as it later certainly was, remains doubtful.[41]

All the time Themistocles was pursuing his fundamental idea of creating a strong Athenian navy. The harbour of the Peiraeus must by then have been ready to shelter a fleet of triremes. Clearly Themistocles saw in the navy an instrument not only for ending the eternal war with Aegina, or increasing the power of the lower classes, but above all for meeting the Persian attack which was bound to come. At the same time he will have recognized that only as a sea-power could Athens become a really great power within the Greek world; no land army could ever hope to compete with Sparta. In the Aegean, on the other hand, there was a great deal of trade, or rather piracy, and no power to keep the sea routes safe. For all these reasons, Themistocles came to pursue his naval policy, and gradually he was able to convince the people as well. The main difficulty in realizing his plans was expense. Then, in 483–482, a stroke of good luck occurred. In the district of Laurium, where Athenian owners worked the silver mines by slave-labour, an unusually rich mine came to light, from which a surplus of no less than a hundred talents went to the state. If that sum is right, it was more money than was needed at the moment; but the citizens would have to forfeit their customary claim for the money to be distributed among them. Themistocles, thinking of Persia but speaking of Aegina, persuaded the assembly to relinquish the money to the state for the building of a fleet of (200?) triremes.[42] This success led to the last ostracism of those years, that of Aristeides (probably 482–481), whose moderate conservatism was opposed to naval policy. The hoplites of Marathon, after all, had proved their worth.

Themistocles called two of his daughters Sybaris and Italia (Plut. *Them.* 32, 2). That shows beyond doubt that he had some connexions with *Magna Graecia*. What they were, we are not told; but it is more than likely that he – a nobleman of doubtful descent who was always eager to make money – had been engaged in trade, and in particular in trade to the west. Herodotus (8, 62) reports that on a later occasion Themistocles threatened to abandon the Greek cause and to make all Athenians emigrate to Siris in Italy, 'which is ours as from old', probably because it was an old Ionian foundation which had been destroyed by its Achaean neighbours. There may have been a connexion during those years with events in Italy and Sicily. Most of the Greek cities there were ruled by petty tyrants of whom the most notorious was Phalaris of Acragas (before the middle of the sixth century). Round about 500 two rulers gained greater stature, Anaxilas of Rhegium and soon also of Zancle-Messana, and Hippocrates of Gela. They had risen to power in the face of conflicts with the previous aristocracies and they gave their cities the military protection which was always necessary on Sicilian soil; although most of the fighting was between the various cities and their rulers, it was sometimes also directed against the native peoples, or possibly against Carthage. As we have mentioned before, interest in the Greek west was strong among the eastern Greeks (see p. 106), who regarded it as a region of refuge. It must have made a strong impression when the rise of city rulers culminated in even more powerful men such as Theron of Acragas and Gelon, the successor of Hippocrates, who in 485 made himself master of Syracuse; there the ruling class of the gamori, the big landowners, had been expelled by a revolution, and Gelon restored order and property. The two rulers were closely connected by intermarriage and relied on the wealthy classes rather than the demos. For their expanding power it is significant (as before for Hippocrates) that they kept other cities subdued under the rule of dependent tyrants, often a member of their families or a faithful friend; Gelon made his brother Hieron the ruler of Gela. It is too early to speak of territorial empires, but the trend towards larger units of power is evident.

The wealth and grandeur of these tyrants were brought home to the Greeks in the motherland by their splendid victories in chariot races, as, for instance, the one in 490 of Theron's brother Xenocrates to whom Pindar dedicated his sixth Pythian ode; two years later Gelon won an Olympic victory with his chariot, and in the seventies his brother Polyzelus a Pythian victory of which the great, column-like bronze statue of the charioteer, part of a lost chariot-group, still stands at Delphi as a magnificent memorial. Horse-breeding was easy in the Sicilian plains, and the use of cavalry, mostly mercenaries, was a successful weapon in the hands of the tyrants. It was most likely the need to pay the mercenaries that compelled the tyrants to introduce coinage. But Gelon's Syracuse with its excellent harbours was also to be the home of a formidable navy. It provided a firm basis for Gelon's expanding power, but was also directed against the threat of Carthage, which had hung over the western Greeks ever since the battle of Alalia in 540. As Persia largely relied on the Phoenicians for her fleet, it was only natural that there should be also some link with the Phoenician naval power in the west. To Carthage, the Greek cities, especially in Sicily, were a natural enemy, and a constant menace to the western part of the island, which was in Phoenician hands. The situation grew more dangerous when there were strong rulers to stop the mutual quarrels among the Greeks themselves, especially after Theron had captured Himera, and the previous ruler Terillus had fled to Carthage. It is unlikely that, as Ephorus maintains (*FGrH* 70 F 186), Xerxes and Carthage had concluded an actual alliance, but if Herodotus does not mention any connexion, it is nevertheless almost certain that the coincidence of the events in Greece and Sicily was the result of some understanding between the two powers.[42a] It is equally certain that the growing tension between the Sicilian Greeks and Carthage was not a matter of racial enmity, rather the outcome of economic and political rivalry.

With this general background in mind, it is perhaps more than a mere conjecture to assume that Themistocles had approached Gelon, even before the Greek council of 481 sent envoys (see below). Themistocles' creation of a harbour and fleet for Athens is essentially the outcome of his imaginative foresight.[43] He did not know beforehand that he was to save Greece, but he must have known about the Persian preparations, in 493 as well as in 483. It cannot have been difficult to find out that the coming attack would have to be met on sea as well as on land.

The Persians made that quite clear. Xerxes, young, ambitious, and surrounded by advisers who were mostly also young and ambitious and among whom Mardonius as well as some Greek emigrants were prominent, was master of an enormously powerful empire which he first restored to peace and order. Egypt was reconquered, and Babylon crushed. One prominent feature in these events was Xerxes' severe treatment of temples and priests, a result of his intolerant orthodoxy.[44] He certainly was neither a fool nor an overbearing, megalomaniac despot, both views which were held by later Greeks; he could be cruel, but also magnanimous. Nor, indeed, was he an incapable wretch as he appears in Aeschylus' *Persae*. But he was impetuous and overconfident, perhaps even conceited, as a man in his thirties, flushed with power and success, might easily be.

The conquest of Greece was a task inherited from Darius, but fervently taken up as his own by Xerxes. To what extent Herodotus' story (7, 46 ff.) of Artabanus' warnings and Xerxes' vacillation between his grand plans and his fears contains any historical truth, remains doubtful. Anyway, Xerxes made far-reaching preparations. Probably even before he heard of the growing Athenian sea-power he decided not to risk another Marathon. Mardonius' campaign of 492 was to be the model, and in order to avoid a second naval disaster, the Persians began to dig a canal through the isthmus of the Athos peninsula; they also built bridges over the Hellespont and Strymon, and had stores of foodstuffs set up along the land route through Thrace and along the coast. These were major achievements in engineering and organization, technological ventures which to the Greeks seemed acts of *hubris*.

They, on the other hand, fully aware of the threatening onslaught, convened a conference, not later than in summer 481, on the Corinthian Isthmus of all Greeks willing to resist. A confederacy for the war, usually called 'the Greeks', and a general alliance (*symmachia*) with inter-state truce were established; thus, for instance, the war between Athens and Aegina came to an end. The Greeks also decided to send spies to Asia, and envoys to Gelon as well as to some states not yet prepared to join (Hdt. 7, 145 ff.). Under the leadership of Sparta and with the stimulating example set by Athens, the Greeks made the attempt to create, as far as possible, general unity against Persia.[45] It remained imperfect, but even so it was the beginning of a strong surge of anti-Persian 'Hellenism' which naturally grew much stronger after victory was won. The position of the Ionians in Asia Minor made clear what the Greeks had to expect if the Persians conquered their country. It would not mean cruel tyranny nor economic suffering; but Greece would be a new satrapy in the great empire, and the freedom of the Greek states would be lost with all their independent policy. Those who took the other side were henceforth stigmatized as 'siding with the Medes' (*medizontes*).[46] Fear, bribery, or egotistic and short-sighted policy kept a number of states away; many had offered Xerxes' envoys the tokens of submission. Among those which did not dare to take sides was Delphi, and naturally its cautious, even pessimistic attitude influenced others. However, when early in 480 the Persian forces, after wintering in Asia Minor, moved towards the Hellespont, the scene on both sides was set for the great war.

4 · *The Great War in East and West*

The army with which Xerxes invaded Europe was of great strength.[47] Herodotus (7, 58 ff.) provides a detailed account of both its numbers and its contingents with their respective commanders and equipment. For this catalogue he must have had a written source, probably of the peoples of the empire rather than the actual participants in the war. There is a good deal of correct knowledge, e.g. in the names of the generals, many of whom were related to the royal family; but the numbers are simply fantastic. For the fleet Herodotus accepted the figure in Aeschylus' *Persae*, 1,207 triremes, to which he added later contributions of 120 ships from the Greeks in Thrace. It is likely that the 1,207 included the 207 fast ships mentioned (*Persae* 343); then the whole account is based on the round figure of 1,000, which is probably too large. As Herodotus gives a catalogue of naval contingents, again in round figures, it has been suggested that his numbers may be potential rather than actual levies. The army total amounts to no less than 5,283,220 men! Although exactly half the total sum is reserved for non-combatants, even so, any theory trying to make sense of these figures or to explain them by some rational scheme is futile. Any reasonable guess – and that is the only thing we can aim at – must take into account the enormous difficulties of providing food and water for men and horses. If the crossing of the two bridges over the Hellespont (Hdt. 7, 53 ff.) really took seven days and seven nights, a number of about 200,000 men and 75,000 beasts has been regarded as a possible maximum, and that would imply not more than 150,000 combatants. With a fighting fleet – sometimes reduced by storms, but partly replenished by allied ships – of 600–700 triremes, the total would still be impressive enough, though now at least manageable.[48]

After a review of army and navy at Doriscus in Thrace, the Persian forces moved westward. Progress on land was slow as the way frequently had first to be cleared through forests and mountains, though the route, accurately described by Herodotus, was probably the best possible.[49] The Thracian tribes kept aloof, though some were forced into service (Hdt. 7, 115), while most of the Greek coastal cities were simply bypassed. The navy successfully sailed through the canal of the Athos peninsula and then rounded the Chalcidice. Army and fleet met again, as arranged, at Therma (Saloniki today). By then it was summer, probably July.

Several months earlier Thessalian envoys had reached the Greek *probouloi*, who acted as a permanent council on the Corinthian Isthmus, and had asked for help. As Macedon had submitted to Persia, Thessaly was to be the first part of Greece proper to suffer an attack. At that time, however, the most powerful family in Thessaly, the Aleuads in Larissa, had already been in contact with Persia; it has been shown that most likely from 492, when Mardonius had marched through Thrace, the Aleuads had used coins of Persian standard, and as early as then had submitted to Persia.[50] The envoys to the Isthmus could only have represented a loyal section of the Thessalians. They persuaded the Greeks, who were probably induced to see in them representatives of the majority, to dispatch a force to the Tempe valley, the entrance from Macedon into Thessaly. Herodotus (7, 172 ff.) tells us that an army of 10,000 hoplites was at once sent out, first by sea to Halus in Achaea Phthiotis, and then to march north in order to occupy the pass, where they were joined by Thessalian cavalry. At that time Xerxes was still in Thrace, but the troops were sent in great haste.[51] A Spartan, Euaenetus, was in charge, but Themistocles led the Athenian contingent. After only a few days of reconnoitring, and receiving advice from the Macedonian king Alexander – who had no interest in seeing the Persian army held up on his side of the frontier – the whole force returned by the same route, and Thessaly was left open to the enemy.

This is in many ways an odd story. To send out such a considerable force, though not under a Spartan king, could mean either merely a demonstration or a serious defence scheme; the presence of Themistocles speaks for the latter, although he was the champion of naval defence; it is likely that most of the ships used were Athenian. How could such an effort be abandoned long before Xerxes reached Macedon? In fact, why was it made at all at such an early stage? Did the Greeks hope for a general rising of the Thessalians against the Aleuads? Did they hope for assistance from frontier tribes or even from the Macedonians? We do not know, though Thessalian apathy and possibly hostility will have played its part, as is maintained in a different story found in Diodorus (11, 2, 5 f.). Herodotus explains the prompt return by the discovery that the Tempe pass was only one of several passes, and therefore not a safe position for the defence. This is true, but the Thessalians at least must have known it before. There can be no doubt, however, that whatever hopes the Greeks had held were disappointed.[52]

To keep the Thessalians now on the Greek side was impossible. Despondency spread throughout Greece, and at this time, if not even earlier, the members of the congress are said to have bound themselves by an oath (Hdt. 7, 132) to punish all states which submitted to Persia, and to give a tithe to Delphi; that would come from the loot from the sacked cities. If this move was an attempt to deter anybody, or in fact to try to get the support of Delphi, it failed; it is quite possible that the oath was a later invention, born from that 'nationalist' feeling of which we shall speak in a different context.[53] Most Greek states had undoubtedly asked Apollo for advice, and the two oracles given to Athens stand as examples for the rest unknown to us.[54] The first was utterly pessimistic and advised the Athenians to flee to the west; the second had the famous ambiguous reference to the wooden walls (Hdt. 7, 140 f.). Many Greeks must have realized, among them of course Themistocles, that resistance on land could not be decisive, that the greatest hope centred on the fleet.[55] Herodotus is convinced that the Spartan idea of defending the Isthmus line was futile, at least without strong naval protection – for which the waters round the Isthmus were quite unsuitable. That is why he calls – after the gods – Athens with her large fleet the saviour of Greece (7, 139). Naturally this is a verdict after the event, but Themistocles knew, and he was not the only one. Anyway, he persuaded the majority of his fellow citizens to accept his interpretation of the second oracle, that the saving wooden walls were the ships. Perhaps it was after all on his instigation that Delphi produced the second oracle. Even so, the tension between the Peloponnesians who wished to protect their homeland on the Isthmus and the other Greeks never quite ceased.

That became manifest again on the first occasion. Northern Greece was lost, but central Greece might still be saved. At that time the Greeks knew that they could not hope for any substantial support; neither Corcyra nor Argos nor, above all, Gelon of Syracuse was willing or able to help. The Greeks of the motherland, who were determined to fight, stood alone, and they had finally to decide where to meet the enemy. The Oeta massif separated Thessaly from the rest of Greece, and the Greeks did agree on a defence line which would protect the countries south of Thessaly. It was an absolutely necessary step, if only for maintaining the general morale of the Greeks. Defence was possibly only by a combined operation by land and sea. The pass of Thermopylae, with its sea flank through the narrow waters of the Malian gulf reaching as far as Artemisium, the northern cape of Euboea, provided the best possible position for an extended defence. An army under the Spartan king Leonidas went to Thermopylae, and a fleet of both Athenian and Peloponnesian ships was to hold the position between the northern end of the Euripus and Artemisium. The two forces were to keep in close contact by swift boats (Hdt. 8, 21).

Leonidas' Peloponnesian army consisted, according to Herodotus, of 300 Spartiates, 2,120 Arcadians, 400 Corinthians, 200 Phliusians, 80 Mycenaeans, i.e. a total of 3,100. Simonides in his epitaph (Hdt. 7, 228) speaks of 4,000 Peloponnesians fighting against 3 million (!) enemies.[56] From central Greece came 1,000 Phocians and the full force of Opuntian Locris, from Boeotia 700 Thespians and 400 Thebans. Thespiae, like Plataea, was in south Boeotia and tended towards Athens rather than Thebes; the Plataeans this time sent hoplites to man the fleet. In Thebes, on the other hand, views were severely divided, though the ruling oligarchy was eager to come to terms with Persia and to save the city from destruction; the 400 at Thermopylae were not a kind of hostage, as Herodotus suggests, but men from the minority in favour of resistance, as is confirmed by their final massacre at the hands of the Persians. All in all, Leonidas' army numbered between six and seven thousand men,[57] a small force, though probably strong enough to hold the Persians in a narrow pass for some time. That Sparta as well as the congress practically neglected the danger of turning the pass – even after the experience of Tempe – can only be explained by the belief that the narrow and difficult mountain paths over the Oeta were impracticable for any larger military force; even so, Leonidas was advised, either then or later, to make sure that he would not be taken by surprise. We cannot say to what extent Peloponnesian misgivings about any defence north of the Isthmus played a part, but more likely than not they did influence the decision to send only a small force. Herodotus (7, 206) assumes that Sparta and the Peloponnesians intended to strengthen the army later, after the festivals of the Carneia and the Olympics. This view is generally disbelieved by modern scholars, but it seems by no means unlikely, though the question must remain open. Even the small contingent of Spartiates was sent out, despite their religious scruples; the main strength of the Peloponnesians, on the other hand, was reserved for the unfinished fortification and defence – a defence in depth – of the Isthmus line.

We know too little of what was done and thought in all the states concerned. We have mentioned Thebes, and a great patriot and aristocrat such as Pindar confirms her defeatist attitude. Only of Athens do we know more. It seems likely that here preparations were made for evacuating at least the non-combatants. Details are contained in a decree of Themistocles, of which a later copy has recently been found.[58] If it throws some new light on the events, it poses at least as many new problems, and some of the most important facts mentioned are likely to be later invention.[59] An official decree on any evacuation before Artemisium would have revealed a frightening state of affairs to friend and foe alike. Nevertheless, something was done. The short time in which, according to Herodotus, the evacuation actually took place, the days between the arrival of the Greek fleet in Athenian waters, and that of the Persian fleet at Phaleron, cannot have been sufficient unless some preparatory action had already taken place.[60] It was also decided to allow the ostracized men to return home.[61]

The Greeks went into position. Leonidas was early enough to

strengthen his defence line at the 'Middle Gate' of Thermopylae, the best part of the pass for defence. It seems that he was even able to make a night raid into the flat country of the Spercheius valley, in order to get provisions and perhaps also to make a show of strength which might deter the inhabitants from helping the enemy. The fleet assembled at about the same time near Artemisium;[62] according to Herodotus, it amounted to a total of 271 triremes, of which Athens provided more than half, apart from a squadron of 53 which was to protect the rear, i.e. the southern end of the Euripus. Themistocles waived the claim to Athenian leadership, and the Spartan Eurybiades was the admiral in command of the whole fleet.[63]

Xerxes left Therma with his army early in August and marched through Macedon and Thessaly to Malis; for this march he needed twelve to fourteen days. The Persian fleet sailed from Therma on the twelfth day after the army had left; some fast boats will have previously made sure of the nautical conditions. In the evening the fleet anchored along the Magnesian coast, which had few and small beaches.[64] It was here that they were hit by one of the strong northeasterly gales not uncommon in those parts, and suffered heavy losses, especially among the smaller boats and corn ships (Hdt. 7, 188 ff.). The storm lasted for three days; after that the Persian ships reached Aphetae and the protection of the gulf of Pagasae, which included the channel north of Artemisium. The Greeks had, for one day at least, retreated into the Euripus, obviously to be protected from the storm, while watchers were posted on the Euboean heights.[65] When the storm ended, a squadron of 200 ships was sent by the Persian commander round Euboea, in order to attack the Greek fleet from the rear.[66] Once more the gods interfered. The squadron sailed into a violent local thunderstorm with heavy blinding rain. The tradition is that all the 200 ships perished at the 'Hollows' (koila) of Euboea, probably on the south-east coast. At any rate, they were completely put out of action, and the 53 Athenian triremes now joined the main fleet. There were several skirmishes in the waters north of Artemisium; although the Persian ships were more numerous and 'better sailing', clever tactics and nightfall saved the Greeks, after they had done more damage than they suffered.[67]

At Thermopylae, meanwhile, Xerxes had been waiting for four days (Hdt. 7, 210). It was natural that the army after its long march should need a rest before attempting to force the pass. Moreover, Xerxes had to wait for news from his fleet; no less than the Greeks, he needed co-operation between army and navy, which for him was more difficult to maintain. On the two following days the Persians attacked, suffering and inflicting severe losses, but making no progress. Sheer weight of numbers was ineffective in the narrow pass against defenders who at the same time used clever tactics and made a heroic stand. Xerxes found the situation far more frightening than he had expected, especially as he must have found it difficult to feed his army. It was then that he learned from Ephialtes, a man from Trachis, about a path on the Oeta mountain, which would lead into the rear of the Greek position.[68] During the night this man led a force of Xerxes' best soldiers, the 'Immortals', under Hydarnes, along the mountain path.[69] Leonidas had heard about that path and posted the Phocian contingent, 1,000 men strong, to guard it; they would at the same time guard the tracks leading directly to their own country. When in the middle of the night these troops heard the steps of the approaching Persians,[70] they seized their arms; both sides were equally surprised at the sight of the enemy. The Phocians were met by showers of arrows and fled to the peaks, taking up a position to protect themselves as well as the entry into Phocis. Their cowardice sealed Leonidas' fate. The Persians took no further notice of them and continued on their way to the eastern end of the pass. Leonidas heard from deserters and his own scouts what had happened, and he prepared for the last stand. In the early hours Hydarnes and his men reached the 'East Gate', and the Greeks were trapped.

There has been a good deal of controversy about Leonidas' final actions. Quick decisions had to be taken before the door to escape was closed. Most of the allies decided to go home, or were ordered by Leonidas to do so. Herodotus (7, 219 f.) regards the latter version as more likely, because Leonidas must have realized that they were no longer really willing to stay. As the situation was desperate, it was natural to save as many lives as possible for the continuation of the war. Thus all the Peloponnesians left, most of whom had probably never whole-heartedly supported the defence of Thermopylae, as well as the Locrians, whose homeland was the nearest to be invaded. The remainder of the 300 Spartiates with their helots, together with the Thespians and Thebans, probably still well over 1,000 fighting men, were determined not to surrender. Herodotus thinks that Leonidas acted as he did for the sake of Sparta[71] and for his own honour. Modern scholars believe that there were strategic reasons, mainly to give the fleet sufficient time to retreat. It is not impossible that this was one of his considerations, but hardly the decisive one. We need only think of the situation which would have resulted from a complete withdrawal of the Greeks, in order to realize that he simply could not act otherwise. The Persians with their strong cavalry would have at once pursued the retreating Greeks, and they would all have perished in an ignominious flight. Their retreat had to be protected by the determined stand of a rear-guard. Moreover, for a Spartan king, even more than for any other leader, there was no choice. That is the truth contained in the famous epitaph that the Spartans died according to Sparta's laws.[72] The Thebans, for other reasons, had probably no choice either, while the Thespians acted out of pure patriotism. That morning of the third day's fighting saw a wild heroic struggle in which Leonidas and all the rest were killed, not without inflicting new and heavy losses on the Persians. It is more than understandable that legend took hold of the event. It was a Spartan legend which Herodotus heard; it was one-sided and forgot the Thespians, to say nothing of the Thebans.[73] We repeat the two epitaphs mentioned before which Herodotus copied (7, 228):

> 'Here once against three million men
> Four thousand fought from Pelops' land'

and:

> 'Let, stranger, those in Lacedaemon know
> That here we lie, obedient to their laws.'

On the same day as the disaster at Thermopylae the fleets met for their first major battle.[74] The Persians staged a full-scale attack, while the Greeks defended the entry to the Euripus, their line of retreat. Severe fighting, largely from deck to deck, lasted through a hot day from noon to sunset. Both sides suffered, and when they separated, the Persians at least intended to renew the battle the next morning. However, the Greeks learned in the evening the news from Thermopylae, and during the night they retreated down the Euripus. All through the days of fighting Themistocles had backed up the Greek morale which sometimes wavered. Now, resistance was no longer useful, if at all possible; but while Thermopylae had a great effect on the morale of both Greeks and Persians, the naval fighting, though undecisive, had – with the help of the weather – considerably reduced the strength of the Persian fleet. Henceforth it could not risk any diversion, a factor which later prevented any action against the Peloponnese. The Greeks found the time and the means to restore their battered fleet and the flagging spirit of the crews. Some years later Pindar, the Theban, said in a dithyramb to the glory of Athens (fr. 77 Snell. 65 Bowra) that at Artemisium 'the sons of the Athenians laid the bright foundation of freedom'. This may be poetic exaggeration, due to the poet's theme; but it was more than mere flattery. Themistocles had well prepared for Salamis.

The Persians were surprised when they realized that the Greek fleet had gone, but soon they heard about Thermopylae. They occupied the town and territory of Histiaea in Euboea, and then a large part of the crews went on an arranged sight-seeing tour to Thermopylae. After a few days' rest, Xerxes, puzzled that at such a moment the Greeks should be celebrating the Olympic games, moved south to occupy central Greece; but only Phocis, largely because it was the hated enemy of Thessaly, was devastated. Otherwise, there was no resistance, and it was in the Persian interest to welcome any state willing to become an ally. Delphi, with all its riches, was spared. To the Greeks, this was due to a miraculous intervention by two local heroes; but it is quite possible that the Delphic priests, who had been defeatist all the time, had negotiated with Xerxes, and that he, on the other hand, did not wish to rouse the feelings of the Greeks, especially his allies, by ravaging the sacred place, and withdrew his troops.[75]

The Boeotian cities, partly by the mediation of Macedonian agents, surrendered peacefully; only the people of Thespiae and Plataea fled to the Peloponnese, and the towns were burnt down. A large part of Xerxes' army probably marched on without delay and reached Attica where they were joined by the fleet. How long this march took is a matter of dispute, though Xerxes must have tried to be as quick as possible. At any rate, Athens was in the middle of evacuating her people to Troezen, Aegina, and Salamis. Many Athenians had hoped that a Peloponnesian army would meet the enemy in Boeotia, and thus delayed their departure; but Mt Cithae-ron did not provide a safe position for defence, and in any case the Peloponnesians relied only on the Isthmus defence (cf. maps 1 and 3). Whether a partial evacuation of Attica had occurred before or not, now it was a hasty *sauve-qui-peut*, a flight partially financed by the members of the Areopagus.[76] Not every Athenian actually left. There must have been a fair number in distant parts of Attica, quite apart from those who interpreted the oracle's wooden walls verbally and took position behind hastily erected palisades on the Acropolis. These people were not only Herodotus' 'treasurers and poor' (8, 51).[77] It probably took Xerxes some time to seize the citadel, which must have been defended by some kind of garrison.[78]

The Peloponnesian army was concentrating on fortifying the Isthmus line, while the Greek fleet assembled at Salamis. At least some of the Peloponnesian leaders must have realized that the fleet in the open waters off the coast of the Argolis would be unable to protect the rear of the army. At Salamis, while the Persian fleet could not risk bypassing them, it might be possible to stop it. It reached Phaleron bay on the ninth day, it seems, after the fall of Thermopylae; about the same time the advance groups of Xerxes' army must have entered Athens, as Herodotus says, three months after they had crossed into Europe. The palisades and the temples on the Acropolis went up in flames, all the brave defenders were killed, and Xerxes could send a message of victory to Susa; at last the Persians had taken their revenge. Or, at least, so it seemed. To the Greeks at Salamis, the burning of the Acropolis came as a warning signal. We need not believe Herodotus, who as so often speaks of a panic; but the voices clamouring for withdrawal to the Isthmus area must have grown stronger again.

It was by now early September. The date of the battle of Salamis depends on the fact that shortly afterwards, on 2nd October, a solar eclipse occurred.[79] What happened in the interval of roughly four weeks is by no means certain. Herodotus had no longer a firm time-table as for the earlier stages of the campaign. He fills the period (8, 56–75) with several Greek councils of war, a council on the Persian side, a miracle at Eleusis, and the story of Themistocles' message to Xerxes. This message was to induce the Persians to attack; it may indeed be historical, although to carry it out must have been a daring venture. The main reason for the interval, how-ever, was the time needed for the conquest of the Acropolis,[80] though there may have also been delays before the Persian com-mand came to a decision. We can be sure that Themistocles had great difficulty in persuading the Greek fleet not to leave for the Isthmus; he acted not only from Athenian interest but also because he knew that the narrow waters at Salamis provided a good chance, probably the only one, of a naval success. The Persians, on the other hand, eager to finish the war before the winter, must have realized (as Artemisia does in Herodotus' story) that the tactical position round Salamis concealed many dangers. To what extent they tried to improve it remains unknown. It is possible that it was then that Xerxes started building a mole, obviously in order to bridge the narrows and cut off the Greek fleet. Herodotus (8, 97), quite unconvincingly, dates this after the battle.[81] It is certain, on the other hand, that it was in the Greek interest not to leave the favourable position along Salamis, while the Persians, if they wanted a decision as they must have done, had to start the battle.

The Greek fleet was hardly stronger than about 300 ships (cf. Aesch. *Pers.* 337 ff.), with the largest contingents coming from Athens, Aegina, and Megara; they all naturally favoured the Salamis position, and in the end the Peloponnesians had to agree. During the deliberations Themistocles, whom his opponents, be-cause of the destruction of Athens, could call a man without a polis (Hdt. 8, 61), is said to have threatened that if the Greeks left for the Peloponnese, the Athenians would not fight and would sail for Italy. However legendary that story may be, the real trouble for Themi-stocles all the time was the fear of the Peloponnesians that the Isthmus line might be left unprotected.

Our evidence for the battle of Salamis, as is well known, comes from two sources, Herodotus and Aeschylus.[82] The latter was not only contemporary but took part in the fighting himself. The messenger's report in the *Persae*, however, is not a historical document. Aeschylus, probably serving on one of the Athenian ships, had no wide experience of his own, and for many aspects had to rely on what other people told him. Moreover, the messenger is one

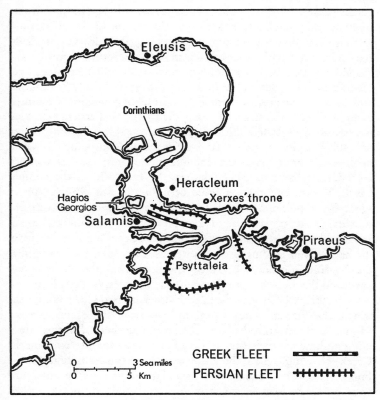

7. Battle of Salamis

of the *dramatis personae*, and his words are shaped by the needs of the dramatic situation rather than the desire to paint a true picture. Even so, the Athenian audience would notice any serious misstatements; within the limits of poetry and drama, Aeschylus' evidence is invaluable. Herodotus, on the other hand, with his usual

mixture of fact and legend, lacks military knowledge. It is understandable that modern descriptions of the battle differ greatly.

The Persians, whether on account of Themistocles' message or
not, went into action. Their ships outnumbered the Greek ones,
though hardly by the traditional number (see above, p. 152).[83] The
details of the battle are highly controversial. It is certain that at one
moment the Greeks, that is to say, the whole island of Salamis,
were encircled, with no outlet left open; they learnt this from
Aristeides, who with other ostracized men had returned from exile,
evaded the Persian blockade, and reached Salamis; his story was
confirmed by a deserter ship from Tenos (Hdt. 8, 78–82). The
Greeks were prepared to meet the Persians, but could not be tempted
to fight outside the straits. During the night the Persians occupied
the island of Psyttaleia (Hdt. 8, 76. Aesch. 447); according to the
prevailing opinion, this island is modern Lipsokontali, which
divides the entry into the Salamis straits into two channels.[84]
Herodotus tells us that Psyttaleia lay 'in the path' of the coming
battle. Xerxes sent there a force of noble Persian youths (Aesch.
441); he must have regarded the action as important. Both our
sources say that it was done to save shipwrecked Persians, and to kill
any Greeks. We may add: to prevent any Greek ship fleeing from
the battle from landing there. In the same night of late September
the Persians, in order to break the deadlock, took the offensive and
advanced through the two channels east and west of Psyttaleia.

At daybreak both sides faced each other in battle lines within the
straits, the Persians lined up along the Attic shore; the Greeks,
having emerged from the bay of Salamis, met them with their right
wing pushing ahead.[85] The decisive fight, however, occurred on the
Greek left wing, where the Athenians and Aeginetans engaged the
Phoenicians. The Persians soon got into difficulties because they
were unable to manoeuvre their ships in the narrow waters; when
some took to flight, there was soon chaos, and the losses became
heavy; ships were rammed not only by the enemy but in the general
panic by friends as well. Still, the battle lasted all through the day.
Xerxes, sitting on a throne at the foot of Mt Aegaleus near the
shore, saw the disaster from which nevertheless a considerable part
of his fleet escaped to Phaleron. The final chapter was fought on
land when Aristeides with a mixed force from the boats landed on

Psyttaleia and destroyed the Persians there.[86] As the Persians at Artemisium, so now the Greeks prepared for a further fight the next day; having suffered heavy losses themselves, they were not aware how complete their victory was. The Persian fleet, without further delay, returned to Asia – we are told, to secure the bridges over the Hellespont; Xerxes hastened back himself by land, escorted by a small force. This march gave rise to many novelistic or horror stories, reflected in both Aeschylus and Herodotus. We do not know why Xerxes chose the long route overland; perhaps he wished to remain among his Persians, or was afraid of the Greek fleet pursuing his own ships. Most of the army was put under Mardonius' command and withdrew to Thessaly for winter quarters. The Greek fleet advanced as far as Andros and levied payments on several of the islands.[87]

Victory was won, and Themistocles was generally honoured for his wisdom and cleverness (Hdt. 8, 124). The battle of Salamis was not the end of the war, but it ended once and for all Persian naval aggression and with it the strategy of combined land and sea operations. It made final victory possible.

During that summer of 480 the Greeks in Sicily fought their own war against an invader.[88] It is unlikely, as we stated before, that the simultaneous attacks in east and west were a chance coincidence. A Phoenician city like Carthage would, at any rate, have some kind of political obligation towards Persia, though without a formal treaty of alliance. Self-interest alone would bring it about. In the west, Greeks and Phoenicians had for a long time been rivals in trade, and with the growing power of Carthage, more than once enemies in war. The Carthaginian trading empire had been consolidated by treaties with Etruscans and Romans. Greek and Phoenician colonies existed side by side, though rarely on a friendly basis.[89] Nowhere was co-existence so precarious as in Sicily, where the Greeks had generally been the aggressors, and Carthage became the protector of the Phoenicians in the western part of the island. Still, the struggle remained on a comparatively small scale, until Gelon of Syracuse and Theron of Acragas succeeded in creating strong and expanding powers, including most of Greek Sicily. When in 483, as mentioned before, Theron expelled the ruler of Himera, Terillus, and the latter went to Carthage asking for help, war became inevitable. For not only was Terillus a friend of the suffete Hamilcar who belonged to the ruling family of the Magonids; Himera was also the Greek outpost on the Sicilian north coast, and its capture meant the isolation of the pro-Carthaginian Anaxilas, tyrant of Rhegium and Messana and son-in-law of Terillus. Moreover, Carthage might wish to hold the town the situation of which in the north equalled that of Selinus in the south, and Selinus had become an ally of Carthage. Three years passed before the Carthaginians acted, and that is an additional reason for assuming that they wanted to synchronize their enterprise with Xerxes' campaign, so that the Greeks were prevented from giving help to one another.

Carthage had by then become a strong military power with an army of mercenaries and dependent allies, and a fleet manned by Carthaginian crews. The expedition which went out under Hamilcar's command comprised 200 warships and a large number of soldiers, which, however, is exaggerated in our sources as is Xerxes' army.[90] Carthage knew that her aim in restoring Terillus implied war against the powerful Gelon, and they prepared for that. It was the present threat that made it quite impossible for Gelon to help the motherland. It may be added that even the western Greeks outside Sicily, from Corcyra to Cumae, did not join the struggle.[91] Neither in Greece nor in Sicily was there a Panhellenic war.

A storm damaged the Carthaginian fleet as it crossed from Africa to Sicily, but most ships arrived safely at Panormus. After three days of rest Hamilcar moved army and fleet eastwards against Himera. Theron hastened to help the city, which was under strong pressure; at the same time he sent for Gelon, who soon arrived with a formidable force. By a ruse he succeeded in putting his cavalry behind the enemy's stockades, where Hamilcar was killed while sacrificing. According to Herodotus, he threw himself into the altar fire and his body was never found. The general battle was on, though it did not all go one way. Eventually, however, the enemy took flight, and the fleet was destroyed; a large number of men, surrounded on a waterless hill, soon surrendered. Of Gelon's fleet we hear nothing. He may have sent it near the straights of Messana to keep an eye on Anaxilas.[92] No fighting occurred, it seems, and no mention is made, for instance by Pindar, of Anaxilas, who later gave his daughter in marriage to Gelon's brother Hieron. Anaxilas must have made his peace in good time with his great rivals and opponents.

Carthage had lost an army and a fleet as well as an important general; but if the war was lost, the peace was not, as long as the west of Sicily remained Phoenician.[93] Carthage at once started negotiations, and Gelon was quite satisfied to conclude peace under moderate conditions. He was by then an old and tired man and died two years later, leaving his realm to Hieron. Still, his leniency towards Carthage as well as Anaxilas was not simply an outcome of old age. It was a wise decision which granted Sicily decades of peace and prosperity, although some danger remained. In Italy it took Hieron's victory at Cumae (474) over the Etruscans to secure the freedom of the Greek cities; it even opened the way for the growth of Rome.[94] Still, Pindar (N. 9, 28) warned the general Chromius, who helped Hieron in founding Aetna, not to endanger the city by a war with Carthage, and that was in the late seventies, after the battle of Cumae; thus, the threat still remained.

In the motherland the Greeks, by many offerings and dedications, thanked the gods for the miraculous turn the war had taken. Autumn saw the Peloponnese free from any menace, but Athens was still in danger. Mardonius' army, however, was no longer supported by a fleet and depended for its supplies mainly on Thessaly, and possibly on the long route through Thrace and Macedon. The fleet had gone to Samos and remained inactive; in fact, it soon began to disintegrate. The initiative on sea was now with the Greeks, and Mardonius had to fear a combined attack.[95] He took a surprising step; he tried to win Athens over to the Persian side. Alexander of Macedon, for some time past a guest-friend of the Athenians, was to persuade the city, that same city which had been burnt and sacked. It seemed the only chance for Mardonius to get hold of a strong fleet which might enable him to force the Isthmus. His proposals were quite generous, naturally enough. If the Athenians joined the Persians – as so many Greeks had done – they would not only save Attica from new destruction but could also gain any land they wished; their temples would be restored and they would be free in their domestic affairs, which meant that the Peisistratids would not return. The people had just come back to their land and city. Now, if they refused the offer they would face again occupation and devastation. They were determined to refuse; the Spartans, however, were not so sure about it. They might easily have had some doubts on account of the permanent 'isolationism' of the Peloponnese. When Spartan envoys turned up at Athens, the Athenians had not yet given a reply to Alexander; they now made sure that a Greek army would arrive as early as possible to meet the enemy in Boeotia; then they sent Alexander home. Herodotus (8, 140 ff.) tells us of high-sounding speeches made by all the parties; they (or something like them) may easily have been spoken, but behind them and a genuine patriotism were sound politics and sound strategy.[96]

The Greek fleet which in spring 479 assembled at Aegina and later moved as far as Delos numbered only 110 ships, far too small a force to use in an offensive move against Ionia. We are told that such a move had been Themistocles' original suggestion. But too many men were needed for the army. Now the whole fleet was under the command of the Spartan king Leotychidas, and the Athenian contingent under Xanthippus; the Athenian army was commanded by Aristeides. Whether Themistocles was still one of the ten strategi, we do not know; but his passive role may have been a result of the general change in strategy, which had become necessary on account of the enemy's actions. Land warfare was now the main issue, and that was true for Athens even more decisively than for Sparta, which could send out a king with the navy, as the Isthmus was no longer threatened. Anyway, there was again some friction between the two states. Whether it was the right thing to do, not to send the fleet to the Malian gulf in order to make Mardonius' position untenable, is another question.

The Persians meanwhile had to deal with a revolt in the Chalcidice, which could become dangerous if it spread. Artabazus, who had escorted Xerxes as far as the Hellespont, besieged Potidaea, though he could not take it; but by massacring the population of Olynthus, he prevented any further rising in Mardonius' rear. The latter had some trouble with other Greeks during the winter and, perhaps for the sake of his allies, consulted several Greek oracles (Hdt. 8, 133 ff.). Persian gold also played a part in attempts at gaining more allies. At that time Mardonius was probably still hoping for a peaceful settlement north of the Isthmus. The two fleets remained inactive, and 'fear reigned over the area between them'.

At last, tired of waiting, Mardonius neglected the Theban advice to continue winning supporters while remaining in Boeotia, and marched into Attica; the Athenians had again to evacuate their country. That was at the end of June. Once more Mardonius tried to persuade the Athenians to change sides. They refused, but the Spartan army had not yet left Sparta. They were celebrating the Hyacinthia, and we should not look upon their religious scruples as a mere pretext. While an Athenian embassy was urging them to march out, an alleged number of 5,000 Spartiates suddenly left overnight, followed by 5,000 perioeci the next day; a vast number of helots accompanied the army, and at least some of them served as light-armed soldiers. The army was led by Pausanias, Leonidas' nephew and regent for his infant son. The Peloponnesians joined in full strength, and hostile Argos could do nothing but inform Mardonius of the departure of the army.

The Persians, after further destruction and devastation, left Attica and withdrew to Boeotia,[97] where Mardonius could hope to make full use of his cavalry, and had the backing of Thebes; in her territory he built a fortified camp and held the line of the river Asopus, with his main forces probably on its north bank. He faced, but did not defend, the passes over the Cithaeron, trying to get the Greeks into the open plain. The Greeks advanced on the main road from Eleusis, where the Athenians under Aristeides joined them, via Eleutherae to Erythrae, spreading out along the northern slopes of the mountain (see map 3). The battle which followed lasting for about three weeks was really, within a small space, a complicated campaign with constant fluctuations between success and failure. Herodotus was aware of the character of the fighting and did his best to present a full and clear picture. He knew the topography and had a great deal of second-hand information. Even so, much remains obscure.

From a later moment in the battle (Hdt. 9, 28, 2) we know the contingents of the Greek army in the order of their positions, with their numbers of hoplites, whether actual or – more likely – merely nominal. The total amounts to more than 35,000, apart from the very large number of light-armed troops – the biggest army so far in Greek history, even if the actual numbers were smaller. As to Mardonius' army, no exact estimate can be made, but with a large number of allied Greek forces it must have been considerably larger than the Greek army.[98] Its great strength was the cavalry, both Greek and Asiatic, while the infantry was weaker than their opponents', both in numbers and in armour. The Greeks on the Persian side, henceforth called the 'medizing', acted from short-sighted self-interest rather than as traitors. We have stressed before, and shall come back to it, that there could be in this war no high treason as long as there was no full Greek unity.

We can easily distinguish several phases in the fighting. The first was when the whole Persian cavalry made frontal attacks on the Greeks who refused to come down from their elevated positions (Hdt. 9, 20 ff.). The leader of the Persian cavalry was killed, and after some serious fighting the attack finally failed. Then Pausanias decided, mainly because of the need for a better water supply, to move slightly to the north-west, to a low ridge south of the Asopus and nearer to some springs and the fields of Plataea, which was to give its name to the battle. The Greeks now covered another pass through Mt Cithaeron, the road called after Dryoscephalae, the 'Oaks' Heads'; it was to serve as a supply route. The move by the Greeks started the second phase (Hdt. 9, 24 ff.); for more than a week there was hardly any real fighting. Meanwhile more Greeks were coming up from the rear, but both sides were reluctant to take the offensive. The Persian cavalry was again active and destroyed a column of men and beasts which were bringing supplies over the mountain (Hdt. 9, 39). One night, however, if the story is true, a horseman approached the Athenian line and told the commanders that a general attack was planned for the next day. This was Alexander of Macedon, who may have tried to atone for his earlier ambiguous attitude; it may just as well be a later invention to clear his reputation.[99]

The Greeks even now suffered from lack of food and water supplies, and after a raid by the Persian cavalry on the springs near the Spartan position, the situation became desperate; Pausanias decided on a new move which would bring the Greek line to the 'island' (nēsos), an area between small streams just north-east of

Plataea. With that withdrawal during the night and its various difficulties begins the third phase of the battle (Hdt. 9, 51 ff.). As that 'island' was too small for the whole Greek army, some troops were to be posted on the Cithaeron slopes to secure the supply route. Actually the centre of the Greek front is said to have used the withdrawal as a chance of evading further cavalry attacks, and to have gone back as far as Plataea; even so, there was no panic, as Herodotus characteristically thinks, but clearly a planned movement. The Spartans on the right wing and the Athenians on the left still held their former positions and began to withdraw only at daybreak, while they were partly sheltered from view by the hills.[100] At last the final phase began (Hdt. 9, 58 ff.), when Mardonius became afraid that the Greeks might completely evade a pitched battle. He must have known that no support could be expected from the fleet, and he will have had his own troubles with his mixed army of Asiatics and Greeks, and also difficulties in getting supplies.

He launched the attack. Since the Athenians were prevented from joining forces with the Spartans, there were two separate areas of fighting. The Athenians were up against the Thessalian and Boeotian cavalry as well as the Theban hoplites, while the Lacedaemonians and the men from Tegea fought the Persian infantry. In both places the Greeks had a hard stand. Then the Greek centre advanced from their rearward position, the Corinthians and other Peloponnesians moving towards the Spartans, and others, especially the Megarians, saving the Athenians who were in grave danger. Losses were heavy in general, but the hardest hand-to-hand fighting took place between the Persian *élite* troops and the Spartans and Tegeans. Here Mardonius was killed and the whole battle decided. The Persian army fled, protected by the cavalry. Artabazus with the centre had no part in the final struggle and retreated to Phocis and farther. He had warned Mardonius all the time; now he reached the Bosporus and Asia – avoiding the Hellespont, where he might encounter the Greek fleet – and was well received by the king. His withdrawal, on the other hand, sealed the fate of the rest of Mardonius' army. The Persians fled to the stockade, where the Athenians soon broke through; almost all the enemies were slain. The minute figures of the Greek dead, as given by Herodotus (9, 70), are, to say the least, incomplete and untrustworthy.

Victory was due to intelligent leadership as well as great courage and discipline by almost everybody on the Greek side. Most of the Greeks regarded the final victory as a Spartan achievement, though each of the other states claimed at least second-place honours. Only the men from Mantinea and Elis came too late to take part in the battle; they later blamed their generals for that, but it may have been deliberate opposition to Sparta's leadership; when victory was won, they rejoined the rest.[101] The story (Plut. *Arist.* 21) of a common Greek decision to create a permanent force for the continuation of the war is hardly authentic. The Greeks had not yet found a way of making 'national' policy.

For ten days after the fighting a vast amount of booty was collected, the dead were buried, and the desecrated shrines round Plataea purified. Pausanias rightly refused to pursue Artabazus, but turned against Thebes, the most powerful Greek ally of the Persians. The town, whither all the Boeotians had fled, was put to siege, but no progress was made. Eventually the leaders responsible for Theban policy offered themselves in surrender, but were refused trial and executed at the Isthmus. No other Greek states were punished, and the overwhelming feeling was that of grateful joy for the liberation of the motherland. Rich offerings were given to many temples.[102] The most famous dedication was the golden tripod at Delphi, which stood on top of a column of three intertwined bronze serpents; the trunk now stands in the hippodrome at Istanbul. The story is that Pausanias put an arrogant, self-laudatory epigram on it, which was later replaced by the Spartans; they put instead on the coils of the serpents the names, still legible today, of those Greek states that had taken part in the battles of Salamis and Plataea, under the simple heading: 'These have fought the war.'[103]

The Greek fleet was at Delos. We are told that even before the battle of Plataea, envoys from Chios and Samos had come and asked Leotychidas to advance farther and to liberate Ionia. He agreed and crossed the sea. The Samians, so far ruled by a pro-Persian tyrant, joined the Greek fleet when it arrived at the island. The Persian fleet was no longer fighting fit nor were its leaders sure of Ionian loyalty. They decided to beach their ships on the promontory of Mycale, north of Miletus, disarmed their Ionian troops, and entrenched their own forces near the ships. The ensuing battle was supposed to have been fought on the evening of the day of the final battle of Plataea, and we learn that a rumour of the defeat of Mardonius ran through the Greek fleet before its landing. Herodotus (9, 100 ff.) regards this as an intervention by the gods; it is much more likely that Mycale was fought some time after Plataea. The Greeks, led by the Athenians, who were best in overcoming fortifications, broke into the Persian entrenchment and after hard fighting put the enemies to flight. The victors were joined by all the Ionians in the Persian army. So it came about, says Herodotus (9, 104), that 'Ionia for the second time revolted against the Persians'.

The Persian ships were plundered and burnt, and the Greeks, reassembled at Samos, sailed to the Hellespont.[104] The bridges had gone, whereupon the Peloponnesians sailed home. The danger of a new invasion seemed remote, but Xanthippus with his Athenians and those Ionians who had revolted against Persia (Thuc. 1, 89, 2) were determined to liberate 'the Hellespont and the islands' (Hdt. 9, 101). That meant capturing the stronghold of Sestus, which once, under Miltiades, had been Athenian and now was defended by Persian troops. The town surrendered after a long siege, and the Persians were killed, one way or another. 'After that, they returned to Greece, taking with them their spoils and among them the cables of the bridges, to offer them in their sanctuaries. And this year nothing more happened' (Hdt. 9, 121).

The war of defence was over with the year 479, and ever since Thucydides (1, 89) this has been regarded as the end of the Persian wars. But the next year was to show that the war with Persia was not finished. The capture of Sestus, and even earlier the battle of Mycale, not only ended an epoch but started a new one. These events can be understood as completing the defence of the motherland, but they implied more. In fact, the Greeks went over to the offensive. This was to bring other great changes with it, of which we shall speak later. For the moment we end, where Herodotus ends.

But do we? The sentences quoted end the last but one chapter of Herodotus' work. What follows (ch. 122) is a story about the great Cyrus, who warned his Persians not to leave their hard and poor country for a better land which would make them soft and slaves to other people. Apart from leading back to the initial parts of his book, concerned with Cyrus, and contrasting him with the sensuous and cruel Xerxes of whom Herodotus had just told a few shocking stories (9, 108–13), at the same time contradicting the often repeated view of the softness and luxuriousness of the Persians, the chapter also contains a warning. In ending his work, he was thinking of what happened during the next fifty years up to his own time. That was a new period on which he would not and could not write; but he had it in mind.[105]

5 · The War Generation

Herodotus, who wrote the history of the Persian wars, was at that time a small child in far-away Halicarnassus. Later he travelled far and wide, came to Greece, and settled first at Athens and afterwards in Pericles' Panhellenic colony Thurii in Italy. He still knew personally some of those who had been in the Great War, and he must have done a good deal of inquiring. While he saw the events in the light of both divine order and human history, he naturally wrote as a man of the middle of the century, and his historical picture is coloured by the thoughts and feelings of his own time. Even so, he reports impartially on the heroic deeds and savage cruelties which occurred on either side. It is even more difficult for us than for Herodotus to get under the skin of that generation which perhaps more than any other decided in the long run the course of European history. Still, in some ways the greater distance makes things easier as well, and though we shall have to struggle all the way with the scarcity and vagueness of our sources, we shall try to trace some essential trends and aspects of the war generation.[106]

A few words must be said on the economic effects of the war years. It goes without saying that the occupation of north and central Greece and the double evacuation of Attica caused serious difficulties in feeding the population.[107] The Peloponnese was more or less self-sufficient even during the war, but from where did, for example, the refugees on Aegina and Salamis get sufficient food, to say nothing of the fleet and army? There can be little doubt that overseas trade continued even in wartime, though it must have been largely confined to the routes between Greece and the west.[108] When the war was won, the greatest immediate economic advantage was the opening of the trade routes to the Black Sea by the captures of Sestus and shortly afterwards Byzantium. With Persia and the Phoenicians gone, Miletus severely crippled, and Megara of little influence, the field was open, and Athens was soon able to exclude potential rivals. The war trade to and from the west was probably mainly in the hands of Corinth, but Athenian silver and pottery were again available for export, while wine and especially oil must have been scarce for years. In the whole question of Greek trade it is essential to realize that it was a matter of individual enterprise, frequently financially supported by private loans, when the considerable risk of any seafaring venture was shared by the lender and the trader. No trade policy by the state ever existed.

In considering the nature of the war generation we may first think of a few works of art. Vase-painting reached its highest level in the red-figured style of c. 500–480. Mythological scenes still prevailed, but the life of aristocratic youth and Dionysiac revelries played a big part. Traditional features survived; for example, faces were always still shown in profile, and there was still no perspective, but the vividness of the scenes and their exquisite composition show the great progress made. There is, however, very little to show a special spirit of the war generation.[109] The serpent column, on the other hand, reminds us of the fact that in the Peloponnese recently the art of bronze sculpture had reached a very high standard. Argos, Sicyon, and Aegina were the leading cities, and bronze technique tended to influence marble sculpture as well. An outstanding example are the groups in the pediments of the Aphaea temple at Aegina. Scenes of the Trojan war are here brought to life as hardly anywhere else, both in the earlier and stiffer west pediment and in the later east pediment with its freer style. If the former belongs to the time from 500 to 490, the latter is certainly contemporary with the Great Persian War, and its lively realism had its models in the men and the spirit of the Persian wars. To the same kind of sculpture belongs after the war the groups of the tyrannicides by Critias and Nesiotes at Athens, and the impressive statue of a chariot driver at Delphi. If we compare these virile and severe statues, for instance, with the masterpiece of Ionian art, the Ludovisi throne, or, on the other hand, with the wonderful metopes of the Heraeum at Selinus or those of the temple of Zeus at Olympia (all of which are a decade or so later), we can feel something of the breadth and the depth of the art of that one generation, but we may also realize how difficult, if not impossible, it is to establish close connexions between any special features and the war generation as a whole. Greek civilization reached new aspects in and through the war, but it had flourished before, even in Asia Minor under Persian rule, and it was to go on flourishing afterwards. There was no sudden break.

This statement is strongly confirmed by the literature of the period. Aeschylus fought both at Marathon and at Salamis; in 484 he gained his first victory on the stage. He represents the war generation more fully than anybody else, even better than his contemporaries Themistocles, who was older, and Cimon, who was younger. Moreover, he is almost the only man, and certainly the only Athenian, of his generation who still speaks to us as he spoke to his fellow citizens. The Athenian theatre was very close to the people, their lives and thoughts. 'The theatre was the polis.'[110] At whatever heights and depths of thought and imagination tragedy aimed, it remained in intimate contact with its audience of citizens. Aeschylus was too great a man to be typical, but just because he was great and a tragic poet he can tell us more about his time and place than about himself. Of his early years we know nothing; he was in his fifties when his tragedy of the war, the *Persians*, was performed in 472 B.C., with the young Pericles as choregus. It is the earliest of the extant plays,[111] and that means that nothing is known of Aeschylus' work before and between the wars.[112] The *Persians* followed Phrynichus' *Phoenician Women*, which was probably performed a few years earlier and of which we know next to nothing. In both plays the tragedian shows the effects of the late war on the enemy, though naturally as a fervent testimony to the glory of Greece and especially of Athens. By setting the scene in Persia he substitutes for the lacking distance in time the distance of space and foreign surroundings. The audience will have had certain general ideas about Persia and the king's court, but Aeschylus added to the usual concepts, and made at the same time such deviations from reality as either dramatic necessity or the deliberately Greek interpretation demanded. Taken as a whole, we can understand the *Persians* (and probably the *Phoenician Women* as well) as a kind of epilogue to the war, and it may be significant and inevitable that in general the picture in our minds will be largely formed by witnesses after the event.[113] We shall see that we have a few utterances from the war years, and at any rate, with the experience of our own recent past, we might be able to distinguish the war generation from the post-war generation.

In describing the war generation we must, of course, go beyond the one play by Aeschylus, about which we shall say more later. It should also not be forgotten that tragedy was a comparatively new art form which was to dominate the literary scene for the seven or eight decades after the war. Lyric poetry, on the other hand, in general originated and flourished in the past; the branch of literature most closely bound to the pre-war and the war years is choral lyric. Again we have to face the fact that much of the work is lost. Enough, however, is extant to teach us something about the period with which we are concerned. I am not writing a history of literature, and I feel justified in selecting those poets and poems which are of particular significance in our context. We turn to Simonides and Pindar, the former born about 555 on Keos, the small Cycladic island nearest to Attica, the latter about 520 into an aristocratic family in Thebes in Boeotia. Both stayed for a time in Athens, Pindar as an apprentice of his art, Simonides on several occasions during his life. They both lived to a very old age; Simonides died about 468 and Pindar about 438. These dates make clear at once that the two poets belonged to different generations. Only Pindar was really of the war generation, but Simonides was still very active during the war, although an old man. He and his nephew Bacchylides were on various occasions Pindar's rivals, and (what is more) Simonides was most definitely regarded, both in ancient and modern judgement, as the outstanding poet of the war. Under his name went, for instance, a bitter and sarcastic epitaph for Timocreon, Themistocles' enemy (99 D). Above all, however, Simonides was the poet who wrote poems on the Greek deeds in battle, and epitaphs for those killed in the war. In that respect he was *the* poet, and many epigrams on the war dead went under his name, though they were of later origin. However, he wrote a hymn on Artemisium, of which only a few words survive (1. 2 D. 28 P); he probably wrote the poem

when a sanctuary of Boreas, who had helped the Greek fleet, was inaugurated there (Hdt. 7, 189).[114] Simonides' true voice emerges in
the dirge turned *enkomion* (5 D. 26 P) for those who died at Thermopylae, whose fate and fame are glorious and lasting. 'An altar is
their grave, instead of laments there is memory, compassion becomes praise.' 'This burial place of brave men has as its guardian
the fair fame (*eudoxia*) of Hellas.' These are words of a proud
patriotism which is also expressed in numerous famous epitaphs.
We shall have more to say about this new patriotism and the new
consciousness of the Greeks of their own existence as Greeks.
'Hellas' is any Greek land, though especially the motherland. We
have an indication of a new meaning of the word 'barbarian' in lines,
probably from an elegy (65 D), in which Simonides praises Democritus of Naxos as one of the three men largely responsible for the
victory of Salamis, who excelled in personal bravery and 'saved
Doris (= the Peloponnese) from being conquered by barbaric
hand'.

It is well known that it took time before the names Hellenes and
barbarians came to mean what they did later.[115] Homer's Trojans
speak Greek and do not differ from the Greeks; they even worship
the same gods. If in the *Iliad* (2, 867) the Carians are called *barbaro-
phonoi*, it indicates that the onomatopoetic word *barbaros* means
incomprehensible language as, in fact, it did in various early languages, both Aryan and Semitic.[116] If the Carians are picked out, it
is probably because for a long time they were to the Greeks the best
known non-Greek people. It was only natural that a man who could
express himself merely in such sounds (or perhaps in such bad
Greek) was regarded as uneducated, a view often confirmed by the
kind of foreign people the Greeks came to know, for instance, most
of their slaves. So far, however, the barbarians were not regarded
as savages or something similar but simply as non-Greeks. The great
nations and civilizations of the Near East, Egypt, Babylon, Persia,
Lydia were barbarians in this sense only, and even in Aeschylus'
Persians and in Herodotus the word still kept its general meaning,
free from any deprecation. The Greek superiority complex was to
come, but it was not a direct result of the Persian wars, though it
became usual to call the Persians by the singular 'the barbarian', and
that could only mean 'the enemy'.

The whole development is the less surprising as the Greeks themselves had for a long time no common name for themselves. They actually found it later than the common name for the non-Greeks. Homer calls the Greeks indiscriminately Danaans, Argives, and Achaeans, thus confirming that there was not one common name. Hellenes and Hellas were local Thessalian names, and 'Panhellenes', which occurs in Homer (Il. 2, 530), Hesiod (*Erga* 528), and Archilochus (54 D), is nothing but an extended tribal name. The identification of Hellenes and Greek was probably a creation of the sixth century. Maybe the Hellenic games had something to do with it, as the word must have been in general use there when the judges were called *hellenodikai*.

Pindar, 'prince of poets and poet of princes', whom alone we can follow almost step by step through the first decades of the century, may teach us more about these matters.[117] In the tradition of his forerunners, but with particular emphasis, he valued his art as a divine gift and a source of wisdom. He sings for those who have excelled in life, not only for the athletic victors, though they certainly played an outstanding part, and his voice was heard in all parts of the Greek world. In a sense, Pindar was a Panhellenic poet, just as Simonides and Bacchylides were; for him, his aristocratic connexions were of special significance. Yet he was not a Greek patriot. In the earliest of his odes (P. 10 of 498 B.C.) he speaks of a Thessalian family that had won victories at Olympia and Delphi, as 'having gained not a small share of the joys in Hellas' (19). In 490 – the year of Marathon! – he celebrates a flute player from Acragas because 'he has defeated Hellas at his art' (P. 12, 6).[118] In the short song for the Alcmaeonid Megacles (P. 7, 8; 486 B.C.), who had just been ostracized, Pindar praises his family as the most illustrious in Hellas; in support of his praise, he naturally cannot mention Marathon,[119] when the Alcmaeonids played a dubious part, but he speaks of their rebuilding of the Delphic temple. Later he was to sing the praise of Athens, but in a dance song of 480, when Xerxes was about to invade Greece, Pindar advised Thebes (fr. 109 Snell. 99b Bowra) to keep domestic peace; that was at a moment when the internal strife meant pro- and anti-war policies opposing each other. Pindar took no side, and that implied no share in the war either. Many Greeks at the time must have felt like that,

especially among the aristocrats. The poet, for instance, who wrote
some part of the *Theognidea*, says (757), 'May the gods give us the
right kind of speech and mind, but let us drink and make music,
and not fear the war with the Persians.' Was neutrality a possible
way out? Certainly not for a city on the very route which the Persian
army was bound to take. Anyway, Pindar pleaded in vain, in spite
of his warning of discord, 'giver of poverty, hostile nurse of the
young men'. Still in the same year, in the spring of 480, in *I.* 6 he does
not even mention the threatening danger and says (23) that 'no
polis is so barbaric or foreign in speech' as not to know about
Peleus or Ajax, whose deeds are known as far as the Aethiopians
and the Hyperboreans. These, and not the Persians, are the 'barbarians', living at the ends of the earth, and they are described just
as Homer's Carians. Pindar was no politician, and his neutralism, a
form of pacifism, was practically defeatism or at least blindness. He
was personally not involved, however much he suffered for his
beloved Thebes, and it is unlikely that he was at Thebes during the
war. The city was in a very dangerous position, resistance would
mean destruction, and there was no outlet overseas as at Athens. A
Persian victory, on the other hand, seemed more than likely, and the
attitude of Pindar's most revered god, the Delphic Apollo, made it
clear that discretion was the better part of valour. In the end,
however (in the words of William Blake), 'prudence is a rich, ugly,
old maid courted by incapacity', and in the months between Salamis
and Plataea, Pindar must have become very sad and almost desperate. In 478 the tune has changed.[120] He had to face reality, though
he did so without giving up any of his deeper convictions or in fact
his traditional conventions. When Aegina, who was so dear to him,
has excelled at Salamis, he can praise her sailors, but he suppresses
any exultation (*I.* 5, 48). In *I.* 8 he is still 'sad in his heart' (5), but
grateful that he can sing again, 'freed from overwhelming evils',
that 'a god has turned aside the stone of Tantalus over our heads, an
unbearable burden for Hellas' (10). This burden was the threat by
the Greeks to destroy Thebes, unbearable for Thebes as well as for
the others, in fact, for 'Hellas'. It is significant that in the myth of
this song Zeus and Poseidon, both eager to win Thetis, follow
'well-counselling Themis' (who does not belong to the original
myth) to let Peleus marry her (32). It was wise to abstain from a

disastrous decision, after the threat to Thebes had paralysed Pindar's poetic power (12). The freedom (16) that enables him to gain new hope is not that from Persian rule (though that may be meant too) but the freedom from fear. Those Greeks who had gone over to the Persians, however strongly under pressure, had now to suffer the recriminations from others as well as from their own conscience. For by now, after victory, Hellas was the country of freedom, and in the following years Pindar, though less expressly than Simonides, celebrated the deeds of 480 and 479, when 'the fate of Hellas had been on razor's edge' (Simonides 95 D). The passage which shows perhaps most clearly the new meaning of Hellenes and barbarians is Simonides' epigram on Gelon and his brothers (106 D) who, 'having defeated the barbarian hordes, fighting together with the Hellenes, had helped them towards liberty'.[121]

Hellenes defeated the barbarians, but not all Hellenes were involved. It is remarkable that all of them, also those who did not fight or even fought on the other side, the *medizontes*, were henceforth Hellenes. There could be no doubt that Greeks everywhere belonged to the same people, were 'Hellenes'. It was a concept which was to a large extent geographical, but at the same time it had a good many undertones of cultural and religious unity. Tribes still remained tribes, and cities remained cities, that is to say, independent states; but the forces of unity gradually gained more strength. Even after war and victory, however, it would have been a mistake to speak of a Greek nation. Nationalism, even in opposition to Persia, was practically non-existent. The war had not been a national war, and was not so even in its after-effects. If it slowly led to a greater awareness of 'Europe' as contrasted with 'Asia', the world of the small city-state contrasted with imperial power and glory, freedom of the citizen with despotism, neither the idea nor any reality of 'Europe' had yet come to stay, but perhaps it can be said that their first foundations were laid.

Anyway, a great historical decision had taken place, and if Simonides and Pindar more or less realized this fact, it must have been even clearer to others. The two poets were both steeped in sixth-century views; for them the 'people' did hardly exist. Earning their living, as they largely did, by serving the religious and athletic spirit of an aristocratic upper class and, more recently, also the upstart splendour of the Sicilian and other tyrants,[122] they could only vaguely feel and express what men like Themistocles and Aristeides and many of their generation in Athens, Sparta, Aegina, and other places must have felt very strongly, that victory was due to the free citizens as a whole. It is a widespread view that the experience of the war strengthened, or even created the concept of a Greek nation. There had been much before to make the Greeks realize that they were one people. The same gods, the same language, the same aristocratic ethical and social standards, the uniting influence of Delphi, the Panhellenic festivals which gave evidence that Greeks everywhere excelled in athletics and in poetry, both more than tinged by the predominant passion of paederasty, all that counted, and yet there was no idea of political unity. Without that, I feel, it is misleading to speak of a nation. This remains true even during and after the experience of the Persian wars – in fact, if anything, political disruption and local patriotism became stronger. The *poleis*, and not a Greek nation, had defeated the Persians. No greater justification of the polis as the community of free citizens was indeed possible than their victories by sea and land, and this fact, with increasing strength, penetrated the Greek mind. The aristocratic Pindar, on the other hand, who could call his Muse a 'worker' (*ergatis*) and 'gain-loving' (*I.* 2, 6), who was no politician, and only for personal reasons declared (*P.* 11, 52) that he loved the middle line and neither tyranny nor democracy, was quite unable to see the deeper meaning of the Greek victory. We can be sure that most of his fellow aristocrats and even others were in the same position.

The simple will for self-preservation and the nebulous ideas about the war crystallized into the fundamental conflict between freedom and slavery or despotism, and that conflict was identified with the contrast between Greeks and barbarians. The world was still practically confined to the Greek world. To Pindar, we have seen, the Hyperboreans remained fairy-tale people almost beyond the frontiers of the world (*P.* 10, 30. *I.* 6, 22. *O.* 3, 16), the Scythians were a strange people of whom he had heard some curious stories (fr. 105. 203 Snell. 94. 192 Bowra), but the known world ended at the Pillars of Heracles; to go beyond, that is, to venture into the Atlantic, became a symbol for going beyond the limits set for man (*O.* 3,

44. *I.* 3–4, 30. *N.* 3, 22. 4, 69). Pindar really does not think in space, nor, as to that, in time. Aeschylus, on the other hand, is greatly interested in world-wide distances, in wanderings and travels; equally, in the framework of his trilogies, time plays a major part. The Mediterranean, with Greek cities and their enemies in Asia and Africa, was of course well known, and Pindar could call Africa 'the third root of firm land' (*P.* 9, 7), the third continent. Geographical knowledge was no longer the privilege of a few merchant-adventurers or of Ionian learning. The beginnings of medical science showed similar trends. Asclepius was for Pindar not a god (*P.* 3, 6. *N.* 3, 54) but the son of Apollo, who knew all about fighting disease, from magic formulas and soothing potions to bandages of healing herbs and even operations (*P.* 3, 50).

These matters, however important in the long run, are peripheral to the theme of this chapter. But the concept of the world was the framework for the contrast between Greeks and barbarians, and that was increasingly seen as a contrast not only of language and religion but of political and cultural standards generally. The contrast, however, was by no means absolute. Interest in geographical and ethnological knowledge increased among the Greeks, as is clear from Aeschylus no less than from Herodotus. While barbarians were described in appearance, customs, countries of origin, and so on,[123] it became, on the other hand, a common feature to put foreign concepts into Greek dress and vice versa; best known is the acceptance of barbarian gods under the names of Greek deities, the *interpretatio Graeca*. Particularly significant is the famous dream of Atossa in Aeschylus' *Persians* (181 ff.), as in fact is the whole play.[124] Atossa, the old queen, saw two beautiful women, one in Persian, the other in 'Doric', that is to say, the normal Greek dress, 'sisters of the same descent' – the ancestors of Kipling's 'twains'. One lived in Hellas, the other in barbarian land. As they began to quarrel, Xerxes (in order to placate them!) yoked them both to his chariot. While the one prided herself in obeying his reins, the other revolted, tore the yoke asunder, and dashed the whole vehicle to pieces. Xerxes fell to the ground, and there stood Darius, his father; in view of him, Xerxes broke down and rent his robe. The dream is really an oracle, and it is followed by a bad omen when Atossa makes a sacrifice. All this is typically Greek. The Persians, in their own speeches, are again and again called barbarians, without the slightest thought of degradation,[125] and the dream confirms that the poet regarded Greeks and Persians as equal in status. But Asia's effort against Hellas has been futile (268 ff.). It was Xerxes' attempt to put Greece under his yoke which caused the conflict and his own disaster. That is the theme dominating the whole play, however unhistorical it may be. Atossa is a dignified motherly person, Darius a hero full of wisdom, the chorus of elders are loyal and human servants. It is very remarkable how Aeschylus was able to combine such a noble attitude towards the enemy with the pride of the victor and the free citizen; it is likely that his audience appreciated the former as much as, naturally, the latter. Even the belief in a malignant daemon who was ultimately responsible for the Persian disaster is probably more Greek than Persian. At any rate, the poet felt strongly that it was the gods who had saved Greece – even the city of Athens (346), which had in fact been sacked and destroyed. In 472, the year the *Persians* were performed, Athens was again safe and whole, but if the gods had saved her, it was through her citizens. The sacking of Athens is being played down; so are other things.[126] The story of the battle of Salamis is the central theme of the play, and the only one in which Aeschylus is really interested. Plataea and Sparta's part in it are foreshadowed (806 ff.); dramatically they are irrelevant. What mattered was the idea that Xerxes had led Persia into ruin, as Atossa tells Darius (714), 'The realm of the Persians is utterly destroyed.' 'Round Athens, the whole army has perished' (716); the same has been said before by the messenger (255).[127] Nobody in 472 could think of Persia as completely ruined – why does Aeschylus time and again stress the enormity of the disaster? To some extent it is merely a dramatic device in order to enhance the greatness of the Athenian achievement. Xerxes, on the other hand, the real culprit, changes in the last scene from the wretch in torn clothes into the king whose rule is reasserted. Darius' wisdom, his whole person and rule, are absurdly idealized, in order to make him the mouthpiece of the poet's own ethical thoughts, and at the same time, to emphasize his advice never again to invade Greece (790 ff.). That clearly was something the audience liked to hear. Above all, however, by simplifying and to some extent falsifying the historical facts, Aeschylus raised the story of the recent past to the realm of myth, where alone the true tragic measure could be taken of gods and men and events. He followed Phrynichus' example, and we must not forget that for the Greeks no sharp demarcation line existed between myth and history. Myth was their early history. Even so, however, those who like Aeschylus had fought in the last war would regard this recent experience with less detachment than, for instance, the Trojan war; but they would regard the Persian war less in its historical aspect than as a proof of divine help, that is to say, in mythical terms.

In spite of all the intrusions of Greek concepts into the Persian world of the play, the master–slave relationship between king and subjects is frequently stressed, and it is opposed to the Greek concept of liberty. It is said of the Athenians (242), 'As no man's slaves or subjects are they spoken of.' It is as a victory of free men, and not the expression of national pride, that the events of the war give the people of the seventies their self-confidence. The difference in their ways of life and their fundamental political and social ideas, even more than the experience of the war itself, has raised the barrier between Greece and Persia, between Europe and Asia.

Victory would be complete if the east accepted the freedom of the west. That is the conclusion which the chorus reaches in the most ahistorical passage of the play (584 ff.):

> No longer will the people throughout Asia be ruled by the Persians, no longer will they pay tribute at their masters' commands nor prostrate themselves before their rulers. For regal power has perished. No longer is the tongue of men under guard; the people have been loosed to speak freely, since the yoke of power was loosed.

That was pronounced from the stage when for years Xerxes had continued to be the absolute ruler of the Persian empire. The last sentence of this astonishing description can mean only one thing: *parrhesia*, freedom of speech, the symbol of Greek democracy. What is the idea? Was it a poet's wishful thinking? Was it in the mind of those who then, as we shall see, waged an offensive war against Persia? Both would still be more likely than that this was an expression of genuine Persian fear. However, I feel that any 'realistic'

interpretation of these lines leads astray. Just as Darius could say
(781), 'I never did so much harm to the polis', meaning the Persian
empire, so here the frontiers between east and west have no longer
a meaning. Aeschylus did not think of the Persia of 480 or of that
of 472, nor of its possible future. This is myth, and nothing in that
context was important to him but the idea of freedom, as it was
realized in Greek democracy.

Before we try to trace in Aeschylus as well as in Pindar the depths
underlying all merely political thought, it might be fitting to point
out some examples of simple human relationships in the *Persians*,
reflecting the moods of ordinary people during the war. In their
first song the chorus lament for the women at home (133 ff.); each
one is longing for her husband, and their lonely beds are filled with
tears. Later on Atossa thinks of the parents whose sons have gone to
war (245). The theme is repeated and varied. The messenger speaks
of 'the Persian city, longing for the beloved youth of the country'
(511). It is, of course, not only the absence of the men, it is their
death in battle which frightens the Persian women everywhere
and causes endless grief (532 ff.). The heavy Persian losses in the war
are emphasized throughout by the accumulation of names of those
killed. Aeschylus certainly had not a pacifist mind; but he, like his
audience, had gone through the terrors and sorrows of war, even
though the Greek losses were smaller, and the home-coming of the
men earlier and easier than for the Persians. The vase-painters of the
time, more and more inclined to describe scenes of everyday life
beside their mythical stories, found a favourite theme, that belonged
to both spheres, in the warrior's parting from his wife or his father.
Aeschylus would be the last to avoid the heroic gesture, but in putting himself into the camp of the defeated, his genius could realize
the fullest possible impact of war. Pindar, on the other hand, has
hardly anything to say about this human–inhuman aspect of war,
apart from calling it generally 'the hostile nurse of young men'
(above, p. 179). He often speaks of mythical wars to show examples
of heroic deeds, and he even frequently compares an athletic victory
with the real thing as a true test for a man. He lived in the world of
the aristocratic polis, for which a victory at the games was an
achievement enhancing the glory of the state. Pindar did not really
know what war could mean. All the time he speaks of goddesses

and heroines, including the girls loved by gods, but he hardly speaks of wives at all, and he calls 'mother' his city (*I*. 1, 1) or Aegina when he identifies himself with the Aeginetan chorus (*P*. 8, 98), or his Muse (*N*. 3, 1); once, in the early sixth Paean (12), he compares his own relationship with Delphi to that of a child to his mother. When in *P*. 8, 85, the boys who were unsuccessful in the games are seen creeping home to their mothers, the latter mean little more than home and cannot be regarded as confirming 'an acknowledged position of Theban women'.[128] On the contrary, in this aristocratic and heroic world loving wives and mothers play no part, and their suffering in war is never mentioned. In old age Pindar remembers the pleasures of youth and love; then he can sing (*N*. 8, 1): 'Divine youth, herald of Aphrodite's immortal caresses, you who lie on the eyelids of girls and boys.' However lovely these lines are, they do not show any human attitude beyond his own personal feelings and social convention. Another reference (*P*. 11, 24) is to adulterous young women whose sins cannot escape other people's gossip. Instead of Aeschylus' humanity, here is social pride and prejudice. And the direct experience or non-experience of war may have something to do with it.

Pindar and Aeschylus belong to the same generation, and to a phase in the history of the Greek mind which is characterized by a highly ethical approach to religion and myth. With Pindar, this leads – in contrast to the hostile rationalism of Ionians such as Xenophanes – to a cautious and reverent revision of the traditional stories wherever they were crude or cruel. 'It becomes man to speak fair words about the gods' (*O*. 1, 35). Sometimes he even alters a mythical story in order to please his patrons, and usually he tells it to teach a lesson. Even earlier poets had 'humanized' the ancient myths, as, for instance, Simonides does in his moving song on Danae and her baby (fr. 13 D. 38 P). To Pindar it is not so much the human aspect of the myth which he emphasizes, rather the divine one; divine myth shows the greatness of the gods, their overwhelming power, and the attitudes of their conventions. In that respect he and Aeschylus belong together, at least to some extent. The often expressed view that Pindar is looking back to the past, and Aeschylus towards the future, contains a good deal of truth. To both, the most decisive matter is the relationship between man and god. That, of course, is at the core of all non-rational ethical beliefs. For Pindar the tragic tension is between the glamour of man's noble achievements and his short-lived existence, for Aeschylus the conflict is rather between man's aims and his own conscience, or if that is putting it on too personal a level, between his aims and the will of the gods. His concept of deity goes beyond Pindar's awe of Zeus' all-embracing mastery (*I.* 5, 53) to a spiritual height far above any traditional religion. He believes in that Zeus whose name is the first word of the *Suppliants*, and also of its last chorus song (1064), that Zeus 'whoever he may be' (*Ag.* 160), whom words cannot describe, 'who guided men to think' (*Ag.* 176), who can be identified with 'air, earth and heaven, as he is all that because he is something above it' (fr. 70). This was not a god of rational scepticism like that of Xenophanes nor the lord of the Olympian Pantheon, but the object of a fervent faith in divine wisdom and justice.[129] Aeschylus was, in the meaning of his age, a 'modern' man.

The two poets are separated in spirit as well as in social life, just as Athens and Thebes represented different, almost contradictory atmospheres. As Pindar grew older, his voice became fuller and deeper, his mind richer and wider, but essentially he remained the same. Dionysiac ecstasy (*dithyr.* 2, 70b Snell. 61 Bowra), or Orphic eschatology to which Theron adhered (*O.* 2, 56), or the hope for a life on the blessed islands (*O.* 2, 71) remained outside Pindar's own religion, however strongly he felt the depth and beauty of such beliefs. To him, man's free will and fate entirely depend on the gods, both in happiness and misfortune. His religion is traditional, far away from all intellectual theology or philosophy, though he likes to turn abstract concepts into divine persons. His last song (*P.* 8, of 446 B.C.) significantly begins with the call to Hesychia, a deity straight from the poet's mind whom he had once invoked for his fellow Thebans as that 'Peace' that prevented discord and war (fr. 109 Snell. 99b Bowra), that 'Quiet' 'that holds the keys of war and councils'. The poem ends in the magnificent lines which were the fundamental theme of his beliefs throughout his life: 'Creatures of a day – what are we, what are we not? The dream of a shadow is man. But when god-given radiance comes, there is a shining light for men and a sweet time.'

Aeschylus, in his greatest works, belongs to a new era, for

unlike Pindar he moved with the times. If Pindar was, above all, a traditionalist and Aeschylus a revolutionary, that could hardly be otherwise, for with Pindar choral lyrics found their culmination and end, while tragedy was largely created by Aeschylus and launched by him on its glorious journey. Aristotle says (*poet.* 1450a, 16. 23): 'tragedy is representation, not of men, but of action and life, and of happiness and unhappiness', and 'without action, there could be no tragedy, but there could be without characters'. That may be true, or it may not. The persons on the Athenian stage were not puppets, though neither characters in the Shakespearean sense. Aeschylus' characters were, true to an Athenian tradition going back to Solon, at the same time creatures of God and citizens of their community. The deepest contrast between Darius and Xerxes in the *Persians* is that of responsibility and egotism; the latter the Greeks called *hubris*, the overbearing attitude of man towards both the gods and his fellow men. Thus, responsibility was of a twofold nature too. Actually, we may say, it amounts to the same thing, for the polis is a human community under divine direction and protection. This remains the underlying theme of Aeschylus' later plays as well, and it is clearly the democratic polis that dominates the scene. Eteocles in the *Seven against Thebes* is from the first line of the play the responsible leader of the citizens, Pelasgus in the *Suppliants* a king by the grace of the demos, who refuses to make any decision as king and master. The tragic conflict arises when men, individually or as a group, challenge the divinely imposed order. In a different sense, even Prometheus' revolt against a tyrannical Zeus belongs to the same kind of tragic conflict.

It cannot be our task to discuss the meaning and development of Attic tragedy, though we shall have frequently to refer to its testimony on later occasions.[130] It must be said, however, that of all the branches of literature it was tragedy that victoriously overcame the long-lasting influence of sixth-century tradition, tragedy which received its predominant incentive from the experience of the war, and the part played in it by the polis. And the polis stood for freedom. The field for freedom was widened in and by tragedy, covering political freedom as well as inner freedom. In the more ample space provided by the introduction of trilogies it was also possible to show freedom working through the changes of time. Whether

freedom included the freedom of the individual was at first undecided. In the transition from *tyrannis* or aristocracy to the democratic
state, which at Athens and not only at Athens took place in the
decades before and after the turn of the century, the transition from
eunomia to *isonomia*, the question of the relation between individual
and community changed its character. Lust for power is innate in
man, but the man who became a tyrant in opposing the aristocracy
was different from the man who tried to become the supreme leader
of a democracy, or let us rather say (in order to include, e.g.,
Sparta), of a community of free men.

The tragedy of individual *hubris* was most clearly exemplified in
the sphere of political reality by the fates of Pausanias and Themistocles, of which we shall speak later; we can well imagine that the
dramatic lives and ends of these great men, on their part, influenced
the stage. Was Xerxes' part in the *Persians* intended also as a warning to contemporary men and their actions, the aspirations of his
great enemy Themistocles, for instance, and possibly even to
Cimon's offensive warfare against Persia? We do not know, but it is
not impossible, and the events which belong to the following
period immediately emerged from the war; the men in question
were outstanding members of the war generation. It is easy to see
that the war, with which one epoch ended and a new one began, had
solved some problems and created others. The certainty that free
citizens had defeated the Great King and his 'slaves', finally created
the Greek superiority complex over the 'barbarians'. It is as the
democratic champion of freedom that Athens grew into her new
powerful role. Later she destroyed her own image, but at first it was
at Athens that new ideas were loosed and new aims evolved, which
Sparta was neither willing nor able to pursue herself. Thus, from the
united effort in the defence of freedom, there derived not only the
rise of that culture which we call classical but also the dualism which
was to be fatal to the greatness of Greece.

It was the Athenian war-leaders who more impressively than
others formed the flower of the war generation, no one more than
Themistocles, whose naval policy determined the history of the
whole century. The greatness of the man is reflected in a famous
chapter of Thucydides (1, 138). He describes Themistocles' outstanding intellectual power and political foresight, but not the

diplomatic skill which he displayed during the war, nor the faults of his moral character. These must be added to the picture. In contrast to Aristeides, who was an honest patriot, but no genius, Themistocles was brilliant, but not a great character.[131] Tradition rightly groups him with Pausanias. The victors of Salamis and Plataea both came, as we shall see, to a bad and sad end. They represent that generation which brought about the triumph of their cities, but at the same time set the ambition of great individuals against the polis, foreshadowing the trend of times to come.

VI

THE ASCENDANCY OF
ATHENS

1 · *Growing Imperialism*

The period from 478–477, the year following the end of the Persian
invasion, to 431, the beginning of the Peloponnesian war, bears the
name of the *Pentekontaetia*, the 'time of fifty years', although it
actually, even given the Greek method of counting inclusively, falls
a little short of the full number.[1] Thucydides wrote a famous excursus (1, 89–118) about this period, with the main purpose of revealing
the growth of Athenian power as the chief reason for, the 'truest
cause' of, the outbreak of the great war (1, 23, 6). Obviously he
treated those fifty years only as a prelude, and therefore from a one-
sided point of view. Even so, the excursus shows astonishing omissions, and it has to be supplemented from other sources. It is strictly
confined to the relations between Athens and Sparta, which, of
course, includes the growth of Athenian imperialism; but, for
instance, of its economic side nothing is said.[2] The shortcomings of
Thucydides' account may be due, at least partly, to the fact that it
had never been given its final shape; but that question leads into the
more general question of the composition of Thucydides' work,
'a vain and insoluble problem',[3] which is entirely outside the scope
of the present book. Anyway, whatever gaps there are to be filled,
those thirty chapters of Thucydides' first book remain the basis of
any description of the inter-war years.

During the time of the siege of Sestus (479–478; above, p. 173),
the Athenians in Greece had returned to their city and begun to
rebuild their houses and the city walls, including those of the
Peiraeus (Thuc. 1, 90–93). The Spartans disliked the idea of a fortified city and harbour just outside the Peloponnese; their friendly

insistence hardly disguised their selfish feelings, and Athenian opposition was roused. It was essential for the position of Athens among the Greeks that their city, without walls far more vulnerable than Sparta, should be safely walled in. Sparta, on the other hand, as the leading or 'guardian' power of Hellas, might see a threat to her own position, which some of the Greeks, and certainly Sparta herself, regarded as a necessary guarantee for a firm and united peace. Themistocles, still the leading man at home, went to Sparta, where he was regarded as a friend, and by clever tactics protracted the negotiations while the walls were hurriedly being built.[4] When they were high enough, he proclaimed Athenian independence, which had been threatened by Spartan interference, and Sparta gave way, surely with some bad feeling. This was the first time that her leadership on land was seriously challenged by Athens.[5]

At the same time Athens had to overcome the grave difficulties caused by the loss of two harvests and of much property in city and country. It also seems certain that, after the losses in the war, the population of Athens quickly increased far beyond its previous numbers; thus the feeding of the people must have been the foremost need. Our sources are silent on this point, though it may be significant that Athenian coins have been found, especially in the West; we can be sure that the silver mines were soon producing again, if only after 478; the fleet may also have collected more levies than were needed for its maintenance,[6] and some food must have been imported on Athenian merchant vessels. Most important of all was to reopen the Black Sea route as early as possible. Moreover, the cities of Aeolis and Ionia would never join, unless the Greeks continued the war along the shores of Asia Minor.[7] In spring 478 a fleet of moderate size under Pausanias' command started the offensive in earnest; Aristeides was in charge of the Athenian contingent (Thuc. 1, 94). Cyprus and Byzantium were taken, and thus the Persian threat to the Asiatic Greeks was thrown back, both in the south and in the north. For the Greeks themselves, and especially the Athenians, the capture of Byzantium was of far greater, and certainly more lasting, importance than that of Cyprus.

Whether and to what extent Pausanias had to persuade the ephors to agree to this campaign, we do not know, though it seems certain that Sparta still desired to lead in the war. Once in a position to act, Pausanias began to pursue his personal aims. According to Thucydides (1, 128, 3), he wanted 'the rule of Hellas'; his attitude towards the Greeks was one of 'tyranny rather than military leadership' (Thuc. 1, 95, 3). Moreover, once master of Byzantium he began intriguing with Persia. He behaved like an oriental despot, and is even reported to have had a bodyguard of Persians and Egyptians (Thuc. 1, 130). He was recalled to Sparta, punished, but acquitted of conspiring with Persia. At the same time, and at least partly because of Pausanias' behaviour, the allies, apart from the Peloponnesians, asked Athens to take over the naval command. When Sparta, in spring 477, sent a new commander, Dorcis, with a small force, he was rejected by the allies and had to go home. No Peloponnesians were left to fight the naval war. Up to this moment Sparta had obviously not thought of giving up the leadership in the war against Persia, and Thucydides' view (1, 95, 7) that Sparta was more or less glad to leave it to Athens seems to go too far.[8] Whether Pausanias' attitude served as a pretext or not, the Ionians and the Athenians had come to some sort of agreement. After all, it was obvious that the Greeks on the islands and in Asia Minor would readily entrust their future to the strongest naval power, and the Athenians certainly did everything to encourage them. The change in naval command did not yet break up the war alliance itself, but it lost a great deal of its importance.

Pausanias returned to Byzantium, we are told, as a private person to continue his intrigues with Persia. Thucydides (1, 128-34) knows the text of some letters exchanged between Pausanias and Xerxes; there is no indication how they could have been preserved, and we might easily suspect them to be fakes, published after Pausanias' death.[9] Did he return to Asia with the tacit consent of the Spartan government? Anyway, after some time he was once more called back to Sparta and obeyed, probably in the hope of getting away as easily as the last time.[10] The ephors, after many attempts to acquire reliable evidence, which seem to have taken several years,[11] found that he had started to conspire with the helots, and that sealed his fate. He was starved to death in the temple of Athena Chalkioikos, but brought out before he died, in order not to pollute the sanctuary. He had still been the regent of Sparta, and there are indications that he had supporters among the Spartiates. But like Cleomenes he found the power of the ephors too strong.

The Athenians, with the good will of, and possibly a direct invitation by, the majority of the Greeks, had begun (in 478–477; *AP* 23, 5) to create a new body, the so-called Delian League. They concluded treaties of alliance, both defensive and offensive, with each of the states concerned. The main purpose was aggression against Persia, and to inflict vengeance by devastating the King's land (Thuc. 1, 96, 1). The chief organizer was Aristeides, who, with his well-known integrity, was the right man to discuss with each state the amount of tribute to be paid into a common treasury. This was to be installed on Delos, probably in the temple of Apollo, a religious centre for all Ionians and therefore well suited to unite the eastern Greeks with Athens, perhaps also to act as a counterpart to Delphi and its all too cautious policy. The Ionian islands were prominent in the whole development. It is not known whether the old Ionian league still survived – more likely it did not. The question arises whether the new league had any other aims than to take vengeance and gain plunder.[12] No doubt such purposes will have been popular, and in agreement with the feelings of that age, but the leaders must have looked further ahead. Later in the fifth century the liberation of the Asiatic Greeks was regarded as the main purpose of the league, and the whole situation in the early 'seventies was simply asking for an extension of Greek against Persian power. As to the Ionian and Aeolian cities, it is known that Persian rule had not directly been oppressive; even so they would, to say the least, follow the lead of Miletus and join the Greeks, if and when they could do so without endangering themselves. To what extent that was possible, we cannot say, and the idea of an enthusiastic acceptance of 'liberation' is probably a misconception. Still, Athenian policy aimed at bringing all Ionians together.

Delos was intended as the meeting-place for the council of the league. The tribute was to be given in money, except for some states, especially the big islands, which provided ships and crews of their own. How many of this type were in existence in the first years of the league, we do not know; but their number soon declined. It was Athens which selected the states which gave ships instead of money, and it was in her interest, at least after a few years, to get the money in order to increase her own fleet; permission to keep a fleet soon became a privilege. In each case the amount of money and the number of ships were fixed by agreement between Aristeides and the state concerned.[13] Though the league was primarily intended for the maintenance of a large fleet and the continuation of the war, no time limit was set, and nothing was said about what would happen if and when Persia was finally beaten. Obviously, the league also served in securing food and other supplies both for Athens and the navy, and to suppress piracy. The leading position of Athens was made clear at once by the bilateral oath she took with every individual city to have the same friends and foes (*AP* 23, 5), while the allies were not allowed to conclude treaties among themselves. A clear sign of the situation was also that the treasurers of the league, the *hellenotamiai*, were Athenian officials. Their name corresponded to the unofficial name of 'the Hellenes', which was used for the league at least as long as the war with Persia lasted.[14] There is, on the other hand, no sign that Athens had more votes in the council than each member state; an organized opposition was not to be expected, and the council anyway was of little importance. The official name of the league, 'The Athenians and their allies', did not indicate (as with 'The Lacedaemonians and their allies') a constitutionally exceptional position of the hegemonic state, though it did imply its actual position of power. Hegemony for Athens was no longer a merely military matter, but, like Sparta in the Peloponnesian League, she was now the political hegemon as well, while in contrast to the Peloponnesian League the new organization was very much stricter, and bound to become even more so. Soon the overriding problem was how to combine Athens' hegemony of the league with the autonomy of each member state (cf. Thuc. 1, 97, 1).[15]

No evidence exists as to which states, or even how many, were the original members of the league, though a good deal can be inferred. It is, for instance, no mere guess that the league at first included only cities on the islands and perhaps the eastern shores of the Aegean sea, including the area of the Straits as far as Byzantium. Retrospective conclusions from the quota lists are possible, but frequently remain uncertain. Naturally all cities whose entry is known to have been later cannot have been among the original members. A moderate estimate would be that about 150 cities joined in 478–477.[16]

At home, at the same time, things had changed a good deal. The council on the Areopagus had regained some of its old prestige and power (*AP* 23, 1. *pol.* 1304a, 20), though not by a special decree or law. Since the majority of the urban lower classes were away as oarsmen of the fleet, the upper classes again gained more influence, and the leading families once more came into their own. We hear little of Themistocles, though Plutarch tells us of opposition to him and even to Aristeides. The latter, however, found a supporter, who soon replaced him in the command of the fleet, in Cimon, son of Miltiades, then in his early thirties. He captured Eion in Thrace, a Persian stronghold at the mouth of the river Strymon, and the island of Scyrus, where the non-Greek inhabitants, notorious for their piracy, were sold into slavery. At both places colonists were settled, probably as cleruchs, that is to say, they remained Athenian citizens. The foundation of cleruchies was one of the most effective means of providing for the land-hunger of the lower classes; later they became of political importance as well, as an instrument of imperialism. In those early years of the league the economic advantages for Athens were generally on a small scale, but soon opportunities increased; there were spoils of war, ransom for captives, and of course increased trade. Even so, life for a cleruch was never easy, though their loyalty to her old city seems never to have wavered.[16a]

The capture of Scyrus had nothing to do with the war against Persia, except that it would help Athenian rule of the seas.[17] Cimon's next move was even more clearly made for the sake of Athens' position within the Delian league. Carystus had not joined the Greeks in 480, and now understandably she did not join the league either. Situated on the south coast of Euboea, it was too close to Attica and to the route across the Aegean to be allowed to keep aloof; it was forced to enrol.[18] Military leadership and economic prosperity began to work hand in hand to increase the political power of Athens, and this worked at least equally the other way, that is to say, politics fostered economy. Athenian policy was moving towards imperialism, an imperialism different from the modern concept, and yet leading to similar results.

Compared with the successes of Athens, Sparta went through a difficult period. Some time after 479 the king Leotychidas started a campaign to punish the pro-Persian Thessalians and to remove the feudal 'tyranny' of the Aleuads. This attempt to continue the war, if not against Persia, at least against 'medism', was a complete failure, and Leotychidas was later accused of having been bribed; he died in exile.[19] During these years Sparta also lost temporarily her full hegemony over the Peloponnese. Argos in particular recovered some of her former power, and recaptured Tiryns and Mycenae, which were severely punished for having defected. Elis succeeded in creating by synoecism a unified and democratic polis; soon after, the same thing happened at Mantineia. Her rival Tegea was allied to Argos and had tried to found an independent Arcadian league, but was beaten by Sparta in two battles, at Tegea and Dipaea. Mantineia had remained loyal to Sparta, whose position in Arcadia was again fairly strong; but on the whole, Sparta had lost ground in the Peloponnese.[20]

In some way or other Themistocles was involved in these events. He had pleaded for an anti-Spartan policy, since he regarded Sparta as the main obstacle to Athenian greatness; but he met with strong opposition, and was forced into the background by such men as Aristeides and Xanthippus whom once he had driven into exile.[20a] In spring 476 he was still at Athens, acting as choregus for Phrynichus (Plut. *Them.* 5, 5). After that (we do not know the date) he was ostracized and lived in Argos. How the ostracism came about, we never learn, but ever since Cimon's successes, Themistocles' popularity had been on the decline; in fact, for several years he had been out of power.[21] It is possible that Aristeides, back home after Cimon had taken over the naval command, found sufficient support, especially with the Alcmaeonids, to have Themistocles removed; the fact that both men worked together in the battle of Salamis, and are praised for their activities in Aeschylus' *Persae*, does not prove that they were friends. While at Argos, Themistocles must have been involved in anti-Spartan activities. Before long, Sparta retaliated (Thuc. 1, 135) by conveying evidence to Athens that he had conspired with Pausanias. Whatever truth the accusation may have contained, Themistocles had to leave Argos; he escaped arrest, went first to Corcyra, and then was hunted from place to place till he eventually reached Ephesus. Later he approached the

Persian king (now Artaxerxes) and was given not only asylum but an honourable rule over Magnesia and two other towns in Asia Minor.[22] At Athens he was apparently accused of medism, and condemned. Whether he really hoped to be called back to Athens or not, and whatever it meant to be a vassal of the Great King, his last years must have been a struggle between self-reliance and self-torment. He died many years later, perhaps by suicide. Thucydides (1, 138, 6) reports a rumour that his body was later secretly buried in Attica. The parallel between the fate of Themistocles and that of Pausanias has been obvious, ever since Thucydides compared them. It is therefore hardly sufficient to speak of the ingratitude of Athenian democracy. More likely, Themistocles fell a victim to his own difficult character and the hostility he had aroused among other Athenian politicians. It probably also counted that he was a *homo novus* among the aristocratic families who usually provided the political leaders. Behind all that, however, as with Pausanias, was the fact of a very personal policy, and the fact that no Greek state at that time could come to terms with a great individual who, on account of his merits, had become a law to himself.

Cimon, the successful admiral, was at the same time a popular man at home. In many ways a typical aristocrat, rich, related to several outstanding families, and a guest-friend of Sparta, he was a natural opponent to Themistocles. He called his three younger sons Lakedaimonios, Eleios, and Thessalos, thus indicating a whole programme of foreign policy. He was a *grandseigneur*, genial and generous. Cratinus (fr. 1) describes him in glowing terms, as 'divine, most hospitable, in every way the best of all Greeks'. Many stories survived about his magnificence and liberality, and many buildings as witnesses of his wealth. He certainly lived an unconventional life, and naturally became the object of much gossip, both favourable and hostile.[23] He was, however, a great patriot who never tried to gain personal power beyond that of a legally elected *strategos*. Like Aristeides, who must have died during the 'seventies, Cimon was no diehard, no extremist in politics; he became one of the builders, indirectly of democracy and directly of Athenian rule over the Aegean. To him, however, the naval power of Athens was only the counterpart to Sparta's supremacy on land, so that a balance of power and peaceful co-existence might be possible.

Athens, in these years, began to assume a position of increased supremacy over her allies, and Thucydides (1, 98 f.) makes it clear that it was chiefly the exacting methods of collecting the contributions of the allies and the lack of equal status between Athens and the allies which caused misgivings and led to desertions. We can add that the apparent, though perhaps deceptive, inactivity of Persia may have played its part in the feelings within the league.[24] The first state to secede, and to be forced back into membership, was Naxos, according to Thucydides 'the first allied polis to be enslaved against the established law', i.e. against the covenant of the league that guaranteed autonomy to each member state. 'Enslavement' is an exaggeration, caused by later developments, but it must have implied some serious restrictions of political independence; whether that meant an Athenian garrison or the dissolution of the Naxian fleet, or both and something else, we cannot say.[25] At any rate, it is a fact that no state was allowed to leave the league, and that in these years Athens was gradually approaching a position of monopoly and domination.[26] Thucydides (1, 99) provides, as it were, an excuse for Athens: 'The allies themselves were responsible for that. For . . . in order not to be away from home, they had agreed to pay a tribute in cash instead of ships. Thus the Athenian navy grew from the payments they contributed, and when they tried to secede, they were unprepared and inexperienced for warfare.' The process of change from providing ships to paying tribute went on for a considerable time, but we know of no date for any individual state. When large fleets of Athenian and allied ships were sent out during the 'fifties (e.g. Thuc. 1, 104, 2. 105, 2. 110, 4. 112, 2) the change may still have been at an early stage, while in the Samian war of 440 B.C. only squadrons from Chios and Lesbos joined the Athenian fleet (116, 2); they were by then the only two states left in the empire with navies of their own.

The process of building up the league and the position of Athens as its leader had led to a slackening of the war effort, though it is likely that a Greek fleet remained in eastern waters, if only for the protection of the Asiatic Greeks. The Persians had, in fact, collected forces again, and to forestall an offensive on their part, Cimon, some time after the subjection of Naxos, in 469 or 468, sailed with a large fleet to Pamphylia and gained a crushing victory by land and naval forces near the mouth of the Eurymedon river.[27] It was a decisive event, especially when soon afterwards Xerxes was murdered by his brother and successor Artaxerxes, who had then to quell various revolts within the Persian empire. The Greeks rightly celebrated the battle of the Eurymedon as one of their outstanding victories. The important city of Phaselis had joined the league before the battle, and soon concluded a judicial treaty with Athens, which granted the Phaselites some privileges.[28] Cimon's success soon persuaded the cities of Caria and Lycia farther west to follow suit. Apart from gaining important new allies, this also meant that the Phoenician fleet was prevented from advancing beyond Cyprus. That island remained in Persian hands, but Greek rule over the Aegean was now uncontested.

All the time the Spartans had kept quiet, though they will have regarded the rising power of Athens with increasing misgivings. For some years, as we have seen, Sparta had been concerned with her own weakened position in the Peloponnese; but the battle of the Eurymedon and its consequences must have appeared to the Spartans as a serious threat to any balance of power. Was Greece to be led as before by the strongest land power, which Sparta still was, or by the adventurous state whose navy was stronger than all the other fleets together? Rivalry between the two powers grew into enmity which threatened to tear the Greek world into two.

The first threat of a possible direct clash occurred after the people of Thasos revolted in 465. Cimon won a naval victory against them, landed on the island, and besieged the city, whereupon the Thasians sent a message to Sparta asking for help in the shape of an invasion of Attica. Thasos, with her rich mines both on the island and in Thrace, and with flourishing wine and timber trades, was a commercial power, important enough to explain both the revolt and the immediate and strong Athenian reaction. Sparta, according to Thucydides, secretly promised help, but at that moment Laconia was shaken by an earthquake, and that was immediately followed by a revolt of the helots, of which we shall have more to say. Sparta was unable to give Thasos any help, and the island surrendered after two years of siege; she had to raze her walls and give up her fleet as well as her possessions on the mainland.[29] The last fact probably explains why the tribute which Thasos paid in the following years was moderate. About the same time the Athenians sent a large group of colonists to a place called Enneahodoi ('Nine Ways'), at the site of the later Amphipolis in the country of the Edonians, a Thracian tribe. The exact date of the expedition is not known; it is possible that the Thasians had heard about it, and that it was one of the causes of their revolt. However whether this colony near the mouth of the Strymon was actually directed against possessions of Thasos is not clear; part of the settlers went farther inland and perished in an attack by the Edonians near Drabescus, and the whole colony was withdrawn.[30] There may have been other setbacks to expanding Athenian imperialism; more, at any rate, were to follow, but the present event was the beginning of the end of Cimon's popularity.

The helots in Laconia, and especially in Messenia, had been restless before, but even the secret leadership of Cleomenes and Pausanias had not led to any improvement in their situation. The difficulties Sparta had to face in her Peloponnesian policy will have increased the threat of a helot revolt, though our sources do not give any indication of open unrest before the year 464, when an earthquake destroyed part of Sparta and killed a large number of Spartiates.[31] That event gave the helots the opportunity of starting a full-size revolt. It involved both Laconia and Messenia, and even some towns of the perioeci in Messenia. It was a very serious challenge to Sparta, the more so as the helots seem to have had efficient leaders. We know hardly any details, but Herodotus (9, 64, 2) mentions the death of three hundred men from Sparta at Stenyclarus in the centre of Messenia. The Laconian helots were fairly soon suppressed, and we can be sure it was done with the utmost ruthlessness. Still, the Messenians were able to raid and ravage even the Laconian countryside, and the war against them lasted for years. The Spartans, unable to take their palisaded headquarters on Mt Ithome, asked their allies, among them the Athenians, for support. The latter, well known at least since Plataea and Mycale for their ability to overcome fortified positions, sent a strong force of hoplites under Cimon's leadership. He, in fact, had pleaded for this action, which met with resistance in the assembly, especially by a man of whom we shall hear more, Ephialtes. We learn from Thucydides (1, 102, 4) that the alliance against Persia still included both Sparta and Athens; but could that alliance be the basis for Athenian help against the Messenians? It sounds odd, though the alliance still existed, at least in theory, as late as 427 (Thuc. 3, 63, 2), that is to say, in the middle of the Peloponnesian war. The alliance of 481 was legally the reason for calling in the Athenians 'as allies'.[32]

The following events are introduced by Thucydides (102, 3) with the words: 'From this campaign resulted for the first time an open disagreement between Lacedaemonians and Athenians.' We are further told that the former feared the bold and revolutionary spirit of the Athenians, and also that these might be tempted by the helots to change sides. Sparta's fear of Athenian independence and freedom is mentioned by Herodotus (5, 91, 1), when it was used, as early as 510, as a reason for bringing Hippias back to Athens. Herodotus worked on his *Histories* in the decades of the middle of the century; he will have reflected later fears which were better founded. Without showing their mistrust, the Spartans sent away Cimon and his men, alone among the allies. It is a remarkable story. Thucydides neglects earlier friction between the two states, but that is not surprising. It had never led to such an open outrage; moreover, relations had been fairly good when Sparta asked for Athenian help. For Thucydides anyway, this was the first of several events leading to the Peloponnesian war.

We must ask what Sparta really feared. Athens stood on the brink of a democratic revolution (see below, p. 211f.), and that may already have shown some of its power and attractiveness. There may have been other indications of a disquieting attitude, even among Cimon's middle-class hoplites. What was really at the bottom of Sparta's suspicions, and what came to the surface through the pressure of Athens' growing power, was the fundamental difference in outlook between the two peoples – Thucydides even refers to their ethnic difference as Dorians and Ionians. It was to some extent an irrational attitude on the part of the Spartans, but not entirely so. The Spartans wished to maintain their power, Athens to increase hers. Sparta had become ultra-conservative, the more so as the danger of unrest and revolt of the helots was never very far from the thoughts of the Spartiates. They were also urged on against Athens by some of the Peloponnesians such as Corinth and Aegina, suffering from the growing expansion of Athenian naval power and sea trade, which more and more included also the Greek west, Corinth's special sphere of interest. Political and economic reasons coincided, and we can be sure that Sparta feared most of all the advance of democracy.

It did not only advance politically, but produced a unique atmosphere in the cultural field. During the 'sixties Cimon, among other things, built the south wall of the Acropolis, which in the end was to provide the large platform for the Parthenon. Into the gap between wall, rock, and earlier foundations, the Athenians threw all the 'rubbish' left from the Persian sacking, the *Perserschutt*, while architectural pieces, and even some of the lovely archaic statues now in the Acropolis museum, had been built, in the emergency after 479, into the rebuilt north wall of the Acropolis (see note 4). The Greeks in general never thought of preserving old works of art, especially if damaged, unless they were figures of high religious importance; but the sweeping act of 'cleaning-up' in Cimon's time was on a scale unknown from other places or times. If the Athenians, as was natural, did not think in terms of museum pieces, one would still have thought that some scruples of piety might have intervened.

Cimon brought Polygnotus from Thasos to Athens, the first great painter of whom we know, though we know very little. He painted large frescoes on mythical subjects, and was famous for a certain 'naturalistic' approach. He was said to have painted men with *ethos*, that is a deliberate stress on character. Art, like literature, we can guess, was invaded by standards neither purely aesthetic nor religious, though the latter were still predominant.[33] Little of Athenian sculpture from the 'seventies and 'sixties has survived, but we have the wonderful large bronze statue of a spear-throwing Zeus, which was rescued from the sea near Artemisium and was probably dedicated after the victory there. We may add the lovely miniature relief of the 'mourning' or rather 'pensive' Athena.[34] There is little that is archaic about that Zeus full of vitality and strength, or the divine humanity of Athena, but otherwise we still find the artists battling against, of even lovingly continuing, archaic traditions.

The process is reflected in one of the masterpieces of Greek sculpture, the pediments of the temple of Zeus at Olympia. The subject on the east side is the preparation for the chariot race between King Oenomaus and Pelops for the hand of the king's daughter and the rule of the country. The west pediment, later in date, depicts the struggle between the Lapithes and Centaurs. Like Athena in the pediments at Aegina, but far more impressive, Zeus is in the centre of the earlier, Apollo of the later, pediment. Zeus is the majestic central figure of a row of isolated quiet statues, Apollo dominates, with a grandiose gesture, the turbulent events on his left and right. The arrangement of the Pelops scene is archaic, but of a wonderful and striking harmony, and instead of the archaic smile there is a lifelike expression on every single face and in the easy attitude of every body. These people are no longer types, but individuals, and, for example, the signs of old age in the seer are just as prominent as the differences in social status in some of the figures. It is, however, easy to see that the artist is far from simply copying nature. In the west pediment, which can be regarded as a further development of the east pediment at Aegina, all is movement and passion, even violence, though marshalled by the artist into lively symmetrical groups. Faces and bodies clearly reflect the events, the resistance and the fear of the women, the quiet heroism of the men, the lust and the savagery of the centaurs. There is still archaic tradition, but naturalistic and individualistic trends are breaking through. A new future is foreshadowed.

The Olympian pediments were not made by Athenian artists, but it is quite clear, as they are the predecessors of Pheidias' work, that Athens had a share in the same developments. In fact, it is believed that the sculptors of the Olympian west pediment were influenced by the great painters working at Athens, who reached achievements which we can only faintly trace in some vase paintings. The changes in style and the liberation from earlier conventions amount almost to a revolution. Sparta, of course, was completely out of all this, while the Athenian spirit, apart from the all-important politics, was manifest in particular in the uniquely Athenian form of art, the theatre. It was in those years that tragedy reached new heights, and comedy started on its career as a form of high literature and a new poetical and entertaining form of public discussion.[35]

If Aeschylus has been called the creator of tragedy, this is true in more than one sense. To the traditional one actor, identical with the poet, he added a second actor to reply to the chorus and to answer the other actor.[36] That not only created a new and more dramatic situation on the stage, it changed the character of the play from the religious spectacle of choral singing and dancing with interspersed speeches into true drama ('action') in which the tragic suffering of man could become that of an individual hero. Moreover, Aeschylus invented the form of the trilogy. The scheme of three separate tragedies and one satyr-drama, all performed in one day, had existed for some time, and when Aeschylus produced the *Persians*, this play had no connexion whatsoever with the other plays of the same day. But in the *Seven against Thebes* of 467, the *Suppliants* of a slightly later date, the *Prometheus Bound* of late but unknown date, and the *Oresteia* of 458 we have in each case clear evidence of a coherent story which enabled the poet to show more than one generation under the impact of fate.[37] Gods and men sometimes play curious and dangerous parts in the eternal struggle with fate. The issues are different, but men or women are always in the midst, and the gods behind and above them. In the *Danaid* trilogy the idea of marriage as ordained by Zeus leads to the most horrible human errors and misdeeds, though finally there must have been some solution providing peace and harmony.[38] In the Theban trilogy it is the struggle of both family and city against a cruel fate that counts; in the *Oresteia* the bonds between husband and wife, between parents and children, are stressed to the point of inhuman deeds and seemingly divine misdirection. Always, however, there is the assurance that force and violence can be redeemed, whether for men or gods. This was revolutionary religion, and in a world in which religion and cult traditions played an outstanding part, that meant a great deal; but there was something even more immediately threatening, the conflict between individual and community.

The strong individual (like Eteocles in the *Seven*) battles against a fate that is stronger than he, stronger than his ideals, stronger than his gods. Eteocles is convinced that he and his brother are both condemned by their father's curse, that the gods have forgotten them (702). For even they are ultimately helpless against fate; Eteocles has learnt to doubt their power and their justice. He is far away from the *hubris* of the enemies of Thebes, but he rebels against a destiny that is beyond personal guilt. He no longer believes in traditional religion, but he cannot free himself from its bonds. He fears that with the kings the polis is threatened (764), just as in the first lines of the play he describes his own position as separate from the old beliefs and from the fickle people of the polis. As a soldier and commander he is the leader of the state, and many in the audience might think of their own leaders who faced similar ordeals. The polis, often mentioned as the 'ship of state', is the framework for the tragic happenings; it is saved in the end by 'Zeus and its guardian gods'; but the individual suffers the tragedy of standing between the demands of family ties and those of the polis, between past and future.[39] By accepting the inevitable, the hero attains truly tragic stature; his own free will is submerged in his destiny. This is also true of Aeschylus' greatest play, the *Agamemnon*. Personal responsibility and free will are there, in the man who killed his daughter for the common cause, in Clytaemnestra, who kills Agamemnon. Behind it, however, is the will of Zeus, and independent of either are the dark powers of ancient curse and the punishers of human crime, whether a daemon or the Erinyes. The most tragic fate, however, is suffered by those who have the foresight of what is to come, such as Cassandra or Eteocles in the *Septem*. When free choice is hardest, but equally inevitable, the human mind reaches its pinnacle, man's stature is greatest and most tragic.[40]

What is the last play of the Theban trilogy becomes frighteningly clear, and is also indicated in the political and, as it were, arbitrary justification of Orestes in the *Eumenides*, is hidden from us in the *Prometheus Bound*, which was followed by a lost play *Prometheus Liberated*. The struggle of the defiant, man-loving titan against a tyrannical Zeus will be dissolved in the future; Prometheus' redemption is foreshadowed by his own prophecy on Io, Hera's victim driven over the earth. The solution will show a different Prometheus, belonging to that ordered world, ruled over by Zeus' justice, in which the poet believed. How that happened, we do not know; what we know and see is the spectacle of a demi-god, son of Themis, who has taught mankind a civilized life; he is the creator of human communal life and its laws.[41] Suffering for his knowledge, which is greater than that of Zeus, he suffers for suffering humanity. Prometheus was the first great symbol of man's revolution, and the impact of this formidable figure and his fate was to continue throughout the centuries.

Man is bound to reach knowledge by suffering only, and man suffers because he acts. No other theme appears so frequently in Aeschylus as the inevitable connexion between action and suffering. It is the formula by which in some mysterious way the will and the rule of Zeus are bound up with man's free will. The transfer into the divine world – in reversed order – of action and suffering may have sounded strange to the audience; it is unlikely that the average Athenian shared, or even understood, such views of a poet who at the same time was a religious genius. Still, the theatre was open to the whole people, and we know how intent the Athenians were on going there. Something of those lofty thoughts will have settled in the minds of ordinary people. There was an atmosphere in which new and dangerous ideas could be born and grow, an atmosphere, a spiritual climate, full of the 'fondness of innovation' which Sparta might easily fear.

The insult which Cimon and his men had suffered was not only a blow to Athenian pride, it also meant the collapse of his foreign policy, which was based on friendship with Sparta. Almost immediately Athens went into action and concluded treaties of alliance with Sparta's two chief enemies, Argos and Thessaly (Thuc. 1, 102, 4). The war against the Messenians dragged on for some time,[42] till they were eventually forced to surrender, but allowed free departure, on condition that they never returned to the Peloponnese. Athens settled them at Naupactus, which had only recently been taken from the Ozolian Locrians; thus the Athenians gained a loyal stronghold at a place that dominated the Corinthian gulf.[43]

Athenian imperialism had been growing for a considerable time. The allies must have feared the danger of a situation which would have nothing in common with the defensive aims of the Delian league. The threat from Athens was not to be checked by the friction with Sparta; actually the first consequence was that Megara, on account of a quarrel with Corinth over some frontier land, left the Peloponnesian League and joined Athens (Thuc. 1, 103, 4), which now held Megara's two harbours, Nisaea and Pagae; the former was soon connected with Megara by long walls, while Pagae at the Corinthian gulf was of outstanding importance for the connexion with Naupactus. The succeeding years showed more Athenian expansion and even bolder adventures, a fact essentially due to the change of leaders and constitution, which followed, or coincided with, Cimon's ignominious return. At the same time, at least at Athens herself, the tendency grew of making her deeds in the past the excuse for, or rather the justification of, present politics. A symbol of this trend is the institution of official speeches on the occasions of the annual burial of those killed in war.[43a]

2 · Democracy and Dualism

Aeschylus' *Suppliants*, according to a recently published papyrus, was performed in the 'sixties.[44] The stage is set in mythical Argos, which is ruled by Pelasgus, a king of astonishingly democratic convictions and position. He and his people have to face the question, both religious and political, whether to accept as refugees the daughters of Danaus, and thus to risk a war. The question of refuge will have been in many minds, as Themistocles had been a refugee in the same Argos that was Pelasgus' city. The women of the chorus have fled from marrying their cousins, the fifty sons of Aegyptus. He and Danaus stand for the two peoples, but Aegyptus' sons are never called barbarians. The dresses of the chorus may be barbarian (234 f.), and Egypt or the Egyptian herald's voice are described by a rare synonym *karbanos*.[44a] The women's appearance is compared with that of other foreign women, an ethnographic excursus without reference to barbarians (877 ff.). If the poet avoids extending the contrast of Greeks and barbarians beyond the mere appearance, the plot may have prevented him from using the usual terms, since the women are refugees, claiming to be true Argives.

Pelasgus faces a difficult situation; he cannot act without the consent of the people, and if the central question of the play is that of asylum, its essential background is the polis as a democratic community and its constitution. Pelasgus' position is strongly contrasted with the image the chorus has of a monarch: 'Thou art the state, thou the people' (370). This is not the personal leadership of an Eteocles, but monarchy as an institution. Pelasgus refuses it: he is acting as the *prostates*, the guardian of the people, the unofficial title which was to become normal at Athens for the democratic leader.[45] Though Pelasgus has no illusions about the people's weaknesses, everything is decided by a decree of the people (601, and elsewhere), and by the voting method usual in the Athenian assembly, the show of hands (*cheirotonia*). The word *demokratia* does not occur, but time and again the fact is stressed that 'the demos rules' (*demos kratei*). That seems to show that the abstract and significant word was actually in use by then. Cleisthenes' *isonomia* had lost its half-constitutional meaning, and democracy had received its eternal name. In Aeschylus' play, as we should expect, democracy is founded on divine protection and the maintenance of divine law. A famous passage of the chorus, who want to express good wishes for Argos, mentions various future blessings, ending with the hope that the three laws, 'written on the foundation stones of justice' (701 ff.; *thesmia dikes*), may always last. They are the three rules of popular ethics, to honour the gods, parents, and strangers; sometimes they are called 'the unwritten laws', or by modern scholars 'the three Greek Commandments'.[46] In fact, they are simply traditional prescripts of polis life. Pelasgus' decision, on the other hand, to accept the suppliants, and thus rightly to set a religious duty above all political consideration, is based on the vote of the citizens (942) and a true unwritten law (946); it leads – in the later plays of the tragedy – to disaster when the suppliants murder their husbands. Perhaps 'Pelasgus was wrong to have done the right thing',[47] but the rule of the demos prevailed. Mythical Argos reflects both contemporary Argos and Athens. Democracy under the gods' blessing is the basis of both states, and Pelasgus' realm, reaching as far as the Strymon (254 f.), is a reflection of Athenian imperialism.

The play not only contains our earliest description of democracy, a democracy, as it were, in full swing, despite its mythical features; there is also a warning that pious justice may lead to a conflict with politics. Democracy was in the air when the play was performed;[48] in those years it gained power in Sicily and Cyrene (see below, p. 254) Sparta had trouble enough with the Peloponnesian democracies, and the play about democratic Argos, if the Spartans knew of it, will not have pleased them. They will meanwhile also have heard what new moves had started at Athens. They feared the Athenians, but their own mistrust only accelerated and intensified a process by which Greece was to be divided into two. Imperialism and democracy worked hand in hand against Sparta's old *prostasia* and oligarchy; the Greeks were forced into the position of taking sides, neutrality was no longer really possible, and among the ruling oligarchies of some of the allied states the fear of Athenian rule must have grown. The great division, the dualism, of the Greek world became inevitable, and if a man like Cimon had believed in an ideal of balance between the two great powers, and even some kind of Panhellenism, that had lost its meaning for a long time.

Through almost twenty years, ever since it played an important part in supervising and supporting the evacuation of Athens in 480, the ancient council on the Areopagus had been, according to Aristotle, the predominant factor in Athenian politics. The ex-archons who were its members, though no longer directly elected (see above, p. 146), belonged to the two upper income classes; their outlook was by necessity generally conservative. They caused no trouble to a man like Cimon, and whole-heartedly supported Athenian imperialism; but the prestige and influence of the Areopagus were chiefly concerned with domestic policy. We know hardly anything about the way in which such influence was exercised, and the fact that its members were no longer active politicians must have reduced that influence. Still, its prestige stood high, and Aristotle (*AP* 25, 2) even speaks of its 'additional', more recently acquired rights, which seem to have been the basis of its 'guardianship' of the state; this mainly implied the supervision of the officials.[49] The institution, with its life-long membership, had obviously become an obstacle to the development of democracy, though less on legal than on prestige grounds. Propaganda had been going on for some time against privileges assumed by the Areopagus. Under the umbrella of democracy the struggle continued between conservatives and progressives, usually called oligarchs and democrats. In 462, when Cimon was in Messenia and with him thousands of hoplites who might oppose any radical policy, attacks in the ecclesia started in earnest, under the leadership of Ephialtes, son of

Sophonides. He was an honest, if ruthless, partisan of democracy, but that is about all we know of him. Those 'additional' rights of the Areopagus were abolished, and the council of the Five Hundred, the assembly, and the popular courts shared the activities so far exercised by the Areopagus, in particular, all secular jurisdiction. Only jurisdiction bound to unchangeable religious rules, such as cases of homicide and a few minor matters, remained with the ancient council. Its political influence was reduced to a minimum.[50]

When, in 458, Aeschylus produced the *Oresteia*, he gave the Areopagus a decisive role in the last scenes of the *Eumenides*. We are in a mythical Athens where there is no king. Instead, Athena herself rules the city, and it is she who creates the council as a sacred and venerable institution (681 ff., 949), though essentially as a judicial court only for capital crime. It was supposed to be the first court of its kind in the Greek world, and its early importance in Athenian history is followed up by the homicide laws of Dracon. While admonishing the people – the people listening on the tiers – not to remove from the city 'everything awe-inspiring' (698), while reconciling 'the ancient and the new deities', Athena persuades the Erinyes to become the Eumenides and thus help in making Athens, 'as years go by' (1000), a pious and peaceful community. Athena at the same time acknowledges the work of 462 and warns against further steps in the same direction, keeping to the general and non-political principle of pious awe as well as to avoiding the political extremes of anarchy and tyranny.[51] With Athena – in contrast to Apollo – divine ethics are supreme and decide man's fate. The relation here between Athena and Apollo to some extent reflects the supremacy held by Athens at that time over the Delphic oracle. Athena is Athens, but through her voice the poet speaks himself, and it has frequently been thought not unlikely (we cannot say more) that Athena's warning refers to the idea carried out in the following year, of admitting the zeugitae to the archonship, and thus indirectly to the Areopagus. It was a move to reduce its prestige, and to 'democratize' it. Athena's general warning not to destroy that awe which prevents human crime may also refer to the right, ascribed to Solon's legislation and now no longer restricted by the Areopagus, of every citizen to act as a prosecutor; it is from this law that the race of sycophants was to derive.[52] Athena particularly abhors civil strife (861 ff.), and the chorus confirms the horror of vengeance and murder (976 ff.).

There can be little doubt that Aeschylus, who was not involved on one side or the other of the political strife, but stresses the importance of the alliance with Argos and clearly accepts the present domestic situation, is thinking of the murder of Ephialtes, which occurred soon after the move against the Areopagus, and which must have shocked a large section of the people. The murderer was a man from Tanagra, a hired killer, and behind him was an oligarchic group. Who was to continue Ephialtes' policy? His laws are once (*AP* 35, 2) connected with a certain Archestratus of whom nothing whatsoever is known. Anyway, Pericles was not his official or unofficial 'lieutenant',[53] though, if there was a successor to Ephialtes as the leader of the anti-oligarchic and anti-Spartan policy, it could, as far as we know, hardly have been anybody but Pericles, who was then in his early thirties. It is, however, by no means certain that he at once gained a position of leadership. What Plutarch (*Per.* 7) tells us about his early career is retrospective and often misleading conjecture, and Aristotle's chronology is very much at fault.[54] It is difficult indeed, on the other hand, to find a leading politician at Athens, whether democrat or oligarch, for the years, say 461 to 457. Perhaps we can assume a slowly increasing prominence of Pericles.[55] He seems to have been on fairly good terms with Cimon, although he became one of his elected prosecutors. Pericles had an Alcmaeonid mother, and Cimon a wife from the same clan, but neither of them, however much they might differ otherwise, seems ever to have made Alcmaeonid policy. It was much later that Pericles was burdened with the old Alcmaeonid crime, and that was done by Sparta. It is quite possible that the young Pericles, especially in domestic issues, used his several connexions with aristocratic families, and at first avoided constitutional questions. The people, however, would hardly have agreed for any length of time to be without a leader. We may also refer once more to the almost contemporary picture of a democratic *prostates* in Aeschylus' *Suppliants*. Democracy, though there was not a democratic 'party', needed a leader, a *demagogos*.

We can at least be sure that the new democratic measures a few years later were taken under Pericles' leadership; it is less certain

whether the adventurous expedition to Egypt in 460 was Pericles'
idea. Inarus, a ruler in Libya, revolted against Persia at a moment
when, after the murder of Xerxes, the domestic situation of Persia
and her empire had been unsettled for several years. He asked for
help from Athens, the prominent anti-Persian power. If Diodorus
(11, 71, 4) were right, Inarus offered Athens common rule over a
liberated Egypt, but even without such an unlikely offer, the Athenians might like the idea of gaining a foothold in Egypt, and thus
try to close the ring round the eastern Mediterranean. But whose
idea was it? Cimon, after his humiliation by Sparta, was ostracized
in 461. Anti-Persian strategy had been the essence of his policy,
but there is no sign that this kind of policy was not vigorously continued after he had left the scene.[56] Who then was in a position, after
Ephialtes' death, to gather the necessary votes for the ostracism, and
even for the adventurous decision on the Egyptian expedition? The
new leader of the oligarchs, Thucydides, son of Melesias, seems to
have been only building up his position in those years.[57] Athens, at
a dangerous point of her history, as we shall see, was guided, if at
all, by a man whose imperialist ambitions went even beyond
Cimon's, and who risked the position of Athens at home by pursuing a policy of a rapid progress both in power politics and in
democratization. Surely this was a young man's policy, and it is no
argument against this assumption that Pericles' policy later was
different.

The first steps to widen the gulf between Sparta and Athens had
been taken, more cautiously by the former, far more definitively
by the latter. In the *Eumenides*, that curiously political final play of
one of the greatest tragic stories, the emphasis on an alliance between Athens and Argos (287 ff., 671 f., 762 ff.), conforming with
the idea in the *Choephoroi* (1046) of Orestes liberating Argos, shows
the strong feelings of the poet, and probably also of the audience, in
favour of an anti-Spartan policy. Athenian war activities are dramatically illustrated by the war-casualty list of one single phyle,
Erechtheis, inscribed on a stele erected in 459 (or possibly 458).
'The following died in the war on Cyprus, in Egypt, in Phoenicia,
at Halieis, at Aegina, at Megara in the same year.' Then follow the
names of two strategi, one seer, one hundred and seventy hoplites
(and perhaps citizen sailors), and four archers.[58] The losses were

heavy indeed, but Erechtheis may have suffered more than other tribes, and we should not simply multiply the figure of 177 by ten for Athens as a whole.

The places mentioned in the inscription cover two different theatres of war. Cyprus, Egypt, Phoenicia – that is the result of the war against Persia and the alliance with Inarus. Thucydides (1, 104) speaks of a fleet of two hundred going to Cyprus. The inscription shows that Athens was involved in fighting there and in Phoenicia; only a section of the two hundred triremes, though probably a large one, will have gone to Egypt and begun a successful campaign, until after several years a Persian army under Megabyzus reversed the destiny of war. The expedition ended in disaster, and a relief force of fifty ships was also involved; that was probably in 454. The loss of men and ships as well as of prestige was great, though perhaps not as formidable as Thucydides (1, 110) indicates. It was not very long before military relations between Egyptian rebels and Athens were taken up again (Thuc. 112, 3), and Egyptian 'kings' were soon again active, at least in the delta.[59] Even so, the end of the great campaign was a serious setback, it reversed the success of the Eurymedon, and the immediate consequence was that the Phoenician fleet threatened again the Aegean. That was the reason, though perhaps only a pretext, for transferring the treasury of the league from Delos to Athens. There is a tradition that Samos suggested the transfer. It was also probably from Samos that about that time, if not in the same year, the cult of a new version of Athena Polias, together with that of the four Ionian tribal *eponymoi*, spread round the islands. She was called the guardian goddess (*medéousa*), which may have been one of Aphrodite's titles at Cyprus (*h. hom.* 10, 4); as Athena's new title it became popular even at Athens. Unless the movement followed Athenian imperialism, it may have been a kind of 'religious propaganda of the Delian League'.[60] The general need for Athens to strengthen the ties within the League became urgent. With the treasury in hand, Athens held the reins of inter-state power more firmly than before, and any meetings of the League council, of which we hear nothing even in previous years, were now completely abandoned.

Meanwhile important things had happened in Greece. The second group of places in the Erechtheis inscription deals with the war caused by the enmity of Corinth, an enmity largely due to the Athenian predominance over Megara. Near Halieis in the Argolis the Athenians landed, but were beaten by the Corinthians and Epidaurians; soon afterwards they defeated a Peloponnesian fleet at Cecryphalaea, between Epidaurus and Aegina (Thuc. I, 105), and again the Peloponnesians in a famous battle when Aegina itself was invaded. The Corinthians had at the same time attacked Megara, but the Athenians sent a last levy of the young and the old under Myronides, who, after a first indecisive fight, completely defeated the enemy.[61] Thucydides expressly mentions that both sides in this war had been joined by allies, that is to say, the Peloponnesian and Delian Leagues were actually at war with one another. It has become fairly common to speak of the First Peloponnesian War (459–446).

All the time the Athenians had been building the two 'Long Walls' to Phaleron and Peiraeus (Thuc. I, 107, I. 108, 3), which secured the connexion between the city and its harbours, and provided at the same time a large area of refuge for the population of Attica in case of an invasion (see map 8). Years later, after Phaleron ceased to be a harbour of any importance, a third wall was built between the two to strengthen the direct connexion with the Peiraeus.[62] Athens, even more definitely than before, was a maritime city. That also implied a considerable strengthening of the democratic forces, and Pericles proved to be a deliberate follower of Themistoclean policy.

It is justifiable to speak of an almost feverish Athenian activity in these years. If we take it at the highest level, it can perhaps be explained by a will to power based on the genuine conviction of having to fulfil a task given to Athens, and to Athens alone, a task that would give greatness and prosperity to the Greek world in general, and to Athens in particular. Almost certainly in 458–457 a treaty of alliance was concluded even with the Elymian town of Egesta (Segesta) in western Sicily; ever afterwards the domination of Sicily was in the Athenian mind among its political aims. There was not one reason alone which increased the tension among the Greeks, but a complex combination of political, economic, and also religious forces, with Athens as their chief, though not their only source. Obviously Sparta could not simply let things go on without displaying some of her old strength.[63] We know very little of the particular aims and means of Spartan policy, but we can assume that much of her hesitancy was due not only to the innate character of the people but also to the lack of determined leadership and the differences of political opinion, especially in foreign policy, among kings and ephors. The best-known example of such a clash was to

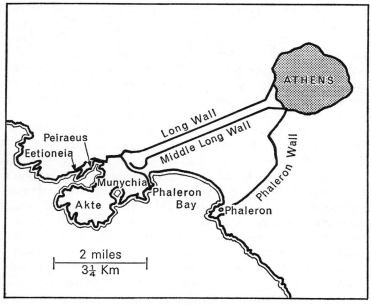

8. Athens and her Harbours

occur just before the outbreak of the Peloponnesian war (Thuc. I, 79 ff. 86). Meanwhile, when the Phocians, who were generally on the side of Athens, attacked the Doris and took one of its small cities, an army of Spartans and Peloponnesians rushed to help their 'motherland', and compelled the Phocians to withdraw (Thuc. I, 107, 2). The army had crossed the Corinthian Gulf; the transports will have returned, probably to Corinth, before Athens sent a fleet to cut them off. It is certain that the Spartans intended to do more than to intervene in a quarrel in central Greece.[64] They entered

Boeotia, where they renewed the alliance with Thebes, although it then had a democratic constitution; Athens was threatened by the restoration of a united state in Boeotia. Moreover, it became known that the Spartans were in touch with a number of Athenian exiles who were prepared to submit to Sparta in order to destroy democracy and its new source of strength, the Long Walls, even before they were completed.

The Athenians, still engaged in Egypt and Aegina, met the threat with greatest determination. They marched out in full strength to meet the enemy, supported by a thousand Argives and other allies.[65] One of the chief reasons for quick offensive action was the fear that democracy might be overthrown if the Peloponnesians invaded Attica.[66] At Tanagra, where the enemy held the Asopus line, the armies met (457 B.C.). Athenian aristocrats, eager to prove their patriotism in view of the traitors on the other side, were foremost in the fighting and many were killed; but the day belonged to the Peloponnesians after the Thessalian cavalry changed sides. It is difficult to find sense in the contradictory attitudes of Greek aristocrats and democrats, though mistrust of Athens was a strong force. Losses on both sides during the battle were heavy, but the Spartan commander made no use of his tactical victory; he marched home, devastating the Megarid on the way. Thus he deserted the Boeotians, and Athens, her courage unbroken, seized the opportunity. Only two months later another Athenian army under Myronides marched out and defeated the Boeotians at Oenophyta, probably not far from Tanagra. All Boeotia, apart from Thebes, as well as Phocis joined Athens, and the Opuntian Locrians were forced into submission. This was more than a tactical victory; the Athenians were masters of most of central Greece, masters of a land empire as well as of a naval one, and Myronides remained in Athenian memory as one of their great leaders.

There is a tradition (Theopompus, *FGrH* 115 F 88) that Cimon, on Pericles' instigation, was recalled after Tanagra, but the facts speak against it. Neither foreign nor domestic policy was changed. The war against Sparta, and especially against Corinth, was now waged by naval expeditions, the first round the Peloponnese under Tolmides (456–455); he burnt down the harbour installations at Gytheion and won new allies in western Greece. Aegina, after a long siege, was captured and became a member of the Delian League with a high tribute. After the failure of the Egyptian expedition, the treasury, as already mentioned, was moved from Delos to Athens, a more than symbolic action, in fact, a really great opportunity, in the direction of turning the Delian League into an Athenian empire.[66a]

It has become usual to speak of an empire into which the league of 477 gradually changed in the 'fifties and 'forties. The expression is convenient, and I sometimes use it myself; but it is to some extent misleading. There was no longer an alliance of independent states, but there was never a unified state with, say, overseas provinces and a full central organization, nor was there ever a colonial empire in the modern sense.[67] The Greeks spoke of 'rule' (*archē*). The earlier 'hegemony' as a free leadership of free states, especially in war, turned into a system in which increasingly by various means, sometimes not without the collaboration of the local demos, the 'allies' became 'subjects'. Though that was never legally nor completely brought about, the rule of Athens was established by garrisons, tributes, Athenian inspectors, the presence of the Athenian navy, various decrees imposing political or economic or jurisdictional dependence, and possibly the introduction of a democratic constitution in the allied state. The intermingling of democratic and imperialist policies created an atmosphere in which neither the democrats in the cities could whole-heartedly accept Athenian rule nor their opponents easily stage revolts. It was an atmosphere of war or near-war. At the same time the rule of Athens had now only one sacred centre, Athens and her goddess on the Acropolis, though that did not mean that the Athenians were trying to found an 'Attic amphictyony'.[68] Peace among the allies was a natural supposition. It was secured and enforced by the Athenian fleet, and that alone – and the resulting economic advantages – sufficed to keep the league going. If the allies just like the colonists contributed to the Attic festivals, that signified the religious basis which any political organization among the Greeks was bound to have. Athens was the flourishing centre of a political as well as an economic empire; her people – on all levels – shared in the growing wealth, and the numbers of metics and slaves increased.

In 453–452 a campaign to punish Thessaly, though supported by

Boeotia and Phocis, was a failure, while Pericles made a naval expedition into the Corinthian Gulf, which was at least partly successful. It is the first time that Pericles is mentioned by Thucydides (1, 111). The son of Xanthippus and an Alcmaeonid mother was now the most important political leader in Athens. He clearly continued the domestic policy of Ephialtes. Among the measures taken in the 'fifties was, as already mentioned, the admission of the zeugitae to the archonship (457–456; AP 26, 2); they had so far only served in the lower offices. This was not a revolutionary action, for the archons were figureheads rather than an effective board; but it gave to a much larger section of the people the honour of what was still regarded in the public mind as the highest office. Not much later, pure if double sortition of the archons must have been introduced in the place of 'sortition from pre-elected' (klerosis ek prokriton). Henceforth all magistrates except the military ones were appointed by lot, and (as stressed before; see p. 98) that was by no means as senseless as people sometimes thought it to be. Combined with the principle of non-iteration in office, i.e. rotation among large numbers of citizens, and an ever-increasing number of administrative boards, sortition secured the participation in administration and government of a very large part of the citizen population. Outstanding among the 'offices' was the council of the Five Hundred; though a man could become its member twice in a lifetime, its composition followed the same radical principles. The Athenians avoided both powerful magistrates and a bureaucracy, while they found their political leaders among the strategi. Most other magistrates, with the help of slaves or freedmen as secretaries, did chiefly routine work. As long as assembly and council were able to make sensible major decisions, and as long as responsible leaders were elected, the price paid by the chance of sortition was not too high.[69]

Some magistrates, and especially the Areopagus, had been responsible for a great deal of jurisdiction. Now the popular courts, the dikasteria, took over, and the number of courts as well as their members went up with the increasing amount of litigation; the latter was largely caused by the rapidly growing intensity of economic life, especially of trade, also by the trend, soon to be legalized, of transferring the more important legal cases from the allied states to Athens. Ps. Xenophon (1, 17) gives an amusing description of the minor advantages of that move for the Athenians. One law on jurisdiction is dated (453–452; AP 26, 3), the revival of Peisistratus' thirty travelling rural judges, perhaps abolished by Cleisthenes. Apart from travelling about, they decided petty cases in each deme, up to the value of ten drachmae. Later their number was raised to forty. These deme judges were, of course, a blessing for the rural population; at the same time they served as a relief for the overburdened city courts. For these had not only to deal with litigation but also to decide on the legal qualifications of all office holders (*dokimasiai*), and to prosecute those whose examination at the end of their term of office (*euthynai*) had been unsatisfactory.

How many of the courts that existed later were introduced in this period, and whether their numbers were already as large as in the fourth century, we do not know; but there can be no doubt that a vast number of citizens was engaged in daily public business, in particular in the courts whose members were jurors and judges at the same time. It proved necessary to give them some compensation for their loss of time and income. Pericles therefore introduced a moderate daily payment of two obols (third of a drachme) for the *dikastai* (*AP* 27, 3 f.). The measure was attacked by his opponents as an attempt at winning popular favour, possibly even in order to counteract Cimon's wealth and generosity. That is obvious propaganda, but the fact remains that, however necessary, it proved the thin end of the wedge. Payment for public service was soon extended to the members of the council and to most officials. It enabled the poorer classes and the peasants to attend state business. We cannot say how swiftly and to what extent the social composition of the council and the boards of officials actually changed, though it is fairly clear that among the large numbers of jurors the lower classes soon were the majority. When more and more political decisions were going to be made in the courts, the way was prepared for the rule of the masses, in both ecclesia and courts. This means at the same time that the frontier zone between legislation and jurisdiction grew narrow and vague, a fact which led to an increasing part being played by professional informers, the sycophants. In the long run it destroyed the very basis of the polis as a state founded on law. Aristotle (*AP* 9, 1), speaking of Solon, but from a fourth-

century viewpoint, could say, 'When the people are the master of
the vote (in the courts), they are the master of the state.'

For the time being, however, assembly and council remained the
ruling bodies. Within the law, and since the demos could always
give new rules even above the law, the people was king. All essential questions, such as foreign and empire policy, not forgetting all
matters of state cult, were decided by the assembly; so were financial matters, but never without previous advice from the council.
If we consider that there were always several thousands assembled
on the Pynx, the hill where the ecclesia met, and that for some decisions a quorum of 6,000 was needed, we realize that the supreme
power of such a large assembly had to be controlled and directed.
That was generally done by the council of the Five Hundred, the
only political council left after 462, elected by sortition from all parts
of Attica and also subject to the principle of rotation – a committee,
as it were, of the people. Divided into ten prytanies, according to
the ten tribes, which served in turn during the year, the fifty prytans did all the current work of co-ordination and administration,
including the all-important financial supervision. The main task of
the full council was to provide a *probouleuma*, a preparatory draft, for
every important decision of the people. The latter could accept or
reject, but also alter a *probouleuma*; they could even demand that the
council would submit one on a particular subject, though in general
the council's advice prevailed.

The co-operation of assembly and council was to a large extent
due to the leadership of Pericles, not only to his person but above all
to the institution of the *strategia*. Ever since the archons were no
longer elected by direct election, i.e. since 487–486, the part played
by the ten generals had grown in political importance. With the
exception of the secretary of each prytany, the strategi were the
only important officials who were elected and could be re-elected
for an indefinite number of years; thus they were free from the duty
of rendering annual accounts. Primarily a military job, the office
was soon open to non-military men, though very few would have
no military qualifications at all. A board of ten, normally one from
each tribe, they were equal in theory, though it was quite usual for
one of them to hold a leading position; Miltiades in 490 is the earliest
example. Later in the century we know of cases where a leading

figure like Pericles was elected together with another man of the same phyle; he was chosen from the whole people.[70] Politically, a strategos would exercise his influence by personal appearance in council or assembly. Naturally he had to be a good speaker. Probably during these years, free speech, *isegoria*, as Herodotus once calls Athenian democracy (5, 78), or *parrhesia*, probably introduced at the time of Cleisthenes (if not by Solon), became a political necessity. While the number of regular assemblies held during the year increased (from ten finally to forty), the principle that any ordinary citizen was allowed to speak in the ecclesia must have been not only proclaimed but also practised (cf. Plat. *Protag.* 319d). It is doubtful whether a special law or decree was needed to do that. It will have become possible – though surely very rare – for the president of the prytans (*epistates*), who was also president of the assembly, to admit anybody, and not only the members of the upper class, to take part in a discussion.[71] Athenian democracy was based on free speech, as is said in the Funeral Speech (Thuc. 2, 40): 'In our view it is not words that impede action, rather the lack of knowledge learned beforehand by discussion.' Whether the people always followed the most sensible speaker is, of course, another question; frequently it was the last speaker rather than the best one. Anyway, the development of Greek rhetoric is closely connected with that of political leadership. The day was not far off when politicians were simply called 'orators'.

On an earlier occasion we noticed the connexion between democracy and navy. No doubt the part the thetes played as oarsmen gave them a political weight they had never had before. However, the more important navy and sea-power became, the more involved were the whole people. Not only were the thetes not alone in manning the ships (there were also hoplites, metics and exceptionally even slaves), but sea-power was also the basis of the flourishing Athenian trade, commerce, and to some extent of agriculture. In the assembly the urban middle and lower classes were generally the most numerous group, and though they included many thetes, the 'naval crowd' must frequently have been absent from Athens.[72]

It is important to realize that this was one of the factors which for the time being prevented democracy from becoming 'radical'. There was no urban proletariat; the majority of the assembly or the courts

were *petits bourgeois*, craftsmen, traders and peasants, who generally
were keen on, and proud of, doing their public duties. For the smooth
working of this democracy, it was essential that most of the strategi
should still be elected from the noble and wealthy families. A firm
tradition was established, while members of the middle classes gradually got used to political responsibility. Those upper-class families
were another factor working against sudden radicalism, since they
clung firmly to the sacred traditions, even if some of their leaders
personally tended to take a secular attitude. The noble 'guardians
of the people', on the other hand, a Cimon, a Pericles, knew well
enough that they could be deposed, i.e. not re-elected, by the demos.
There was never any danger either then or later that a *strategos*
might turn tyrant.

In 451–450 a five years' truce was concluded between Athens and
Sparta (Thuc. 1, 112, 1), and in the same year a thirty years' peace
treaty between Sparta and Argos (Thuc. 5, 14, 4. 28, 2). What the
connexion was between the two moves, we do not know, though
there must have been some. The political somersault by Argos is
most remarkable; it will have been caused by disillusion with the
self-centred policy of Athens. Cimon had returned from exile; the
tradition that he was recalled because he was to help Athens to come
to terms with Sparta is probably untrue. Anyway, Greece badly
needed a breathing space, the more so as it seemed necessary to
oppose certain Persian moves. The end of the Egyptian campaign
had led to increased dissatisfaction among the allies, especially in
Caria and Ionia, where they again felt threatened by Persia. It seems
possible to conclude from the absence of some states from the tribute lists that they had ceased to pay.[73] Athens had to regain her
absolute rule over the Aegean. Cimon sailed to Cyprus with a strong
fleet, and even sent a detachment to Egypt in support of some rebel
ruler in the delta (Thuc. 1, 112, 2 ff.). While Citium was under siege,
Cimon died, but shortly afterwards the Athenians won a decisive
victory near Salamis on Cyprus, and the way was now open for
peace with Persia, a peace badly needed by Athens to secure her
position at home and in the Aegean.

We have an inscription (*ML*, no. 44) which shows that Athens
decided to introduce a priestess for life of Athena Nike, and to build
a temple to the goddess. That was after the Peace of Callias (prob-

ably in 449) had been concluded. The peace treaty is mentioned only in later sources, but modern research has made it as likely as possible that peace was officially restored at that time.[74] Whether a formal treaty was concluded is another question. The essential point of the agreement between Athens and Persia, if we may believe some of the later sources, was a definite separation of the spheres of military action and interest. The Aegean sea became a forbidden area to the Persian fleet; Phaselis and its surroundings were the limit in the south and the Bosporus in the north; Cyprus was back in Persian hands, and so, of course, was Egypt. If it is true that on land a neutral zone of three days march from the shore was established, it freed the Greek cities in Asia from Persian garrisons; the latter must have happened at any rate. The treaty was a compromise, and not a victory for Athens as it was regarded there; but it gave the Athenians the chance to fight the threats nearer home, and to emerge eventually as the great centre of culture. If anything proves the existence of established peace, it is the activity of Athens in the following years.

Among Pericles' measures of domestic policy even before the peace was one of particular significance, though difficult to explain. In 451–450 a law was accepted confining Athenian citizenship to those whose parents had both been Athenians (*ex amphoin astoin*. AP 26, 3. Plut. *Per*. 37, 3).[75] Aristotle says of this measure, which at first glance looks very undemocratic, that it was caused by the increase of citizens. That is probably only a guess. Was there, in view of the rapidly growing number of metics (resident foreigners) and slaves, any sense in limiting the ruling people to a relatively small minority? Did not Athens need more rather than fewer citizens in her ambitious struggle against the Peloponnesians and the extension of her rule? Could it be, on the other hand, a move to reduce the number of those who were to be paid by the state, and thus to please the egotist instincts of the masses?[76] It seems certain that the law was not generally retrospective nor was it immediately put into effect. It seems even more certain that it was directed only against sons of marriages between Athenian men and foreign women (*metroxenoi*); the opposite would hardly occur. It is a curious coincidence that Cimon, who was the son of a foreign mother, had recently returned from exile. Was there a connexion between his return and the new law? Modern views differ.[77] Perhaps it is more important to find out how the law fitted into Pericles' democracy.

It was in those years that Athens started sending out cleruchies on a larger scale. Cleruchies and colonies chiefly served to control the empire as well as to improve the economic standards of the lower classes, and to provide places where ships could stop in order to take on water and other supplies.[78] No doubt most of the colonists, who only exceptionally would be 'absentee landlords', belonged to the lower classes. There was no need to restrict their numbers by a special law. In fact, intermarriage with non-Athenian women had been fairly frequent only in the upper classes. The poorer people would have found it very hard to marry, or even to meet, foreign women apart from slaves; possibly some naval expedition or cleruchy might create an opportunity. However, the number of people concerned cannot have been large, and the immediate legal effects must have been negligible. More likely, the law was a weapon, or perhaps only the threat of a weapon, in the internal struggle against the oligarchs. There was Cimon, who probably died shortly afterwards; there was Thucydides, son of Melesias, who was probably married to Cimon's sister, and thus his children would descend from a foreign woman.[79] There will have been others. In those years, when Pericles was pursuing the most determined policy both at home and abroad, he met with the strong opposition of the aristocracy; the law on citizenship was most likely directed against them.

In spring 453 Cratinus, the 'father' of Old Comedy, and three years later Crates, gained their first victories on the stage. Fun and satire had reached full stature. In a far more realistic, though less elevated and spiritual manner than in tragedy, politics and politicians could now be openly discussed and ridiculed. Reality and fantasy are inseparably mixed in comedy, a mixture particularly suitable to an audience largely composed of ordinary people, well acquainted with the traditions of Dionysiac exhilaration as well as the troubles of day-to-day life. Aeschylus had recently died in Sicily; Sophocles had produced a number of plays and was soon to write his great tragedies; Euripides was learning his craft. Painting flourished. With Anaxagoras and Protagoras philosophical teaching had entered Athens. It is necessary to keep such facts in mind, at least as the background to an increasingly self-centred and harsh policy.

The story of the late fifties and early forties is the story of a crisis in the Athenian empire, largely, though not exclusively, caused by the disappearance of the Persian menace through the Peace of Callias. The allies no longer felt they needed Athenian protection. Thucydides (1, 112–15) mentions the main revolts and their consequences, and a number of inscriptions tell us about Athenian policy towards her allies.[80] Both Athens and Sparta maintained the truce, but indirect clashes were inevitable. It all started again with a 'Sacred War', when Sparta first freed Delphi from Phocian rule, and soon afterwards the latter was restored by Athens. This, however, caused a revolt of Boeotia, in the course of which an army of Athenians and allies under Tolmides was completely destroyed at Coronea (447); no Boeotians were any longer subject to Athenian power. There followed revolts in Euboea and Megara. A Peloponnesian army invaded Attica, but its leader, the Spartan king Pleistoanax, a son of Pausanias, withdrew again, and was later charged with having been bribed; it may be that he was sent out to help Megara, but was to avoid battle with the Athenians, since the period of truce had not yet come to an end, and that later the event looked rather different. Megara nevertheless changed sides again and became one of the most determined enemies of Athens, but Pericles was able to concentrate on the all-important Euboea which he conquered. The land-owning aristocracy of Chalcis was expelled; otherwise both Chalcis and Eretria were treated leniently (see below), while the people of Histiaea in the north of the island were driven out and replaced by Athenian cleruchs; Plutarch (*Per.* 23) mentions as the reason for the severe treatment of Histiaea that they had killed the crew of an Athenian ship; moreover, more land was needed for cleruchs. Anyway, though Euboea was recovered, the attempt at establishing Athenian rule over central Greece, and cutting off Sparta from her connexion with Boeotia, was over, and Athens, abandoning any foothold she still had in the Peloponnese, no longer aimed at a land empire. Sparta, back again as the strongest power on land, was willing to acknowledge Athens as the head of her sea empire. Only for Aegina, autonomy was specially stipulated, though she remained a tribute-paying member of the Athenian alliance. On this basis peace was concluded in 446–445 for thirty years, which, according to the standards of the time, was as long a fixed period as conceivable.[81] It was actually to last for less than fifteen years, and its real result was the complete division of Greece. On either side the allies were firmly bound to the leading state. They, on the other hand, accepted arbitration in cases of disagreement. The dualism in the Greek world was finally established on a balance of power between the aristocratic land power and the democratic naval one; it determined Greek politics till the end of the Great War, and even beyond it.[81a]

About this time, probably a few years earlier, Pericles had issued a decree, to be sent by special envoys to all Greek states, that a Panhellenic congress should be held at Athens (*Plut.* 17 = *ATL* D 12).[82] Its objects were to restore the temples burnt by the Persians, to establish the sacrifices vowed to the gods in 480, and to secure the freedom of the seas. The plan came to nothing, because Sparta opposed it, understandably enough, as the true purpose of the congress was clearly a *Pax Atheniensis*. The Peloponnese had no interest in paying for the rebuilding of temples which would all be outside their territory and, in fact, included little else than damage done in Attica. Still less were they willing to confirm the freedom of the seas, guaranteed and policed by the Athenian navy. Pericles' Panhellenism was to serve the greater glory of Athens, but his general desire for peace was genuine, influenced as it was by the troubles the Athenians had with their allies, and the increased activity of Persia in Asia Minor.

To illustrate this we shall briefly discuss a few of the relevant inscriptions.[83] The most general one is the decree of Cleinias (*ATL* D 7. *ML*, no. 46), according to which the tributes of the allied states were to be collected more strictly by several Athenian officials; moreover, all the allies were requested to send 'a cow and a panoply' to the Great Panathenaea, as previously only colonies had done. This could still be called a privilege, though it concerned a purely Athenian festival; it was part of that religious propaganda we have mentioned before. However, it was imposed with the threat of the same penalty as for the failure to pay the tribute. Ever since peace with Persia had been established, the allies were bound to ask why they should still pay their tribute, and Athens was at pains to enforce, if not to justify, the continuation of the payments. There was little left of the autonomy of the allies, and the rule of Athens was firmly established. The date of the Cleinias decree has been much discussed,[84] and the same is true of that of Clearchus, the 'coinage decree' (*ML*, no. 45. *ATL* D 14; cf. *SEG* 24, no. 2), of which fragments were found at various places. However the epigraphists may finally decide, if at all, on the dates of the two decrees, these bear witness to the harsh and strict Athenian rule, to Athens as the mistress of an 'empire'. Clearchus' decree imposes Athenian coinage, weights, and measures on all allied cities. The local mints are to be closed, and local coins are to be changed at Athens into Athenian money. As usual, penalties are threatened, and a copy of the decree was to be set up in each city – if not by the cities themselves, then by Athens. The decree continued an economic policy which put the resources of the allies more and more at the disposal of Athens; unity was to become uniformity which was probably also required for the administration of the treasury. There may have been some economic advantages for the allies as well, but many were clearly reluctant to lose the most significant symbol of political autonomy, and Samos, for instance, defied the coinage decree.[84a]

Earlier decrees show a similar tendency in the relations with individual cities, such as that which dealt with Erythrae in Asia Minor.[85] Its date is uncertain, and so is much of the text. But it is possible to understand the chief points, and they are of the utmost importance, because the decree is certainly the earliest of its kind. The first section after the prescript deals with religious duties for the Erythraeans, in particular with contributions to the Panathenaea; this is a precedent to the general rule in the Cleinias decree, though less harsh. A second part (vv. 7–19) contains regulations about a new council of 120 members who must be natives and over thirty years of age; they will be appointed by sortition and will hold office for four years. This council is like a smaller copy of the Athenian model; it is significant that the (Athenian) inspectors and the phrurarch, the commander of the Athenian garrison, are responsible for the first sortition; even in future the latter will act together with the existing council, so that Athens always has her finger in local politics. Rules about the taking of an oath and the oath itself follow. The councillors swear to serve the people of Erythrae, of Athens, and of the allies, and not to harbour any fugitives fleeing to the Persians, without permission by the Athenian council and the demos of Erythrae. Finally, penal laws are fixed, prescribing exile outside 'the whole Athenian alliance'. The Erythraeans promise not to desert to the enemy, and the death penalty, extended as it often is to the descendants,[86] is pronounced for anyone betraying the city to the tyrants (vv. 29–37). Erythrae had seceded under pressure from the Persians, who tried to install a tyrant. Now after Athens had forced the city back into the alliance and under her control, a democratic constitution was imposed, which does not exclude the possibility that there had been a democracy before, and that Athens had intervened to help the suppressed democrats.[87]

Some time later, perhaps in 447–46, it was the turn of Colophon (*ML*, no. 47. *SEG* 25, no. 13). The quota lists seem to indicate that the city had not paid tribute for several years. The decree, of which only a section can be restored, mentions 'settlers', probably Athenian colonists, not a commission of 'founders'.[88] Colophon was one of a number of colonies or cleruchies, all founded in the forties. The whole move, as has been said before, served the *land-hunger* of the poorer people at Athens, and at the same time helped against the spreading of dissent and revolt among the allies, who had to provide land for the colonists and therefore usually got a reduction of their tribute. The Colophonians took an oath to act as best they could for the good of Athens and her allies, and never to secede from the Athenian demos. 'And I shall be a friend to the demos of the Athenians, I shall not desert it, nor destroy democracy at Colophon.' The usual assurances follow. Neither Persia nor a tyrant are mentioned, but colony and oath show that the situation had looked precarious. The promise of friendship (*philia*) refers to the usual peaceful relations between city-states, as for instance, insisted upon by the Melians, but regarded as a sign of weakness by the Athenians (Thuc. 5, 94 ff.). The impression remains that Athens could not rely on the Colophonian demos, and friendship seemed rather an enforced sentiment.

The revolt of Euboea was followed by decrees concerning Eretria and Chalcis (*ATL* D 16. 17. *ML*, no. 52. *DSDA* nos. 154. 155). Of the former only a fragment is extant, but as we learn from the practically complete Chalcis decree (v. 42), the other one served as a model for the mutual oaths; the fragment does not teach us anything more. The Chalcis decree, on the other hand, is of the greatest significance and deserves more detailed treatment. A short prescript is followed by the oath, taken by 'the council and the courts at Athens' (vv. 4–16). They swear to abstain from any kind of punishment without trial either of the state of Chalcis or of any individual, and promise 'as far as possible' not to delay the hearing of envoys for more than ten days.[89] However, 'I shall uphold this oath to the Chalcidians, as long as they obey the Athenian demos.' The strategi are made responsible to see that all concerned will take the oath. We first ask: why *boulē* and *dikastai*? Some scholars have assumed that they simply represent the people; but an oath by the members of the assembly would have been at least as easy to administer. Moreover, at the end of the paragraph on the main punishments, we read 'without the demos of the Athenians', that is to say, the people remain sovereign even to the extent that under certain conditions they can override the oath; that is why they could not take the oath themselves. It is the only time we know of Athens binding herself to an ally by an oath, and that oath is certainly not worthless; in most cases the binding of council and courts would suffice, but a loophole has been kept open.[90]

The oath of the Chalcidians follows (vv. 21–39), with the usual promises of loyalty; they will pay the tribute 'to which they can persuade the Athenians to agree', and they promise to be obedient allies. All adult Chalcidians are to take the oath, and strong penalties threaten those who evade it. Obedience rather than friendship is the decisive word, although the Athenian attitude is not openly aggressive. However mutual the oaths, their balance is clearly one-sided. An amendment moved at the same meeting of the assembly (vv. 40–69) deals with procedure, but also refuses to change the present position of the Chalcidian hostages held by Athens. Then follows a sentence, which has caused much discussion, about 'the foreigners at Chalcis' who do not pay taxes to Athens and those who have been given freedom from taxes there; all the rest are to pay taxes at Chalcis like the Chalcidians. The foreigners will have been Athenian cleruchs, also some other privileged persons, and they were to be saved from double taxation.[91] Finally, a rider to the amendment (vv. 70–79) adds that Chalcidian officials are to be judged by Chalcidian courts, except for cases involving exile, death, or loss of citizenship, which are to be transferred to the heliaea at Athens, over which the thesmothetae presided.[92] Thus, any 'polical' case would be decided by an Athenian court.

The decree was originally preceded by a treaty, no longer extant, between the two states; it is alluded to in the text (vv. 49, 76). That shows that our decree is no mere dictate, and that the autonomy of Chalcis was formally upheld. But behind a fairly smooth façade there was all the time the imperial will of Athens, and that means that of Pericles. He was a much younger man than the one Thucydides admired, and his ambition, though for Athens rather than for himself, was not yet restrained by misfortune and advanced years. The decree, together with that on Eretria, reflects an important moment in the history of Athenian rule. It was the last time before the thirty years peace that a city had to submit. There were still troubles to come, but it can be said that the crisis of the empire was over – for the time being. Athens was free for those things no other community could perform.

3 · The Age of Pericles

Ever since Thucydides wrote Pericles' Funeral Speech, and Plutarch his eulogist Life of Pericles,[93] and again since nineteenth-century liberalism, especially George Grote, discovered its ideal predecessor in ancient Athens, Pericles and his times have been regarded as the very fulfilment of human endeavour and cultural harmony. More recently a reaction has set in and scholars have tried to see that period in a more realistic light, and if the pendulum has sometimes swung to the other extreme – as, in fact, it had already done with Plato's bitter criticism[94] – this is, in view of the widespread and popular idealization, a healthy move. The greatness of the man and his age will emerge even more convincingly if shadows show off the light, and men of flesh and blood replace the pale idols of pure harmony and perfection.[95]

To call an era that of Pericles had been an early device. Our sources are inclined to limit it to the years when Pericles was the practically unopposed ruler of Athens, that is to say, from the ostracism of Thucydides, son of Melesias (443), till Pericles' death (429), or at least to the outbreak of the Peloponnesian war (431). But the erection of the Parthenon was started in 447, and its planning must have begun at least two years earlier. It seems impossible not to include the Parthenon in the Periclean age, and it is obvious that its time limits are by no means clearly fixed. More important still is another aspect of the whole concept of that Periclean age. When we use the phrase we try to indicate that the man shaped his time, politically as well as culturally. That is, at any rate, an ambiguous concept, and from our ancient evidence the figure of Pericles emerges as that of a wise and strong-minded statesman, a great an even clever political leader, a wonderful and persuasive orator; but very little is said about any involvement in the artistic and intellectual life of his time.

The peace of 446–445 had given both sides a free hand within their own spheres of power. It was a pact of non-aggression which removed the fear of a renewal of war from the mind of most people, though the Greek situation was by no means so tranquil that a future war seemed impossible. It is true that both Sparta and Athens during these years strengthened their power, but at least for some time it was not a deliberate preparation for a new war. Thucydides (1, 18, 3) speaks with the knowledge of what happened in 431. Pericles, at any rate, while intent on securing the position, and extending the power, of Athens, at the same time aimed at making Athens a paragon of beauty and culture. The question how to finance this became urgent indeed. Enormous sums were spent on buildings, both religious and profane, on festivals, and cult. The wealthy had a large share in these expenses, though we may doubt whether it was always quite voluntarily that they took over the various forms of 'liturgy' (trierarchy, choregy, gymnasiarchy, and others); often enough, nomination by a magistrate or even free choice may have happened under the pressure of public opinion. Above all, however, it was the allies, more than ever, who felt the pinch. The organization of Athenian rule was strengthened when, in the late 'forties, the whole realm was divided into five districts, Thrace, Hellespont, Ionia, Caria, and islands. It would be a mistake to speak of provinces; they were hardly more than subdivisions for the purpose of collecting the tributes. The cause of the allies was taken up by the oligarchic and anti-imperialist conservatives whose strong and active leader was Thucydides, son of Melesias. He was the political heir to Cimon, perhaps his brother-in-law, but as far as we can see, he was a very different kind of person, much more of a politician.[96] The situation too was different. Friendship, or at least peaceful relations, with Sparta was no longer an urgent issue, and for the time being, Greek dualism calmed down to a balance of power. What now was at stake was the survival of Athenian aristocracy, and at the same time the situation of the allies. They, soon to be called 'subjects', were suppressed and exploited, and therefore very discontented, while Athens, with dangerous optimism and egotism, seemed to waste their and her own money on public salaries, temples and other buildings, and similar 'democratic' achievements. She was 'like a shameless woman with her precious stones, her statues, and her 1,000-talent temples' (Plut. 12, 2). Thucydides seems to have been the man to take a strong line; he organized his followers, most of them probably members of hetaeriae, into something like a political party, and fought Pericles in the assembly as hard as he could. It is more than doubtful whether he ever was *strategos*, and Aristotle (*AP* 28, 2. 5) mentions him only as one of the outstanding oligarchic leaders.

During these years Sophocles produced his *Aias*. It is a matter of recent dispute to what extent it might be possible to see in the tragedy of Ajax and the magnanimity of Odysseus a reflection of contemporary political strife, or, on the other hand, to find in characters such as Teucer and Tecmessa a protest against Pericles' law of 451–450.[97] Such theories actually neglect the main issue of the play, or rather the two issues of its two halves: the tragedy of the man who is the victim of his own pride, the aristocratic individual thrown into the conflict between the genuine tradition of his nobility and the 'modern' world of bourgeois morality, and, on the other hand, the problem of burial as a test for the ancient sacred laws versus tyrannical and rationalist egotism. On simpler lines, the main issue of the *Antigone* was anticipated. In a general way the *Aias* did reflect the struggles, in fact, the spiritual revolution, of the time, also the teaching of Protagoras (see below, p. 340) in the use of antithetic speeches; it equally reflected the hatred of war by ordinary people (chorus, 1185 ff.), but that is all we dare say. There is no pro- or anti-Periclean tendency in the *Aias*, though the poet's intense participation in the spiritual, and to some extent also the political, world around him is manifest.

The son of Melesias put up a good fight against Pericles, but it was either (depending on our point of view) premature or a rear-guard action; it ended in his ostracism (443). For the next fifteen years, according to Plutarch (16, 3), Pericles was the unopposed leader of the state; he was elected *strategos* year by year, and therefore never had to give account for the past year, as all officials had to do.

Shortly before Thucydides' ostracism an enterprise was carried out which had been under preparation for several years, the sending out under Athenian leadership of a Panhellenic colony to Italy to resettle the people of Sybaris, which had been destroyed by Croton for the second time.[98] The survivors had sought help in Sparta and Athens; Sparta refused, Athens accepted. The plan followed aims similar to those of Pericles' proposal for a Panhellenic congress; earlier alliances with western cities (see below, p. 256) tended in the same direction. The decisive idea was to make Athens the leading state of an all-Greek enterprise, the true *prostates Hellados*. The aims had by now become more modest and more realistic, but the spirit was the same. Men from all over Greece joined, though officially no other state took part. A small expedition seems to have gone out in 446–45 and founded a 'third' Sybaris, but shortly afterwards that city broke up, and what followed was the foundation of Thurii near the old site of Sybaris. With all means of propaganda, oracles, and special soothsayers (the *Thouriomanteis* of comedy), the enterprise was introduced, and various great men shared in it, men such as Hippodamus, who did the town-planning, and Protagoras, who wrote the laws for the new state. There was also the prophet and politician Lampon, a partisan of Pericles. Politics and religion, progressive and conservative forces went hand in hand, but both were clearly and exclusively Athenian; the Delphic Apollo had no say in this all-Greek colony.

The foundation of Thurii was an outcome of Pericles' imperialist policy. With Hippodamus and Protagoras, the new colony reflected the rationalist and 'modern' approach, equally characteristic of Pericles; but the more conservative forces were not entirely excluded. At the same time great building activity was in full swing, above all, the monumental gateway of the Propylaea and the temple which was to shelter Pheidias' gold-ivory statue of the goddess. Through the Propylaea to the old temple of Athena and the Parthenon would move the procession of the Panathenaea, the central feature of the festival to the glory of Athena and Athens.[99] It was this glory, and not a deeper religious feeling, that inspired those great new buildings. No other power, no oracle, no god was allowed to sanction Pericles' enterprises, and if we should hesitate to speak of any personal desire for glory, as far as Pericles was concerned, he certainly did everything possible, and even impossible, for the greatness of Athens. Even more decisively, and of course much more lastingly, than by her imperialist policy, Athens gained a unique position by her intellectual and artistic brilliance. Wherever centres of culture arose in the Greek world as, for example, in the west, the spiritual prevalence of Athens was beyond any doubt. Thurii, in the long run, proved a failure, but the Acropolis still speaks to us of Athens' greatest time.

Pericles' building programme was at the same time a matter of economic importance, both because of its enormous costs and because it provided labour on a comparatively large scale. Plutarch, in two of his seemingly most factual, though partly anachronistic, chapters (12–14, 1) gives a lively picture of these aspects of Pericles' policy and of the reactions of his opponents. For the attacks of the opposition had centred especially on his imperialist and financial policy. The people, says one of the comedians (adesp. 41 = Plut. 7, 8), were 'like a horse, no longer willing to obey, but biting Euboea and leaping upon the islands'. Whether the comedian wanted to distinguish between the people and their leader, we do not know, as we do not know the context; but it is far more likely that he meant both. As another contemporary comedian says (Telecleides 42 = Plut. 16, 2), everything was left to Pericles' discretion, 'the tribute of the cities, and the cities themselves to be bound or unleashed; the walls of stone to be built or cast down again; treaties, power, mastery, peace, wealth, and happiness'. With Thucydides' ostracism, the direct attacks more or less ceased, and the great orator was able to put his policy into effect and lead his people along the road which was bound to lead to glory but also to war, and after his death to disaster.

He had, however, still to face some sort of opposition, in fact
two sorts – the growing criticism of 'middle-class' democrats against
the cautious and yet overbearing aristocrat who was in sympathy
with the modern spirit of rationalism, and, on the other hand, the
ill-will of many of the oligarchs and the allies against the imperialist
democrats. Criticism, otherwise practically mute, found as before
a mouthpiece in the irony and satire of comedy.[100] Cratinus, as well
as a few other comedians, the creators of 'Old Comedy' as a special
branch of theatrical poetry, wrote either mythological parodies or
political satire. They talked about the great orator, that it could mean
'words, not deeds', at least with reference to the third Long Wall
on which work had started in 445. The 'Zeus who sends thunder
and lightning' – a reflection of Pericles' oratory as well as his reserved 'Olympic' attitude – was also the 'big tyrant', born from the
union of Kronos and Stasis, the child of civil strife, just as his mistress Aspasia was called a tyrannical Omphale and a child of de-
bauchery. These and other quotations from comedy are not mere
fun; they disclose a deep hostility or, to say the least, the lack of any
enthusiasm, and that is reflected in the words of other contemporaries as well.[101]

The most outstanding among the latter were two men who were
friends and at the same time voices to be heard: Sophocles and
Herodotus. In spring 442 Sophocles' *Antigone* was performed.[102]
I firmly believe that Creon, the tyrannical and self-righteous ruler
of the play, mirrors essential features of Pericles' character and
position. There is naturally no question of some kind of portrait
or a drama *à clef*. The man who proclaims a programme of excellent
principles, but acts differently and in defiance of the 'unwritten
laws', is not a hypocrite but a slave to his political convictions. His
standards never go beyond the state, and the state is himself! That
means that nothing could be more mistaken than to accept Hegel's
view that Creon represented the polis, and Antigone family and
religion. In fact, such a conflict would never have made sense in
fifth-century Athens. The theme really is that absolute political
power overrides even the demands of tradition and religion. There
is a clear parallel as well as a contrast between the man who fought
Antigone's wide and divine 'unwritten laws', and the Thucydidean
Pericles (and almost certainly the historical Pericles) who speaks of

the unwritten laws as something specifically Athenian and, at the same time, human and secular only. This is not political opposition but a conflict of spiritual attitudes, to which we shall return later. For a personal point of view we have the testimony of Ion of Chios, who knew both men, apart from being a friend of Cimon's. Of Sophocles he said that 'in politics he was neither clever nor active, but like any of the worthy Athenians'; that probably means like an ordinary Athenian gentleman. Pericles, on the other hand, in Ion's view, showed boastful arrogance and contempt for others (*FGrH* 392 F 6. 15).[103] Sophocles' *Antigone*, however, is rightly famous, not for the portrait of Creon, but for the high regard to human nature as represented in the lovable person of Antigone and, as it were, theoretically in the famous chorus song about man's achievements (332 ff.). Far from being a 'humanist', Sophocles combined genuine piety with the awareness of man's intellectual and technical progress as well as his mortal limitation.

Herodotus,[103a] it can be assumed, was 'on the side of the gods', and thus essentially in agreement with Sophocles. Politically he admired Athens for her deeds in the Persian wars, but was fair and impartial towards other states, especially Sparta, though not towards the Ionians. He was indeed the last outstanding heir of the Ionian tradition of story-telling, and of their creative interest in foreign places and peoples; but he had discovered the secret of the historian's task as distinct from the curiosity of the geographer and ethnographer, and equally from the politician's propaganda. He was not the first to realize that truth had to be the writer's guide; even Hesiod knew that, and no less did Herodotus' predecessor Hecataeus, both in his attempts at rationalizing myth and in his geographical work. Truth, however, can be an ambiguous concept, and for Herodotus it is often of greater importance to mention all possible reports than to find out which version is the true one. Still, he changed the meaning of the word *historíe* from 'research' into 'history'. He had, in a way, three souls, though to some extent they may represent various stages of his development. He was an excellent and charming story-teller of the kind that is known in the east; at the same time he was the keen traveller searching for the true conditions of foreign peoples and places, and also the factual reporter of the battles of the Persian war and the man who realized the

historical importance of the conflict between East and West, in
particular between despotism and freedom.[104] The *pater historiae*
had an inkling of the 'scientific' aspect of writing history, of the
basic importance of the sources, and the interconnexion between
personal, social, and political causes – all that without giving up his
firm belief in the power of the gods and the significance of oracles
and dreams.

Herodotus' relationship to Pericles has been the subject o. recent
research and changing views.[105] Herodotus mentions Pericles only
once (6, 131): when Xanthippus' wife Agariste was pregnant, she
had a dream that she would give birth to a lion, and a few days later
Pericles was born. Lions figure in Greek imagination as a frequent
symbol of formidable greatness, but also of dangerous savagery.
They are, in particular, associated with the idea of kingship or
tyranny. That may have been the underlying idea for Herodotus'
story, though it seems to have been fairly common to praise a new-
born boy as a lion (Aristoph. *Thesmoph.* 514), and in a comic oracle
(Ar. *Eq.* 1037) the lion born to an Athenian woman is supposed to
have fought for the demos. That looks (in 424!) like an allusion to
the story about Pericles.[106] If there was respect, and even awe, in
Herodotus' words about Pericles, he never showed any sign of
affection or political support. Otherwise Herodotus, apart from an
occasional incidental remark, never touches on events later than the
'seventies, and we are left guessing at what he thought about the
Athenian rule over the Aegean, about Cimon, or about Pericles.
One fact may be important, but remains ambiguous. Herodotus
went to Thurii, and in one branch of the tradition (Arist. *rhet.*
1409a, 28, Plut. *mor.* 604 F) his work begins with the words 'This
is the published research of Herodotus of Thurii', while in all our
manuscripts he is called after his birthplace, Halicarnassus. At one
time or another he must have been a citizen of Thurii, but we do
not know when he went there, whether with the first colonists in
444/43 or later, and in view of the changing political climate of Thurii,
there is no certainty about his motives. The Panhellenic nature of the
colony must have pleased him, but we wonder whether that can also
be said of that special brand of Athenian Panhellenism.

If Hippodamus of Miletus was the town-planner for Thurii as he
had been for the rebuilding of the Peiraeus, this remarkable man

must have been attracted by the growing cultural importance of Athens, and perhaps a personal invitation by Pericles. The spirit of a new age revealed itself in Hippodamus, not only in his famous rectangular street plans with their emphasis on a central market-place but also in the fact that as a true disciple of sophist thought, he developed an abstract political theory. He divided the citizens of his ideal city into three classes and the land into three parts, though there was no direct connexion between the two systems; it was a highly artificial picture, and he was the first, as Aristotle tells us, 'of non-political men to deal with the question of the best *politeia*', and thus a predecessor of Plato's Utopia.[107]

Hostile feelings against Pericles were roused when Samos, one of the most faithful and strongest allied cities, seceded. That followed one of the usual border quarrels between Miletus and Samos, which had territory on the Asiatic mainland. Miletus was a democracy, Samos was not, but both were supposed to be autonomous. Nevertheless, Athens intervened, and after Samos had refused to accept arbitration (which anyway would not have been impartial), Pericles in spring 440 went to war (Thuc. 1, 115–17). One of the strategi was Sophocles, who had been elected after, and possibly because of, his *Antigone*; he was given a special task which made no demands on his non-existent military qualifications. In a way it can be said that Pericles no less than Sophocles, by fighting this war, betrayed their ideals; but patriotism meant polis-egotism. Samos was taken by surprise, made a democracy under an Athenian garrison, and had to give hostages. But the Samian oligarchs were supported by the Persian satrap; they returned and overthrew the democrats. A small Athenian fleet was crushed; the efficient leader of the Samian fleet was Melissus, admiral and – in true Ionian fashion – philosopher, a disciple of Parmenides. Pericles at once sailed again, and with the help of contingents from Lesbos and Chios, the strong Athenian fleet in spring 439 eventually defeated the Samians. They had hoped for, and Pericles in fact expected, an intervention by the Phoenician fleet, but it never turned up, and Persia did not break the peace treaty. Byzantium too had revolted, but returned to the fold as a tributary state after Samos was defeated. Pericles held the Funeral Speech in honour of those who had died in the war.

He had acted with great speed and efficiency. He was lucky, as the two possible threats, an attack by the Phoenicians or an intervention by the Peloponnesians, never materialized; the latter decided, on the initiative of Corinth, not to interfere and to keep the peace which by then was only six years old. The special part played by Corinth can be explained by the fact that she had no more political demands east of the Isthmus, wished to concentrate on her western interests, and was aiming at keeping Athens away from the west as far as possible. After the war the naval supremacy of Athens and her sway over the allies were more formidable than ever. 'Where Samos had failed, no other state was likely to succeed.'[108] The losses, however, in human lives, and the thought of having lost the friendship of Samos, gave rise to strong misgivings. The ironical words of Cimon's sister Elpinice, as recounted by Plutarch (28, 6), that under Pericles Athenian citizens were killed in a war, not as in Cimon's time against the Persians but against an allied and related city, undoubtedly reflected the feelings of many. The critics did not wait for the return of the son of Melesias from exile six years thence in order to attack Pericles, if only indirectly. It was probably in 438-437 that Pheidias, who had made the chryselephantine statue of Athena in the Parthenon, was accused by one of his fellow workers of embezzling either gold or ivory. It seems that he somehow evaded the penalty and later worked in Olympia on the statue of Zeus.[109] By then the Greeks, and not least the Athenians themselves, had realized that the 'empire' was a *tyrannis*, and the man responsible for Athenian power politics was the man who was the ruler, if not the tyrant, of Athens.[110]

His position was based on his annual re-election as one of the strategi. In most years another man from his phyle, the Acamantis, was also elected, and that meant that Pericles was elected from all phylae together, i.e. from the whole people (*ex hapanton*), while one phyle that year was without a representative on the board of strategi. It also sometimes happened that another phyle, Pandionis, provided two strategi (in 440-439 and 430-429), Phormio and Hagnon, who were the best military leaders in Pericles' time.[111] To what extent and by what means Pericles influenced the elections is difficult to say, though there can be little doubt that he did. We can assume that he was eager to have some outstanding unpolitical generals among his colleagues. Phormio, in particular, made some brilliant campaigns in western Greece during the early years of the war. Otherwise it is remarkable that so many of the strategi, e.g. his colleagues from Acamantis, were re-elected several times without having shown any distinction; it is obvious that the elections were somehow directed.

What sort of man Pericles really was is very hard to discover. Neither Thucydides' nor Plutarch's portrait can be called unbiased and authentic; in particular, neither of them distinguished between the earlier and the later Pericles. It was only the latter they knew, and that is more or less true of our knowledge too. We have tried, as far as possible, to sketch the policy and the character of the Pericles of the 'fifties and the early 'forties, and it is perhaps possible to say that he grew steadily more cautious as well as more autocratic. The 'Olympian', no doubt, was a lonely man. Among the politicians, including his supporters, he had no friend. He avoided all social activity, he did not leave any written records, he only went out for official business, and his speeches were always impressive. He had, of course, Aspasia as his companion, who held the first place in his heart and in his house. She was probably his equal intellectually. He liked occasional talks with men such as Protagoras and, above all, Anaxagoras. He was on friendly terms with Pheidias, whom he made superintendent of all the architectural and artistic work on the Acropolis; as in the case of Aspasia, he was above the widespread prejudices of his fellow citizens who saw in her only the hetaera, and in Pheidias a mere manual craftsman, a *banausos*. How far did Pericles live in the world of beauty which he helped to create? We cannot say for certain, but it seems equally clear that he had an understanding of art, and that it did not dominate his mind. Love of beauty, after all, must have been strong among the Athenians generally, even among the *petits bourgeois* as we know them from comedy, but they took it more or less as something self-evident. No Greek was ever an aesthete. 'We love beauty without personal luxury, and we love wisdom without unmanliness.'[112]

Perhaps Aspasia's trial, too, is to be dated in the years after the Samian war. Popular gossip later connected her with the outbreak of both wars, the Samian and the Peloponnesian (Duris, *FGrH* 76 F 65). In the former case it was her Milesian origin and Pericles'

siding with Miletus which made tongues wag.[113] Pericles had become
Aspasia's lover during the 'forties, and there can be no doubt that the
role the former hetaera played in Pericles' house and life caused a
good deal of surprise and even anger. She was charged with *asebeia*;
in what her impiety consisted, we are never told. Certainty about
the date of the trial cannot be attained, but the story is that Pericles
persuaded the jurors to acquit her, even by shedding tears.

Actually Aspasia was a woman not only of beauty but also of
great intellect and higher interests. That explains the unconventional
union which lasted till Pericles' death. If there was one aspect which
interested him apart from politics it was the new spirit that put
reason and intellect in the place of religion and tradition. It was
this attitude that caused the people to regard Pericles and his personal circle of friends as impious.[114] The use Pericles made of
Lampon, the popular soothsayer, shows that he avoided going
against general beliefs and feelings, but also that he tried to use
religion in support of his policy. We do not know to what extent,
if at all, such an attitude was more than political, though we might
say that Pericles was above popular superstitions, but neither a
hypocrite nor an atheist. As we know so little of his thoughts, we
must draw conclusions from his relations with other people. There,
Anaxagoras is outstanding.[115] He lived at Athens for about thirty
years, without taking any interest in public affairs. He brought there
the legacy of Ionian philosophy, though under the influence of
Parmenides he turned monism into dualism, that is to say, he
distinguished between matter and its moving cause. The latter he
called 'mind' (*nous*); that was more than mere reason and intellect,
but it gave his reasoned picture of the world its meaning and unity.
It was the original creative force, and also the permanent ruler, of
the world, like Xenophanes' 'god' (see frs. 12–14). Pericles, though
not the Athenians in general, accepted the secularization of the
kosmos, in which sun and moon were stone and earth, and its ruler
a rational force. The statesman would conclude that the same
principle should rule the state; to the Greeks the order of the
universe and that of the polis seemed always parallel, if not identical,
phenomena. Pericles was a 'humanist' and a realist; whatever the
truth of Plutarch's anecdotes, the portrait which emerges in its
factual lines seems true to life. That is confirmed by the speeches

which Thucydides puts into Pericles' mouth.[116] Thus, we come to
the conclusion that our two main sources, despite all their idealization, tell us something about the real Pericles. He did not speak
of the gods, nor indeed of any traditional beliefs. He showed reverence where and when it was needed, but had no piety in the sense
in which the people understood it, and it was this aspect which
played a decisive part in the attitude of his opponents. He did, however, believe in Athena as the divine symbol of Athens; in fact,
state and goddess were one for him no less than in a different way
for the people.

The only passion in Pericles' austere and reserved mind was
statesmanship, which included day-to-day politics. The people in
general trusted him, not least because of his integrity in financial
matters, a quality comparatively rare among Greek politicians. He
was not a man to make friends easily, and that was also revealed in
his policy. As Thucydides says in his eulogy (2, 65), 'he rather led
the people than was led by them', and summarizing this leadership
in one famous sentence, 'it was in name a democracy, but in fact
the rule by the first man'. Leadership had become personal rule, and
that tended increasingly to become autocracy, that is to say, *tyrannis*.
Comedy could refer to the personal autocracy of Pericles (see above,
p. 237) as well as to the tyranny of the *archē* when 'the demos rules'
(Cratinus, fr. 162 A Edm.). That was the *tyrannis* Pericles himself
mentioned when speaking to the people (Thuc. 2, 63, 2), and there
is no reason to doubt that he actually used the word. There was,
however, a distinction between using the word against an enemy
of democracy and using it in referring to the assumption by the
leading state of a position in which the autonomy of the allies had
lost its meaning, to say nothing of the demos in the subject states;
they sometimes, at least, might prefer the rule by the Athenian
demos to that of their own oligarchs. Still, what could be called
tyrannis was domination. No attempt was made to organize the rule
of Athens on more federal lines; Athens did not learn the lesson,
already practised at the time, e.g., in Boeotia and the Chalcidice,
till she made her second naval alliance a century after the start of
the Delian league (i.e. 377 B.C.). There was no moral justification
for that kind of Athenian rule, except that Pericles still avoided too
extreme measures against the allies.[117] Pericles believed in power,

and even in the Funeral Speech, a document intended equally to honour and to idealize Athens and her ruler, the power (*dynamis*) of the state is regarded not simply as a necessity but as the basis for the citizens to become her 'lovers' (2, 43, 1). Pericles' endeavours to make Athens beautiful were to a large extent dictated by the wish to display to citizens and foreigners alike the unique greatness of Athens.

For as long as he was at the helm of the state, Pericles followed pure power politics. He had not succeeded on the Greek mainland. So he was the more determined to exercise Athenian power over her allies. One of the most offensive measures was the coercion to bring all major cases of litigation before Athenian juries. It burdened the allies with much extra expense, and at the same time subjected them to the prejudice of the popular courts. Heavy penalties were imposed on the allied state when an Athenian was killed in its territory, and with all that and the strict and regular collection of the tributes, it was no longer possible to maintain the fiction of the autonomy of the allies. They were subjects and could be called so even in official documents; their cities were those 'in which the Athenians ruled'.[118]

At the same time expansion within the Aegean area continued. The Thracian coast was of particular importance, both politically and economically. In 437–436 Amphipolis was founded by one of Pericles' fellow generals, Hagnon, at the same place of Enneahodoi where an earlier attempt had failed (above, p. 202). It was, like Thurii, a colony of mixed Greek population, many from neighbouring places, where the strengthening of the Greek position against the Thracians was probably welcomed; but it was not regarded as a Panhellenic colony. Amphipolis soon became an important place, not least by its export of timber and probably by mining concessions, and thus by its contribution to Athenian revenues (Thuc. 4, 108, 1), but above all, by its strategic position near the mouth of the Strymon, dominating the bridge of the important east–west route. Amphipolis was one of several independent colonies founded in those years at the Thracian shores; another one was Brea. We do not know its exact position, but we have the second decree about its foundation.[119] Both colonies were privileged, paying no tribute; both, on the other hand, were members of the 'empire', and at least for Brea we know of a degree of dependence on Athens, not dissimilar from that of a cleruchy.[120] In Asia Minor a number of smaller places ceased to pay tribute, and in eastern Thrace the native kingdom of the Odrysians had grown quite powerful, though Athens in general was on good terms with them, if only by various concessions. It was also of importance that the relations between Athens and Macedon, which included western Thrace as far as the Strymon, were always under considerable strain. This gave Amphipolis additional importance. The details of the general situation remain obscure, but it seems possible to accept the foundation of Brea as an example of other similar actions. A rider to the decree mentions the colonists as taken from the two lower classes only. It was an afterthought which confirms that the provision of land for those without it was an important, but not the primary, task of the new foundation. Athens strengthened her position, strong as it already was, along the shores from the Chalcidice in the west to the Chersonese in the east.

Pericles went even further, and in a naval display in the Black Sea he paraded Athenian power, especially for the sake of the barbarian kings and peoples, and in order to strengthen the position of the Greek cities there.[121] Our main source is Plutarch (20), who tells us that Sinope received Athenian colonists. In other literary sources other colonies are mentioned, Amisus farther east from Sinope, even beyond the mouth of the Halys, and Astacus in the eastern Propontis. There can be little doubt that politics supported, and were influenced by, trade and economy, and Ps.-Xenophon (2, 7 ff.) knows what he is talking about when he describes Athenian sea-power as the source of all sorts of imports from all sorts of places, luxuries no less than timber, iron, copper, and flax. The extent to which Athens still relied on her rural economy must by then have become comparatively small, even though some production of corn remained important, and the cultivation of olive trees and vines flourished, especially on marginal land; oil and pottery remained the chief articles of export. The Peiraeus was the economic centre of Athenian rule, and trade in control of the whole Aegean area and beyond was 'the milking cow of public revenue'.[122] Athens had long given up the old polis ideal of autarcy; financially she was living on her silver mines, her outward possessions, her harbour and custom duties, the duty of a tenth (*dekate*) to be paid, e.g. by ships passing through the Bosporus, and last not least the tributes. Her imperialism had grown no less economic than political.

Ever since the Persian wars, the possession or the acquisition of money had become a factor of the first importance, and its influence can be traced in public no less than in private life. Herodotus speaks a great deal of money, though he does not yet show like Thucydides its overriding power. Pericles was able to accumulate in the public treasury a very large amount of money, in fact several thousand talents; much of it was in the Parthenon under the guardianship of the goddess. Apart from Thucydides' survey of the financial resources of Athens (2, 13), we have two decrees under the name of Callias (*ATL* D 1–2, *ML*, no. 58), which are usually dated in 434–433.[123] Without trying to discuss the details, highly disputed as they are, we can state that to the best of our knowledge it was the first time that a Greek state had a permanent state treasure which could be used, with the consent of the demos, in peace and war. Since even Athenian economy did not know a budget, this ready money was of particular importance. Pericles took part of it for the buildings on the Acropolis, and kept a reserve fund against the possibility, in fact the probability, of war. That idea was behind the regulations of the Callias decrees by which the treasurers of the goddess were granted greater, though limited, power, both over the *hellenotamiai*, the treasurers of the alliance, and over the 'treasurers of the other gods'. The whole financial apparatus was being simplified and strengthened. At the same time the military power of Athens, both naval and land forces, was being built up.

An interesting feature of the Brea decree is that places among the colonists were reserved for a month for citizens returning from active service (26 ff.), and that in a rider (32 ff.) the colonists are confined to members of the two lower classes, the thetes and the zeugitae. It is clear that many discharged soldiers would need employment or land, and not everybody was suitable for agriculture. In this context we remember Plutarch's story (13) that Pericles' building programme was largely influenced by the need to fight unemployment. The argument may not have been without some foundation, but skilled men for architectural and sculptural work would be available in small numbers only, and the more menial tasks in building work would probably be refused, at least by the zeugitae. Plutarch's description is largely anachronistic, and Pericles' plans had nothing in common with the idea of a welfare state. There was, it is true, the problem of the returning soldier citizens, and the colonies served that second need as well as strategic and political demands.

The composition of the Attic population, especially in the city, had by then greatly changed. It could be said that Athens had become a cosmopolitan town. We have no reliable figures, but it is likely that the number of citizens with their families was hardly more than equal to that of metics and slaves.[124] It is obvious that both groups of non-citizens were needed for labour – in home and workshop, in trade, to some extent in agriculture, and even in naval service, though many metics and even a few slaves were wealthy, and many of the artists and thinkers of the period were foreigners. The citizens had many privileges, above all, that of doing paid public service as officials, counsellors, and jurors. But there was no question of the state taking care of its citizens; the modest payments provided little more than a minimum of personal maintenance costs, a compensation for the unavoidable loss of a day's earnings. The introduction of the *theorikon* (two obols for visiting the theatre during the great festivals) was very popular; if Pericles introduced it, it reveals his shrewdness as well as the people's love for tragedy and comedy. With the rise of building activity and the growth of trade, wealth was generally increasing, but private living standards remained low. The residential quarters of Athens showed poor housing and dirty streets, and the people, with few exceptions, led a frugal life.[125] In the country, on the other hand, a gradual transformation took place; farming became a commercial activity, supporting, and supported by, the trade in oil and wine. Many of the citizens, had a great deal of leisure, and that was needed both for political and juridical activities and for the enjoyment of the theatre and the arts.

The eternal question arises to what extent the privileged position of the citizens was made possible by slavery. It is certain that slaves, both Greek and non-Greek, did much of the manual labour, but it is equally certain that many citizens did the same. The fixed Marxist concept of a society of slave-owners is, if not quite wrong, at least completely misleading, though the existence of slaves was generally taken for granted, especially in an advanced economy like that of Athenian democracy. Tragedy can show close bonds between mistress and slave girls, for instance, in Euripides' *Alcestis* or *Medea*, while comedy's slaves, though caricatured and funny, share in the daily life of a citizen's family. It is, however, true that in either case the slaves never reach full human status. There was still a long way to go before theoretical thought opened the way to the realization, always shared by a minority, that slaves were as human as free people.[126]

The most significant, and the most expensive, witnesses to the Periclean age are, of course, the buildings on the Acropolis, in the town, and the Peiraeus, with the Parthenon as the most outstanding example.[127] During the 'forties and 'thirties the metopes, the frieze, and the pediments were being sculptured and put into place; in 438 Pheidias' gold and ivory statute of Athena was erected inside the temple, which was finally completed in 432. Many hands joined in the work, but the general concept and the essential unity point to one dominating mind, that of Pheidias. The Parthenon shows in its very construction a new spirit. It was built according to very subtle mathematical devices, and it can essentially be maintained that in this building of apparently simple and effortless design there is no straight line, neither in the stylobate on which the columns rest nor in the columns themselves, nor in the architrave above them. The graceful 'refinements of curvature and inclination'[128] and the harmony of the proportions generally, with the unique number of columns,[129] are dictated by a thorough knowledge of mathematics and optical theory – a clear, if easily unnoticed, example of that rational spirit which combined art and science.

These facts go together with the religious aspect of the Parthenon. It is a monument *in maiorem gloriam* of Athens and her virgin goddess Athena, and not of cult and worship, which still concentrated on the ancient site of the Erechtheum. The pediments show the birth of Athena from Zeus' head,[130] and her competition with Poseidon for the rule over Attica, olive tree versus spring, both so essential for the life of the country. The pediments show the most advanced ('individualist') style of all the Parthenon sculptures which, as a whole, display the development of a decade particularly rich in artistic trends and personalities. The metopes represent mythical fights between Greeks and barbarians, a symbol of the fact that Athena saved her city in the Persian war. The 'barbarians' of myth were Centaurs, giants, Amazons, and Trojans. The frieze – a unique feature so far in a Doric temple – depicts, however incompletely, the solemn procession at the Great Panathenaea, that is to say, a contemporary human event, celebrating the unity of Attica and the devotion of the Athenian people to their goddess. The reality of the subject, with all its details, is elevated into an ideal sphere in which the young cavalrymen or the girls attending to their cult duties are not aristocrats, and the old men and attendants not democrats, though some of the outstanding men may be heroes. They all do honour to the gods who appear sitting (invisibly) on either side of the central scene, the offering of the new garment, the *peplos*, to the priest of Athena. The frieze represents that ideal which Pericles describes in his Funeral Speech.

The *peplos*, renewed every fourth year and the work of noble Athenian girls, was to be worn by the ancient wooden statue of Athena Polias, the guardian of city and state. Pheidias' statue in the Parthenon was the triumphant armed goddess with Nike in her outstretched hand, with the theme of the metopes repeated on shield and sandals. The impression of the huge gold and ivory statue on anybody entering the cella of the temple must have been tremendous, but the intimate love of the people belonged to a different kind of goddess.[131] Pheidias' statue was not an object of worship but a symbol of Athens. The two statues of the same goddess, and the two temples, represented the two trends of thought prevailing at Pericles' time, the traditional beliefs and what has been called 'the thinking religion'.[132] Athena was at the same time Polias, the wise guardian of land and city, of crafts and art, and Parthenos, the expression of political greatness and ambitious policy. The same spirit created the magnificent entrance gate to the Acropolis, the Propylaea, the first building to combine Doric and Ionic columns. Its original planning was upset by the need to complete the little temple of Athena Nike on the south-west corner of the Acropolis, a gracious building in purely Ionic style, with a frieze depicting turbulent scenes from the fighting against the Persians. These and other buildings, some of which were completed long after Pericles' death, fulfilled an essential part of the programme of the Panhellenic congress which Pericles had failed to convene. He taught his people a new kind of patriotism in which belief in the gods and belief in the greatness of Athens were insolubly bound together, and at least for a minority founded on a rational, if not rationalist, attitude. Athenian leadership was summarized in Pericles' expression of the 'School for Hellas'.

Still, Athens was not the only place in Greece where the arts flourished. There were plenty of sculptors at Athens besides and after Pheidias, and he actually created his most famous statue, that of Zeus at Olympia, as an exile. The most important development outside Athens, however, took place at Argos, where Polycletus founded a school of sculpture. His best-known statues, the *Diadumenos* and the *Doryphoros*, illustrate his theory of human proportions which he laid down in a treatise called the *Kanon*. He rather than Pheidias is the ancestor of the flourishing creation in the fourth century of individual statues, both male and female.

Probably about 433 a son was born to Pericles and Aspasia, who was called Pericles, but according to Athenian law, in fact to Pericles' own law of 451–450, was illegitimate. Also in 433 Thucydides, son of Melesias, returned from exile, and it is more than likely that he intensified the attacks on Pericles and his friends, and that he re-organized his followers into something like a 'party'. The 'democrats' more or less followed his example, and in Ps.-Xenophon's pamphlet (probably early in the war) the existence of two parties seems a fact. Pericles was outside any party policy, and it is probably natural that some of the radicals joined with the oligarchs in the attempts of attacking him and his circle. Even if we think that not all the trials for 'impiety' belong to the years immediately before the war, the decree of Diopeithes, condemning atheism, has to be dated in 433–432 or 432–431 (Plut. *Per.* 32, 3). Diopeithes, one of the charlatan soothsayers who were trusted by the people, acted on the instigation of Cleon, the emerging middle-class opponent of Pericles. The decree was most likely directed in particular against Anaxagoras. He was perhaps the only man who could be called Pericles' friend, but Pericles could not protect him, and had to ask him to leave Athens. No doubt the action was inspired as much by the hostility to Pericles personally as to the 'modern' spirit as represented by the great philosopher. That would explain why the attack did not, or at any rate not exclusively, come from the oligarchic side. In matters of traditional beliefs the ordinary people were most conservative, and the trial of Anaxagoras was, in a sense, a predecessor of that more famous trial one generation later, the trial of Socrates.

The Periclean age, in spite of its appearance of 'classical' harmony, was an age of transition in more than one respect. Athenian power reached, and passed, its highest point, and at the same time the struggle had started between the old and the new ways of thought and belief. Pericles was clearly on the side of the modern trend. We have mentioned his moralism devoid of traditional religion, and his reliance on the human intellect. Sophocles, on the other hand, so often regarded (together with Pheidias, and with even less justification than he) as a true representative of the Periclean age, was neither a moralist nor an intellectual; yet he was no mere reactionary. His warm humanity went together with a passionate belief in the greatness of the gods, and raised him above the level of pure traditionalism; it also prevented him from sharing the rational humanism which during his lifetime had made such a great progress. It is this mixture which made him the great poet he was, different from his revolutionary predecessor and his revolutionary contemporary, Aeschylus and Euripides. What nevertheless united the two attitudes personified in Sophocles and Pericles was the common belief in man's possible perfection, and in the final goal of human harmony.[133]

It is equally significant that in this period Euripides had started on his career as a tragedian, though for quite a time he had little success. His plays increasingly reflected the man-centred concept of life, and the deeper conflicts within the mind of man – or, for that matter, woman. Euripides' early plays are all, in a sense, family tragedies. In spring 438 he produced the *Alcestis*, the earliest play extant and a kind of semi-tragedy. A woman played the supreme part, and in a very different sense from, e.g., Antigone. The door had been opened to the psychology of the female mind, its magnanimity and courage, frequently contrasted with the egotism of man. Still, we must not overemphasize this aspect. The world of myth is there, and the gods play an essential part; but myth has become a kind of human parable in which even a child has a voice, and the half-burlesque, half-heroic figure of Heracles as well as the happy ending point towards the place of *Alcestis* as the last play of a tetralogy, standing for a satyr-play. The decisive facts are, of course, Alcestis' self-sacrifice, and its effects on Admetus, who learns late, though not too late ('I see it now', 940), that to be alive in unhappiness may not be preferable to death. This is not the place to discuss the intricate mixture of character, action, and theatrical effects; but with *Alcestis*, Euripides for the first, though not the last, time created a woman who performs 'the greatest of human achievement, the complete renunciation of herself in an act of sacrifice'.[134] The figure of Alcestis dominates the play, different also from Deianeira in Sophocles' *Trachiniae*. Though that play was clearly written under Euripides' influence, Deianeira's fate and character serve only as a foil to Heracles, who is most of the time absent from the stage. Slightly later, Euripides produced a first version of *Hippolytus*,[135] in which, it seems, Phaedra played with a difference the Potiphar's wife part as the seductress of a chaste youth. *She* probably rather than *he* was the central character. The helplessness of unhappy love was a theme well known to the Greeks. Phaedra's state of mind may also have been an expression of revenge on her husband Theseus. In contrast to Aeschylus' Clytaemnestra, Phaedra is an adulteress out of weakness (or intended to be so). The Athenians disliked the play, in the main probably because of Phaedra's complete and shameless submission to her desires. It is less likely that Hippolytus' chastity was a real problem for the audience, though it must have had an air of unreality.[135a] Euripides later wrote a new version (the one we have) in which the two forces of lust and chastity – in the shape of Aphrodite and Artemis – fought for the soul of Hippolytus, and Phaedra put up a desperate fight against her own infatuation. The reaction of the people is to be seen against the background of family life, which included the domestic slaves and is revealed in many of the sculptured grave stones. Anyway, women were to join the male world with problems of their own, and they were to shape anew the great issues of life. A new epoch in the history of the human mind was beginning; it was to show the victory of the spirit of Athens over her political misfortunes.

4 · The Western Greeks

The situation in the western Mediterranean, after the defeat of Carthage in 480 and that of the Etruscans in 474 (see above, p. 166f.), was not dissimilar to that of the motherland. The external enemies had been beaten off, while the internal struggles never ceased. At the same time the economy and the arts flourished. There were, however, differences in the external situation, as the Sicilian and Italian Greeks had to deal not only with one another but also with the native peoples. And it made an important difference that the victories over Carthage and the Etruscans had been won not by the people and their elected leaders but by tyrants.[136]

It was the figure of Hieron, in particular, that dominated the 'seventies. He had followed his brother Gelon, the creator of the Deinomenid dynasty, as the ruler of Syracuse and Gela, and founded the new city of Aetna, in the place of Catane, which was later restored. It was also he who had gained that victory in Italy over the Etruscans which secured Roman independence. In many ways described as a typical powerful ruler, Hieron is known to us in particular from Pindar and Bacchylides, who, like Simonides and Aeschylus, were for a time honoured guests at his court.[137] Pindar calls him 'king', and if that means anything, and not only the same as 'tyrant', a title the poet might like to avoid, it reflects the extension of power over a number of Greek cities, and at the same time the splendour of a man whose ambition was at least as much to gain a victory in the chariot race at Olympia, and to act as a patron of the great poets of his time, as to exercise absolute power, relying on his mercenaries and even employing secret agents in the cities. In many ways he was the type of old-fashioned tyrant who pursued a strong family policy; he married the daughter of another tyrant, Anaxilas of Rhegium. Hieron was, in fact, one out of several, if the most brilliant; Theron of Acragas was his strongest rival. The fluctuations of monarchical rule in the Sicilian cities are of minor interest, if we keep in mind that they were going on all the time, and that *tyrannis* held the scene till as late as the 'sixties of the fifth century. When the tyrants were expelled and democracy and independence introduced, about the same time as the rule of the Battiads in Cyrene was also overthrown, there still remained in Sicily the mercenaries to deal with, and the increasing danger from the native Siculi under their leader Ducetius. The mercenaries were eventually given the city of Messana. Ducetius led a kind of national revival in the interior, but was in the end defeated by Syracuse. Exiled to Corinth, he had a come-back when a war between Syracuse and Acragas raised his hopes, but soon afterwards he died, and with him died all resistance of the Siculi against the Greeks.

For several decades, the relations between Greeks and Carthaginians were quite friendly; we find evidence of mixed population in some places, and bilingual coins testify to mutual trade. Sicily prospered greatly. All over the island the ruins still bear witness to a glorious past, though it was at that very time that the large estates and the rural slavery began to develop which in succeeding centuries were to become such great economic and social dangers. Culturally, in a world of mixed populations and a high degree of political instability, Selinus, the most western of the Greek cities, and its eastern neighbour Acragas were of special significance; both were able to extend their temple areas by new and impressive buildings. The metopes of the Hera temple (E) at Selinus are among the most beautiful pieces of archaic sculpture, combining in their figures physical quietness with deep emotion. Selinus had not been at war with Carthage; that fact, together with its position between Segesta (or Egesta), city of the native Elymians, and Acragas, made the place, though by no means a haven of peace, yet a centre of deeply Greek and more than provincial art. It radiates an atmosphere of astonishing serenity, such as cannot be found, at least not so early, either at Olympia or at Athens. In Acragas the enormous size and heavy proportions of the Zeus temple with its giant figures supporting the roof contrast with the fine harmony of the so-called Concordia temple and other fifth-century buildings. Here Empedocles was born, and we may think that somehow the place lived up to his half-mystic, half-materialistic philosophy of Love and Hatred. Out of their strife, together with the doctrine of the four elements, all mentioned by earlier thinkers but never before seen as equals, Empedocles developed a cosmology of his own, under the rule of the mythical force of necessity (*ananke*) as well as the 'holy mind'. He opposed Parmenides' monism, and the competition between Love and Hatred owes something to Heraclitus. But he was more than an eclectic. He also was a physician, though not of the scientific school of which we shall speak later; for him, medicine was as much a matter of philosophical insight into nature as of religious beliefs. Still, he developed various physiological theories, based on his fundamental axioms of the four elements, the divine roots of life, and of Love and Hatred as its moving forces. He was even a man of action. On his advice democracy was introduced at Acragas; he was a spiritual leader not of an exclusive circle like the Pythagoreans (with whom, as is shown in his poem 'Purifications' (*Katharmoi*), he had much in common) but of the whole people with their strength and their foibles; to them, as he says himself, he became an immortal (fr. 112 f.). In a sense, he combined the part played by Pericles as the leader of democracy with that of a prophet such as Epimenides, who is supposed to have purified Athens in the sixth century from the Cylonian sacrilege (see p. 56), and again that of a rational thinker with that of a mystic. It can be said that this astonishing man combined in himself Nietzsche's two fundamental aspects, prior to the rise of scepticism, of the Greek mind, the Apollinian and the Dionysiac.

Local wars, as mentioned before, hardly ever ceased among the Sicilian cities. We have an inscription (*ML*, no. 38) in which in about 450 or later Selinus gives thanks to all the gods for a victory. No mention is made of the defeated enemy, but it is possible that by that victory a long struggle ended between Selinus and Segesta.[138] Another inscription (*ML*, no. 37. *DSDA* no. 139. *SEG* 25, no. 3) is supposed to belong to 454–453 or even 458–457. It contains fragments of an alliance between Athens and Segesta. If the treaty is rightly dated,[139] it is the earliest evidence for active interest of Athens in the west, even with a non-Greek city far west; real military or economic support will hardly have come forward, as Athens had her own troubles nearer home. We have spoken of an almost feverish activity during the fifties, and of the change from the hegemony into a full *archē*; in this, as in the interest taken in the west, Pericles followed Themistocles' example and aims.

Perhaps even more surprising than the Athenian attitude is that the Elymians turned to Athens. Though the lovely temple at Segesta and its theatre are witnesses to its early and fundamental hellenization, we still ask: why Athens? For one thing, of course, nobody but a maritime power could possibly send help, and Dorian Corinth was out of the question; for she would be on the side of her colony Syracuse, formidable by her ever-growing power. Here democracy – restored very much after the Athenian model[140] – tended to resume the expansive imperialism of the tyrants. Predominant in trade and commerce, Syracuse had a strong army and navy, and threatened the independence of the other cities. They could not ask for help from any other state but the great Ionian power. It was for the same reason that the Athenians time and again seemed to show genuine anxiety that Syracuse might support Corinth and indirectly Sparta.

In Italy the situation of the Greek cities was similar, though apart from Rhegium, which anyway, with its twin city of Messana, belonged as much to Sicilian politics as to Italian, they were not ruled by tyrants but by aristocracies, the heritage of the Pythagoreans, or by moderate democracies which had revolted against Pythagorean principles and cliques.[141] The struggles among the Greeks did not even cease when attacks by Italian peoples, such as the Iapygians and Messapians, seriously threatened the Greeks, no city more than Taras, Tarentum. In western Italy, Campania, with Cumae, Capua, and Neapolis, became the leading Greek area. The temples of Poseidonia (Paestum), and the recent excavations at Foce del Sele, are witness to the grandeur and the elegance of a Greek world that claimed to be *Magna Graecia*. This Greek culture fertilized the soil from which grew the later Etruscan civilization and indeed the emancipation of Rome.

The appearance of the Athenians in Thurii naturally had its impact on cities that so far had kept away from the dualism of the motherland. It was, however, soon after the former treaties, mentioned above, that Rhegium and Leontini concluded alliances with Athens.[142] That again meant Sicily rather than Italy. Thurii, on the other hand, was in for a good deal of trouble, in external wars with Taras, which was victorious, and with the Lucanians and Bruttians; but the main trouble was internal. The Athenian scheme did not work; at that time the leading man in Thurii was Cleandridas, a Spartan exile. The city, with its strongly mixed population, ceased to have a primarily Athenian character, and chose to accept the god of Delphi as its founder; at the same time the democratic constitution underwent various changes. Thus, Pericles' original plan came to nothing, but Thurii itself declined and lost most of its importance. The whole situation, however, changed when Athenian naval expeditions reached Sicily and Italy during the Peloponnesian war. It was Athens that brought practically the whole Greek world together, although only as her united adversaries.

Taking, as it is reasonable to do, the fifth-century civilization of the western Greeks as a separate, but more or less uniform, branch of Greek civilization, the fact of a comparatively late development (as in politics) seems obvious. Trends of the sixth century in the motherland, such as mystical religion and thought, or the discovery of new forms of literature, for instance, the writing of history,[143] find their parallels in the west during the course of the fifth century. Life in general was more luxurious, and literary, especially theatrical, art (mime, farce and comedy, rhetoric) represented, it seems, a curious mixture of crude traditions and new beginnings. Outstanding in original creativeness was Epicharmus, who wrote short witty comedies, often burlesque parodies of mythical persons such as Heracles or Odysseus; food and drink played a large part, but there were also literary and philosophical allusions. Our fragmentary evidence does not allow us to draw definite conclusions, though it is likely that his plays had no chorus. To what extent he influenced Attic Old Comedy is disputed; but it can be said that the literature and philosophy of the western Greeks in general did have considerable influence on the classical civilization of the motherland.

VII

THE PELOPONNESIAN WAR

The period from 431 – with the preliminaries of 433–432 – till 404, though divided into several periods of war and peace, was first recognized as a unity by the great contemporary historian of the war, Thucydides son of Olorus. He is by far our most important source. His theme is the war, and the war only, though we get a few glimpses of the social, economic, and spiritual background; naturally the description of the war is as much a piece of political as of military history; in fact, Thucydides was chiefly interested in the nature of political and military leadership. His work, ending in 411, was continued in the *Hellenika* of several writers, of which only Xenophon's book survives. Other sources come into their own, above all inscriptions, but also comedy and tragedy, and the earliest extant prose book, the so-called 'Old Oligarch', a pamphlet on *The State of Athens*, preserved among the writings of Xenophon, but probably written in the early years of the war.[1] In addition there are several speeches by orators such as Antiphon, Andocides, and Lysias.

Thucydides (1, 1) calls his subject, which he considers the greatest war ever fought by Greeks or even non-Greeks, 'the war between the Peloponnesians and the Athenians', or that 'of the Athenians and Peloponnesians' (2, 1); with slight variations this remained for a long time the name given to the war. Seen from the Athenian side, it was 'the war against the Peloponnesians' (e.g. Ar. *Ach.* 620, 623. *AP* 27, 2), while the other side could speak of the 'Attic war' (Thuc. 5, 31, 3.5), and the Argives (5, 28, 2) discussed the approaching 'war of the Lacedaemonians'. These and other examples show that there was no fixed name, until much later it became the 'Peloponnesian war'.[1a] The one remarkable thing about these variations is that, with two exceptions,[2] the war was never named after Sparta, rather after the Peloponnesian League, and this in spite of the fact that later some Peloponnesians actually fought on the Athenian side. It seems obvious that it was never a 'Spartan' war, whereas nobody was ever in doubt that, seen from the Peloponnesian side, it was an Athenian war. In this contrast, the differing characters of the Peloponnesian League and the Athenian rule are clearly reflected, and indirectly the role of Corinth and other allies of Sparta is indicated.

It is an outcome of later ancient scholarship that the 'Peloponnesian war' became the usual name for the war from 431 to 404. We cannot say how and why that happened, though it reveals the predominance of the Athenian point of view. It is surprising that modern historians accepted the name without questioning or doubt.[3] Now, of course, it is established for all time.

In a famous chapter Thucydides (1, 23, 5) distinguishes 'the truest cause' of the war from the more immediate 'grievances and conflicts'.[4] The former, as already mentioned, is Sparta's fear of the growing power of Athens, a fear to some extent deliberately fostered by Athens herself. To the other reasons we now turn.

1 · Prelude to War

There were three major events which Thucydides mentions as immediate causes of the war: Athenian participation in the struggle between Corinth and Corcyra, the fight for Potidaea, and the Megarian decree.

Corcyra, a Corinthian colony which at an early time had grown hostile to its mother-city, was important both by its geographical position and by its navy. The two states are reported to have fought in the seventh century the first naval battle among Greeks (Thuc. 1, 13, 4). Their hostility, with all its vicissitudes, was mainly a result of their rivalry in the north-western area, above all over the entry to the Adriatic, where Corcyra seems to have dominated the trade with the non-Greeks. It was at the same time the last stop before the crossing to southern Italy and Sicily, a route of major importance for Corinthian trade. In the Adriatic, Corinth had founded a number of colonies along the west coast of the Greek peninsula, all of them in different degrees dependent on the mother-city.[5] Although Corinth and Corcyra sometimes acted together, and now and then kept up friendly relations on the whole their interests clashed, just because their aims and methods were so similar. The most disastrous trouble started in 435 over Epidamnus (later Dyrrhachium–Durazzo), which was a Corcyrean colony, but had a Corinthian as the original founder (Thuc. 1, 24, 2). The Epidamnians, their power reduced by barbarian neighbours, overthrew their oligarchic government, and when the exiled oligarchs tried to regain power with the help of the barbarians, the people asked Corcyra for help, but were refused. On the advice of Delphi they then sent to Corinth. Hatred of Corcyra and their own self-interest induced the Corinthians to send colonists and troops from other colonies as well as a force of their own, and they succeeded in entering Epidamnus. Thereupon the Corcyreans took up the cause of the exiled oligarchs, besieged Epidamnus, and Corinth prepared for war. The Corinthians proclaimed that a new great colony was to be founded in Epidamnus where old and new settlers would have equal rights;[6] even such people who would not sail themselves but would pay fifty drachmae each were to be included in the new foundation. From other cities they acquired ships, men, or money, and thus assembled a strong force. The support Corinth received not only from her colonies but also from states such as Megara, Thebes, and various Peloponnesians, shows that many of Sparta's allies were on her side, and also that her power in the Adriatic might be regarded as a factor for strength and stability.[7]

Corcyra was not yet prepared to risk a major war, and together with Sparta and Sicyon suggested arbitration by some Peloponnesian states or by Delphi. In case of refusal, the Corcyreans threatened to get new friends, and that could only mean Athens. Corinth refused all concessions; it is clear that her aim was to make sure of her position in the north-west, while Sparta and, for that matter, Delphi did not think of war at all, but were afraid of a widening of the conflict. The Corinthians, however, sailed and were completely defeated by the Corcyrean fleet near Leucimne, the southern promontory of Corcyra; on the same day Epidamnus surrendered. Corcyra was in control of the Ionian sea, until in summer 434[8] a new Corinthian fleet was sent out to protect their allies, though there were no more attacks from either side.

The Corinthians could not leave things at that. For two years they prepared another fleet, and Corcyra, so far neither in the Athenian nor in the Peloponnesian League,[9] decided to seek an alliance with Athens. Thucydides (1, 32–43) describes the situation in two speeches, made at Athens by envoys from Corcyra and from Corinth; they may be composite work, and they are part of an *agon* (*antilogia*), but the arguments in either speech will be very near to those actually used. In different ways, they are both based on the sophists' concepts of the 'useful' and the 'just', that is to say, on power politics and their moral cover. Corcyra, with the largest navy after the Athenian one, could appeal to Athenian self-interest; war seemed rather near, though Athens, by accepting Corcyra as an ally, would not break the treaty of 445. The Corinthians, on the other hand, appealed rather to Athenian emotions and were at first successful; but in a second assembly the people resolved to conclude an alliance with Corcyra, though only a defensive one.

A small naval squadron – too small, in fact, to be decisive – was dispatched to Corcyra (Thuc. 1, 45. *ML*, no. 61), with orders not to attack but only to prevent Corinth from landing on places in Corcyrean possession. Cimon's son Lakedaimonios was one of the admirals, very much against his own wish, a fact which confirms that the Athenians were trying to avoid even the appearance of breaking the treaty (Plut. 29, 2). It was probably at the end of the summer of 431 that the Corinthian and Corcyrean fleets met again near the Sybota islands, at the entrance into the waters round Corcyra. The Athenian squadron had joined the Corcyrean line on its right. Since the two left wings were successful, the Athenian ships were involved in the fighting, which was severe and caused many losses in dead and prisoners on both sides. In the end, after more setbacks for the Corcyreans, the Corinthians suddenly began to retreat, because they had noticed another fleet approaching, and rightly believed it was Athenian, though it was only a supporting squadron of twenty ships (Thuc. 1, 50f.) and not, as the Corinthians feared, something like the full fleet. After another day, during which the fleets faced each other without fighting, the Corinthians went home. Both sides claimed to have won, but Corcyra had the better of the war, and regained Epidamnus. The Corinthians, however, on their voyage home not only occupied Anactorium, an important place inside the Gulf of Ambracia, near its entrance, and resettled it with their own men, but could also claim that Athens, having fought against them, had broken the peace treaty. Still, neither Sparta nor the Peloponnesian League was so far involved, but the balance of power was seriously threatened, and Corinth's hatred of Athens had increased dangerously. Sparta was soon bound to come into the open.

Shortly after the events mentioned, a new cause of contention emerged between Corinth and Athens. Potidaea, situated on the isthmus of the western peninsula of the Chalcidice, and important for the trade with Macedon, was a Corinthian colony, still receiving two annual 'supervisors' from the mother-city;[10] at the same time it paid tribute as one of the Athenian allies. The ambiguity of that position became dangerous when Athens found that Perdiccas, king of Macedon, previously a friend and ally, had turned enemy. Made unsafe in his own rule by the rival aims of his brothers, he was alarmed when they joined the Athenian alliance. He contacted Sparta and Corinth, and tried to rouse the northern neighbours of Potidaea, the Bottiaeans and Chalcidians, into revolt. Athens sent out a body of a thousand hoplites against him, with the order to force Potidaea to break off her relations with Corinth, to raze her walls, and to give hostages. Potidaea, true to her double allegiance, but in fact prepared to defy Athens, sent envoys to Athens as well as to Corinth and Sparta. Lengthy negotiations at Athens were without result, but the 'officials' in Sparta promised to invade Attica if Potidaea was attacked.[11] In spring 432 Potidaea and her neighbours revolted. A second expedition went out from Athens, while Corinth sent troops under Aristeus in support of Potidaea. Sparta did nothing. The Athenians, after some successes, diverted their first force away from Macedon against the city. Perdiccas, an opportunist of the first order,[12] was glad to get them out of Macedon and made no trouble, though he soon again joined Potidaea. Events now centred on the isthmus of Potidaea, where the Athenians gained a victory[13] and blockaded the city, first only from the north; when they received new reinforcements they could build a wall on the southern side as well, and they left troops to devastate the regions round Olynthus and Spartolus, the cities of the Chalcidians and Bottiaeans. The siege of Potidaea continued, and Athenian and

Peloponnesian troops there faced each other; but 'the war had not yet broken out, and truce still prevailed; for the Corinthians had acted on their own'.[14]

Athenian policy all the time was, of course, directed by Pericles. So far the situation had forced his hand, now it was the other way round. He 'saw the war coming up from the Peloponnese' (Plut. 8, 7) and he was sure that Athens, with her military and financial resources, could stand a longer war than any of her enemies. The Athenian army was by then of considerable strength, and it is significant that Perdiccas changed sides again and provided troops against the Chalcidians. The Athenian navy was not yet involved in any significant way, but Pericles knew, and so did the people, how it reigned supreme, militarily as well as economically. There will have been another factor which influenced Pericles, the fear that revolts in the empire might spread if Athens showed herself weak. Now, he deliberately tried to force Sparta into war before she was really ready. By the 'Megarian decree', in winter 433–432, Athens excluded the Megarians from the Athenian market and the harbours of their empire (Thuc. 1, 67, 4. 139, 1 f.). The reasons given for this harsh measure are negligible; it actually followed a number of minor actions, due to the central and critical situation of Megara as the outpost for any Peloponnesian threat against Attica. Thucydides never gives a real explanation; he practically omits all possible reasons – personal or otherwise – why Pericles enforced the decree. Popular opinion, on the other hand, inside and outside Athens, regarded the Megarian *psephisma* as the deliberate and final cause of the outbreak of the war. Otherwise, it would hardly have been possible for Aristophanes later, in 426–425 and even in 422–421, to make it the result of a deliberate provocation on the part of Pericles.[15]

Megara, just like Corinth and (secretly) Aegina, had made complaints to Sparta, where the question of declaring war became the predominant issue under dispute. Corinth was the driving force. Ever since the Athenian occupation of Naupactus, her vital interests as a naval and trading power had been threatened, and the Athenian intervention at Corcyra and Potidaea was the last straw. After much hesitation, Sparta summoned her allies to a meeting, and Thucydides (1, 67–87) gives an account of that meeting in which, after a speech by the Corinthian envoys, an Athenian embassy, which rather surprisingly happened to be in Sparta, was invited to reply; this meant one speech for and one against a declaration of war. Sparta was under strong pressure, especially from Corinth, which threatened to look for other allies, and that meant Argos – the worst thing that could happen to Sparta. When the Spartans afterwards held a meeting of their own, the king Archidamus gave a realistic warning of the dangers Sparta would have to face, and pleaded for time; the ephor Sthenelaidas said in a short address that Sparta must help her allies. After that, the assembly decided by a large majority that Athens had broken the treaty of 445. At a later meeting of the Peloponnesian League (Thuc. 1, 119-25) it was decided to declare war (c. August 432), though in a diplomatic offensive which was not really genuine, Sparta still tried to find more ground to stand on. More embassies were exchanged, and the demand for the autonomy of the allies emerged as Sparta's fundamental point. It would mean, if not the dissolution of the Delian League, certainly the destruction of Athenian rule. Pericles replied by a demand for the full autonomy of Sparta's allies, and the request to renounce the Megarian decree was answered by the demand that Sparta should abolish the expulsion of foreigners. The debate had now an air of unreality, and when the Athenians offered arbitration (Thuc. 1, 145), this was no longer a possible way out, in fact it was not a genuine offer. Now, if not earlier, war had become inevitable.[16]

It was in spring 431 that Euripides produced his *Medea*, perhaps the most intensely tragic of all his plays. Once again a woman in despair is at the centre, but she is a sorceress whose vengeance on the unfaithful Iason destroys not only his new bride Creusa but also Medea's own children. In hostile Corinth Medea has been deprived of homeland and city, she is *apolis*. Athens, in the person of Aegeus, offers her a new home to which she turns even after her dreadful deed. She is not the victim of a curse by divine powers, she is the victim of her own passion and fury. Athens, however, is praised by the chorus in some of the most beautiful lines (824 ff.) as the home of beauty and wisdom, the alleged birthplace of the Muses, and the place where Aphrodite sends forth her Loves (*erotes*) as 'companions of wisdom, the helpers in every kind of valour'. This seems an

Athens far away from the reality of the time; Athena is not mentioned, though the Parthenon had just been completed. Rightly the chorus may ask (846) how the sacred and hospitable city can protect a murderess. But the song of praise is the poet's answer to all the charges made against his city; he may also have thought of the old charge of sacrilege against the Alcmaeonids, recently renewed by Sparta in order to undermine Pericles' position. *Medea* is an essentially unpolitical play, but it moves on the human (and inhuman) level in which neither gods nor daemons play a part. What matters are only the forces in the souls of men or women. It is for them to decide what to make of a situation threatening their own lives as well as their city. This was a new challenge, though we must not forget that Euripides did not express the feelings of the people in general.

Thucydides uses various speeches to describe the situation and the psychological reactions on either side. It is not a complete story, and, for instance, the discussion to what extent Pericles' own position was involved will probably go on for ever. The trials of members of his circle show, at any rate, that the opposition had gained strength. Ultimately, however, the theme of all the debates, whether recorded or not, whether *pro* or *contra*, was Athenian power politics, her imperialism. Thucydides' final résumé is given in a speech by Pericles (1, 140–4) in which, above all, the economic and military prospects of the war are discussed. If the picture, as is natural, is favourably biased, it is nevertheless sensible. If Athens followed Pericles' leadership and avoided all hazardous risks, the prospects were good. Invasions into Attica were expected, but would do no serious harm, while a naval blockade and a war of attrition would soon exhaust the enemies' slender resources. We must add: if nothing unforeseen happened; but that can never be assumed in war, and it was indeed to happen early enough. Both sides claimed to be going to war for reasons of justice, but the Spartan claim of fighting for the freedom of all Greek states had the greater force of attraction, despite the fact that Sparta was the first to break the arbitration rule of the treaty of 445. On the other hand, it is hardly justifiable simply to see in Athens 'the aggressor'. Her dynamism and expansive imperialism had the justification, or perhaps only a genuine pretext, that it was not an end in itself but went together with the aims of social progress and cultural supremacy. Against the conservative forces represented by Sparta, Athens was the champion of new and even revolutionary ideas.[17]

2 · The Archidamian War

The name of the ten years' war from 431 to 421 derives from the name of the Spartan king who led the invasions into Attica. It is clearly of Athenian coinage, and we find it first used by Lysias (fr. IX Th.). When Thucydides decided to write the history of the war, he knew only of the Archidamian war which he once (5, 25) calls the 'ten years' war'; later he discovered the unity of the whole war from 431 to 404, that is to say, it included the time of official peace after 421. At what moment this new concept was conceived, and to what extent it influenced the earlier stages already written, is part of the intricate question of the composition of Thucydides' work; it is outside the scope of this book.

The war started rather surprisingly in spring 431 with a Theban attack on Plataea (Thuc. 2, 2 ff.). That small Boeotian town near the Attic border, closely bound to Athens ever since the Persian war, was a thorn in the flesh of Theban supremacy over Boeotia, which was based on a complicated federal constitution (*Hell. Oxyrh.* 16).[18] With the help of some partisans among the Plataeans, a small force of Thebans entered the town by surprise, hoping that they could create a *fait accompli*, and that the obvious violation of the peace treaty would be forgotten in the coming war. The majority of the Plataeans, however, had no wish to defect from Athens, and when they found out how small the Theban force was, they fell upon them during the night, chased them through the streets, and killed many; the rest surrendered, the reinforcements from Thebes came too late, and the Plataeans put their prisoners, 180 in number, to death. The Athenians had tried to prevent this massacre, but their message did not arrive in time. Committed, as they were, to defend Plataea, they first imprisoned all Boeotians then in Attica.

The news soon spread through Hellas, and almost everywhere there was great excitement and enthusiasm for the war. Athens, the ruling power in the eastern Mediterranean – only Melos and Thera were outside Athenian rule – had additional allies in Corcyra,

Zacynthus, and even in Sicily, apart from the Acarnanians, Thessalians, and others on the Greek mainland. Sparta held the Peloponnese, except for Argos and Achaea, which remained neutral; Corinth, Megara, and Boeotia practically encircled Attica, but the Athenian navy had no serious rival. Against Athenian raids on their shores the Peloponnesian army was helpless, though it was at least three times stronger than the Athenian land forces. If, however, 'money is the sinews of war' (a view contested by Francis Bacon), Athens was much better prepared and had much larger resources.

With these facts in mind, Pericles had planned Athenian strategy. The Long Walls now came fully into their own, for in the space between them as well as in other free space within the city, even in some of the sanctuaries, the country population was to assemble, with women and children, household goods and farm implements;[19] only cattle and sheep were sent to Euboea and other islands. Against the expected invasions of the countryside nothing was to be done, except some harrassing by the cavalry; the fleet was to make raids on important harbours on the Peloponnesian shores, and to interrupt the trade routes, in particular of Corinth. This strategy did not make for swift and outstanding successes, and the removal of the peasants must have caused a great deal of misery. It is significant for the general mood that Pericles offered his country estate to the community, in case Archidamus, who was his guest-friend, might spare it.

Archidamus with the Peloponnesian army was, in fact, on his way, but moving slowly, too slowly for the feelings of his own troops. After an unsuccessful attempt at taking the fort of Oenoe near the Boeotian frontier, he at last, 'on the eightieth day after the Theban occupation of Plataea' (Thuc. 2, 19, 1), i.e. late in May, invaded Attica as far as Acharnae, destroying the harvest everywhere. He seems at first to have hoped that Athens would still come to terms, or at least meet the invaders in the field. Neither of these happened, but there were a few cavalry skirmishes, after a Thessalian force had unexpectedly arrived to help the Athenians. Naturally many citizens longed to save the country from devastation, and to expel an enemy so close to the city itself. Pericles had to realize that there was danger in the people's attitude, the more so as their discontent found a leader in the tempestuous Cleon. For some time Pericles refused to summon a meeting of the assembly, a remarkable fact revealing the leader's power in a democratic state. But a fleet was sent round the Peloponnese, and another smaller one to Locris; they had no spectacular success, although the former was strengthened by a special force of hoplites; on one occasion the Spartan Brasidas, who was to play a unique part in the war, excelled in saving the town of Methone from capture. More important was the fact that the Athenians expelled the people of Aegina and sent there settlers of their own,[20] thus removing what Pericles called the eye-sore of the Peiraeus (Plut. 8, 7); Sparta resettled the Aeginetans in the Thyreatis, near the Argive sea. About that time the Peloponnesians, lacking in supplies and anxious to work their own fields, went home and dispersed. Athens then started on a series of annual invasions into the Megarid without meeting any resistance.

Pericles decided on several new measures, such as establishing garrisons in important spots within Attica, and putting every year the best hundred triremes under three trierarchs in reserve. The latter certainly was an expression of confidence, though it emphasized the defensive character of Athenian policy. That is also true of the decree by which a reserve of 1,000 talents was secured, not to be used unless the city was directly attacked by a fleet. The raids on the Peloponnesian and other coasts will have had a certain effect on the enemies' economic situation, but they would not lead to the disruption of the Peloponnesian League. In all this we recognize the hand of the prudent statesman who expected the war to last long and foresaw unexpected dangers; he could not reckon with the disaster that was to come.

The first year of the war also brought an alliance with Sitalces, king of the Odrysians (see above, p. 246), and Perdiccas was once more reconciled with Athens. All the time the siege of Potidaea was maintained, and most of the large expenses recorded in inscriptions, probably belonging to 431–430, will have occurred in that connexion.[21] There were several successful raids; Cephallenia was won, the important island on the way to Corcyra, and a later attack by the Corinthians on the island was defeated. The Megarid was invaded by a major expedition, navy and army in full strength, under Pericles' leadership. Among the hoplites a large number of metics served, henceforth a fairly common practice. Thucydides (2, 28) also reports that an eclipse of the sun took place; that was on 3rd August. In the few words of the historian nothing indicated that it was a portent, good or bad; he is aware of the natural cause, though not certain of the astronomical conditions. He records the event like others, and we can only guess what the reactions of the ordinary people were.[22]

In winter 431–430 the public funeral of those killed in war was held as usual, and Pericles made the traditional eulogy.[23] Pericles had actually delivered the solemn speech after the first year of the Samian war, and now he was chosen again 'by the state', which was an honour for him and for the occasion, although he was the obvious choice. The number of slain in 431 must have been very small indeed, but Pericles made the funeral a great occasion. In Thucydides' rendering (2, 34–46) this *Epitaphios* or Funeral Speech has become the most famous document of Periclean policy. In fact, it is an idealizing, though in a deeper sense truthful, picture of everything Athens stood for, or at least was to stand for in minds such as Pericles' and Thucydides' own. Pericles never made a speech like this, though Thucydides did use certain important phrases and ideas which had been expressed by Pericles; Thucydides may have listened to the oration himself. What we have, however, is, like most speeches in Thucydides, a matter for reading rather than listening to; much of the rhetoric, with its Gorgian touches and its subtlety of thought, may have been fashionable, but would have been more or less lost on the audience. Among genuine Periclean concepts is the idea that the citizens should be lovers of their city, the existence of 'unwritten laws' as the result of public opinion and convention,[24] and of course the democratic constitution, based on freedom and equality, and contrasted with Sparta's reliance on obedience and training. Ultimately this was the difference between trust and distrust in human nature.[25] In a different way the rather hollow and empty exhortations directed to the relatives of the dead (ch. 44 f.) have also the appearance of genuineness, significant for the austere and lonely nature of Pericles.

The *Epitaphios* proves, if proof were needed, that a literary composition can have far greater effects than the original words. The immortality of this speech as written by Thucydides is due in equal measure to the greatness of Thucydides' mind and to that of Pericles which inspired him. Ultimately that means to the greatness of Athens; its main theme is the combination of power politics with the genuine love of art and wisdom; it is what made Athens 'the school of Hellas'. In Thucydides' *History* that speech, 'a possession for ever' like the whole work (1, 22, 4), is witness to the last moment of undiminished splendour in Pericles' life and in that of the Athenian people.

Early in summer 430 Archidamus again invaded Attica, prepared for a long stay. Then the plague broke out at Athens, swiftly spreading from the Peiraeus over the whole city. Thucydides (2, 47–54) is our impressive witness; he fell ill himself, observed what happened to him and to others, and survived to tell the story. Neither medical care nor prayers were of any avail, and many thousands from every walk of life died a miserable death. Despite Thucydides' careful description of the symptoms – he was fully acquainted with the advanced medical writing of his time – modern views still differ as to the nature of the disease; most likely it was typhoid fever. Soon conditions became terrible, especially due to the crowding within the walls, corpses filled the streets and temples, and the people in general abandoned all standards of religion and lawful order. The plague lasted for two years, and broke out for another year in winter 427–426 (Thuc. 3, 87). About one in three of the hoplites and horsemen died, and a vast unknown number of old men, women and children, metics and slaves. The reduction in population was felt for a long time, and it was not until 415, according to Thucydides (6, 26, 2), that a new generation had grown up to fill the ranks of the army and the city.

The effects of the disaster on the war were immediate and far-reaching. The Peloponnesian invaders had moved to the shores of Attica in the east and north-east, reaching as far south as Laurium, though we do not hear of any damage to the mines. When they heard of the plague, the enemies left 'after the longest time they ever stayed', i.e. forty days. Meanwhile a strong Athenian fleet was ravaging some of the Peloponnesian shores, using even horse transports. Pericles was in command. The same fleet, after its return, went straight out again to the Chalcidice and Potidaea, now under different commanders. They tried in vain to take the city, but had brought the plague with them and lost a quarter of their soldiers. The infectious nature of the disease, whether recognized or not, influenced some of the military events; for instance, Plataea and Potidaea, while besieged and thus cut off from the outer world, remained free from the plague. Thucydides calls the leaders of the Potidaean expedition, Hagnon and Cleopompus, 'fellow strategi of Pericles' (2,58, 1); this unique description refers to the year 430–429,[26] and the wording points to the fact that Pericles was soon afterwards to lose his position.

War and plague together had been too much for the Athenians. Pericles was blamed for their misfortunes, and they were prepared to come to terms with Sparta. Envoys were sent there, but achieved nothing. The attempt must have been made against Pericles' advice, though 'he still was *strategos*',[27] proof enough that even under a strong leader the will of the assembly was supreme. However, Pericles' position was in grave danger, and he now called an assembly and tried to change the people's mind. His speech, his last in Thucydides (2, 60–64), is both a self-defence and an accusation. Though more remote, it seems, from the actual speech than any other, it certainly reflects Pericles' unbroken vigour, and repeats some of his words. He turned, in particular, against those who put private above public activity, the *apragmones*, and he warned the Athenians not to let go the rule 'which you hold like a *tyrannis*' (63, 2), which it may have been unjust to acquire but would be dangerous to surrender. In fact, the rule of Athens, her empire, was at stake. Behind the generalizations and theories of the speech there is Pericles, the great realist.

The assembly was persuaded, once again, to follow his political lead, though not without much grumbling in private, and first subjecting him to a heavy penalty. Thucydides says nothing more than that, but he implies that Pericles was dismissed from office. He was almost certainly charged in an *apocheirotonia*, the usual form of deposition of an official during his term of office, but we do not know what was the charge.[28] Soon he was back as *strategos*, though again we do not know how soon; anyway, he was once again 'entrusted with everything'. A few weeks later, still in 429, he was dead, having caught the plague and been unable to recover. His two legitimate sons had died earlier, but one of his last actions had been to legitimize his son by Aspasia, the younger Pericles.

The swift change of fortune confirms not only the fickleness of the people but in fact the hold Pericles had on them. His death meant the end of an epoch. Thucydides emphasizes the greatness of the man and his unique position in a few famous sentences, mentioned before (p. 244); his kind of leadership was just what his successors could not achieve. If Thucydides blames them, he has forgotten that the death of the great leader left a gap which was at least so much Pericles' own fault as that of his inadequate successors.[28a] The war went on much as before, though moods and actions on either side became more and more grim and cruel. Still, in 430 the friendship with Sitalces, which, by the way, may have brought the cult of the Thracian goddess Bendis to Athens, had led to the seizure of Peloponnesian envoys on their way to Persia. Sparta, from the beginning of the war, had thought of getting from Persia the two things she did not have herself, ships and money. She was never successful, but nobody blamed her for treason to the Greek cause. Sitalces sent the envoys to Athens, where they were executed, after the Spartans had killed every man, whether Athenian or ally, and all of them civilians, whom they captured on board ship mostly in neutral harbours.[29]

Athens, under Phormio's generalship, had successes against Corinth; several campaigns and naval battles took place, Naupactus was held, and with that the interference with Peloponnesian trade went on.[30] Potidaea surrendered during the winter 430–429 because of the complete lack of food; the Athenian generals allowed the inhabitants and foreign troops free departure, and were promptly blamed for that at home. Later, Athenian colonists settled at the place, and Potidaea as an Athenian colony paid no more tribute.[31] During the summer the Athenians suffered a defeat by the Chalcidians near Spartolus. In the battle light-armed troops gained superiority over hoplites, in military tactics an indication of things to come about a generation later.[32] Later events (Thuc. 2, 95–101) showed a display of strength on the part of Sitalces who invaded Macedon and Chalcidice, without meeting resistance either from Macedon or from Athens.

The political leaders at Athens were now partly men of the commercial middle class, outstanding among them Cleon, the owner of a tannery. He was the first who no longer held the office of *strategia*. His political programme was the continuation of the war to the utmost, and he had the ear of the assembly. In comedy as well as by Thucydides he is described as a boisterous and brainless demagogue, or at least as 'the most violent of the citizens'. A demagogue he certainly was, who tried to flatter the people, but he had courage, great power of speech, and quite good brains. The contrast to Pericles was very great, and that was probably the chief reason why the traditional picture is biased and unfair.[33]

In summer 429 the Peloponnesians avoided plague-ridden Attica, and Archidamus put Plataea to siege (Thuc. 2, 71–78). For the sake of an important ally such as Thebes, and in spite of the obligations the Greeks had to Plataea, Sparta decided on the attack, and negotiations broke down. Thucydides describes in great detail the methods of the beleaguers as well as the effective counter-measures of the Plataeans, partly at least because he wished to explain why the enemy was unable to overcome the small Plataean garrison. During the winter about half of these managed to escape to Athens, and it was not before summer 427 that the town, without help from Athens and practically starved, surrendered. Thucydides (3, 52–68) reports a debate in front of the Spartans between Plataeans and Thebans, which is a specimen of his art, but has little, if any, historical value, though one interesting point is that the Thebans defended themselves against the reproach of medism by blaming the ruling oligarchs, having neither democracy nor a 'democratic oligarchy' (*isonomos oligarchia*); that probably refers to Athens and Sparta respectively. The outcome, anyway, was that all Plataeans unable to affirm that in this war(!) they had done something for Sparta or her allies were executed. Later the town was destroyed. If Athens sent no help, it is quite possible that she simply was not able to do so.

To Thucydides the fate of Plataea was chiefly a case to be used as a parallel and partial contrast to the simultaneous event of the revolt of Mytilene, or rather of Lesbos with the exception of Methymna (3, 2–18, 25–50).[33a] Lesbos, apart from Chios, was the last more or less independent ally of Athens, with a navy of her own; the ruling oligarchs seized the opportunity when Athens was in a seemingly bad position. It was a shock to the Athenians, who were reluctant to start a new theatre of war, while they were still under the shadow of the plague, and the Peloponnesians had again invaded Attica. Mytilene, they feared, might give an example to other allies and strengthen the forces of the enemy. The revolt was at first successful, though Mytilenean envoys at Olympia clamoured in vain for Peloponnesian help. Thucydides reports their speech; it is effective, full of sophistic antitheses, but with clear traces of the genuine argument. It ends in an explanatory summary, definitely overstating their case.[34] Mytilene was accepted as an ally by Sparta, but the attempt at attacking Athens by land and sea came to nothing, and Mytilene was besieged by an Athenian force under Paches. Among the great efforts Athens made at that moment was the introduction of a capital tax (*eisphora*) of 200 talents, a big sum, even though paid by citizens and metics alike.[35] The procedure proves the need of money for the war, but at the same time the possibility of getting a good deal out of the wealthy. It was the work of Cleon, as the comedians indicate and as we should suspect; Thucydides' silence on this point remains remarkable.

Early in 427 Mytilene surrendered, after her demos, not out of loyalty to Athens, but because of lack of food, had turned against their rulers; the Peloponnesians again devastated Attica, but the fleet they had promised to help Mytilene never arrived; its admiral displayed the typical Spartan lack of initiative in naval matters. There was a number of incidents, all showing the cruel harshness of warfare on either side; this came to a head when the leaders of the revolt had been sent to Athens, and the assembly had to decide on their fate and that of Mytilene. The first decision was to kill all men, and to sell into slavery the women and children; with that order, a trireme was at once dispatched to Paches. Views, however, had been divided, and the next day another assembly was called; that was the occasion for perhaps the most famous duel of speeches in Thucydides, between Cleon, who defended the action taken, and one Diodotus, otherwise unknown, who spoke for a more moderate course.[36] It is anything but an authentic report, though the prevailing theme of what is just and what is useful, however common to sophist thought, may easily have played its part in the actual debate. Cleon's attacks on the sophists were largely intended to contrast him with Pericles, while at the same time there are allusions to words used by the Thucydidean Pericles, an indication to what extent Thucydides used the speeches in his work as a means of revealing subtle facts below the surface. On the other hand, it has always been noticed that even Diodotus does not plead for mercy or justice, but for expediency. The mind of the people was dominated not so much by pity and humanity – put by Cleon on a level with their 'pleasure in speeches' – as by the reluctance to punish the Mytilenean demos together with the oligarchic leaders of the revolt. The former decision was revoked, and another trireme dispatched which arrived in time; Paches seems to have hesitated, and now only the Lesbians already in Athens were executed.[37] Athenian cleruchs went to Lesbos to occupy the land of the oligarchs.

The Spartans at Plataea, the Athenians against the Mytileneans – the parallel is as obvious as it is terrible. Probably about the same time Sophocles produced his *Oedipus the King*.[38] It is the tragedy of a great man and a great ruler, whose search for the truth about himself destroys him. He is wiser and greater than the Creon of the *Antigone*, and it is the very irony of his tragic fate that he believes in the gods and their oracles, and yet tries to evade them. Throughout the play all evidence turns out to mean the contrary, and this tragic irony reveals the eternal conflict between the will of man and the course of fate. In a final sense Oedipus too, seeking 'to be master in everything' (1522), puts human standards and his own intellectual power over the divine world order, and that without showing *hubris*. At the same time he is essentially a ruler. The kings of myth are common figures on the stage, but to Sophocles, who himself never went to a prince's court as Aeschylus and Euripides did, the relation between the ruler and the ruled was an additional serious problem. It seems, after all, not too bold to see in the tragic figure of Oedipus some reflection, however distant, of Pericles and his tragic end.[39] The pious poet, who believes in the eternal 'laws set up on high' (865), turns against man's self-reliance as taught by the sophists, and accepted by many of his fellow citizens. He teaches 'the defencelessness of human nature', and that all human happiness is built on an illusion.[40] The basic issue is the conflict of opposing attitudes to life; it is remarkable how Sophocles turns his back on the events of the day, steadily clings to tradition, and yet takes sides in the spiritual struggle of the time. Curiously enough, his anti-sophist attitude seems to make him an ally of Cleon; but his deepest beliefs belong to a different sphere: the gods are cruel, man stands alone, persuasion is powerless. The great play shows most clearly that no simple formula can adequately cover the spiritual world of Athens at war.[41]

Thucydides' narrative of the war in 427 centres on the horrible events of the civil war in Corcyra, in which even slaves and women took part; it led to two murderous massacres by the democrats, the last one as late as summer 425 (Thuc. 4, 46–48). Corcyra was of major importance, and at first, fleets of both the Peloponnesians and the Athenians tried to intervene, but without success. The civil war (*stasis*), in fact, spread to other parts, a result of the general dualism of divided Greece. Sparta and the oligarchs, the upper-class families of noble descent and wealth, on the one side, and Athens and the democrats, that is to say, the peasants, tradesmen, and artisans of the demos, on the other, those were the two camps which fought each other not only in the war between the two leagues but also within each single polis. War proved indeed to be 'a violent teacher'. Thucydides, in two famous chapters (3, 82–83) on the effects of war and civil strife on human nature,[42] realized the changes taking place in the minds of the people, the hunger for power, the new meaning of words and slogans, the sectional spirit and the increase of lawlessness, jealousy, and perfidy – in short, the breakdown of all moral standards.

Much of this disruption is reflected in the early comedies of Aristophanes, of which we shall speak later, and in the pamphlet on the *State of the Athenians*, already mentioned.[43] The author attacks democracy by showing how consistently it has been built up to the advantage of the ordinary people. This earliest extant Attic prose-book is full of the pride of the 'good' over and against the 'bad' men, of the oligarchs – and that means those capable of ruling – against the masses of the people. The author is a 'civilized' man whose chief weapon is irony; nevertheless, the book is an expression of that savage struggle which was going on inside most of the Greek states. It ends with the statement that Athenian democracy has nothing to fear from the exiled oligarchs, proof that at that time there was no danger of a revolt at Athens such as had happened in other states.

The spirit of Athens was unbroken, although the city was hit by a new outbreak of the plague. In contrast to Pericles' cautious strategy, Athens was at the same time engaged in several aggressive actions. There were two main theatres of war. One was Sicily, where the Athenians helped Leontini, an Ionian colony, against Dorian Syracuse. It is remarkable how strong the influence of ethnic allegiances was in Sicily, far stronger than in the east. Athens, in 433–432, had renewed treaties of alliance with Rhegium and Leontini (ML. nos. 63, 64. SEG 25, no. 22), and an embassy from Leontini had reached Athens. Its main speaker was the sophist Gorgias, who made an enormous impression on the Athenian public.[44] The Sicilian war spread to Italy, a new fleet went out the following year, and fighting continued in 425 and 424. The other area of warfare was in western Greece, centred on Naupactus. The general here was Demosthenes, one of the most brilliant military leaders in this war. After a first setback against the Aetolians, after which he did not return to Athens, he gained two victories with the help of the Acarnanians; the city of Ambracia suffered what Thucydides (3, 113, 6) calls 'the greatest disaster to any single polis during the war', obviously meaning the Archidamian war. Even so, the whole campaign had little general importance, except in strengthening the Athenian position at Naupactus. About the same time Sparta made a move more adventurous than usual. In Trachis, not far west of Thermopylae, a colony was founded, Heracleia, which might have considerable strategic value, both by securing the position of the Dorians in central Greece and by countering Athenian forces going up to Thrace (Thuc. 3, 92) The Spartans could not yet know that the place was to become the base for Brasidas' campaign in the north (Thuc. 4, 78).

Meanwhile, politics at Athens were in the hands of Cleon, who had the people behind him. He met public criticism from an unexpected quarter. Aristophanes, still in his late teens or early twenties, had produced his first comedy, the Banqueters (Daitalēs), in spring 427, and brought out another play, the Babylonians, the following year.[45] We know little of that comedy, but enough to say that the young man criticized Cleon's policy and the officials of the state; as the play was performed at the Great Dionysia, it took place in the presence of foreigners and allies. That had the effect that Cleon brought the poet to trial on the charge of slandering the state. Most of our knowledge derives from Aristophanes' next play, the earliest extant, the *Acharnians*, and a *scholion* (to v. 378). Political comedy had for some time been a voice of uninhibited and possibly critical satire, largely concerned with the leadership of the state. For three years at the time of the Samian war there seems to have existed a kind of censorship;[46] otherwise, the freedom, or even licence, of comedy, towards gods no less than men, was unbridled, as a part of democratic *parrhesia*, freedom of speech. Cleon's strong reaction – soon after the Mytilenean debate – probably means that he was displeased by such a young man's daring rather than by the freedom of comedy generally. In the *Acharnians* (February 425) Aristophanes was more cautious; moreover, it was performed at the Lenaea when no foreigners, in particular no allies, were in the theatre.

The play nevertheless discloses the deep divisions in public opinion about the war.[47] The whole play is dominated by the poet's passionate longing for peace. Since real peace seemed unattainable, the farmer hero of the play, Dicaeopolis, makes his private peace. This was, of course, a flight of absurd fancy, and the man a truly comic hero, but there is a manifest deeper meaning.[48] The whole comedy is permeated by an atmosphere of defeatism, in which the true enemy was not so much Sparta but the Athenian political leaders. 'I do not speak of the polis,' Dicaeopolis, 'the man of a just city',[49] repeatedly stresses, but of those 'men of ours', responsible for the war and for all the misery it brought about. They are Pericles, who inaugurated the Megarian decree, the people in the assembly, who were always prepared to go to war and elect the wrong leaders, Lamachus, the funny caricature of militarism, and of course, Cleon, who is personally challenged. Most of the play is fun and farce, but the chorus of the old Acharnian Marathon-fighters, who at first want to fight the war through to absolute victory, are converted by Dicaeopolis' courage and commonsense, and by the very materialist advantages of his private peace which leads to his final triumph.

The *Acharnians* was awarded the first prize, and it seems certain that this was not a merely aesthetic verdict. The longing for peace was widespread, though there was no 'peace party' at Athens. Just because Dicaeopolis' complaints are more or less trivial (destruction of vines, difficulties of trade, scarcity of some foodstuffs), and do not even mention the real disasters of war, the audience of ordinary citizens would feel that their lives were concerned. We have here an authentic picture, almost free of caricature, though not of fancy.

All that, though not Aristophanes' hostility to Cleon, was changed by the events of the summer. On board one of the ships which were on their way to Corcyra and Sicily was Demosthenes, at his own request, but with the official permission to act at his own discretion. He advised the generals to land at Pylos, the rocky headland at the narrow northern entrance to the 'harbour', the bay later named after Navarino. The weather was bad, and therefore favourable to his plan for fortifying the place unmolested by the enemy. Hereby, he initiated a policy which, in contrast to his offensive against Aetolia, could still be regarded as a natural consequence of Periclean strategy, which included naval raids on the shores of the Peloponnese; but it was an important step further to build a more or less permanent fort in the enemy's country, from which it would be possible to incite the helots.[50] Demosthenes was left at Pylos with a fairly strong force of soldiers and five ships, while the fleet sailed on. So far the Spartans had not interfered, though they had broken up their invasion of Attica. They now concentrated on Pylos, and the Peloponnesian fleet soon arrived.

From Thucydides' topographical description it is clear that he never saw the place; but we can establish the main facts of the situation (see map). In front of the large bay lies an island, Sphacteria, wooded and uninhabited; it was not a safe barrier since the southern entrance to the bay was wide and deep, and could not be blocked. The Spartans, nevertheless, placed a force of several hundred hoplites on the island, and then attacked Demosthenes' position from the sea with no effect. When the Athenian fleet, recalled by two of Demosthenes' ships, arrived, it was able to enter the bay by both entrances and to defeat the Peloponnesian fleet, part of which was taken by surprise. Thus, the hoplites on Sphacteria were cut off, with little water or food, while Athenian ships controlled the island by continuous patrols. A truce was concluded to allow food to be transported, while the Peloponnesian fleet was for the time surrendered to the Athenians. Then Spartan envoys went to Athens, offering peace and friendship in return for the liberation of the men on Sphacteria. At that moment the whole war situation seemed changed. Athens was near victory, if – but only if – the Spartan proposal was genuine. The most damaging point was that Sparta acted

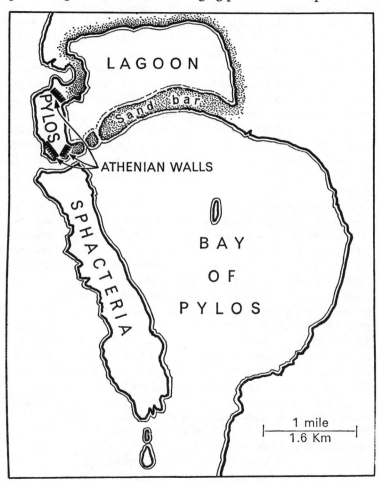

9. Pylos and Sphacteria

without consulting her allies. Her peace offer would remain meaningless unless the Peloponnesian League was behind it. The Athenian
refusal, therefore, was perhaps not unjustified, though a wiser policy
would have gained something out of that unique situation.[51]

Such a policy could hardly be expected as long as Cleon was at
the helm. Thucydides (4, 21), on this occasion, solemnly reintro-
duces him as 'the leader of the demos' (*demagogos*) and 'most
trusted by the masses'. The truce at Pylos ended, but the Athenians
broke their word and refused to return the Peloponnesian ships.
The blockade of Sphacteria proved difficult, since food was secretly
brought over, especially by helots who were promised their freedom. The Athenians on the spot were full of misgivings, and so
were the people at home. Cleon challenged his opponent Nicias,
who was a general, but did not like military adventures, to lead a
fleet to Pylos and capture Sphacteria, whereupon Nicias resigned
and offered his post to Cleon, who was forced to accept, and then
boasted he would bring home the Spartans within twenty days,
alive or dead.

If that was a boast at which the people might laugh, Cleon knew
what to do. He asked for, and was given, a force of light-armed
troops, and he chose Demosthenes as his colleague. He had good
luck as well, for a fire had recently destroyed the woods on
the island; that made an attack much easier. A few days later the
Athenians landed and by a kind of guerrilla warfare reduced the
Spartans to a last stand; soon they surrendered. Of the original 420
hoplites, 292 were still alive, among them 120 Spartiates. The
blockade had lasted for more than ten weeks. Now the prisoners
were brought to Athens, and the armies withdrew from Pylos;
the place was held by Messenians from Naupactus, who continued
to stir up the helots. It was they who dedicated to the Olympian
Zeus the famous statue of Nike, sculptured by Paeonius, a marvel
of bold and accomplished art. The goddess, standing on a high
triangular base, seemed not to stand at all but to fly down from
Olympus, borne on the back of an eagle, with the wind blowing
her dress behind her. It was a figure worthy of the occasion of a
victory won by daring courage and clever planning.

Cleon's bold promise was fulfilled, thanks to his energy and
Demosthenes' good generalship. Throughout Greece, people were

amazed at the fact that Spartiates had given up their arms instead of fighting to the last. The prisoners were held as hostages, and threatened with death in the case of another invasion of Attica. The Spartans tried in vain to negotiate for their recovery. Athens had reached the peak of her war efforts, and Cleon was the undisputed political leader.

He was, however, prudent enough to leave the military tasks to others. They were aristocrats and had a good deal of experience in the field and on sea, men such as Nicias, Demosthenes, and Lamachus. Expeditions went out in 425 and 424, against Corinth and Anactorium in the gulf of Ambracia, also to Chios and Lesbos, and even – though not successfully – to the Black Sea. Cythera was captured, and became a permanent menace to Sparta, more dangerous even than Pylos; actually the whole Peloponnese was more or less blockaded, and Sparta's allies suffered. In Sicily a truce was concluded on the basis of the *status quo*; Thucydides (4, 59 ff.) puts a speech into the mouth of the leading Syracusan statesman Hermocrates, who, while recognizing the power of Athens, pleaded for peace in Sicily under the slogan 'Sicily for the Siceliots'. The Athenians – or at least many of them – had dreamt of plans of expansion, reaching as far as Carthage (cf. Arist. *Eq.* 174); they were disappointed when the fleet came home, and the generals were penalized by the people. There was a growing tendency at Athens to distrust the high officials, most of them members of the upper class. Democracy, with the growing self-confidence of the people, became more radical, and Cleon's leadership, to say the least, did nothing to tame that spirit. With their light-hearted optimism, which derived from a great power of resilience and courage, the Athenians went from strength to strength. They even captured Nisaea, but could not prevent an oligarchic counter-coup in Megara; the Spartan Brasidas was involved there, and he was soon to change the general war situation.

During this period negotiations were going on between Sparta and Persia. Since Sparta could not openly renounce the freedom of the Asiatic Greeks, and that was Persia's *conditio sine qua non* for any help, the negotiations came to nothing. Athenian sea-power, on the other hand, impressed the Persians so strongly that in 425 the new king Darius confirmed the peace treaty of Callias.[52]

The intensive activity of Athens naturally cost a lot of money. Direct personal tax, though never common among Greek states, had been introduced before (*eisphora*); it had been increased during recent years, and it is hardly unfair to give Cleon the chief credit for a measure necessary for the state, though a heavy burden on the wealthy (cf. Arist. *Eq.* 923 f., also 774 f.). Financially still more important was a new assessment of the tributes. Such assessments were, as a rule, made every four years, and when the money was urgently needed, as happened frequently, the tributes were collected by the notorious 'silver-collecting ships' which Thucydides mentions several times,[53] even before the allies brought the tributes to Athens, usually at the Dionysia. These collections emphasize the difficulties which Athens experienced in securing the tributes which, with every new assessment, will generally have grown, though not in each single case. The assessment of 425–524 is the only one of which we have the decree regulating present and future procedure, and it has been found that the total of tributes now amounted to 1,460 talents, or even more. The devaluation of money had something to do with such a sum, which also led to an increase in the jurors' pay from two to three obols; but there can be no doubt that the pressure on the allies had been greatly intensified. Pericles' moderation in dealing with the allies, although it had been energetic and harsh enough, gave way to an exploitation which foreshadowed disaster. Cleon was 'watching like a tunny watcher the tributes coming in' (Arist. *Eq.* 312).

He was the man who 'surveys everything himself' (*Eq.* 75). That is the main theme of the *Knights*, the comedy Aristophanes produced – this time under his own name – at the Lenaea in 424 B.C. Cleon appears as a Paphlagonian slave, all-powerful in the house of Demos, and dominating his fellow slaves Nicias and Demosthenes. He is a scoundrel who is being beaten by a greater scoundrel, the sausage-seller, who rather surprisingly is to become the city's saviour (149), and in the end rejuvenates the old doddering and gluttonous Demos (1321) and makes him 'king of the Hellenes' (1333). Perhaps the most remarkable thing in this ferocious political comedy is the strange alliance between the noble youth of the chorus and the sausage-seller, who first does not even know how to become 'a man' (179), that is to say, one who fulfils the main task of being an active citizen.[54] The alliance is based on the common hostility to Cleon, the common aim of fighting war policy and political corruption; it does not mean an anti-democratic attitude. The polemics against Cleon could hardly be more outrageous, and sitting, as he did during the performance, in the first row on account of the *prohedria* bestowed upon him after his Pylos success, Cleon must have listened with rather mixed feelings. Like the audience he will have laughed at many of the coarse jokes, but he cannot have liked the insinuation that at Pylos he 'served a cake to Demos, which another man had baked' (54), or only reaped what others had sown (392; cf. 742. 845). He will, on the other hand, have enjoyed the repeated allusions to his war policy and his refusal of any peace offer. The *agon* of the two shameless and corrupt demagogues, the absurd obscenity and poor wit of their exchanges, make the political scene a mere grotesque; almost the only true fact that emerges, apart from occasional asides, is the poet's savage hatred of Cleon.[55] Aristophanes again got the first prize with the *Knights*, and Cleon made no attempt to punish him; but it is mistaken to speak of a peace party behind the poet. In the play the council shouted 'with one voice' (670) that, when the sardines were cheap, there was no chance of peace: 'Let the war go on!' And the war did go on.

During these years, between 430 and 424, Euripides wrote a number of plays which reflect, one way or another, the climate of war.[56] In that sense they were 'political', and in the main highly patriotic, plays. Allusions to Sparta were sporadic and generally peripheral, though in the contempt for Sparta expressed in the *Andromache* we feel political poetry deteriorating into mere propaganda. The *Heraclids* and *Suppliants* are both dominated by the relations of Athens with Argos, but even more prominent, though in a different spirit, are the horrors and the sufferings of war, and the failure of man to live up to its moral challenge. Apart from the (limited) righteousness of the democratic ruler Theseus and the Athenians generally, it is the women who, through their love and self-sacrifice, raise each play above the usual conflict between Right and Might, or between freedom and tyranny, and above the frequent appeal to the common laws of Hellas. The latter are, in fact, for Euripides the laws of humanity, the laws of a human world in which the gods have no real place. The actual secularization of the state is strongly reflected, and the 'first commandment' of honouring the gods, or the mentioning of cults or personal actions by divine persons, are no longer truly pious allusions; they seem no longer real. Small wonder that Euripides, in spite of his love for, and his frequent praise of, Athens – which could sometimes almost equal Pericles' Funeral Speech (cf. *Suppl.* 427 ff.) and make Theseus the ideal representative of democracy – failed to win the favour of an audience that was generally still dominated by traditional religion; very rarely he won a first prize.[57] The audience, with their old-fashioned standards, did neither take any real interest – as shown by the failure of the first *Hippolytus*–in the psychology of erotic passions and the aberrations of female love, which Euripides was the first to introduce into drama. In a different way, such an attitude on the part of the people may be confirmed by the fact that Aristophanes' attempt in the *Clouds* (spring 423) at discussing, and making fun of, Socrates and the sophists was a failure. He later wrote, but never produced, a second version, the one extant, which contained a more definite condemnation of Socrates. We shall talk about it in the next chapter.

The centre of the war had meanwhile (summer 424) moved north where Brasidas had entered Thrace. He was supported by Sparta's wish to break out of her hard-pressed situation and her fear of the helots. Actually, Brasidas had taken seven hundred helots into his army as hoplites, that is, as freed men. There is no reason to doubt Brasidas' honesty, which he showed on many occasions, but for the Spartan government it was only another opportunity of getting rid of some of the Messenians who saw in occupied Pylos a chance of revolt.[58] The situation in the north was as confused as it could be, and Athenian rule was hardly anywhere as vulnerable as in that economically highly important area. Perdiccas, king of Macedon, and the Chalcidian cities were frightened by the Athenian forces in Thrace, and wanted Spartan help; the Athenian allies, on the other hand, were often in precarious situations among hostile Thracians and Macedonians, while Arrhidaeus, king of the Lyncestrians in northwest Macedon, was an obstacle to Perdiccas' policy of aggrandizement; with him, against Perdiccas' wish, Brasidas began to negotiate. In the cities pro- and anti-Athenian groups were usually at loggerheads. Brasidas himself was more than merely an efficient and courageous general, even more than 'not a bad speaker for a Lacedaemonian' (Thuc. 4, 84); he was an honest and moderate man, though naturally a Spartan patriot. He soon had success among the Greek cities, but refused to support any single party, and gave solemn pledges to grant full liberty to the cities. Whether he genuinely believed in Sparta's unselfish programme of liberation and anti-imperialism is difficult to decide; but it is significant that he was soon to lose the support of his own government. Brasidas was surprised when some of the Athenian tributaries were not willing to revolt; he then threatened them with punishment, for the sake of Sparta's programme of general freedom. He had entered the city of Acanthus alone, and persuaded the people to surrender; but even Thucydides says that happened largely because of their fear for the harvest (4, 88). During the winter the king of the Odrysians, Sitalces, was killed in a local fight, and was succeeded by a nephew who was Perdiccas' brother-in-law and anti-Athenian. Brasidas, strengthened by allied forces, suddenly marched against Amphipolis, taking the Athenians completely by surprise. The historian Thucydides was in charge of a small fleet near Thasos, and was only in time to save Eion, the harbour of Amphipolis. The city itself, with its mixed population, surrendered when Brasidas offered moderate terms. The loss of Amphipolis decisively changed the situation in the north, and deprived Athens of an important source of money and timber, and also of the direct route to her allies farther east. To what extent Thucydides or the Athenian commander at Amphipolis was at fault cannot be decided. The people at home condemned Thucydides to exile, which was to last for twenty years; it gave the historian new and unexpected opportunities of collecting material for his great work.

In the meantime, late in autumn 424, an intrigue between some Boeotian democrats and leading Athenians, especially Demosthenes, had been discovered; therefore it miscarried (Thuc. 4, 90 ff.). While the Athenian army was already retreating towards Attica, they were pursued by the Boeotians and forced to a stand at Delium, near the sea and near the Attic border. The Boeotians were stronger in numbers, above all in light-armed troops, and for the first time the new oblique Theban phalanx, up to twenty-five men deep, went into action. At nightfall the Athenians were routed though many escaped by sea. It was the first and only real land battle of the war, and Pericles' strategy to avoid all pitched battles was fully justified by the defeat. For seventeen days afterwards the two sides wrangled about the collection of the dead, one of the most cherished and established traditions of Greek warfare. Soon nothing of religious or moral feelings seemed left to save the war from its full bestiality. It was under the impression of these events that Euripides wrote the *Suppliants*.

During the winter, probably as a consequence of the Boeotian campaign, Megara recovered and destroyed the Long Walls which made an Athenian attack on the city from Nisaea possible. At the same time Brasidas had more successes in the Chalcidice; in particular, the important city of Torone fell into his hands, with the help of some anti-Athenians among the citizens. The Athenian garrison had a rather inglorious escape (Thuc. 4, 110 ff.), and the allies farther east began to turn to Brasidas. Thus, the war situation became more and more favourable for Sparta, and yet the ephors, partly out of personal jealousy and partly because of the precarious situation in the Peloponnese, refused Brasidas the reinforcements he had been asking for. The desire for peace was spreading on both sides, and it led in spring 423 at least to a one-year truce (Thuc. 4, 117 ff.). Neither side, however, was at that moment ready for a genuine peace.

The news of the truce interrupted Brasidas' campaign, just after the town of Scione had submitted and crowned him as the 'liberator of Hellas'. Thucydides (4, 121) compares this crowning with that of an athlete, words which do not express irony but reflect the genuine enthusiasm for Brasidas. Scione's revolt, however, happened two days after the conclusion of the truce, the Athenians demanded the city's surrender and prepared to act, and more trouble arose, both with several Greek cities and with Perdiccas, who once again changed sides, concluded an alliance with Athens, and stopped a Peloponnesian force from marching through Thessaly. Nicias was operating with some success from Potidaea, which Brasidas failed to take by surprise. Still, nothing of real importance happened during the winter, till in spring 422 the truce ended.

Shortly before, Aristophanes produced the *Wasps*. While, like the *Clouds*, it stressed the contrast between the generations, which had become one of the major problems of Athenian society and of which more will be said, the play also continued the poet's attacks on Cleon and on demagogy, this time chiefly in their effect on the law-courts. The old man Philocleon is taught the necessary lesson by his son Bdelycleon, the 'Cleon-lover' by the 'Cleon-hater'. Between father and son the natural order of things is reversed; the son is well-off, and the father is waiting for his death in order to make a flute-girl his legal concubine. The chorus, old men and jurors like Philocleon, share his enthusiasm and later his conversion. This witty and wicked play is not only one of Aristophanes' best comedies, it is also, though fair-minded, one of the strongest attacks on one of the people's chief faults, their love of litigation and their pleasure in the 'sting of the wasps'. It is also no mere chance, but a result of the war situation, that the jurors are old and poor. The poet, who is on the side of the sensible son and his hatred of the self-seeking demagogues, depicts the character of the old men, while stressing their bad temper, in a kindly and good-natured way. Philocleon is the hero of the play, not an ordinary citizen in a quasi-heroic action like Dicaeopolis, rather a reflection of Demos himself, who, as in the *Knights*, is rejuvenated in the end. Hardly anything is said of the longed-for peace, or of that imperialism which was more or less the same whether Cleon or Nicias was leading. Fun was more easily and less dangerously to be got from the fickle yet lovable people at home; the political events of the moment were outside the play's scope.

The outstanding event after the end of the truce was Cleon's expedition to the Chalcidice. After a first success he sailed to Eion, and on the whole showed more sense and better leadership than Thucydides will concede (5, 2 ff.). In the final battle, however, Cleon made serious mistakes, and together with several hundred of his troops, he was killed. Brasidas too was severely wounded, and died after having learnt that the Athenians were defeated. Amphipolis was lost to Athens, and Brasidas was worshipped there as the heroic founder of the city (5, 11). Thus ended the most outstanding Spartan, who might have saved Sparta from temporary defeat, and the Athenian, who had nearly brought victory to his state. With the two most aggressive leaders out of the way, the road towards peace lay open.

Sparta, in view of the fact that the treaty with Argos was coming to its end, and with the urgent need to get back the men from Sphacteria, was even keener than Athens to finish the war. Both sides had lost confidence. The Spartan king Pleistoanax, who some years earlier had returned from exile, and Nicias in Athens were the right men to start negotiations and to achieve consent. In spring 421 peace was concluded for fifty years, the 'Peace of Nicias', as it is called, not without justification. Its main condition was the return of cities or men captured during the war. Among the former was Amphipolis, and though Sparta even allowed Brasidas' newly won allies to return to Athenian rule, if they wished, new trouble was to arise. In case of dispute both sides had agreed on a peaceful solution, whether by direct negotiations or by arbitration of a third power. The treaty was ratified and sworn, but some of the major members of the Peloponnesian League rejected it. The peace was a compromise, though with a favourable bias towards Athens. Afraid of Argive hostility and a possible helot revolt, Sparta even concluded a treaty of defensive alliance with Athens which promised help against the helots (5, 22 f.). The time of Cimon seemed to have returned. For the moment, in both states alike a feeling of great relief prevailed. Plutarch (*Nic.* 9, 7) tells us that the people joined in singing the chorus of Euripides' *Erechtheus* (fr. 369), which began: 'Down with my spear, let it be covered with spiders' webs!'

The mood of the weeks when peace was certain, but not yet concluded, finds expression in Aristophanes' *Peace*. At last the struggle was over, or so it seemed. The goal was reached, and the poet could describe Trygaeus' achievement of gaining peace as a fantastic and burlesque, but generally acclaimed, deed; only soothsayers and armourers, both of them war-profiteers, or a politician who wanted to become a strategos, such as Alcibiades (450; cf. Thuc. 6, 12, 2), still objected. As in earlier plays, peace appeared as the condition for a peasant's quiet life, for the pleasures of sex and harvest, and for the fulfilment of religious obligations long neglected. And it was a peace for all Greeks.[59] The ideal – in comedy as in reality – was the restoration of the *status quo ante*, an impossible and empty ideal. The importance given by both sides to the sacred rules and divine sanction of the treaty could not prevent it from being concluded in a kind of vacuum and an atmosphere of wishful thinking, almost like Trygaeus' flight to heaven on a dung beetle, in order to 'excavate' peace. The end of the ten years' war did not mean a stable peace. The war was not yet over.

3 · Between Peace and War

Thucydides wrote a new prooemium (5, 26) when he started his narrative of further events; now he makes it quite clear that the whole war of twenty-seven years is one and the same. He also tells his own private story of his exile from Athens for twenty years. This chapter is one of the crucial passages for the discussion of the way in which Thucydides wrote this book. Here it will suffice to say that 'the war', which previously could sometimes mean the Archidamian war only, henceforth cannot mean anything but the whole war from 431 to 404.[60]

The aftermath of the Peace of Nicias was, for several years, a confused and confusing diplomatic tug-of-war, full of trickery and inefficiency.[60a] The political constellations changed all the time, and there was little difference in the methods of Sparta, Athens, Argos, or Corinth. Nicias tried to save his peace, while a new leader of the anti-Spartan group at Athens emerged in the person of the young and brilliant Alcibiades, son of Cleinias, an aristocrat of the purest blood, and a complete individualist and egotist at that. His actions show little, if any, influence of his guardian Pericles, in whose house he was brought up, or of Socrates, who was his beloved teacher. In spite of his youth, he had a greater influence with the people, thanks to his charm and brilliance, than the moderate and hesitant Nicias. He was elected general for several successive years.

It seems hardly worth while to follow the diplomatic actions in detail, but it ought to be mentioned that now at last the Peloponnesian League was broken; Corinth turned to Argos, which emerged as a strong power, hoping to gain the hegemony over the Peloponnese. Mantineia and Elis, Corinth and the cities of the Chalcidice joined Argos in a new alliance. Some states, however, refused, partly because their oligarchic governments distrusted democratic Argos. Athens, under Nicias' steady and cautious leadership, kept aloof for the time being; the radical leaders, who had succeeded Cleon, were soon to be replaced by Alcibiades. Sparta, on the whole rather helpless, made a few counter-moves, such as an expedition to free the Parrhasians in Arcadia from Mantinean rule, and the settlement of Brasidas' helots and *neodamodeis* at Lepreum in Triphylia, the stronghold of Spartan policy against Elis.[61] The first indication that all was not well between Sparta and Athens was provided by the refusal of the local commander to return Amphipolis to Athenian rule; in consequence, the Athenians retained Pylos. Another centre of trouble was Boeotia. After such breaches of the peace treaty, apart from all the negotiations marked by mutual distrust between the various states, Alcibiades succeeded in persuading the Athenians to conclude a defensive alliance for a hundred years with Argos, Mantineia, and Elis.[62] Sparta had a bad time. Elis could exclude her from the Olympic games, Heracleia in Trachis was defeated by neighbouring tribes and finally fell to Boeotia, and Argos began a war against Epidaurus; a late and weak attempt by Sparta in winter 419–418 to help the beleaguered town was regarded by Athens as a definite breach of the treaty of 421.

At last, in summer 418, Sparta realized the serious danger of her position and made a full-scale expedition, 'they themselves and the helots altogether', led by King Agis.[63] Those allies who had remained loyal joined, but in a confused situation in which neither side knew who was endangered, the army leaders agreed to a truce for four months (5, 58 ff.), very much to the anger of their troops and indeed their governments. Thus, what Thucydides (5, 60, 3) calls 'the finest army till that day' was kept out of action, largely by the over-cautious, though clever, tactics of King Agis. Eventually Alcibiades, acting as ambassador in Argos, brought about a new offensive in which Orchomenus was taken and Tegea threatened. That meant an indirect threat to Laconia, and once again the Spartans marched out in full force, asking their allies to join them. The two armies met in the Mantineian plain, and after some vicissitudes Sparta gained a complete victory.[64] This battle restored Sparta's reputation, and caused an oligarchic revolution at Argos, followed by a defensive alliance for fifty years between the two old enemies.[65] The anti-Spartan coalition, and Alcibiades' double-edged intrigues, had broken down, the Peloponnesian League was practically restored, and some of those who were usually sitting on the fence, such as Perdiccas and Mantineia, now joined the new Spartan alliance.

In summer 417, however, democracy was re-established at Argos, and soon her relations with Sparta became cool again, while Athens, and especially Alcibiades, became more active and aggressive. That policy culminated in an attack on the island of Melos, which, though regarded as a Spartan colony, while assessed for tribute by Athens in 425 B.C., had remained neutral all through the war. Athens gave the island city the choice between becoming a tributary subject and being destroyed by force. The negotiations are compressed by Thucydides (5, 85–113) into the famous debate which, though unhistorical, reflects the principles or lack of such of, and the spiritual forces behind, the mutual political attitudes. Melos conformed with the traditional standards of trusting the gods and of human decency, while the Athenians argued with the sophistic contrast between the just and the useful, and finally and cynically proclaimed the Right of the Stronger. This time there was no Diodotus, as in the Mytilenean debate, to oppose the extremist policy of Athens, nobody to remind the Athenians of what kind of policy was in their true interest. It is no mere chance that Thucydides puts at this point his elaborate dialogue, for the 'hubris' of Athens was the main cause of the decisive change which took place in the following years. Thucydides was undoubtedly worried about Athenian policy, and the dialogue, if he wrote it himself as most likely, is an example of his condemnation of the disastrous imperialism of Athens, which goes together with his admiration for Pericles' policy, even his imperialism.[65a] Melos was blockaded, remained without help from Sparta, and after brave resistance surrendered (winter 416–415). All adult men were killed, the women and children enslaved, and five hundred Athenian colonists sent to the island.[66] The ruthlessness and violence of warfare, though practised by all belligerents, had reached a culminating point. The fact that Sparta had not intervened caused alarm among her allies, while it gave Athens, and especially Alcibiades, a feeling of security and even of predominance that was finally to lead to disaster. Athenian policy caused more hatred than ever before; she had not won the war, and was now losing the peace.

In the midst of all these events, economics and culture at Athens remained strong and vigorous. The political strife among the people's leaders also went on. Hyperbolus served as a weaker kind of Cleon against the conservative Nicias and the erratic genius of Alcibiades. Nicias, middle-aged, wealthy, modest, was not without military efficiency, but too diffident and cautious. Significantly, a comedian says of somebody that he was 'a good citizen who did not walk about timidly like Nicias'.[67] He was the very opposite of Alcibiades, the youthful, dashing *homme à femmes*, who had both genius and complete egotism, in fact such a mixture of contrasts that it is almost impossible to draw his portrait.[68] The pupil and friend of Socrates was also a man whose megalomania and ambition excelled equally in racing victories and in politics. His policy in the Peloponnese had gone astray, but so had Nicias' peace policy. Alcibiades could rely on the support of some, though by no means all, of the hetaeriae, the aristocratic clubs, which at that time had acquired considerable strength. Nicias might have a fair amount of followers among the middle-aged and the old, while Hyperbolus, the leader of the demos, was unable to impress or to excite the masses. He was frequently ridiculed by comedy, but so were the two other politicians, and Hyperbolus was never seen as a danger in the way Cleon had been portrayed. In his *Maricas*, Eupolis described the demagogue Hyperbolus rather than one of his noble opponents as a paedarast prostitute, a commonplace charge which did not fit the man. Hyperbolus was not taken very seriously even by the people, and when, probably in 417, he tried to expel Alcibiades by ostracism, his two opponents joined forces, and the man ostracized was Hyperbolus himself. That was a farce in which the people played an absurd part. It was the end of ostracism no less than of the politician Hyperbolus; ostracism was never practised again. As another weapon against individual claims to power, the 'charge of unlawfulness' (*graphē paranomon*) was introduced, by which the case was put before a court instead of the assembly.[68a] It is well known what the courts were like, and it remained to be seen how far the new measure could protect the constitution; for the moment, at any rate, the leadership of Athens remained strongly divided between Nicias and Alcibiades.

Economically Athens had few worries as long as she ruled the

seas, and the necessary imports, especially of food and timber, regularly reached the Peiraeus. The Peace of Nicias had restored security
to the Attic peasants, and their products, above all oil and wine, still
reached distant countries – a valuable source of income. Athenian
artisans and artists never ceased to work. More and more metics
settled at Athens, and the city benefited from their skill and enterprise. At the same time the number of slaves increased, while the
number of citizens, after the losses by war and plague, slowly rose
again. The beautiful little temple of Athena Nike was built, over-
looking the slopes of the Acropolis, before anything like a true
victory could be claimed. At the same time the building of the
Erechtheum continued, which, if not 'great' architecture, largely
because of its cramped position, and the accumulation of elements
demanded by different cults, displayed what perhaps can be called
the finest details of decoration, and in the porch of the *korai* a
masterpiece of combined architecture and sculpture. All that would
not have been possible if Athenian finance had not been, on the
whole, fairly healthy again. It is known that loans were repaid to the
goddess, and the number of ships in the navy was increased.[69]

For those who, like Aristophanes, had hoped for final peace,
these years must have been full of disappointments. He left it to others
to attack such a minor figure as Hyperbolus, and wrote unpolitical
comedies, for instance, mythological parodies. Tragedy, much less
concerned with actuality, still flourished. Sophocles, impressed by
some of the new features of Euripides' plays, laid increased stress on
human psychology and less on the role played by the gods and by
fate. This can be seen from tragedies like the *Trachiniae* (the date of
which is quite uncertain) and the *Electra* (later, but also undated).
Euripides wrote, as it were, parallel plays – whether before or after
Sophocles, is an undecided question – the *Heracles* and *Electra*, the
first a document of pathological psychology, the latter significant
(though not only for that reason) for bringing myth more than ever
down to earth.[70] The terrible story of Heracles' madness, which was
caused by the cruel amoral forces called gods, ends in a discussion
between Heracles and Theseus, which is a weak anti-climax arti-
stically, but proclaims the great truth that man must rely on man,
defying the blows of fate. The heroine in *Electra* has been forced to
marry a poor peasant. Persons of lower social status had appeared in

earlier tragedies, the messengers in Aeschylus, the shepherds in *Oedipus Rex*, even the nurse in *Hippolytus*, but they were all servants. Now a simple husbandman (*autourgos*) plays a part on the same level as the members of the royal house. He is a noble character who leaves Electra a virgin. If he is said to descend from noble forefathers (35), that is of no significance, though perhaps a minor concession to traditional prejudices. In fact, Euripides no longer discriminates between the 'good' and the 'bad' as social classes. Electra has become a hard-working housewife, 'for it is a joy for the worker to come home and see the house in good order' (75). These are the standards of the lower classes, which had never before been portrayed in myth and tragedy. Orestes (367) reveals the intellectual background behind the social change; he realizes that wealth and nobility are no true criteria for a man's value; the only criterion is his 'nature' (*physis*). Repeatedly we hear that 'many of noble descent are bad men' (551). It goes without saying that the change in social conscience does not apply to slaves whose loyalty belongs to those who win the day (632). All these things are, of course, peripheral in the play. What the poet really aimed to do might be called to improve on Aeschylus, not only in small matters such as means of recognition (*anagnorisis*) but also in the essential point – Apollo's guilt. It is not the murderers who are guilty but the god (1296).

In spring 415 Euripides produced the *Trojan Women*. Athens was in the midst of the preparations for the Sicilian expedition when this passionate anti-war drama was performed. It can hardly be called a drama, it is a kind of oratorio on the destruction of Troy, and on the disasters which struck the conquered and will strike the conquerors. The stage is filled with suffering and cruelty, inflicted by a destiny both meaningless and pitiless, but there is no plot or action. The fate of the Trojans, the men and even the boys being killed and the suffering women led into slavery, reflects what happened time and again during the war. 'The great city' (*megalopolis*) is a city no more (*apolis*), 'Troy no longer exists' (1291). 'The name of the land will vanish. Her children shall widely be scattered' (1322). A woeful warning, a dirge before the event, that was the poet's prophetic reflection of his own time.[71]

It is also in this play that Euripides reveals more strongly perhaps than anywhere else his fundamental belief. Hecuba's prayer (884), is an invocation of that power called Zeus 'whosoever thou art', deliberately taking up the theme of Aeschylus' *Agamemnon* (160). But while Aeschylus seeks for words worthy of divinity, Euripides seeks the god as 'nature's necessity or the mind of man', referring to philosophical theories of his time, may be the deification of the ether by Diogenes of Apollonia or Anaxagoras' supreme power of *nous*, human reason and intellect. Hecuba's prayer is an isolated intrusion into the play, but the more significant as an expression of the poet's mind, influenced by contemporary philosophy, and wrestling with the problems of divine power – though not divine persons –, a witness to the growing secularization of Greek thought. The prayer is followed by a rhetorical *agon* between Hecuba and Helena, in which the contrast between human responsibility and the mythical part played by the gods is finally put to the test. To Helena's excuse that she was the victim of Aphrodite (*Kypris*), Hecuba replies (988): 'Thy mind, when it saw him, became Kypris.' That mind, called *nous*, is clearly more than mere intellect; it is her inner self – we might say, her character or even her soul –, and that alone is responsible for her adultery and all its consequences.[72]

At the moment of the performance of the *Trojan Women* the plans for the great expedition to Sicily overshadowed everything else. Most of the Athenians knew hardly anything about Sicily, though Leontini was an ally, and they probably knew that the Ionian city was in danger from its powerful neighbour, Dorian Syracuse. There was undoubtedly a strong trend in Syracusan policy, aiming at a hegemonic position over the Sicilian Greeks as a whole. We do not know to what extent Athens was influenced by the fear of such a development, though the idea that Syracuse might help Sparta against Athens was hardly taken seriously. Anyway, the situation of Leontini only served as a pretext. Thucydides dedicates two books of his work (6 and 7) almost exclusively to the Sicilian expedition. These two books are unique in character; style and composition are of a coherence and unity found nowhere else in his war history. With all their wonderful variety the two books have the build-up of a tragedy.[73] He makes it quite clear that the true reason for the expedition was the widespread wish to conquer Sicily (6, 1), that is to say, that Athens and her people were completely dominated by their imperialist ambitions, which found no satisfaction in small and not very successful raids to help Argos, or in fighting the Thracians. Domination over the west had been one of the Athenian aims ever since Pericles, if not earlier, though Pericles would never have thought of a large diversion of forces as long as the situation at home was still unsettled. The expedition of 427 had been on a small scale only, not to be compared with what was to happen now. While Pericles' and even Cleon's main object had been to consolidate the existing Athenian rule, Alcibiades in 415 was dreaming of its extension over the whole Mediterranean, and of himself as the great leader and conqueror.

Things began to move when the Elymian city of Egesta in northwest Sicily, an old ally, sent envoys asking for help against Selinus which was strongly supported by Syracuse; the latter had also occupied Leontini. The Athenians were prudent enough to send an embassy of their own, in order to find out whether Egesta was able, as promised, to finance the expedition. In summer 415 these envoys returned and brought evidence, as Thucydides says (6, 8, 2), equally 'seductive and untrue'. Egesta offered sixty talents for the monthly pay of the crews of a fleet of sixty triremes; that meant one drachme a day for each man, a fairly, but not unreasonably, high wage. The Athenian envoys had been made to believe, by various tricks, that Egesta's wealth was enormous. The assembly therefore decided on an expedition, and appointed three generals with full and equal power (*strategoi autokratores*), Nicias, Alcibiades, and Lamachus, the last a professional soldier, the *miles gloriosus* of Aristophanes' *Acharnians*. Their task was described in modest terms, but it really meant the conquest of Syracuse and Sicily.[74] Another meeting of the assembly took place four days later; according to Thucydides, it was then that the two leaders Nicias and Alcibiades opposed each other's policy, Nicias giving a serious, though rather late warning 'not to aim at a new *arche* before having secured what we have',[75] and turning against the youthful adventurer Alcibiades, who only thought of himself. Nicias proposed a new vote, but he could not sway the people, who, after an emphatically optimistic and clever speech by Alcibiades, maintained their earlier decision. The people of 415 had really recovered from plague and war, and a generation had grown up who liked Alcibiades' adventurous ardour far better than Nicias' cautious conservatism. Many also, among them Alcibiades himself, whose style of life was too expensive even for his wealth, were looking forward to becoming rich from the war. Those who doubted the wisdom of the decision did not dare to oppose it for fear of looking unpatriotic. Nicias made a last attempt, changing his tactics and stressing the need for the greatest military strength for the expedition. Instead of frightening the people, he only made them more determined; they asked him to state what he wanted, and thus forced him indirectly to support Alcibiades' policy. Frivolous egotism and imperialism defeated common sense and realistic patriotism. In a further decree from which Thucydides (6, 26) quotes, the three generals were again given complete power to make what arrangements they thought necessary, and the final preparations got under way.

In midsummer 415 the fleet left amid great enthusiasm. Prayers and libations accompanied the departure. Thucydides (6, 31 f.) assures us that it was the most magnificent spectacle, and the best prepared and most expensive expedition ever sent out. Yet, in view of the far-reaching aims of most people and the possible setbacks, the effort was far too weak. In spite of Nicias' warnings, few Athenians realized the dangers of failure. The whole atmosphere was so full of elation and excitement that no reasonable argument could prevail. That had become particularly manifest when shortly before the fleet left, many of the hermae, the figures of Hermes standing all over the town, were found to have been mutilated. The sacrilege had obviously been organized beforehand, and was not simply the work of a band of drunken revellers. People regarded it very seriously, not only as a bad omen for the expedition but even as a sign of an oligarchic conspiracy. Some opponents of the war in Sicily may have been involved. Moreover, evidence was produced of the profanation in some private houses of the Eleusinian mysteries. Greek religion knew of no heresy, and comedy provides many examples of how gods and even mysteries could be parodied, but the people, particularly at that critical moment, were very sensitive to any serious act of irreverence. The two sacrileges were obvious signs of growing scepticism, if not the complete negation of the gods. It is not certain whether there was a connexion between the *hermocopidae* and the private mockery of the mysteries. It is, however, certain that political use was made of both events. One or another of the oligarchic 'clubs', the *hetairiai*, was certainly involved, and Alcibiades was named as one of the participants, though he had nothing to do with the mutilation of the hermae, which endangered the sailing of the fleet, the main object of his policy at the moment.[76] However, the whole affair provided the great opportunity for which his many enemies had been waiting. He pleaded for an immediate inquiry, but his opponents, hoping for a better result later in his absence, managed to convince the people that the expedition should sail without delay. Even the offended religious feelings did not prevail.

Rumours of the expedition naturally reached Syracuse, but seemed almost incredible (Thuc. 6, 32 ff.). In an assembly Hermocrates pleaded for immediate preparations, while a demagogue, Athenagoras, with much rhetoric, denounced Hermocrates and his like for trying to overthrow democracy. One of the strategi then closed the debate, promised to acquire information, and assured the people that what was necessary would be done. Meanwhile, the great fleet crossed over from Corcyra to Italy, where they found an unfriendly, sometimes actually hostile, reception. Even Rhegium, where the ships finally assembled, did not join the expedition, in spite of the alliance of 433–432 with Athens (*ML*, no. 63. *DSDA* no. 162), though it showed a fairly friendly noncommittal attitude of 'wait and see'.[77] The main disappointment was Egesta, which provided only thirty talents (half the sum promised for each month); it now became clear that city owned nothing like the wealth the envoys had been shown.

Thucydides then reports a council of the three Athenian generals at which the question how to proceed was discussed. It seems unlikely that the question had not been discussed before, though it was probably only then, when the military and financial conditions were clear and, as to that, far less favourable than originally believed, that a final decision was taken. Each of the three generals had a plan of his own, and the plans were very much in accordance with the nature of the men. Nicias wanted to confine action to Selinus and Egesta; Alcibiades first to win over as many states as possible, Greek or Sicel, and then to attack both Syracuse and Selinus; Lamachus pleaded for an immediate attack on Syracuse, unprepared as it was, from a new base at Megara (see map 5). Only the last plan was conceived by a military expert; but neither of the other two plans seemed to demand anything impossible. Lamachus, to avoid dead-

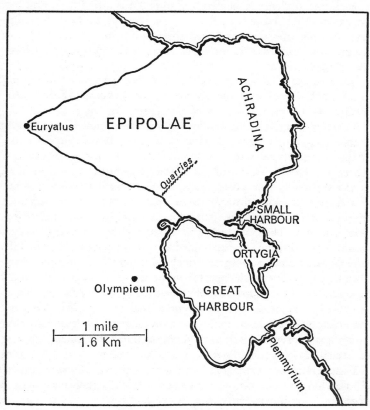

10. Syracuse

lock, agreed to Alcibiades' idea. It became clear from the start how mistaken it was to have three supreme commanders, and Alcibiades' plan, which foresaw Messana as a base, miscarried at once, as he failed to take the town. Nothing had yet been achieved when the *Salaminia*, the official trireme, arrived to fetch Alcibiades and some other noblemen home to stand trial for the profanation of the mysteries. The recall of the initiator of the expedition had disastrous consequences. At Athens the excitement over the suspected conspiracy seems to have overshadowed all the hopes and fears for the expedition. In Sicily it seemed best to make as little fuss as possible, and to keep Alcibiades' recall more or less secret; he was allowed to use his own ship, and managed to escape from Thurii. He went to the Peloponnese, a traitor to his home city, and was sentenced to death *in absentia.*

During the winter 415–414 the Athenians succeeded in getting a strong foothold near the temple of the Olympian Zeus in the centre of the great harbour of Syracuse. Thus it was, after all, Lamachus' plan which was followed, at least to some extent. A first battle took place near Cantane, and after heavy fighting the Athenians emerged victorious (Thuc. 6, 64–71). That victory proved to be the fatal *peripateia* of the whole expedition. The Syracusan army was badly in need of reorganization; for the fifteen generals previously in office three with full powers were now elected, a curious imitation of the Athenian example; one of them was Hermocrates. They at once sent envoys to Corinth and Sparta, asking for help; they also extended the walls of Syracuse to include the deserted place of Megara which Lamachus had intended to use as a base. Next came an appeal from both sides to Camarina, an old foundation of Syracuse, but for some time an ally of Athens (Thuc. 6, 75–88). Camarina decided to send a small force to help Syracuse, but openly to remain neutral, sitting on the fence till it became clear who was to prevail. Sicels in the interior joined the Athenian forces, especially as horsemen. Envoys even went as far as Carthage and the Etruscans; the latter sent some troops, the former, as far as we know, did nothing. On the whole, the reception of the Athenians remained cool and restrained.

The most important event during the winter occurred at Sparta (Thuc. 6, 88–93). Syracusan envoys, joined by Corinthians, pleaded for help, and they found an unexpected ally in Alcibiades. His personality carried the day even in that difficult situation of an Athenian exile advising the enemies of Athens. Sparta was little inclined to give Syracuse more than moral support, but Alcibiades persuaded them to send an efficient commander with some troops to

Sicily, while at the same time they were to occupy Deceleia in Attica, an action greatly feared by Athens. His advice was accepted, though Sparta as so often moved very slowly. Alcibiades' speech in Thucydides' rendering is a masterpiece. We can assume that some of the effects he foretells, especially of the occupation of Deceleia, were formulated by Thucydides when he knew what these effects actually were; the wild plans, on the other hand, of occupying Italy, Carthage, and finally the Peloponnese belonged to the Alcibiades of 415 rather than to later Athens. Essentially Alcibiades must have said what Thucydides makes him say. Although a speech *post eventum*, its combination of clever self-defence, practical advice, and fake honesty is masterly and has the ring of truth.

The people at Athens remained in suspense. Money and horsemen were sent to Sicily, where horses could easily be found, but otherwise mutual distrust, a great amount of litigation, and a general emotional and unreasonable atmosphere prevailed. Democracy flourished dangerously, both in the patriotic enthusiasm for the Sicilian expedition and in the struggle among the people at home. The news of Alcibiades' desertion must have come as a shock to his friends and followers, and served as a source of new indictments for his enemies. It was, however, more than that. Denunciations and informing were the order of the day, metics and slaves – with or without torture – came forward to give evidence and to produce long lists of men who were supposed to have taken part in one or both of the sacrileges. Inscriptions contain lists of the property confiscated from those condemned as *hermokopidai*, and those charged with impiety against the Eleusinian goddesses, including Alcibiades.[78] Trial followed trial, and to most Athenians these affairs seemed, at least for the time being, more important even than the whole expedition. At the same time economic conditions deteriorated and discontent spread throughout the empire. It was in this kind of atmosphere that Aristophanes wrote the *Birds*, the gayest, the most poetic, and perhaps the most cynical (or wise?) of his comedies.

Peithetaerus, the 'persuasive friend', and his *alter ego*, Euelpides, 'the man of good hope', both 'citizens among citizens', with phyle and clan behind them (33), find life in their home city unbearable. They have left Athens to escape from debts, lawsuits, and the whole setting of Athenian society. They do not hate Athens, that happy city 'common to all to pay fines', nor are they oligarchs hating democracy (125). They are looking for a 'comfortable', 'quiet' polis, a *topos apragmon* (44), where one is free from politics and violence. Then the flight into Utopia begins. A chorus of birds was a traditional feature,[79] but it is unlikely that the main theme had ever before been the realm of the birds, described as free and easy and a haven from contemporary Athens. Peithetaerus, as the leader and as an Athenian, cannot imagine life except within a polis; he therefore aims at a city in the air, and soon orders walls to be built. The new city arises, between earth and heaven, between men and gods, the 'city of the birds in the clouds' (*Nephelokokkygia*, Cloudcuckooborough) (818). The whole process is depicted in a delightful mixture of fun and poetry, with innumerable puns, many allusions to contemporaries, and plenty of literary parodies. It has rightly been stressed what a decisive part the 'language of absurdity' here plays, even more than in any other of Aristophanes' comedies,[80] but it is Peithetaerus' general 'sophism and subtlety' that defeats all mistrust on the part of the birds and makes him their saviour (545) and king.

The two Athenians have been given wings; on the stage they no longer differ in their appearance from the birds, who are also winged men. A whole mythology of the birds is being developed, an *ornithogony* to beat all theogonies. Birds were prior to gods (477, 701), birds now replace the gods (723), and there will even be a 'holy war' against Zeus (556), and a customs frontier between heaven and earth. The birds as ancient providers of *omina* are 'Ammon, Delphi, Dodona, Phoebus Apollon to men' (716). There will be lots of good things for men under the birds' rule, there will not be Nicias-like delays (640), no promises broken by the demagogues of providing grain (580), no need for expensive marble temples (612), and what is bad or forbidden in Athenian law will be permitted and good with the birds (755).

The light-hearted praise of the birds' city is interrupted by visitors from Athens, who have heard of the new foundation. They are generally unwelcome, and only trying to make money. Peithetaerus deals with each of them, for the most part very drastically. There is the priest who wishes to pray for the city, there is the poet who sings a parody of Pindar, comparing Peithetaerus with Hieron, there are the soothsayer, the astronomer and land-surveyor Meton, the public inspector (*episkopos*), the decree-trader[81] – they all are treated as quacks and forcibly expelled. Later a second batch appears, wanting wings for themselves, a father-striker (representative of the conflict of the generations), Cinesias, a feeble poet, a sycophant who wants wings to denounce the allies in court before they can reach Athens. Again Peithetaerus knows how to deal with them. The meaning is obvious: at Athens there are too many official and un-official parasites preying upon the state's money, and nothing of the sort is to happen in the birds' ideal state.

But is it ideal, even among all the poetic fancy and the beautiful pastoral songs? The city is called rich and radiant (*liparon*, 826), just like Athens, its god will not be Athena Polias, but the *peplos* will be there, and the wall of the storks is the *Pelargikon* or *Pelasgikon* on the Acropolis – it is a second Athens that is being built in the clouds. At its gates it will have custom duties ('seal and signet', 1213), it sends out a vast expedition when a god is said to have crossed the frontier (1173), and worse, the birds promise in case of victory never to let men fail to have enough Laurium owls (1106), and to help them to steal when they hold office – one of the very things the enthusiastic founder wanted to do away with. The city has begun to destroy the birds' innocence, they proclaim war (1189), they have even threatened the gods with 'Melian famine' (186). They fall into the faults of Athenian imperialism, and from this point of view the whole great adventure seems rather more than a flight of fancy or an escape story; it becomes a satire not only on domestic conditions but also on schemes of conquest such as the Sicilian expedition still in progress at the time.

If that is true, the *Birds* is, in fact, a highly political comedy. The fun with the gods in the latter part is pure comedy of an almost incredible irreverence, from Prometheus' saying that 'Zeus is lost' (1514) to the surrender of Zeus' envoys – Poseidon, the gluttonous Heracles, and the barbarian Triballian god –, the transfer of Zeus' sceptre to Peithetaerus, and the latter's marriage to Basileia. This Basileia is not merely a lovely girl but in charge of Zeus' thunder-bolts, of his wise counsels (*euboulia*), his good order of the world (*eunomia*), his moderation and – of the shipyards, the slander, the finance officials, the triobolon for the jurors (1538). What can that

mean if not that the new city will be Athens all over again? When
Peithetaerus appears with his bride, he has reached his full triumph,
he is 'tyrant',[82] he has conquered Zeus and rules everything. The
marriage with Basileia is an allegory, at the same time affording the
usual *finale* of a sexual union, and the fantastic rise of the great individual. What in the *Knights* had happened to Demos himself was now
bestowed upon a single political leader, whose name perhaps points
to the hetaeriae. Alcibiades *redivivus*? Anyway, Athens remains
Athens, men remain men. The poet has clad his pessimism in fanciful and colourful dress, but it is nevertheless a deep pessimism. There
is no glorification of the idea of monarchy, as has sometimes been
thought. It is a dream that leads *ad absurdum*.[83]

Meanwhile, in spring and summer 414, activities round Syracuse
increased. The main battlefield was now Epipolae, the plateau in the
north-west of the city as a dominating, though uninhabited, citadel
(*Fluchtburg*). Walls and counter-walls were being built to blockade
the city and, on the other hand, to break the blockade. Some fighting
took place, in which Lamachus was killed, the fleet entered the great
harbour, and the Athenians had, on the whole, the better of the
struggle – in fact, victory might have been in sight; but Nicias, now
the only commander, was not up to his task. Gylippus, the Spartan
general, who with a small force had reached Tarentum, heard alarming rumours about the situation at Syracuse (Thuc. 6, 94–104). He
was the right man for the job, an energetic and inventive soldier,
and at the same time a man of tact. In Greece the war between
Athens and the Peloponnesians had broken out again, since an
Athenian fleet had landed on the Laconian coast to help Argos
against a Spartan invasion. It was important for Sparta's genuinely
conservative and pious spirit that it was Athens that had openly
broken the treaty of 421. Now, Sparta prepared for the occupation
of Deceleia, and Athens faced the double threat in Greece and in
Sicily; the 'Peloponnesian war', even more than ever before, was
a 'Greek' war.

Gylippus and a Corinthian squadron reached Sicily, found allies
in Himera and elsewhere, and could not be prevented from entering
Syracuse. This soon proved to be the turning point of the Sicilian
war. The Athenians had never fought another democracy; now they

got to know what a democratic people could achieve under great leadership, such as they had not experienced since the days of Pericles. Gylippus not only strengthened the will to resist among the Syracusans and restored military discipline; after some successes and misfortunes he was soon able to break the blockade once and for all and to regain Epipolae. Nicias' occupation of the fort Plemmyrium at the southern entrance of the great harbour defeated its purpose, made supplying the fleet more difficult, and led to a grave demoralization of the sailors and to many desertions. While more help arrived for Syracuse, the Athenian situation deteriorated, and Nicias saw no chance of regaining the initiative, either on land or sea. He sent an alarming report to Athens, which was read to the assembly.[84] It made it clear that the situation was desperate, that Nicias himself was a sick man, that a quick decision was needed, either to withdraw from Sicily completely or to send a substantial force under a new commander (Thuc. 7, 10–15).

The people reacted swiftly. The great general Demosthenes, and Eurymedon who had been to Sicily in 424, were elected commanders of a new force of citizens and allies. Eurymedon left in mid-winter with ten ships and some money, while Demosthenes prepared a larger expedition for the spring. At that time the Peloponnesians under King Agis, son of Archidamus, had already invaded Attica and begun to fortify Deceleia. The consequences were very serious for Athens. For several years the countryside was devastated, many cattle lost, and the supply route from Euboea blocked; it had to be replaced by the longer sea route. Slaves were running away in their thousands, and money became scarce, as the home revenues, especially the Laurium silver, no longer reached the city.[85] It was then that Athens renounced the tributes, irregular as they were, in favour of a 5 per cent duty (*eikostē*) on all imports and exports within her rule. It was hoped, perhaps rightly, that this tax would bring more money in. Athens was like a fortress under siege, though not yet fully blockaded; the strategy of the war, in a complete reversal, had come full circle. It was Sparta and her allies who now tried to turn Pericles' policy against Athens.

At that time large reinforcements, having succeeded in diverting Athenian attention, sailed to Sicily. There, in spite of an Athenian victory, Plemmyrium was taken with its considerable stores of

supplies and armaments, and Syracuse was hoping for victory
before any Athenian reinforcements arrived. A fierce battle lasted
for several days and ended in great Athenian losses. At that moment
Demosthenes' large fleet entered the harbour, a heavy shock for
Syracuse. Once again the balance was changed, and Athens gained
supremacy by land and sea. Demosthenes, determined to avoid the
mistakes made by Nicias, decided on a speedy attack; it would mean
either the capture of the city or immediate and complete withdrawal.
In a furious nocturnal battle, which Thucydides describes in great
detail, the Athenians were beaten. Demosthenes now insisted on
withdrawal, northwards towards Catane, but Nicias stubbornly
refused; he set his hope on his knowledge of a supposed Fifth
Column inside Syracuse. At last he gave way, when an eclipse of the
moon occurred (27th August, 413). All his superstitions were
aroused, and he followed the advice of the soothsayers to postpone
the departure for a full month. That was the beginning of the end.
The Athenians tried in vain to prevent the enemy from sealing the
harbour, and the decline in the health and morale of army and navy
made the final retreat over land inevitable. It became an ordeal
caused as much by Nicias' hesitations as by Gylippus' efficiency in
blockading roads and river crossings. Lacking in discipline and
leadership no less than in supplies and even water, harrassed by
the enemy's cavalry, the Athenians reached the sea in the south in
a deplorable state. Demosthenes, leading the rear of six thousand
men, was the first to be overtaken; he surrendered against the
promise that none of his troops would be killed. Two days later,
after a dreadful massacre, Nicias too surrendered. The prisoners, in
so far as they were not privately sold into slavery, were thrown into
the notorious quarries, where many died. The two generals, against
Gylippus' wish and the promise given to Demosthenes, were
executed.

The greatest military enterprise had ended in complete disaster.
The disbelief of the Athenians soon turned into fury against their
generals, orators, and soothsayers, 'as though they had not voted
themselves for the expedition' (Thuc. 8, 1). It was like a tragic irony
that in the following year when Hermocrates sailed to Greece to
fight Athens there, the victorious Syracusans, under the leadership
of the demagogue Diocles, introduced radical democracy with

sortition and reduced power of the officials – an event largely due to the fact that Syracuse was a great naval power, but at the same time a surprising tribute to the defeated enemy.[86] The indomitable spirit of the Athenian people rose again, but the fatal end could only be postponed not averted.

4 · The Last Act

The final phase of the Peloponnesian war, the ten years from 413 to 404, had started with the occupation of Deceleia and the Sicilian disaster. It is therefore often called the Deceleian war, but the full impact of the new situation came with the entrance of Persia into the war, the new theatre of war in Ionia, and the gradual break-up of the Athenian empire. Athens lacked men and money, but she decided to build a new navy; her most important ally was now Euboea. Soon ships were being built, Cape Sunion was fortified to protect the corn-ships, and general expenses were cut down. The first indication that the methods of pure democracy were to be changed came when the people elected a board of ten counsellors (*probouloi*) to advise the council and the assembly; they were old men, among them the octogenarian Sophocles. Thucydides, with a mixture of admiration and contempt, states (8, 1, 4) that 'as the demos likes to do, as long as they were full of fear, they were prepared to keep discipline'.

Their fears were well-founded. Everywhere, within and without the empire, anti-Athenian feelings vehemently increased, together with the hope for an early conclusion of the war, and for freedom under Spartan leadership. It was, however, the latter that was greatly amiss. While Agis in Deceleia held a powerful position, collecting money from as far as Thessaly, and was asked for help from Athenian allies such as Euboea and Lesbos, both of the first importance, he was at loggerheads with his own government. Moreover, the order by Sparta to her allies to build a fleet of a hundred triremes was never fully carried out; the naval efforts of the Peloponnesians were getting weaker and weaker. Sparta's main hope was the fleet which was to come from Sicily and Italy; the fleet from Syracuse under Hermocrates was one of the strongest contingents of the allied fleet. Handicapped by lack of money as well as of experience in naval warfare, Sparta was a weak enemy in the new theatre of war, and it was only the promises of support by the two rival satraps, Tissaphernes in Ionia and Lydia, and Pharnabazus in Phrygia and Bithynia, which kept things moving. They both induced the Greek cities in Asia Minor to pay their tributes no longer to Athens but again to Persia, and it is likely that much of it would fill their own pockets. These satraps had gained more power while the Persian kingdom had weakened. Most remarkable is also the fact that the satraps, whatever their political attitude, had to some extent accepted Greek civilization. Tissaphernes issued coins with his own portrait, modelled on Athenian coins with the owl. Another strong influence was Alcibiades, on whose initiative, and through the good services of his friend Endius, one of the ephors who was equally hostile to Agis, the ephors eventually sent him and the nauarch Chalcideus, though only with a tiny squadron of five ships, to Chios, which revolted against Athens; the support for Chios meant at the same time that the Peloponnesians concentrated on the area ruled by Tissaphernes.[87]

In the early years of the Deceleian war, while the outcome was still in the balance, though the scales were beginning to favour Sparta, Euripides produced several plays, such as *Iphigeneia in Tauris* (*IT.*), *Ion*, and *Helena*.[88] They were all variations on the old theme of recognition (*anagnorisis*), and at the same time they let human cleverness or innocence triumph not only over barbarian foes but also over the gods. None of the plays is a tragedy, though there are moments of tragic tension in every one, and they all have complicated melodramatic plots. There is a happy end, a natural one, as it were, and not only due to the slightly awkward intervention of a *deus ex machina*. In *IT.*, the story of the human sacrifices to the Taurian Artemis, whose priestess Iphigeneia is, provides the predominant theme of the contrast between Greeks and barbarians. There is nothing new about it, except perhaps for King Thoas' remark that matricide, Orestes' crime, could never happen among barbarians (1174). The story of the flight with the Artemis statue is a story of cunning and deceit on the part of Iphigeneia; as in *Helena*, the barbarian king is fair game for deception by the heroes of the play. Still, to generalize on the treacherous nature of all women comes easily to the messenger who reports the flight (1298). In the end an Athenian audience would gain natural satisfaction from the fact that the personal appearance of Athena only serves the purpose of having Artemis and her cult transferred to Attica. In *Ion*, the theme which throughout the play is stressed again and again is the 'autochthony' of the Athenians, and their abhorrence of any foreign intruder into the ruling family of Erechtheus.[89] Ion, trying to find out who his mother was, hopes she will be Athenian, for otherwise he would not have citizenship at Athens (671).[90] Athens is not praised in this play; she is not, as in earlier tragedies, a refuge for exiles, rather a source of undefined fears for the various people concerned, and in particular contrasted with Delphi, the place of Ion's peaceful existence. Any hint of contemporary Athens, such as Ion's denunciation of democratic politicians (598 ff.), is so general that we cannot speak of a political trend. The play has been called a kind of romance, and that covers at least most of it. Apollo's part in fathering Ion is, in the end, justified by making the Greek people descend from Ion and his half-brothers; but there is no moral justification, and Athena must act for Apollo, who is blamed, even by his faithful servant Ion, for lack of humanity! There ought to be no different laws for men and gods (442). Creusa, a pathetic figure, however melodramatic, is an example of women's misery, and she cries out against Apollo's shamelessness. What kind of god is he really? There is no simple answer. The gods are there, and their actions are important, even decisive, for men; but they are no longer the traditional Olympians nor Aeschylus' moral powers. They were, so it seems, as enigmatic to Euripides himself as in his plays they are to us, whatever that wisdom that is often attributed to them, may mean.[91] The gods and their servants play an even more preposterous part in *Helena*, the light-weight among the three plays, in which Stesichorus' old story is taken up that Helen was never at Troy, that a phantom took her place, and that all the time she herself was in Egypt.[91a] It is there that Menelaus finds her again after seventeen years, not much the worse for being at least middle-aged. Like any decent woman, she has been longing for her husband, her daughter, and for Sparta, which receives much praise in this play. For once there is no Athenian patriotism; on the other hand, there is an element of comedy in the various confrontations of different people, sometimes bordering on the absurd. Myth is taken lightly, the gods are praised as better and safer than the seers (759), a view which cannot be taken seriously as the only person who is always right is the priestess and seer Theonoe. The chorus reflects modern thought when they sing that men exploring even the farthest reaches of the world cannot decide 'what is god or not god or something in between' (1137). Could any phrase make more obvious Euripides' uncertainty about the gods, and is it mere chance that the words so strongly remind us of Protagoras' famous saying?

The three plays reveal Euripides as very remote from the contemporary scene. That goes together with a kind of routine playfulness, intended probably to cause entertainment rather than emotion There is a good deal of poetry in choral and individual songs, and young Ion remains a creation of subtle design and wonderful charm. We have, it is true, one more play belonging to the same period, the *Phoenician Women*. It is different indeed from the other plays, 'full of Ares' like Aeschylus' *Septem*, on which Euripides tried to improve. It is also under strong influence from Sophocles' *Antigone*, and in a sense seems to approach the atmosphere of *Oedipus Coloneus*, written about three years later. Euripides has burdened his play, which proved to be very popular in antiquity, with every possible kind of Theban myth, including the newly invented story of the self-sacrifice of Creon's young son Menoecus. Contemporary problems, or at least political aspects, are reflected in the allusions to Carthage (see below, p. 329), and in the conflict between the power-drunk ruler Eteocles and the exile Polyneices, though we must not think of anybody in particular; there were many analogies which would enter the minds of the audience. Polyneices is in a condition 'against nature', and has lost his right of free speech (391); that reminds us of a similar utterance in *Ion* (see above). The question of political equality is discussed between Eteocles and his mother (499 ff., 531 ff.), he the defender of tyranny and she proclaiming equality as 'right by nature', all that of little importance in the context of the play.[92] The general trend is the condemnation of individual ambition and strife, though that is a frequent theme in Euripidean tragedy, and we need not draw comparisons with the contemporary actors on the political stage. What matters is that human characters of very different kinds are displayed, though none, perhaps with the exception of Antigone and Iocaste, is full and convincing; all, however, except Menoecus, are self-centred, with no concern for the state. Melodramatic theatre, though perhaps at its best, that is the main impression. The long and crowded play is a problem for the historian of literature rather than the general historian.

The poet, though naturally always *of* his time, was no longer really *in* his time. How different with comedy! In the year when Euripides produced his semi-comedy *Helena* (412), old Eupolis brought out his last and most famous play, the *Demoi*. Enough fragments are extant to enable us to reconstruct its main features. Athens, at that time, had no great leader, and Eupolis conjured back from Hades the great statesmen of the past, from Solon to Pericles, to help the state in its plight. Their guide, rather surprisingly, is Myronides, who represents, if as an ideal of the past, the honest citizen and good general who keeps away from day-to-day politics. He is the opposite of the poet's contemporaries, of those generals who were also politicians. This is a truly political comedy with the very serious purpose of attacking present conditions. Its background is provided by the chorus of the 'demes', the villages and boroughs that were the home of the rural section of the citizens. Closely attached to their land and their neighbours, they were, however narrow-minded and *petits bourgeois*, the true foundation of state and society.

The war by then had acquired a new aspect, and Athenian rule in the Aegean was definitely threatened. Persia, without entering the war, had become an important factor with which both sides had to reckon. Although the Peloponnesian squadrons were all very small, their presence in Ionian waters, the connexion with Tissaphernes, and last but not least Alcibiades' unique power of persuasion caused the open revolts of Chios, Erythrae, and Clazomenae. The Athenians rightly feared that Chios, 'the greatest allied polis', might induce many others to follow suit. Counter-measures were taken; above all, the thousand talents which had been the last reserve, forbidden to be used except in the utmost danger (Thuc. 2, 24; cf. above, p. 269), were now used, while the hundred reserved triremes seemed no

longer to have been in existence. At any rate, a strong fleet was
collected in order to recover Chios, and the Chians soon suffered a
minor naval reverse. However, other cities did revolt, the most
important Miletus. Alcibiades and Chalcideus, together with the
Chians, did everything in their power to make a success of their
campaign; partly, at least, they did so to counteract Agis and his
followers at Sparta. A first attempt was also made at concluding
a treaty of alliance with Persia, though that document remained
incomplete and most unfavourable to the Greek side; it was never
ratified.[93]

The command of the Peloponnesian fleet was taken over by the
nauarch Astyochus, who proved an admiral of little capability and
not up to the task of fighting against the energy and resourcefulness
of the Athenians. A great success for Athens was the democratic
revolt at Samos, which was supported by Athenian sailors. The
Samians regained their autonomy, lost since 440, and took strict
measures against their own oligarchs. Samos now became the base
for the Athenian navy, a base of greatest strategic importance. Then
Lesbos revolted, but the Athenians recovered it and carried out
several successful attacks on Chios and a raid against Miletus, when
Chalcideus was killed (Thuc. 8, 21–24). Even in Chios a pro-
Athenian move was started, but Astyochus heard of it, and took
hostages away. At the end of summer strong forces – with Dorians
and Ionians on either side – battled for Miletus; it was also the only
time that Alcibiades actually fought against Athenians. Eventually,
after a strong Syracusan and Peloponnesian fleet had arrived, the
Athenian general Phrynichus brought his army back to Samos, while
their Argive allies went angrily home (Thuc. 8, 25–27).

It was then that Alcibiades' policy began to break down. All
his promises were either only half fulfilled or not at all. Tissaphernes
played the master rather than the ally, though he provided some
help by his mercenaries and by reluctantly paying the crews of the
Peloponnesian fleet. The war went on through the winter (412–
411), though hampered by bad weather. The Peloponnesian efforts
were weakened by the tension between Astyochus and the Spartan
commander at Chios, Pedaritus; the Athenians held a fortified
place there, and the Chians, divided by differing fears and loyalties,
remained inactive.[93a] Shortly afterwards large numbers of slaves

deserted the city; Chios was notorious for the part slavery played in her economy, and the present event throws a significant light on a society which had moved from early democracy to an unstable oligarchy. Cnidus, on the other hand, joined the number of allies who had defected from Athens. Meanwhile, Pharnabazus' agents had been busy at Sparta, and as a result, a new Peloponnesian fleet went out, and with it eleven Spartiates to serve as counsellors (*symbouloi*) with Astyochus; that was clearly an indication of mistrust on the part of the ephors, caused by Pedaritus' complaints and the slow progress of the war. The new fleet arrived at Caunus, far in the south-east, and after an Athenian attempt at causing trouble had failed, the two Peloponnesian fleets joined forces. Soon afterwards Rhodes revolted, and provided the Peloponnesians with a considerable sum of money. That was badly needed, since Tissaphernes, especially in view of the unexpected strength of Athens, was easily persuaded that his own interest lay not so much in supporting Sparta as maintaining a balance of power between the two Greek states. The moment had come for Alcibiades to change his policy. He had quarrelled with the Spartans, and eventually received information that Astyochus had orders from Sparta to kill him; he escaped to Tissaphernes, and was soon preparing for a return to Athens.

Exercising the power which his friendship with Tissaphernes gave him, Alcibiades refused to allow financial help to those cities which had revolted from Athens; then he made contact with the fleet at Samos. He was faced with the fact that, at least among the generals, the oligarchs were beginning to gain the upper hand, and Alcibiades promised them Persian support if Athens would put down democracy. Alcibiades was no oligarch, as soon enough became evident, nor did he love the democrats, who were largely responsible for his exile from Athens. More than ever his policy was purely opportunist. At Samos a real conspiracy developed in which a newly established hetaeria played the decisive part. Only one of the leaders, Phrynichus, mistrusted Alcibiades. He realized that all Alcibiades wanted was his return to power, and that he was no more concerned than Persia or the Athenian allies with the constitutional question. The allies only wanted their freedom, and that was no less secure with the democrats than with the oligarchs. Thus, while Peisander and others were sent to Athens to prepare the revolt there, Phrynichus is reported to have denounced Alcibiades in a letter to Astyochus, who on his part at once related everything to Alcibiades and Tissaphernes. According to Thucydides, Phrynichus even went so far as to write a second letter; he was prepared to sacrifice Samos and the fleet, but when his action became public, he managed to convince the troops that the whole intrigue was Alcibiades' alone, and he actually strengthened his own position. The story sounds almost unbelievable, and we are tempted to regard it as a fabrication by Alcibiades.[93b] He retained a strong influence on Tissaphernes, and the latter's relations with the Peloponnesians remained in suspense (Thuc. 8, 45-52). In judging his vacillating policy, it must not be forgotten that his own military strength was almost negligible; his mercenary force was small, and the fleet supposed to be prepared in Phoenicia never turned up.[94] The one effective weapon in the hands of the satraps was money, of which both Greek sides were badly in need; but even that did not flow abundantly enough.

Meanwhile, the oligarchs at Athens under Peisander's leadership began to move, though there were difficulties, even apart from popular opinion. For instance, the two ancient families connected with Eleusis, the Eumolpids and the Ceryces, strongly opposed Alcibiades' return on account of his involvement in the affair of the mockery of the mysteries. Peisander, however, a clever politician and a turncoat like Alcibiades, won over all those hetaeriae 'which managed trials and elections'. That meant bribery, illegal influence, and terrorization. The cause of the oligarchic revolt was flourishing, and Peisander was able to overcome all resistance against Alcibiades' return. Phrynichus was deposed by the army; but when Peisander was sent to Alcibiades and Tissaphernes, he found that he was being duped. Exorbitant demands were made by Alcibiades, who acted as Tissaphernes' spokesman. The change in Alcibiades' attitude is not quite clear, but Peisander departed in anger, and Tissaphernes once again approached the Spartans. After a second draft (B) in autumn 412 (Thuc. 8, 37), now at last, in spring 411, a final treaty (C) was concluded between Persia and Sparta (Thuc. 8, 58).[95]

The document, as reproduced by Thucydides, whose knowledge may derive from Alcibiades' archive, begins with an elaborate prescript containing the date, the place, the purpose, and the parties of the treaty; the last are the Peloponnesian League, on the one side, and the satraps, on the other.[96] The first item deals with formerly Persian land that is to be returned to the king. Compared with the dangerous vagueness of the earlier drafts, the area is now strictly confined to Asia. Even in this mitigated form it implies that Sparta, the potential 'liberator' of the Greeks, sacrificed the Asiatic Greeks; that was, as before, the *conditio sine qua non* for any agreement with the Persians. The parties mutually promise not to interfere in their respective countries, and both sides declare that they will together fight the Athenians to the very end. Only in the final treaty is anything said about Tissaphernes' guarantee of maintaining the Peloponnesian fleet; he is supposed to pay 'till the king's ships arrive', which they never did. We do not know whether Tissaphernes himself believed that the king would send the fleet and lighten his financial burden; anyway, the Greeks were to repay all the money after the war. The general impression of the treaty is still that it favoured the Persians, and in particular Tissaphernes. For Alcibiades the agreement must have been a setback, and he made new promises to the oligarchs, who, he still hoped, might bring him back to Athens.

The winter ended badly for the Athenians when Oropus was betrayed to the Boeotians; the Peloponnesians, on the other hand, were not able to relieve Chios until May 411, when a small force under the Spartan Dercylidas at last approached the Hellespont. Abydus and Lampsacus revolted, though the latter was regained by the Athenians, who also built a fort at Sestus to protect the sea route. The war began to move into the vital area of the Straits. Chios succeeded in regaining partial superiority at sea. A remarkable fact is that the new Spartan commander at Chios came from the ranks; just as the occasional employment of perioeci in responsible posts (Thuc. 8, 22), it shows that the number of Spartiates was dangerously diminishing.

While Athens was making the most strenuous efforts in the war, Aristophanes, in spring 411, produced the *Lysistrate*, the play of the woman 'who disbands the army'. The poet had no part in the party struggle, though he makes fun of the recently appointed *probouloi*, and seems to disapprove of the oligarchs, and of Peisander in particular. To Aristophanes, the only issue that counted was to end the war. By the very feminine method of a sex strike, Lysistrate and her womenfolk force their men to make peace, and a truly Panhellenic peace it was to be, based on the alliance between Lysistrate and the Spartan woman Lampito. A good deal of courage was needed for such a plea at that moment, though the political climate in 411 was very different from that of 415 when the poet produced his *Peace*. It is significant that he proclaims his largely Utopian ideas through a woman, which meant through a source of warm humanity which shines through all the obscenity and the fun of this comedy. *Lysistrate* is a masterpiece; the *Thesmophoriazusae* of the same year is less so, though it is very good fun. It is one of several comedies, all of them lost, which were concerned with literature, but then Athenian literature, and especially tragedy, was always part of political and social life. The main target in the *Thesmophoriazusae* is Euripides, but not as a representative of the modern spirit, rather as a woman-hater. Still, it is not the poet, however parodied, but the women and their festival that are really held up to derision, and the play has hardly any political overtones, though both plays were revolutionary enough in pronouncing their message by women.

By then the oligarchs' revolt was under way.[97] Peisander was the most active leader, and he found matters at home well prepared. Some of the democratic leaders were murdered, and a programme was announced foreseeing the creation of a citizens' body of five thousand and the abolition of all public payments except for the soldiers. In fact, however, a small number of oligarchs ruled by terror and fear. By a special election, four hundred men were appointed as the real government, and they gave to the revolt the name of the 'Rule of the Four Hundred'. In the difference between programme and reality, the deep division is reflected between the moderates and the extremists, the former under the leadership of Theramenes trying to steer a middle course, the latter displaying very radical aims and methods. The Four Hundred created a guard of 120 'Greek' youths who served as an instrument of terror; they were called Greek in order to distinguish them from the Scythians who served as policemen at Athens. After assembly and council had been dismissed without resistance, largely because a substantial section of the people had either died in Sicily or were with the fleet at Samos, the arbitrary and violent rule of the oligarchs was established. Among the leaders were Antiphon, whose personality is greatly admired by Thucydides, and Phrynichus, who was equally hostile to Peisander and to Alcibiades. The latter was rightly regarded as 'not suitable for an oligarchy'; his name was officially not mentioned, and to prevent his return, there was no general recall of the exiles (Thuc. 8, 63–70). Sophocles, it seems, who had first supported the Four Hundred, now withdrew.[97a]

The Four Hundred, however, failed to get what they most wanted, better conditions of peace. Alcibiades' promises proved to be without basis, and the break between him and the oligarchs became inevitable. An equally great disappointment for the latter was that the allies most decisively preferred the freedom promised by Sparta to any Athenian rule; they wanted liberty, and not *eunomia*, the fake signboard of oligarchy (Thuc. 8, 64). Worst of all for the rebels was that, after first the exiled Hyperbolus had been murdered, the democratic attitude of the fleet at Samos was firmly and finally established. The oligarchs tried in vain to persuade the soldiers that it was really the Five Thousand, and not the Four Hundred, who ruled. The 'navy crowd' in whose ranks the lower classes predominated, whose envoys to Athens had received a bad reception and on their return gave an exaggerated description of the oligarchic terror at home, could be restrained from violence only by their two new leaders, Thrasybulus and Thrasyllus, the former a trierarch, the latter a simple hoplite, but both convinced democrats and now elected strategi. In fear of the oligarchs as well as the Peloponnesians, the soldiers voted for the recall of Alcibiades; in him and Tissaphernes' friendship, in which they believed, they saw the only chance of salvation.

Alcibiades went to Samos. He was still a man in his prime, and had not lost his charm and his power of persuasion. He must also have learnt something from the many reversals of fortune he had suffered.[98] Anyway, he at once adapted himself to a situation in which he had to acknowledge the democratic attitude of the fleet instead of entering an Athens ruled by his friends. He still hoped to return there later, and meanwhile again promised more than he could ever expect to achieve. He was elected general, but refused to lead the fleet to the Peiraeus, thus saving Athens from a full civil war and from finally losing her last allies in the east.[99] He went back to Tissaphernes, 'frightening him with the Athenians, and them with Tissaphernes' (Thuc. 8, 82). However amoral, for the moment this policy proved to be the right one.

The oligarchic revolt at Athens began to peter out, as the Four Hundred were disunited among themselves, and their leaders were rivals for the leadership of the state. The extremist side started to build a fort at Eetioneia, north of Peiraeus harbour, as a stronghold and refuge; they were prepared to admit the Peloponnesian fleet and to destroy their own state in order to save their lives. In a general upheaval Phrynichus was murdered, and Theramenes with a crowd of angry soldiers destroyed the fort. When a Peloponnesian fleet appeared near Aegina and seemed to approach the Peiraeus, everybody rushed to the defence. The fleet, however, sailed round Attica to Oropus, defeated a hastily collected Athenian fleet, and caused the revolt of Euboea, which 'meant everything to the Athenians, shut in, as they were, within Attica' (Thuc. 8, 95, 2). No ships, no men were left. If the Spartans had shown initiative, they could then have finished the Athenian empire and the war. They did not dare follow up their naval victory, but at least their reluctance in helping the oligarchs was fully justified. The rule of the Four Hundred broke down after only four months, the leaders fled to Deceleia, and Theramenes created a government based on the Five Thousand as those who were able – both physically and financially – to bear arms. Thucydides calls this the first good constitution in his lifetime because it was 'a mixture of oligarchy and democracy' (Thuc. 8, 97, 2). It is likely that it was largely based on what we might call 'the middle class', artisans and traders of some standing, and above all the peasantry. Theramenes' constitution remained in force during the winter 411–410, and prevented unnecessary bloodshed. The Five Thousand were a theoretical number, and it took time for a full list to be established; it seems that then the actual number was 9,000 ([Lys.] 20, 13). These were the citizens with full citizenship, and the outcome was a very moderate oligarchy; we cannot be certain whether the thetes were back as members of the assembly and the courts, though the real power anyway was with the council. The constitution was regarded as a return to

what was called 'the ancestral constitution' (*patrios politeia*).[100] The
idea was popular, although different people understood different
things by that slogan. The fleet at Samos, however, remained democratic and independent; its sailors defended the crumbling empire,
and soon Theramenes joined Thrasybulus with a small fighting
squadron, acquiring the nickname of the *Kothornos*, the boot that
fitted either foot. At that time his constitution, which had still
maintained a board of strategi apart from those at Samos, was
quietly replaced by a return to democracy. The state was again
unified. It was not likely that at that moment the people at home
would favour Alcibiades' return. What he needed, more than ever,
was an impressive success in the war.

The Peloponnesians, meanwhile, had difficulties of their own,
especially in maintaining a large fleet. Still, a squadron got through
to Pharnabazes and caused the revolt of Byzantium, a severe setback
for Athens. In the main fleet of the enemy, however, unrest increased; its chief causes were the weak leadership of Astyochus and
the doubtful attitude of Tissaphernes, who neither paid them
enough nor brought, as he had promised, the Phoenician fleet to the
Aegean. Thucydides (8, 87, 4) is convinced that Tissaphernes was
never honest in his policy, and only aimed at paralysing both Greek
sides. The situation changed when a new Spartan nauarch, Mindarus,
arrived with a strong fleet and entered the Hellespont, after avoiding
the Athenians at Samos by creeping along the coast. After several
skirmishes the two fleets met in full force at Cynossema, opposite
Abydus, and the Peloponnesians suffered a heavy defeat; the
Athenians under Thrasyllus captured the important city and harbour
of Cyzicus. The second Peloponnesian fleet, sailing from Euboea,
ran into a severe storm and was almost completely destroyed. Hopes
rose again at Athens, and Alcibiades, who had escaped from
temporary imprisonment by Tissaphernes, was now practically
in charge of the whole Athenian fleet, even after Theramenes and
Thrasybulus had joined him. He was soon to prove his outstanding
ability as a naval commander. First, he had some success in the
south, and Tissaphernes again fell out with the Spartans; he planned
to outrival Pharnabazus and showed friendship once more to the
Athenians.[101] Spartan squadrons gathered at the Hellespont, and
Alcibiades went north for the decisive fight.

In two great battles by sea and land, at Abydus (late in 411) and at Cyzicus (May 410), the Peloponnesians were defeated and practically annihilated. Mindarus was killed, and the Athenians seized a letter which his second-in-command had sent to the ephors: 'Gone are the ships. Mindarus is dead. The men are starving. At a loss what to do' (Xen. 1, 1, 23). This pathetic message vividly contrasts with the new strong confidence felt at Athens. Alcibiades was prominent all the time and had proved his worth; the chances for his return were rising. He received much money for the fleet from Cyzicus, he secured the sea route through the Bosporus, he was on good terms with Pharnabazus. The situation was still uncertain, but when Agis declared that the occupation of Deceleia was useless without a naval blockade, Sparta offered peace on the *status quo*, though with the exchange of Pylos and Deceleia. The restored democracy at Athens, with Cleophon as the leading demagogue, refused.[102] Without Euboea and Oropus, with the vacillating events of the war in Ionia, with Calchedon and Byzantium not yet back in Athenian hands, the refusal seems less arbitrary and senseless than it is frequently regarded. Still, a few years of peace might have been a blessing, restoring much of Athenian strength; but Cleophon as well as Alcibiades had higher aims. The democrats at Athens tried to secure the future of democracy, and at the same time to restore order and peace. In summer 410 a decree by Demophantus prescribed the death penalty for any attempt at overthrowing the existing constitution, or only obtaining office under a non-democratic government. Trials and banishments of many of the adherents of the Four Hundred followed; Critias was one of those who went into exile. Payment for officials and jurors had been reintroduced, and Cleophon created the *diobelia*, a payment of two obols daily, as a help for the growing number of poor people. Where the money came from, we are not told, though we know that the temple treasurers contributed a good deal; soon the golden statues of Nike on the Acropolis were melted down. It is clear that the state was in a bad financial situation, and at the same time large sections of the population were more or less destitute.

Even so, when lasting peace was not yet in sight, the successes and needs of the moment revitalized Athenian building activities. The

Erechtheum was nearing completion, and its construction provided many artisans and workers with an opportunity of earning a modest living. Also a parapet was erected round the platform of the Nike temple, displaying reliefs in a new style. There are the figures of a number of winged *Nikai*, with their garments draped in the double task of veiling and unveiling their beautiful bodies; the most famous is the one removing her sandal.

In 409 Sophocles, well into his eighties, produced his *Philoctetes*. The story had been known ever since Homer, and had been repeated several times. The Greek leaders on the way to Troy exposed Philoctetes on Lemnos because of the smell of a snake bite; but according to a later prophecy, he was needed together with his, i.e. Heracles' old, bow to conquer Troy. Thus, the embittered man had to be brought there, by force or persuasion, and the right person to do that was Odysseus. He did so with his usual cunning in a play by Aeschylus, and in a different way in Euripides' *Philoctetes* of 431, who made the story, as far as we can see, more reasonable, at the same time stressing the conflict between personal feelings and patriotic duty, by introducing a Trojan mission as well.[103] Euripides' play could perhaps be regarded as one of his political tragedies, while the Sophoclean *Philoctetes* is essentially a battle of characters. There is clearly general Euripidean influence, even to the extent of a *deus ex machina* being introduced, though of a different, more integrated kind. Philoctetes here is an outcast on a deserted island, 'a friendless, lonely, stateless man, dead among the living' (1018), and he remains so even when he returns to the army, which stands for the polis, that polis represented by Odysseus, a dishonest man and a sophist, who hopes to achieve his ends – which are also those of the polis – by amoral tricks of persuasion. An even more decisive change from the other plays on Philoctetes is the introduction of Neoptolemus, the youthful and noble son of Achilles, whom Odysseus uses in his aim at deceiving Philoctetes. In Neoptolemus' soul the fight is fought between truth and falsehood, between his nature (*physis*) and what can be regarded as his duty towards the Greeks before Troy. 'All is disgust when a man betrays his own nature, and does things that are not fit' (902). Thus, we have here a reflection of the sophists' teaching on *physis* and *nomos* (see p. 346f.), but the loyalty to one's nature is stronger than the loyalty to a polis, and in the end Neoptolemus breaks through the net of lies to which he had reluctantly submitted. With a reconciled Philoctetes, the two noble souls obey the will of the gods. That is as we should expect in a play by Sophocles, but the question remains open whether, or to what extent, he was thinking of Athens when he described the polis and its leaders. When Neoptolemus exclaims that 'war never takes a bad man but by chance, though always the good men' (436), it may be a more or less conventional statement; but it could also be a *cri-de-coeur* of the old poet. It is not unlikely that Sophocles despaired of his own polis, disrupted and corrupt as it was in those years.

In the following year Euripides' *Orestes* was performed, the most melodramatic of his extant plays, full of theatrical effects, and in its later parts a story of violence and crime. The well-known myth of the matricide becomes an object of argument which naturally remains inconclusive. All the characters are under the strongest possible emotional stress, but the ever-changing plot seems more important than the personalities, whose psychological reactions largely derive from their typical natures. Helena is wicked, Menelaus a coward, Orestes and Electra are loyal to each other, and Pylades is a staunch friend. The breakdown and revival of Orestes, however, are shown as the result of his own conscience as well as of the hatred of his grandfather Tyndareus, and the complete lack of help on the part of Menelaus. The charge against Orestes is put before the assembly of Argos (866 ff.), and this assembly is a true picture of the Athenian ecclesia with its opposing parties, its honest or dishonest politicians, and the easily swayed people. A new intrigue develops. Under the threat of death by the vote of the people of Argos, the young people embark on a path of criminal plotting and vengeance. We cannot say whether the audience accepted the wild story as a warning against the hatred and violence rampant in their midst. Anyway, in the end all is well. Apollo, the real culprit, solves all the problems, and the happy ending is even secured by a double marriage. Did they live happily ever after? Even the Athenians, used to the poet's distortion of myth, would hardly believe that, nor would they accept Orestes' excuses for his matricide, by which he claims to have rendered service to all Greece in saving husbands from their wives' murderous plans (565). There was a gulf between the poet's and the people's feelings, and that is confirmed by the fact that in the same year, 408, Euripides left Athens for good and went to the court of the Macedonian king. Aeschylus had done something similar when he went to Sicily, and yet it does not seem the same. With Euripides, it was not so much a question of patronage as of a disillusioned man leaving his homeland.

The war was not going well for either side. Sparta recaptured Pylos, and the Megarians Nisaea, but the Spartan colonists at Heracleia Trachinia were massacred by neighbouring tribes. The defeated Peloponnesians were to give money and timber to build a new fleet, but soon Byzantium and Calchedon were captured by Alcibiades. Selymbria, at the northern side of the Propontis, was brought back to Athenian rule under very conciliatory terms (*ML*, no. 87. *DSDA* no. 207); it seems that Alcibiades as well as the people at home had learnt their lesson, as far as imperialism was concerned. Pharnabazus, in order to protect his satrapy, came to terms with the Athenians; Tissaphernes remained entirely inactive. A serious setback for the Spartan side was the recall of the most active section of their fleet, of Hermocrates who had been exiled from Syracuse, with the Sicilian and Italian ships; that happened after the destruction of Selinus by the Carthaginians (see p. 328). The various vicissitudes of the war only show that it had reached a stage of attrition. Alcibiades and his colleagues, it is true, were able to secure some more places in Asia and Thrace, also to collect much-needed money; to the people at Athens the situation must have looked much more hopeful than it was, and the need for reconciliation with Alcibiades seemed urgent. Cleophon, the only political leader of importance and Alcibiades' personal enemy, could hardly object to the return of a general so conspicuously successful, and Critias, nobleman and sophist, of whom we shall hear more, did what he could to rehabilitate Alcibiades (*DK* 88 B 4. 5). Thus, in 407 Alcibiades returned home. He entered Peiraeus not without some misgivings, but was soon surrounded by his friends and found enthusiastic crowds to greet him. Together with Adeimantus of the same phyle who had shared his fate in 415, and with Thrasybulus and Conon, the most promising military man at the moment, Alcibiades was elected strategus, obviously by all the phylae.[104] Neither Theramenes

nor even Thrasyllus was among the ten elected. After a brilliant
speech in the assembly to clear himself of the old charge of violating
the mysteries, while nobody dared mention his actions during his
exile, he was given the supreme command, that is to say, *plein
pouvoir* in the leadership of the war. To pacify his special enemies
and the religious feelings of many, he led a procession, protected by
his soldiers, to Eleusis (Xen. *hell.* 1, 4, 11–20). It was the first time
since the occupation of Deceleia that the solemn procession on the
Sacred Road had taken place. Its peaceful completion must have
vastly raised Alcibiades' prestige. His reconciliation with the
people of Athens and the holy goddesses of Eleusis was complete.[105]

After four months at Athens, Alcibiades had collected sufficient
forces, and went out to reconquer Ionia. His base was again Samos.
The enemy's fleet was still comparatively weak, but its leadership
and its spirit had changed. The initiative was now being taken by
two new men, the young Cyrus, brother of the Great King, who
was given supreme power over all satrapies in Asia Minor, and
Lysander, the new energetic Spartan nauarch, a great strategist as
well as a diplomat. Both became famous through later events, but
even then, at the beginning of their respective careers, they caused
a decisive change. Their meeting led to a strong personal friendship
which made Persian financial help more secure. Cyrus full-heartedly
supported Sparta, and refused to see Athenian envoys. Lysander
appeared with a strong fleet at Ephesus, and Alcibiades seems
quickly to have realized that the enemy was under new and efficient
leadership. When he went to meet Thrasybulus who had finished
a brilliant campaign in Thrace and was now trying to blockade
Phocaea, Alcibiades committed a serious blunder. Instead of giving
the temporary command of the fleet to one of his colleagues, he
put his helmsman Antiochus, a personal friend, in charge, though he
expressly forbade him to sail out, an order that Antiochus promptly
neglected. At Notium, north of Ephesus, he was defeated and lost
at least fifteen ships (winter 407–406).[105a] Alcibiades was unable to
renew the battle, since Lysander refused to come forward. At Athens
disappointment and resentment led to covert and open attacks on
Alcibiades, and at the next election of strategi neither he nor Thrasybulus was re-elected; Conon was now the leading admiral. Alcibiades, once again out of favour with the Athenians and in danger of

having to appear before a court,[106] went to one of his castles in Thrace. There he still had influence, and might have had new plans, but his historical role had come to an end. During the next year he tried in vain to warn the Athenian fleet of the dangers of the position at Aegospotami (see p. 329), and fled to the court of the same Pharnabazus with whom he had had dubious dealings before, and this man, on Lysander's instigation, put him to death. Alcibiades ended as he had lived, as a great adventurer, a man without home, a man without principles, and yet the same man who had proved to be a military genius, who, though utterly unreliable, had time and again charmed all kinds of people, and continued to do so even after his death; proof of that is Plato's *Symposium*. He was an outstanding example of that generation in which the great individual broke the bonds of the community. Lysander was to follow him in playing a similar part in Sparta.

The year 406 was in many ways a tragic year for Athens, though it only foreshadowed the final catastrophe. It even brought about that sudden change (*peripeteia*) that belongs to tragedy, a victory with disastrous consequences. It was also, as it were, ominous that early in 406 Euripides died, as a few months later did Sophocles, in his nineties. In his last production of a play he dressed his chorus in mourning for his rival's death. They both left remarkable plays which were performed posthumously, Sophocles the *Oedipus Coloneus*, Euripides the *Iphigeneia in Aulis* and the *Bacchae*. We shall return later to these plays, examples of unbroken creativeness, culminations, and at the same time witnesses of the end, of Attic tragedy, coinciding with the downfall of the city.

In accordance with constitutional rule, Lysander was succeeded as nauarch by Callicratidas, who first fell out with Cyrus, but soon established the powerful force of a fleet of 170 ships. Conon was powerless against such an enemy and was blockaded in the harbour of Mytilene. After he had sent a secret message to Athens, the city once more rose to the occasion. With the help of Archelaus of Macedon, who provided timber and equipment (*ML*, no. 91), a new fleet was built; it was manned with men from all age groups and classes, including knights as well as slaves. They were in time to save Conon, and to meet the enemy near the Arginusae islands, south of Lesbos. The Peloponnesians were heavily defeated, and Callicratidas was killed, but losses were very large on both sides. At about the same time Agis made a strong attack against the city, but troops under the protection of the walls were out in time, and Agis withdrew. Even so, the strain on the garrison was greatly increased, and that may partly account for the events that followed. The losses in the naval battle had been particularly heavy because a storm prevented the rescue of many shipwrecked sailors. This fact led to the notorious trial of the six generals – two others had fled – who were accused of criminal negligence. At the first trial they were acquitted, but a second one was demanded after a general outburst of hysteria, and the men were condemned and executed. Socrates was the only one among the prytaneis to vote against a decision which was immoral and even illegal. Theramenes played a sinister part in the whole affair, and the demos claimed that 'it were terrible if they could not do what they liked'; thus the charge of illegality (*graphē paranomon*) had to be dropped (Xen. 1, 7, 12). Democracy had deteriorated into mob rule, and the anti-democratic forces were strengthened.[107]

It was in the same year that Athens, once again, took an interest in events that happened in Sicily. The Greeks there, after the victory over the Athenians, had returned to the party-strife and the easy life of peace and prosperity. When in 410 Egesta was threatened with final destruction by her old enemy Selinus, the Elymian town turned to Carthage. After seven decades of non-intervention in Sicily, the Carthaginians decided to support Egesta and thus to protect their own possessions in western Sicily.[108] The invasion in 409 was led by Hannibal, the grandson of that Hamilcar who had died at Himera in 480, a member of the leading family of the Magonids. He was entirely successful; first, Selinus was almost completely destroyed, and then Himera; Syracusan help was too late and too weak. The two cities had been the most western outposts of the Greeks in south and north; their destruction meant that the Greeks were pushed back, and at the same time Hannibal had taken cruel vengeance for the death of Hamilcar. Without trying to punish Syracuse, the Carthaginians then went home. They were provoked into a new expedition only when the exile Hermocrates had made dangerous raids from Selinus into the territories of Motye and Panormus, the main Carthaginian strongholds in Sicily. Now the war party in Carthage – which always existed side by side with a more reluctant group among the ruling merchant aristocracy – was determined to secure western Sicily as a united Carthaginian province. A large army and fleet were prepared, and it was then that Carthaginian envoys appeared at Athens; it seems that a treaty of alliance was concluded.[109] They had a common enemy in Syracuse, but for the moment neither side could hope to gain much by their connexion. Even though the Chalcidian cities of Naxos and Catane followed Athenian advice and did not join the Greek side, that fact was hardly responsible for the sweeping campaign of 406–405 when the Carthaginians took Acragas, Gela, and Camarina. Once again, however, they desisted from pushing their success to its limits, and offered peace, perhaps because a plague had decimated their army, but probably also because by then the fate of Athens was decided, and Sparta was free to help Syracuse. At the same time a new efficient general had risen in Syracuse, Dionysius, who overthrew democracy, had his opponents executed, and became the master of the city. For the moment he was forced to accept peace terms which made Carthage and their native allies the rulers of the larger part of Sicily. Just as Sparta had sacrificed the Ionian Greeks in order to secure Persia's help, so Athens had given up all Panhellenic pretences in Sicily and was on the side of Carthage. In the years to follow, the rule of the great Dionysius, however, was to save the Sicilian Greeks from Carthaginian rule, and his *tyrannis* rested on the response of a people who hero-worshipped their great ruler.

Meanwhile, Lysander came on the scene again, not as nauarch (repetition was illegal) but as *epistoleus*, a vice-admiral who was actually soon in command again, dominating the Ionian coastline and the Straits. The strong Athenian fleet took up its position at the mouth of a small river, Aegospotami, in the Chersonese peninsula opposite Lampsacus, which had been taken by Lysander. It was an unfortunate choice, as it gave little chance of free movement, and caused supply difficulties. The clever delaying tactics of Lysander completely deceived the Athenian generals, who refused to listen to Alcibiades' warning. Lysander's final attack came as a surprise when most of the crews were foraging on land. The whole fleet was captured, only Conon escaped with nine ships; all Athenians taken prisoner were executed. Soon Byzantium and Calchedon fell to the Peloponnesians; many Athenians were sent off to Athens, and increased the danger of famine in the city. Athens had lost her last fleet. All her allies revolted, with the one exception of Samos, where the oligarchs were slain, and envoys sent to Athens to provide for common action. It was too late.[110]

At the Lenaea of 405, midway between the battles of Arginusae and Aegospotami, Aristophanes had produced the *Frogs*, once again a highly political comedy, written under the impact of the knowledge that the state and society of Athens were on the verge of disintegration. Other writers of comedy before had used the idea of a descent to Hades in order to fetch some great men of the past back to the world; we have spoken of Eupolis' *Demoi* (p. 313), when the great statesmen were to stop the decline of the polis. But now the mission is performed by the god Dionysus, funny and farcical in his disguise as Heracles, an anti-hero accompanied by a slave, who is his second *ego*, though cleverer than the god. Dionysus wants to find the poet who might save the state, and he thinks of Euripides. Naturally, it turns out differently. If his descent, as has been maintained,[111] is a variation of the myth of Dionysus fetching his mother Semele from Hades, it would add to the far from comic meaning behind the god's enterprise. It is also relevant that the chorus consists of the souls of initiates in the Eleusinian mysteries to which Dionysus belonged as identified with Iacchus, the god revealed in the ecstatic cries of the mystic procession. The chorus of the initiates is strangely contrasted with the other chorus of the frogs. They make it clear (211) that they belong to the cult of Dionysus, and to that part of the festival of the Anthesteria that was celebrated in Limnae ('the swamps'), not far from the theatre. Otherwise, their *brekekekex koax* provides the rhythm for Dionysus' clumsy attempt at rowing. In the end he shouts them down, adapting himself to the demands of 'rowing', which in every Athenian mind would mean the fleet of which they used to be so proud. As the god of the theatre, Dionysus represents the Athenian audience, and they would enjoy the fact that Charon's fare is two obols (142. 270), which Theseus, the mythical hero of Athenian democracy, is said to have introduced instead of the traditional one obol which was put into the mouth of every corpse; it was, of course, a reminder of Cleophon's *diobelia*. The audience might also be impressed by the chorus' plea in the *parabasis* (686) for equal rights for all citizens; when the slaves who fought at Arginusae had become free citizens, those who, like their ancestors, had often fought for Athens should not be deprived of their citizenship 'for one mishap'. That was rather an understatement for the revolt of the Four Hundred, but the poet did not speak for the oligarchs, rather for the restoration of unity among all citizens. We may wonder whether the poet could really hope for a response from a hysterical and blind democracy.

The *agon* of the play is between Aeschylus and Euripides, that is to say, between a return to the unspoiled simplicity and the moral standards of the Marathon-fighters, or the acceptance of the sophistic and sophisticated views of the modern mind. In a sense, each side is shown to have good and bad points, and the outcome is not fully justified by the preceding contest. An outstanding example of Euripides' 'pupils' is Theramenes, who is depicted as a sly, versatile, and smart man, clearly not a favourite of the poet. More important is the question of what should be done with Alcibiades, who had actually gone, but whom the city 'loves, and hates, and wants to hold' (1425). Euripides makes it clear that he regards Alcibiades a man clever for himself, but useless for the state. Aeschylus speaks the famous line about the lion's whelp 'whom it is best not to rear, but having reared him, one must serve his ways'.[112] He seems to express the view that Athens has made Alcibiades great, and thus brought about her own ruin. In spite of all its literary allusions, its plays on words, its stylistic remarks, its parodies, all of which show the people's interest in literary matters, remarkable enough at that time of distress, in spite of all that, the *agon* is not a literary contest, not an attempt at finding who is the better poet but a purely political matter, though political in the widest sense of the word. The tragedian was generally regarded as a teacher of his people, not in the way of deliberate education – that was the business of the sophists – but as the poet who, like Homer, set intellectual and social standards. No earlier generation would have made 'the poet a teacher, consciously chosen and consciously carrying out his task'. Aristophanes did so as a child of his time, as a pupil – however indirectly and however hostile – of the sophists himself.[113] Aeschylus is eventually chosen, not for any special wisdom or art but because he represents a period of Athenian greatness, and thus will be able 'to save the state' (1501). The poet's fear of the present situation breaks through all the fun and farce of comedy; it provides a background that is very serious, indeed tragic.

Athens was now under siege by land and sea. Famine was threatening, despair was spreading. Even so, any demand to pull down the Long Walls was strictly refused. Theramenes then managed to be sent as a peace envoy to Sparta (Xen. 2, 2, 16. Lys. 13, 8). He first went to Lysander who was beleaguering Samos, and later led an embassy to Sparta, delaying his return for several months, while at Athens the famine grew worse and worse. It was then that Cleophon, fanatic demagogue and fanatic patriot, was condemned on a trumped-up charge of desertion. In an assembly at Sparta her allies demanded the full punishment of Athens – massacre and enslavement – just as she had treated Melos and other places. Sparta, however, was unwilling to destroy the city which had done so much for Greece; it might also be sound policy not completely to give way to states such as Corinth and Thebes. Sparta's terms of peace were the destruction of the Long Walls and those of the Peiraeus, the surrender of the fleet except for twelve ships, the return of the exiles, and the conclusion of an alliance which made Athenian policy dependent on Sparta. A large majority of the Athenian assembly accepted these terms, probably with relief. Lysander entered the Peiraeus, and to the accompaniment of flute players, the Long Walls were pulled down, 'in the belief that that day meant the beginning of freedom for Greece' (Xen. 2, 2, 23).

This, of course, was far from the truth. But it was the fault of Athenian democracy that in its imperialist policy it had denied the very principles of democracy and freedom. And that was Pericles' legacy.

VIII

'KNOW THYSELF'

The phrase 'Know Thyself' (*gnothi seauton*), inscribed on the temple wall at Delphi, and repeated as a slogan of some of the Seven Sages, had been one of the *Leitmotifs* of Greek thought, ever since the Apollinian religion of Delphi had spread among the Greeks, even among some non-Greeks, infusing ethical elements into life and myth. The true meaning of the saying, as we have seen, was 'know thyself as a human being, and follow the god'. It implied the pious contrast which played such an important part in Greek ethics, the contrast and conflict between wisdom and moderation (*sophrosyne*), on the one hand, and presumption and arrogance (*hubris*), on the other. It was an idea close to the heart and mind of Pindar as well as of the Athenian tragedians. In the fifth century, however, it was given a new meaning, the knowledge by man of himself.[1] Heraclitus had said, 'I have searched myself,' and 'character (*ethos*) is man's dae-mon'. Words such as these heralded a new era in which man, even individual man, became the object of investigation, and human reason the decisive factor over and against divine guidance. We have mentioned before some evidence for this development, but it is de-sirable to describe it independently, and to see it as a whole. This is not easy, because it was never a straightforward, clear-cut move-ment. Rational and irrational elements frequently intermingled, and even the great agnostic minds acknowledged forces and pri-mary causes of a mythical, or at least non-rational, nature. Still, the general trend is clear. The problem of cosmogony and cosmology gradually lost their preponderance, and man moved into the centre of thought.[2] That might be any individual man, but increasingly the idea of mankind and its unity gained force. The discussion that follows is an integral part of the story as told so far.

1 · The Birth of Science

Perhaps the most determined and most significant attack on pre-rational thinking was in the field of medicine, where the human individual was quite literally the thing to be treated. Hippocrates, born about 460, founded a medical school in his native island of Cos; a rival school developed in Cnidus. Medical books appeared in great numbers. Fifty-eight are collected in the vast *Corpus Hippo-craticum*, many of them of later date; it is an open question which, if any, go back to Hippocrates himself, or at least to his immediate pupils. It is, however, agreed that some of the most important works belong to the fifth century, and most of them to the firmly empirical school of Cos; its library was probably the nucleus of the whole collection.[3]

The most famous document is, of course, the Hippocratic oath, which may belong to the late fifth or early fourth century. It was sworn 'by Apollo, Asclepius, Health, and all the powers of healing', that is to say, by divinities and abstract forces alike. The contents of the oath reveal the close bonds of son and father, pupil and teacher relationship among the physicians, which may easily go back to Hippocrates himself, who was a member of the family of the Asclepiads. Their name indicates a traditional connexion with the god of healing; but they were practitioners of medicine rather than priests of Asclepius, though the two may once have coincided. The main content of the oath, however, is a code of behaviour of very high ethical standards indeed. Although it was for a long time not generally accepted, its influence was widespread, and it has proved its value throughout the centuries till the present day.[4]

Among the other Hippocratic writings one or two books are of a more general significance. We learn of the close connexion between medicine and natural philosophy, and on the other hand, of the emphasis on empirical knowledge. As to the influence of philosophy, it determined the beginnings of scientific medicine by abandoning religious rituals and magic. 'Prayer is good, but in invoking the gods, one must help oneself.' Philosophy also provided simple theories and doctrines which soon roused the resistance of the empirically minded. Alcmaeon, physician and philosopher, applied the doctrine of opposites, which had dominated parts of natural philosophy, e.g. in Heraclitus and Empedocles, to the constitution of man. It has rightly been said that natural philosophy and empirical medicine met, or rather clashed, in the one fundamental question 'what is man?'

The empirical physician's point of view is clearly put in the book *On Ancient Medicine*, especially chapter 20.[5] This essay, written late in the fifth century, is partly retrospective, but concerned with the ways of scientific research, stressing the discoveries past and present, such as the importance of a correct diet, of which the author has much to say. He refuses to accept any *a priori* principle as suggested by different concepts of the philosophers; but he does discuss, e.g., the effects of hot and cold, even the causes of the common cold. 'I do not believe,' he says, 'that any clear knowledge of nature can be obtained from any other source but medicine.' He refuses to accept the view of human nature expressed by men like Empedocles and others, 'doctors and sophists'. He knows a good deal about the working of the human body, and draws his medical conclusions from it. When his experience is insufficient, he is helped by his rational common sense. We meet a similarly sober and experimental approach in other essays as well, for instance, in *Prognosis*, a book in which the significance of the various symptoms of a disease are discussed in great detail. For the development of all sciences or near-sciences the new medical methods were essential.

Another empirical approach of great originality is made in the book *On Airs, Waters, and Places*, which could reasonably be called 'On Man and his Surroundings'. It was probably written by, and for the use of, a travelling doctor who would find natural conditions very different at different places. The first part (chs. 1–11) speaks of the effects on man's health of the winds, the geographical position (*thesis*), the various kinds of drinking water, the seasons, and the weather in general. Chapter 12 starts a new section on the difference between Asia (i.e. Asia Minor) and Europe, and its effects on the nature of people. Medicine is combined with geography and ethnography. Personal observation, description from hearsay (for instance, of the northern tribes), and theories such as the *nomos–physis* contrast of sophist teaching (about which more later) are all put together by a very ingenious mind which tries to discover the causes of everything. Even the *shamans*, the asexual wonder-doctors of the

Scythians, mentioned by Herodotus (1, 105. 4, 67), are explained on medical grounds. The strengthening influence of a moderate climate and of rigorous surroundings is contrasted with the weakening effects of a 'soft' country, a theme repeated by Herodotus in the last chapter of his work. We realize how the general intellectual atmosphere is changing; science is on the march.

The book on *The Sacred Disease*, sometimes ascribed to the same author as the one *On Airs, Waters, and Places*, makes this, if possible, even clearer. The so-called sacred disease is epilepsy, but there is nothing sacred about it. The writer passionately attacks the charlatans who prescribe purifications, incantations, and a senseless, if harmless, therapy. Instead, the illness is closely observed and described, and the central part played by the brain is emphasized, also the hereditary character of diseases in general. The real cause is found in an overpressure in the blood vessels of phlegm, one of the four 'humours' in the human body.[6]

These doctors do not deny the gods, but they try to explain man and his diseases without referring to supernatural forces. In that respect as well as in others they are the true contemporaries of the sophists. They are also the first to try something like experiments. The physicians led the way, but they were not alone. It was a general trend. Natural science, sometimes still as the handmaid of natural philosophy, found the way to secular and rational explanations, for instance, in astronomy. Mathematicians discussed among other things the problem of the infinitely smallest, paving the way for the atomist theories of Leucippus and Democritus. The scientists had to fight the mythical and religious foundations of common beliefs; but they also fought against natural philosophers, not only mystical miracle-workers like Empedocles – who, after all, was a physician as well – but above all the paradoxical and influential scepticism of the Eleatics who denied any reality in human observations. The only philosopher about the middle of the century who was definitely on the side of rational science was Anaxagoras (see p. 243); his pupil Archelaus was the first Athenian among the early thinkers, and perhaps the teacher of Socrates. His position, as it were, may have been symbolic on the way from the philosophy of nature to that of man.[7]

Natural philosophy culminated in the theories of the atomists at about the same time as humanist philosophy reached a first peak. Both were agreed on the prevalence of moral standards over divine forces. An exception was probably Diogenes of Apollonia, whose explanation of the cosmic order was essentially theological; in general he seems to have been an eclectic of sorts. It is his theory of the air, as being both a god and the human mind, that underlies Aristophanes' caricature of Socrates praying to air and clouds (*Clouds* 264). The atomism of Leucippus and Democritus is pure materialism, based on a world composed of the smallest possible particles, so that they were truly 'indivisible' (*atoma*). Their number is infinite, and their shapes vary indefinitely. They move, or are moved, fighting each other in an infinite void. This astonishing theory, in which Ionian and Eleatic monism is combined with the plurality of matter, is matched by the assumption of unlimited numbers of cosmic systems, ruled over by a completely de-mytho-logized, practically incomprehensible notion of necessity (*ananke*). Similar 'physical' explanations cover man's thoughts and sensations as well. Among Democritus' hundreds of fragments are many – if they are genuine – of an ethical or political nature; it is not clear to what extent he really was more than a physicist of genius. Living towards the end of the period of the sophists, he naturally realized the importance of education (*DK* 68 B 242). It may be significant of the hesitant acceptance of science at Athens that the man from Abdera, in contrast to the other Abderite, Protagoras, never felt at home in Athens, though Anaxagoras did. 'For I came to Athens, and nobody knew of me' (B 116), Democritus said; he would not have done so if he had not been 'somebody' at that time. As a philosopher of human ethics, at any rate, he was not original, though he reflected the climate of his age, and it remains significant that the great atomist was a contemporary of Socrates.[8]

Science extended its realm to subjects not necessarily belonging to its field. We have spoken of the beginnings of ethnography and history. We have drawn some parallels with Herodotus, while the pre-Herodotean tradition found its zenith and its end in Hellanicus of Lesbos (*FGrH* 4), who was roughly contemporary with Thucy-dides. A large part of his work is concerned with mythological genealogies, and their place in a reconstruction of early history. He took great interest in non-Greek countries and peoples as so many did, but he was less of a geographer than an ethnologist and at the same time a bold etymologist; he also dealt with various regions of Greece, thus preparing the ground for many local historians to follow. With his *Atthis* he was the first of a long line of 'Atthido-graphers'; that book was used by Thucydides, whose own debt to science will later be discussed. He criticizes Hellanicus' chronological inaccuracy for the time after the Persian wars (1, 97, 2). Hellanicus' historical books were largely in the nature of chronicles; apart from reconstructed genealogies, he used – a remarkable methodical advance – lists of kings or officials (e.g. the Athenian archons), or of athletic victors, or the priestesses of Hera at Argos; no doubt he had to do some research in reconstructing the lists, although he manipu-lated them with a great deal of irresponsibility. He was not a great historian, but he has his place in the history of the growing interest in, and the growing knowledge of, the development of man.[8a]

2 · The Sophists

The decisive steps, however, in that direction were made by the sophists. The word *sophistes* originally meant a wise man, also a teacher of wisdom, and in particular an expert in any sort of art or craft (*techne*). He could be an artisan or an artist, a physician or even a prophet, but above all he was a poet and thinker. Solon, Pythagoras, and many others, even Homer and Hesiod, could be called sophists. Those whom we call in particular by that name belong to the fifth century, and made teaching on a higher level their profession. It was then that the name of sophist gradually acquired a less honourable meaning. Once Simonides (53 D) had said 'the polis educates man'. That was no longer quite true, since the bonds of the community had weakened. The sophists were the first to make the education of young men an aim deliberately pur-sued; they were the first to travel about and give lessons for pay.[9] Men who could hardly be called citizens of a polis wanted to teach the young citizens their business. It was Plato, by his hostile de-scription of the sophists as charlatans, who finally brought the name into discredit, and it was only during the nineteenth century that the value of their teaching was recognized, first by George Grote in chapter 67 of his *History of Greece*.[10] There is still a good deal of discussion going on about the true nature of the sophists' teaching, and it seems hardly possible to deal with the question without some prejudice, or at least some strong feeling.[11]

The problem has been made more difficult by the fact that Plato and Aristotle were hostile not only to the sophists of the fifth century, but under the same general name they also attacked philosophers of their own time. Still, we do know a certain amount about the sophists. They were not a school of philosophy but individual teachers, differing in their views as well as their standards, but agreeing on man as the central subject of their teaching, and in particular man as a political animal. They could be called the heirs of the poets who down to Solon were regarded as the teachers of the Greek people; but they were also strongly influenced by the early philosophers. They wrote books, but for most of them the direct approach to living persons was more important than the idea of future readers. To this end they studied and taught, each in his own way, the conditions of human life, with special emphasis on man's speech and thought. They held certain philosophical views, and some of these had lasting influence, as, for example, the claim that virtue and value (*aretē*) was founded on knowledge, and therefore could be taught. It is, however, not so much their philosophy that counted historically. They were, above all, a social phenomenon, professional teachers of middle-class origin, who educated the young sons of the wealthy and noble.[12] That meant political education, and it largely boiled down to rhetorical education, as was needed in political life generally, and in democracy in particular. At the same time the sophists included in their teaching a large variety of facts and questions, often of astonishing breadth and variety. They were true professionals. 'Polymathy' was a characteristic quality, though it might differ greatly in its components; Protagoras (Plat. 318d) protested against it, and confined himself to the teaching of the art of politics which, however, included a number of subjects. Dominated as the sophists' teaching was by the wish to use the means of persuasion, their education, at least at its best, aimed at a comprehensive and civilized personal culture. There is no doubt that this education responded to a real need of society; the sophists were an expression of their age, and also guided its spirit.

They were, at the same time, largely responsible for a widening of the gap between the generations. This divergence reached its critical stage during the war, as is reflected in Aristophanes' *Clouds* and *Wasps*. The older generation had suffered severe losses through war and pestilence, and the ruling class was giving way to the influx of men of comparatively little education and still less tradition and experience. The ways of life and the beliefs of the older people had to a large extent been wrecked by developments which put new demands on, and opened new possibilities for, each single citizen. The young could look to a new future. The new education gave them the chance of emancipation from a world which was left behind by the stormy and revolutionary times. The younger generation hoped to respond to the requests of a changing society by active participation. The sophists who provided the new education came from all over the Greek world, though in general not from Ionia, the homeland of natural philosophy.[13] They centred on Athens and created, or at least made important contributions to, the atmosphere and the substance of the first 'age of enlightenment'.

The earliest and also the greatest of the sophists was Protagoras of Abdera, who came to Athens about the middle of the century, and visited the city often and for long periods, thus becoming part of the Periclean age. He soon became famous; we have heard of his relationship to Pericles. Still, for our knowledge of his thoughts and teaching, we have to rely, apart from the usual late biographies such as Diogenes Laertius and Philostratus, chiefly on two genuine quotations and on the great speech put into his mouth in Plato's *Protagoras*, which we accept as an essentially genuine mirror of Protagoras' views. Others of Plato's dialogues, in which he appears, reflect – with one exception (see below) – the author's own views rather than those of Protagoras.[14]

The two quotations are the *homo – mensura* – sentence, and the equally famous words about his knowledge of the gods (*DK* 80 B 1. 4). 'Man is the measure of all things, of those being, that they are, of those not being, that they are not.' The phrase seems to have been the first sentence of a book called either *Truth* or *Destructive Arguments* (*Kataballontes*).[15] Nobody can pretend that the sentence or its translation is clear and meaningful. It needs further explanation, and that is by no means obvious. The 'things', as explained in Plato,[16] cannot be matter as such, but only matter as seen, felt, or believed by the human mind. The sentence refers to the question, frequently asked and differently answered ever since Parmenides, to what extent reality coincides, on the one hand, with the perception of our senses and, on the other, with ethical standards. It is likely that Protagoras went beyond the meaning of mere sense perception. The main point, the one clearly positive and the one which impressed people at once and for all time, is the *metron anthropos*, the central position given to man. Then the question arises at once whether it is man in general or man as an individual. From the two passages in Plato, it seems clear that it means neither mankind nor each man, rather 'any man you choose', which definitely points to individual man. Whatever explanation we accept, there is either way a distinct expression of a strong subjectivism and relativism. Whether Protagoras himself regarded the truth of ethical values and beliefs as purely dependent on the will and mind of the individual or not, they are at any rate not absolute, whether individual or collective. They may depend on tribal or other customs, on the laws of a state, or possibly on personal conscience. Traditional laws and customs are put in question, that is to say, the ground is prepared for the opposition, not yet strictly formulated, between nature and convention, *physis* and *nomos*. The general trend towards relativism and scepticism found its most important champion in Protagoras. He had, at the same time, found the *Leitmotif* of all sophist thought – man as the centre and the subject of knowledge – indeed, as the master of the world.

That follows even more clearly from the other quotation. 'As to the gods, I have no possibility of knowing that they are, nor that they are not, nor what they are like in appearance. Many are the obstacles to such knowledge, their invisibility no less than the shortness of human life.' This is not a proof of atheism but an admission of inevitable ignorance. The surprising last part of the quotation sounds like a *captatio benevolentiae*, implying that if life were longer, he might still find out something more certain. Protagoras was an agnostic, and that still meant being in opposition to everything most people believed. If he nevertheless wrote a book *On the Gods*, which began with that quotation, he will have criticized existing beliefs and myths rather than religious practice and rituals. He must also have answered the question how men first believed in the existence of gods. That was the main reason for him to expound in a myth his beliefs in the origin of human civilization. It is well known that the Greeks had two contrasting versions of that story, a 'pessimist' and an 'optimist' one, the myth of the Golden Age with its deteriorating further ages being the most outstanding among the former, the Prometheus saga among the latter. Naturally Protagoras was on the optimistic side, on the side of man. He narrated the origin and development of all animals, including man; but the latter is the victim of Epimetheus' distribution of protective and aggressive qualities, since Epimetheus ('after-thought') forgot man till he had nothing left to provide, except the ability to worship and the gift of language (*Prot.* 322a). Then his brother Prometheus ('fore-thought') intervened, stole fire from the gods, and taught man the crafts of Hephaestus and Athena. 'Thus men had the wisdom to keep alive, but political wisdom they had not, for that was with Zeus.' Having learnt to live in cities, but unable to keep peace among themselves, they were granted a share in justice (*dike*) and reverence (*aidōs*). Thus man, and man alone, was enabled to lead a civilized life within a community. Protagoras clearly acknowledged the polis as the state based on law, but (to see his view without the myth) all 'progress', all civilization was man's own work. This is the first rational theory of progress, which was to become one of the leading ideas of political philosophy. In Protagoras' thought it was firmly bound to the idea of a 'social compact', the development of the human community by consent. Man, having learnt to know what is just and what is venerable, created tradition and convention, custom and law, that is to say, *nomos*. Everybody should be able to reach a high degree of perfection (*aretē*), but it is not given to man by nature (*physei*). The well-known contrast seems close at hand, but Protagoras did not yet find the simple formula which became famous or notorious, the opposition of convention and nature. To him, the essential thing was that *aretē* had to be taught; he says that 'teaching needs nature and training' (B 3). Education is his chief concern, as other evidence confirms; he has no doubt that 'virtue' is teachable.[17] Former generations had been proud to descend from the gods; now men learnt that their individual human nature –

physical as well as spiritual – was what they had to value and to perfect.

The 'art of politics' involved the 'art of rhetoric', and its primary purpose, as of any kind of speech, is persuasion. However, in order to persuade, it was not enough to give an oration expounding one's own views (although that might be important too). Protagoras was not a narrow and dogmatic thinker, rather a sceptic, and that is why he proclaimed (B 6a) that 'there were two contradictory *logoi* about everything'. Perhaps a different version of the same idea is contained in the phrase (6b) 'to make the weaker *logos* the stronger one'. That does not necessarily mean, although it could be understood in that sense, to inflate a morally or intellectually weaker cause, and thus to deceive the audience.[18] The phrases probably belonged to a work called *Antilogiai* (or 'Opposing Arguments'), and to see a thing from two sides is not mere sophistry, but can be an expression of the desire for greater knowledge, and therefore indicate the value of the contents of the sophist's teaching. It can be assumed that Protagoras in this book discussed the advantages and disadvantages of various political constitutions. If that is true, he may have been the source, or at least one among others, for the debate of the Persians on the best constitution in Herodotus, and perhaps also of many theoretical discussions in Euripides, in which democracy carried the day against monarchy.[18a] Protagoras was perhaps not the first to establish political theory as an independent branch of philosophical studies, but he was certainly among the first, and surely the most influential. Both the lawgiver and the town-planner of Thurii, Protagoras and Hippodamus, were deeply interested in the theoretical aspects of the life and the form of the community. What to earlier generations, from Hesiod to Solon, from Anaximander to Aeschylus, was the divinely determined 'justice' was largely replaced by new, rational, and secular theories. They might be applied to the practical needs of the moment or to an ideal construction, but they centred on developing a constitution, whether more democratic or more aristocratic. Thus a new kind of philosophical thought was created, which was Greek to the core, the pure product of the polis.

Protagoras' famous phrase of the two contradictory *logoi* implies that it ought to be possible to argue both sides of a statement in turn, and that a clever speaker would be able to persuade his audience to accept anything. Here lies the root of a dangerous 'revaluation of all values' and of the belief in the relativity of values, whether Protagoras intended such an effect or not. It might be put to use in practical life, in particular in politics. It was at the same time the beginning of a method of investigation by discussion, which we call dialectics. That was to turn out to be the Socratic method, but it could, and did, easily deteriorate into mere eristics, serving a rhetorical and logical triumph rather than the truth.[19]

The second great sophist was Gorgias from Leontini. He was, above all, a rhetor, whether in speech or in writing. He brought to Greece the Sicilian art and technique of words, an ancient feature of his homeland, which he raised to a new level of artistry. When in 427 B.C. he headed an embassy to Athens to ask for help for Leontini against Syracuse, the brilliance of his speech made a great impression, and soon many pupils gathered round him. His share in philosophy consisted in a book On Non-Being, most likely a pamphlet against Parmenides and the Eleatics, culminating in a threefold paradox that is quoted verbatim (DK 82 B 3): 'Nothing exists. If something does exist, it is incomprehensible to man. If it is comprehensible, it cannot be explained to another man.' It seems probable that this was not a serious treatise, rather a satire, though with a serious purpose. The reversal of the paradox could, and perhaps did, mean that speaking is more important than thinking, and thinking more than being. That was a philosophy of nihilism, and therefore a repudiation of all dogmatic thought, while at the same time a complete justification of rhetoric. This is what we should expect as a genuine expression of Gorgias' thought.[20]

He practised all the branches of rhetoric, speeches in court no less than political and epideictic orations. They cannot be clearly distinguished, for his style with its rhythm and antitheses, the variety of his linguistic formulas and mannerisms, and his playing with words appears in all of them.[21] As examples of this style may serve phrases like 'Xerxes, the Zeus of the Persians', and 'vultures, living tombs', both from the Epitaphios in which soon after 421 he praised the deeds of the Athenians (B 5a). Much more remarkable, however, is that this funeral speech openly proclaimed the Panhellenic idea. 'Victories over the barbarians call for hymns of praise, those over the

Greeks for laments of mourning' (5b). A similar tendency was obviously expressed in speeches he made at the Panhellenic festivals at Olympia and Delphi (B 7–9). This one trend apart, the contents really mattered little; it was the form which gave his words both brilliance and the power of persuasion. Poetry was to him merely part of rhetorical art, and he is well aware of its effects on human emotions. He displays a mixture of prose and poetry especially in speeches, written for readers rather than listeners, such as the *Eulogy of Helen* (B 11) and the *Defence of Palamedes* (B 11a). Both of these defend a much maligned mythical person. He calls the former a *paignion*, a plaything or jest, though it is rather a serious, if paradoxical, examination of the nature of a weaker person over and against various possible stronger forces. Even so, we should regard the speech also in the light of Gorgias' disarming remark (B 12) that it is necessary 'to destroy the earnestness of opponents by laughter, and their laughter by earnestness'. Palamedes, on the other hand, who was believed to have been the inventor of all human arts and intellectual activities, is defended against the reproach that his inventions had bad effects; he is shown as the true benefactor of Greece. There is no very deep thought in these writings, rather a firework of words and a display of great formal art. Accordingly, Gorgias influenced literature more than philosophy. He made prose an art, and rhetoric a dangerous weapon of possible misuse; through his follower Isocrates he became the father of a school which fought philosophy in the field of education. Gorgias' ethical duplicity made him at the same time a teacher of sophistry in the bad sense of the word.[22]

It is difficult to say to what extent the Gorgias in Plato's dialogue of that name is the historical person, whether, for instance, he held the view that rhetoric 'is the greatest good which brings freedom to mankind, and at the same time to each man the rule over others in his polis' (452d). The 'will for power', expressed in that sentence, is, however, the main theme later in the dialogue, and what we know of Gorgias' pupils confirms his teaching on that point. Xenophon, for example, tells us (*Anab.* 2, 6, 16) of one of them, Proxenus, who was ambitious, but refused to use unjust means to achieve his aims; also of Menon, whom Plato (*Menon* 70e) calls Gorgias' disciple, who is described by Xenophon as using perjury, lies, and deceit in order to gain money and glory. The former was Xenophon's friend, the latter his worst enemy; we may doubt whether his description is impartial. Nor does this pair of pupils necessarily prove, as is sometimes thought, Gorgias' ethical indifference; that may have been a fact, but where should we end if we took Socrates' various followers as an indication of his lack of ethical interest?

It is not necessary for us to deal in great detail with other figures among the sophists. They are, on the whole, of minor stature, though most of them represent important trends within the whole phenomenon. There was Prodicus of Ceos, with his famous 'Heracles at the crossroads' as told by Xenophon (DK 84 B 2), a preacher of serious, if somewhat trivial, ethics. The story, which was to become famous throughout the ages, offered man a free choice between good and evil.[23] 'Eritis sicut Deus . . . .', but to the sophists the way did not start from the paradise of the Golden Age, rather from a state of primitive savagery, to lead to the final freedom of civilized man. Prodicus, like others, had his ideas about the origin of the gods; he thought they were man-made, but an expression of gratitude for the gifts of nature. In that gratitude Prodicus saw the origins of religion. The identity between deities and their gifts (wine – Dionysus; water – Poseidon; fire – Hephaestus; grain – Demeter, etc.) gave his theory a backing that could easily be understood. Another well-known man was Hippias of Elis, the first sophist of Dorian origin, whose main characteristic seems to have been his polymathy, including all sorts of practical abilities. He proclaimed the complete self-sufficiency of the individual. Though not an original thinker, he was certainly a clever eclectic who boasted of having drawn his knowledge from Greek as well as barbarian writers (DK 86 B 6). In 'performing' at the great festivals he continued the tradition of the rhapsodes. He also composed a list of the victors in the Olympian stadium race, though he did not yet use it for historial chronology. From Plato's Protagoras (337c) we learn that Hippias regarded all men as kinsmen 'by nature, though not by convention', that nomos is the tyrant of man, compelling us to do many things against nature (physis).

Here we approach one of the most significant issues, or rather formulas, of the sophists' thought, in which Pindar's enigmatic fragment on 'Nomos, king of mortals and immortals' (169 Sn., 152 B) plays a predominant part, although its meaning varies from quotation to quotation.[24] We cannot discuss the long prehistory of the two concepts of *nomos* and *physis*, which originally developed separately, though their contrast was influenced by the Eleatic one of truth and illusion. It can, however, be said that, in a way, both concepts prevailed in the two types of myth on the origin of man. The two versions, mentioned before and going back to early times (Hesiod's five ages and his Prometheus), were represented in the 'optimistic' tale by Protagoras, when the story starts with primitive 'nature', and progress is made towards 'custom' and 'law', while in the 'pessimistic' story we have the fairy-tale of a golden age ('nature' again), from which man gradually declines to lesser ages of deteriorating customs and laws (*nomoi* again). In either case, the part (if any) played by the gods was questionable; agnosticism and even atheism were spreading. Still, the people involved were a minority; today they might be called 'the intelligentsia'. Equally, in ethnographic writings from pre-sophist times to books under sophist influence, we can trace the knowledge of the varying, and therefore 'relative', *nomoi* of different peoples, and the varying influence of natural surroundings. The curious double character of the two concepts remained typical of philosophical discussion and its effects on life and politics.

We have seen that the concept of the antithesis of *nomos* and *physis* was being prepared, though it was not yet reached, in Protagoras' thought. What he made clear was that he believed in the equality of men as created by nature, and also that *nomos*, secured by justice and awe, was essential for the community. Nomos and Dike were one. Among Gorgias' pupils we find one Lycophron, who accepts Protagoras' high esteem of *nomos*, which to him is 'the guarantor of mutual rights' (*DK* 83 B 3). Aristotle (*pol.* 1280b, 10) took this as the earliest evidence of the doctrine of the social contract; but the idea may be older, for it was implied in the theories of man's rise from primitive to civilized life, e.g. in Critias' *Sisyphus* (*DK* 88 B 25), a remarkable fact in view of Critias' general attitude, of which more later. Something similar is the *eunomia* of the Anonymus Iamblichi (*DK* 89, 7); for him, too, *nomos* and justice are identical, and he even includes the possibility of a superman who rules by law and justice (6, 2). He warns against the menace of *tyrannis*, which derives from the doctrine of the Right of the Stronger, of which again more later. For this kind of sophist the rule of justice is established by nature. This seems to bridge the gap between the two concepts. The final formula of the conflict between *nomos* and *physis*, it is generally agreed, was also found by one of the sophists.[25] It is possible, but can hardly be proved, that Parmenides' contrast between truth and opinion, between being and seeming was the primary cause of the sophists' formula; it would mean a transfer from the sphere of perception and knowledge to that of ethics and politics.

In order to trace the contrasting couple of concepts, we shall not continue to follow the lines of historical development, which, in any case, remain obscure. We shall start at the other end and discuss what may be called the final forms of the theories based on that contrast. Most sophists and their followers are agreed on the relativity of *nomos*. What once – for Heraclitus or Pindar or Empedocles – was the highest possible norm of all was, on the other hand, or at least was supposed to be, as 'the laws of the state' the guide for the citizens' life. Now *nomos* was regarded as a mere human convention, usually of no real value, or even, as with Hippias, as a tyrant to be destroyed. We have all, in our own lifetime, come to know of conventions as contemptible as tyrannical. Its opposite, *physis*, became the leading force, either as an expression of the natural equality of men, and thus a justification of democracy, or as the opposite, an expression of the natural uniqueness of the individual, in particular the great individual, and thus a support for monarchy or tyranny. Taken as a whole, the theory was an answer to the belief, whether pious or rational, in the 'unwritten laws'.[26]

For most of the sophists the question of *nomos* was insolubly connected with that of usefulness. The latter (*to xympheron*) became the yardstick for measuring the significance of *nomos* for human life. Antiphon, for instance, is an important witness. Fragments show that in his *Aletheia* (*Truth*) he wrote about various aspects of natural and cultural philosophy; our evidence, however, is fragmentary, and the text is often doubtful. It came as a decisive, if surprising, addition to our knowledge when large sections of Antiphon's book were found in a papyrus.[27] He speaks of justice as the rule not to violate the laws of the state. That is hardly his own view, as the further context shows.[28] Led by the idea of usefulness or advantage, Antiphon draws the conclusion that before witnesses a man should show respect for the state's lawful rules (nomima), but when alone he should follow those of nature. 'For those of the laws are arbitrary, those of nature necessary.' 'The advantages established by the nomoi are fetters of nature, but those by physis are free.' This means that natural law is put above state law, even though, by the cowardly rule of secrecy, man is advised not to act accordingly in public. While English common sense and fairness require justice not only to be done but also to be seen to be done, the sophist preaches that not justice, but only the appearance of it, is useful. Freedom from the nomoi means negation of the polis, although as far as Antiphon is concerned, it probably does not yet mean the complete liberation of the individual; but it did mean liberation from conventional rules which had become meaningless.

In his book On Unity (homonoia) Antiphon stresses the importance of education, and declares that anarchy is evil, and therefore obedience essential (B 60 f.) This positive attitude towards the community contrasts to some extent to those views mentioned, but the concept of homonoia, which Antiphon traces back to the unity of the family (B 49), had at that time generally begun to be acclaimed as the remedy for social troubles within the state; it grew in importance as an ideal that had nothing to do with constitutional issues. Antiphon's belief in natural law compels him to oppose class distinctions and Greek superiority, 'for by nature we all are in every way similar, whether barbarians or Greeks'. While Thrasymachus (DK 85 B 2) could still complain: 'are we to slave for Archelaus, Greeks for a barbarian?', Hippias had taken a cosmopolitan point of view, and Antiphon's emphasis on equality is probably reflected in numerous passages from tragedy, especially Euripides.[29] The emphasis is not only on barbarians but also on slaves; they were often enough the same people.

Another of Gorgias' pupils was Alcidamas, whom Aristotle frequently quotes in his Rhetoric, disapproving of his highly artificial style. Alcidamas pleads for the rule of the wise, whether poet or philosopher or statesman, and regards philosophy as a 'barrier against the laws', the 'kings of cities', an allusion again to Pindar's 'King Nomos'.[30] A gap in the text (1373b, 18) is filled by the scholiast's sentence which essentially derives from Alcidamas, 'God created all men free, nature has made no man a slave.' This is one of several voices raised at that time against an institution which to most Greeks was no problem at all. Alcidamas, it is true, is a contemporary of Isocrates, but even as a slightly later witness he completes the picture of a trend of thought which made the law of nature a weapon against slavery, and the basis of cosmopolitanism and the concept of mankind, ideas for which the Hellenistic age was to provide a fertile soil.

Another trend led to the opposite conclusion. It is first represented by Thrasymachus, who was well known at Athens in 428–427, when Aristophanes in his earliest comedy, the *Banqueters* (*Daitales*), made fun of him as an expert in rhetorical expressions (fr. 198). We know of Thrasymachus from Plato's *Republic* (338c), where he claims that 'justice is nothing else but the advantage of the stronger' (*DK* 85 B 6a). That is the theory of the Right of the Stronger, based on his 'nature' and on the facts of the political world; it culminates in the praise of injustice exercised by a great man – a full justification of tyranny. If Thrasymachus is little more than a mouthpiece of extremist views, pleading that justice and right have to give way to might, another man takes the final step and maintains that might *is* right. This is Callicles in Plato's *Gorgias*, not a sophist but an upper-class Athenian who learnt his rhetoric from Gorgias, and shaped his views and his life on the doctrine of the Right of the Stronger.[31] It is he who claims (483d) that men like Xerxes and Darius acted 'according to the nature of justice, and indeed according to the law of nature'. The same claim is made by the Athenians in the astonishing display of sophistic methods in Thucydides, the Melian dialogue (5, 105 ff.); they are acting from a natural necessity that those rule who have the power – a law received from ancient times and existing for ever. This law of nature is not the natural law of later times, rather the forerunner of Nietzsche's *Herrenmoral*,[32] a law nevertheless, the law of unlimited individualism, the law lived by such men as Alcibiades, Lysander, and Critias. They were enemies not only of democracy but of the polis itself. The self-knowledge of the strong man implies, at the same time, the complete reversal of the meaning of the Delphic word with which we started this chapter.

The concentration on man's nature, as implied in different ways in so much of the sophists' teaching, led many minds away from public life to some kind of intellectual introspection or a generally theoretical approach to life. Social and political reasons alike favoured a trend away from active life. The contrast was born between theory and practice, or rather between contemplation and activity, as ideals by which to live one's life. It frequently went together with the opposition of aristocrat and democrat, and we have an example in fragments of one of Euripides' later plays, the *Antiope*.[33] The art of the same period, though as usual more conservative than thought and drama, shows an exaggeration beyond the standards of Pheidias, as, for instance, at Phigaleia and in the Nereid monument. Easier in movements and more open emotionally, art reflected also the various aspects of domestic life and its underlying emotions, in particular the role of wives and mothers, as we can see it portrayed on tombstones, white *lekythoi*, and some red-figured vases. The farcical pictures of the Italiote phylax vases, on the other hand, depicting a crude kind of comedy, are 'tinged with the spirit of Aristophanes'.[34] The fourth century, with Praxiteles and Scopas, was to start a new style of art, just as new forms of politics or thought, of practice or theory.

3 · Political Events

It is clear from what we have said about the scientists and sophists that intellectual life at Athens, and even at some other places, had become very lively indeed. It was not merely a lot of professional quibbles, but to a large extent the life and strife of the people, and that was closely bound up with the upheavals of politics and warfare. Society was changing in character, and outstanding individuals reflected the sophists' teaching. Thucydides, in two magnificent chapters (3, 82 f.), speaks of the devastating effects of war and civil strife on moral and society life. Just as some sophists exaggerated the power of the individual, thus Athens had overestimated her power. The warning of 'Know Thyself' was true in a wider sense.

After war and defeat came tyranny. The democratic forces were to make a final major effort, but under the impact of the post-war atmosphere, and as education spread and provided new interests, political consciousness in general was on the wane, despite the fact that deliberate political education spread. It is part of the story that there was active opposition to rationalist attitudes. Not only were the old gods still alive; even more significant was the introduction or revival of numerous foreign cults, such as those of Cybele and Attis, Adonis and Bendis and Sabazius. Their worship contained mystic and ecstatic tendencies, though they were gradually tamed and hellenized.

Sparta, together with her allies, especially Corinth and Thebes, and with Persian support, had won the long war. She had promised to bring freedom to the Greek states. In so far as this meant the destruction of Athenian rule, her aims were fulfilled. Beyond that, however, she had no ideological programme, but only a policy of establishing her own hegemony, a programme of pure power politics. It had to be the hegemony of an exhausted and disordered world, and it required economic and psychological leadership. Sparta was incapable of either. There was no second Brasidas at Sparta, who would believe in an idealistic policy of liberation, and though there still were forces to object to an expansive and aggressive attitude, they were too weak. It is possible to doubt whether any other policy was really open to Sparta. Anyway, the legacy of imperialist Athens, or the power of leading individuals such as Lysander, or both, were responsible for another case to prove, if proof were needed, that power corrupts.

Lysander had captured Samos, discharged the Peloponnesian fleet, and returned in triumph to Sparta (Xen. 2, 3, 3. 6 f.), while Agis went home from Deceleia. Lysander, who had brought to Sparta a vast war booty, now directed the policy of the state; more than any other nauarch it was he who caused Aristotle to say (*pol.* 1271a, 40) that at Sparta 'the nauarchy is almost a second kingship'. What had begun in some captured cities even during the war was now happening all over the Aegean world. Oligarchs were put into power, usually a group of ten (decarchies), Spartan commanders (harmosts) were installed together with garrisons, and high tributes were imposed. Many of the commanders, none more than Lysander, outgrew the discipline of their own state and society; love of personal gain and cruel tyranny spread. Soon, disappointment and resentment were ripe among the 'liberated' Greeks.

At Athens, under Lysander's pressure, five ephors were at first appointed (Lysias 12, 43), an unheard-of office after the Spartan model; then the decree of Dracontides formally established oligarchy. Under the pretext of aiming at restoring the 'ancestral laws', thirty men were elected to be masters of the state.[35] The two outstanding leaders were Theramenes and Critias. The latter, banished from Athens after the fall of Alcibiades, had returned from exile in Thessaly. He had by then turned into the most cynical and vindictive extremist, while Theramenes still tried to pursue a moderate line. Critias, a relative of Plato, was a nobleman and a gifted poet and prose writer. He even wrote *politeiai* in verse, and highly praised Sparta's constitution and way of life. He had swallowed the most extreme doctrines of the sophists; in fact, he was himself one of them, although as a rich aristocrat and politician he never taught. Still, he knew that 'more people are valuable (*agathoi* – aristocrats?) by training rather than by nature' (*DK* 88 B 9). He described the gods as the invention of a clever man to prevent others from secretly doing wrong (B 25). Above all, he *lived* the doctrine of the Right of the Stronger, the theories of Thrasymachus and Callicles; with the latter, in particular, he had much in common.

The rule of the Thirty began quietly. They filled the council and the boards of officials (among them ten men to govern the Peiraeus) with their followers, repealed the laws of 462, and deprived the popular courts of their power. They also engaged – an ominous sign of things to come – three hundred 'whip-bearers', a kind of stormtroopers, and made no effort to establish a new constitution. Even so, they soon felt uneasy and asked for help from Sparta; an harmost with seven hundred men arrived and held the Acropolis. The government by the Thirty now became a reign of terror; they fully deserved the name of the Thirty Tyrants. Rich men, especially metics, and men of democratic convictions were the main victims, and the number of the executed soon exceeded 1,500. Theramenes protested, and the people, when they heard of it, took his side. In order to pacify them, the Thirty drew up a list of three thousand who were to have full citizens' rights; but the list remained secret, and Theramenes protested again, especially against the limitation in numbers.[36]

Early in the winter of 404–403 Thrasybulus, with a handful of loyal democrats who had fled, occupied the fort of Phyle in northern Attica; soon more people flocked to his leadership, and when the Thirty marched against him they were defeated. Shaken and fearing the threat of wider opposition, they decided to get rid of Theramenes. It was Critias in particular who accused him of many previous misdeeds, and demanded his death. Theramenes' defence was of no use, the others did not dare raise any objection, and Theramenes was even dragged from the altar. He died nobly. As so often later, 'the revolution, like Saturnus, devoured its own children'.[37] The list of the three thousand was published, after Theramenes' name had been removed; all those not on the list were disarmed, and many fled to Megara or Thebes. Thrasybulus, whose force had been growing all the time, made a successful raid on the camp of the Thirty. They were now seriously frightened, and to have a safe refuge, they occupied Eleusis and forced their followers to kill all the hoplites they had captured. Thrasybulus, with now about a thousand men, made a night attack on the Peiraeus, but was met by the full force of the Thirty including the Spartans; he managed, however, to occupy Munichia. Eventually a full-scale battle followed in which the Thirty were defeated; many were killed, among them Critias. It has been said that he 'had ranged himself . . . under the triumvirate of Theramenes, Alcibiades, and Thrasybulus; of these he executed Theramenes, got his foreign friends to execute Alcibiades, and was himself killed by Thrasybulus. The quisling's progress.'[38] Actually, all of them, with the exception of Thrasybulus, were opportunist turncoats who all, at one time or another, used Spartan help. They became traitors because they thought only of themselves, but nobody was personally responsible for the death of more of his fellow citizens than Critias. Xenophon (2, 4, 21) reports that the Thirty – and that meant, above all, Critias – had killed more Athenians within eight months than the Peloponnesians had done in ten years of war. Critias, a smaller man than Alcibiades and far more vindictive, hardly deserves the respect paid to him by Plato.

The rest of the Thirty were deposed by the assembly of the three thousand and went to Eleusis, while ten men were elected to end the war. However, they belonged to the extreme oligarchs (Lys. 12, 54), though they had opposed Critias; now, they asked for Spartan help and ruled Athens very harshly. More and more of the people turned to the exiles, who by then held the whole of the Peiraeus.[39] In Sparta, Lysander temporarily lost some of his status, but in summer 403 he was once more at the top, himself as an harmost, his brother as the nauarch, and they blockaded Thrasybulus and his men at the Peiraeus. Athens was saved by inner dissension at Sparta. Lysander found himself put out of action by the Spartan government. King Pausanias was sent out by the ephors with allied forces; he had some minor fights with the exiles, but eventually decided to negotiate. It was with Sparta's help that civil war at Athens was stopped, and under the archonship of Eucleides (403–402) reconciliation was made.[40] A Spartan commission came to assist Pausanias, and a treaty was concluded; the Thirty were to remain at Eleusis, where anyone wishing to join them was free to do so within a short period. No connexion, except for the Eleusinian mysteries, was to be allowed between those at Eleusis and the people at Athens, where democrats under Thrasybulus and moderates under Archinus succeeded in acting together. Both 'states' were to be independent, but swore to keep peace with one another, to repay the loans Sparta had previously granted, and to submit to Spartan foreign policy. Pausanias and his troops went home, and the democrats from the Peiraeus marched in armed procession to the Acropolis. Amnesty was proclaimed for all past events, except for the Thirty, the Ten who had governed the Peiraeus, and the notorious *Hendeka*, the Eleven, who had acted as executioners for the Thirty. Civil war was avoided, thanks just as much to the moderation of the Spartans as to the admirable attitude of the Athenian people.[41] With the restoration of a democratic constitution, Athens was to return to the laws of Solon and, in so far as homicide was concerned, those of Dracon. Two years later the Thirty broke the agreement and made an attempt to regain power with the help of mercenaries; the enterprise failed, the leaders were killed, and the rest persuaded to return to Athens under a mutual agreement with the demos. The ridiculous division into two states came to an end, and democratic unity was restored. It was also in

401–400 – if a much damaged inscription (Tod, no. 100) is rightly interpreted – that metics who had marched with Thrasybulus from Phyle received full citizenship; others who had joined later were granted generous privileges.

Meanwhile Sparta, though generally reluctant to continue an expansive foreign policy, was forced by circumstances to be active in various parts. We know little about such activities in the years 404–400 except that she was unable to cope with the task of keeping the Greek world free and safe. On the seas, freed from Athenian rule, pirates were increasingly endangering all peaceful trade. Sparta herself, corrupted by the influx of wealth, lost most of her austerity; social differences widened, and many were impoverished, lost their *klaros*, and hence full citizenship; they were called *hypomeiones*, inferior citizens. Moreover, Lysander had completely outgrown the boundaries of Spartan constitution and society. He was honoured in many states and temples, even worshipped as divine, anticipating the ruler-cult of Hellenistic times. At home he met with growing opposition, and for a short time he disappeared from the public scene; but soon he regained his influence with Cyrus in Asia Minor.

Even without Lysander, Sparta found herself in a position where imperialist policy could not be avoided, for instance in Thessaly. Sparta became involved in events there concerning Larissa. The city had unsuccessfully fought against one of the local tyrants, Lycophron of Pherae; that was about the time of the eclipse of the sun on 3rd September 404 (Xen. 2, 3, 4). In consequence of the defeat, strife broke out among the Larissaeans, and when Sparta decided to wage war against Larissa's northern neighbour, Archelaus of Macedon, the citizens had to face the question whether to join. That situation is discussed in a speech on which views still differ to some extent, though it is more or less agreed that it is a sophist's speech, and a quite impressive one at that, reflecting the contemporary situation in the years before 400 B.C.[42] The speaker is strongly in favour of joining Sparta against Archelaus, who had remained sitting on the fence during the great war, but had inflicted some damage to Larissa. The former fact was reason enough for Sparta to make a show of strength, with the possible aim of extending her power northwards from her colony, Heracleia Trachinia. A war

nearer home against Elis strengthened Sparta's position in the Peloponnese.[43] Elis had long played an independent part. Sparta deprived her of her perioeci, but left her in possession of Olympia,
for that was a religious rather than a political matter.

A new field of foreign policy – new at least in the situation of that
time – opened in Asia. Darius had died in 405–404 and was succeeded by his son Artaxerxes Mnemon, a weak ruler. His younger
son Cyrus, who ruled Asia Minor almost independently, aimed
at the throne, and in summer 401 he marched with an army of
natives and Greek mercenaries against his brother. At Cunaxa,
north of Babylon, the two armies met; the Greeks, on their wing,
were victorious, but Cyrus at the centre was killed, and his army
ran away. The campaign is described in detail in Xenophon's
Anabasis; its most famous section is the retreat of the 'Ten Thousand', part of the time led by Xenophon, through the difficult
mountains of Armenia, harrassed by hostile natives, till the Greeks
got their first sight of the Black Sea: *thalassa, thalassa*! In these shouts
of the soldiers the eternal attachment of the Greeks to the sea found
its most famous expression. Xenophon's book is not a work of art,
but its character as a military journal, written in very simple language, made it unique. The author, it is true, exaggerated the part he
himself played in the adventure. Cyrus' mercenaries soon joined
the Spartan forces in Asia Minor; for ever since Sparta had favoured
Cyrus' expedition, she had been at war with Persia. Both the battle
of Cunaxa and the heroic march of the Ten Thousand confirmed the
view (still prevalent with Alexander, and truly justifiable) that
Greek hoplites were immeasurably superior to the Persians and
other Asiatic soldiers. Sparta began a series of campaigns against the
re-installed satraps Tissaphernes and Pharnabazus. It was the start
of new fighting both in Asia and in Greece, here against an anti-
Spartan coalition. Lysander played a part in both theatres of war,
till he was killed in battle in 395.

A significant feature of the *Anabasis* (cf. 3, 2, 26) is that, perhaps
for the first time apart from Thurii, the idea of a Panhellenic colony
occurred, though now in Asia, within the territory of the Persian
empire. Social conditions in Greece after the war were rather bad,
and the need to reduce the number of the poor and unemployed
was urgent. As a remedy, the sending-out of a colony, even if it

succeeded, would probably have been insufficient; but combined with the idea of Panhellenism, an idea growing among the intellectual upper class, and also with the popular wish to get land within the Persian empire, the scheme began to take root in the Greek mind. It found its most eloquent advocate in Isocrates, and more than its fulfilment in the conquest of Asia by Alexander. Far more effective for the time being, and of wider immediate importance, was the fact that in growing numbers Greeks served abroad as mercenaries, a profession regarded as entirely respectable, and taken up even by Spartan kings. It meant a real revolution that Greek citizens, apart from those subject to Persia who had been employed in Egypt and Mesopotamia, no longer served their own polis, but foreign powers.

4 · The End of Tragedy

On various occasions we could point to the influence of the sophists' teaching on political events and on the spirit of the age. Nobody more than Euripides reflected their philosophy of man, their rhetoric, and their scepticism. To describe him as a rationalist is by no means sufficient, as we have found before and shall find confirmed again. He was the great innovator of dramatic psychology and theatrical design, but he was also the grave-digger of Attic tragedy. It is time to look at the last tragedies of Sophocles and Euripides which, after the restoration of democracy, were performed posthumously; they can be regarded as their legacies to Athens. When Aristophanes wrote his *Frogs*, he knew none of these tragedies. Sophocles' *Oedipus at Colonus* (*OC*) is, above all, about the blessed death of the tormented sufferer, whose grave – or rather place of disappearance from earth –, the sacred precinct of the Eumenides, will bring blessings to the country and people who received him, to Athens and in particular to Colonus, Sophocles' own birthplace. The old men of the chorus know what old age means, that he is a fool who craves for more than the normal length of life. These words were written by the poet in his nineties, when his creative force was still undiminished, though clearly he was aware of his approaching death. Those blessings to come are the old poet's farewell to his beloved city whose praise is sung again and again by the chorus, and whose ruler Theseus is seen as the ideal Athenian, not so much a king as 'a man' (567). By his polis and its gods, Oedipus, the man expelled from his own polis, is finally received; in fact, Theseus promises to establish him as a fellow citizen.[44] Oedipus enters immortality on Athenian soil; the Theban myth and the hero of a Theban cult has become an Athenian myth and an Athenian cult. He is no longer the parricide and husband of his mother, although he speaks of that himself, and the chorus is duly horrified when they first learn who the old man is. The idea of Oedipus' 'guilt' or 'innocence' was never touched upon in *Oedipus Rex*; now he himself assures us many times that his frightful sins were not his fault. It seems clear that Sophocles tried to deal with a theme that was being discussed at that time – and, in fact, ever since. The pious poet could not accept that the fault was with the gods. Oedipus himself invokes 'Justice of old fame, sitting with Zeus by ancient laws' (1382); above all, his mysterious end means that, in the words of the chorus (1567), 'a just god will raise him' to enter immortality. Divine justice is beyond human understanding, but it has the final word.

And yet the play is anything but a peaceful farewell to life. The oracle which had promised the blessings for Athens, at the same time foreshadowed ruin for those who had expelled Oedipus. The fighting world outside sends its envoys – Creon, Polyneices, who both want Oedipus' return for purely selfish reasons. His bitter reply to Creon, whom he regards as a man 'who would borrow a crafty device from any just speech' (761), sounds like an answer to the methods of the sophists of the day, and his passionate curse on his sons, who are fighting each other for the Theban throne and will both die by each other's hand, reveals an Oedipus so implacable and irate that we must ask whether he is really prepared to enter the peace of another world. It is a deep contrast, and we feel that the man Oedipus has, after all, suffered also for his own tempestuous and pitiless nature. Within the play, the contrast means that Oedipus had once more to go through his former life's misery before he was to find peace.

The parallel between the dying Oedipus and the poet who stood on the threshold of death has often been drawn. Sophocles' life

had been without major troubles; he was regarded by his fellow
Athenians as a very happy man. But he must have suffered often
and intensely in his love for Athens. Although the chorus says (726)
that they may be old men, but 'this country's strength has not
grown old', he must have known better, especially after having been
elected one of the *probouloi* in 413, who were to save what still could
be saved. Sophocles will have been in favour of a moderate policy;
he must have been intensely perturbed by the events of 411. He will
have foreseen the final disaster; fortunately for him, he would then
no longer be alive. He also must have suffered from the growing
dissolution of the ancient beliefs. He himself never lost the close
connexion with the forces of piety, and he accepted in his house the
holy snake which represented the god Asclepius, newly brought to
Athens. That is why after his death he was made a hero Dexion,
'the one who receives'. In the *OC* he reminds his people of the
greatness and the beauty of a place where the gods dwell; they have
given to Athens all the bounties of nature, as proclaimed by the
chorus in the first beautiful *stasimon* (668). It was right that the
Athenians made the poet a hero – like the Oedipus of his last play.

There could hardly be two more different plays than the two
Euripides left more or less finished when he died. It is difficult to
speak about *Iphigeneia in Aulis* (*IA*), as the text is corrupt and the
end, perhaps also the beginning, are later additions. The story of
how Iphigeneia was to be sacrificed to Artemis according to the
seer's demands is the centre of a complex and confusing drama in
which psychology seems to overreach itself. Every character is depicted as caught up in the conflict of opposing forces, and thus in the
throes of almost incomprehensible changes. The inner conflicts
typical of so many of Euripides' characters have become an unconvincing theatrical device. There is the great leader Agamemnon,
an irresolute mind wavering between his duty to Hellas and the love
for his child. There is Menelaus, intent on Iphigeneia's sacrifice, and
the next moment nobly submitting to Agamemnon's grief. There
is Iphigeneia, a loving child who is desperate when she hears of her
father's decision, but then surprisingly and heroically rises to the
occasion.[45] There is a chorus of girls from Chalcis, whom mere
curiosity to see the army has brought to the scene, singing lovely
songs, but playing no part in the plot. That plot, on the other hand,

with a noble, if somewhat inhibited, Achilles, a horribly deceived Clytaemnestra, an old servant who always comes at the right moment to keep the story going – all this, in an almost operatic style of endless orations and long songs, seems to herald a new form of theatrical drama that has little to do with the earlier tradition of the 'theatre of the polis'.

Yet there are certain 'political' themes, in fact two which are in many ways significant, and keep the restlessly changing aspects of the plot together. One is the Panhellenic idea, contrasted with the private tragedy of the Atrides; the other is the frequently expressed contempt for the rabble of common folk in the army.[46] The war against Troy is truly Panhellenic; it is for Hellas that Agamemnon must agree to have his child sacrificed. The old theme of Greeks versus barbarians is repeatedly stressed, and Iphigeneia is eventually proud to die 'as the saviour of Greece'. Events are bound to reach this end, not only owing to the cruel will of Artemis but also to the evil power of the masses, which even Achilles is unable to overcome. There is not the slightest hint of that ideal democracy so frequently depicted before by Euripides. Both themes reveal how disillusioned by his native city the poet was – the one theme as the usual idealistic escape from disappointed polis patriotism, the other as the reflection of the depraved democracy of those years. Besides, the play shows the strong influence of the sophists' teaching, both positively and negatively. If it is said generally that tragedy was overcome by philosophy, this play shows the effects of other forces, such as the denial of traditional form, and the demands of rhetorical and musical entertainment.[47]

How different is the *Bacchae*! This is perhaps Euripides' greatest play, and the most disturbing of all Athenian tragedies. Its form and style look back to almost archaic models, and it is difficult to think of the two plays as written about the same time; once again Euripides' mind remains enigmatic. The contents of the *Bacchae* are based on the long history of Dionysiac religion and rituals, as they appear on many vases from the late sixth century onwards. Euripides was in his seventies when he wrote this play, and he wrote, or at least completed it, in Macedon. Most likely he was influenced by his new surroundings to which he sometimes alludes; in fact, much of the play's extraordinary force in picturing Dionysiac ecstasy and primitive rituals, their beauty no less than their brutality and savagery, will be due to the impressions Euripides received in Macedon. Even so, he must have written for an Athenian audience, and it has rightly been stressed that orgiastic and ecstatic cults had been reintroduced in Athens.[48] The real theme of the play, the fight between the unbeliever Pentheus and the god Dionysus, the *theomachia*, to which the text frequently refers, is described in terms which create no true sympathy for either side. The god, at first patient and benevolent, shows the utmost cruelty later; the young king is foolish, arrogant, and full of sexual curiosity, though his final fate arouses pity. The god's worshippers are represented, on the one hand, by the chorus of Asiatic women who are very active followers of the god, sharing in the plot; they sing many most beautiful songs in honour of Dionysus, songs which flow from the poet's undiminished lyrical creativeness. There are, on the other hand, the Theban maenads who in their religious drunkenness commit the most outrageous deeds. Dionysus, it has been said, is both devilish and divine, or simply beyond good and evil. His cult, barbarian and Greek alike, of fierce animality as well as genial festivity, brings to its initiates extreme rapture and extreme liberation, mass hysteria no less than individual happiness. A most remarkable parallel occurs with Sophocles' *OC* (*Bacch.* 1078 ff. ~ *OC* 1622 ff.), when nature was hushed to complete stillness, before the god's voice was heard. However different the situation, there is a similar expression of awe by both poets.[49] Euripides was deeply impressed by all the aspects of the cult, and it is this which created the play, and no intention of imposing on his audience either religion or its opposite. It is, as it were, an impartial picture; he shows the blessed peace of the initiates just as well as their savage ecstasy. The 'wisdom' of which the persons of the play speak again and again[50] oscillates between truth and self-deceit, between old-fashioned belief and modern rationalism. The play does not represent an escape of the poet's *ego* into mystical experience, rather a poetical and dramatic reflection of that experience. There is also a subtle treatment of the demented minds of those, like Pentheus and his mother Agave, into whom the god has entered, just as the two old men, Teiresias and Cadmus, are treated with understanding irony, although Cadmus is also the instrument of the psychical cure applied to Agave who has murdered her son.[50a] Throughout his life Euripides had tried to find an answer to the problems of man, and he had found faith neither in divine order nor in human reason. But he realized the immense power, and thus the danger, of inspired emotion and of its conflict with the law and order of polis life; he pleaded for the right understanding of such worship. His last play makes it particularly clear that he is not simply the poet of an age of enlightenment but of the mutually opposing forces which gave that age its real depth.

Tragedy had come to its end. There followed only minor poets of little significance, though in great numbers. Theatres were built in many Greek cities. The stage saw repeat performances of the three great tragedians, above all of Euripides. Tragedy, as the fifth century knew it, was kept alive, largely by the increased reputation of professional actors. As a creative art it no longer existed. Only comedy lived on, as a popular entertainment, whether of the people as a whole or a bourgeois majority; but it had changed its character and its social significance. Otherwise, the world of rational thought caused every kind of poetry to give way to philosophy and rhetoric. Plato, the great philosopher of the next generation, was at the same time a poet and a tragedian.

5 · Thucydides

There was one man who combined the new spirit of rational and exact inquiry with the methods of the sophists' dialectics and his own deep feeling for human tragedy, though he refused to give way to the mysterious or divine. That was the historian Thucydides.[51] The prevailing feature of his work is, no doubt, his ability, not to say genius, for applying logical and rational considerations throughout the field of history, past as well as contemporary. It is by now an established fact that he learned from the sophists, the medical writers, the natural scientists – actually more than he did from earlier historians such as Hecataeus, Herodotus, and Hellanicus. He continued, it is true, Herodotus' *History*, or rather *Histories*, and we have tried to show that Herodotus was more than a charming story-teller, that in fact he had discovered the secret of writing history. Even so, the difference between Thucydides and his forerunners is enormous, although he is reluctant to criticize them openly. Both he and Herodotus knew what it meant to look for historical sources, but their search for, and their use of them, differed widely. If Herodotus was the *pater historiae*, he still continued the epic tradition with all that it involved in the way of the mythical and the interest in personal motives and activities. Thucydides' scope was narrower, but he was far more impersonal, and intent on gathering impartial information; he was, in brief, far more scientific. He was the creator of political and critical history, and that on a purely human level, using the methods of scientific observation and investigation, including a deep psychological insight. At the same time he employed the means of deliberate literary art and craft; his model in that respect, if there was one at all, was tragedy rather than epic poetry.

The first impression any reader gets of Thucydides' work is of his difficult, closely knit language, a language and style without parallel in Greek literature. To understand this we must try to go deeper than mere vocabulary and syntax; it really is a matter of contents and method. For that I can refer to several recent careful investigations.[52] The primary demand on an historian's work is regard for chronology. After giving an exact date for the outbreak of the war (2, 2), Thucydides follows a strict scheme, divided into summers and winters, fitting for a story of war, since warfare was practically impossible in Greece during the winter. Thucydides probably knew of Hippias' reconstruction of the list of the victorious runners at the stadium at Olympia, but was wiser than later historians who accepted as their chronological framework a scheme which was the first attempt at a generally acceptable chronology, but with its four-year Olympiads was unwieldy and cumbersome. Thucydides' own chronology, as well as leaving room for a certain vagueness of dates, is frequently interrupted and neglected, sometimes by repeated parallels, echoes, and reminders of earlier passages, and sometimes by the disruption of the natural trend of the narrative for reasons of style and composition. Thus, details are often not mentioned until they become relevant, or they are simply left out. Since the author hardly ever makes a personal appearance, every explanation has to be read in or between the lines, and careful combination and understanding are constantly demanded. There are plenty of examples of this kind of writing, especially of isolated stories breaking the chronological order. In general, the facts speak for themselves, though Thucydides' silences can be most irritating. Some of the gaps, especially in the history of the Pentecontaetia, remain virtually unexplained. Sometimes it can be shown that the omission of an event contributes to the dramatic tension of the story, as can be seen in various parts of the work. Thucydides was indeed as far away as possible from writing a mere chronical. To say it once again, he was an historian who was both a scientist and an artist, and therefore neither the one nor the other exclusively.[53]

We know that Thucydides had accepted the main principle of the Hippocratic school of medicine that observation and experience, not philosophical theories or general hypotheses, lead to the discovery of truth. What was right for the human body might also be right for the human mind and for human actions; but it was a sort of intellectual revolution to transfer an attitude and a method, suitable for the discovery of nature, to the investigation of a contemporary political struggle. A word frequently used by the physicians, *prophasis*, to indicate the real external cause of an illness was contrasted, we may assume, with what even the observing doctor might find 'invisible' or hidden. Accordingly, Thucydides pointed to 'the truest cause' of the war (1, 23, 6), 'rationally not obvious'.[54] His primary aims were to find out what Ranke, over twenty-three centuries later, expressed in the words 'how it had really been'.[55] Thucydides had turned to the medical writers because no better teachers of rational impartiality could be found.

In his incessant search for historical truth, Thucydides did not accept the intervention of any superhuman power. When he speaks of Tyche he means mere coincidence, the inexplicable event which overcomes human prediction and planning; he never speaks or thinks of a divine force. The events of history are determined by human strength and human weakness, by the acquisition and use of political power, by the interests (real or imagined) of states and individuals. We cannot go far wrong when we describe Thucydides as a realist. But the historian of the greatest war in Greek history realised at the same time the greatness and the evils of war and its effects on humanity. In the course of his work he describes with obvious horror a number of atrocious murders and massacres, among them the important civil war at Corcyra and the completely irrelevant massacre at Mycalessus (7, 29); such crimes were committed by any one of the combatants, and they increased as the war grew older. Thucydides does not blame any special party, though his horror is plain. It seems paradoxical that he started with his work at the very moment when a war was to begin, which he knew would be of unparalleled magnitude. We may conclude, without going beyond our limited knowledge, that the young man of 431 (he was hardly more than thirty then) was aware of the awesome greatness of the event rather than of its terrible symptoms. He may not yet have realized that, though war was of man's making, it might escape human control.

There are a great number of particular subjects or episodes in which Thucydides' art is at its best. It will be sufficient to remember the terrifying picture of the factual and moral results of civil war (3, 82 f.), the story and the portraits of Pausanias and Themistocles (1, 128 ff.), the fight for Pylos and Sphacteria (4, 3 ff. 26 ff.), and above all, the tragic drama of the Sicilian expedition, which fills two books (6 and 7 to 8, 6). The last item is far more than an episode, however important; it is the dramatic peripeteia of the whole war, caused by a complex array of human endeavours and failures, and foreshadowing the end.

Some special remarks are needed about the two 'excursusses' in the first book, the *Archaeologia* (2–19) and the *Pentecontaetia* (89–117). The former is a compressed sketch of the early history of Greece, that is, of the change from a largely mythical story to historical reality. Here more than anywhere else the necessity of selecting the facts taught Thucydides the critical method; at the same time he displayed his deep insight – less obvious in most of the narration of the war – into the geographic, demographic, and economic foundations of history. About the Pentecontaetia, something has been said in an earlier passage (see p. 192). Here it will be sufficient to stress the fact that this survey of fifty crowded years, though often incoherent and too selective, is a remarkable introduction to the situation which led to the outbreak of the Peloponnesian war. Even so, it can be said that the greatness of the historian is proved less by his exploration of the past than by his writing on the events of his own time. When we mentally review the historiography of later times, ancient and modern, it may be worthwhile to ponder on that remarkable fact.

A special device of Thucydides is, of course, the speeches. They have been an obstacle to those who regard him as a pure scientist, but even for the rest it remained a problem to bring them into harmony with Thucydides' claim to tell the truth and, if not the whole truth, yet nothing but the truth. In a special chapter (1, 22) he explains his own position, and tries to defend it:

> 'As to the speeches made either before or during the war, it was difficult, for myself as far as I have listened to them, as well as for others who reported to me, to remember the exact words. I have therefore let each speaker express what in my view would be most suitable under the prevailing circumstances, myself following as closely as possible the general meaning of what actually had been said.'

In contrast, Thucydides continues, the facts of the events of the war have been described after careful and detailed examination. This distinction between the narrative and the speeches does not yet explain what his intention was in writing the speeches. One point is clear at once. Made by various persons, frequently only called 'the Athenians', 'the Corinthians', and therefore in fact anonymous, based on knowledge of very different kinds and from different sources, whether direct or hearsay, the speeches are nevertheless all uniformly in Thucydides' own language and style; the claim to have reproduced 'the general meaning' must be related to the fact that the Greeks never felt it a duty to copy a text, even a document, completely *verbatim*. The speeches generally share the same rhetorical technique; even if it existed at the supposed time of the speech, it does not prove (against the view of one outstanding Thucydides scholar) that it was used alike by different men from different states on different occasions. We can only guess at what time Thucydides wrote each of the speeches, but in composing them throughout his work,[56] he cannot be called a realist, though he was still a historian, and it cannot be maintained that he abandoned his principles. While he put ideas and even words of the original into his version, he also included matters which he almost without exception refused to include in his narrative – general descriptions of peoples and situations, the discussion of causes and motives, the psychology and pathology of power, of democracy, of imperialism, in fact everything we might call the 'history of ideas', and even more than that.

Thucydides uses either single speeches or antithetic pairs. In either case he learnt from the sophists. That is particularly clear from the antitheses, which obviously follow Protagoras' method of discussing every question from two opposite angles. For Thucydides, if not for Protagoras as well, this was a means of discovering the truth. It is significant that in the Mytilenean debate (3, 37 ff.) Cleon attacks rhetoric, while Diodotus, whose views Thucydides more or less shares, frequently uses antithetic arguments. Such opposing speeches occur on many occasions, from the speeches by the Corcyrean and Corinthian envoys (1, 32 ff.), and the debate in two pairs of speeches in the Spartan session before war was declared (1, 68 ff.), down to the pep talks by generals on either side (2, 87 ff. 7, 61 ff.), from the Mytilenaean and Plataean debates in the third book down to the oratorical *agon* of Nicias and Alcibiades (6, 9 ff.), that of Hermocrates and Athenagoras (6, 33 ff.), or of Hermocrates and Euphemus (6, 76 ff.) all during the Sicilian expedition.

It is obvious from this catalogue that antithetic speeches are a major feature in Thucydides; closer investigation of the speeches, which would be out of place in our context, will reveal their great variety and psychological subtlety. Thucydides employed a technique which we can see at work, for instance, in Antiphon's *Tetralogiai*, but the historian has immeasurably improved on the rhetor, both in thought and in language. A technique, grown from rhetorical theory and practice, could serve forensic needs as well as the illumination of history; it could equally develop into a rhetorical game and an instrument of logical dispute. It was bound finally to lead to pure dialogue, and thus beyond the aims and methods of the sophists. In Thucydides' work the climax is reached in the dialogue between 'the Athenians' and 'the Melians' (5, 85 ff.), which intrudes as an awkward piece upon the stylistic coherence. Here the reality of mutual argument has gained its most unrealistic form. While the historian was working on his book as an exile away from Athens, the dialogue between individuals, as a means of investigation, as an expression of the recognition of one man by another was practised by Socrates in the streets and houses and palaestras of Athens.

A few speeches in Thucydides have no counter-speech, foremost three made by Pericles, and intended to characterize the man and his policy – the first by which he prepared his people for the inevitable war (1, 140 ff.), the last one in which, after the outbreak of the plague, he defended his policy (2, 60 ff.), and in between the Funeral Speech (2, 35 ff.), that famous oration written by Thucydides to express his love for Athens and his admiration for her great leader. We have spoken of it before (p. 270), also of another single speech, that of Alcibiades in Sparta; there are a few others, like that of Hermocrates at the Pansicilian congress in 424 (4, 59 ff.). They were all written in order to underline the nature of the speakers, all of them important men, and the significance of the moment. We now understand how the speeches, whether single or in pairs, fulfilled a serious and fundamental task in Thucydides' work. The man who was the first to write political and military history from a purely human point of view, and endeavoured to attain the ideal of almost perfect objectivity, was able to show his own deeper insight into human affairs without seriously impeding the order of events or the unity of his work.

There are many more questions about Thucydides, but they cannot be answered here, even if the present author felt more competent. We must, however, ask one essential question. What, apart from writing the history of the war, was in Thucydides' mind? We have mentioned the scientist and the artist, and that must be enough to characterize his way of working. We still ask what, if anything, in Thucydides' intentions went beyond the immediate and limited purpose? Descended from an aristocratic family, he had, as far as we know, kept out of politics, even before his exile, but he naturally held political views. He praised Pericles and hated Cleon; that is to say, he knew about the limits and dangers of democracy. On the other hand, he was not an oligarch, though he went out of his way to praise the moderate constitution of Theramenes, which lasted only for a few months. This looks rather like a theoretical approach to constitutional questions, in favour of a moderate middle-line. In general, he had the attitude of his times in thinking of man as the centre of events, and man was to him the 'political animal'.

He did not believe in human progress, except for the emergence of early man from primitive conditions, but he did believe that man could learn from history. That is what he tells us in the famous programmatic chapter (1, 22). His book, he knew, was not suitable to be read aloud before a large audience, as Herodotus' work had been, 'but if those who really wish to know past and also future events which, according to human nature, will happen in the same or a similar way, regard my work as useful, then I shall be satisfied. I have written it as a possession for ever rather than an object of competition, which is heard and forgotten.'

The 'programme of Thucydides' has been discussed again and again, and it must be admitted that no one single interpretation has victoriously emerged.[57] Thucydides' claim to have written a work useful for future generations has clearly been justified, up to the present day, by those generations themselves. That claim, however, did not imply the idea of pragmatic history, written with the intention of presenting examples for future actions, still less the concept that there are laws of history, repeating themselves and thus valid for all times. Thucydides was a realist, not a determinist. He has, by the force of his great intellect, revealed human behaviour on all levels of political, military, and social experience. He knows that in general men will always behave according to their nature, and the usefulness he is hoping for is the information of those, in particular politicians and statesmen, who have read and understood the implications of his story, and may learn to avoid the worst.

In that respect we may call him an optimist. But as far as his experience of men and their actions goes, he is as much a pessimist as Euripides. His view of man and of history, just like much of the composition of his book, has more than a touch of tragedy. He may have believed in Pericles, and he tries to show that defeat was not inevitable, if Pericles' successors had adhered to his policy; but that is a rational and objective verdict. If he strongly admires Pericles, that emotion cannot be understood without his feelings about the decline and the disaster that followed. To believe in one man who, after all, could not prevent the radicalization of democracy, and whose work fell to pieces after his death, would make a man a pessimist rather than an optimist.[58] Thucydides had accepted the concept of 'human nature' (*physis*) from medical literature, but his impartial aloofness was impaired by his pessimist view of man's nature. If he knew that sometimes the right man at the right moment could prevent disaster, he knew of no way to avoid it for ever.

6 · Socrates

We come, at last, to Socrates, the greatest, and the least known, among the great men of that unique period. Least known he is because he left no written word, and those who did write about him were not historically minded, and all except one wrote after an interval of several years. It was their hostility or loyalty to Socrates which prevented them from describing the real man, quite apart from the fact that they wanted to express views of their own. Thus, we have several portraits in each of which a different Socrates appears; the original was to be ridiculed, defended, attacked, idealized.[59] It is necessary to say a few words about those sources of ours. The only contemporary one is Aristophanes' *Clouds*, first produced in spring 423, but unsuccessfully and therefore revised later, perhaps much later, and not performed again; this second version is the one we have. The two writers whose works are most important for our knowledge, or non-knowledge, of Socrates are Plato, who belonged to the inner circle of his pupils, and Xenophon, who did not, despite his statements to the contrary. Finally there is Aristotle, who was born after Socrates' death, but could learn something from his teacher Plato and the Academy. None of the four writers created the real Socrates, but there are considerable differences in the historical value of the four portraits.

The Socrates of the *Clouds* displays a few features which will fit the historical person, such as, for instance, his (exaggerated) poverty, which distinguished him from the sophists. Nevertheless, he is depicted as the foremost of the sophists, reflecting the type rather than individual men, the combination of a poor wretch and starveling, a star-gazer, and an amoral rhetorician. It is a type, or a combination of types, the people had in their minds when they thought of the sophists. The comedian is, in fact, not concerned with Socrates as a person, and he leaves out numerous real traits which might have been good material for caricature. To Aristophanes, what mattered was his own fight against the new education, such as it is depicted in the antithetic speeches of the Just and the Unjust Logos. He regarded the sophists as corrupters of the noble youth – a charge very likely raised against Socrates by some people as early as the time of the *Clouds*. Rightly or wrongly, as is usual with generalizations, the sophists were regarded as propagating the means of distorting the truth by 'making the weaker case the stronger one', and that for the sake of personal interests and individual self-assertion. The fact that Aristophanes picked on Socrates as the protagonist is easily explained, since he, and probably he alone, was known among ordinary people through his questioning in public anybody who interested him for one reason or another. Actually the Socrates of the *Clouds* is a comparatively harmless figure, though his irreligious and immoral materialism is a symptom of the time, and to Plato the attacks by comedy were the main source of the charge at Socrates' trial (*apol.* 19b). However false Aristophanes' picture of Socrates was, it did reflect trends in public opinion that came forth when he stood in court.[60]

It is likely that 'Socratic' literature did not start before his death. A few years later, however, a real storm of writing about Socrates broke loose. Apart from Plato and Xenophon, we have only fragments and allusions. Most important, perhaps, was the literary success of an attack by a 'sophist' Polycrates, a radical Athenian democrat. He wrote (probably not before 394) a fictional speech of accusation (*kategoria*), put into the mouth of the chief prosecutor in 399, Anytus. It is likely that Polycrates was provoked by some writing in defence of Socrates; he, on the other hand, caused a flood of further defence, such as Plato's *Apology* and Xenophon's Socratic writings, especially the first two books of his *Memorabilia*; the 'accuser' who appears in Xenophon was most likely Polycrates. Plato and Xenophon, like others, e.g. Antisthenes and Aeschines of Sphettus, wrote 'Socratic' dialogues, not only apologies, and each of them described the Socrates of his own insight and his own dreams. It is by the means of such different portraits that a large number of anecdotes reached later writers, some of which have the ring of truth. We have too little evidence on which to work, but even if we had more, it would not be possible to separate the historical substance from what is fiction or at least deliberate construction.[61]

Plato, of course, is our most important witness. Since the chronology of his dialogues has been roughly established, and at the same time reveals the change from a more 'independent' Socrates to one of clearly Platonic nature, there is a real chance that the earliest group of dialogues contains a good deal of historical truth. Even Plato, however, started writing several years after Socrates' death, though he may have made notes while he belonged to the inner circle round Socrates; he himself was then in his thirties. The question of what exactly is historically true in the Socrates of Plato's early writings cannot finally be answered; we shall never know for certain where Socrates ends and Plato begins. Even so, however, before Plato developed his own philosophy, the love for his teacher and his own genius are fairly safe guarantees that, despite the interval of years, the essential Socrates is reflected in those dialogues which, at any rate, display method rather than results. What is true of dialogues such as *Laches*, *Charmides*, *Euthyphron*, and *Lysis*, perhaps also *Protagoras*, may, or may not, be true of the two works on Socrates' trial and death, *Apology* and *Crito*. The view that we learn most about Socrates from these writings is accepted by many scholars, though by no means by all. No doubt Plato created the most beautiful portrait of Socrates; through him, and as the man he described, Socrates became immortal. But if, as in fact happens, dialogues such as *Phaedrus* and *Symposium*, or even *Phaedo*, are also taken as historical sources, Socrates will have anticipated the ideas of Plato himself. It has often been said that Plato's genius went deeper than others, as it certainly did, and that therefore he provided a truth more profound than reality. That is dangerous ground for the historian. He is bound to remain sceptical; he must try, as best as he can, to separate history from the infiltration by another, even the greatest, mind.

It is different with Xenophon who was not a great mind. His Socrates is a reasonable, commonplace bourgeois, a virtuous philistine whose mind reflects the intellectual level and the interests of Xenophon himself. Apart from a few details, we learn from Xenophon's Socratic books little, if anything, about the man who changed the direction of human thought and history. We may learn something of the unimportant, practical ways of his life and character, and more perhaps of the thoughts and interests of the average

Athenian. Xenophon had known Socrates personally, though rather superficially, and his so-called *Memoirs* are no memoirs at all. We may believe that Socrates impressed him strongly, and he may have remembered a few occasions when he actually heard him; but on the whole his *Socratica* are largely based on other people's books, and he probably worked by excerpting them and shaping them 'in his own image'. In more than one sense his evidence is second-hand, though it speaks for him that he had no philosophy of his own to impose on his Socrates, as most of the other Socratics did. He probably reports some ideas as correctly as he was able to understand them, but his overall picture more or less omits the thinker Socrates.

Aristotle mentions Socrates in a few passages which, in view of their author and his lack of bias, cannot be neglected; but he is chiefly interested in contrasting Socrates with Plato and his theory of ideas. Nobody, I think, any longer believes that Socrates had a real share in that theory. Still, Plato's early dialogues point to a Socrates who tried to find definitions of abstract concepts, and that is what Aristotle confirms.[62] In a way Socrates inaugurated the philosophy of language. However, to build our own picture on a logical theory towards which little more than the first steps have been taken, or, on the other hand, on Aristotle's short and abstract remarks, would be perverse. There is more historical evidence hidden in Plato and Xenophon, though we can extract very little. In view of the nature and variety of our sources, it can easily be understood that any picture that may emerge is bound to remain hypothetical. There is no want of variety among modern portraits; in fact, it can be said that, at least since the eighteenth century, every generation has produced its own picture of Socrates.

The present writer is not in the position to make a final decision one way or another, or even only a final attempt at clearing the jungle. One particular trend, however, ought, I think, to be excluded. The attempt has recently been made to trace a philosophical development from the early to the later Socrates. This is in itself a legitimate task, but it involves the Socrates of the *Clouds* being seriously regarded as a step in this development. In his early career he would than have either started as a physical scientist under the influence of Anaxagoras or followed the teaching of some of the sophists.[63] Theoretically, something like that could have happened, and naturally Socrates' mind will have undergone changes, though I doubt that he ever went through a real 'conversion'. At any rate, with the evidence we have, the stages of a spiritual history of Socrates simply cannot be reconstructed; Aristophanes' comic figure anyway reveals too little of the real man. Other sources for the early Socrates are even less safe. If it has been asserted that Plato, who never knew the early Socrates, wrote pure fiction in his *Apology*, it ought to be impossible to accept at the same time as historical, for instance, the story of Socrates' conversion in *Phaedo* (96a), a dialogue of much later date.[64]

We shall now point to the few facts practically incontestable, and then proceed a few steps on less safe ground. Socrates, son of Sophroniscus, of the deme Alopeke, was born round 470 B.C. He was brought up in his father's profession as a stone-mason; his mother was a midwife. He thus belonged to the class of small artisans, and therefore to that majority of the Athenian people, who were neither rich nor starving. He married, rather late in life, Xanthippe, probably a woman of good family, as her name indicates, who will have brought some money with her dowry. Her reputation as a shrew and a terror is probably undeserved; Socrates cannot have been an easy husband to live with, and neither side will have been able to lead a married life of tender fondness, anyway rare among the Greeks, although we have seen signs of it in contemporary art. There were three sons, still small in 399.[65] Socrates was a townsman (cf. Plato, *Apol.* 30a) who left Athens only when he served in several campaigns as a hoplite. In 406 he held office as a prytan; in fact, he was chairman on the day of the trial of the generals who had been in command at the Arginusae, and he was the only one to protest against their condemnation.[66] He clashed with the Thirty when he refused to assist in the arrest of an innocent rich metic. On both occasions he showed remarkable courage and independence. In general, however, he kept away from public affairs. He will have learnt from Anaxagoras, whether through Archelaus or not (see p. 336); but his interest will have tended towards the ruling 'mind' (*nous*) of Anaxagoras' philosophy rather than his natural science. The Socrates whom we know was no longer young. He was all the time busy questioning all sorts of people, and conversing with them.

We can be sure that his satyr-like appearance and his unusual activity (or lack of it) made him a well-known figure, whether he was loved or hated or ridiculed. His main friends – for so he called the young men who wished to learn from him – were among the aristocratic youth, that is to say, those most likely to become members of the governing class. In his person, Socrates bridged the gulf between the classes as well as that between the generations. In spite of the *Clouds*, Socrates cannot have been without means, though his property dwindled away during the many years when he earned nothing. The picture of the poverty-stricken man was largely caused by his habit of walking through the streets without a warm coat and barefoot, a shocking sight by bourgeois standards. In the end he was accused by three men of whom only one, Anytus, was of any importance; he belonged to the moderate democrats who had gained influence after the fall of the Thirty.[67] Socrates was charged with introducing new gods and corrupting the young. He was condemned to death and, serene and sublime to the last moment, he drank the cup of hemlock. The Socrates of those last days, when execution was delayed for external religious reasons, is described in Plato's *Crito* and *Phaedo*; he is a figure of such greatness and humanity that no purely historical approach, unsupported by any other evidence, could improve on that picture.

These are the few historical facts about Socrates' life. Many details, even of his trial, are open to doubt. Plato's *Apology* is one of many that existed. It survived because of Plato, but it was probably also the deepest and most beautiful of all the versions of Socrates' speech of defence. Though it has become the version firmly fixed in our minds, it has no monopoly. We should like to regard as historical Socrates' provocative demand for public honours, which increased the votes for his condemnation; but we cannot be sure, and some modern scholars even deny that he made a defence speech at all. The facts taken as historical do not tell us much about his spiritual life; that is largely hidden behind the screen of the writings of the Socratics. The screen itself, however, is a fact of the greatest importance. It shows that this man of modest origin and ugly appearance, who left not a single written word, caused a tremendous stir in Greek intellectual life. The name of 'the Socratics' covers a number of disciples and their philosophical schools, all different from and often hostile to each other. It is a unique example of the effects of one man's life and death; it has often been compared with the story of the Gospels. No description of Socrates can be regarded as serious which does not take into full account the widespread consequences of his activities.

In a frequently quoted passage Cicero (*Tusc.* 5, 4, 10) says, 'Socrates was the first to bring philosophy down from heaven; he took it to men's cities, and introduced it to their homes; he forced it to inquire about life and morals, about good and evil.' Cicero naturally drew from Socratic literature, and we find a similar statement in Aristotle (*Metaph.* 978b, 1) that Socrates 'disregarded the physical universe and confined his study to moral questions'.[68] He was not the first to do that, as we have seen in dealing with the sophists, but in his case it meant at the same time that he no longer looked for the beginnings – of nature, of man – but for the end, the meaning of man's life. Contrary to most of the sophists, he despised polymathy and aimed at true wisdom. The old contrast, felt so intensely by Heraclitus (*DK* 12 B 40 f.), was revived in a new form. In order to understand Socrates, our own starting point is perhaps best to be found in the charges brought against him at his trial. They are reported in almost identical terms by Plato (*Apol.* 24b) and Xenophon (*Mem.* 1, 1), and probably preserved as an original transcript in Diogenes Laertius (2, 40); their explanations differ widely, but these are historically irrelevant. As we briefly mentioned before, there were two indictments, one that he corrupts the youth, the other that he does not believe in the gods of the polis, but has introduced new divine powers (*daimonia*).

To take the second, probably the more difficult one, first, it must be remembered that there had been numerous trials for irreligion (*asebeia*) at Athens, such as for denying the gods; but it was not a crime – on the contrary, a frequent event of which people might be proud – to introduce new, i.e. foreign, gods. The first part of that accusation could therefore be well explained; with the second it is much harder. The picture of Socrates in Aristophanes, who had ridiculed him as a sophist and a natural philosopher, praying to the aether and the clouds, was a popular concept, and could easily be the basis of the charge of denying the gods. To the man in the street, a real knowledge of what Socrates was and taught was practically unattainable. Moreover, in wartime the people's religious feelings were far more intense and more easily roused; that was made clear by the hysterical attitude pervading the city after the mutilation of the hermae. There was a revival of superstition and magic, of ecstasy and mystery, of prophecies and oracles. It is quite possible that this atmosphere had contributed to the hostility against a man who was friendly with aristocrats who were involved in the scandal, and on the other hand, with scientists and sophists; his real thoughts remained obscure and enigmatic to the ordinary people, and perhaps even to some of his friends.

But Socrates was not an atheist. What about the new gods? We believe – till the contrary has been proven – that the accusers in 399 primarily acted from a genuine fear, and that they probably shared many of the popular feelings. In Plato's *Euthyphron* (3b) Socrates says that Meletus (the acting prosecutor) called him a 'maker of gods' who invents new gods. In all our tradition there is only one 'god' who could be called Socrates' own creation, and that is the inner voice to which he refers as his *daimonion*, a divine force warning and directing him throughout his life, ever since he was a child. He mentions it fairly often in our sources.[69] It is hardly mere chance that the same word, unusual in this sense, and not the word 'gods', is also used in the official charge. This divine voice was more than moral conscience; it was an irrational force of intellectual as well as moral nature. To a simple, and certainly to a hostile, mind the divine power of which Socrates spoke both with reverence and with self-confidence will have looked like a form of secret revelation outside the realm of traditional religion.

In this context we must ask about Socrates' relations with Delphi. He never claimed – how could he? – to be Apollo's mouthpiece. In Plato's *Apology* (33c) he says that he acted under the command 'of the god', and mentions all sorts of ways in which he received such commands. In other passages the god is Apollo; it can therefore hardly be the *daimonion* which this time gives the command. Perhaps the god is Apollo, and at the same time an expression of Socrates' belief that he is acting in a divine mission. Plato (*Apol.* 20e) also tells the story of Chaerophon, Socrates' friend, who went to Delphi, to ask the god whether anybody was wiser than Socrates, and the Pythia replied: nobody. This is no command, and Socrates only concludes: what the god meant was that he, Socrates, knew that he knew not. If the story is genuine Socrates must have drawn further conclusions about the way to find knowledge. Thus, by a detour, the oracle became a command indeed. It seems safe to say that Socrates thought of the Delphic god with a reverence that did not prevent him from combining it with that irony simulating his own ignorance. Another connexion with Delphi is mentioned by Xenophon (*Mem.* 4, 2, 24) when Socrates refers to the inscription 'Know Thyself'. We can, indeed we must, see Socrates as a decisive force within that tradition which we are trying to describe in the present chapter.

The charge of irreligion seems, after all, rather far-fetched. The accusation that Socrates had corrupted the youth is a different matter. Everybody knew that he had his endless talks, above all, with young men of promise, largely of the upper class. Many of them might turn out to be harmless citizens, though their fathers will have resented some of the things they claimed to have learnt; Pheidippides in the *Clouds* is an example, if a caricature. Above all, however, there were among the disciples men like Alcibiades and Critias who had proved to be enemies of democracy. Moreover, the charge might contain more than was said. Socrates' essentially apolitical attitude, with his occasional criticisms of the sortition of officials,[70] or of radical democracy in general, as in the case of 406 when he opposed the masses clamouring for the death of the generals – all that might be sufficient to confirm the mistrust of the politicians and the fears of the people. Not to be concerned with politics was usually interpreted as hostility against the state. It is significant that Socrates twice clashed with the authorities, first with the Thirty, and finally with democracy.

The question arises whether, as has been said, the religious indictment was only a smoke screen for the political charge, that is to say, that Socrates fell as an opponent of democracy.[71] Because of the amnesty law of 403, a purely political charge was impossible. Anytus, as far as we know, was a moderate man and not a religious fanatic. We must assume that he only wanted to get rid of a man who was a 'gadfly' for the present state, and whose disciples might again turn against it. He wanted to silence the voice of Socrates, and he expected him to go into voluntary exile, as others had done before, for example Anaxagoras. He is supposed to have said (Plato, *Apol.* 29c) 'that either Socrates should not have come into court or, since he was here, it was impossible not to execute him'. If Socrates was accused, and by Anytus, the version that he should not have appeared in court at all can only mean that he should have gone into exile. We know how completely mistaken Anytus was. If Socrates kept silent he was no longer Socrates. Moreover, he was one with Athens, all his friends were Athenians, and his loyalty to the laws of the state is stressed again and again. No individual has the right to weaken their authority; Socrates would never flee from their verdict. The great individualist was far removed from the type of individualist hostile to the state.

Yet it is possible to find some justification for democracy condemning Socrates. His greatness, his unconcern, and the force of his ideas, his way of life, on the other hand, and the part played by his disciples, made a clash with the existing authorities almost inevitable. That was also Hegel's view. Even then, however, we ask whether this is the full story. If political fear and hostility were the only, or at least the chief, cause of Socrates' condemnation, it would have been simply a crime just like the many executions by the Thirty. We have mentioned the background of religion and superstition. It is the traditional union of politics and religion in the polis, and in addition the contrast of the generations, that led to the final tragedy. No doubt Socrates was a seducer, and the whole trend of his influence on the younger generation is revealed not only in Plato's dialogues but also in the fact that all Socratic schools, the Academy no less than the Cynics and Cyrenaics, and even Xenophon, stood outside or even against the polis tradition, whether that led to an Utopian state, or to radical individualism of one sort or another, or even to turning against Athens. The democratic polis, supported by the beliefs of the people, condemned the man who seemed to teach the freedom of the individual. Just as the doctrine of the 'Right of the Stronger' has grown in Attic soil, and suited the extremist politicians at Athens, so its complete opposite, the moralist's view of the individual's obligations within the state, had come to life in Socrates. It is the tragic paradox that democracy confused the two concepts.

Socrates has been called 'the greatest teacher in European history'.[72] What did he teach? In fact, did he teach at all in the usual sense of the word? Education is more than teaching, and Socrates' chief aim was not to impart information but to make the other man think, and thus to make him a better person. Socrates did not believe, as the sophists had done, that anybody could 'teach virtue', but he could search for the way leading towards that end, for himself as well as for others. He says that, acting according to divine will, he had 'to philosophize' (Plato, *Apol.* 28e), which does not mean 'to be a philosopher'. All the early Platonic dialogues show that by his questioning he does not try to get final results, and thus in the end a systematic philosophy of his own. He looks for definitions of ethical concepts, in order to clear his own and the pupil's minds. He founded no school, he left no philosophical system. Not the weakest weapon in his armoury was his irony, largely exercised against himself. He practised 'midwifery', his mother's profession, in bringing men's hidden thoughts to life. We may perhaps say that he was himself the living urge for philosophy.

All the Socratics learned from Socrates to write dialogues. He who never wrote lived them. This was something new, although we have noticed preparatory steps made by the sophists and Thucydides. Perhaps the influence of tragedy, with its *stichomythia*, also contributed. Dialectics, the art of the dialogue, became the instrument of men's way of thinking, until Aristotle replaced it by the philosophical treatise. Socrates discussed the highest aims of moral education without ever lecturing. He investigated ethical concepts, but he did not teach them. He never felt like a teacher, his 'pupils' were his 'friends', and 'virtue' emerged, if at all, from the dialogue between two persons; it could not be directly transferred from one to another. The pupils were the opponents in their conversations, though they played very much the weaker part. One thing held both sides together, and that was Socrates' *eros*. It may at first have been an ironical suggestion of the Athenian pre-occupation with homosexual love, but in fact it was the mutual relationship in the common search for truth.

The highest aim of man is the supreme good which the Greeks called *aretē*, the word which is usually translated by 'virtue', but better by 'perfection'. Socrates, heir to an essentially rational tradition, wanted to reach the goal by deeper knowledge. Not *aretē*, as the sophists thought, but the way that might lead to it could be taught. This is regarded also as the only way towards true happiness, which alone mattered. On a high level Socrates was an eudaemonist. He did not aim at a theory of knowledge, but based man's perfection on his knowledge of himself as well as of good and evil. Nobody does wrong willingly and knowingly. It was Socrates' task not to teach perfection but to investigate man's concepts of perfection, and that included practical advice to people how to live their lives in the right way. This remained essential, although the *aretē* he proclaimed was, in fact, unobtainable but for the few. Thus, it became true that 'perfection is knowledge', the knowledge of one's self.[73]

Socrates' aims were clearly and exclusively ethical, and whether deliberately or not, he initiated the distinction between ethics and politics. By exhortation as well as examination, by encouraging his opponents to think for themselves, he opened the only door to true values – knowledge from insight instead of information from others. Like the sophists he could identify the 'good' with the 'useful', but he raised the issue far beyond the individual and utilitarian level. Justice as the useful knowledge of good and evil was to Socrates 'nature' in need of human wisdom. He solved, I believe, the problem of *physis* and *nomos*. He established his ethical standards, independent of religious tradition and of the rules of society. If Socrates said that the only thing he knew was that he knew nothing, his natural scepticism prevented him from overestimating the intellect, however firmly he believed in its power. He did not want to appear, nor indeed to be, wiser than others. He did not teach philosophy (to say it once more), but he showed by his life and his conversations what it meant to philosophize, that is, to think freely and unreservedly. Thus, the freedom of the individual became a question of morality; the ethical autonomy of man was established.

It was essential to find one's own way to one's soul. That meant that body and soul were clearly to be distinguished. The concept of *psyche* had gone through many changes which cannot be discussed here, but Socrates was the first to speak of it as being in command of the body. It was the intellectual and emotional force, and therefore lastly true wisdom. To learn to know that was Socrates' final aim.[74] That could be done by discussion, but also by quiet contemplation.

This is the advice, rather surprisingly given in the *Clouds*, by the chorus (700) and by Socrates himself (740); there is also the famous story of how Socrates stood for hours on the same spot, without noticing anything outside himself. The man whose restless questioning of people made him notorious was at the same time the man who led a life of inactivity and was the first to preach the beauty of contemplation. He had realized the distinction between mere opinion and real knowledge in a far more personal sense than Parmenides. In the field of rational thought he was the true anti-sophist. More thoroughly than anybody else before him, and more single-minded, he lived the wisdom of the Delphic advice 'Know Thyself'.

We reach the conclusion that Socrates was not a teacher nor a philosopher in the ordinary sense of the words. He was neither a poet and theoretical thinker like Plato, nor a man of practical life like Xenophon. He was unique, yet a product of his age, an intellectual and a saint, above all a humanist before all humanism. His only true interest was man. He was at the same time the clearest intellect and the most passionate explorer, 'a physician of man's soul'. Socrates overcame the relativism of the sophists, which endangered the unity of a civilization gradually losing its centre, the unity of the polis. The sophists had paved the way towards the knowledge of man, but it was Socrates who finally broke through the wall of tradition, prejudice, and superficiality. He tried, perhaps in vain, to find the powers of unity in man's soul. His acceptance of death followed from an ultimate desire for self-fulfilment. With Socrates the centuries of the polis ended, and the centuries of individual man began. Whether for mankind that was to the good or to the bad, his historical position is the final proof of his greatness.

CONCLUSION

There is no need to say more, except perhaps to explain why I have limited this book to the time down to 400 B.C. If 'classical' were a historical concept – which it is not – its era would end then. The Greece of the fourth century is different from that of the fifth. I have described it before[1] – as a period of transition, which means that it continued to some extent the past and to some extent prepared for the future. It did so in a more express way than most other historical periods, all of them by necessity 'transitional'. What the fourth century was in itself and of its own is indicated by names such as Plato and Aristotle, Isocrates and Demosthenes, Praxiteles and Lysippus, though there is more to it than that. Socrates' legacy spread, and so did that of the sophists in the flowering of rhetoric. Political theory was the one creative trend that sprang from the polis, which itself continued with occasional ups and downs – along its path of self-destruction. Witnesses are the apolitical bourgeoisie, enjoying the great art and mild excitement of New Comedy, a continued growth of individualism, a widening social gap between rich and poor, the final failure of hegemonic leadership among Greek states, and the general longing for inter-hellenic peace. On the positive side the decline of the polis showed remarkable retardments and even great moments while, on the other hand, it led to the creation of larger political units in the shape of confederations, federal states, and territorial monarchies. More-over, the idea of the unity of mankind and the brotherhood of men grew in the minds of the educated. All this prepared the way for Alexander and the Hellenistic age.

NOTES

1. (p. 3) The account of early Greek history as given in the text is by necessity so brief that any discussion of detailed questions and of the vast literature would be out of place. The sources are mainly archaeological, to some extent also linguistic; mythology comes in, but it is not a safe source. The decipherment of the script used in Mycenaean times for Greek texts, known as Linear B, is an important addition to our source material, though it has proved less rewarding historically than one might have hoped, and a good deal is still uncertain. Cf. J. Chadwick, *The Decipherment of Linear B* (Cambridge 1962²). There are several excellent books on Minoan and Mycenaean art. For the traditions connecting the Minoan and Mycenaean civilizations with the later Greeks cf. M. P. Nilsson, *The Minoan–Mycenaean Religion and its Survival in Greek Religion* (Lund 1950²); for the period of the declining Mycenaean Age and its aftermath cf. the outstanding book by V. R. d'A. Desborough, *The Last Mycenaeans and their Successors* (Oxford 1964); for the connexions with the Near East cf. T. J. Dunbabin, *The Greeks and their Eastern Neighbours* (London 1957), and A. Severyns, *Grèce et le Proche-Orient avant Homère* (Brussels 1960). A reconstruction of the various invasions is attempted by R. J. Buck, *Historia* 1969, 276.

1a. (p. 3) Cf. D. L. Page, *The Santorini Volcan and the Destruction of Minoan Crete* (Soc. of Hell. Studies 1971).

2. (p. 4) Thus, e.g., G. L. Huxley, *Achaeans and Hittites* (Oxford 1960), and Desborough, loc. cit., 217. That view is particularly contradicted by the arguments for regarding Aḥḥijava as situated on the Asian mainland or even on one of the Asiatic islands, e.g. Rhodes. In general, cf. C. G. Thomas, *JHS* 1970, 184, with whom I largely agree. On the Hittites see *Neuere Hethiterforschung* (ed. G. Walser). *Historia*, Einzelschrift 7 (1964).

3. (p. 4) Cf. the short, illuminating, if naturally hypothetical, discussion by F. H. Stubbings, *CAH²*, vol. 2, ch. 27, also the debate by M. I. Finley and others in *JHS* 1964, 1, and above all, C. V. Blegen and others, *Troy* (Princeton 1950–8), also Blegen, *CAH²*, vols. 1 and 2. On the catalogue of ships, see recently R. Hope Simpson and J. F. Lazenby, *The Catalogue of Ships in Homer's Iliad* (Oxford 1970).

3a. (p. 5) On Linear B and its historical importance cf. V. Ehrenberg, *HZ* 180 (1955), 1 (= *Belfagor* 1956, 148) and, above all, S. Dow and J. Chadwick, *CAH²*, vol. 2, ch. 13.

4. (p. 6) On this much discussed subject cf., e.g., E. Akurgal, *AJA* 1962, 369; J. M. Cook, *The Greeks in Ionia and the East* (London 1962). It is, however, only partially true that Greek civilization was born on the periphery of the Greek world. The high standards of colonial civilization were accompanied, or even preceded, by remarkable achievements in the motherland and the Aegean islands. The Ionian migration is dealt with in a wider context by G. L. Huxley, *The Early Ionians* (London 1966).

5. (p. 6) Cf. V. Ehrenberg, 'The Greek Country and the Greek State', *Aspects of the Ancient World* (Oxford 1946), ch. 3.

5a. (p. 7) Cf. F. Gschnitzer, *Chiron* I 1971, 1.

6. (p. 8) Cf. below, ch. III, on Athens, where the development of the tribal order is best known to us.

6a. (p. 8) F. Gschnitzer, *Festschrift f. L. C. Franz* (Innsbruck 1965), 99.

7. (p. 8) For any further general reading it will be best to look into one of the many histories of Greece. It will always be worth while to consult the *History of Greece* by George Grote (many editions). Not a history, but a spirited and provocative account of the essence of Greek life and culture is H. D. F. Kitto, *The Greeks* (Harmondsworth 1951); a sounder and yet very stimulating picture is given by M. I. Finley, *The Ancient Greeks* (London 1963) and more recently by A. Andrewes, *The Greeks* (London 1967). Otherwise, J. B. Bury's short *History of Greece* (revised by R. Meiggs, London 1951³) and N. G. L. Hammond's *History of Greece* (Oxford 1967²) should be useful (together with the latter's *Studies in Greek History* (Oxford 1972)). Of non-English histories I mention (after the great works by Ed. Meyer and K. J. Beloch): H. Bengtson, *Griechische Geschichte* (Munich 1969⁴) (ample recording of modern literature); G. Glotz, *Histoire grecque*, vols. 1 and 2 (Paris 1925–31); G. De Sanctis, *Storia dei Greci*, 1. 2 (Florence 1961⁶, with bibliographies by A. Momigliano). For maps see *Grosser Historischer Weltatlas* (Munich 1953), Part 1, with full index, and M. Grant, *Ancient History Atlas 1700 B.C. to A.D. 565* (London 1971); for some maps and excellent photos see *Atlas of the Classical World* (ed. by Van der Heyden and Scullard) (London 1959).

8. (p. 10) Books on Homer and the Homeric question are legion, and views differ widely. There is not one book which could be singled out

as a safe guide, but many recent books convey interesting aspects and a knowledge of the difficult problems. A penetrating brief survey of Homer 'as history' is given by G. S. Kirk in *CAH²*, vol. 2. On the catalogue of ships, see above, note 3. The American school of Homeric scholars, initiated by Milman Parry, is firm in believing that Homer did not write; cf., now M. Parry, *The Making of Homeric Verse* (ed. A. Parry) (Oxford 1971). It is not my task to discuss an attitude which other scholars find unacceptable, in spite of the strong points made by Parry, Lord, and their disciples. Some reasonable strictures on their methods: J. B. Hainsworth, *Greece and Rome. New Surveys*, Oxford 1969; *JHS* 1970, 90. A. Lesky, 'Homeros', in *RE* Suppl. XI and his *History of Greek Literature* (London 1966), 18, also F. Dirlmeier, *SB Heidelbg. Akad.* 1971.

9. (p. 11) Cf. J. M. Cook and R. V. Nichols, *BSA* 1958–9. F. H. Stubbings, *CAH²*, vol. 2, ch. 27.

9a. (p. 12) Cf. my *Rechlsidee im frühen Griechentum* (Leipzig 1921, repr. Darmstadt 1966), esp. 67 ff.

10. (p. 13) I am not convinced by J. -P. Vernant's ingenious theory (*Myth et pensée chez les Grecs* (Paris 1965), 20) which co-ordinates the Heroic Age with the Bronze Age, and makes the Iron Age the odd one.

11. (p. 13) For the transitional period (eleventh to eighth century) see especially Desborough (above note 1), also V. Ehrenberg, *Society and Civilization in Greece and Rome* (Cambridge, Mass. 1964), ch. 1, and the literature mentioned there. Recently: G. Maddoli, Δαμος e Βασιληες (Studi Micenei ed Egeo-Anatolici xii, Rome 1970).

12. (p. 13) The latter is only partly true; cf. C. J. Classen, *Historia* 1965, 385.

13. (p. 14) For the Ionian League cf. J. A. O. Larsen, *Representative Government in Greece and Rome* (Berkeley 1955). He thinks of a federal state, which at such an early date is unlikely.

14. (p. 14) For the whole question of Greek expansion cf. J. Boardman, *The Greeks Overseas* (Penguin 1964), covering the vast archaeological evidence.

15. (p. 15) Cf. J. Seibert, *Metropolis und Apoikie* (Diss. Würzburg 1963), and above all, A. J. Graham, *Colony and Mother City in Ancient Greece* (Manchester 1964), also *JHS* 1971, 35ff.

16. (p. 15) For the polis in general cf. V. Ehrenberg, *The Greek State* (London, 1969²).

17. (p. 17) Cf. L. Woolley, *JHS* 1938; Boardman, 62.

18. (p. 17) Cf. T. J. Dunbabin, *The Western Greeks* (Oxford 1948); A. G. Woodhead, *The Greeks in the West* (London 1962).

19. (p. 18) Cf. Boardman, 203: 'In the West, the Greeks had nothing to learn, much to teach'.

20. (p. 18) Cf. F. Chamoux, *Cyrène sous la monarchie des Battiades* (Paris 1953). Important for the whole era down to Solon is the survey by E. Will in *Deuxième conférence internat. d'hist. économique* I (Paris 1965), 41.

20a. (p. 19) Cf. Graham (note 15), ch. IV; his discussion includes the Brea decree (see below, p. 454, note 119).

21. (p. 19) Cf. Huxley (see note 4), 67. Archaeologists now stress the poor character of Ionian material civilization before *c.* 650 (though they cannot deny the evidence of epic poetry).

22. (p. 20) Cf. J. Huizinga, *Homo Ludens*. Paperback, Boston 1955.

23. (p. 23) The attempts at turning the main lawgivers of the seventh century into gods or heroes belong to the past; cf. the good refutation by F. E. Adcock, *CHJ* 2 (1927), 95.

24. (p. 23) On the tyrants cf. the brief but comprehensive survey by A. Andrewes, *The Greek Tyrants* (London 1956). Cf. also W. G. Forrest, *The Emergence of Greek Democracy* (London 1966), and especially H. Berve, *Die Tyrannis bei den Griechen* (München 1967) (see my review *Gnomon* 1969, 48).

25. (p. 24) On his date see ch. II, note 30.

26. (p. 24) Cf. A. J. Graham (see note 15), 118, who, against misleading statements, puts the relationship between Corinth and her colonies on a reasonable basis.

27. (p. 25) Cf. M. A. Levi, *Political Power in the Ancient World* (London 1965), 68.

28. (p. 25) A bundle of spits has been found in the Heraeum of Argos, where Pheidon is supposed to have dedicated it; cf. C. T. Seltman, *Athens, its History and its Coinage* (Cambridge 1925), 117. There have been such dedications at other places as well (cf. W. L. Brown, *Num. Chr.* 1950, 190). The Perachora inscription δραχμὰ ἐγό, hέρα λευϙ[όλενε (*SEG* 17, no. 156) is of later date and has nothing to do with the creation of a new coinage.

29. (p. 26) On ancient slavery cf. e.g., M. I. Finley (ed.). *Slavery in Class. Antiquity* (Cambridge 1960); J. Vogt, *Sklaverei und Humanität* (*Historia*, Einzelschrift 8) (Wiesbaden 1965); *Die Sklaverei un utopischen Denken der Griechen* (*Riv. storica dell'antichità* I, 1971, 19).

30. (p. 26) *ML*, no. 8. Chios had electron and silver staters at an early date, probably before 600; C. T. Seltman, *Greek Coins* (London 1955²), 31, has, as generally, an even earlier date.

II · EARLY SPARTA

1. (p. 28) Cf. F. Ollier, *Le mirage spartiate* I. II (Paris 1933–45); P. Janni, *La cultura di Sparta arcaica* (Rome 1965); E. N. Tigerstedt, *The Legend of Sparta in Class. Antiquity* I (Stockholm 1965); E. Rawson, *The Spartan Tradition in European Thought* (Oxford 1969).

2. (p. 28) The history of early Sparta has been a kind of battlefield for modern historians. The scarcity and/or unreliability of our sources is well described by F. Jacoby, *FGrH*, vol. IIIb, LXXI, p. 613 ff. Only the contemporary poets, Alcman and Tyrtaeus in particular, and the document known as the Great Rhetra in Plut. *Lyc. 6* can count as primary sources. All later evidence, including Aristotle, is shaped by the Lycurgus legend and some non-Spartan attempts at giving credit to a number of foreign influences. The only coherent history among our sources is in Pausanias III; but it seems a hopeless task to extract from it more than a few glimpses of any historical value. The same can be said of Ephorus (*FGrH* 70 F 113 ff.). Recent discussion started with L. Pareti, *Storia di Sparta arcaica* I (Florence 1920). This was followed by many other books and articles from various scholars, most of them struggling with imaginative theories as well as with learned detail. At one time the present writer took part in this kind of intellectual gymnastics; he is now convinced that many, though by no means all, of his earlier suggestions must be abandoned. The game is still on. A full survey of most of the writing up to 1969 is made by P. Oliva, *Sparta and her Social Problems* (Praha 1971); his own views are generally sound, if not always as certain as he believes. His book is essential for all future work on Sparta; I shall not specially refer to it later on. Other recent works, full of interesting ideas, are W. G. Forrest, *A History of Sparta* (London 1968) and A. J. Toynbee, *Some Problems of Greek History* (London 1969), 152 ff.

On the Rhetra (see p. 33) in particular cf. A. Andrewes, *CQ* 1938, 89; H. T. Wade-Gery, *CQ* 1943–4 = *Essays in Greek History* (Oxford 1948), 37; N. G. L. Hammond, *JHS* 1950, 42; A. H. M. Jones, *ASAI*, 165; also J. H. Oliver, *Demokratia, the Gods, and the Free World* (Baltimore 1960), cf. A. Momigliano, *JRS* 1961, 235; D. Butler, *Historia* 1962, 385, who relies too much on Oliver's hazardous reconstruction. See also note 11.

3. (p. 28) This equation is by no means self-evident. It is possible that Lacedaemon was the original name, either of central Laconia or of part of what was to be Sparta.

4. (p. 30) Some of the noble Achaean families seem to have survived, such as the Aegidae (Hdt. 4, 149: φυλὴ (!) μεγάλη), and the Talthybii, the heralds' clan (Her. 7, 134). Their genealogies, however, may be a later invention, when it became usual for Spartans in general to regard themselves as descendants of Agamemnon (Hdt. 7, 159). Did, in fact, exiled Achaeans lead the Dorians into the Peloponnese? (cf. M. A. Levi, 'Studi Spartani' I. *Rendiconti Istit. Lombardo* 1962, 479)? The break between Dorian Sparta and everything Mycenaean seems too definite to allow such a view. The traditions connecting the two more closely will have originated in the sixth century. The most famous evidence is to be found in the words, recorded by Herodotus (5, 72), of the king Cleomenes to the priestess of Athena Polias at Athens, who barred the entrance to him as a Dorian: 'O woman, I am not a Dorian, I am an Achaean.'

5. (p. 30) For the latter route, and against the former, see Kiechle, *Lakonien und Sparta* (München 1963), 55. Cf. also Rhys Carpenter, *Discontinuity in Greek Civilisation* (Cambridge 1966), 48 ff.

6. (p. 30) Cf. J. Boardman, *BSA* 58 (1963) 1.

7. (p. 31) It seems to me very doubtful (in spite of Paus. 3, 12, 9) whether this was the beginning, and not the end, of the full conquest of Laconia.

8. (p. 31) On the perioeci see above, p. 42. Melos: Thuc. 5, 84, 2. 89, 1. His date (112, 2): 700 years before his time, i.e. in the eleventh century, is quite impossible, and the story of a late writer, Conon (*FGrH* 26 F 1, XXXVI), that Gortyn in Crete was founded by the same expedition in which Spartans and Achaeans from Amyclae joined hands, is fantastic and derives from the occurrence of the name Amyklaion as belonging to Gortyn (*Law of Gortyn* III 8; cf. Bücheler and Zitelmann, *Das Recht von Gortyn* (Frankfurt 1885), 21; Kiechle, 78); if that name was imported from Laconia – which is quite uncertain – it points to a pre-Dorian colony. Thera: Her. 4, 147 ff. – "Sparta was no trading power in the late 8th century" (J. N. Coldstream, *Greek Geometric Pottery* (London 1968), 365).

9. (p. 32) This similarity was noted by the Greeks themselves. They, as well as modern historians, drew diverse historical conclusions, and there are legendary stories about the mutual relations between Sparta and Crete.

There is, however, no certain historical connexion, apart from the common Dorian heritage.

10. (p. 32) We cannot be quite sure whether Tyrtaeus in that poem, of which only parts are extant, refers to his own generation or to the army of two generations earlier as well (see below). The three phylae as formative elements of the state reappear again when Hieron founded Aetna according to the Dorian 'laws of Aegimius' (Pind. *P.* 1, 61 ff.).

11. (p. 32) The kings held the priesthoods of Zeus Uranios and Zeus Lakedaimon (Hdt. 6, 56), both unique cults which may have reflected the transition from the migrant tribe to the people settled in Lacedaemon. Nothing else is known, but it is tempting to bring the double cult into connexion with the double kingship; cf. H. Schaefer, *Probleme der alten Geschichte* (Göttingen 1963), 280; Ehrenberg, *The Greek State* (London, 1965²), 16. I cannot believe (contrary to Miss L. H. Jeffery, *Historia* 1961, 144) that the title *archagetes* must mean (as it sometimes does) the 'first leader' or 'founder'. The word may just as well simply stress the concept of leadership, especially in war. In the Rhetra it would be far-fetched indeed to call the kings 'cult-founders', an alleged reference to the cults of Zeus Syllanios and Athena Syllania, mentioned in the first section of the Rhetra. Cf. also Kiechle, 157 ff.

12. (p. 32) It cannot be proved, and is unlikely, that they were the same class of 'serfs' that may have existed in Mycenaean times. On the other hand, a number of modern historians believe that the helots were Dorians like the Spartans, who were forced into dependence by the gradual loss of their own land. But the original helots must have been there soon after the occupation. Neither they, nor their masters' position, could otherwise be explained and the linguistic evidence proves nothing, especially as we have none of their utterances. Thucydides (3, 112, 4. 4, 3, 3. 41, 2) speaks only of the Messenians when he says that they spoke Dorian; he even seems to emphasize this fact as though he wished to stress a difference from the Laconian helots.

13. (p. 32) Taenaron and the helots: see Bölte, *RE* IV A, 2043. Kiechle, 109, has doubts about that special connexion.

14. (p. 33) The name of apella appears in the verb *apellazein* in the Rhetra and in late evidence (Hesych., inscriptions of first century B.C.). In the fifth century we find, even officially (Thuc. 5, 77, 1), the use of the common Greek word *ekklesia*. Cf. also the μικρὰ ἐκκλησία, mentioned only once (Xen. *hell.* 3, 3, 8). Even so, I find it difficult to believe that the common

expression was the original one in Sparta; a later origin of the name 'apella' seems most unlikely. But see A. Andrewes, *ASAI* 17, note 3.

15. (p. 34) A council of the elders must have existed before; what was new was the limited number of its members and the inclusion of the kings. Naturally this indicated a change in position and power. The kings were to be *primi inter pares* (cf. Tigerstedt, 55).

16. (p. 34) This last is expressed in a corrupt sentence which has been widely discussed (see note 2). The most likely text runs: δήμῳ δ' ἀνταγορίαν ἦμεν καὶ κράτος, 'the damos shall have the right of refusal (rather than of criticism) and the power'. We cannot say for certain what the last word implied.

17. (p. 34) The Tyrtaeus versions of the Rhetra in Plut. *Lyc.* 6 and Diod. 7, 12, 5, refer not only to the last line but also to the rider. Cf. below, note 35.

18. (p. 34) Cf. Ehrenberg, *RE* 17, 1701 ff. This view has been questioned after the discovery of an inscription (probably *c.* 500 B.C.) in which an ὁ Fὰ Ἀρκάλον is mentioned (*SEG* 11, 475a. 22, 296) – if the reading is correct. Cf. Beattie, *CQ* 1951, 46; Kiechle, 119 ff. The latter rightly rejects Beattie's attempt at putting it among the later Eleutherolaconian cities. He believes in a synonymity between *oba* and *genos*, but in our evidence, however late and confused, the local meaning is clearly predominant. The identity of the obae with the κῶμαι of Sparta seems to me beyond doubt, even if their location, at least that of Pitane, is not equally certain. See also note 46.

19. (p. 34) It is not necessary for the φυλάζειν and ὠβάζειν of the Rhetra to imply exactly the same procedure concerning phylae and obae respectively. Kiechle, 150, is too pedantic on this issue. The Amyclaeans were made citizens (1) by including them into the three phylae, and (2), in view of the distance between Sparta and Amyclae, by creating for them a new oba.

20. (p. 34) This, of course, would be natural if the Rhetra belonged to the ninth century (as Hammond maintains). Such a date and its combination with 'Lycurgus' seem to me out of the question. Neither can I accept the view of A. H. M. Jones, *ASAI* 171, that 'the ephors, being at this time a revolutionary body, are ignored in a document evidently drafted for the nobility'. The Rhetra was concerned with all constitutional aspects, including damos and assembly; if the ephors had been of political significance then, they could not be ignored.

21. (p. 35) I am not competent to decide whether it really meant that lunar and solar years then coincided; cf. G. Thomson, *Studies in Ancient Greek Society*, vol. 2 (London 1955), 127.

22. (p. 35) The same could be true of an allegedly early ephor Asteropus, the 'star-gazer' (cf. Ehrenberg, *Philol. Wochenschrift* 1927, 27). A similar meaning will have been implied when high officials in Aegina (Pind. *N.* 3, 70 and schol.) or Mantineia (Thuc. 5, 47, 9) were called *theoroi* (or *thearoi*) a title normally used for envoys to a sanctuary or a religious festival. The early existence of some kind of ephors seems confirmed by the fact that Thera as well as Cyrene, her daughter-city, had an office of that name; cf. Busolt-Swoboda, *Griech. Staatskunde* 2, 1270. Cf. Kiechle, 220, on the ancient theories about the origins of the ephorate – theories which all are without a true background in the early past of Sparta.

23. (p. 35) I cannot believe that as early as the middle of the eighth century the ephors could be 'inspectors of the life of the citizens'. Clearly that was a feature of the later reforms.

24. (p. 35) Cf. Ehrenberg, *Hermes* 1924, 49 = *PI* 182.

25. (p. 36) About the conquest of Messenia and the later troubles there cf. F. Kiechle, *Messenische Studien* (Munich 1957); but I disagree with his view (56 ff.) that the Messenians were only made helots at the end of the second war.

26. (p. 36) Cf. note 20, and Gomme, I, 218 ff.

27. (p. 36) It must be admitted that Aristotle's ὑπὸ τὸν Μεσσηνιακὸν πόλεμον leaves room for doubts. I dare not express any opinion on the alleged pacification by the poet Terpander (Arist. fr. 545).

28. (p. 37) In this respect, I am close to the views expressed by W. G. Forrest, *Phoenix* 1963, 157.

29. (p. 37) On the *partheniai* see the sources, e.g., in H. Michell, *Sparta* (Cambridge 1952), 85, who rejects all the different ancient stories about them, but does not explain their name; cf. Kiechle, 176 ff., and now S. Pembroke, *Annales* 5 (1970), 1265. – Pottery at Tarent: E. A. Lane, *BSA* 1933–4, 181; F. Pelagatti, *Annuario d. scuola archaeol. di Atene* 17 (1955), 7; F. G. Lo Porto, ibid., 37–38 (1960), 7. Cf. generally, A. J. Graham, *Colony and Mother City in Anc. Greece* (Manchester 1964), 7.

30. (p. 37) The date of Pheidon has been much discussed; cf., e.g., Lenschau, *RE* XIX (1939); Den Boer, *Laconian Studies* (Amsterdam 1954), 55 ff.; A. Andrewes (see ch. I, note 24), 39; H. Chantraine, *Jhb. f. Numism.* 8 (1957), 70; Huxley, *BCH* 1958, 588; *Early Sparta*, 28. The choice is roughly between the middle of the eighth and the first half of the seventh century. I accept the second date, though not without some misgivings. J. N. Coldstream (see note

8) regards (p. 218) Argive and Laconian vase styles as more or less contemporary – that would be in favour of an earlier date.

31. (p. 37) There is today almost unanimity among scholars that the Rhetra and the 'Lycurgan' reforms imply changes in state and society during the seventh century. Divergence of opinion mainly exists with regard to the place of either event within Spartan history. I believe the solution lies in the following chronological order: the Rhetra is earlier than Tyrtaeus, and Tyrtaeus is earlier than the full realization of the 'Lycurgan' reforms. Moreover, the constitutional issues of the Rhetra are of a different character from the social reforms, and there seems no serious reason why they should not be separated in date. The phrase 'alternative to tyranny' belongs to A. Andrewes, (note 30), ch. 6.

32. (p. 38) The date derives from Tyrtaeus fr. 4 D and the list of Spartan kings; but it is really uncertain. H. T. Wade-Gery dates the war before 650 because of 'the fathers of our fathers' (*ASAI* 296).

33. (p. 38) He also speaks of the broad shield (8, 22) and the individual fighting which belong to earlier tactics. If the introduction of the phalanx tactics took time, as it is only reasonable to assume, it is just possible that Tyrtaeus lived through that process. Cf. the discussion in Tigerstedt (note 1) 47, and about Tyrtaeus' phalanx A. M. Snodgrass, *JHS* 1965, 115, who speaks of 'confused tactics and reluctant hoplites'. The γυμνῆτες in Tyrtaeus 8, 35 (who have nothing to do with the festival of the Gymnopaedia) fight close to the hoplites; their position is analogous to that of the Sciritae, whom Xenophon (*rep. Lac.* 13, 6. *hell.* 5, 4, 52) mentions together with the cavalry. Both kinds of troops existed, but were of small importance; it is quite mistaken to think that the γυμνῆτες were helots.

34. (p. 38) Against a much earlier date, as suggested by some scholars on account of Mycenaean or post-Mycenaean heavy armour, cf. Kiechle, 266 ff. Recently armour of enormous strength has been found at Dendra (fifteenth century) which could never have been worn by an ordinary hoplite; cf. E. Vanderpool, *AJA* 1963, 280. The military features of the festival of the Carneia (μίμημα στρατιωτικῆς ἀγωγῆς, Dem. Sceps. in Athen. 4, 141) should not be used to date the reform. The essential nature of that festival was one of harvesting and expiation. Even the σκιάδες in which the soldiers had their meals were not military tents but country huts ('*Laubhütten*'), as at other Laconian festivals or in the cult of Dionysus (Hesych. s. σκιάς). It is quite possible that the particular military aspects, anyway only part of the whole festival, were added at a later time. Cf. M. P. Nilsson, *Griech. Feste* (Leipzig 1906), 120; Ziehen, *RE* III A, 1513.

35. (p. 38) There seems a change of emphasis between the Rhetra and Tyrtaeus' reference to it (fr. 3 D) on the parts played by kings and elders. If that is not only due to the demands of poetical form, it could well be understood as a change in the political climate during the intervening years. Nobody need expect that Tyrtaeus covered every point of the Rhetra, but he referred to it.

36. (p. 39) Tyrtaeus (fr. 8, 14) repeats a Homeric phrase (*Il.* 14, 522), but the 'tremblers' (τρέσαντες) became a fixed concept in Sparta; cf. Ehrenberg, *RE* VI A, 2292.

37. (p. 39) For general reasons we should like to date Alcman before Tyrtaeus, but there is no certainty. A fragmentary papyrus (*Oxyrh. Pap.* XXIV (1957), no. 2390, II) with a commentary on Alcman, does not really help. It mentions Leotychidas, who was king about the middle of the seventh century (cf. Hdt. 8, 131), and it seems certain that Alcman refers to several members of the royal houses; I am at a loss to know what kind of poem that was. Two fragments are quoted: νῦν ἴ ομε τῶ δαίμονος and παίδων ἀρίσταν, followed by the comment: Λεοτυχίδας Λακεδαιμονίων βασιλεύς. Whether δαίμονος refers to the dead Leotychidas (Davison, *Proceed. IX Internat. Congress of Papyrol.* 1958, publ. Lund 1961, 33) is most doubtful, since we have no idea what was said between the two fragments. In general, cf. also Kiechle, 185, note 2. M. L. West, *CQ* 1965, 188, cleverly pleads for a late date (*c.* 600); but if it is possible that Alcman reached that time in his old age, there seems no evidence against putting most of his poetry before the Second Messenian war.

38. (p. 39) The only lengthy piece of Alcman's poetry is a choral song for girl singers; cf. D. L. Page, *Alcman. The Partheneion* (Oxford 1951). Beginning and end are missing, and the rest is difficult to understand. Even so, the beauty of the song, and the vivid freshness of its spirit, are unmistakable. On another fragment (49 D), and Alcman's Sparta in general, cf. Ehrenberg, *Hermes* 1933, 288 = *PI* 202; on his ethical standards and origin, P. Janni (see note 1), chs. 3 and 4.

39. (p. 40) Cf. E. Homann-Wedeking, *Antike und Abendland* VII (Hamburg 1958), 63; J. Boardman, *BSA* 1963, 1.

40. (p. 40) Pottery; cf. E. A. Lane, *BSA* 1933-4, 99. Roughly to the (late?) sixth century belongs the magnificent Vix crater (cf. R. Jeffroy, *Le trésor de Vix* (Paris 1954); A. Rumpf, *Charites* (for E. Langlotz) (Bonn 1957), 127), but its alleged Laconian origin has been disputed; cf. C. Rolley, *BCH* 1958, 168; M. Gjødesen, *AJA* 1963, 335.

41. (p. 40) 'Leonidas': cf. E. Langlotz, *Frühgriech. Bildhauerschulen* (Nurnberg, 1927), 89.

42. (p. 40) The economic importance of the trade in fine pottery has been exaggerated; cf. R. M. Cook, *AJhb* 1954, 114. A change in taste, however, took place; it hit in particular the Corinthian pottery.

43. (p. 40) The final verdict on the development of Laconian art is a matter for the archaeologists. Much to the point, though leaving out a good deal, is a short paper by R. M. Cook, *CQ* 1962, 156. The inscription (mentioned by Cook) of Damonon (*IG* V 1, 213; before 431 B.C.), who in about a hundred lines celebrates his own and his son's many victories in chariot and horse races, continues a long story, starting in the sixth century, of Spartans rich enough to keep and to train horses. Cf. Kiechle, 190.

44. (p. 41) ἡ ἀρχαία μοῖρα, Heracleides Pont. *FHG* II, p. 211. Aristotle, fr. 611, 12 R. The land of the Spartiates was generally known as ἡ πολιτικὴ χώρα; cf. e.g., Polyb. 6, 45, 3, and the discussion of the problems of Spartan land tenure by F. W. Walbank, *Commentary on Polybius* I (Oxford 1957), 728. Cf. also Kiechle, 203.

45. (p. 42) Kiechle, 133 ff., rightly points out that this aristocracy, in contrast to the Cretan, had no special legal or political rights.

45a. (p. 42) Critias' (B 37) sweeping verdict that in Sparta "the free were most fully free and the slaves most fully slaves" is biased, probable in both aspects.

46. (p. 42) The fact that the figure 'five' played an important part in sixth- and fifth-century Sparta does not necessarily imply that all the 'fives' were based on one and the same institution, i.e. the obae. These may have been the basis for the ἀγαθοεργοί (Hdt. 1, 67, 5), who were taken from the ἱππεῖς (300 according to Thuc. 5, 72, 4, therefore deriving from the old three phylae). The new organization of the army in five *lochoi*, of course, might be based on the local principle; but the names of the *lochoi* except one differ from those of the obae. H. T. Wade-Gery, *Essays in Greek History*, 71, nevertheless distinguishes between a 'tribal' and an 'obal' army; in that I cannot follow him. The twenty-seven phratries, once mentioned at the festival of the Carneia (see note 34), do certainly not prove that there were nine obae (Huxley, 48).

47. (p. 45) Our main source for state and society of fifth-century Sparta is despite its idealization, Xenophon's *Respubl. Lacedaemoniorum.*

48. (p. 45) See above p. 390 (4).

49. (p. 47) Cf. F. Kiechle, *XIIe Congr. internat. des sciences hist. Rapports* 1965, 279 (though he overstates his case).

50. (p. 47) Cf. A. Andrewes, *Probuleusis* (Oxford 1954). More cautious: E. S. Staveley, *Greek and Roman Voting* (London 1972), 18 ff., 73 ff.

51. (p. 47) Cf. A. Andrewes, *ASAI 6*, who also refers to eight passages in Xenophon.

52. (p. 48) Sparta as a totalitarian state: Ehrenberg, *Aspects of the Ancient World* (Oxford 1946), ch. 7. Some scholars disagreed with that definition. As the ideal was never attained, it may be better to use the word 'authoritarian' instead. On Spartan government in classical times see A. Andrewes, *ASAI 1*.

53. (p. 48) Dr J. P. Barron pointed out to me that Samos held the balance of maritime power during the time between Persia's acquisition of the Phoenician fleet and her conquest of Egypt.

54. (p. 48) The epigram was by a little-known poet, Ion of Samos (Diehl, *Anthologia Lyrica*, fasc. 1, p. 87). He calls Sparta Ἑλλάδος ἀκρόπολιν, καλλίχορομ πατρίδα.

III · ATHENS BEFORE AND UNDER SOLON

1. (p. 50) Most of the later tradition does not go further back than the local historians of the fifth century, the Atthidographers (cf. F. Jacoby, *Atthis* (Oxford 1949), and *FGrH*), the first of whom was Hellanicus of Lesbos; much of their reconstruction, especially that by Androtion, is contained, though in parts contradicted, in the early chapters of Aristotle's *Athenaion Politeia* (*AP*). This book, first published from a papyrus in 1891, is a unique source, though its value is frequently contested, even to the extent of denying Aristotle's authorship. In general cf. my short remarks in *The Greek State* (London, 1969²), 255. Commented edition by J. E. Sandys (London 1912²); recent translation with introduction by K. von Fritz and E. Kapp (New York 1950). Critical, often too sceptical, discussion of the early history of Athens: G. de Sanctis, *Atthis* (Turin 1912²); C. Hignett, *A History of the Athenian Constitution* (Oxford 1952). Not a very safe guide is J. Day and M. Chambers, *Aristotle's History of Athenian Democracy* (Berkeley 1962). Against them (and F. W. Gilliard, *Historia* 1971, 430) it must be stressed that the *AP* cannot be treated in isolation; it belongs to the *corpus* of 158 constitutions which can hardly be regarded as philosophical treatises, even though we know so little about the whole lot.

2. (p. 51) The existence of an independent Eleusis with her own history (cf. *h. h. Dem.* 96 f.) is neglected.

3. (p. 52) In the case of Syracuse it may be that the union of Ortygia and the mainland settlement was responsible. The plural is easier to explain, e.g., in Megara, a union of several palaces (*megara*).

4. (p. 52) The names are: *Geleontes, Hopletes, Argadeis, Aigikoreis*. To explain them as occupations (farmers, warriors, artisans, shepherds), as already some ancient writers did, seems mistaken both linguistically and historically. The analogy of the Dorian tribes seems to prove that it is also a mistake to take the 'Ionian' phylae as territorial units. The attempt by D. Kienast, *HZ* 200 (1965), 272, to reconstruct an early local division from the four(!) names of each phyle in Poll. 8, 109, seems to me more than doubtful. The phylae were part of the personal structure of the tribe, even though the name 'Ionian' was first coined in Asia Minor, and thence returned to Athens from where, as mentioned before (p. 6), the 'Ionian Migration' originated; cf. C. Roebuck, *Ionian Trade and Colonisation* (New York 1959); a good survey of modern views: H. Gallet de Santerre, *REA* 64 (1962), 20 ff. As to the radical denial of the Ionian migration by F. Cassola, *La Ionia del Mondo Miceneo* (Naples 1957), cf. F. Schachermeyr, *Gnomon* 1960, 207. The Athenians thought of themselves (mistakenly) as 'autochthonous', not as early invaders, and Solon (4D) called Athens 'the oldest land of Ionia'.

5. (p. 52) The details and the nomenclature of the early social structure are by no means clear. The matter has been made more complicated by Aristotle's belief in two different stages of development, one under Ion, the mythical ancestor of the Ionians, himself surely a comparatively late invention, the other under Theseus. Cf. the penetrating studies by H. T. Wade-Gery, *CQ* 1931, 77 ff., 129 ff.=*Essays in Greek History*, 86 ff., 116 ff., but also K. Latte, *RE* XX, 746 ff., 994 ff., and A. Andrewes, *JHS* 1961, 1 ff.

6. (p. 53) Aristotle believes that the office of archon was a later creation than basileus and polemarch, because he had only additional, no traditional, functions; but that is a wrong conclusion. Even after the other two had taken over most of the old regal duties, the first archon was still the highest official in the state.

7. (p. 53) Chronology of archons: T. J. Cadoux, *JHS* 68 (1948), 70 ff.

7a. (p. 53) Against a very late date for the introduction of the *thesmothetae*, as suggested by E. Ruschenbusch, see *HZ* 210 (1970), 664.

8. (p. 54) It seems certain that there was also an individual clan (*genos*) called Eupatridae; Alcibiades belonged to it (Isocr. 16, 25). Some modern scholars have denied the existence of that clan, others that of a noble class

of the name. I believe both assumptions are unnecessary. Whether we should call the nobility a 'legal class' is another question. We cannot discuss here the complex question in detail; important contributions to such a discussion are, e.g., J. Toepffer, *Attische Genealogie* (Berlin 1889), 173. 175; H. T. Wade-Gery, 86 ff.; Hignett, *passim*; R. Sealey, *Historia* 1960, 178.

9. (p. 54) The last are those 'who worked for the demos'. In Homer they include all sorts of professions, such as seers, physicians, shipbuilders, heralds, and bards (*Od.* 17, 382 ff. 19, 134 f.). They originally did not belong to the demos, but were mostly migrants. Under settled conditions, they would be the landless class. Cf., in general, K. Murakawa, *Historia* 1957, 385 ff. Some scholars, e.g. J. Hasebroek, *Griech. Wirtschafts- und Gesellschaftsgeschichte* (Tübingen 1931), 47, doubt the authenticity of the three classes as a whole; there is no serious reason for supporting such a theory.

10. (p. 54) For the 'natural background' and the difficulties of Attic agriculture see A. French, *The Growth of Athenian Economy* (London 1964), chs. 1 and 2.

10a. (p. 54) It is noteworthy that the Greeks never drank their wine if not mixed with water (a point overlooked by Andrewes (*The Greeks*, 122)).

11. (p. 55) The meaning and significance of the *orgeones* are still disputed; cf. A. Andrewes, *JHS* 1961, 1. On the phratries (post-Mycenaean ?) cf. Andrewes, *The Greeks*, 79 ff.

12. (p. 55) Well shown by Sealey (see note 8), an article which combines some excellent ideas with some wild guesses. Regional and social struggles are by no means exclusive contrasts.

13. (p. 56) The relation between phratry and trittyes, both parts of the phylae, is obscure; the one is a personal and religious unit, the other one of local administration. If there were twelve phratries – and their military side demanded a fixed number – then the trittyes may be a substitute for administrative purposes. At any rate, there is no historical value in the construction (*AP.* fr. 5=Arist. fr. 385) that originally the four phylae were subdivided into three parts, the trittyes or phratries, and each section into thirty clans containing each thirty men!

14. (p. 56) Holt, 5, 71. Thuc. 1, 126. Paus. 7, 25, 3, and others. In general, the most important sources for seventh-century Athens are Solon's poems, Aristotle, *AP*, and Plutarch, *Life of Solon*. The first, of course, is the most authentic one, but still leaves much unexplained; the two others are largely based on Solon's poems, of which much is quoted, but they had some, if

unknown, evidence besides. Plutarch, or his source, used *AP* as well as
the Atthidographers (Androtion). To some extent the poems going under
the name of Theognis (see p. 180) seem to be of Athenian origin; they would
reflect feelings of the Athenian aristocrats, though rather of the sixth century.

15. (p. 57) Date of Cylon: Jacoby, *Atthis* 366, note 77. Slightly different
versions of the story: Hdt. 5, 71; Thuc. 1, 126; Paus. 7, 25, 3; *AP* fr. 8,
ch. 1; Plut. *Sol.* 12; Schol. Aristoph. *Equ.* 445.

16. (p. 57) Law on homicide: Tod, no. 87. It was finally reinstated in the
general restitution of 403. Cf. D. M. MacDowell, *Athenian Homicide Law*
(Manchester 1964).

17. (p. 58) Cf. E. Ruschenbusch, *Historia* 1960, 129 ff. Other important
issues raised in this article cannot be dealt with here. Cf. also next note.

18. (p. 58) Aristotle, *Pol.* 1274b, 15, expressly states that Dracon gave
laws, but 'added them to the existing constitution'. It is likely that *AP* 4
reflects views of the oligarchs of 411 or the fourth century; cf. A. Fuks
The Ancestral Constitution (London 1953), 84 ff.; E. Ruschenbusch, *Historia*
1958, 421 f. It is probably an interpolation, perhaps by Aristotle himself.

19. (p. 58) Cf. R. J. Hopper, *ASAI* 139, who asks the right questions about
the social crisis, even though his answers (in a short article) do not cover the
ground.

19a. (p. 59) M. I. Finley, in a short article (*Eirene* 1968, 25), shows that the
question of alienability of land is very complicated, but he does not distinguish between nobility and peasantry. Andrewes (see note 11) strictly denies
that land was not alienable.

20. (p. 59) *AP* 2, 2 (cf. 5, 1): ἡ δὲ πᾶσα γῆ δι' ὀλίγων ἦν. The problems of
land tenure in seventh-century Athens are discussed in every book on Solon.
A special difficulty derives from the fact that Aristotle and those who
followed him spoke in the legal terms of fourth-century economy. I very
much doubt that anything as formal as the πρᾶσις ἐπὶ λύσει (sale with op-
tion of redemption) existed in the seventh century. Also the *horoi* of Solon's
times are not the same as those of the fourth century; cf. especially Wade-
Gery, *Mél. Glotz* (Paris 1932), 2, 877 ff.; J. V. A. Fine, *Horoi* (*Hesperia*
Suppl. 9, 1951); M. I. Finley, *Land and Credit in Ancient Athens* (New
Brunswick 1951); J. Pečirka in Γέρας, Studies presented to G. Thomson
(Prague 1963), 183; also the many books on Solon's person and work, e.g.
Ch. Gilliard, *Quelques réformes de Solon* (Lausanne 1907); I. M. Linforth,
Solon the Athenian (Univ. of California Publ. in Class. Philol. 6, Berkeley
1919); K. Freeman, *The Work and Life of Solon* (Cardiff 1926); W. J.

Woodhouse, *Solon the Liberator* (Oxford 1938); K. Hönn, *Solon* (Vienna 1948). Cf. also A. French, *CQ* 1956, 11 ff.; *Historia* 1963, 242 ff.; D. Lotze, *Philol.* 102 (1958), 1 ff.; D. Asheri, *Historia* 1963, 1 ff.; F. Cassola, *Parola del Passato* 94 (1964), 26 (the interpretation of Solon, fr. 3, 12 f. is not convincing); M. I. Finley, *Rev. hist. de droit franç. et étranger* 1965, 159 (important). W. G. Forrest, *The Emergence of Greek Democracy* (London 1966). I have not seen A. Martina, *Solone* (1968).

21. (p. 60) Pelatae and hectemorii: *AP* 2, 2; hectemorii and thetes: Plut. *Sol.* 13, 4. It is certain that the hectemorii paid one-sixth, and not five-sixths; cf. K. v. Fritz, *AJP* 61 (1940), 54. 64 (1943), 24. Even one-sixth is anything but a light burden, especially in view of the generally poor land the small farmers held. The common charge of a tithe (= one-tenth) was often bad enough.

22. (p. 60) Cf. A. French (see note 10), 11.

23. (p. 60) This probably means 'by decision of judges or without it'. In a higher sense the sale of a fellow citizen into slavery was, at any rate, unjust, also for the Greeks.

24. (p. 61) A. French, *Historia* 1963, 242, has well refuted the view of N. G. L. Hammond, 157, that the first group were impoverished noblemen (*gennetae*), and the other non-nobles ('guildsmen'). Relying on Plutarch, Hammond forgets that the 'hectemorii and thetes' cannot have been of noble origin.

25. (p. 62) In this context it ought to be remembered that, according to a reliable tradition, Athens towards 600 B.C. founded Sigeum near the Hellespont, her first and, at the time, only colony; it was led by Phrynon, an Olympic victor, and the foundation caused a long war with Mytilene on Lesbos. The choice of place indicates that the colony was to provide both fertile land and a site close to an important trade route. If the enterprise was an attempt at alleviating the domestic situation, it can only have been on a small scale and of little effect, but it seemed important enough to be fought for through many years. Cf. also R. J. Hopper, *BSA* 1962, 212; *ASAI* 143.

26. (p. 63) It is not certain that the Salamis elegy preceded Solon's archonship, but our tradition maintains it, and it is likely in itself.

27. (p. 63) It is usually called the elegy εἰς ἑαυτόν. It begins with the traditional solemn invocation of the Muses, and then deals with the life of man under the impact of good and evil forces sent by fate.

28. (p. 64) These lines, it is true, also appear in Theognis (315 ff.; cf. 57 f., 1109 f.), but Solon is the 'onlie begetter'. What to Theognis is bitter sarcasm and disappointment is to Solon a moral fact.

29. (p. 64) Cf. F. Solmsen, *Hesiod and Aeschylus* (Ithaca 1949), 107.

30. (p. 64) fr. 24, 15 f. For the interpretation of these lines see *Athenaeum* 1965, 458.

31. (p. 64) In ancient tradition, the date of Solon's archonship wavers between 594–593 and 592–591. For a full discussion see T. J. Cadoux, *JHS* 1948, 93; he deals at length with the sources as well as their modern interpretations; cf. also G. V. Sumner, *CQ* 1961, 49. Whether the legislation (as contrasted with *seisachtheia* and constitution) belongs to 592–591, as indicated by *AP* 14, 1, and as, e.g., N. G. L. Hammond, *JHS* 1940, 71, tries to show, we do not know; at any rate, it is difficult to see how that date could survive, if Solon was not archon then, as he certainly was not. However, some way was probably found to extend Solon's term of office, or at least his activity. Hignett, 316 ff., is very good in his criticism, but makes the bold and unconvincing attempt at dating Solon's legislation between 570 and 560; cf. also R. Sealey, *Historia* 1960, 159 ff. Such a late date would clash with more or less everything we know or believe we know. A. E. Raubitschek, *CP* 1963, 139, on the other hand, speaks of Solon's ἀρχή as covering his ἀποδημία and thus lasting till 576–575. I cannot accept an ἀρχή without archonship. Cf. also the hypothetical time-table for Solon's activities by M. Miller, *Arethusa* 1 (1968), 62.

31a. (p. 65) For a recent discussion of the *seisachtheia* see D. Asheri, *Legge greche sul problema dei debiti* (*Studi Class. e Orient.* 18, 1969), 9.

32. (p. 65) Cf. Homer A. Thompson (and others), *The Athenian Agora. A Guide* (Athens 1962²).

33. (p. 65) The *zeugitai* can be explained either as those who own a pair of oxen under the yoke (*zeugos*) or those who are joined to their neighbours in the ranks of the phalanx. For the first meaning might be significant the description in comedy of the small farmer as the 'two-oxen man'; cf. my *People of Aristophanes* (New York 1962³), 76. The thetes sometimes did service as light-armed troops or as oarsmen in the fleet.

34. (p. 66) Later sources equate the *medimnos* with the *metretes*, the measure for liquid stuff, and both as well as a sheep with one drachma in money. But wine and oil were of different value, and at a time of money economy, Solon's agrarian division would no longer hold good as an economic frame-

work. In the whole complex question I owe much to an essay by G. E. M. de Ste Croix (not yet published). Although a good deal remains hypothetical, he says what is necessary about Plut. *Sol*. 23, 3 (and Wilcken's ingenious but mistaken conjecture οὐσιῶν for θυσιῶν), and about the fantastic evidence of Poll. 8, 130, on the taxes each class was supposed to pay. Cf. also C. M. A. Van den Oudenrijn, *Mnemos*. 1952, 19.

35. (p. 66) Poll. 9, 61: εἰκοσάβοιον, Pollux further describes the use in sacred language (ἐν τῇ παρὰ Δηλίοις θεωρίᾳ) of a βοῦς as equal to two drachmas. Dracon's laws were essentially traditional laws; his use of the ancient money symbol and the Homeric word (*Od*. 1, 431) does not exclude an Athenian barley currency before Solon, though it makes it unlikely.

36. (p. 67) Therefore, I cannot share Schaefer's view, expressed in a lecture unfortunately never printed, that Solon aimed at a return to the old aristocracy (cf. *Probleme der alten Geschichte* (Göttingen 1963), 287, 2. 313 f.).

37. (p. 67) On the ὅπλα παρεχόμενοι see p. 320.

38. (p. 68) This is certain for the treasurers who had to belong to the richest people; for it was a common, if mistaken, view that the rich would be more honest than the poor in dealing with public money. Naturally it was also easier, in case some public money had 'disappeared', to get it back from a wealthy man. Whether the archons came from the first class only, or the two upper classes, is disputed; cf., e.g., Hignett, 99 f. Staveley (see ch. II, note 50), 33.

39. (p. 68) κλήρωσις ἐκ προκρίτων, *AP* 8, 1; differently: *AP* 22, 5; Arist. *pol*. 1273 b, 40. 1274a, 16. Did Solon use election by lot at all? It is almost certain that the members of the popular court were appointed in this way from the people (*pol*. 1274a, 5). About the council see below. In *AP* 47, 1 (cf. 8, 1), we read that at the time of Aristotle the treasurers 'were elected by lot . . . from the pentacosiomedimni according to Solon's law which is still in force'. The last clause refers probably to 'from the pentacosiomedimni' only, and does not concern the manner of election. For a more detailed discussion see my article 'Losung', *RE* 13, 1468 ff. There I have taken the κλήρωσις ἐκ προκίτων of the archons in *AP* 8, 1, as historical, but I could do so only by assuming that there was a change in the form of electing the archons between Solon and Cleisthenes (probably under Hippias); for that there is, of course, no evidence. Cf. more recently R. J. Buck, *CP* 1965, 96. D. W. Knight (see ch. IV, note 34), 25. Staveley, 34.

40. (p. 68) Was there a special law by Solon against tyranny, possibly even one before him? It seems unlikely; but cf. M. Ostwald, *TAPA* 86 (1955), 103 ff.

41. (p. 69) K. Freeman (see note 20), 79, 1, suggests that the paragraph in Plutarch (19, 2) with its partly poetical expressions may derive from a poem by Solon. That seems quite possible, though it cannot be proved. The Athenian local historians of the fifth and fourth centuries believed in Solon's council of the Four Hundred as a sign of early democracy. The inscription from Chios mentioned before (*ML*, no. 8), with its clear features of a democratic constitution (δήμο ῥήτρα, βουλὴ ἡ δημοσίη, with special powers), is now dated *c.* 575–550 (and not *c.* 600); cf. L. H. Jeffery, *BSA* 51 (1956), 157; also J. H. Oliver, *AJP* 80 (1959) 296 (with some rather bold supplements of missing parts). Chios was notorious for its large numbers of slaves at an early time, mainly barbarians (Theopomp. *FGrH* 115 F 122a. Nymphodorus, *FGrH* 572, F4; cf. A. Fuks, *Athenaeum* 1968, 102). Was democracy responsible for that, or was it the other way round?

42. (p. 69) Cf. H. J. Wolff, *Beiträge zur Rechtsgeschichte*, etc. (Weimar 1961), 1; E. Ruschenbusch, *Historia* 1965, 381.

43. (p. 69) G. Vlastos, *CP* 41 (1946), 69.

44. (p. 70) Hignett, 313, 318 f., has doubted the authenticity of the wording – not without some good reasons. But as it was quoted as 'the eighth law of Solon's thirteenth axon', we cannot seriously question that in essentials it was Solonian. We only must keep in mind that quotations in Greek literature need never have been verbatim, and usually were not.

45. (p. 71) Some archaic expressions have been preserved; they definitely go back to the sixth century. About the laws and their history cf., apart from general books on Solon (note 16), recently: E. Ruschenbusch, Σόλωνος Νόμοι (*Historia*, Einzelheft 9, 1966).

46. (p. 72) The comedian Cratinus (fr. 276, Kock), about the middle of the fifth century, speaks of Dracon's and Solon's laws 'now used to parch our barley', a comic exaggeration for saying that they were no longer good for anything but firewood. The joke would have been senseless if wooden tablets were no longer in existence. The word used by Cratinus is *kyrbeis* (cf. *AP* 7, 1; Plut. 25; see L. B. Holland, *AJA* 45 (1941), 346; F. Jacoby, *Atthis* 309, 64). Holland is mistaken in assuming that *axones* were not used before the fourth century. What about the 'first axon' of Dracon's law (*ML*, no. 86)? Cf. A. R. W. Harrison, *CQ* 1961, 3. ἐν τῷ ἄξονι in Dem. 23, 28. 31 (usually corrected to ἐν τῷ ⟨ά⟩ ἄξονι) could also point to Dracon, but the crucial test is the inscription (see note 48). Most quotations refer to the *axones*, among them one to the thirteenth *axon* (law of amnesty) (Plut. 19, 4), and another to the sixteenth, referring to price limits for sacrifices

(Plut. 23, 4). Lys. 30, 17 f., speaks of a sacrificial calendar ἐκ τῶν κύρβεων, but we do not know for certain that these are genuine Solonian laws; the reference to prices (§20) goes far beyond anything possible in Solon's time. What the difference was between the two expressions κύρβεις and ἄξονες has been discussed since ancient times; only one thing is certain – axon is a revolving slab. The find of a wedge-shaped fragment of marble at Chios proves that axones need not have been of wood. Plutarch (25, 2) mentions the view of 'some' that the kyrbeis contained 'sacred laws and sacrifices', and axones the rest; this view has been taken up again by S. Dow, *Proc. Mass. Hist. Soc.* 71 (1953-7), 3; he bases his argument on a very careful discussion of the renewed code of 410-399 of which parts are extant (cf. S. Dow, *Historia* 1960, 270). Even so I cannot believe in such a division by Solon, as it would interfere with the distribution of the constitutional competences among the various magistrates. Moreover, a definite division between sacred and profane law would be alien to sixth-century thought. Later, τὰ ἱερά was the first item at each meeting of the ecclesia; but that meant cult, not law. The only solution to the whole problem seems that ἄξονες and κύρβεις are two words for the same thing. Ruschenbusch (note 45) believes in a purely technical difference.

47. (p. 72) Main evidence: [Dem.] 46, 14. 44, 63. 66 ff.; cf. Dem. 20, 102. The law was far from being clearly worded, and caused many lawsuits. It is likely that it was only concerned with adoption *inter vivos*, and that later it led to adoption by last will. It is clear from some passages (e.g. [Dem.] 43, 51) that the law was later revised. In general see the detailed discussion by L. Gernet, *Droit et société dans la Grèce ancienne* (Paris 1955), 121. He maintains that all Athenians once belonged to a *genos*, but as I have said before, that is true only of the nobility. With Solon, however, the family in a narrower sense came into its own as a legal unit.

48. (p. 72) The inscription mentioned in note 46 (*ML*, no. 86) contains on the 'first axon' (Dracon's axon, surely) Dracon's law about unintentional killing only, beginning with the word καὶ, which cannot have been the original beginning. Cf. A. R. W. Harrison, *CQ* 1961, 3. What happened to the law on wilful murder? Did Solon repeal it? There is no evidence for that; on the contrary, Demosthenes knows Dracon as the author of all extant homicide laws (20, 157 f. 23, 51). In cases of premeditated killing, clan and phratry would undoubtedly have insisted on their ancient rights even more strongly than they did in the case of unintentional killing. A faint δεύτερος ἄξων has recently been detected on the inscription (see *SEG* 25, no. 39), but we do not know what it contained. Generally, cf. R. G. Stroud, *Univ. of Calif. Class. Studies* 3 (1968); see D. M. Lewis, *CR* 1971, 390.

49. (p. 72) The last rule was either post-Solonian, or, less likely, it referred to weight-value.

50. (p. 73) This translation differs from the usual ones on account of the interpretation given by K. Kraft, *Jahrb. f. Numism. u. Geldgesch.* X (1959–60), 21 ff. I am glad to see my view confirmed by E. Will, *2e Conférence internat. d'hist. écon.* (Aix 1962) (1965), 79, who accepts and supports Kraft's theories. It is essential to realize: (1) that at Solon's time there was no coinage, though there may have been pieces of silver of a certain weight; (2) that Aristotle's order of subjects thoughout is that of measures, weights, coinage. The whole tradition has gone wrong ever since 'the idea of coinage had crept into it' (C. M. Kraay, *N. Chr.* 1956, 67). Difficulties remain; one of them is provided by the different report of Androtion (in Plut. *Sol.* 15, 3), but Androtion had also misunderstood the seisachtheia (Plut. 13, 3 f.).

51. (p. 74) On Aegina see above, p. 25 (Pheidon), and W. L. Brown, *N. Chr.* 1950, 177. On Athens: Kraay, 43. General aspects of early coinage: C. M. Kraay, *JHS* 84 (1964), 57; K. Christ, *Saeculum* 15 (1964), 214.

52. (p. 74) This is the theory of Kraft (note 50) whose complicated discussion cannot be repeated here. He distinguishes *inter alia*, between a trade-weight of 100 drachmas and a coinage-weight of 105. It must be left to the experts to explain the double standard and its economic significance.

53. (p. 74) Cf. M. Gigante, Νόμος Βασιλεύς (Naples 1956). Cf. also W. Theiler, *Mus. Helv.* 22 (1965), 69, and generally, M. Ostwald, *Nomos and the Beginnings of Ath. Democracy* (Oxford 1969).

54. (p. 74) On the nature of Solon's justice see G. Vlastos, *CP* 41 (1946), 65, and E. Wolf, *Gegenwartsprobleme des internationalen Rechts*, etc., *Festschrift f. R. Laun* (Hamburg 1953), 449.

55. (p. 75) Cf. A. W. H. Adkins, *Merit and Responsibility* (Oxford 1960), ch. 4; G. Ferrara, *La politica di Solone* (Napoli 1964).

56. (p. 75) Cf. G. F. Else, *The Origin and Early Form of Greek Tragedy* (Martin Lectures, Cambridge, Mass. 1965), 35.

57. (p. 75) Cf. S. Lauffer, *Abh. Akad. Mainz* 1955, 1956.

58. (p. 76) Cf. A. Bonnard, *Greek Civilization* I (London 1957), ch. 7. Among Marxist scholars, Bonnard is a moderate and comparatively free from dogmatism. A. W. Gomme, *Essays*, 89, in a witty article, argues that the position of women (in Athens) was not 'greatly different from the average in mediaeval and modern Europe'; but that is misleading in spite of a few sound arguments.

IV · THE SIXTH CENTURY

1. (p. 77) Solon's travels provided soil for the growth of many legends, among them the famous Croesus episode (Hdt. 1, 29 ff. 86 ff.), which, if only for reasons of chronology, cannot be historical.

2. (p. 77) Two men appear in our sources as having been archons μετὰ Σόλωνα, which could, but need not, mean the year 593–592; cf. Cadoux, *JHS* 1948, 79 ff. The two names are Dropides, who is supposed to have been a friend of Solon, and Phormio. Nothing more can be said about them, though it seems possible that they were in office in succeeding years. Cadoux mentions other possible names for the years 592–591 to 588–587.

3. (p. 77) *AP* 13, 1. This was called *anarchia*, a time without archons, and therefore without government. Hence the modern concept of anarchy.

4. (p. 78) This is the most likely, in my view the only possible, interpretation of *AP* 13, 2. The ten were neither to fill the nine offices of archonship nor were they chosen, ten from each phyle, to act as a body of πρόκριτοι. Cf. Ed. Meyer, *Forschungen* II (Halle 1899), 537; Ehrenberg, *Neugründer des Staates* (Munich 1925), 76; Cadoux, 103. The reading of the Berlin Papyrus on the number of the Eupatrids has been finally established as πεν]τε, and not as τεττάρ]ας. A different opinion on the ten archons is expressed, e.g., by L. Gernet, *RPh* 1958, 216; but despite great ingenuity, his arguments carry little conviction, and I cannot share the belief that the whole thing is a 'philosophical construction' of the fifth century, as, e.g., D. Kienast, *HZ* 200 (1965), 267, maintains. For another hypothesis see Staveley, 35 f.

5. (p. 78) On the other hand, I cannot quite share H. T. Wade-Gery's view (*Essays in Greek History* (Oxford 1958), 102) that 'the arrangement is made within the scope of the Solonian law'. Economic standards played their part, but they were not the decisive factor.

6. (p. 79) That, I believe, was largely due to the fact that of the three names at least the Paralii, and above all a tripartition of Attica, occur again in Cleisthenes' order (see p. 94), in which the three parts were clearly, though not always logically, separated.

7. (p. 79) Cf. the important paper by R. J. Hopper, *BSA* 56 (1962), 189; he is, I believe, mistaken in taking the tripartition as a later construction. For what follows, I have learned a great deal from his article as well as those by A. French, *Greece and Rome* 1959, 46, and D. M. Lewis, *Historia* 1963, 22. Cf. also R. Sealey, *Historia* 1960, 178, and, on the other hand, Ch. Mossé, *L'antiquité class.* 33 (1964), 401.

8. (p. 80) Cf. also Ps.-Plato, *Hipparchos* 228 B. 'Brauron as a port of dia-cria' relies on an emendation in Heysch. s. διακρεῖς, and on I. Bekker, *Anecdota Graeca*, vol. I (Berlin 1814), 242: διάκρια τόπος ᾿Αττικῆς ὑπὸ Βραυρῶνα ᾿Ελευσίνιον Δήμητρος καὶ Φερσεφάττης ἱερόν.

9. (p. 80) It is not impossible, as French suggests (note 7), that the capture of Salamis and the opening of the trade routes to the west brought economic depression to eastern Attica and to the trade centred on Prasiae.

10. (p. 81) Hopper in his article (note 7) has too confidently assumed that each of the three men had the same aim of seizing full power personally.

11. (p. 81) D. M. Lewis, *Historia* 1963, 24, makes a case for the Philaids belonging to the pediaei.

12. (p. 81) The history – and that means to a large extent the chronology – of Peisistratus' exiles and reign is uncertain and partly obscure. Recent literature: e.g., F. Cornelius, *Die Tyrannis in Athen* (Munich 1929); F. Schachermeyr, *RE* 19, 164; Cadoux (note 2), 104; F. Jacoby, *Atthis* (Oxford 1949), 152. 188; F. Heidbüchel, *Philol.* 1957, 70; Berve (ch. I, note 24), ch. 2. It seems impossible to find a completely satisfactory solution for the diverg-ing views in Hdt. I, 59 ff.; Thuc. I, 20, 2. 6, 55–59; and *AP* 14, 1. 17, 1. 19, 6 (also *pol.* 1315b, 31 ff.), as well as in later sources, but in the main points Herodotus is most reliable. cf. also G. Gottlieb, *Das Verhältnis der ausserherodoteischen Überlieferung zu Herodot* (Diss. Frankfurt 1963), ch. 2.

13. (p. 81) The story of the girl Phye who, acting as the goddess Athena, led Peisistratus to the Acropolis as his charioteer was even for Herodotus (1, 60; cf. *AP* 14, 4) more than he could believe. But there is no reason to doubt the close relationship between Peisistratus and the goddess of Athens. Phye may even have followed an ancient religious tradition of divine incorporation by humans (cf. Kiechle, *Historia* 1970, 263).

14. (p. 82) For the economic conditions cf. A. French, *The Growth of the Athenian Economy* (London 1964), ch. 3.

15. (p. 82) A joint rule in which Hippias, the elder son (Thuc. I, 20, 2. 6, 54, 2), was the politically minded and therefore the real ruler is the version in *AP* 16, 7. 17, 3. 18, 1 (cf. also Hdt. 1, 61, 3); it is likely to have been true. Hipparchus was little more than a 'playboy', interested in literature and art, the host to a number of famous poets.

16. (p. 82) Cf. my *Aspects of the Ancient World* (Oxford 1946), 116=*PI* 221. H. Bengtson, *S.B. Bayr. Ak.* 1939; E. Will, *La Nouvelle Clio* 1954, 424.

17. (p. 83) The so-called *Wappenmünzen* with their different symbols belong, according to recent research, to the time of Peisistratus. Was their issue one of the gestures of conciliation towards the nobles? Cf. Ch. G. Starr, *Athenian Coinage 480–449 B.C.* (Oxford 1970), 5.

18. (p. 83) *AP* 16, 4 – Thuc. 6, 54, in dealing with the rule of Peisistratus' sons, describes their rule in terms such as seem suitable for the whole period of *tyrannis*. He mentions a tax of 5 per cent only (εἰκοστή); we do not know whether that is a correction of the view which we have in *AP*, or means a reduction of Peisistratus' tax by Hippias. I cannot believe that the rural taxes were such a heavy burden on the peasantry, and so important for the state economy, as A. French (see note 14) maintains.

19. (p. 84) The history of the early temples on the Acropolis is very complex. The favoured view today seems that the ἀρχαῖος νεώς was the one just south of the Erechtheum, and that Peisistratus provided it with a peristyle and sculptures. Cf. R. J. Hopper, *Parthenos and Parthenon* (*Greece and Rome*, Suppl. to vol. 10, 1963), 14.

20. (p. 85) ἵππαρχος ἀνέθε[κεν ho Πεισισ]τράτο. That would probably have been during one of Peisistratus' exiles, as we find there an Alcmaeonid dedication as well, most likely to counter the Peisistratid one. Cf. L. Bizard *BCH* 1920, 228. 238. J. J. E. Hondius and F. Hiller v. Gaertringen, *Hermes* 1922, 475. *ML*, no. 11.

21. (p. 85) Cf. the extensive 'Notes on the Panathenaea', by J. A. Davison, *JHS* 1958, 23 (and 1962, 141). Eusebius' date of 566–565 for the first *agon gymnikos* is roughly confirmed by the archaeological evidence of the Panathenaic amphorae.

22. (p. 85) In historical times the name of the festival meant 'celebrated by all Athenians', and that would stand even if there had once been a goddess Panathena (cf. Davison, loc. cit.).

23. (p. 85) For its refutation cf., e.g., J. A. Davison, *TAPA* 1955, 1.

24. (p. 86) I cannot deal with the question of the origin of Greek tragedy, which has been recently discussed in an over-bold manner, though very ingeniously, by G. F. Else (ch. III, note 56).

25. (p. 87) *ML*, no. 6; Cadoux, T 6, p. 109. There are six names partially extant, the first quite uncertain . . .]ετο[. . ., the last . . . . .]στρατ[ος, almost certainly Peisistratos, the eldest son of Hippias (cf. Thuc. 6, 54, 6) whose own name appears in the second place. The most astonishing name is, of course, the third, that of K]λεισθέν[ες; for the Alcmaeonids had been

exiled before, and were exiles again later. Even so it is generally agreed that
M. Guarducci's restoration Π]λεισθέν[ες is most unlikely, as that is
not an Athenian name at all. The following name is that of M]ιλτιάδες, and
this makes a dating possible; for he is known to have been archon in 524–523
(Dion. Hal. 7, 3, 1). Cf. the detailed discussion of the dates and names by
Cadoux, also of the question whether this is the elder or the younger
Miltiades. I have no doubt that it is the latter, the later victor of Marathon.
Another surprising fact is the non-appearance of Hipparchus. There is room
enough for him in the years after 522–521; but even if he was archon then,
the predominance of Hippias over his brother is manifest.

26. (p. 88) M. Amit, *L'antiquité class.* 39 (1970), 414, dates the alliance of
Athens with Plataea in 509, i.e. after Hippias' expulsion.

27. (p. 88) On the different traditions about the tyrannicides in Herodotus,
Thucydides, *AP*, and Ps.-Plato, *Hipparchus*, cf. M. Hirsch, *Klio* 20 (1926),
129, although her discussion deals with literature rather than history.

28. (p. 89) Cf. my article *WSt* 1956, 57=*PI* 253, also *Historia* I (1950),
530=*PI* 264. I cannot really maintain the view that it was perhaps the
Alcmaeonids who created or at least favoured the legend. [This sentence
was written long before I read the paper by A. J. Podlecki criticizing my
earlier articles (*Historia* 1966, 129). I am not convinced by the rest of his
conclusions.] See also note 42.

29. (p. 89) According to Hdt. 5, 55 ff., both Harmodius and Aristogeiton
belonged to the family of the Gephyraei. It is likely that this was originally
a Boeotian family; cf. J. Toepffer, *Attische Genealogie* (Berlin 1889), 293.
There is in our sources no hint of any connexion of the Gephyraei with the
exiled opponents of the tyrants; but Herodotus, who was generally in
favour of the Alcmaeonids, overemphasizes their part in the act of liberation;
thus the *argumentum e silentio* does not prove much.

30. (p. 89) Hdt. 5, 63, 1; *AP* 19, 4. Another similar case: Hdt. 6, 66.

31. (p. 89) In *AP* 20, 1, it is true, Isagoras is called φίλος ὢν τῶν τυράννων
but that is probably a view resulting from Isagoras' opposition to Cleisthenes. See also note 49.

32. (p. 90) It was, at least partly, a struggle of the people against the noble
hetairiai, as Hdt. 5, 66, reveals by the unusual expression that Cleisthenes
τὸν δῆμον προσεταιρίζεται (translated into more common Greek by *AP*
20, 1).

33. (p. 90) This view is contested, but the fact that Cleomenes handed hostages from Aegina over to Athens (Hdt. 6, 73) makes it very plausible.

34. (p. 90) I therefore cannot accept theories (though I held one myself many years ago) of an exact chronology of the events, such as is attempted by F. Schachermeyr, *Klio* 1932, 334, and D. W. Knight, *Some Studies in Athenian Politics* (*Historia*, Einselschrift 15, 1970, 13). Pollux 8, 110, tells us that Cleisthenes' ten phylae were introduced under the archon Alcmaeon. His year is unknown, and may be any of the years between 507–506 and 502–501, except 504–503 when Acestorides was archon (Dion. Hal. 5, 37). Alcmaeon's name makes him a relative of Cleisthenes, possibly his brother or cousin (Schachermeyr, 336). Perhaps Cleisthenes, though as an ex-archon a member of the Areopagus, wanted to make sure that the highest official supported his ideas. He will have learned that much from Peisistratus. Cf. also Cadoux, 114 and note 35.

35. (p. 91) Apart from the general history leading to the reforms in Hdt. 5, 66. 70 ff., which tells us next to nothing about their exact nature, our only source is Aristotle, both *AP* 21 f., and *pol.* 1275b, 36. 1319b, 21. Modern works concerned with Cleisthenes include V. Ehrenberg, *Neugründer des Staates* (Munich 1925), esp. 60. 88; 'Origins of Democracy' (*Historia* I (1950), 537 = *PI* 286); H. T. Wade-Gery, *CQ* 1933 = *Essays*, 124; D. M. Lewis, *Historia* 1963, 22; W. G. Forrest (ch. III, note 20), esp. ch. 8; M. Ostwald (ch. III, note 53), part III; F. Ghirati, *I gruppi politici ateniesi fino alle guerre persiane* (Rome 1970). Most of the divergences among scholars are due to differing verdicts on Aristotle's sources (apart from Herodotus), on whether or not he relied on any documents (any νόμοι of Cleisthenes?). An impressive collection of essays by P. Lévêque and P. Vidal–Naquet, *Clisthène l'Athénien* (Paris 1964), shows sound common sense as well as bold imagination. The latter is stronger than the former in J. P. Verdant, *Mythe et pensée chez les Grecs* (Paris 1965). The view held by some German scholars (e.g. Berve, Schaefer) that it was all a matter of gaining personal power and creating a loyal body of followers (*Gefolgschaft*) does not do justice to the statesmanlike, rational ideas which dominated the work of Cleisthenes.

35a. (p. 92) Rightly stressed by W. E. Thompson, *Symb. Osloenses* 46 (1971).

36. (p. 92) Hdt. 5, 69, 2, must be read: δέκα τε δὴ φυλάρχους ἀπὸ τεσσέρων ἐποίησε, δέκα⟨χα⟩ δὲ καὶ τοὺς δήμους κατένειμε ἐς τὰς φυλάς. There never were exactly 100 demes. We have evidence from an inscription dated at least before 460 (*IG* I², 188) that the officials of the deme were accountable to the deme's assembly. New evidence on δημαρχία: S. Dow, *BCH* 89 (1965), 180. With the creation of the demes as the smallest

political units, the naucraries soon disappeared, though of this process we know nothing in detail.

37. (p. 92) The register is known from later sources as ληξιαρχικὸν γραμματεῖον. Cf. U. Kahrstedt, RE 12 (1925), 2430.

38. (p. 92) Aristotle (see note 35) speaks of φυλετεύειν or φυλοκρινεῖν (the latter originally had the meaning of finding out the origins of a man), and that Cleisthenes made new citizens out of 'foreign metics and slaves' (or perhaps 'foreigners, slaves (and) metics', though cf. Eur. Suppl. 892: μετοικοῦντας ξένους). Against mistaken interpretations of the ambiguous passages in Aristotle, especially by F. Wüst, Historia 1957, 176; 1964, 370; J. H. Oliver, Historia 1960, 503, see D. Kagan, Historia 1963, 41.

39. (p. 93) It is significant that on the many extant ostraca (see below, note 48) men of noble origin usually have also the father's name, and people of lower origin the demotikon. Although there are exceptions, and sometimes both expressions are used, the general tendency is clear. Plut. Sol. 12, 4 (cf. AP 1), speaks of three hundred aristocratic judges who condemned those who were 'cursed' (ἐναγεῖς) because of the murder of Cylon's followers; the accuser was Myron of Phleius. The 'three hundred' seem to date this to the time when Isagoras was in power (see p. 90). It is, however, quite uncertain whether the mentioning of Myron and his deme derives from an official document. Quite apart from the fact that in both sources the event belongs to Solon's or even earlier times, an official use of the demotikon in 508 (and by Cleisthenes' opponent!) is so unlikely that it is a mistake to conclude that Myron is the earliest example of the official use of Cleisthenes' order.

40. (p. 93) On the 'acrophonic' system, i.e. the system using the first letter of the numeral as sign (e.g. Π = πέντε, Δ = δέκα, Η = ηεκατόν, Χ = χίλιοι), see A. G. Woodhead, The Study of Greek Inscriptions (Cambridge 1959), 107. On the history of the decimal system in general cf. Lévêque and Vidal-Naquet (see note 35), 92 ff.

41. (p. 94) On the distribution of the trittyes and its meaning, scholars still disagree. The most important recent studies are by C. W. J. Eliot, 'The Coastal Demes of Attica', Phoenix Suppl. 5 (Toronto 1962), with a full bibliography, also Historia 1967, 279; D. M. Lewis, Historia 1963, 22; W. E. Thompson, Historia 1969, 1; Mnemosyne 1969, 137; P. J. Rhodes, Historia 1971, 385. See map 4.

42. (p. 96) Isonomia, Herodotus' 'most beautiful name of all' (3, 80, 6), was the word in use before 'democracy' became the current concept.

Cf. Ehrenberg, *RE* Suppl. VII, 293, *Historia* 1950, 530 = *PI* 279; G. Vlastos, *AJP* 1953, 337; Lévêque and Vidal-Naquet (note 35), 25; M. Ostwald (ch. III, note 53) who convincingly, at least so far as Athens is concerned (in spite of Ruschenbusch, *Gnomon* 1971, 414), dates the change-over from *thesmoi* to *nomoi*, to the time of Cleisthenes; but cf. also F. Quass, *Nomos und Psephisma* (Zetemata 55, 1971), 17, 98.

43. (p. 97) Whether this division of the year led to a special calendar year of 360 days (or leap years of 390) is disputed. The study of the Athenian calendar (the religious year was a lunar year) is so complicated, and such a battlefield for the specialists, that the ordinary historian would do better to keep out; the creation by Cleisthenes of a 'political' year, however, seems obvious.

44. (p. 97) A few sentences before, it is true, Aristotle says that it happened 'in the fifth year after this establishment (of the new order)'. If that expression means, as is likely, the main feature of Cleisthenes' reforms, the creation of the ten phylae (and not the last mentioned, ostracism), this would fix the archonship of Alcmaeon (see note 34) to 505–504. The ten phylae, at any rate, must have been established before the council of the Five Hundred, and that would imply that, in spite of all practical difficulties, the task was completed in, say, two years; then Alcmaeon belongs to 507–506. Cf. also the discussion by Cadoux, who, however, does not allow enough time for the task of reconstruction.

45. (p. 97) Cf. C. Pelekides, *Histoire de l'ephébie attique* (Paris 1962), esp. 78 f.

46. (p. 98) Since there can hardly ever have been four treasurers, it is unlikely that the phrase 'one from each phyle' was already Solon's; cf. *RE* XIII, 1470. On κλήρωσις ἐκ προκρίτων, and Solon's use of the lot, see above, ch. III, note 39.

47. (p. 99) Cf. R. J. Hopper, *The Basis of the Athenian Democracy*, Inaugural Lecture (Sheffield 1957).

48. (p. 99) Extant ostraca: *ML*, no. 21; cf. O. Broneer, *Hesperia* 7 (1938), 228; H. A. Thompson, *Hesperia* 17 (1948), 193; E. Vanderpool, *Hesperia*, Suppl. 8 (1949), 394, and vol. 17 (1948), 193. 21 (1952), 1; J. P. Barron, *JHS* 1964, 46, note 61; W. Peek, *Kerameikos* III (Berlin 1941), 51. Literary sources: *AP* 22, 3–6; *pol.* 1284a, 17. 1284b, 22. 1302b, 18. Harpocration *s.v.* Ἵππαρχος (*FGrH* 324 F6). Modern literature on ostracism and the date of its introduction, e.g., J. Cacopino, *L'ostracisme athénien* (Paris 1934²); Ehrenberg, *Gnomon* 1929, 9; *Historia* 1950, 543 = *PI* 293; A. Raubitschek, *AJA* 1951,

221; F. Jacoby, *FGrH* 324 F 6; K. J. Dover, *CP* 1963, 256; G. V. Sumner, *BICS* 11, 1964, 79; J. J. Keaney, *Historia* 1970, 1; E. Vanderpool, *Ostracism in Athens* (Cincinatti 1970); G. R. Stanton, *JHS* 1970, 180.

49. (p. 100) Isagoras could be taken as either the one or the other. While we know him as the leader of the anti-Alcmaeonid faction among the aristocrats and opponents of tyranny, *AP* 20, 1, calls him φίλος ὢν τῶν τυράννων, and Herodotus (5, 74, 1) tells us that Cleomenes wanted to make him a tyrant at Athens. This would, of course, run counter to the usual policy of Sparta, but it may have been in the mind of a man like Cleomenes who wanted a loyal supporter in power at Athens.

50. (p. 100) About the divergence between Aristotle and Androtion see the literature in note 48. The greatest difficulty for any explanation of the original measures is the fact that for the earliest ostracisms, those of the 'eighties, the political situation is anything but clear. Cf. p. 144.

51. (p. 101) It is just possible that there were phylarchs as there were demarchs, and Hdt. 5, 69, 2, speaks indeed of ten phylarchs having taken the place of the former four. But of the latter nothing whatsoever is known, and later in the fifth century phylarchs were introduced as squadron leaders of the cavalry, while the commanders of the tribal hoplite units were the taxiarchs. It seems likely that Herodotus wanted to compare the ten new commanders with the four old *phylobasileis* who, under the kings and later under the polemarch, had led the contingents of the four phylae. 'Strategi', it is true, means army commanders and not tribal ones, but if that etymology has any significance, it would make sense in Cleisthenes' constitution when boards of ten were regularly regarded as units.

52. (p. 101) There are gaps and mistakes in Herodotus' story of this war, or rather several wars. For a possible chronology see A. Andrewes, *BSA* 1937–7, 1; less convincing, N. G. L. Hammond, *Historia* 1955, 406; L. H. Jeffery, *AJP* 1962, 44.

53. (p. 101) The two distichs (Simonides, fr. 100 D. *ML*, no. 15) speak of the enemies as mere tribes (suitable perhaps for the Boeotians, but not for the Chalcidians), and their hostility is called *hubris*. There is an understandable tinge of contempt.

54. (p. 102) Hdt. 5, 89 ff. It seems possible that this is only a double of the earlier event, especially as it is used by Herodotus to produce long tirades against tyranny. The 'peace treaty' with Darius I was hardly more than an informal arrangement, not a legal treaty at all (against A. E. Raubitschek, *GRBS* 5 (1964), 151); it did not prevent Persia from supporting Hippias, nor Athens from sending ships to help the Ionian revolt.

55. (p. 102) Euboea: Hdt. 5, 77, 2. 6, 100, 1. Lemnos (and Imbros): Hdt. 6, 136 ff.; cf. V. Ehrenberg, *Aspects of the Ancient World* (Oxford 1946), 129 = *PI* 232. A bronze helmet found at Olympia has the inscription: Ἀθεναῖοι [τ]ὸν ἐγ Λέμν[ο]. Cf. E. Kunze, *Festschrift f. C. Weickert* (Berlin 1935), 7. Salamis: *SEG* 23, 1. A. J. Graham, *Proceedings of the Class. Assoc.* 1956, 28, thinks that the cleruchs who left Lemnos with Miltiades (Hdt. 6, 41, 4) might possibly have settled at Salamis. But the nature of the Salaminian settlers is still much disputed.

56. (p. 102) Cf. Thuc. 2, 23, 3. 4, 99. Oropus was again and again to change between the overrule of Athens and Thebes. Generally, cf. F. Gschnitzer, *Abhängige Orte im griechischen Altertum* (Munich 1958), 82.

57. (p. 103) Liturgies: cf. N. Lewis, *GRBS* 1960, 175.

58. (p. 104) For the history of Corinth down to *c.* 500 cf. E. Will, *Korinthiaka* (Paris 1955).

59. (p. 104) An inscription (*ML*, no. 16) shows a dedication to Hera by Aeaces, son of Brychon, certainly a relation of Polycrates and a man of importance; it proves that piracy (σύλη) was done with the consent of the state goddess. Cf. Ehrenberg, *JHS* 1937, 149 = *PI* 86, 2. Polycrates and Delos: cf. H. W. Parke, *CQ* 1946, 105.

60. (p. 104) Polycrates: T. Lenschau, *RE* XXI, 1726; A. Andrewes, *The Greek Tyrants* (London 1956), 117. Our main source is Herodotus (3, 39–60. 120–5. 144), but his account has been questioned by the ingenious, if doubtful, theory of J. P. Barron, *CQ* 1964, 210, and *The Silver Coins of Samos* (London, 1966), 37, who distinguishes between two tyrants of the same name, father and son. Among Polycrates' buildings were technical masterpieces, such as the water tunnel running through a mountain.

61. (p. 105) Cf. note 1.

62. (p. 105) The Greeks did not distinguish between the Medes and Persians; in fact, the first name was more common (cf. ch. V, note 46). The two peoples were, of course, almost identical in race, religion, and national customs. After the fundamental work done by Eduard Meyer and others on the rise of Persia, there is now a good short description by A. R. Burn, *Persia and the Greeks* (London 1962), ch. 2. Our main source is again Herodotus. In addition, we have occasional remarks in other Greek writers, and some oriental sources such as the royal Achaemenid inscription, Babylonian records, and some books of the Bible (Daniel, Isaiah).

63. (p. 107) The first quotation is from Guthrie (see below), the second from
G. Glotz, *Histoire grecque* I (Paris 1925, 554): '*la langue propre de la raison
humaine*'. Milesian philosophers; fragments in *DK*, cf. G. S. Kirk and J. E.
Raven, *The Pre-Socratic Philosophers* (Cambridge 1957). Naturally, their
doctrines have been studied in every history of philosophy. Recently:
W. K. C. Guthrie, *A History of Greek Philosophy*, vol. 1–3 (Cambridge 1962–
69); E. Bréhier, *The Hellenic Age* (Chicago 1963). Cf. also S. Luria, *Anfänge
griechischen Denkens* (Berlin 1963), and R. Schottländer, *Früheste Grund-
sätze der Wissenschaft bei den Griechen* (Berlin 1964) (both overstressing the
materialist point of view); D. R. Dicks, *JHS* 1966, 26. Very clear and helpful
is the short book by J.-P. Vernant, *Les origines de la pensée grecque* (Paris
1962).

63a. (p. 108) Cf. K. v. Fritz, *Die griech. Geschichtsschreibing* (Berlin 1967), 1,
79; 2, 331.

64. (p. 108) Hecataeus: *FGrH* 1. *RE* 7, 2667. Cf. also L. Pearson, *Early
Ionian Historians* (Oxford 1939), ch. 2. v. Fritz (last note), ch. III. Hecataeus is
the link connecting Hesiod's *Theogony* with the later histories; his personal
claim as to the meaning of his work and the truth he has to tell is, although a
legacy of the epics, the ancestor of all modern prefaces.

65. (p. 109) Scylax: Hdt. 4, 44; cf. 3, 102. See Jacoby's commentary on
FGrH 1 F 294. 295. On the connexions between Persia and the Greek world
see various articles in *La Persia e il mondo greco-romano* (Accad. dei Lincei
353, Rome 1966) (English or French résumés).

66. (p. 109) Darius I: see A. T. Olmstead, *History of the Persian Empire*
(Chicago 1948). The view that he created taxation districts different from the
satrapies seems unlikely. The relationship between the king and a satrap is
well illustrated by an inscription (*ML*, no. 12), a letter of Darius to Gadatas,
satrap of Ionia. In this case the king interfered in favour of a Greek sanctuary;
cf. Ehrenberg, *Ost und West* (Brünn 1935), 100, also F. Lochner in W.
Brandenstein and M. Mayrhofer, *Handbuch des Altpersischen* (Wiesbaden
1964), 91.

67. (p. 110) The story (Hdt. 4, 136 ff.) that Miltiades, the ruler of the
Chersonese, advised his fellow generals, though in vain, to destroy the
bridge and thus the Persian army, and therefore had to flee to Greece,
sounds very much like a double of his flight almost twenty years later.

68. (p. 111) It was from a combination of ethnological knowledge and
criticism of traditional religion that he could maintain the view that every
race, whether man or animal, would represent their gods in their own
images (fr. 14 ff.).

69. (p. 112) frs. 2, 3. 'But the first inference was not *cogito ergo sum* but *cogito, ergo est quod cogito*'; cf. Guthrie (note 63), 2, 20.

69a. (p. 113) To the Orphics, cf. W. K. C. Guthrie, *Orpheus and Greek Religion* (Cambridge 1935).

70. (p. 114) Plat. *Phaedo* 69c: ναρθηκοφόροι μὲν πολλοί, βάκχοι δέ τε παῦροι. To the whole question of the 'religious revolution' of the sixth century cf. the fundamental work by E. R. Dodds, *The Greeks and the Irrational* (Paperback, Boston 1957).

71. (p. 114) Cf. J. Defradas, *Les thèmes de la propagande delphique* (Paris 1954). (Review by H. Berve, *Gnomon* 1956, 174). The material about the Delphic oracle is fully dealt with by H. W. Parke and E. W. Wormell, *The Delphic Oracle* (Oxford 1956[2]).

72. (p. 114) Aeschines 2, 115. 3, 109 f. Cf. V. Ehrenberg, *The Greek State* (London 1962[2]), 110.

73. (p. 115) N. G. L. Hammond, *History of Greece*, 170.

74. (p. 115) Cf. A. D. Nock, *Proc. Amer. Philos. Ass.* 1942, 472.

75. (p. 116) Cf. T. J. Dunbabin, *The Western Greeks* (Oxford 1948); A. Schenk v. Stauffenberg, *Trinakria* (Munich 1963); J. Boardman, *The Greeks Overseas* (London 1964), 175; M. I. Finley, *The History of Sicily, Ancient Sicily* (London 1968). See also the periodical Κώκαλος (Palermo 1955 ff.). For Spain see, e.g., Rhys Carpenter, *The Greeks in Spain* (Bryn Mawr 1925).

76. (p. 117) P. E. Arias and M. Hirmer, *Spina* (Munich 1958).

77. (p. 118) Stauffenberg (see also *Historia* 1960, 181) seems to overestimate the importance and the consequences of the adventurous career of Dorieus. In particular, I cannot believe in a powerful official policy of Sparta in the west. See *HZ* 200 (1965), 370. A different chronology and emphasis on the rôle of Dorieus' half-brother Leonidas: V. Merante, *Historia* 1970, 272.

78. (p. 119) The history of Carthage cannot be treated here; in general cf. B. H. Warmington, *Carthage* (London 1960). For all details the fundamental work is S. Gsell, *Histoire ancienne de l'Afrique du Nord*, vols. 1–4 (Paris 1912–20).

79. (p. 119) Tartessus, according to recent research not identical with the Tarshish of the Old Testament, was a kind of Cockaigne country to the Greeks, but the trade (especially silver, and tin from Cornwall) was very real, and it seems (Hdt. 4, 152) that the Greeks were first in reaching Tartessus (in the bay of Gades). Cf. A. Schulten, *Tartessos* (Hamburg 1950[2]); Rhys Carpenter, *AJA* 1948, 474.

80. (p. 120) Herodotus tells us on various occasions that the Asiatic Greeks knew of Sardo (Sardinia) as a possible place for emigration (1, 170, 2. 5, 124. 6, 2). Histiaeus even promised to conquer it for Darius (5, 106).

81. (p. 120) Thuc. 4, 24. 6, 62. Cf. V. Burr, *Nostrum Mare* (Stuttgart 1932), 73.

V · THE WARS FOR FREEDOM

1. (p. 123) Cf. K. H. Waters, *Historia* 1970, 504; D. Hegyi, *Das Altertum* 1971, 142.

1a. (p. 124) Hdt. 5, 35, tells the famous story of the slave on whose shaved head Histiaeus had tattooed his message. If it is not historical, it certainly is a good tale.

2. (p. 124) Who warned Naxos? Herodotus says it was the Persians. Most unlikely; much better to assume (with Grundy) that Aristagoras himself did it – if indeed he wanted to start a revolt and would need Greek help. Otherwise, it may have been some of his enemies – but who were they? Chronology of the years after 500: N. G. L. Hammond, *Historia* 4 (1955), 385, though only in parts convincing; for the later years cf. L. H. Jeffery *AJP* 1962, 44. Sources for Ionian revolt; apart from Hdt., bks. 5–6, Diodorus, bk. 10 (fragments only), 19 ff. General works on the Persian wars: G. B. Grundy, *The Great Persian War* (London 1901); A. R. Burn, *Persia and the Greeks* (London 1962); C. Hignett, *Xerxes' Invasion of Greece* (Oxford 1963); for the earlier events see his Prolegomena. These books are henceforth quoted by author's name only.

3. (p. 126) It is unlikely that Cleomenes refused simply because of the distance from the Aegean to Susa (Hdt. 5, 50), though to inquire about it was a shrewd question. Aristagoras can never seriously have had the idea of marching as far as Susa. The story provided a good opportunity for Herodotus (5, 52 ff.) to display his exact knowledge of the 'royal road'.

4. (p. 126) Burn, 199, points out that Aegina kept quiet, largely from fear of Athens and Eretria. That will have been one of many inter-state tensions of the moment. Plutarch, *de malign. Her.* 24, 861C, mentions a historian, otherwise unknown and probably Hellenistic, Lysanias of Mallos, who described a victorious campaign of Eretria against Cyprus – an event which, if historical, would belong to the first year of the revolt. But it remains obscure why Herodotus should have omitted this incident; for the omission has nothing to do with his bias against the Ionians, and a campaign against

Cyprus would have explained why Eretria sent such a small squadron to Ionia.

5. (p. 126) Cf. L. Huber, 'Herodots Homerverständnis'. *Synusia, Festgabe f. W. Schadewaldt* (Pfullingen 1965), 37.

6. (p. 127) We shall have more to say about the contrast of Greeks and barbarians. Cf. the last section of this chapter, esp. 178 ff.

7. (p. 127) Cf. P. Gardner, *JHS* 1911, 151. 1913, 105; C. T. Seltman, *Greek Coins* (London 1954²), 87; *BMC Ionia*, xxiv. The question of an 'Ionian' coinage, however, is still in dispute; cf. M. O. B. Caspari, *JHS* 1916, 102, and the opinion of E. S. G. Robinson, quoted by Burn, 197, 3.

8. (p. 128) It is, of course, a later construction that Cleisthenes invented ostracism for his sake (*AP* 22, 4). Cf. above, p. 99.

9. (p. 128) Either version is purely hypothetical; but the latter is the more likely in retrospect, in view of the history of the following decade. Cf. V. Ehrenberg, *Ost und West* (Brünn 1935), 112, also G. Glotz, *Histoire grecque* II (Paris 1931), 29; F. Schachermeyr, *HZ* 172 (1951), 7.

10. (p. 129) The story in the chronicle of Lindos (*FGrH* III B, 532, p. 512) of a siege of Lindos on Rhodes by the Persians, and the miracle that saved the city, is of doubtful historical value. If it refers to a real event, the date is uncertain; modern scholars differ between 495 (before the battle of Lade) and 490 (before Marathon).

11. (p. 130) Herodotus' much-discussed reference to Artaphrenes' assessment of tribute (6, 42, 2) – ἀεὶ ἔτι καὶ ἐς ἐμέ – has, according to the explanation, surprising but largely convincing, by O. Murray, *Historia* 1966, 142, nothing to do with the later tributes paid to Athens, but was an internal Persian matter.

12. (p. 131) There is no reason to place the event (with Beloch and others) on the return journey in late autumn, simply because Hdt. 6, 44, 3, speaks of ῥῖγος in the sea water. The storm was the usual 'etesiae', which could be cold enough, and the shipwrecked swimmers in the water would easily submit to the cold. Cf. H.-U. Instinsky, *Hermes* 84 (1956), 477 = *Herodot*, ed. W. Marg (München 1962), 471

13. (p. 131) I always had some doubts about Themistocles being first archon as early as 493-2, though I still misunderstood Thuc. 1, 93, 3. (To invent another Themistocles [Gomme, p. 262. P. Bucknell, *L'antiquité class.* 1970, 427 ff.] seems not a satisfactory solution). Now, Chr. W. Fornara, *Historia* 1971, 534 ff., has shown that Thucydides does not

necessarily speak of archonship; the date in Dion. Hal. 6, 34, 1 is probably mistaken, Themistocles undoubtedly held some office then year by year, and probably started building the Peiraeus harbour, though that work was finished much later. What kind of office Themistocles held in the nineties, we do not know (ἐπιμελητὴς τῶν νεωρίων?). If he was ὑδάτων ἐπιστάτης (Plut. *Them.*. 31, 1), that is to say, held the important office of τῶν κρηνῶν ἐπιμελητής (cf. *AP* 43, 1. *Syll.*³, 281), this would have nothing to do with the Peiraeus.

14. (p. 132) Herodotus knows nothing of the poetess Telesilla, who, according to later sources, played the part of a bellicose maiden. However, as he (6, 77) records the obscure oracle 'when the female will defeat the male,' it seems likely that some story of a similar kind was known in his time. Differently: W. G. Forrest, *CQ* 1960, 221.

15. (p. 133) It is, of course, possible that the whole story of the envoys is an invention, though it is not simply the same story as that of the later embassies. We can assume that envoys were indeed sent out before 490, according to Persian custom and in conformity with the position, e.g., of Aegina, but no detail is certain. The meaning of the story in Hdt. 7, 133, is that the envoys were thrown into deep holes, probably wells, to get their earth and water there; but by naming the one βάραθρον (which existed only at Athens) and the other just φρέαρ, the point of the story seems spoiled. With the Spercheius and Bulis story following and the anti-Athenian tendency, the whole seems a purely Spartan story (137, 1: ὡς λέγουσι Λακεδαιμόνιοι).

16. (p. 134) Hdt. bk. 6 is almost the only source, though there are occasional passages of possible relevance in Plutarch, Pausanias, and others.

17. (p. 134) Cf. K. J. Beloch, *Griech. Geschichte* II 2 (1916²), 79, whose scepticism seems in this case to have hit the truth. The first who clearly rejected the numbers of the armies and fleets in the Persian wars, as recorded in Herodotus and later writers, was H. Delbrück (see note 48).

18. (p. 135) Cf. Hdt. 1, 171. 2, 1. 3, 1.

19. (p. 135) The latter is the view of an over-ingenious article by F. Schachermeyr, *HZ* 172 (1951), 1. Valid objections also by K. Kraft, *Hermes* 1964, 153.

20. (p. 135) The view expressed by several modern scholars that the Persians divided their forces – Datis landing in Attica, while Artaphrenes attacked Eretria – is untenable; cf. e.g., Burn, 238, 5.

21. (p. 137) The union of mountain, plain, and sea is frequent in Greece, though not always in such perfect harmony as that which Byron expressed in two famous (today almost hackneyed) lines:

> The mountains look on Marathon,
> And Marathon looks on the sea.

For the topography of the plain of Marathon and the battle see, after Grundy, 163, the detailed exploration by W. K. Pritchett, *University of California Publications in Class. Archaeology* IV (1960), 137. Among the important points he makes is that there was no small marsh (Brexiza) in antiquity between the sea and the road to Athens, that the course of the Charadra cannot be fixed for the time of the battle, that the Heracleum was at the north end of Mt Agrielki (S. Demetrius), and not up in the Vrana Valley, that the final Athenian position was either between Mt Kotroni and Mt Agrielki, or (more likely, as I think) on a slightly elevated level along the foothills of Agrielki, south-east of the Herakleion. See map 6.

22. (p. 137) Thucydides calls the temporary commander, with other strategi at his side, πέμπτος αὐτός, δέκατος αὐτός; cf. Gomme, to 1, 46, 2. In general, cf. M. H. Jameson, *TAPA* 86 (1955), 63, esp. 79; K. J. Dover, *JHS* 1960, 61; also V. Ehrenberg, *AJP* 66 (1945), 115.

23. (p. 138) Fourth-century sources know of the decree proposed by Militiades in the assembly; cf. Dem. 19, 303, and in particular Aristot. *Rhet.* 1411a, 9: . . . ἔφη δεῖν ἐξιέναι τὸ Μιλτιάδου ψήφισμα. There seems no serious reason why we should doubt the authenticity of this decree.

24. (p. 138) There is, however, a tradition (Paus. 4, 23, 6. Plat. *Laws* 692 d. 698d. Strab. 8, 362), perhaps not to be neglected, though by no means certain, that Sparta at that time was involved in another Messenian revolt; cf. L. H. Jeffery, *JHS* 1949, 26; Burn, 272. The small number of Spartiates (2,000) who arrived after the battle seems to strengthen that argument; but H. T. Wade-Gery, *ASAI* 289, makes it very likely that there never was a Messenian war in 490 B.C. The full moon was probably that of August or perhaps of September. The later story of the same 'Marathon runner', bringing the news of victory to Athens and then falling down dead, is romantic invention.

25. (p. 139) This would be what J. H. Schreiner, *Proceedings of Cambridge Philol. Soc.* 1970, in a clever attempt at explaining our diverse evidence, calls battle A, distinct from the decisive final battle B. I prefer to speak of two phases of the same battle, but I doubt whether Callimachus found the time before final action and his death to make a dedication (*ML*, no. 18).

The best description of the campaign and its topography is by N. G. L. Hammond, *JHS* 1968, 13.

26. (p. 139) Suda: χωρὶς ἱππεῖς, meaning 'those who break up the battle formation'. The passage makes sense, as A. W. Gomme, loc. cit., F. Schachermeyr, loc. cit., 21, and Burn, 247, have shown. The latter (after Hammond) points out that ἀνελθόντας ἐπὶ τὰ δένδρα does probably not mean that the Ionians climbed up trees but that they came up to the trees near the battle line, perhaps some defence work made by the Athenians. The explanation of the proverb must be old, though we do not know when it was coined, nor when it was first used in reference to Marathon. A wholly different view on the part played by the Persian cavalry is held by N. Whatley in an article written in 1920 and published as late as *JHS* 84 (1964), 119. Other sources such as Nepos (*Milt.* 4 f.), even though he may depend on Ephorus, or Pausanias' description of the painting in the Stoa Poikile (1, 15, 3), do not, as I believe, add anything historically reliable. Cf. also next note.

27. (p. 140) Their position on the map (p. 136) is only *exempli gratia*. Pausanias (1, 32, 7) speaks, it is true, of many Persians being driven into the λίμνη τὰ πολλὰ ἑλώδης, as it appeared in the Stoa Poikile. It is possible that, in a panic, some of the Persians did flee in the direction of their former landing beach or were simply hunted by the Greeks into the marches; but it seems impossible that an experienced soldier such as Datis left the dangerous outlet along the *schoinia* as the only way of retreat.

28. (p. 140) Hdt. 6, 112: δρόμῳ, naturally not at the double or running, and not for the whole distance.

29. (p. 140) Hdt. 6, 113–15, with more details.

30. (p. 141) In this context we may mention the curious 'Song on Datis' (Δάτιδος μέλος) (Aristoph. *Peace* 289), and the interesting and bold attempt by A. E. Raubitschek in *Charites* (E. Langlotz gewidmet) (Bonn 1957), 234, at an explanation by referring to the attacks on the Alcmaeonids.

31. (p. 141) Διὶ Ἀθεναῖοι Μέδον λαβόντες. Cf. E. Kunze, Ἀρχαιολογ. Δελτίον, 17 (1964), 117 and pl. 133b. *SEG* 22 (1967), no. 346.

32. (p. 141) Of the so-called Marathon epigrams (cf. the literature in *SEG* 21, no. 117, 22, no. 63; *ML*, no. 26; cf. also K-W. Welwei, *Historia* 1970, 295; W. C. West, *GRBS* 1970, 271) the first most likely refers to Salamis, while the second seems a later addition, referring to Marathon. I cannot accept Schreiner's attempt (see note 25) at referring both epigrams to a land and sea battle near Phaleron.

33. (p. 142) It is not justifiable to draw conclusions for 489 from the fact that in 480 the western Cyclades sent ships to join the Greek fleet.

34. (p. 143) For an explanation of the Parian expedition, as far as it can be explained, see my *Aspects of the Ancient World* (Oxford 1946), 137. Burn 259 f., 265 f., in my view, relies too much on secondary and anecdotic source material. The poverty of Paros at that time is also sufficient reason not to accept the view (A. French, *The Growth of the Athenian Economy* (London 1964), 75) that the aim of the expedition was simply plunder.

35. (p. 144) On the question of the introduction of ostracism see above, p. 99.

36. (p. 145) It is hardly possible to sort out the changing position of Aegina in her relation to Sparta or Athens. Valuable attempts, e.g., by A. Andrewes, *BSA* 1936–7, 1, and D. M. Leahy, *CQ* 1954, 232.

37. (p. 146) This was clearly a κλήρωσις ἐκ προκρίτων, though the number of 500 seems very doubtful. Cf. E. Badian, *Antichthon* 5 (1971), 1, an ingenious, if not entirely convincing, reconstruction.

38. (p. 147) Cf. G. M. A. Richter, *Greek Portraits* I (*Coll. Latomus* 20 (1955)), pl. 1; H. Lichtermann, *Gymnasium* 71 (1964), 348.

39. (p. 147) The number of ostraca found by archaeologists gives little evidence as to the actual results of the voting. Themistocles heads the list, though many sherds with his name will belong to later years; some unknown names appear frequently, especially that of Callixenus (cf. G. A. Stamires and E. Vanderpool, *Hesperia* 1950, 376), while Hipparchus, Megacles, and Xanthippus are rare.

40. (p. 147) Cf. A. E. Raubitschek, *GRBS* 1964, 152. Perhaps the story of the shield signal (above, p. 140) was due to a similar misconception.

41. (p. 148) It is unfortunately not known to what ostracism the 'prefabricated' ostraca belong which were dumped in an old well. They cannot be imagined without some organized group action, but it seems more likely that they belong to the 'seventies rather than the 'eighties. Cf. my *The People of Aristophanes* (New York 1962³), 340, 4.

42. (p. 148) On Themistocles' naval law cf. J. Labarbe, *La loi navale de Thémistocle* (Paris 1957), a learned and ingenious, but on the whole unconvincing, attempt to harmonize all different traditions. For Athenian naval policy in general cf. M. Amit, *Athens and the Sea* (*Coll. Latomus* 74 (1965)).

42a. (p. 150) Cf. K. Meister, *Historia* 1970, 607, although in my view Aristotle's argument (*poet.* 1459a, 24 ff.) that the naval battle of Salamis and the

land battle of Himera "had not the same aim", is not a decisive argument
against an agreement (cf. Jacoby, *FGrH* 2C, 88).

43. (p. 150) It is an attractive idea of Hignett's (p. 97) that the timber for
the fleet came from South Italy, since the usual sources, such as Macedon,
Thrace, or even Asia Minor, were all in Persian hands.

44. (p. 150) It seems that his Zoroastrianism, with its worship of Ahura-
Mazda, was somehow distorted by the teaching of the magi. Cf. R. C.
Zaehner, *The Teachings of the Magi* (London, 1950).

45. (p. 151) It is a question of debate to what extent, if any, the new confederacy made use of the Peloponnesian League, which by then was fully
established, as a kind of basic organization. I believe that, with Sparta as
προστάτης in command, a certain dependence on the earlier organization
was more or less unavoidable. Nevertheless, the confederacy was – or at
least aimed at being – a brotherhood in arms. Its hegemony was a purely
military matter, and the attempt by Athens at gaining at least the naval
leadership should not be regarded as a manoeuvre which led to a new
organization without Sparta (against the interesting *tour de force*, by H. D.
Meyer, *Historia* 1963, 405). The alleged demand of Gelon to be in command
of all Greek forces, if he came to help the motherland, is either pretext or
mere invention. He needed all his forces at home.

46. (p. 151) The only attempt of which I know at explaining the fact that
the Greeks spoke frequently of the Medes when thinking of the Persians,
and that they used only the words μηδίζειν and μηδισμός for collaboration with the Persians, was made by J. L. Myres in *Poetry and Life*. Studies
presented to Gilbert Murray (Oxford 1936), 98. He traces the matter back
to the time when in the seventh century Miletus was allied with the Medes
against Lydia; it became an expression of treason when later the Ionians
betrayed Croesus. If this sounds rather far-fetched, there seems to be no
other explanation.

47. (p. 152) Main sources: Hdt., bks. 7–9. Diodorus, bk. 11. There are
also the Persian sources for the peoples of the empire; cf. G. Walser,
Die Völkerschaften auf den Reliefs von Persepolis (Berlin 1966).

48. (p. 152) The wild exaggeration of the Persian numbers (cf. also note 17)
may reflect genuine Greek fears or, on the other hand, later glorification of
victory. The first sharp reaction against Herodotus' figures came from
a German military historian, H. Delbrück (*Die Perserkriege und die Bur-
gunderkriege*, 1881; later: *Geschichte der Kriegskunst* I³ (Berlin 1920)). He
overstated his case, but he made reasonable guesses possible. For a moderate

estimate cf. F. Maurice, *JHS* 50 (1930), 210. In general see Burn, 322; Hignett, 40. 345.

49. (p. 153) Cf. W. K. Pritchett, *AJA* 65 (1961), 375: 'a much more feasible military way than any of the possible alternatives'. Mardonius, after all, knew the country, and naturally his advice was taken.

50. (p. 153) Cf. H. D. Westlake, *JHS* 56 (1936), 12.

51. (p. 153) The way by sea was quicker, and the Greeks always preferred it to travelling overland. Fear of the doubtful attitude of Boeotia can hardly have been the reason, though Halus was chosen as the port of landing because of the friendly disposition of the people there.

52. (p. 154) It seems to me out of the question that the expedition was made simply as a fake display of goodwill; in that case the prompt return would have had the strongest possible opposite effect, and not only on the Thessalians.

53. (p. 154) There were other oaths and decisions actually invented in a similar way, especially when the curiously patched-up story of Delphi's policy was involved.

54. (p. 154) The Cretans later made a Delphic oracle the excuse for their refusal to help (Hdt. 7, 169).

55. (p. 154) A significant anecdote (Plut. *Cimon* 5, 2) tells us that a group of young noblemen under the leadership of Cimon, son of Miltiades, deposited the reins of their horses on the Acropolis, as a symbol that it was no longer the time for cavalry fighting, and they joined the hoplites on board ship.

56. (p. 155) The gap of 900 between the two figures has been filled either by perioeci or even by emancipated helots; of the latter several hundred (non-emancipated) were in the battle (cf. Hdt. 7, 229. 8, 25, 1), but they would not count among the troops, although many were killed (Hdt. 8, 25, where the figure of 4,000 dead, most of them obviously from the last day's fighting, is quite unreliable). It seems doubtful whether the round and rhetorical number in Simonides is reason enough to come to such conclusions as those just mentioned, but Isocrates and Diodorus actually mention 1,000 Lacedaemonians. A. Daskalakis, *Problèmes historiques autour de la bataille des Thermopyles* (Paris 1962), takes 700 perioeci for granted and tries to explain why Herodotus never mentions them. I do not think his arguments (Sparta's pride in her citizens, etc.) are fully convincing, though his book as a whole is sound and helpful. A few hundred perioeci may, of course, have been sent out with the Spartiates. The latter were all men with

sons living (Hdt. 7, 205, 2) – sufficient proof that Sparta realized the formidable danger which the small force had to face.

57. (p. 155) Diod. 11, 4, 6 f., speaks also of 1,000 Locrians and adds 1,000 Malians, but his figures are generally open to doubt, and the Malians, whose country was not protected by the defenders, are unlikely to have been able to provide any troops.

58. (p. 156) The Themistocles decree was first edited, with translation and commentary, by M. H. Jameson, *Hesperia* 29 (1960), 198; cf. *Hesperia* 31 (1962), 310; now: *ML*, no. 23. Much has been written about this inscription, largely on the question (wrongly put, I believe) whether it is a forgery or genuine. Cf. *SEG* 24, no. 276. 25, no. 376. The arguments against forgery are particularly strong, but they do not confirm that all essential points are historically true; cf. next note.

59. (p. 156) Without going into too much detail (which would be out of place here) it may suffice to state that in my view, which I share with others: (1) The inscription, dating from the early third century B.C., goes back to a text of the fourth century (cf. Dem. 19, 303). (2) This text was neither a forgery nor a literary transmission of the original of 480, as the Greeks never knew literalness in that sense. (3) The history of the text cannot be fully reconstructed, though it is likely that it was included in Craterus' collection of decrees (third century). However, B. D. Meritt, *Greek Historical Studies* (Cincinnati 1962), 28, and J. P. Barron, *JHS* (1964), 42 have made it clear that the use of the expression (v. 4 f.) of Athena as Ἀθηνῶν μεδέουσα (perhaps east Greek for Polias) goes back in Athens to at least 424 (Aristoph. *Eq.* 585. 763), and probably to *c.* 450 (*SEG* 10, no. 17, cf. 25, no. 13). This makes it easy to accept parts of the decree as genuine. Even so, it must have undergone considerable 'editing', and probably more than that. (4) Apart from a number of differences from Herodotus, there seem to be two major difficulties. The first is that by June 480, the assumed date of the decree – unless that date is mistaken and the decree really belongs to the winter 481–480 – the Athenian fleet should not yet have had its captains and crews; therefore practically no time was left for training. The number of only ten ἐπιβάται on each trireme, on the other hand, seems at first unbelievably small; but cf. H. Berve, *SB München* 1961, 16; Jameson, *Historia* 1963, 385. The second difficulty lies in the fact that the evacuation should have started before Artemisium, while our literary tradition has no trace of that date (or is there one in Hdt. 8, 142, 3?). At that moment the evacuation – except perhaps for most of the women and children, though even that would contradict Hdt. 8, 41 – would have been a panic-measure, and no Greeks would ever have been sent to Thermopylae if Athens and Themis-

tocles had taken such desperate action. Incidentally, I cannot believe that either the Tempe expedition or the defence at Thermopylae and Artemisium were only fake actions to show some goodwill, and were never intended to be taken seriously (Schachermeyr, *ÖJh* 46 (1961-3), 169). It would, at any rate, mean that the defence at Thermopylae–Artemisium was nothing but a delaying action. That seems to be refuted by the leadership of a Spartan king at Thermopylae, and by the fighting strength of the Greek fleet at Artemisium, which withdrew only after Thermopylae was lost. Cf. also J. A. S. Evans, *Historia* 1969, 389.

60. (p. 156) This point has rightly been made by J. F. F. Lazenby, *Hermes* 92 (1964), 264.

61. (p. 156) That must have happened in spring 480 (cf. J. Labarbe (note 42) 90). When Aristeides in the battle of Salamis conquered Psyttaleia, he was in command of a strong hoplite force. He may have returned earlier, though it is doubtful whether he had been elected *strategos*. The reference in the Themistocles decree to the ostracized men as first having been confined to Salamis seems an invention on account of the Aristeides story.

62. (p. 157) I do not think we can be sure whether the army or the fleet was first in position. If the fleet moved faster, it may have been ready later. The essential thing is that they were both there when the Persians arrived.

63. (p. 157) In the short description of the two battles I have not discussed the topographical questions, although they are important for the reconstruction; an extensive discussion can be found in every book on the Persian war, ever since Grundy.

64. (p. 157) It will have taken a few days to move the whole fleet; it assembled at various places along the coast, from Meliboea in the north to Cape Sepias in the south. For the actions of both armies and navies, Herodotus (7, 179-228. 8, 6-25) maintains a simultaneity of events, a timetable which does not completely cohere. Several scholars have tried to trace Herodotus' mistake or mistakes, but no solution has been generally accepted. Historically the question is quite unimportant; the essential thing is that the course of events is generally parallel, beginning on the day (no. 1) when the Persian fleet finally left Therma, and ending with the day (9) of the final struggle at Thermopylae and the retreat in the evening of the Greek fleet from Artemisium.

65. (p. 157) This is the only reasonable explanation for the temporary withdrawal, and not the story in Hdt. 7, 183, about a panic among the Greeks (one of his favourite, often repeated, tales). There is, however, no reason why the withdrawal itself should be doubted.

66. (p. 157) The figure of 200 is probably too high, but to maintain that the whole diversion did not take place (thus, after Beloch, Hignett, 386) seems unreasonable. It was, after all, an obvious strategic move. It is equally obvious that the Persian losses so far had not been too heavy to prevent the diversion.

67. (p. 157) There are good remarks by a nautical expert on the battle of Artemisium in A. Köster, *Studien zur Geschichte des antiken Seewesens. Klio*, Beiheft 32 (1934), chs. 4–6.

68. (p. 158) Ephialtes has gone down in history as the prototype of a traitor. Of course, he was a traitor, but to understand him we must see him as a 'collaborator' under foreign occupation. There were many, governments as well as private persons, in a similar position, and Ephialtes had at least the excuse that he 'liberated' his homeland from an oppressive occupation army. The part played, e.g., by the former Spartan king Demaratus as Xerxes' adviser – a frank and honest adviser at that – shows that the word treason does not really fit the situation. Ephialtes was responsible for one of the most tragic events of the war, and that gave his action the most sinister significance. We have only to remember the policy of Delphi, in order to be careful with the term treason. It was the legend of succeeding years that made the Persian war a national war, Thermopylae the greatest sacrifice, and Ephialtes' deed high treason.

69. (p. 158) The figure of 10,000 is traditional for the 'Immortals', but they must have numbered very much less on this occasion.

70. (p. 158) A pretty detail, probably true, is mentioned by Hdt. 7, 218, namely that the Phocians heard the rustling of the leaves under the feet of the Persians before they could see them. The leaves could have fallen long before, but there may have been additional ones on account of the three days of storm.

71. (p. 159) He tries to confirm that by quoting (7, 220) a Delphic oracle that 'either Sparta will perish or one of her kings die'. This oracle was certainly made after the event.

72. (p. 159) A. Daskalakis, in the book mentioned note 56 (cf. *Studi Classici* 1964, 57), makes it clear that orderly withdrawal of an army was not against the Spartan *côde d'honneur*; but flight from the battlefield, and the danger of being slain from behind, definitely were. Cf. also J. A. S. Evans, *GRBS* 1964, 231.

73. (p. 159) Later evidence speaks of five stelae at Thermopylae (Strab. 9, 425), of which one recorded the Spartan seer Megistius (Hdt. 7, 228), one the Locrians, and one clearly the Thespians.

74. (p. 159) It is usually called the third naval encounter round Artemisium.

75. (p. 160) It is not impossible that it was only a band of plunderers who were dispersed by some Delphians sending a shower of rocks upon them from above (Grundy, 350).

76. (p. 161) According to *AP* 23, the Areopagus paid eight drachmas to each man boarding a ship. Aristotle makes this contribution to the victory at Salamis the beginning of the ascendancy of the Areopagus after the Persian wars. That makes the story suspect; but it may be true nevertheless, since the men probably had to buy food during the days of waiting. In a different story Cleidemus (*FGrH* 323 F 21; cf. F. Jacoby, *Atthis* (Oxford 1949), 75) tells us that the Gorgoneion from the statue of Athena was stolen, and Themistocles had all the baggage searched. This is a later 'democratic' invention directed against the Areopagus.

77. (p. 161) It is just as unlikely that 'the treasurers and priestesses' of the Themistocles decree were the only ones left. It seems that no clear knowledge about these people survived the war.

78. (p. 161) A different view is expressed by A. R. Hands, *JHS* 1965, 56.

79. (p. 161) Hdt. 9, 10, speaks of the eclipse in connexion with an intended advance of a Peloponnesian army under Cleombrotus, which then held the Isthmus, but was disbanded soon after. That must have happened shortly after the battle of Salamis when the Persians were no longer an immediate danger to the Peloponnese.

80. (p. 162) Hdt. 8, 52, says: ἐπὶ χρόνον συχνόν.

81. (p. 162) Other sources have the earlier date; cf. Burn, 436. Neither the place nor the purpose of the mole are certain; at any rate, it was never finished, and work probably stopped before much progress was made.

82. (p. 162) At least one single item of importance is preserved by Diodorus (11, 17), concerning the Egyptians who blocked the passage north of Salamis. This corresponds with Aeschylus, *Pers.* 368 (the third στοῖχος [?]), and it is possible that Ephorus, Diodorus' source, worked out a scheme based on Aeschylus. Cf. H. Bengtson, *Chiron* 1 (1971), 89. The manoeuvre of encirclement was necessary, while to dispatch a squadron to the channel east of Hag. Georgios (Hignett, 223) would have been risky indeed. There were ears to hear on Greek scout boats, and probably also on the island itself.

83. (p. 164) A. D. Papanikolaou, *RhM.* 1971, 217, defends the traditional figures of 310 and 1207 for the Greek and Persian fleets.

84. (p. 164) Against the identification (by Beloch and Hammond) of Psyttaleia with the island of Hag. Georgios deep in the narrows, see, e.g., W. K. Pritchett, *AJA* 63 (1959), 251, and Hignett, 396.

85. (p. 164) Why did the Persians wait till the Greeks were in formation? We do not know. It could be that they were waiting for a signal from Xerxes, who, from his throne, wanted to see the battle, and naturally in full daylight.

86. (p. 165) Cf. C. W. Fornara, *JHS* 1966, 51. There can be little doubt that the importance of this event has been greatly exaggerated by Aeschylus (447 ff.), probably to point out, within the framework of his play, a disaster which did not concern the Persian fleet, which was mostly non-Persian, but the Persian élite itself. He does not mention Aristeides, just as he never mentions the name of Themistocles.

87. (p. 165) It is doubtful whether any Greek leader, even Themistocles, ever suggested that the fleet should advance to destroy the Hellespont bridges. Still more doubtful is (Hdt. 8, 109 f.) Themistocles' approach to Xerxes in order 'to have a safe retreat if mischance should befall him by the Athenians' – here speaks the Herodotus of the mid-century. When in spring 479 the fleet sailed as far as Delos, Herodotus (8, 132) described the eastern Aegean, which was still in Persian hands, as frightening ($\delta\epsilon\iota\nu\acute{o}\nu$) and unknown (!), and Samos as far off as the Pillars of Heracles ! – It was probably in connexion with the advance of the fleet to the Cyclades that a contemporary poet, Timocreon of Rhodes, blamed Themistocles for taking bribes (Plut. *Them.* 21 = fr. 1 D; cf. Hdt. 8, 111 f.). Greed for money was to become a repetitive item in the Themistocles story.

88. (p. 165) Herodotus (7, 166) records the view that the battle of Himera was on the same day as Salamis (Diod. 11, 24, as Thermopylae). This is the kind of synchronization the Greeks liked so much.

89. (p. 165) On Carthage and its rising power see B. H. Warmington, *Carthage* (London 1960).

90. (p. 166) The expedition is more extensively treated, if with many adornments, by Diod. 11, 20 f. Herodotus is mainly interested in Hamilcar's personal fate. Diodorus, born in Sicily and using the work of the sound Sicilian historian Timaeus, is here on the whole better than usual.

91. (p. 166) Corcyra, an important link on the sea route between east and west, was known for her non-commital attitude; her fleet, sixty ships strong and therefore of real importance, remained near the western coast

of the Peloponnese (Hdt. 7, 168). Croton, it is true, according to Hdt. 8, 47, the only state outside Greece to help, sent one ship to Salamis, under Phayllus, three times victor at the Pythia. It almost looks like a private enterprise. Anyway, Croton is not mentioned on the serpent column (*ML*, no. 27), just as indeed Seriphus and Pale (Hdt. 8, 46 ff. 9, 28. 31). See below note 103.

92. (p. 166) Cf. T. J. Dunbabin, *The Western Greeks* (Oxford 1948), 425.

93. (p. 167) There was, however, a dedication at Olympia by Acragas after a victory over Motye (Paus. 5, 25, 5), and the arms of Acragas appear on some west Sicilian coins (Dunbabin, loc. cit., 430). Greek influence will have expanded to the west after Himera.

94. (p. 167) Cf. Pind. *P.* 1, 72. *ML*, no. 29.

95. (p. 167) No attempt was made to send part of the fleet up the Euripus or round Euboea to harass, at least, Mardonius' supply lines. Probably the Greeks were not sure whether the Persian fleet might not embark on a new offensive; thus, all ships were needed to meet such an occasion.

96. (p. 168) Some time before these events the Greeks are reported to have sworn a common oath to fight the barbarians, which we know from fourth-century sources (Tod, no. 204. Burn, 512. Hignett, 460). The document cannot be genuine.

97. (p. 169) An attempt at interfering with the Peloponnesian vanguard in the Megarid (Hdt. 9, 14) came to nothing, if it ever took place or ever was more than a cavalry reconnaissance raid.

98. (p. 170) Artabazus, according to Hdt. 9, 66, fled from the battle with 40,000 men. Even if this figure included many non-combatants, no conclusion as to the total of Mardonius' army can be drawn from it. Equally irrelevant are the exaggerated figures, mentioned before the battle (Hdt. 9, 32), of 300,000 barbarians and about 50,000 Greeks, all these without the cavalry!

99. (p. 170) The story lacks point, for the next day there was no general attack, only cavalry assaults. Hdt. 9, 46 f., reports a twofold interchange of positions between Athenians and Lacedaemonians, caused by Alexander's message and followed up by corresponding moves in the Persian army. No modern rescue action can save that story.

100. (p. 171) The delay in the tactical withdrawal of the Spartans is explained by the story of Amompharatus, who, with his Pitanate *lochos*, refused to retreat. For its possible truth cf. Hignett, 328 f. See also v. Fritz 1, 271. The Athenians had been held up for a long time by enemy horsemen.

101. (p. 172) Herodotus' narrative is full of biased insinuations, largely of Athenian origin. As to Elis and Mantineia, cf. A. Andrewes, *Phoenix* 1952, 2.

102. (p. 172) Cf., e.g., Dorothy B. Thompson in *The Aegean and the Near East* (Studies for H. Goldman) (1956), 281.

103. (p. 172) *ML*, no. 27. *DSDA*, no. 130. The list of names provides some unanswerable questions; for certain omissions cf. note 91. The omission of other states, I believe, makes it more likely that the dedication was really for Salamis and Plataea, and not for the whole war; but no solution is completely satisfactory. Lemnos joined the Greeks at Artemisium (Hdt. 8, 11), Mantineia was at Thermopylae, but too late at Plataea (9, 77); the latter is also true of Elis. Samos fought at Mycale (9, 92. 103). With the exception of Elis, none of them is inscribed. Phocis, Locris, and Thebes fought at Thermopylae, but are not mentioned because at Plataea they sided with the enemy. Pausanias 5, 23, enumerates the corresponding dedication at Olympia of 'those Greeks who had fought at Plataea against Mardonius and the Medes', but he includes some of the islanders who fought only at Salamis. He mentions twenty-seven names instead of thirty-one at Delphi, though they appear roughly in the same order. Surprisingly, Pausanias does not mention Thespiae (cf. Hdt. 9, 30), and calls the Plataeans the only state from Boeotia. Elis (see above) could probably not be left out at Olympia, and thus entered also the list at Delphi.

104. (p. 173) Here, according to Hdt. 9, 106, a war council took place about the safety of the Ionians. The Peloponnesians suggested that all Ionians should emigrate and settle in seaports in Greece where the people had medized. The Athenians, claiming the Ionians as their colonists, refused to accept that senseless proposal. The story is probably apocryphal.

105. (p. 174) As should be clear from my text, I cannot share the view that Herodotus' last chapter shows that he did not finish his work. Another question is whether he had finally revised it; v. Fritz *l.c.* shows that gaps and contradictions remained. We are faced with a 'Herodotean question', regarding the composition of his work and his possible development.

106. (p. 174) A chapter in my book of 1935, *Ost und West*, deals with the generation of Marathon. The task sounds similar to the present one, but I hardly use the earlier paper now, partly because the new dating of Aeschylus' *Suppliants* (see note 111) has removed one of the main sources I used then, and partly because some of my views now differ from those I had thirty years ago. In a way I have set myself an impossible task. The 'war generation' includes people born, say, between 530 and 500, and living at any possible place. How can there be a common denominator, for instance,

for an Athenian who was fifty in 490 and a Spartan who was thirty in 480? I do not pretend to have found it. It is impossible to depict what is typical of fathers and sons, of Ionians and Dorians, of noblemen and commoners, of east and west. I shall only be able to show up some highlights, and try to put them in a more general framework. The Greeks themselves never had the idea of one particular generation that had lived through the two decades of 500–479. What they did realize was that things were never again the same after the wars.

107. (p. 174) Cf., in general, A. French, *The Growth of the Athenian Economy*, chs. 6 and 7.

108. (p. 175) For the question how far trade existed between Athens and Egypt when it was a Persian province cf. French, loc. cit., 191, note 9.

109. (p. 175) The greatest names are those of Sosias, the Brygos painter, and Duris; but there are others as well. Cf. P. E. Arias and M. Hirmer, *A History of Greek Vase Painting* (London 1962), pl. 108–59. In general cf. T. B. L. Webster, *Greek Art and Literature*, *530–400 B.C.* (Oxford 1939).

110. (p. 176) See my *People of Aristophanes*, 37. For a detailed description of the community's concern, even financially, for the theatre cf. H. C. Baldry, *The Greek Tragic Theatre* (London 1971), esp. ch. 4.

111. (p. 176) Until the discovery of a *didaskalia* (*P. Oxyrh.* 20, 2256), which puts the trilogy of the Danaids (of which the *Suppliants* is a part) after Sophocles' first victory (468), hardly anybody had doubted that the *Suppliants* was Aeschylus' earliest extant play, belonging to the 'eighties or even the 'nineties. Cf. now H. Lloyd-Jones, *L'antiquité class.* 33 (1964), 356.

112. (p. 176) Cf. *IG* II², 2318. Hill³, B 7, for the date of Pericles' choregy.

113. (p. 177) The only great attempt I know of to present a general picture, that by Ed. Meyer (*GdA* 3, bk. 2, ch. 3), deals with 'the effects of the war', that is, with events and conditions immediately afterwards. Actually he rightly includes, at least to an equal extent, the earlier movements from which those effects derive. Meyer's general views differ a good deal from those expressed in the text, but that is natural as we belong to two, very different, generations!

114. (p. 178) Cf. U. v. Wilamowitz-Moellendorff, *Sappho und Simonides* (Berlin 1913), 207; C. M. Bowra, *Greek Lyric Poetry* (Oxford 1961²), 345; W. Kierdorf, *Erlebnis und Darstellung der Perserkriege* (*Hypomnemata* 16, Göttingen 1966), 16 (see my review, *Gnomon* 1967, 517); A. J. Podlecki, *Historia* 1968, 257.

115. (p. 178) Cf. J. Jüthner, *Hellenen und Barbaren* (Leipzig 1923); *Entretiens Hardt*, vol. 8 (1961); H. C. Baldry, *The Unity of Mankind in Greek Thought* (Cambridge 1965). Thucydides (1, 3 f.) knew already all the essential facts.

116. (p. 178) Cf. H. Frisk, *Etymolog. griech. Wörterbuch* (Heidelberg 1960), s.v.

117. (p. 179) The quotation is the title of a fine chapter in A. Bonnard, *Greek Civilization*, vol. 2 (London 1959). For Pindar is still fundamental, though very subjective: U. v. Wilamowitz, *Pindaros* (Berlin 1923); very helpful, e.g. J. H. Finley, *Pindar and Aeschylus* (Cambridge, Mass. 1955). I have said something about Pindar in *PI* 337. C. M. Bowra, *Pindar* (Oxford 1964), is now the most comprehensive work, and a very sound one at that. Enough dates for the odes are certain (cf. Bowra, 406) to show the poet's progress as far as there was any. For *P*. 11 Bowra (402) pleads for a late date (454 instead of 474); the case seems as yet undecided.

118. (p. 179) Similar use of Hellas and the Hellenes in connexion with the games, e.g. Pindar, *P*. 11, 49. Bacchyl. 7, 7. 8, 22.

119. (p. 179) Marathon is mentioned three times in the extant poems of Pindar, each time only as a place of local games (*O*. 9, 89. 13, 110. *P*. 8, 79).

120. (p. 180) The dates of *I*. 5 and 8, which I mention in the following sentences, are not quite certain; cf. J. H. Finley, *HSt* 1958, 121. With *N*. 5 they all were written for the sons of the Aeginetan Lampon. I believe that *N*. 5 belongs before the great war (*c*. 483); the others reflect the events of 480 and 479, though we cannot be sure whether *I*. 5 was written before Plataea, as assumed by Bowra, 113.

121. (p. 181) Other relevant poems: Simonides' epigrams (whether genuine or imitations): 62–65. 88–96 D. Pindar, *I*. 5, 48. frs. 75–78 Snell. 63–66 Bowra. *P*. 1, 72. In a kind of apology Pindar says in 474 (*P*. 9, 90 ff.) that 'by action he has avoided silent helplessness'; whatever his fellow citizens may think, 'what good has been done in a common cause' must not be hidden, in accordance with Nereus' word that 'one must praise an enemy (Athens?) if he has done worthy deeds'.

122. (p. 182) It is significant that Pindar stresses the old family descent of the tyrants; thus he can see their states as examples of *eunomia*, as though they were aristocracies.

123. (p. 183) Cf. H. H. Bacon, *Barbarians in Greek Tragedy* (New Haven 1961).

124. (p. 183) In general cf. the edition and sound commentary by H. D. Broadhead (Cambridge 1960), also S. M. Adams and L. J. D. Richardson in *Studies in Honour of Gilbert Norwood* (*Phoenix* Suppl. 1) (Toronto 1952).

125. (p. 184) Perhaps the most surprising passage in that respect is when the chorus, praying to the nether gods to send Darius up, are not sure whether 'the blessed godlike king can hear our barbarian laments' (633).

126. (p. 184) Marathon is referred to (244), but on the whole Darius' misfortunes are forgotten, and he appears only as the moderate and wise ruler. As to the events after Salamis, there is only the fantastic story of Xerxes' terrible return.

127. (p. 184) 714: τὰ Περσῶν πράγματα, an expression frequently used in the fifth century for state or government; 255 and 716: πᾶς στρατός. To the following cf. H. C. Avery, *AJP* 1964, 173.

128. (p. 187) See J. H. Finley, *Pindar and Aeschylus*, 163. When Eteocles (*Sept.* 16) calls his homeland 'mother, beloved nurse', he thinks of Mother Earth rather than of the state.

129. (p. 188) I cannot accept Lloyd-Jones' refusal (*JHS* 1956, 55 ff.) to see anything new in Aeschylus' Zeus. He has gone beyond Hesiod's beliefs, and not only by the intensity of his beliefs. Even so Aeschylus never approaches monotheism. It is sufficient to point to the greatness of other deities in his plays, and – perhaps less well known – to the claim of Aphrodite in the *Danaids* (fr. 44).

130. (p. 189) It seems hardly necessary to mention some of the good general books on Greek tragedy, such as those by Wilamowitz, Kitto, Lucas, and Pohlenz. Probably the best short book in English is A. Lesky, *Greek Tragedy* (London 1965).

131. (p. 191) I do not think that this traditional contrast is seriously at fault, although the two men worked well together. Aristeides, of course, was never the conservative and anti-democratic politician of later sources, but even he was a politician, and not that paragon of absolute honesty and – smugness.

VI · THE ASCENDANCY OF ATHENS

1. (p. 192) Thucydides, though he really created the concept, only says (1, 118, 2): ἐν ἔτεσι πεντήκοντα μάλιστα. The word πεντηκονταετία is used for the period in question once and late only, in schol. Thuc. 1, 89; to chs. 42 and 97 the scholiast uses the word πεντηκονταετηρίς.

Otherwise πεντηκονταετία can stand for a period of fifty years generally, sometimes for a man's age of fifty (Dion. Hal. 4, 32. Philo, *de fuga et invent.* 37, *de congressu erud. gratia* 89, *de spec. legibus* 2, 113. 114). I was unable to find out who among modern scholars was the first to call the period 479–431 by that name.

2. (p. 192) Some of the gaps may be explained by the fact that Hellanicus' chronicle of Athens was well known, and Thucydides, despite his polemics against Hellanicus' uncertain chronology, might think that matters less relevant to himself were sufficiently known by that chronicle. Cf. A. Momigliano, *Athenaeum* 1966, 134. The best, though by no means final, treatment of Thucydides' excursus is by A. W. Gomme, *Historical Commentary on Thucydides* I (Oxford 1945), 256. 361. The most important supplementary sources are inscriptions, among them the quota-lists of the allies tributes (*ATL*). A collection of the sources is G. F. Hill, *Sources for Greek History 478–431*, new edn. by R. Meiggs and A. Andrewes (Oxford 1951) (quoted: Hill[3]). There the later literary sources too are collected, especially *AP*, Diodorus and Plutarch. The book should be used to supplement Herodotus and Thucydides; later sources may contain some facts not recorded by the two historians, but in general they must be treated with some caution. The place of Athenian imperialism in the work of Thucydides is the theme of the important book by J. de Romilly, *Thucydides and Athenian Imperialism* (Oxford 1963; original French edn. Paris 1947).

3. (p. 192) de Romilly, loc. cit., 6.

4. (p. 193) Parts of the walls in which all sorts of architectural and sculptural pieces were inserted can still be seen today. Cf. Gomme on 1, 90 ff., esp. 93, 8.

5. (p. 193) During the war there had been arguments on the question of naval leadership, but Athens had always submitted to Sparta's προστασία, which had the backing of the other Greeks (Hdt. 8, 2 f.).

6. (p. 193) Cf. Starr (see ch. IV, note 17), and generally, A. French, *The Growth of the Athenian Economy*, ch. 6.

7. (p. 193) For modern works on the following period, apart from general Greek histories (above, ch. I, n. 7), see, e.g., M. Laistner, *A History of the Greek World from 479 to 323* B.C. (London 1936). We are looking forward to a book by R. Meiggs on the Athenian empire. F. Schachermeyr, *Die frühe Klassik der Griechen* (Stuttgart 1966) is an attempt not dissimilar of the present book. It contains many good ideas and splendid illustrations. A detailed discussion would hardly be useful.

8. (p. 194) Cf. H. D. Meyer, *Historia* 1963, 434, who overstates the case for early friction between Sparta and Athens, and confuses hegemony = military leadership on land or sea with hegemony = political leadership of a league. Thucydides uses the same word for both forms. *AP* 23, 2, says that the Athenians 'obtained the leadership at sea ἀκόντων Λακεδαιμονίων'. It is a matter of dispute whether that means 'Sparta being unwilling to keep it' (Gomme) or 'against the will of the Lacedaemonians' (v. Fritz and Kapp). Dr. Barron pointed out to me that the genitive absolute depends on λαβεῖν, and therefore the first translation could not be right. Anyway, it remains true that Sparta did not withdraw of her own will.

9. (p. 194) J. Vogt, *Gesetz und Handlungsfreiheit in der Geschichte* (Stuttgart 1955), 61, is strongly in favour of the authenticity of the whole affair, putting it into the context of oriental dynastic as well as Persian anti-Greek policy. I have my doubts; cf. also A. Lippold, *RhM* 1965, 320. According to A. Blamire, *GRBS* 1970, 295, our choice is between adherence to Thucydides and ignorance.

10. (p. 194) Thuc. I, 131, says that the ephors sent him an official letter (σκυτάλη); that suggests that Pausanias was still regent, although not commander of the army. Again according to Thucydides, he was threatened with war if he did not obey. It is difficult to imagine how Sparta would wage war against Pausanias, though it might mean a declaration to put him outside the law, similar to the regular declaration of war on the helots (cf. H. Schaefer, *RE* 18, 2574). In fact, the whole story as told by Thucydides raises doubts, and it it possible that the opposition of the ephors to the kings played a part (cf. J. Wolski, *Eos* 1954, 75).

11. (p. 194) Cf. M. E. White, *JHS* 1964, 140, but also W. G. Forrest, *A History of Sparta*, 99 ff.; C. W. Fornara, *Historia* 1966, 257. The chronology of these events is as uncertain as that of the whole Pentacontaetia. It is a curious fact that Thucydides, who claims (I, 97, 2) that one of the reasons why he wrote his excursus on that period was that Hellanicus did the same τοῖς χρόνοις οὐκ ἀκριβῶς, left himself so many dates open, though he generally did follow a chronological order. Cf. Gomme (I, 389 ff.), and e.g., H. D. Westlake, *CQ* 1955, 53.

12. (p. 195) An important contribution to that question is by R. Sealey, *ASAI* 233. He is very sceptical, and has his doubts about any aims of 'liberation' at that early date; against his own solution (piracy) cf. A. H. Jackson, *Historia*, 1969, 12.

13. (p. 196) The total sum of the first tribute, according to Thuc. I, 96, 2, amounted to 460 talents, a sum larger than any annual amount in the years

after 454, when we have the evidence of the tribute lists. The Athenian *archē* then was larger than the league in 477, though fewer states provided ships, and money in the meantime had lost in value. Thus the total at the later date ought to have been higher, not lower. The contribution in ships even in 477 seems not to be quite sufficient to explain the high total of 460 talents (cf. *ATL* 3, 235) maintained by Eddy, *CP* 1968, 184), and it is most unlikely that the provision of ships was included in the cash total of the *phoros* (cf. M. Chambers, *CP* 1958, 26). Nor can we assume (with Gomme) that later assessments were lower, especially after the battle of the Eurymedon for Athens then needed, in fact, more rather than less cash. An attempt at an explanation of Aristeides' assessment as well as of certain later fluctuations of the tributes was made by H. Schaefer, *Hermes* 74 (1939), 225 = *Probleme der alten Geschichte* (Göttingen 1963), 41. He thinks that the original assessment referred to the economic potential of each state, and the tribute was a fixed quota of that; the total of these quota then amounted to 460 talents, but when the income and property of a state changed their value the quota would change too. Most of the tributes between 454 and the new assessment of 425 remained static; that is why one could still speak of ὁ ἐπ' Ἀριστείδου φόρος. A few sudden and big changes of a tribute may have been due to political reasons, but the majority not. This seems, on the whole, a sound argument, though rather artificial; it cannot be proved, and there were additional reasons as well. It is possible that Aristeides' assessment of 460 talents was a sort of ideal figure, if not only a mistake in the text just as the six hundred talents of Thuc. 2, 13, 3, probably are, though this view of Chambers, loc. cit., means cutting rather than solving the Gordian knot. Anyway, there must have been increasingly other sources of revenue besides the tributes, and that is also at the core of the argument by French (see note 6, and *Historia* 1972, 1).

14. (p. 196) The united forces of the league represented 'the Hellenes' against the Persians, while the official title was 'The Athenians and their allies'.

15. (p. 196) This is the type of 'hegemonic symmachy', on which cf. my *Greek State* (London 1969²), 111.

16. (p. 197) For a cautious detailed discussion see *ATL* 3, 194.

16a. (p. 197) Bowra, (note 95), 65, points out that the 'Lemnian Athene' was a gift by the cleruchs at Lemnos.

17. (p. 197) Later sources, especially Plutarch, report that Cimon brought from Scyrus the bones of Theseus to be reburied at Athens. Whatever the tomb which he unearthed, following an ancient oracle, may have contained,

his action caught the imagination of the Athenian people and added to his popularity. At least from the later part of the sixth century Theseus had become the representative mythical hero of Athens and her democracy.

18. (p. 197) The events of Scyrus and Carystus occurred during the 'seventies, though hardly in one continuous campaign, as appears from Thuc. 1, 98. He reports them as immediately following the defection of Naxos, which will not have happened before 469 (see below).

19. (p. 198) This is neither the first nor the last example of the low esteem in which some of the kings, or even the institution of monarchy, were held in Sparta. That was entirely due to the policy of the ephors.

20. (p. 198) A different, rather hypothetical account of the Peloponnesian events is given by W. G. Forrest, *CQ* 1960, 229.

20a. (p. 198) Cf. D. W. Knight (see ch. IV, note 34), 25 ff.

21. (p. 198) Was he already ostracized when Aeschylus (with Pericles as the choregus) produced the *Persians* in spring 472 and praised him for what he had done at Salamis? It is by no means improbable – keeping in mind what kind of man Aeschylus was and that young Pericles was perhaps in sympathy with Themistocles' policy. It is also possible that Aeschylus made a 'pre-ostracism defence' (Forrest, 221) and that Themistocles' fate at that moment was still in suspense; cf. F. Sartori, *Atti dell' istituto Veneto etc.* 128 (1969–70), 771 ff.

22. (p. 199) Forrest, 227, tries to show that Themistocles' flight coincided with the collapse of democracy in Argos. Thucydides (1, 135–8), who shows a biographical interest in Themistocles, otherwise alien to the austere historian, reveals a few significant facts about Themistocles' later years, e.g. that for one year he learned to speak Persian and became acquainted with Persian customs, before he decided to approach the king. However, more likely than not he was also waiting for the death of Xerxes. The evidence of Thucydides cannot be reconciled with the views of those scholars who put the date of Themistocles' flight later, and the end of Pausanias earlier, so that the time gap is between these two events rather than after Themistocles' entry into Persia. Cf. the full discussion by R. J. Lenardon, *Historia* 8 (1959), 23, and the rather sceptical treatment by P. J. Rhodes, *Historia* 1970, 387.

23. (p. 199) On the many versions of Cimon's life story cf. Ed. Meyer, *Forschungen zur alten Geschichte* II (Halle 1899), 1, still the fundamental discussion.

24. (p. 200) If we can believe Plato, *Menex.* 241 d, Persia was all the time preparing for a new attack.

25. (p. 200) On ἐδουλώθη (Thuc. 1, 98, 4) cf. *ATL* 3, 155; J. de Romilly (note 2), 99; Gomme 3, 646.

26. (p. 200) Cf. *ATL* 3, 244.

27. (p. 201) The battle is dated by *ATL* 3, 160, in 469, because of the story (Plut. *Cim.* 8, 7) that, when in spring 468 Sophocles was victorious over Aeschylus, Cimon and his fellow strategi had been asked to act as judges, instead of the usual sortition. Such a departure from custom could be explained by the prestige they had won by the victory of the Eurymedon.

28. (p. 201) *ML*, no. 31. *DSDA* no. 149. Cf. the important article by H. T. Wade-Gery, *Essays in Greek History*, 180, but also G. E. M. de Ste Croix, *CQ* 1961, 100. Wade-Gery dates the decree between 469 and 462, but it might belong to the 'fifties.

29. (p. 201) It is likely that about that time an Athenian embassy under a Callias had gone to Susa to try to come to terms with the new Persian king Artaxerxes (Hdt. 7, 151; cf. note 74). The embassy will have been a simple act of diplomacy, not a change of policy. On his return from Thasos, according to Plutarch (*Cim.* 14, 5. *Per.* 10, 6; cf. *AP* 27, 1), Cimon was accused of having been bribed by the king of Macedon; his main prosecutor was the young Pericles. Cimon was acquitted. If the story is genuine, and not just a reflection of the events of 462–461, it is significant for the inner tensions at Athens.

30. (p. 202) Thuc. 1, 100, 2. 4, 102, 2; cf. Hdt. 7, 115. 9, 75. The details of the story are rather ambiguous; cf. Gomme 1, 296; *ATL* 3, 106. For the chronology of these years cf. F. Jacoby, *FGrH* 328 F. 117. See also note 42.

31. (p. 202) The effects of the 'big earthquake' (Thuc. 1, 128, 1) are not known in any reliable detail; in the later tradition (Diodorus, Plutarch, etc.) they are undoubtedly exaggerated. That, I believe, can also be said of the view of L. Ziehen, *Hermes* 68 (1933), 218 (cf. W. H. Porter, *Hermathena* 49 (1935), 1), that the losses in human life (Diodorus' 'more than 20,000') were the main cause of Sparta's increasing ὀλιγανθρωπία; cf. H. Michell, *Sparta* (Cambridge 1952), 231; Gomme, 298; Forrest (see note 11), 102 f.

32. (p. 203) It is in my view out of the question that at that time Athens was still a member of the Peloponnesian League, whether or not she had once been (which is possible); cf. above, p. 90.

33. (p. 204) I abstain from discussing the development in vase-painting and its various styles, important though it is (cf. T. B. L. Webster, *Greek Art and Literature 530–400 B.C.* (Oxford 1939)). It certainly reflected the art of Polygnotus and his school. It may suffice to remember the works of the Pan and the Niobid painter, and the famous Achilles–Penthesilea cup; cf. P. E. Arias and M. Hirmer, *A History of Greek Vase Painting* (London 1962), pl. 160–81.

34. (p. 204) Cf. M. Detienne, *Parola del Passato* 1965, 443.

35. (p. 205) W. Jaeger, *Paideia* I (Oxford 1939), 252, regards the Olympian pediments as reflections of tragedy. Any such verdict must be subjective; I feel they rather depend on epic tradition.

36. (p. 206) ὑποκριτής, as the word for the actor, traditionally translated by the 'answerer', is nowadays understood as the 'explainer', perhaps the 'speaker of the prologue'. See A. Lesky, *Ges. Schriften* (Bern 1966), 239; H. Schreckenberg, Δρᾶμα (Diss. Münster 1959) (cf. H. Patzer, *Gnomon* 1965, 118). For Schreckenberg δρᾶμα means dance or pantomime.

37. (p. 206) It is the old and widespread belief of 'visiting the iniquity of the father upon the children, and upon the children's children, unto the third and the fourth generation' (2 Mos. 34, 7).

38. (p. 206) See R. P. Winnington-Ingram, *JHS* 1961, 141.

39. (p. 207) In 1919 I wrote a student's essay on Aeschylus in which I spoke of Eteocles as a man tragically caught up in the process of transition from one age to another. I recently found confirmation of my views on the *Septem* in an essay – not yet printed – which Professor R. P. Winnington-Ingram kindly let me see.

40. (p. 207) Cf. Ed. Fraenkel, *Aeschylus' Agamemnon* (Oxford 1950), *passim*; N. G. L. Hammond, *JHS* 1965, 42.

41. (p. 207) It is true that according to Plato, *Protag.* 320 ff., Prometheus, by stealing the fire, gave men only τὴν περὶ τὸν βίον σοφίαν, and that it was Zeus who added αἰδῶ καί δίκην, but in Aeschylus that will have been the result of the reconciliation between Prometheus and Zeus. I do not think we should assume a development of Zeus' character, rather his overwhelming greatness in which friendly and hostile forces alike are united. It is the Zeus of the *Agamemnon* (160), 'whoever he is'. About possible relations between Aeschylus and Protagoras cf. J. A. Davison, *CQ* 1953, 33; *ASAI* 93.

42. (p. 208) According to Thuc. 1, 103, 1, the war lasted for nine years; but that seems almost impossible to accept, although several attempts have

been made to explain it. For δεκάτῳ ἔτει various corrections have been suggested, though none has been generally accepted: τετάρτῳ (Δ̄ for Δ), ἔκτῳ (Gomme), πέμπτῳ. Cf. *DSDA*, no. 138, and the methodical remarks by R. A. McNeal, *Historia* 1970, 306.

43. (p. 208) It is interesting to see from the inscription of the Nike of Paeonius in Olympia (*ML*, no. 74; about 421 B.C.) that Messenians and Naupactians – which included the former Locrian colonists – were on the best of terms with each other, without giving up their own communities.

43a. (p. 209) The date of the first official 'Epitaphios' is disputed. The first of which we actually know was Pericles' after the first year of the Samian war. Cf. W. Kierdorf (see ch. V, note 114) and my review in *Gnomon*, 1967.

44. (p. 209) See ch. V, note 111. The exact date is unknown, but it is after 467, possibly 463, and that would mean shortly before the alliance between Athens and Argos. My discussion of democracy in that play, though it must refer to a much later date than I assumed, is in itself still valid; cf. *Historia* I (1950), 516 = *PI* 266. I had actually written: 'The evidence . . . seems in general to a surprising extent to conform to certain features . . . as we know them from sources fifty or more years younger.' In the text I borrow a good deal from that earlier paper of mine, called 'Origins of Democracy'.

44a. (p. 209) 'The weighty word', E. Fraenkel, *Aeschylus' Agamemnon*, vv. 1051, 1061.

45. (p. 210) For a more detailed discussion of that title cf. my *Sophocles and Pericles* (Oxford 1954), 99.

46. (p. 210) Cf. ibid., Appendix A. Cf. J. de Romilly, *La loi dans la pensée grecque* (Paris 1971), 26 ff.

47. (p. 210) L. Pearson, *Popular Ethics in Ancient Greece* (Stanford 1962), 95.

48. (p. 210) In a line like 401: 'In honouring foreigners thou hast destroyed the polis', one could possibly see a reference to Cimon's acceptance of Sparta's request; that would mean a date just after 462, a few years before the *Oresteia*. The artistic and spiritual distance, however, between the *Suppliants* and the great trilogy seems enormous; on the other hand, we know hardly anything about the trilogy of which the *Suppliants* were a part, and anyway, the reference to Cimon is by no means certain.

49. (p. 211) I am doubtful whether that really included a censorship on good moral behaviour by all citizens (Isocr. 7, 46; cf. Hignett, 201). If there was general supervision it was political and religious, i.e. in the name and spirit of the Polis, not on moral grounds.

50. (p. 212) E. Ruschenbusch, *Historia* 1966, 369, argues that the essential thing about Ephialtes' reform was to gain legal power against Cimon's pro-Spartan policy, and not the question of a stronger democracy. I doubt whether it is possible to separate the two issues so strictly. That seems also the view of F. Schachermeyr, *Pericles* (Stuttgart 1969), 32 ff., who sees in Ephialtes a fanatical believer in the Athenian people as an 'élite', who at the same time prepared for a war on two fronts. Do we know enough about Ephialtes to say so?

51. (p. 212) Cf. K. J. Dover, *JHS* 1957, 230, and, above all, E. R. Dodds' paper on 'Morals and Politics in the Oresteia', *Proc. Cambridge Philol. Soc.* 1960, 19. I cannot agree with all their conclusions, but in general, their views on Aeschylus' political attitude are close to my own. A. Lesky, *Greek Tragedy* (London 1965), 85, maintains that 'no question of topicality' was involved.

52. (p. 212) Cf. G. de Sanctis, ᾽Ατθίς (Torino 1912²), 424; Hignett, 202.

53. (p. 213) The absurd story in *AP* 25, 3, which makes Themistocles the helper of Ephialtes, has rightly found no acceptance, if only for chronological reasons. However, together with that naming of Archestratus, it shows that Ephialtes had no outstanding 'lieutenant', neither Pericles nor anybody else.

54. (p. 213) Cf. E. Meinhardt, *Perikles bei Plutarch* (Diss. Frankfurt 1957), 29. *AP* 25–27, 1, does not make chronological sense; any traditional dating has been destroyed by the Themistocles episode (see last note).

55. (p. 213) R. Sealey, *Hermes* 1956, 234, rightly warns (with Gomme, p. 70, 2) against taking for granted that Pericles was at once the leading politician; but, on the whole, I still believe that what I said in *Sophocles and Pericles* (Oxford 1954), 75 f., is essentially right. If Athens 'owed her empire above all to the imperialists of the 'fifties' (R. Meiggs, *JHS* 1943, 33), the leader of that 'vigorous and resilient generation' can hardly have been anybody else but Pericles.

56. (p. 214) We hear of expeditions made by Pericles and Ephialtes (in this order!) to the south coast of Asia Minor, where they did not meet any Persian force. This story comes from an unexpected source, Callisthenes (*FGrH* 124 F 16), the Alexander historian. It is difficult to find a date for these expeditions which ought to belong to the years after Eurymedon and before 460. Pericles, anyway, was very young then to lead a major expedition (fifty ships, while Ephialtes had only thirty!). Wade-Gery, *Essays*, 203, note 2, thinks, however, that the order of the names may be rhetorical, and that Pericles' expedition is that of the Samian war in 440.

57. (p. 214) Cf. A. E. Raubitschek, *Phoenix* 1960, 81.

58. (p. 214) *ML*, no. 33. Hill³, B 14. Two generals from the same phyle occur more than once (see below, note 70), though in this case they may belong to two civil years (459–458 and 458–457). The one year mentioned in the inscription is almost certainly the campaigning year, or as we can put it: from one official funeral to the next (i.e. November).

59. (p. 215) Thuc. 1, 110, 2; cf. Hdt. 3, 15. Philoch. *FGrH* 328 F 119 (see below, note 76).

60. (p. 215) That is the title of an interesting paper by J. P. Barron, *JHS* 1964, 35, in which the *horoi* from Samos (Hill³, B 96d) are well, though perhaps not finally, interpreted. On the appearance of Athena's title μεδέουσα in the Themistocles decree see above, ch. V, note 59.

61. (p. 216) For Myronides – there probably were two strategi of the name – cf. *RE* Suppl. VII (1942), 510.

62. (p. 216) This wall, τὸ νότιον or τὸ διὰ μέσου τεῖχος, is frequently mentioned in literature (Andoc. 3, 7. Aeschines 2, 174. Plato, *Gorg.* 455 d/e). I cannot agree with Gomme, p. 313, 1, that Plato refers to the building of the Long Walls in general, though the attribution to Themistocles is somewhat confused.

63. (p. 216) Pausanias (1, 15, 1. 10, 10, 4) is the only source to speak of a battle at Oenoe in the Argolis, in which Argive and Athenian forces defeated a Spartan army. The battle must have been famous as it was supposed to be the subject of one of the paintings in the Stoa Poikile, and of a remarkable Argive dedication at Delphi. Its date is unknown, but most likely about 460. The event can thus be regarded as the opening of warfare between Athens and Sparta, and therefore of special patriotic interest. Its omission by Thucydides is not more peculiar than the many omissions in his sketch of the Pentecontaetia. Recent full discussion: L. H. Jeffery, *BSA* 1966, 41.

64. (p. 217) This farcical Sacred War may have been the cause (or the effect) of an alliance of Athens with Delphi, of which a fragmentary inscription is preserved (*DSDA* no. 142. *SEG* 21, 6, 22, 2). In view of the generally cool relations between Athens and the oracle, and of the fact that Delphi could never show any military strength, the alliance seems most remarkable.

65. (p. 218) We do not know who these allies were; but as events had very swiftly come to a head, the forces were more likely from Plataea, Thespiae, Megara, and, as we are expressly told, from Thessaly than from allies overseas.

66. (p. 218) Thuc. 1, 107, 6 speaks of καί τι καὶ τοῦ δήμου καταλύσεως ὑποψίᾳ. How serious the threat was is another question. There is little doubt that the conspirators who had joined the enemy were a mere handful of extremists, but they might find support both in Sparta and in Thebes.

66a. (p. 219) An earlier date is suggested by W. K. Pritchett, *Historia* 1969, 17.

67. (p. 219) I have expressed similar views in a review of *ATL* (*HZ* 173 (1952), 547), and at that time, the nearest system with which it could be compared seemed the rule of Soviet Russia over her satellites; since then things have changed but, as Czechoslovakia showed, less than one thought. An ingenious attempt at contradicting the verdict on the 'unpopularity' of Athenian rule, and thus on the prevailing opinion of ancients and moderns alike, was made by G. E. M. de Ste Croix, *Historia* 1954, 1. He minimizes too much the loss of autonomy, whether by an oligarchy or a demos. Cf. also the sound remarks by J. de Romilly, *Thucydides and Athenian Imperialism*, 376, and her more extensive and subtle discussion in *BICS* 1966, 1, where she stresses the 'pressure' which determined the situation of cities and the divisions of the people ('parties') alike. A. G. Woodhead, *Thucydides and the Nature of Power* (Harvard 1970), 6 f., declares the whole discussion, whether 'approval or disapproval', 'is beside the point'. On the empire, cf. p. 39. His discussion, though very impressive, is too much dominated by modern analogies, and his partiality makes Thucydides appear too partial.

68. (p. 219) A. E. Raubitschek, *AJA* 1966, 37. His article is an ingenious, if unconvincing, attempt at dating to the time before 454 the 'reorganization of a league', and such events as, e.g., the congress decree and the Peace of Callias.

69. (p. 220) It cannot be my task to describe in detail the rather complicated machinery of Athenian administration and constitution. For more extensive discussion see – apart from Busolt-Swoboda and Hignett – A. H. M. Jones, *Athenian Democracy* (Oxford 1957); also A. W. Gomme, *More Essays in Greek History and Literature* (Oxford 1962), 177.

70. (p. 223) That was the election ἐξ ἁπάντων. We do not know the procedure, e.g., how it was decided which tribe that year would have no *strategos*. On these and cognate questions cf. Wade-Gery, *CQ* 1931, 89; Ehrenberg, *AJP* 1945, 113; Hignett, 244. 347; also the list in Hill[3], 401. More recently, E. S. Staveley, *ASAI* 275, in a well-argued article, tried to explain the procedure on account of the law in *AP* 61, 1, which he dates about the middle of the fifth century. I am doubtful about the 'double doubles', i.e. more

than one couple of generals from one phyle in one year. The leadership
in a campaign was often given to one man who might have several colleagues with him; Thucydides then speaks of πέμπτος αὐτός, or similar.
In 1, 116, 1, and 2, 13, 1, Pericles is called δέκατος αὐτός, and Hignett,
353, has defined that as a supreme C.-in-C., but there never was a permanent head of the board. On the other hand, I do not believe that the
expression στρατηγὸς αὐτοκράτωρ had any real significance at Athens;
it probably did not exist before 415 (Thuc. 6, 8, 2), when the three(!)
leaders of the Sicilian expedition were given that rank; cf. M. Scheele,
Στρατηγὸς Αὐτοκράτωρ, (Diss. Leipzig 1932). On all the questions involved cf. the extensive paper by K. J. Dover, *JHS* 1960, 61. I believe, however, that he neglects too much the need for a temporary C.-in-C. in each
particular campaign.

71. (p. 223) Cf. the careful investigation by G. T. Griffith, *ASAI* 115. I
agree with much of what he says, though I believe in an earlier tradition
and not in an official 'introduction of *isegoria* into the assembly's proceedings', unless we mean by it the introduction of the herald's question τίς
ἀγορεύειν βούλεται. Cf. also A. G. Woodhead, *Historia* 1967, 129.
J. D. Lewis, *Historia* 1971, 129.

72. (p. 223) Cf. M. Amit, *Athens and the Sea. Coll. Latomus* 74 (1965), 60.
The connexion between navy and democracy was later a theme of anti-
democratic thought, but it was based on facts; cf. Woodhead (note 67),
188, 32.

73. (p. 224) Cf. *ATL* 3, 232; Meiggs, *HSt* 1963, 4.

74. (p. 225) V. Martin, *Mus. Helv.* 1963, 230, is probably right in stressing
that no Persian king could possibly sign an ordinary bilateral treaty; but
a form could be found, e.g., by the interposition of a satrap, to satisfy the
other side and to establish peace; hostilities, at any rate, ceased at that time.
We cannot discuss the difficult questions of the Callias peace in any detail,
neither of its genuineness nor its chronology. The most important recent
contributions are Wade-Gery, *Essays*, 201; Gomme, 331; and, on the other
hand, D. Stockton, *Historia* 1959, 61, and H. B. Mattingly, *Historia* 1965,
273. Thucydides does not mention the peace, and Herodotus (7, 151) speaks
of an embassy 'many years later . . . in another matter'. These obscure words
are explained by the fact that in the context of 481 Herodotus did not wish
to speak of negotiations with Persia. The simultaneous Argive embassy to
King Artaxerxes, asking for the continuation of Xerxes' friendship, shows
that the event was soon after Artaxerxes' ascension to the throne in 464.

We have to assume that a Callias led an earlier embassy, and that Callisthenes (*FGrH* 124 F 15 f.), in dating the peace treaty after Eurymedon, confused it with the earlier negotiations that did not lead to a real peace. Strong views have been expressed that a formal Peace of Callias round about 450 never existed. The problem is largely that of the general chronology of a number of important Athenian *psephismata* (see note 80), but there are other reasons why a peace agreement was concluded at or shortly after 450.

75. (p. 225) The many questions raised by the law are fully, though not always convincingly, discussed by F. Jacoby, *FGrH* 328 F 119, Appendix, p. 471; cf. also A. W. Gomme, *Essays in Greek History and Literature* (Oxford, 1937), 86; Hignett, 343.

76. (p. 225) Modern views were largely influenced by the fact that six years later an Egyptian (or Libyan) prince sent a large amount of corn to Athens for free distribution among the citizens. We learn this from Philochorus (*FGrH* 328 F 119), who gives exact, though quite unreliable, figures for those who received corn, and those who were illegally registered (παρέγ - γραφοι). The latter expression seems to refer to a διαψηφισμός, a formal scrutiny of citizenship, which would have to be held in the demes. Such a lengthy procedure was quite impossible on the occasion of the corn distribution, nor is there the slightest hint in our evidence that it was foreseen in the law of 451-450.

77. (p. 226) Cf., e.g., Jacoby, loc. cit.; R. Meiggs, *HSt* 1963, 13.

78. (p. 226) The traditional view is that *apoikia* was an independent colony, and *kleruchia* a community of citizens owning land abroad. This clear distinction cannot be fully upheld. I have tried to show (*Aspects of the Ancient World*, 128) that there were intermediate forms as well. Recently, P. A. Brunt, *ASAI* 71, has made it clear, first, that the situation of a colony was different within or without the empire; secondly, that it was important whether earlier Greek inhabitants were still or again living there, or had been expelled, if not massacred. Colonists within the empire did not always lose their citizenship, and a cleruchy at a place no longer inhabited would be of greater independence. Cf. also P. Gauthier, *REG* 1966, 64; J. R. Green and R. K. Sinclair, *Historia* 1970, 515.

79. (p. 226) In *AP* 28, 2. Plut. *Per.* 11, 1, he is called Cimon's κηδεστής. Cf. Wade-Gery, *Essays*, 246. The law will not have asked after the grandmother's origin, and we should avoid any idea of 'pure race' policy. I believe ordinary people did not see the idea of the law in the light of 'keeping the family of Athenian citizens together'.

80. (p. 227) For the interpretation of these inscriptions with regard to the general crisis see *ATL* 3, *passim*; R. Meiggs, *JHS* 1943, 21; *HSt* 1963. The whole edifice, erected on a carefully, if hypothetically, constructed chronology of the inscriptions, would tumble down if H. B. Mattingly were right in dating down every one of these sources. His articles are most ingenious, but the counter arguments by Meritt and Wade-Gery are strong indeed. Mattingly has tried to support his theory by more evidence, again very ingeniously (*Historia* 1963, 257; *Proc. of African Class. Ass.* 1964, 35 and especially *Annual of the Brit. School at Athens* 1970, 129), and has restated, partly with new material, his case against 'Periclean Imperialism' under that very title in *ASAI* 193, stressing now, above all, the varieties of spelling as well as those of early letter forms. I do not feel competent to take sides, and must leave the technical discussion to the epigraphists (cf. now R. Meiggs, *JHS* 1966, 86). I reject, however, Mattingly's general result that the change of *symmachia* into *archē* started under Pericles, though not before 443, and reached its full strength only under Cleon. Thucydides' 'clear distinction between Pericles and Cleon' referred to character and statesmanship, not to their 'imperial attitude'; they both knew that the rule of Athens had become a tyranny (2, 63. 3, 37). It seems that Mme de Romilly essentially agrees with such a view (*Thucydides and Athenian Imperialism*, 164 ff. 373). I shall keep in general to what we may call the orthodox chronology.

81. (p. 228) Cf. the treaty between Argos and Sparta (Thuc. 5, 14, 4). It was only later that treaties were concluded for 100 years or even for ever (ἐς ἀεὶ). Naturally, the religious foundations of every treaty implied the idea that it would last (thus, e.g., the founding of the first Athenian League, *AP* 235); but the fixing of a definite number of years was something different.

81a. (p. 228) Cf. P. J. Fliers, *Thucydides and the Politics of Bipolarity* (Louisiana Univ. Press, 1966), an interesting book, though too much of an artificial construction based on modern concepts and the language of modern sociology.

82. (p. 228) Plutarch's source knew the original decree, but confused the enumeration of the various envoys sent round the Greek world. The group sent 'to Boeotia and Phocis and the Peloponnesus, from there by way of the Locrians to the neighbouring mainland as far as Acarnania and Ambracia' follows an impossible route, and at least the Peloponnese has to be cancelled here; on the other hand, envoys *must* have gone to Sparta and the other Peloponnesians. R. Seager, *Historia* 1969, 129, expresses doubts whether the Congress decree is genuine, a radical view I cannot accept.

83. (p. 228) I abstain from any special discussion of the quota lists (*ATL*), which would demand far more space than can be allowed here, and a far better expert than I can claim to be. Cf. note 80. A detailed history, however, of the 'empire' is not possible without using those annual lists. The quota is one sixtieth of the tribute (one mina in each talent), and was given to the treasury of Athena, that was run by the *tamiai* of the goddess.

84. (p. 229) If this Cleinias was the father of Alcibiades (which is quite possible, as the name was rare), we have a certain *terminus ante quem* for the decree, for he died in the battle of Coroneia (447). The date usually accepted now is 449.

84a. (p. 229) Cf. J. P. Barron, *The Silver Coinage of Samos* (London 1966), 91.

85. (p. 229) *ML*, no. 40. *ATL* D 10. *DSDA* no. 134. The archon Lysicrates of 453–452 has been accepted by most editors. The reconstruction of line 2 f. is by no means certain: . . . ἐπέστατε· Λ[υσι]κ[ράτες ἐρχε· γνόμε τον χσυγγραφέον·' Ερυθραί]ος ἀπάγεν, etc., especially as the dating by archon was still a rarity about the middle of the century. But the date seems roughly right, and H. Schaefer's dating to the early 'sixties (*Hermes* 1936, 129 = *Probl. der alten Gesch.*, 11) seems no longer tenable. Whether the fragments *IG* I², 11–13 (see *ATL*, p. 56), belong to the same date, remains uncertain; the latter is almost certainly an oath of allegiance taken by the Erythraeans.

86. (p. 230) Cf. above, p. 206 and note 37.

87. (p. 230) Cf. in particular Meiggs, *JHS* 1943, 23. Similar were the events at Miletus about 450; cf. *ATL* D 11. *DSDA* no. 151. *ML*, no. 43. Miletus was also brought back under Athenian rule. To roughly the same period belongs a fragmentary decree (*SEG* 10, 13; 25, no. 4) in which Sigeum is praised for its loyalty, and protection is promised against 'anybody of those on the mainland'. This will be a reference to the Persians (and some Greek cities?), and the 'mainland' (ἤπειρος) is not contrasted with any island, but indicates the 'continent' of Asia.

88. (p. 230) Whether we read οἰκισταί or ἀπ]οικισταί, they must be connected with the foundation of a colony. Brunt, *ASAI* 77, has doubts whether the colonists were Athenians.

89. (p. 231) Complaints about such delays must have been frequent, mainly because council and demos were overburdened with necessary and unnecessary work (cf. Ps.-Xen. 3, 1 ff.).

90. (p. 231) The words I have translated 'without trial' (ἀκρίτο οὐδενός) are immediately followed by the ominous ἄνευ τô δέμο τô 'Αθεναίον (v. 9); but logic, grammar, and sense speak against the opinion that the two groups of words belong together.

91. (p. 231) That, I feel, will be the meaning of the phrase. It does not make sense if the ξένοι were metics (despite P. Gauthier, REG 1971, 65) and the passage ὅσοι οἰκôντες μέ τελôσιν 'Αθέναζε can only mean 'except those who lived there and paid tax to Athens'. Other sources show that there were cleruchs also at Eretria; cf. Green and Sinclair (note 78). It is remarkable that about that time even small cities displayed an interest in protecting the ξένοι in their states; cf. the treaty between Oeantheia and Chaleion in Ozolian Locris (Tod, no. 34. DSDA no. 146), though the situation there is quite different from that at Chalcis. The isolation of every Polis was no longer practicable, and inter-state agreements were becoming more frequent.

92. (p. 232) *ephesis*, as in Solon's time (see above, p. 69), here means transfer, and not the right of appeal; cf. Gomme, 342, 2.

93. (p. 232) Cf. E. Meinhardt (see note 54).

94. (p. 232) Socrates (*Gorg.* 575 E) says that he had heard that Pericles had made the Athenians lazy, cowardly, talkative, and fond of money. The first two charges were as untrue of the Athenians in general as the two others were true, but they had little to do with Pericles.

95. (p. 232) This, of course, must be discussed within the issue of the 'truth' of what Thucydides has written. An excellent survey, based on very sound views, had been written in the *Times Lit. Suppl.* of 17th February 1966, in a front article reviewing the English edition of Mme de Romilly's book (see note 2) and the brilliant essay by Sir Frank Adcock, *Thucydides and his History* (Cambridge 1963). C. M. Bowra, *Periclean Athens* (London 1971) gives a general picture of the period, especially good on poetry and thought (cf. my forthcoming review in *Gnomon*).

96. (p. 234) Cf., above all, Wade-Gery, *Essays*, 239, also H. D. Meyer, *Historia* 1967, 141. Apart from *AP* and Plutarch, our most important source is the confused *vita anon. Thuc.*; the paragraphs 6–7 do not refer to the historian but to the earlier Thucydides (see Wade-Gery, loc. cit., Appendix A, p. 261). Even so, we learn very little that is reliable. I disagree with Wade-Gery on some points; the position of Thucydides was hardly as prominent as he makes it, and the man's idealistic Panhellenism simply cannot be proved. Still, the memory of the son of Melesias remained strong

in aristocratic tradition (Plato, *AP*). The importance of Theopompus as a link in the tradition is stressed by A. E. Raubitschek (see note 57).

97. (p. 234) Both these views have found defenders, the first in N. O. Brown, *TAPA* 1951, 1, the second in F. Robert, *RPh* 1964, 213. The former's 'socio-historical interpretation' is sufficiently dealt with in my *Sophocles and Pericles* (Oxford 1954), Appendix C; he dates the play in 444. Robert, on the other hand, believes in the impact of Corinthian policy and the law on citizenship ἐξ ἀμφοῖν ἀστοῖν; his date for the *Aias* is 445. The two arguments exclude each other, and the one is as unconvincing as the other. Nor is the traditional figure of Menelaus proof of anti-Spartan attitude; this is, in fact, the view of such a good scholar as J. C. Kamerbeck, *Mnemos.* 1965, 29. A view very close to my own is expressed by F. Schachermeyr, *WSt* 1966, 49, although I feel his identification of Odysseus with the spirit of Pericles' generation goes beyond what we can know.

98. (p. 235) The Italian situation will be discussed in the next section. In general, cf. my article 'The Foundation of Thurii' (*AJP* 1948, 159 = *PI* 306), from which I repeat a few sentences. I doubt whether there is anything in the uncertain story of the *vita Thuc.* to show that the son of Melesias went to Sybaris shortly before he was ostracized. See note 96.

99. (p. 236) See above, p. 85, and notes. Pericles also introduced musical competitions at the Panathenaea, for which he built the Odeion (Plut. 13, 11; cf. note 127).

100. (p. 237) Cf. *Sophocles and Pericles*, 84 (German edn. – slightly extended – Munich 1956, 104). There all the references are given.

101. (p. 237) The attacks by comedy led, if we can believe schol. Ar. *Ach.* 67, even to a law of censorship (τοῦ μὴ κωμῳδεῖν) that is supposed to have existed from 440–439 to 437–436, i.e. during and immediately after the Samian war. Whatever its authenticity, it would fit into the picture of the 'tyrannical' Pericles. The remark, on the other hand, of Ps.-Xenophon 2, 18, does not necessarily point to a law; cf. my *People of Aristoph.* (New York 1962³) 25, 5. About the alleged attack of the comedian Hermippus on Aspasia, cf. note 113.

102. (p. 237) To the date cf. *Sophocles and Pericles*, 135 (German edn. 167), to Creon in the *Antigone*, p. 54 (67), to the Unwritten Laws p. 22 (25). With H. Funke's interpretation of Creon (*Antike und Abendland* 12 (1966), 29) I am largely in agreement, though not completely.

103. (p. 238) On Ion cf. G. Huxley, *GRBS* 1965, 29. I largely agree, except

for Sophocles being 'a latter day Cimonian'. Ion's verdict rightly puts him above a purely oligarchic attitude.

103a. (p. 238) For general literature on Herodotus see, e.g., F. Jacoby, *RE* Suppl. 2 (1913). J. L. Myres, *H., Father of History* (Oxford 1953). K. v. Fritz, *Die griech. Geschichtsschreibung* I (Berlin 1967), ch. 4. Chr. W. Fornara, *Herodotus* (Oxford 1971), also *JHS* 1971, 25.

104. (p. 239) Cf. A. Momigliano, 'Herodotus in the History of Historiography', *Secondo Contributo alla Storia degli Studi Classici* (Rome 1960), 29.

105. (p. 239) Against the firm tradition in modern scholarship of regarding Herodotus as Pericles' admirer and loyal supporter, strong objections have been raised, above all by H. Strasburger, *Historia* 4 (1955), 1, and by W. G. Forrest in a paper read at Cambridge in August 1965, which he kindly let me see afterwards. He rightly maintains Herodotus' favourable inclination towards the Alcmaeonids, but not towards Pericles. He denies that Herodotus had any interest in Pericles' father Xanthippus (hardly right), but stresses his critical attitude towards Themistocles, who was a kind of political model for Pericles. He agrees that the weight of possible hints leads to the general conclusion as expressed in the text. The earlier view is defended by F. D. Harvey, *Historia* 1966, 254. For my own change of opinion see *Sophokles und Perikles* (German edn.), 169, 1.

106. (p. 239) In the *Frogs*, 1431 (404 B.C.), on the other hand, there is a clear reference to Alcibiades: 'one should not rear a lion's cub within the state' (see above, p. 331). It confirms that the lion spells danger rather than reverence. To say of Herodotus' passage that it is 'a compliment to Pericles, not to his politics' (E. N. Tigerstedt, *The Legend of Sparta* (Stockholm 1965), 86) seems to miss the point. A mysterious and irrelevant reference to a famous phrase by Pericles is Gelon's answer to the Athenian envoy who refuses him as commander of the Greek fleet (7, 162) that this refusal meant 'to take the spring out of the year'. Neither can that be a compliment to Pericles nor an allusion to the Archidamian war (Fornara, l.c. 83 f.; Aristotle's quotations (*rhet.* 1365a, 31. 1411a, 2) may refer to any Epitaphios). I cannot explain Gelon's misplaced quotation.

107. (p. 240) Arist. *pol.* 1267b, 22. Cf. R. E. Wycherley, *How the Greeks built Cities* (London 1962²), *passim*.

108. (p. 241) N. G. L. Hammond, *History of Greece*, 315. For more than three decades Samos had lost her autonomy, and therefore did not issue silver coins. Cf. J. P. Barron (see note 84a), 100.

109. (p. 241) Cf. Philochorus, *FGrH* 328 F 121 (a better source than Plutarch), and Jacoby's extensive commentary, against the view, predominant now-

adays, that *all* the trials of Pericles' friends belong to the years immediately before the war. Even Jacoby cannot completely prove his case, but he makes it more than likely. F. J. Frost, *Historia* 1964, 385, *JHS* 1964, 69, on the other hand, goes too far in trying to date all the trials to about 438. Our evidence is generally obscured by the fact that comedy as well as other sources later combined the trials with the more or less funny attempts at finding reasons for Pericles' responsibility in starting the great war.

110. (p. 241) As is well known, it was Pericles who said (Thuc. 2, 65), 'You have your rule ὡς τυραννίδα'; Cleon (3, 37) repeats the phrase, but without ὡς, and the Athenian envoys to Camarina (6, 85) say in general that for 'a tyrant or a polis holding an ἀρχή' only the principle of usefulness (ξυμφέρον) exists. If that means that Pericles made a comparison, while the others identified *archē* with *tyrannis*, the difference in my view is really irrelevant.

111. (p. 241) See note 70.

112. (p. 242) Thuc. 2, 40, 1: φιλοκαλοῦμεν τε γὰρ μετ᾽ εὐτελείας, καὶ φιλοσοφοῦμεν ἄνευ μαλακίας. The famous sentence of Pericles' Funeral Speech is not as easy to understand as is often assumed; cf. Gomme 2, 119. My own translation is based on the view that only the reference to *individual* εὐτέλεια and μαλακία can make sense. The contrast between public and personal conditions dominates indeed the following sentences as well.

113. (p. 243) If the comedian Hermippus was the prosecutor against Aspas a (Plut. 32, 1), the earlier date is unlikely, though not impossible; his lifetime as a writer extended, as far as we know, from *c.* 431 to *c.* 417. However, the accusation of procuring free women for Pericles sounds like a piece of comedy rather than a historical legal charge, just like the brothel girls in Aristophanes' *Acharnians* (526 ff.), whose abduction was claimed to have caused the Megarian decree.

114. (p. 243) Cf. *Sophocles and Pericles*, 91 ff., from where I repeat a few sentences.

115. (p. 243) Others with whom Pericles had some kind of personal relations were, as mentioned before, the town-planner Hippodamus and the great sophist Protagoras, both true exponents of the 'modern', essentially rationalist, spirit; but we do not know whether they can be called his friends. About Damon, allegedly Pericles' music teacher, but probably belonging to a later date, see *Sophokles u. Perikles* (German edn.), 115, 1.

116. (p. 244) To what extent Thucydides used Pericles' ideas or even words is one of the most disputed points in the Thucydidean debate. As I have made

it clear on an earlier occasion (*Sophocles and Pericles, passim*), I believe that in the speeches we can find traces, and even more than traces, of the original Pericles.

117. (p. 244) Cf. J. Vogt, *HZ* 182 (1956), 249 = *Orbis* (Freiburg 1960), 47.

118. (p. 245) *IG* I², 56, v. 5 ff. (*SEG* 12, 23). Cf. Gomme, 1, 382. The slanderous gossip in Stesimbrotus' anti-Athenian pamphlet 'On Themistocles and Thucydides and Pericles' (*FGrH* 107), which was greatly used by Plutarch, has no historical value, whether it represents a voice from the allies' camp, as is the majority view among scholars, or is simply a kind of schoolmasterly example of pre-Herodotean popular attitudes; cf. F. Schachermeyr, *SB. Oesterr. Akad.* 1965.

119. (p. 245) *ML*, no. 49 (probably 446/5 and perhaps abandoned after the foundation of Amphipolis). The colony was mentioned by Cratinus (fr. 395) and Theopompus, and thus its name got into the lexica (Hesych. Steph. Byz. s. v.). There is no other literary evidence, unless we read (with Bergk and A. G. Woodhead, *CQ* 1952, 57) in Thuc. 1, 61, 4: ἀφικόμενοι ἐς Βρέαν κἀκεῖθεν ἐπὶ Στρέψαν (for ... Βέριοαν ... ἐπιστρέψαντες). In that case Brea would be situated on the north-western shore of the Chalcidice, between Therma and Strepsa; but cf. C. D. Edson, *CP* 1955, 169; A. J. Graham, *Colony* and *Mother City*, 34. The decree shows that Brea belonged to the official district ἐπὶ Θρᾴκης within the Athenian area of rule; the names of the five districts appear for the first time in the tribute list of 443–442 (see above, p. 219). Woodhead dates the decree in *c.* 438, Mattingly, *Historia* 1963, 258, as late as 426–425.

120. (p. 246) Cf. my *Aspects of the Ancient World*, 131 = *PI* 234. *CP* 1952, 143 = *PI* 246.

121. (p. 246) For the date of the expedition cf. *ATL* 3, 114, though it seems difficult to accept their date of 450.

122. (p. 246) French, loc. cit., 125.

123. (p. 247) The sum total and its changes are a matter of dispute. The fundamental evidence is Thuc. 2, 13, 2 ff., and its different version in schol. Ar. *Plut.* 1193. Gomme's commentary provides most of the material of the debate; cf. also B. D. Meritt, *Hesperia* 1954, 185, and Gomme, *Historia* 1955, 333.

124. (p. 248) Cf. the table in my *Greek State* (London, 1969²), 31. In general see French, loc. cit., chs. 7 and 8.

125. (p. 248) Cf. in general my *People of Aristophanes, passim.*

126. (p. 249) Cf. the literature, mentioned ch. 1, note 29.

127. (p. 249) We shall concentrate on the Parthenon, without forgetting the large number of other buildings, sacred and profane, which Pericles built, among them (apart from the Propylaea), for instance, the Odeion, a hall for musical and other performances, which Cratinus (fr. 71) thought looked like the helmet on Pericles' 'squill-shaped' head. Outside the city there were, e.g., the Nemesis temple at Rhamnus, the Poseidon temple of Sunion, and the new telesterion at Eleusis.

128. (p. 249) Cf. D. S. Robertson, *A Handbook of Greek and Roman Architecture* (Cambridge 1943²), 115.

129. (p. 249) The numbers of front and side columns at the Parthenon are eight and seventeen, while the average Doric temple has six in front, and anything between twelve and eighteen on the sides.

130. (p. 249) That strange myth, which reveals the close relationship between Zeus and Athena, could become a subject of comedy (Hermipp. frs. 1–6). As so often, awe and laughter went together in Greek religion.

131. (p. 250) Cf. my *People and Aristophanes*, 254.

132. (p. 250) Cf. the excellent small book by C. J. Herrington, *Athena Parthenos and Athena Polias* (Manchester 1955), also various scholars in *Greece and Rome*, 1963, Supplement 'Parthenos and Parthenon'; generally on the two trends also my *Sophocles and Pericles* (Oxford 1954). The fact, however, that there were two temples on the Acropolis, and therefore the vision of Athena in two forms (or originally perhaps two different goddesses), goes back to the sixth or early fifth century (cf. W. H. Plommer, *JHS* 1960, 127), though it seems impossible for the outsider to get from the contradictory reports of the archaeologists a comparatively clear picture of the archaic Acropolis; cf. I. T. Hill, *The Ancient City of Athens* (London 1953), ch. 14. Herrington, 36 f., makes it likely that all the chryselephantine statues of the period were not real cult figures. Athena Promachos had a statue, but no temple; she was Athena Polias in battle.

133. (p. 252) Cf. again *Sophocles and Pericles*, *passim*.

134. (p. 253) Cf. the edition of the *Alcestis*, by A. M. Dale (Oxford 1954), also A. P. Burnett, *CP* 1965, 240; A. Lesky, *Greek Tragedy* (London 1965), 141.

135. (p. 253) Cf. the reconstruction, however doubtful, by B. Snell, *Scenes from Greek Drama* (Univ. of California Press, 1964), ch. 2.

135a. (p. 253) On the question of Hippolytus' (and Phaedra's!) purity cf. Chr. Segal, *Hermes* 1970, 278.

136. (p. 254) We have very few reliable sources for the fifth-century history of the western Greeks. Pindar is the only contemporary source of import-ance, as far as it goes. The only fairly coherent source are sections of Dio-dorus, books 11 and 12; much of it may go back to Timaeus, but even so it is rather poor evidence. Some good material is preserved in the Pindar scholia. As to modern literature, it is best to consult the general Greek histories (see above, p. 386, n. 7), and some nineteenth-century histories of Sicily, such as E. A. Freeman's. Generally important: D. Randall-McIver, *Greek Cities in Italy and Sicily* (Oxford 1931); for particular aspects, e.g., W. Hüttl, *Verfassungsgesch. von Syrakus* (Prague 1929); H. Wentzker, *Sizilien und Athen* (Heidelberg 1956); but cf. K. F. Stroheker, *Gnomon* 1958, 31; a good survey: M. I. Finley, *Ancient Sicily* (London, 1968).

137. (p. 254) Aeschylus died in Gela in 456–455. Nothing more is known about his death. Was he a voluntary exile who had no intention of returning to Athens? It is possible, but unlikely. He was not a politician, but a patriot; when he wrote his own epitaph he spoke of himself not as a poet and trage-dian but merely as one who had fought at Marathon.

138. (p. 256) Diod. 11, 86, 2 (for 454–453), speaks of a war in which Segesta was concerned. Unfortunately the text Ἐγεσταίοις καί Λιλυβαίοις ἐνέστη πόλεμος is doubtful; cf. the discussion by *ML*, no. 37, also *SEG* 25, no. 3. For Λιλυβαίοις (not founded before the fourth century!) we must read Ἁλικυαίοις; Halicyaea is very close to the upper part of the Mazaros river, and the war was about land πρὸς τῷ Μαζάρῳ ποταμῷ. That would mean an unimportant frontier fight between the two Elymian places, usually on good terms with one another. It is unlikely that Diodorus' description refers to such a minor war, and Beloch has suggested to insert ⟨πρὸς Σελινουντίους⟩. That can be justified by the fact that the Mazaros river runs through the western part of the country between Segesta and Selinus; the town of Mazara was situated on the shore, about twenty miles west of Selinus. Naturally, all this reconstruction remains hypothetical.

139. (p. 256) The date depends on the name of the archon, of which only the ending is extant. The attempted readings are Ἄριστ]ον (454–453), or Ἁ]β[ρ]ον (458–457), or even Ἀντ]ιφόν (418–417). No full agreement has so far been reached. Klaffenbach and Meritt (*BCH* 1964, 413) as well as *ML* insist on 'Habron', and a thorough examination by Vanderpool has failed to discover the slightest trace of 'Antiphon'.

140. (p. 257) 'Petalism' (olive-leaf verdict) was a copy of ostracism, but seems to have worked far more disastrously than the Athenian model. Cf. Hüttl, loc. cit., 69, and above p. 308 f.

141. (p. 257) Cf. K. v. Fritz, *Pythagorean Politics in South Italy* (New York 1940).

142. (p. 257) Treaties of 433–432 (*ML*, nos. 63, 64. *DSDA* nos. 162. 163) have prescripts engraved upon earlier ones. The text of the treaties served at the second occasion as it had done at the previous one. The date of the latter is unknown.

143. (p. 258) Cf. F. W. Walbank, Κωκαλος 1968–69, 476.

VII · THE PELOPONNESIAN WAR

1. (p. 259) The date of the book is still being discussed; cf. M. J. Fontana, *L'Athenaion politeia del 5 secolo* (1968).

1a. (p. 259) Πελοποννήσιος πόλεμος: Aelian. 12, 53. Paus. 4, 6, 1. But Strabo 13, 600 (cf. 14, 654: τὰ Πελοποννησιακά) has τῷ Πελοποννησιάκῳ πολέμωι, and Cic. *de rep.* 3, 44. *de off.* 1, 84, *Peloponnesiacum bellum*, while Nepos several times uses the pleasanter form *Peloponnesium*. Anyway, it was not before Hellenistic times that 'the Peloponnesian war' became the usual name.

2. (p. 259) Thuc. 5, 28, 2, just mentioned. Aristot. *pol.* 1303a, 10: τὸν Λακωνικὸν πόλεμον.

3. (p. 260) B. W. Henderson, it is true, gave his book on the war the title *The Great War between Athens and Sparta* (London, 1927).

4. (p. 260) The ἀληθεστάτη πρόφασις looks like a deliberately chosen expression for something that was at the same time ἀφανεστάτη λόγῳ, not spoken of, unavowed, while in 5, 6, 1 it is opposed to the clearly suitable (εὐπρεπές), Gomme 1, 153, maintains that αἰτία and πρόφασις are interchangeable and have the same meaning of 'cause'. While the αἰτίαι were 'grievances', the truest reason was anything but a pretext. It was the true 'motive'. Cf. L. Pearson, *TAPA* 1952, 205. R. Sealey, *CQ* 1957, 1. A. Momigliano, 'On Causes of War in Ancient Historiography', *Studies in Historiography* (London 1966), 116; v. Fritz, I 623 ff.; C. Schäublin, *Mus. Helvet.* 1971, 133. See also above, p. 370.

5. (p. 260) For details cf. A. J. Graham, *Colony and Mother City in Ancient Greece*, ch. VII. He rightly maintains that there was no general legal arrangement in the relations between Corinth and her colonies, but even so speaks

of a colonial empire – with less justification, I believe, than is done even in the case of Athens. Corinth exercised a fairly close, though not uniform, control, but we cannot even speak of a Corinthian ἀρχή.

6. (p. 261) Thuc. 1, 27, 1: ἐπὶ τῇ ἴσῃ καὶ ὁμοίᾳ. It is interesting that the oligarchy of Corinth was willing to accept and to continue the democratic rule at Epidamnus.

7. (p. 261) That is another argument for the fact that her control was not a strict (and therefore dangerous) rule.

8. (p. 261) For the chronology cf. Gomme 1, 165. 196 ff.

9. (p. 262) Seeking Athenian support, the Corcyreans must apologize for having been neutral. They call that ἀπραγμοσύνη, which is usually, but by no means always as Gomme maintains (p. 68), a complimentary term.

10. (p. 263) Thuc. 1, 56, 2: ἐπιδημιουργούς. The powers held by these officials are unknown, but they confirm, at any rate, the close connexion between Corinth and her colony. It is equally unknown whether a similar office existed in other Corinthian colonies.

11. (p. 263) Thuc. 1, 58, 1: τὰ τέλη τῶν Λακεδαιμονίων, probably the ephors or at least some of them. Nothing came of that promise. The progress of events is illuminated by the variations of the tribute; cf. *ATL* 3, 64. 321.

12. (p. 263) Cf. Hermippus, fr. 63, 8 (Kock).

13. (p. 263) In this battle, as Plato tells us, the young Alcibiades, surprisingly serving as a hoplite, was wounded and saved by Socrates (*Charm.* 153 a–c, *Symp.* 220 d/c). For the heavy losses of the Athenians see the fine epigrams of the epitaph (Tod, no. 59. *SEG* 10, 414).

14. (p. 264) Thuc. 1, 66: ἰδίᾳ γὰρ ταῦτα οἱ Κορίνθιοι ἔπραξαν. With some, and against other, commentators (e.g. Gomme), I believe this means a separate, but not an unofficial, action. The Corinthian army at Potidaea included volunteers and Peloponnesian mercenaries (Thuc. 1, 60, 1) – who paid the latter if not the state? It is right, however, that there was no official declaration of war; therefore the citizens enrolled nominally as volunteers.

15. (p. 264) As is well known, Aristophanes (*Ach.* 526) says that the abduction by the Megarians of two of Aspasia's 'whores' caused Pericles' anger and the outbreak of the war. In *Peace*, 605, it was his own weakened position, as shown by the trials of his friends (Pheidias' trial of probably 438 is mentioned), that drove Pericles on to rush into war. However unhistorical the

stories are, some aspects of public opinion, and perhaps even some sort of policy, are reflected in those passages. Plut. *Per.* 30, 3, speaks of the killing at Megara of a herald, Anthemocritus, and of the decree of Charinus threatening with death every Megarian on Attic soil, and letting the strategi swear to invade Megara twice a year. The latter fact is confirmed by Thuc. 4, 66, but the date of Charinus' decree is still disputed; cf. W. R. Connor, *AJP* 1962, 225 (352–349 B.C.!); K. J. Dover, *AJP* 1966, 203 (432–431). Dover is clearly right against Connor (who later revised his theory; *REG* 1970, 305), but I would like (with e.g., Ed. Meyer) to put Charinus' decree *after* that of Pericles, i.e. 431–430.

16. (p. 265) Papers on the prehistory of the Peloponnesian war are legion; most helpful probably are H. Nesselhauf, *Hermes* 1934, 286, and of course Gomme's commentary.

17. (p. 267) Cf. Gomme 2, 9; in general, J. de Romilly, *Thucydides and Athenian Imperialism* (Oxford 1963). For the Athenian dynamism (expressed in the word πολυπραγμοσύνη) cf. *JHS* 67 (1947), 46 = *PI* 466. See also note 9.

18. (p. 267) Cf. my *Greek State* (London, 1969²), 122 f.

19. (p. 268) They even brought the wooden fixtures of their houses, such as doors and window frames – an indication of how valuable any timber was; perhaps it was also the intention to remove as much combustible stuff as possible.

20. (p. 269) The settlers were almost certainly cleruchs; cf. *CP* 1952, 146 = *PI* 248. Aegina could serve as an important base for the Athenian navy.

21. (p. 269) Cf. Gomme 2, 144. *SEG* 25, no. 44.

22. (p. 270) Cf. Gomme 2, 88.

23. (p. 270) According to Thuc. 2, 34, this official burial was a πάτριος νόμος. Marathon (see § 5) and Plataea (not mentioned in this context by Thucydides) would then be exceptions. On the whole question cf. F. Jacoby, *JHS* 1944, 37; Gomme 2, 94.

24. (p. 270) They were different from Antigone's divine unwritten laws (see my *Sophocles and Pericles*, ch. 2). On Pericles, and Thucydides' portrait of him, see also p. 369.

25. (p. 270) Cf. J. H. Finley, *HSt* 1938, 37. On the Greek concept of freedom and its effects on later times see my paper in: *The Living Heritage of Greek Antiquity* (The Hague, 1967).

26. (p. 272) Cf. *AJP* 1945, 127.

27. (p. 272) Thuc. 2, 59, 3. This was immediately before his deposition; why more or less the same is said in 55, 2 (στρατηγὸς ὢν καὶ τότε), is unexplained.

28. (p. 272) Nor do we know who was his accuser. Cf. Gomme 2, 182. See below, note 106.

28a. (p. 273) A modern analogy is Bismarck; he too left a gap that could not be filled by his successors.

29. (p. 273) These stories sound somewhat like the horror stories going round during the two world wars, but they will have contained some truth just as the modern ones. The killing of the envoys by the Athenians is one of the few late events mentioned by Herodotus (7, 137; cf. above, p. 133).

30. (p. 273) Phormio established a close friendship with the Acarnanians, but the story of his later life is obscure. Thucydides is silent on that theme. Androtion (*FGrH* 324 F 8; cf. also Paus. 1, 23, 10) knows of a trial, and Thuc. 3, 8, of an expedition under his son at the request of the Acarnanians; where Phormio was then (exiled, dead, offended?) we are not told. In later memory Phormio lived on as an outstanding soldier (Aristoph. *Peace*, 347, *Lysistr.* 804). The complex questions involved are discussed by myself, *AJP* 1945, 122; F. Jacoby, *FGrH* 3b, 125. 532; Gomme, 2, 234.

31. (p. 273) A dedication (*ML*, no. 66) runs: ἐποίκων ἐς Ποτιδαίαν, and the same word ἔποικοι is used in the later oath (*ATL* D 21) and in Thuc. 2, 70. I have tried to show that Thucydides' use of ἄποικοι and ἔποικοι is indiscriminate (*CP* 1952, 143 = *PI* 245), but the official use in this case must mean that the colonists were 'to supplement the city's depleted population' (Tod, no. 146). Cf. also Brunt, *ASAI* 77.

32. (p. 273) This refers primarily to the victory of an Athenian force of trained *peltastai* under Iphicrates over Spartan hoplites in 390 B.C. (Xen. 4, 5, 13).

33. (p. 274) *Demagogos* is the leader of the demos, natural and necessary in every democracy. In that sense Pericles was a demagogue. Our strongly anti-democratic tradition, however, made them *a priori* despicable seducers of the people. Cf. M. I. Finley, *Past and Present* 1962, 3. Cleon has found defenders, ever since Grote, as well as hostile criticism. For the former cf. A. G. Woodhead, *Mnemosyne* 13 (1960), 289.

33a. (p. 274) Cf. D. Gillies, *AJP* 1971, 38, also T. J. Quinn, *Historia* 1971, 405.

34. (p. 275) Thucydides speaks of πρόφασις and αἰτίαι, as he did in the famous chapter 1, 23, 6; but the words have a different meaning here; both practically mean complaints about Athenian policy.

35. (p. 275) Thuc. 3, 19, 1, speaks of τότε πρῶτον, which may mean the first time in this war, hardly the first time at all; cf. the Callias decree (*ATL* D 2, 15), and other inscriptions (*ATL* D 11, 58. *SEG* 10, 37. 25, 14), all mentioning the *eisphora* as something familiar. In the same year a fleet went out to collect tributes, but perished in Caria. This is in complete contrast to Thuc. 3, 17, where the strength of Athenian naval and financial power is stressed far beyond reality. Cf. Gomme, and my short remark, *Historia* 1958, 252.

36. (p. 275) For the interpretation of the debate cf. F. M. Wassermann, *TAPA* 1956, 32; D. Ebener, *Wiss. Zeitschr. d. Universität Halle-Wittenberg* V (1955–6); A. Andrewes, *Phoenix* 1962, 64; R. P. Winnington-Ingram, *BICS* 1965, 70. The last mentioned stresses in particular the inherent dramatic, even tragic, line of argument. Τὰ δέοντα εἰπεῖν was the principle according to which Thucydides shaped the speeches in his work (1, 22, 1), and τὰ δέοντα was rarely identical with what the speakers actually said. Much can also be learnt from the debate about the views and prejudices of the common man.

37. (p. 276) They are called 'the most guilty'. Thuc. 3, 50, speaks of more than a thousand, a figure which has rightly been regarded as too high.

38. (p. 276) We have no tradition about the date; but the description of the plague, and its likeness to that by Thucydides, make a date soon after 429 (which seems also right for other reasons) probable. Cf. my *Sophocles and Pericles*, 114. From another point of view, that of Attic penal law, the closeness of the play to its contemporary surroundings is stressed by G. Greifenhagen, *Hermes* 1966, 147.

39. (p. 276) Cf. *Sophocles and Pericles*, 34. 66. 153. The question whether the expression ἀνδρῶν πρῶτος (*OR.* 33) can be a hint at Pericles, whom Thucydides calls so, is discussed ibid., 112. E. R. Dodds, *Greece and Rome* 1966, 47, in a very illuminating article, objects to the view ascribed to me that 'the character of Oedipus reflects that of Pericles'. I did not mean to compare 'characters', but rather saw Pericles' position – political and intellectual – to some extent reflected in Sophocles' play. F. Schachermeyr, *WSt* 1966, 60, supports my interpretation.

40. (p. 276) Cf. A. Lesky, *Greek Tragedy* (London 1965), 10; Dodds, loc. cit., 48.

41. (p. 277) Cf. R. P. Winnington-Ingram, in: *Classical Drama and its In-fluence* (London 1965), 31; *JHS* 1971, 119.

42. (p. 277) Chapter 84, partly repeating the points of the two previous chapters, and partly contradicting them, is generally regarded as not genuine. Cf. recently A. Fuks, *AJP* 1971, 48.

43. (p. 277) See above, p. 259. The most likely date for the book is between 431 and 424, i.e. after the beginning of the war (cf. 2, 14. 3, 2), and before the expedition of Brasidas (cf. 2, 5). Nothing is known about the author, or the occasion for which it was written.

44. (p. 278) Cf. Plat. *Hipp. maior* 282 B. We shall have more to say about Gorgias in the next chapter.

45. (p. 278) For some reason Aristophanes did not act himself as χοροδι-δάσκαλος, but left the task of production to a man Callisthenes – not only because of his youth, since the same happened later. However, as events showed, the poet's name was known, even though it did not appear in the official files, which always registered that of the producer.

46. (p. 279) See ch. VI, note 101.

47. (p. 279) Cf. my *People of Aristophanes* (New York 1962), 26. 44.

48. (p. 279) Cf. C. H. Whitman, *Aristophanes and the Comic Hero* (Cambridge, Mass. 1964), 61.

49. (p. 279) In Pind. *P.* 8, 22, Aegina is called δικαιόπολις . . . νῆσος. In giving the name to an individual, Aristophanes makes him, as it were, a polis of his own – very fitting for a man who concludes a peace treaty of his own.

50. (p. 280) The word for it is ἐπιτειχισμός (cf. Thuc. 1, 122, 1), and its most effective occurrence was the occupation of Deceleia by the Spartans (below, ch. VIII, note 30). The events round Pylos: Thuc. 4, 2–41.

51. (p. 282) Cf. Gomme 3, 458. I cannot explain what it means that accord-ing to Aristoph. *Ach.* 652, Sparta had offered peace against the surrender of Aegina, but the offer was refused. There was, as far as I know, no situation before the occupation of Pylos which could have led to such an offer. Was it said only for the sake of the joke about Aristophanes himself? In that case it was an amazing prophecy.

52. (p. 283) Andoc. *de pace* 29. *DSDA* 183. Cf. P. A. Brunt, *Phoenix* 1965, 262.

53. (p. 284) ἀργυρολόγοι νῆες, Thuc. 2, 69, 1. 3, 19, 1. 4, 50, 1; cf. *ATL* 3, 67. Text (often doubtful), translation, and interpretation of the assessment of 425–424; *ATL* A 9. 3, 70; cf. B. D. Meritt and A. B. West, *The Athenian Assessment of 425 B.C.* (Ann Arbor 1934). On the μισθοφόροι τριήρεις (Arist. *Eq.* 555), obviously a joke on the usual ἀργυρολόγοι, cf. my *People of Aristophanes*, 304, 6.

54. (p. 285) Or does he mean to say that he is 'sub-human', and Cleon is 'the superhuman colossus' (Whitman [see note 48], 103)? I am not so sure. Either explanation seems to fit when Demosthenes later (1255) claims that he made him a man, and we only then learn the sausage-seller's name, Agoracritus, the 'pick of the market'. It is different when in the *Clouds* Strepsiades thinks he can make a man of his son, whom he still calls 'little boy' (παιδάριον), by teaching him there are no gods (823). Cf. R. A. Neil's note in his edition of the *Knights* (Cambridge, 1901).

55. (p. 285) It is partly, but not only, the medium of comedy that makes Aristophanes' picture of Cleon so much more hateful than even that by Thucydides, who certainly regarded him as an evil for Athens and, as F. E. Adcock puts it (*Thucydides and his History* (Cambridge 1963), 63), 'if there was a doubt . . . Thucydides would not give Cleon the benefit of it'.

56. (p. 285) Cf., above all, G. Zuntz, *The Political Plays of Euripides* (Manchester 1955). I cannot follow him in all his arguments, and the *Heracleidae* remain for me a bad and incomplete play; but his dates (*Heracleidae* 430, *Suppliants* 424) have much to recommend them; *Hecuba* will be only a little later, *Andromache* probably earlier (cf. P. T. Stevens' edition, Oxford 1971). A passage in the *Suppliants* (1191 ff.) seems to speak of the possibility of an Argive invasion into Attica. That was outside everything we know of the times of the Archidamian war, though 'Argos exploited . . . the profitable position of the *tertius gaudens*' (Zuntz, 92). I cannot believe that the terms of Adrastus' oath were written on a tripod actually extant at Delphi at that time (Zuntz, 77), but doubts about the attitude of Argos may have been in the minds of the Athenians (cf. Aristoph. *Eq.* 465).

57. (p. 286) It is perhaps right to mention in this context that Euripides from the fourth century onwards was the favourite playwright, far outstripping Aeschylus and Sophocles. He was, after all, ahead of his time, especially in thought and psychology.

58. (p. 286) Probably shortly before, Sparta had promised freedom to two thousand helots who were believed to have excelled in the war. After a solemn religious ceremony those two thousand simply disappeared, 'and nobody knew how each of them perished' (Thuc. 4, 80, 4). It seems odd that

Gomme describes Grote's horror of that perfidy as 'old-fashioned'. He probably means that the experiences of our generation reduce those of the past to minor affairs. But the moral issue remains the same and is not changed by being more up to date.

59. (p. 290) The description of the chorus wavers between *Panhellenes*, coming from various states specifically mentioned, and, on the other hand, Attic peasants. It is useless to trace in this inconsistency anything particular; it lies within the limits of poetical licence, but as such it is significant. Cf. *People of Aristophanes* 55, 1, M. Platnauer's edition (Oxford 1963), and J. S. Morrison, *CR* 1965, 272.

60. (p. 291) He speaks (6, 26, 2) of the continuous (συνεχής) war when he refers to the Archidamian war, as contrasted with the time after 421.

60a. (p. 291) For the whole of this chapter cf. Gomme, vol. 4 (ed. by A. Andrewes and K. J. Dover, Oxford 1970).

61. (p. 292) *neodamodeis*: cf. *RE* 16, 2396, and note 63.

62. (p. 292) Here we have the double evidence of Thucydides (5, 47) and an inscription (Tod, no. 72. *DSDA* no. 193) which can be restored with the help of Thucydides' text. There are a number of differences between the two versions, none of them of historical significance. For the text of Thucydides, too much weight should not be attached to these discrepancies, only too common in Greek documents. An impressive illustration of Athenian activities during the years 418–414 is the list of payments from Athena's treasury (*ML*, no. 77).

63. (p. 292) The formula in Thuc. 5, 57: αὐτοὶ καὶ οἱ Εἵλωτες πανδημεί (repeated in ch. 64) is unique. Obviously it indicates a new development of helots serving as hoplites. This is confirmed by the appearance of the *neodamodeis*, who are frequently mentioned together with the helots in the army. They were not 'new citizens' but liberated helots who were called 'men newly attached to the damos' (literary 'smelling of the damos'). Our sources mention them between 421 and 370, that is to say, in a period of military pressure and great need of soldiers (cf. *RE* 16, 2390). It was a source bound to dry up; at any rate, it did not provide first-class hoplites, and later they were replaced by mercenaries. Cf. also Gomme 4, 35 f.

64. (p. 292) Thuc. 5, 65–75. There are many interesting and disputable points in Thucydides' detailed description of the battle. I do not wish to go into the tactical details, fascinating as they are, but I should like to mention that the Spartan army is called ἄρχοντες ἀρχόντων (66, 4), which means, as explained in the previous paragraph, that there were

officers down to the smallest unit, the *enomotia*; this can only imply that responsibility was widespread, and discipline not based on blind obedience alone. The independence of the king as army leader, on the other hand, was limited to the extent that Agis was accompanied by no less than ten ξύμβουλοι (63, 4). In fact, he acted quite independently during the battle; thus the many cooks did not spoil the broth.

65. (p. 292) The text of the treaty (5, 79) is interesting for several reasons. For the two states concerned as well as the other Peloponnesian cities, much emphasis is laid on the ἴσοις καὶ ὁμοίοις δίκαι κατὰ πάτρια, and this rule of equal rights is extended to all allies outside the Peloponnese. Thus, any appearance of Spartan hegemony was avoided. The allies are described as αὐτόνομοι καὶ αὐτοπόλιες, the latter an ἅπαξ λεγόμενον, which only emphasizes the meaning of political independence. Finally, arbitration is prescribed between the states in all cases of dispute. It is doubtful whether the last sentence, τὼς δὲ ἔτας καττὰ πάτρια δικάζεσθαι refers to the justice administered to private citizens (ἔται) in another city.

65a. (p. 293) Cf. A. Andrewes in Gomme 4, 182 ff.

66. (p. 293) Sparta meanwhile destroyed the half-finished Long Walls of Argos, the work of the whole people including women and children, which would have secured the sea connexions, and thus the potential support by Athens (5, 81). Worse still was that the Spartans captured the Argive town of Hysiae, and executed all free men.

67. (p. 294) Phryn. fr. 59: κοὐχ ὑποταγεὶς ἐβάδιζεν ὥσπερ Νίκιας. Edmonds compares the modern concept of the inferiority complex, but it would rather be the result of Nicias' piety and superstition.

68. (p. 294) The best modern book on Alcibiades is by J. Hatzfeld, *Alcibiade* (Paris 1940, later reprinted). On Thucydides as a source for Alcibiades cf. E. Delebecque, *Thucydide et Alcibiade* (Aix-en-Provence 1965), though this is rather hypothetical (cf. H. D. Westlake, *CR* 1967, 24).

68a. (p. 294) For the γραφὴ παρανόμων cf. H. J. Wolff, *SB Heidelb. Akad.* 1970.

69. (p. 295) Andoc. 3, 8 f. (a programme rather than facts). See also Thuc. 6, 12, 1. Cf. *ATL* 3, 346, on the difficult problems of finance during that period, also D. M. MacDowell, *CR* 1965, 260.

70. (p. 295) In a different way Sophocles in his *Electra* did the same, that is, put characters of human strength and weakness in the place of the traditional myth; cf. H. F. Johansen, *Class. et Mediaevalia* 1964, 8. A. Lesky, *Greek*

Tragedy, 169, like other scholars, dates Euripides' *Electra* in 413, because ships in Sicilian waters are mentioned (1347). I am not sure that this is conclusive, and Zuntz, *Political Plays*, 68, makes it fairly certain that the date is wrong. Cf. G. Ronnet, *REG* 1970, 309, but also C. W. Fornara, *JHS* 1971, 30. To the problems of the *Heracles*, on which I could only touch in the text, cf. my 'Tragic Heracles', *PI* 380, especially 391.

71. (p. 296) The prophetic role of Euripides was repeated when in March 1914 the Austrian poet Franz Werfel published his translation (*Die Troerinnen des Euripides*) as 'a sign of the coming revolution'. 'The wretched Hecuba may now return as her time has come again.' Hamlet's question 'What's Hecuba to him, and he to Hecuba, that he should weep for her?' has been answered throughout the ages, recently again by J.-P. Sartre in an impressive reshaping of the play (*Les Troyennes*, Paris 1965); he regards the tragedy as 'une condemnation de la guerre en général, et des expéditions coloniales en particulier'.

72. (p. 297) Cf. A. Lesky, *Entretiens Fondation Hardt* 6 (1959), 132.

73. (p. 297) The special character of the two books 6 and 7 has always been noticed, and ever since W. Schadewaldt, *Die Geschichtsschreibung des Thukydides* (Berlin 1929), they have been at the centre of discussion. Cf. also W. Liebeschütz, *Historia* 1968, 289.

74. (p. 298) Thuc. 6, 8. The original decree, it seems, left the question still open whether one or three commanders should be appointed (*ML*, no. 78b. *SEG* 10, 107).

75. (p. 298) We find here the expression 'let us not have disastrous craving for things beyond our reach' ($\delta\upsilon\sigma\acute{\epsilon}\rho\omega\tau\epsilon\varsigma$ $\epsilon\hat{\iota}\nu\alpha\iota$ $\tau\hat{\omega}\nu$ $\mathring{\alpha}\pi\acute{o}\nu\tau\omega\nu$). Scholars have rightly stressed that this concept has strong emotional meaning for the Greeks. Pindar (*P.* 4, 20) says of Coronis, who is unfaithful to her lover Apollo: $\mathring{\eta}\rho\alpha\tau o$ $\tau\hat{\omega}\nu$ $\mathring{\alpha}\pi\acute{o}\nu\tau\omega\nu$. These are the same words, but Pindar adds a general verdict on the useless sort of people who have far-reaching aims, and at the same time neglect things at home. We find the same on a different plane in Alexander's *pothos* for the unknown; cf. my *Alexander and the Greeks* (Oxford 1938), ch. 2 = *PI* 458. 499.

76. (p. 300) The matter remains to some extent obscure. Thucydides could have little direct knowledge of what was going on behind the scenes. It was different with Andocides, who was the main informer, and probably guilty himself. Thus, Andoc. *de mysteriis*, [Lysias], *In Andocidem* (6), and the *vita Andocidis* (from Plutarch, *vitae decem oratorum*) are important sources, though none of them is impartial in the questions involved. Cf. the full discussions

in the edition of Andocides, *On the Mysteries*, by D. M. MacDowell (Oxford 1962), and Gomme 4, 264 ff.

77. (p. 300) A badly mutilated inscription (*SEG* 17, 7) mentions sums received, obviously in support of the expedition. Apart from the Sicels, who seem to play the greatest role, Rhegium is mentioned with at least seventy-five, and Catane with over thirty talents.

78. (p. 303) Examples of such inscriptions: *SEG* 13, 12–22. 15, 29 (*ML*, no. 79). On the whole evidence, the kind and the amount of property sold, and the possible gains by the state, see D. M. Lewis, *ASAI* 177.

79. (p. 304) Cf. the black-figured oenochoe, Brit. Mus. B 509 (*c.* 500 B.C.), often reproduced, e.g. in my *People of Aristophanes*, pl. IIc.

80. (p. 304) Cf. C. H. Whitman (see note 48), especially 172 ff., though I am not certain whether Aristophanes was actually following Gorgias' 'philosophy of nothingness'.

81. (p. 305) Cf. *People of Aristophanes*², 122, 7. 157, 10. Peithetaerus' actions remind us of the anecdote (Plut. *Alc.* 5) of Alcibiades dealing with the collectors and his metic friend; he even uses the threat of the whip, which in the *Birds* remains no mere threat.

82. (p. 306) The word 'tyrant' (1708) here means no more than 'king' or ruler. A few lines before (1673), Peithetaerus promised to make the bastard Heracles (νόθος) a tyrant. His own name may mean 'the persuasive member of a hetaeria'; cf. F. Sartori, *Le eterie nella vita politica*, etc. (Rome 1957).

83. (p. 306) My interpretation of the *Birds* (cf. note 81) is due to the shock when I realized that it was not simply a story of fanciful escape into an ideal Utopia, as I had believed before. [Is it significant that in the production by the Greek Art Theatre, Peithetaerus appeared in the mask of – Lenin?].

84. (p. 307) The γραμματεύς who read it is neither the clerk of the prytans nor the one τῆς βουλῆς, but a third one, elected by vote (!), whose only duty seems to have been to read documents before the assembly or the council (*AP* 54, 3).

85. (p. 307) The lack of money is drastically illustrated by the fact that Thracian mercenaries were sent back as too expensive (Thuc. 7, 27). This group of barbarians committed one of the worst war crimes in sacking the small town of Mycalessus in north Boeotia. The Thebans pursued and punished them (7, 29).

86. (p. 309) About Diocles' leadership and his famous laws we learn only from Diodorus. Whether the lawgiver is different (earlier?) from the politician, as some modern scholars assume, remains doubtful; but Diodorus' narrative contains several inconsistencies.

87. (p. 310) We do not know the special reason for Endius' enmity, but Alcibiades was suspected to have committed adultery with the wife of King Agis, Timaea. Her son Leotychidas, born in 412, was later excluded from kingship as a bastard.

88. (p. 310) Of the three plays, only *Helena* is firmly dated in 412. *Ion* will be near that date, perhaps a few years later, *Iphigeneia in Tauris* a little earlier. On Euripidean chronology, especially also of the lost plays, cf. T. B. L. Webster, *WSt* 1966; *The Tragedies of Euripides* (London 1967), 184 ff.

89. (p. 311) It is most unlikely that this is an allusion to the present intruder into Attica, Agis at Deceleia. This is a question of origin, not of a contemporary situation. And yet the emphasis, repeated so often, on the theme of the genuine nature of the rulers of Athens seems to ask for some special reason. Perhaps it had something to do with the fact that during those years down to 408 the Erechtheum was being built, and thus the memory of the earliest earth-born king, Erechtheus, was particularly alive. Cf. G. Zuntz, *The Political Plays of Eur.* 64, 1.

90. (p. 311) He naturally hopes that she is no slave woman; that would be worse than not to find his mother at all (1383). It is interesting to notice that, in contrast to this typical Greek attitude, Creusa's old servant maintains (854) that only the name of slave means disgrace, while in every other respect a 'noble' slave is equal to a free man.

91. (p. 311) One particular feature of this play is the 'sightseeing' of the chorus at Delphi (184 ff.), and as a similar feature the long description of tent and tapestries at Xanthus' feast (1122 ff.). It confirms the poet's detachment and secularization of myth. In general, cf. C. Wolff, *HSt* 1965, 169.

91a. (p. 311) The senselessness of the Trojan war, and of war in general, is implied, though not particularly stressed. Cf. the edition by A. M. Dale (Oxford 1967), especially the Introduction.

92. (p. 312) The 'Phoenician island' (204) whence the chorus comes may be Sicily after a Punic invasion, but the allusion would be too vague to be understood by the audience, and anyway does not matter. For the general political aspects of the play – largely negative – cf. D. Ebener, *Eirene* 2 (1960), 71. J. de Romilly, *RPh* 1965, 28, even speaks of Eteocles and Polyneices as 'les successeurs de Périclès'. Cf. also E. Rawson, *GRBS* 1970, 109.

93. (p. 314) This first draft (A) (Thuc. 8, 18) was followed by another one (B) (Thuc. 8, 37), in winter 412–411, and the final treaty (C) of spring 411 (Thuc. 8, 58). The texts are printed side by side, with reference to modern literature, in *DSDA* nos. 200–2. See also notes 95 f.

93a. (p. 314) To the political divisions at Chios cf. T. J. Quinn, *Historia* 1969, 22.

93b. (p. 316) Cf., on the other hand, H. D. Westlake, *JHS* 1956, 99, and U. Schindel, *RhM.* 1970, 281.

94. (p. 316) Unless this fleet never existed, which is unlikely, and contradicted by Thuc. 8, 87.

95. (p. 316) It is very remarkable that Thucydides knows the wording not only of the final treaty but also of the two drafts which were never ratified. He could only have known copies. Whether he got them from Alcibiades, as A. Kirchhoff, *Thukydides und sein Urkundenmaterial* (Berlin 1895), 142, thought, is uncertain, but possible. All three documents are written in Attic dialect, though interspersed with some slight Ionisms, as used among the sophists of that period (cf. *DK* 2, p. 400). We do not know who was primarily responsible for the wording, though it seems likely that the drafts were made by Spartans (Chalcideus, Therimenes, Astyochus) – but why did they in A and B say nothing about the Persian subsidies? And if the text was originally written by Spartans, did they use that dialect as a kind of international language, used in the way French was used in the eighteenth and nineteenth centuries (J. Hatzfeld, *Alcibiade* 222, 3)? We do not know. Cf. also Woodhead (ch. VI, note 67), 138 f.

96. (p. 317) In C the Persian king is mentioned for the date only, while in A he and his sons appear, in B he and Tissaphernes. The satraps in C besides Tissaphernes seem to be included in order to name all Persian rulers in Asia Minor; otherwise these variations remain unexplained. More important is the difference of the title of the treaty, 'alliance' in A, 'articles of agreement' ($\xi\upsilon\nu\theta\tilde{\eta}\kappa\alpha\iota$) in B and C, but in B is added, 'treaty ($\sigma\pi\upsilon\nu\delta\alpha\iota$) and friendship'. The changes seem to indicate a gradual increase in amicable relations.

97. (p. 318) We have two accounts of the revolution of 411, Thucydides' and Aristotle's (*AP* 29–32). They are largely incompatible. For the discussion of the problem cf. C. Hignett, *Hist. of the Ath. Constitution*, Appendix XII, p. 356.

97a. (p. 319) Cf. M. H. Jameson, *Historia* 1971, 541 ff.

98. (p. 319) The story of Alcibiades is most vividly illustrated by the anecdotes and details narrated by Plutarch, *Alcibiades*. I have not used this evidence as it is very doubtful to what extent it can be regarded as historical.

99. (p. 320) Thuc. 8, 86, 4, perhaps rightly, regards this refusal as his greatest service to Athens. If the fleet had left Samos, the rest of the empire would have been lost at once.

100. (p. 321) Cf. A. Fuks, *The Ancestral Constitution* (London 1953). M. I. Finley, *The Ancestral Constitution* (Inaugural, Cambridge 1971). *If* the constitution of the 5,000 ever materialized, and *if AP* 30 is that constitution, i.e. that of Theramenes, however idealized, its most original device is the rule in turn of the four sections of the council. The Boeotian constitution contained a similar feature, but direct influence cannot be confirmed. After all, Boeotia was a federal state (see p. 267). The council, probably the Five Hundred, was elected and not appointed by lot. To this question, and the wider one of the position of the thetes, cf. G. E. M. de Ste Croix, *Historia* 1956, 1. I have not seen C. Domini, *La posizione di Tucidide verso il governo dei Cinquemila* (Torino 1969).

101. (p. 321) At this moment, in the middle of a sentence, Thucydides' work breaks off. It seems certain that he died while writing, probably soon after 400. It is not impossible that a few chapters have been lost, covering some weeks not treated by Xenophon either. The latter's *Hellenica*, however, continued Thucydides immediately; it begins with the words μετὰ δὲ ταῦτα and some items clearly show knowledge of Thucydides (cf. G. E. Underhill, *Commentary on the Hellenica of Xenophon* (Oxford 1900), XVI f.). Xenophon will be our main source for the following years, though a vastly inferior one. The first part of the book deals with the last years of the Peloponnesian war (till 2, 3, 10), followed by a description of the rule of the Thirty and the restoration of democracy. It is likely that these parts were written in the 'nineties of the fourth century. Apart from his many omissions and mistakes, Xenophon has not succeeded in following up, as he tried to do, Thucydides' chronological scheme of summers and winters. His narrative hardly deserves the name of history. Another continuation of Thucydides was the *Hellenica Oxyrhynchia* of which considerable fragments on Papyrus are extant, the earliest concerned with 410 B.C. (ed. V. Bartoletti, *Bibl. Teubneriana* (Leipzig 1959)). From the moment Thucydides is no longer our main source, the doubtful evidence of Diodorus becomes more important; other sources are speeches by Lysias and Andocides.

102. (p. 322) This event is not mentioned by Xenophon. Diod. 13, 52; Philoch. *FGrH* 328 F 139, and later sources date it in summer 410. Only

Aristotle, *AP* 34, 1, puts it after the battle of Arginusae in 406; but his chronology here and in the following chapters is hopelessly confused. Since Sparta obviously regained Pylos in 410 (Diod. 13, 64, 5; cf. Xen. 1, 2, 18), the peace proposal must be earlier. At the same time Athens lost Nisaea, the harbour of Megara (again not in Xen., but Diod. 13, 65 and *Hell. Oxyrh.* fr. Florent. A I).

103. (p. 323) Cf. A. Lesky, *Greek Tragedy* 120; H. J. Mette, *Der verlorene Aischylos* (Berlin 1963), 99. Apart from fragments, we have a comparison of the three Philoctetes plays by Dio Chrys., *or.* 52, and a retelling of Euripides' story, partly in dialogue form, in *or.* 59. To Sophocles' *Philoctetes* cf., e.g., K. Alt, *Hermes* 1961, 141; K. Erbse, *Hermes* 1966, 177.

104. (p. 325) On the election ἐξ ἁπάντων, see ch. VI, note 70.

105. (p. 326) His property was to be restored to him. 'One might well imagine that that would be difficult' (D. M. Lewis, *ASAI* 189), and the restitution will have been made by a grant of land (cf. Isocr. 16, 46). If, as is possible, Aristophanes' *Triphales* was directed against Alcibiades, and if it was performed in 406, it would show that comedy still maintained the right of mentioning what was unmentionable at the moment.

105a. (p. 326) A detailed analysis of our evidence: H. R. Breitenbach, *Historia* 1971, 152.

106. (p. 327) It is not clear whether Cleophon actually accused Alcibiades of treason (Phot. 377a, 18. Himerius, Ecl. ex Photio 36, 15), or whether it was simply a matter of ἐπιχειροτονία, the frequent decision to put a strategos on trial because of his conduct of affairs (cf. *AP* 61, 2).

107. (p. 328) The story of another peace offer by Sparta, and its refusal again by Cleophon, is hardly historical. See note 102.

108. (p. 328) The story of the Sicilian wars was told by Timaeus, the fourth-century historian, who is the main source for Diodorus, bk. 13, in his chapters on the western Greeks. Timaeus, who on the whole was a good and reliable historian, is most likely also the source of the short insertions on the west in Xenophon's *Hellenica* (1, 1, 37. 1, 5, 21. 2, 2, 24. 2, 3, 5).

109. (p. 329) This follows from Meritt's reconstruction (though partly hypothetical) of a much-damaged inscription (*SEG* 10, 136. 21, 56. *ML*, no. 92. *DSDA* 208). Cf. K. F. Stroheker, *Historia* 3, 1954–5, 163.

110. (p. 330) We know this from an Athenian decree (*ML*, no. 94) in which the Samians were granted Athenian citizenship and full autonomy. How differently would the Athenian empire have developed if such a measure had been taken at an earlier date and on a larger scale!

111. (p. 330) By C. H. Whitman, *Aristophanes and the Comic Hero*, 233.

112. (p. 331) This alludes to Aesch. *Ag.* 717, where it means either Helen or Paris. Cf. E. Fraenkel, *Aesch. Agamemnon* to v. 736.

113. (p. 332) Cf. my *People of Aristophanes*, 65.

VIII · 'KNOW THYSELF'

1. (p. 333) U. v. Wilamowitz-Moellendorff, *Reden und Vorträge* (Berlin 1926⁴), 2, 171, surveys the meaning of the sentence throughout the centuries. He reminds us, for instance, of the ironical greeting by the Athenians for Pompey (Plut. *Pomp.* 27), typical for a time of deification of great and less great men. On a different level, the continued impact of the Delphic sentence was revealed by the man I saw in 1925 at the beach of Phaleron, who invited customers to his scales by an inscribed poster: Γνῶθι Σαυτόν.

2. (p. 333) In earlier passages I have referred to literature on the development of Greek thought. It is important not to describe it as one of simple progress. In general, cf. W. K. C. Guthrie, *In the Beginning* (London 1957), and his *History of Greek Philosophy*, vols. 1–3 (Cambridge 1963–69); also F. Wehrli, *Hauptrichtungen griechischen Denkens* (Zürich 1964). On the sophists, Guthrie's third volume is of greatest importance, though I cannot accept the title of 'Enlightenment' for the fifth century. Cf. J. B. S. Skemp's review *JHS* 1971, 178 ff. On political philosophy see T. A. Sinclair, *A History of Greek Political Thought* (London 1951). In general, cf. also the stimulating, if wrong-headed, book by E. A. Havelock, *The Liberal Temper in Greek Politics* (London 1957).

3. (p. 334) *Corpus Hippocraticum*: editions with translation by E. Littré (10 vols., Paris 1839–61), and by W. H. S. Jones and E. T. Withington (4 vols., Loeb Library 1932–31). Text only: *Corpus Medicorum Graecorum* 1 (Lipsiae 1927). A useful selection of important works in English (primarily for medical students): J. Chadwick and W. N. Mann, *The Medical Works of Hippocrates* (Oxford 1950). Among modern literature cf., e.g., M. Pohlenz, *Hippokrates u. die Begründung der wissenschaftl. Medizin* (Berlin 1938); A. J. Festugière's edition of *Hippocrate, L'ancienne médicine* (Paris 1948); F. M. Cornford, *Principium Sapientiae* (Cambridge 1952); R. Joly, *Le niveau de la science hippocratique* (Paris 1966). I cannot discuss the problems of chronology and authorship of the various Hippocratic books; some parts of the *Corpus* are as late as the first century A.D.

4. (p. 334) An interesting particular of the oath is the separation of the physician from at least one kind of surgeon, another one is the prohibition of

abortion. L. Edelstein, *The Hippocratic Oath* (Baltimore 1943), makes it likely that the ideas expressed in the oath go back to Pythagorean doctrine as known to us from fourth-century sources.

5. (p. 335) Cf. Cornford (note 3), 39.

6. (p. 336) The humours of the body are: blood, phlegm, yellow and black bile. Have the four elements of natural philosophy become the real stuff of life in a material sense?

7. (p. 336) According to late sources (*DK* 60 A 1. 2), he was the first to say that right and wrong were οὐ φύσει, ἀλλὰ νόμῳ. Guthrie, 2, 344, is inclined to accept this as a fact. F. Heinimann, *Nomos and Physis* (Basle 1945), 111, is less certain. He thinks that Archelaus has conceived the idea of the human origin of the *nomoi* (also of language, p. 161), but not their confrontation with an absolute norm, i.e. *physis*. Cf. above, pp. 334, 338 f.

8. (p. 337) That is as far as I dare go. I cannot pretend fully to understand Greek atomism, still less its relevance to modern physics. What I have written owes a great deal to Guthrie (2, ch. 8) and S. Sambursky, *The Physical World of the Greeks* (London 1956). For the theory that the soul's balance of atoms, and thus man's character, can be disturbed by envy, ambition, and other bad qualities cf., in particular, *DK* 68 B 191, discussed, e.g., by K. v. Fritz, *Philosophischer und sprachlicher Ausdruck*, etc. (New York 1940), and G. Vlastos, *Philos. Rev.* 1945, 578; 1946, 53. It means the intrusion of materialism into ethics, or of ethics into materialism.

8a. (p. 338) For Hellanicus see Jacoby, *RE* s.v. *FGrH* 4; v. Fritz, (see ch. IV, note 63a), I 476. Roughly contemporary was Antiochus of Syracuse who dealt with the Greek settlements in Sicily and Italy (v. Fritz I 508).

9. (p. 338) In a way they continued the old tradition of migrant bards, craftsmen, physicians, the Homeric δημιουργοί.

10. (p. 339) Grote found a valuable, if slightly critical, supporter in H. Sidgwick, *Journ. of Philology* 4 (1872), 288; 5 (1873), 66. These articles still belong to the best that has been written about the sophists.

11. (p. 339) Apart from the general histories of philosophy, there is M. Untersteiner, *The Sophists* (transl. by K. Freeman (Oxford 1954)), a book partly arbitrary, and to myself largely incomprehensible. Good descriptions can be found in W. Jaeger, *Paideia*, vol. 1 (Oxford 1939); E. Wolf, *Griechisches Rechtsdenken*, vol. 2 (Frankfurt 1952); L. Versényi, (see note 59); and especially W. Nestle, *Vom Mythos zum Logos* (Stuttgart 1940). As examples of 'strong feelings' in the defence of the sophists may be mentioned K. R.

Popper, *The Open Society and its Enemies* (London 1945), and the book by Havelock (see note 2).

12. (p. 339) Young Hippocrates (not of course the great physician!), who wants nothing more than to be taught by Protagoras, is horrified by the idea that he himself would be made a sophist (Plato, *Protag.* 312).

13. (p. 340) Protagoras of Abdera and Prodicus of Ceos were Ionians, but not from Asia Minor.

14. (p. 340) I found G. Vlastos' introduction to the translation (by Jowett–Ostwald) of Plato's *Protagoras* (New York 1956) very helpful. As to the doubts and different views on the myth, see Havelock, 407, and, on the other hand, ch. VI, note 41.

15. (p. 340) Less likely as titles of this book are *The Great Treatise* (μέγας λόγος) or *On Being* (περὶ τοῦ ὄντος). Our tradition mentions far more titles than can be accepted as independent books. Untersteiner, ch. 2, wishes to reduce them all to two, *Truth* or *Kataballontes*, and *Antilogiai*. His particular attributions, however, are uncertain, and partly unconvincing.

16. (p. 341) *Theaet.* 152a and *Cratylus* 385e. In both passages the same language is used to explain μέτρον ἄνθρωπος, and obviously it is Protagoras' own explanation. It would make no sense if it were not.

17. (p. 342) Cf. generally G. B. Kerferd, *JHS* 1953, 42; Guthrie, *In the Beginning*, 84.

18. (p. 343) The familiar interpretation was 'to make the worse appear the better'. That is the meaning for Strepsiades in Aristophanes' *Clouds* (99. 112), when the 'worse' is identified with sophistic thought in contrast to philosophy as the 'better', and used to win an unjust case in court.

18a. (p. 343) Hdt. 3, 80 ff. Eur. *Suppl.* 403 f. *Phoen.* 499 ff. Sophistic influence on these discussions seems to me beyond doubt; I cannot accept a Persian source for Herodotus' debate, in spite of a few (natural) hints at the Persian situation.

19. (p. 344) Eristics were ridiculed, with special reference to Protagoras, in Plato's *Euthydemus* (286c).

20. (p. 344) Nietzsche called Gorgias 'the first complete nihilist of Europe'. I do not know whether Gorgias makes an appearance in more recent philosophies of 'nothingness'. Among classical scholars the question has been much discussed whether Gorgias was a sophist or only a rhetor. In spite of what Professor E. R. Dodds says in his outstanding edition of Plato's

Gorgias (Oxford 1959), 6, I cannot believe that the distinction is really valid, just as it was a mistake to regard (with H. Gomperz) all sophists as mere rhetors. Cf. W. Jaeger, *Paideia* (English edn.) 1, 287, and especially E. L. Harrison, *Phoenix* 1964, 183, and C. M. J. Sicking, *Mnemosyne* 1964, 225.

21. (p. 344) He was regarded in antiquity as the inventor of the σχήματα Γοργίεια with their mixture of poetical and prose styles, and the artificial playing with words.

22. (p. 345) For the duplicity see, e.g., B 23, where the deceiver is regarded as more just than the non-deceiver, and the deceived as wiser than the un-deceived. The concepts of the ἐπιεικὲς and the δίκαιον in Gorgias' *Epitaphios* (B 6) are so nebulous and rhetorical that conclusions such as I tried to draw in an early article (see note 24) are very doubtful.

23. (p. 346) Cf. B. Snell, *Die Entdeckung des Geistes* (Hamburg 1955³), ch. 13 ('Das Symbol des Weges') (not in the English edition).

24. (p. 347) Cf. Guthrie and Heinimann (note 7); M. Gigante, Νόμος Βασιλεύς (Naples 1956); also V. Ehrenberg, *Archiv f. Gesch. d. Philosophie* 1923, 119 = *PI* 359, esp. 369; H. E. Stier, *Philologus* 1928.

25. (p. 348) In that early article of mine I tried to show that Hippias was, or at least could be, the inventor of the phrase. I am more cautious today, but I found that Untersteiner (note 11), 281, shares that view. In general, cf. now A. W. H. Adkins, *From the Many to the One* (London 1970), 110 ff.

26. (p. 348) Cf. my *Sophocles and Pericles* (Oxford 1954), ch. 2, and Appendix A. In the latter Ideal with the 'three commandments', called ἄγραφοι νόμοι in Xen. *mem.* 4, 4, 19. I should not have confined that notion to the Xenophontic Socrates, but should have included Hippias, with whom he is discussing the idea of justice.

27. (p. 349) Ancient writers distinguished two Antiphons – one, 'the Athenian', usually called 'the sophist', and the other, Antiphon of Rhamnus, a politician and rhetor, of whom Thucydides tells us a great deal. He was one of the leaders of the oligarchs in 411 (see p. 319), and he is best known by a number of speeches in court, probably also as the author of some rhetorical exercises under the name of *Tetralogiai*. The sophist wrote several 'philosophical' books, and it is he with whom we are concerned here. The distinction, however, between the two men, and even more the attribution of works to either of them, has not met with unanimous consent; our acceptance of the assumption as described above will at least provide a reasonable basis. Cf. also Guthrie, esp. 292 ff.

28. (p. 349) It is questionable indeed whether, or to what extent, the radical views expressed in the papyrus fragment (*DK* 87 B 44) belong to Antiphon himself or to a discussion of opposing opinions. G. B. Kerferd, *Proc. Cambr. Phil. Soc.* 1956–7, 26, ingeniously pleads even that nothing of importance belongs to Antiphon's views. Most interesting is his statement of a third standard between nature and laws, that of the 'Golden Rule'; that would derive from the typical Greek preference for the middle line. From a general point of view it makes little difference if those views belong to an opponent; in that case, he was another sophist.

29. (p. 349) See Soph. frg. 532 (*Tereus*), Eur. *Hecuba passim*, frg. 52 (*Alexandros*); cf. Nestle (note 11), 377; Webster (see ch. VII, note 88), 165. S. G. Daitz, *Hermes* 1971, 217 ff. The question of slavery is treated in the play from two opposite points of view. The view exemplified in the son of Priam's being brought up as a slave is, of course, *quod erat demonstrandum*, i.e. the poet's view, which is strongly influenced by sophist thought. The opposite view of the innate inferiority of slaves belongs to another character; it is an *agon* of words and views, not a conflict in one and the same mind.

30. (p. 350) Aristotle, *rhet.* 1406a, 22. 1406b, 11: ἐπιτείχισμα τῶν νόμων. In my view, remembering the use of the verb ἐπιτειχίζειν, this cannot mean the opposite, a 'stronghold of the laws'. Liddell–Scott–Jones leave the question open. Cf. ch. VII, note 50.

31. (p. 350) I am in agreement with E. R. Dodds' opinion (see note 20) on Callicles. We know 'nothing beyond what Plato tells in the *Gorgias*'. It is most unlikely that Callicles is an invented character. Dodds believes that Socrates' warning (519a) is a prophecy *post eventum*, and that Callicles died young. At the alleged time of the dialogue (between 425 and 405 – if Plato thought of a fixed date at all), Callicles was 'embarking on an active career' (515a) in the last years of the war, and then still 'too young to be remembered – if Plato had not remembered him'.

32. (p. 350) Cf. the short, but comprehensive, Appendix in Dodds' edition on 'Socrates, Callicles, and Nietzsche' (p. 387).

33. (p. 351) Cf. *PI* 478, where it is shown that the ἀρπάγμων represented the contemplative life, the πολυπάργμων the life of political activity.

34. (p. 351) Cf., e.g., J. D. Beazley and B. Ashmole, *Greek Sculpture and Painting* (Cambridge, reprinted 1966), 503.

35. (p. 353) The following events are described, if rather poorly, by Xenophon, *hell.* 2, 3 f., and *AP* 35 ff.; important also are Lysias' speeches 12, 13,

25. The detailed chronology is uncertain; cf. D. Lotze, 'Lysander und der peloponnesische Krieg', *Abh. Sächs. Akad.* 1964, 87.

36. (p. 354) We remember that his own moderate form of oligarchy had a number of 5,000 citizens, and at the first attempt at establishing it, they amounted to 9,000 (see above, p. 320).

37. (p. 354) A. de Lamartine, *Histoire des Girondins*, bk. 38, ch. 20. Theramenes is the Danton of the Athenian revolution. Xenophon (2, 3, 56) describes his death as a kind of parallel to that of Socrates; he offered a libation 'for the noble Critias'. The record of his political life, however, was anything but blameless; he had, for example, no scruples at the trial of the strategi in 406, or in overthrowing democracy with the help of Sparta. It is mainly because he favoured a moderate form of oligarchy that Aristotle (*AP* 28, 5), like Thucydides, praises him together with Nicias and Thucydides son of Melesias. To Critias and Theramenes, cf. also S. Usher, *JHS* 1968, 128.

38. (p. 354) This is the verdict of Wade-Gery at the end of the article mentioned in note 42.

39. (p. 355) *AP* 38, 3, alone speaks of the election of another board of ten in the place of the former one. The insertion of a set of 'men of the highest reputation' may have been an attempt by Aristotle or his source at giving the moderate oligarchs a share in the making of peace. Cf. F. Jacoby, *FGrH* 324 F 10–11.

40. (p. 355) In the same year the Ionic alphabet was officially introduced for the inscription of new laws and decrees. It had been in use at Athens for quite a time, though in inscriptions down to 403 the old Attic alphabet was normally used.

41. (p. 355) It is significant that no radical proposals were accepted, whether from the one side or the other. Thus, Thrasybulus' motion to give full citizenship to all metics and slaves who had sided with the democrats was rejected just as was the move to deprive of their citizenship al l men without landed property; that would have meant the disenfranchisement of many thousands of thetes.

42. (p. 356) Nobody would doubt this if the speech had not been preserved under the heading: Ἡρώδου περὶ πολιτείας. The text is printed in Ed. Meyer, *Theopomps Hellenika* (Halle 1909), 201; he also discusses the contemporary background, but is strongly opposed by F. E. Adcock and A. D. Knox, *Klio* 1913, 249. I am still inclined to accept the more common view that the speech belongs to the late fifth century. The author is not Herodes

(Atticus), the sophist of the second century A.D., nor is the speech about a constitution (apart from §§ 30–31). Perhaps Dobree's guess was right that the original heading was περὶ πολ (ἐμου), for it is all about war. Most scholars seem to think that the author was Thrasymachus, whose quotations from a speech *About the Larissaeans* (*DK* 85 B 2) is an attack on the 'barbarian' Archelaus (see above, p. 349); cf. M. Sordi, *Rfil* 1955, 175. Wade-Gery (*CQ* 1945 = *Essays*, 271) has made out a case for Critias, who had been living for some time as an exile in Thessaly. The *stasis* at Larissa exploded in 402, when the Aleuad Aristippus asked Cyrus for military help against his local opponents (Xen. *anab.* 1, 1, 10. 2, 1); he later returned the troops under the leadership of Menon, one of Gorgias' pupils (see above, p. 345 f.).

43. (p. 357) Xen. *hell.* 3, 2, 21 ff. The date of this campaign is not certain, but it was probably shortly after the date of the Larissa speech (Wade-Gery, *Essays*, 276).

44. (p. 359) *OC* 637: χώρᾳ δ᾽ ἔμπολιν κατοικιῶ. The text has ἔμπαλιν, but Musgrave's correction is certain. The rare word appears again in v. 1156. It is the appropriate opposite to the equally rare ἀπόπτολις in v. 208.

45. (p. 360) Cf. the verdict of Aristotle, *poet.* 1454a, 31.

46. (p. 361) Panhellenism: 350, 414, 751ff., 1271, 1378, 1384 ff., 1397, 1400, 1407, 1421, 1447. Rabble: 450, 517, 526, 735, 1000, 1030, 1352, 1357 (τὸ πολὺ δεινὸν κακόν).

47. (p. 361) I am afraid I cannot understand, much less share, the view that this is 'one of the finest Greek plays' (H. Strohm, *Euripides* (Munich 1957), 2, 2). But I wish to mention this in order to leave the final verdict to others. A moderate appreciation can be found in Lesky, *Greek Tragedy* (London 1965), 193. Cf. B. M. W. Knox, *GRBS* 1966, 229 ('truly heroic action which spring . . . from a change of mind!').

48. (pp. 362) See above, pp. 113 and 352. The best edition of the play is E. R. Dodds, *Euripides' Bacchae* (Oxford 1960²). His introduction and extensive commentary cover the ground most satisfactorily. He also makes it quite clear that the two contrasting main interpretations of the play by scholars of recent times are equally mistaken, the one that regards the *Bacchae* as a recantation by a former unbeliever, and the other that Euripides wished to point out the evils of religion. Cf. also G. M. A. Grube, *TAPA* 1935, 37; *The Drama of Euripides* (London 1941), 398; W. Jaeger, *Paideia* (Oxford 1939), 1, 352; R. P. Winnington-Ingram, *Euripides and Dionysus* (Cambridge 1948).

49. (p. 362) Dodds, p. 212, shows that this is more than a chance similarity. He thinks that 'if either poet echoed the other, Sophocles was the echoer', and that copies of Euripides' play may have reached Athens in spring or summer 406, when Sophocles was at work on the OC. We shall never know for certain.

50. (p. 362) Cf. R. P. Winnington-Ingram, BICS 1966, 34.

50a. (p. 363) 'A truly psychoanalytic process' (G. Devereux, JHS 1970, 35).

51. (p. 363) It would be senseless to produce a list of the immense literature on Thucydides. Much of it, for instance, the question of unity versus divisionist analysis, does not concern us; that is to say, we abstain from any discussion of the 'Thucydidean question'. The idea of either a scientific or a non-scientific Thucydides can lead to an exaggeration which no longer makes sense. Most useful for our purposes were the various writings by J. H. Finley and J. de Romilly (see next note), also A. W. Gomme, The Greek Attitude to Poetry and History (Univ. of California Press 1954), chs. 6 and 7, and the remarks by A. Lesky, History of Greek Literature (London 1966), 455. A valuable investigation into ancient historiography is: H. Strasburger, Die Wesensbestimmung der Geschichte, etc. (Wiesbaden 1966).

52. (p. 364) I mention in particular J. H. Finley, HSt 50 (1939), 35, and Thucydides (Cambridge, Mass. 1952); J. de Romilly, Histoire et raison chez Thucydide (Paris 1956); RPh 1965, 28; REG 1965, 557. F. E. Adcock, Thucydides and his History (Cambridge 1963). See also ch. VI, notes 2 and 67.

53. (p. 365) It is a remarkable fact that modern historians who proclaimed 'history is a science', no less than those who regard writing history as an art, could both base their arguments on Thucydides. It is both, and we can learn that from Thucydides. Cf. the concluding pages of v. Fritz, I 821 ff.

54. (p. 365) The translation is perhaps unusual, but ἀφανεστάτη λόγῳ can hardly mean 'not openly expressed', since it was expressed more than openly by the Corinthians at Sparta (1, 70). The use of the word πρόφασις is the more remarkable as its meaning is ambiguous, and most frequently it stands for a pretended reason, a pretext. Cf. ch. VII, note 4.

55. (p. 365) 'Wie es eigentlich gewesen ist.' Cf. Aristotle, poet. 1451a, 36: τὰ γενόμενα λέγειν. Today, historians are probably more sceptical than Ranke was, as they have learnt that it is impossible to reconstruct the past in its fullness. It may be easier for the historian of his own time (like Thucydides), although the proximity of his subject makes objectivity even more difficult. That was an obstacle which Thucydides, on the whole, successfully, though not completely, overcame.

56. (p. 367) No speeches appear in bk. 8, and that has frequently and rightly been explained by the fact that Thucydides was not able to finish his work. For the same reason bk. 8 includes more *verbatim* documents than any other section; there was no time to work the documents stylistically into the text.

57. (p. 370) Cf. J. de Romilly, *Entretiens Fondations Hardt* 4 (1956), and the following discussion.

58. (p. 370) Here, for once, I definitely differ from Mme de Romilly, who (*REG* 1965, 557) speaks of Thucydides' profound optimism, though she admits that the word may be misleading (p. 575).

59. (p. 371) Among the vast literature, I mention some books in English, however different in outlook. At the beginning there is Grote's great ch. 68 of his *History of Greece*. Very important: A. E. Taylor, *Varia Socratica* (Oxford 1911); *Socrates* (Edinburgh 1932); F. M. Cornford, *Before and after Socrates* (Cambridge 1932); *Principium Sapientiae* (Cambridge 1952). Further: W. Jaeger, *Paideia*, vol. 2 (Oxford 1944); E. R. Dodds, *The Greeks and the Irrational* (Univ. of California 1951); A.-H. Chroust, *Socrates, Man and Myth* (London 1957); L. Versényi, *Socratic Humanism* (New Haven and London 1963); J. E. Raven, *Plato's Thought in the Making* (Cambridge 1965); N. Gulley, The Philosophy of Socrates (London, 1968), and once again, Guthrie, 3.

60. (p. 372) Did Aristophanes believe in the image that public opinion had of Socrates? We cannot be sure; but it remains significant that Plato in the *Symposium* makes Aristophanes a member of the company, and an important and pleasant one at that, whose speech is central as the target for Diotima's (cf. K. J. Dover, *JHS* 1966, 41). Without trying to disentangle Plato's feelings towards the author of the *Clouds*, it is difficult to imagine that he did not see Aristophanes in a very different light when he wrote the *Symposium*. At that time Aristophanes had probably been dead for a few years.

61. (p. 372) O. Gigon, *Sokrates* (Berne 1947), has dealt with the Socratic literature which he treats as pure fiction (*Dichtung*). He also reminds us that we must not forget about the lost Socratics. His book is very stimulating, even though he is inclined to throw out the baby with the bath-water. Antisthenes, a contemporary of Hippias and Prodicus, was probably the oldest 'Socratic', but as the creator of the Cynic school he does not belong within the scope of this book. His rôle as a loyal disciple of Socrates has been exaggerated by some modern scholars.

62. (p. 374) Aristotle, *metaph.* 1078b, 18. 28. 1086b, 3. He makes it clear that Socrates was not the first to use inductive arguments, but the first to recognize their full importance for the finding of general definitions. Cf. O. Gigon, *Mus. Helv.* 1959, 174, a very thorough, if difficult, paper.

63. (p. 375) The former view is taken by A. D. Winspear and T. Silverberg, *Who was Socrates?* (Gordon Co., U.S.A. 1939), and also held by W. Schmid, *Philologus* 1948, 209; the latter is suggested, more tentatively and more subtly, by B. Snell, ibid., 125. I feel that my view on the *Clouds* (*People of Aristophanes*², 274) still holds good. An ingenious attempt at reconstructing Socrates' life is J. L. Fischer, *The Case of Socrates* (Praha 1969), using arguments of social and psychological analysis. On the other hand, I find it very hard, not to say impossible, to accept the idea that Socrates never spoke at all in court (H. Gomperz, *WSt* 1936, 32; W. A. Oldfather, *Cl. Weekly* 1938, 203).

64. (p. 375) The story in *Phaedo* that the young Socrates started with the aim of that wisdom 'that is called περὶ φύσεως ἱστορία' could, of course, to some extent support the picture of the *Clouds*. But Aristophanes cannot be used as a realistic source; he even described the sophists generally as 'star-gazers'. On the other hand, the fact that all Platonic dialogues before the *Phaedo* (which belongs to the period of *Symposium* and *Republic*) never hint at this early phase in Socrates' life, while *Apology* 19c denies such a phase in the strictest terms, seems to me an argument not to be neglected. Still, cf. Guthrie 3, 417 ff.

65. (p. 375) The story of a first (or second?) marriage to Myrto, supposed to be the daughter (!) or granddaughter of the famous Aristeides, is probably worthless gossip, as is the charge of bigamy.

66. (p. 375) Plato, *apol.* 32b. Cf. above, p. 328.

67. (p. 376) We may ask why the radical democracy before 404 had done nothing against Socrates. The answer is probably that only when Critias had become such a hideous enemy of the people the time was ripe for prosecuting his teacher.

68. (p. 377) Translation after H. Tredennick in the Loeb Library.

69. (p. 378) Taylor's denial (*Socrates*, 108) that the new δαιμόνια are represented by Socrates' δαιμόινον is clever enough, but he reaches the conclusion that this part of the accusation had no meaning at all, not even to the prosecutor. That is in itself a refutation of his theory.

70. (p. 379) Aristotle, *rhet.* 1393b, 3. The criticism of sortition was not specifically Socratic. We find, e.g., a discussion – though, it is true, with a distinctly Socratic flavour – in the Δίσσοι Λόγοι (*DK* 90, § 7).

71. (p. 379) Cf. A. K. Rogers *The Socratic Problem* (New Haven 1933), 58.

72. (p. 381) Cf. W. Jaeger (note 59), 2, 27.

73. (p. 382) Cf. Eva Ehrenberg in my *Aspects of the Ancient World* (Oxford 1946), 251.

74. (p. 382) I dare not decide whether Socrates believed in the soul's immortality, though Plato's *Apology* leaves no doubt about it.

CONCLUSION

1. (p. 384) See *PI* 32.

INDICES

Items which appear throughout the book have usually been omitted. The *italic* figures in brackets refer to the notes.

I General

II Modern Authors